About the cover images

The single most transformative process of early world history was the breakthrough to agriculture. It fostered population growth, required settled communities, and permitted the development of "civilizations" and all that followed from them. The cover evokes this Agricultural Revolution by depicting a grape arbor in ancient Egypt and the harvesting of rice in pre-modern China.

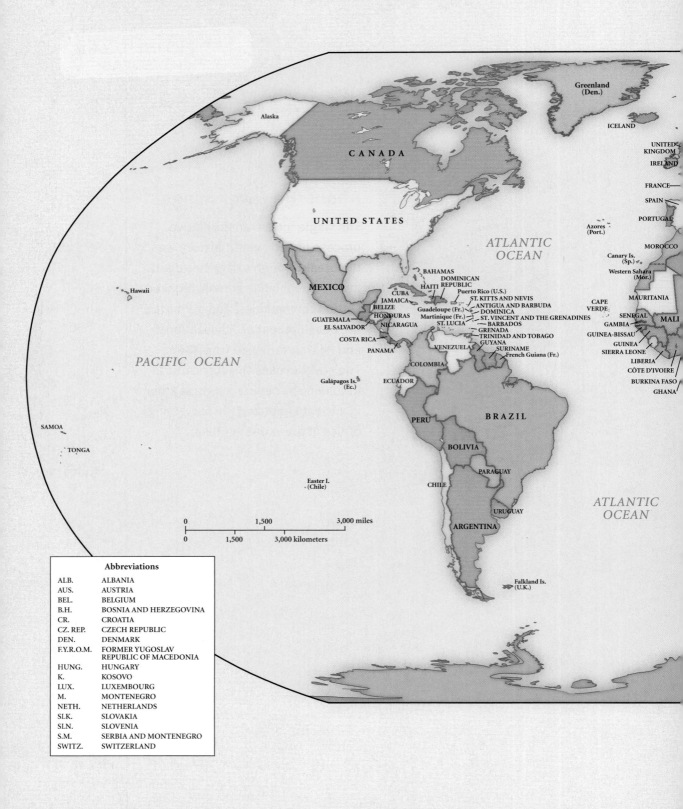

Greenland
(Den.)

ICELAND

UNITED
KINGDOM

IRELAND

FRANCE

SPAIN

PORTUGAL

Azores
(Port.)

MOROCCO

Canary Is.
(Sp.)

Western Sahara
(Mor.)

MAURITANIA

CAPE
VERDE

SENEGAL

MALI

GAMBIA

GUINEA-BISSAU

GUINEA

SIERRA LEONE

LIBERIA

CÔTE D'IVOIRE

BURKINA FASO

GHANA

Alaska

C A N A D A

UNITED STATES

ATLANTIC
OCEAN

MEXICO

BAHAMAS

CUBA

JAMAICA

BELIZE

GUATEMALA

EL SALVADOR

HONDURAS

NICARAGUA

COSTA RICA

PANAMA

DOMINICAN
REPUBLIC

HAITI

Puerto Rico (U.S.)

ST. KITTS AND NEVIS

ANTIGUA AND BARBUDA

Guadeloupe (Fr.)

DOMINICA

Martinique (Fr.)

ST. VINCENT AND THE GRENADINES

ST. LUCIA

BARBADOS

GRENADA

TRINIDAD AND TOBAGO

VENEZUELA

GUYANA

SURINAME

French Guiana (Fr.)

COLOMBIA

Galápagos Is.
(Ec.)

ECUADOR

PERU

BRAZIL

BOLIVIA

PARAGUAY

CHILE

URUGUAY

ARGENTINA

Hawaii

PACIFIC OCEAN

SAMOA

TONGA

Easter I.
(Chile)

ATLANTIC
OCEAN

Falkland Is.
(U.K.)

0   1,500   3,000 miles

0   1,500   3,000 kilometers

Abbreviations

ALB.	ALBANIA
AUS.	AUSTRIA
BEL.	BELGIUM
B.H.	BOSNIA AND HERZEGOVINA
CR.	CROATIA
CZ. REP.	CZECH REPUBLIC
DEN.	DENMARK
F.Y.R.O.M.	FORMER YUGOSLAV REPUBLIC OF MACEDONIA
HUNG.	HUNGARY
K.	KOSOVO
LUX.	LUXEMBOURG
M.	MONTENEGRO
NETH.	NETHERLANDS
SLK.	SLOVAKIA
SLN.	SLOVENIA
S.M.	SERBIA AND MONTENEGRO
SWITZ.	SWITZERLAND

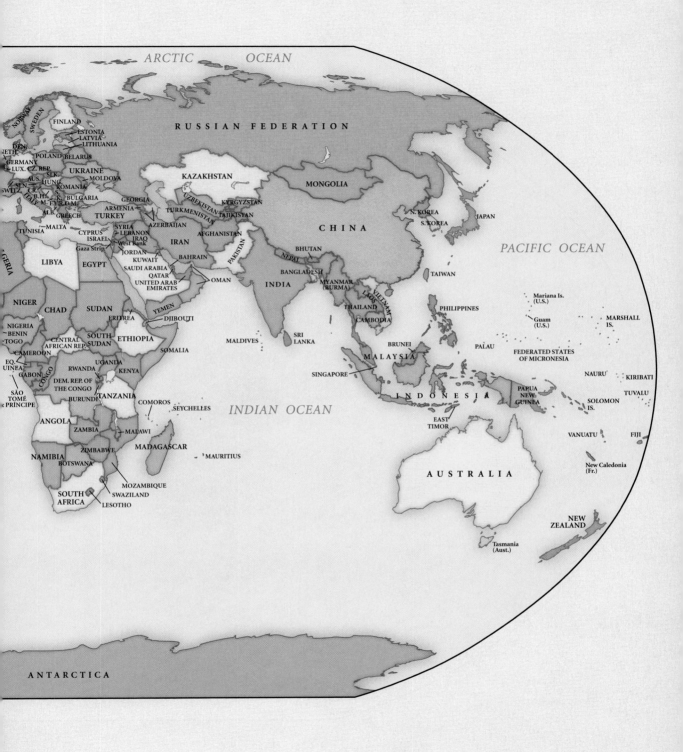

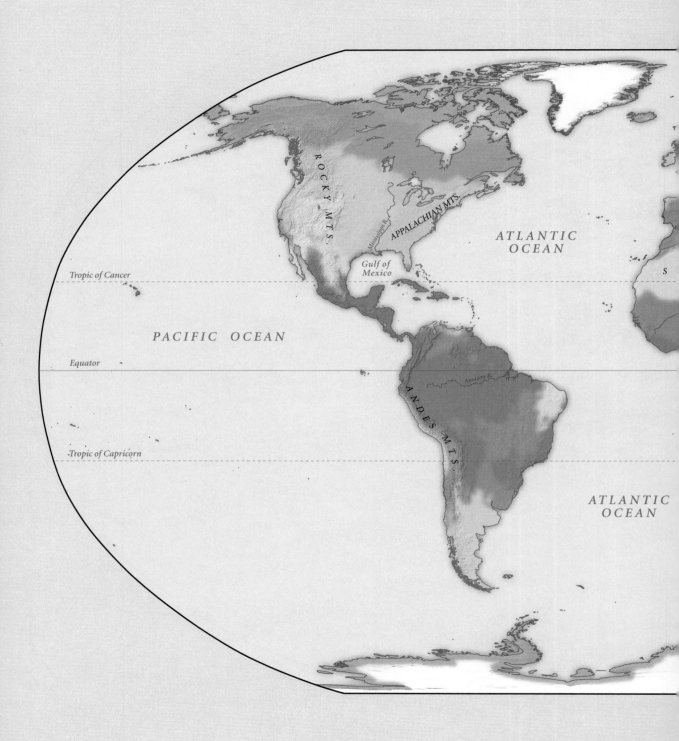

ROCKY MTS.

APPALACHIAN MTS.

ATLANTIC
OCEAN

Mississippi R.

Gulf of
Mexico

Tropic of Cancer

PACIFIC   OCEAN

Equator

A N D E S   M T S.

Amazon R.

Tropic of Capricorn

ATLANTIC
OCEAN

S

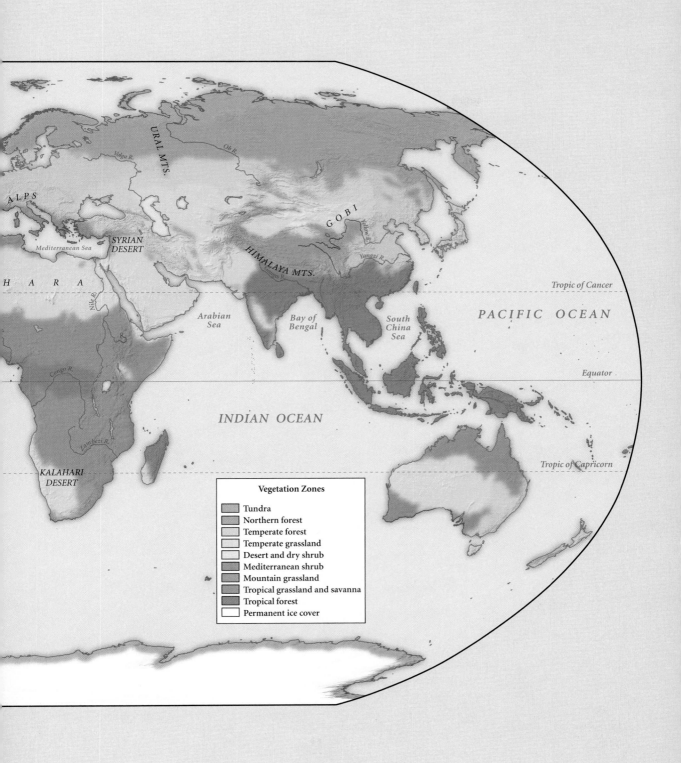

ALPS

URAL MTS.

Volga R.

Ob R.

GOBI

Yellow R.

HIMALAYA MTS.

Yangzi R.

SYRIAN
DESERT

Mediterranean Sea

H A R A

Nile R.

Arabian
Sea

Bay of
Bengal

South
China
Sea

Tropic of Cancer

PACIFIC OCEAN

Congo R.

Equator

INDIAN OCEAN

Zambezi R.

KALAHARI
DESERT

Tropic of Capricorn

Vegetation Zones

- Tundra
- Northern forest
- Temperate forest
- Temperate grassland
- Desert and dry shrub
- Mediterranean shrub
- Mountain grassland
- Tropical grassland and savanna
- Tropical forest
- Permanent ice cover

Ways of the World

A Brief Global History

VOLUME I: TO 1500

Ways of the World
A Brief Global History

ROBERT W. STRAYER

The College at Brockport: State University of New York

SECOND EDITION

Bedford/St. Martin's
Boston • New York

For Bedford/St. Martin's

Publisher for History: Mary V. Dougherty

Executive Editor for History:
   Traci M. Crowell

Director of Development for History:
   Jane Knetzger

Developmental Editor: Kathryn Abbott

Senior Production Editor: Bridget Leahy

Senior Marketing Manager: Paul Stillitano

Assistant Production Manager: Joe Ford

Editorial Assistant: Emily DiPietro

Production Assistant: Laura Winstead

Copy Editor: Lisa Wehrle

Indexer: Melanie Belkin

Cartography: Mapping Specialists, Ltd.

Photo Researcher: Carole Frohlich, The Visual
   Connection Image Research, Inc.

Permissions Manager: Kalina K. Ingham

Senior Art Director: Anna Palchik

Text Designer: Joyce Weston

Cover Art: Top: A detail of a painting from
   the tomb of Nakht depicting the
gathering of grapes from an arbor. West
Thebes, Egypt, 18th dynasty c.1421–1413
B.C. Werner Forman/akg-images.
Bottom: *Rice harvesting,* attributed to
Cheng Chi, Yuan Dynasty, 13th–14th
century A.D., China. Freer Gallery of Art,
Washington, D.C. / The Art Archive at
Art Resource, NY.

Composition: Jouve

Printing and Binding: RR Donnelley
   and Sons

President, Bedford/St. Martin's:
   Denise B. Wydra

Presidents, Macmillan Higher Education:
   Joan E. Feinberg and Tom Scotty

Director of Marketing: Karen R. Soeltz

Production Director: Susan W. Brown

Associate Production Director:
   Elise S. Kaiser

Managing Editor: Elizabeth M. Schaaf

Manufactured in the United States of America.

7   6   5   4   3   2
f   e   d   c   b   a

For information, write: Bedford/St. Martin's, 75 Arlington Street, Boston, MA 02116
   (617-399-4000)

ISBN 978-0-312-44443-3 (Combined Edition)
ISBN 978-1-4576-4729-1 (Loose-leaf Edition)
ISBN 978-0-312-48704-1 (Vol. 1)
ISBN 978-1-4576-4733-8 (Loose-leaf Edition, Vol. 1)
ISBN 978-0-312-48705-8 (Vol. 2)
ISBN 978-1-4576-4732-1 (Loose-leaf Edition, Vol. 2)
ISBN 978-1-4576-2221-2 (High School Edition)

Preface

THE FIRST EDITION OF *WAYS OF THE WORLD* set out to present a coherent, comparative, and brief global narrative focused on the big picture of world history. As the book's author, I have been pleased—and not a little surprised—by its commercial success and immensely gratified that it has proven useful for conveying the rich perspective of world history to so many students. The original book and the subsequent docutext version—with chapter-based sets of written and visual primary sources—have been adopted by world history instructors at over 550 colleges and universities and are used in many high school AP world history courses as well. *Ways of the World* represents for me the satisfying culmination of a long involvement in world history classrooms in Ethiopia, New York, New Zealand, and California. Feedback from instructors as well as from student readers suggests that they have appreciated the book's narrative brevity, its thematic and comparative focus, its many pedagogical features, the clarity and accessibility of its writing, and its musing or reflective tone.

Since the publication of the first edition, technology has continued to transform teaching and learning. This edition of the text includes of a number of electronic dimensions, including LearningCurve, an easy-to-assign adaptive learning tool that helps students rehearse the material so they come to class better prepared. Students receive access to LearningCurve, described more fully below, when they purchase a new copy of the book.

What's in a Title?

The title of a book should evoke something of its character and outlook. The title *Ways of the World* is intended to suggest at least three dimensions of the text.

The first is **diversity** or **variation**, for the "ways of the world," or the ways of being human in the world, have been many and constantly changing. This book seeks to embrace the experience of humankind in its vast diversity, while noticing the changing location of particular centers of innovation and wider influence.

Second, the title *Ways of the World* invokes major **panoramas**, **patterns**, or **pathways** in world history, as opposed to highly detailed narratives. Many world history instructors have found that students often feel overwhelmed by the sheer quantity of data that a course in global history can require of them. In the narrative sections of this book, the larger patterns or the "big pictures" of world history appear in the foreground on center stage, while the still plentiful details, data, and facts occupy the background, serving in supporting roles.

A third implication of the book's title lies in a certain **reflective** or **musing quality** of *Ways of the World*, which appears especially in the Big Picture essays that introduce each part of the book and in a Reflections section at the end of each chapter. These features of the book offer many opportunities for contemplating larger questions. The Big Picture essay for Part Six, for example, asks whether the twentieth century deserves to be considered a separate period of world history. Chapter 4 explores how historians and religious believers sometimes rub each other the wrong way. Chapter 8 probes how and why human societies change. And Chapter 22 muses about the difficulties and the usefulness of studying the unfinished stories of recent history. None of these questions have clear or easy answers, but the opportunity to contemplate them is among the great gifts that the study of history offers to us all.

The Dilemma of World History: Inclusivity and Coherence

The great virtue of world history lies in its inclusiveness, for its subject matter is the human species itself. But that virtue is also the source of world history's greatest difficulty — telling a coherent story. How can we meaningfully present the planet's many and distinct peoples and their intersections with one another in the confines of a single book or a single term? What prevents that telling from bogging down in the endless detail of various civilizations or cultures, from losing the forest for the trees, from implying that history is just "one damned thing after another"?

Less Can Be More

From the beginning, *Ways of the World* set out to cope with this fundamental conundrum of world history — the tension between inclusion and coherence — in several ways. The first is the relative brevity of the narrative. This means leaving some things out or treating them more succinctly than some instructors might expect. But it also means that the textbook need not overwhelm students or dominate the course. It allows for more creativity by instructors in constructing their own world history courses, giving them the opportunity to mix and match text, sources, and other materials in distinctive ways.

The Centrality of Context: Change, Comparison, Connection

A further aid to achieving coherence amid the fragmenting possibilities of inclusion lies in maintaining the centrality of context, for in world history, nothing stands alone. Those of us who practice world history as teachers or textbook authors are seldom specialists in the particulars of what we study and teach. Rather we are "specialists of the whole," seeking to find the richest, most suggestive, and most meaningful contexts in which to embed those particulars. Our task, fundamentally, is to teach contextual thinking.

To aid in this task, *Ways of the World* repeatedly highlights three such contexts, what I call the "**three Cs**" of world history: **change**, **comparison**, and **connection**.

The first "C" emphasizes large-scale **change**, both within and especially across major regions of the world. Examples include the peopling of the planet, the breakthrough to agriculture, the emergence of "civilization," the rise of universal religions, the changing shape of the Islamic world, the linking of eastern and western hemispheres in the wake of Columbus's voyages, the Industrial Revolution, the rise and fall of world communism, and the acceleration of globalization during the twentieth century.

The second "C" involves frequent **comparison**, a technique of integration through juxtaposition, bringing several regions or cultures into our field of vision at the same time. It encourages reflection both on the common elements of the human experience and on its many variations. Such comparisons are pervasive throughout the book. We examine the difference, for example, between the Agricultural Revolution in the Eastern and Western Hemispheres; between the beginnings of Buddhism and the early history of Christianity and Islam; between patriarchy in Athens and in Sparta; between European and Asian empires of the early modern era; between the Chinese and the Japanese response to European intrusion; between the Russian and Chinese revolutions; and many more.

The final "C" emphasizes **connection**, networks of communication and exchange that increasingly shaped the character of those societies that participated in them. For world historians, cross-cultural interaction becomes one of the major motors of historical transformation. Such connections are addressed in nearly every chapter narrative. Examples include the clash of the ancient Greeks and the Persians; the long-distance commercial networks that linked the Afro-Eurasian world; the numerous cross-cultural encounters spawned by the spread of Islam; the trans-hemispheric Columbian exchange of the early modern era; and the growth of a genuinely global economy.

Organizing World History: Chronology, Theme, and Region

Organizing a world history textbook or a world history course is, to put it mildly, a daunting task. How should we divide up the seamless stream of human experience into manageable and accessible pieces, while recognizing always that such divisions are artificial, arbitrary, and contested? Historians, of course, debate the issue endlessly. In structuring *Ways of the World*, I have drawn on my own sense of "what works" in the classroom, on a personal penchant for organizational clarity, and on established practice in the field. The outcome has been an effort to balance three principles of organization—chronology, theme, and region—in a flexible format that can accommodate a variety of teaching approaches and curricular strategies.

This book addresses the question of chronology by dividing world history into six major periods. Each of these six "parts" begins with a **Big Picture essay** that introduces the general patterns of a particular period and raises questions about the problems historians face in periodizing the human past.

Part One (to 500 B.C.E.) deals in two chapters with beginnings—of human migration and social construction from the Paleolithic era through the Agricultural Revolution and the development of the First Civilizations. Each chapter pursues important themes on a global scale, illustrating those themes with regional examples treated comparatively.

Part Two examines the millennium of second-wave civilizations (500 B.C.E. to 500 C.E.) and employs the thematic principle in exploring the major civilizations of Eurasia (Chinese, Indian, Persian, and Mediterranean), with separate chapters focusing on their empires (Chapter 3), religious and cultural traditions (Chapter 4), and social organization (Chapter 5). These Afro-Eurasian chapters are followed by a single chapter (Chapter 6) that examines regionally the second-wave era in sub-Saharan Africa and the Americas.

Part Three, embracing the thousand years between 500 and 1500 C.E., reflects a mix of thematic and regional principles. Chapter 7 focuses topically on commercial networks, while Chapters 8, 9, and 10 deal regionally with the Chinese, Islamic, and Christian worlds respectively. Chapter 11 treats pastoral societies as a broad theme and the Mongols as the most dramatic illustration of their impact on the larger stage of world history. Chapter 12, which bridges the two volumes of the book, presents an around-the-world tour in the fifteenth century, which serves both to conclude Volume 1 and to open Volume 2.

Part Four considers the early modern era (1450–1750), and treats each of its three chapters thematically. Chapter 13 compares European and Asian empires; Chapter 14 lays out the major patterns of global commerce and their consequences; and Chapter 15 focuses on cultural patterns, including the globalization of Christianity and the rise of modern science.

Part Five takes up the era of maximum European influence in the world, from 1750 to 1914. It charts the emergence of distinctively modern societies, devoting separate chapters to the Atlantic revolutions (Chapter 16) and the Industrial Revolution (Chapter 17). Chapters 18 and 19 focus on the growing impact of those European societies on the rest of humankind—on the world of formal colonies and on the still independent states of Latin America, China, the Ottoman Empire, and Japan.

Part Six, which looks at the most recent century (1914–2012), is perhaps the most problematic for world historians, given the abundance of data and the absence of time to sort out what is fundamental and what is peripheral. Its four chapters explore themes of global significance. Chapter 20 focuses on the descent of Europe into war, depression, and the Holocaust, and the global outcomes of this collapse. Chapter 21 examines global communism—its birth in revolution, its efforts to create socialist societies, its role in the Cold War, and its abandonment by the end of the twentieth century. Chapter 22 turns the spotlight on the Afro-Asian-Latin American majority of the world's population, describing their exit from formal colonial rule and their emergence on the world stage as the developing countries. Chapter 23 concludes this account of the human journey by assessing the economic, environmental, and cultural dimensions of what we know as globalization.

What's New?

In preparing this second edition of *Ways of the World*, I have sought to build on the strengths of the first edition, guided by the wise counsel of many reviewers and users of the book. I am especially pleased that this second edition has grown not at all beyond the contours of the first, thus refuting an apparent law of nature that revised books increase substantially in size. To make room for new material, I have made some judicious abbreviations. A revised Chapter 1, for example, incorporates both the Paleolithic and Neolithic eras, which had separate chapters in the first edition.

These and other cuts have made possible the inclusion of much that is new. Latin America and Southeast Asia have been incorporated more fully into the narrative. Gender and environmental issues are treated far more extensively and integrated throughout the narrative more smoothly than before. The discussion of early Christianity now highlights its Asian and African dimensions alongside the more familiar Roman and European aspects, while the eighteenth- and nineteenth-century Atlantic Revolutions are cast in a more global context.

An entirely new feature in *Ways of the World*, entitled "**Portraits**," provides a short biographical sketch of an individual in each chapter. Readers will meet Paneb, a notorious criminal in ancient Egypt whose life contrasts with the better-known history that celebrates the triumphs of Egyptian civilization in Chapter 2; Cecilia Penifader, a fourteenth-century English peasant woman, whose story provides a window into the lives of ordinary rural people, in Chapter 10; Ayuba Diallo, a prominent West African Muslim who was transported into slavery in America and then traveled back to freedom and slave owning at home, in Chapter 14; and Etty Hillesum, an inspiring Dutch observer and victim of Nazi aggression and the Holocaust whose life stands as a testament to the resilience of the human spirit in Chapter 20. These and many other portraits—some of prominent persons but most describing quite ordinary people—provide a glimpse into individual lives often obscured in the larger patterns of world history.

Promoting Active Learning

As all instructors know, students can often "do the assignment" or read the required chapter and yet have nearly no understanding of it when they come to class. The problem, frequently, is passive studying—a quick once-over, perhaps some highlighting of the text—but little sustained involvement with the material. A central pedagogical problem in all teaching is how to encourage more active, engaged styles of learning. We want to enable students to manipulate the information of the book, using its ideas and data to answer questions, to make comparisons, to draw conclusions, to criticize assumptions, and to infer implications that are not explicitly disclosed in the text itself.

Ways of the World seeks to promote active learning in at least four major ways. First, the book includes access to **LearningCurve**, online adaptive quizzing that promotes engaged reading and focused review. Cross-references at the end of every major section and chapter in the text prompt students to log in and rehearse their understanding of the material they have just read. Students move at their own pace and accumulate points as they go, giving the interaction a game-like feel. Feedback for incorrect responses explains why the answer is incorrect and directs students back to the text to review before they attempt to answer the question again. The end result is a better understanding of the key elements of the text.

A second active learning element involves motivation. A **contemporary vignette** opens each chapter with a story that links the past and the present to show the continuing resonance of the past in the lives of contemporary people. Chapter 6, for example, begins by describing the inauguration in 2010 of Bolivian President Evo Morales at an impressive ceremony at Tiwanaku, the center of an ancient Andean empire and emphasizing the continuing importance of this ancient civilization in Bolivian culture. At the end of each chapter, a short **Reflections** section raises provocative, sometimes quasi-philosophical, questions about the craft of the historian and the unfolding of the human story. Hopefully, these brief essays provide an incentive for our students' own pondering and grist for the mill of vigorous class discussions.

A third technique for encouraging active learning lies in the provision of frequent contextual markers. Student readers need to know where they are going and where they have been. Thus part-opening **Big Picture essays** preview what follows in the subsequent chapters. A **chapter outline** opens each chapter, while a **NEW Map of Time** provides a chronological overview of major events and processes. In addition, a **NEW Seeking the Main Point** question helps students focus on the main theme of the chapter. Each chapter also has at least one **NEW Summing Up So Far** question that invites students to reflect on what they have learned to that point in the chapter. **Snapshots** appear in every chapter and present succinct glimpses of particular themes, regions, or time periods, adding some trees to the forest of world history. A **list of terms** at the end of each chapter invites students to check their grasp of the material. As usual with books published by Bedford/St. Martin's, a **rich illustration program** enhances the narrative. And over 100 **maps**, many enriched or redrawn for this edition, provide beautifully rendered spatial context for the unfolding of history.

Finally, active learning means approaching the text with something to look for, rather than simply dutifully completing the assignment. *Ways of the World* provides such cues in abundance. A series of **questions in the margins**, labeled "change," "comparison," or "connection," allows students to read the adjacent material with a clear purpose in mind. **Big Picture Questions** at the end of each chapter deal with matters not directly addressed in the text. Instead, they provide opportunities for integration, comparison, analysis, and sometimes speculation.

"It Takes a Village"

In any enterprise of significance "it takes a village," as they say. Bringing *Ways of the World* to life, it seems, has occupied the energies of several villages. Among the privileges and delights of writing and revising this book has been the opportunity to interact with my fellow villagers.

The largest of these communities consists of the people who read the first edition of the book and commented on it. I continue to be surprised at the power of this kind of collaboration, frequently finding that passages I had regarded as polished to a gleaming perfection benefited greatly from the collective wisdom and experience of these thoughtful reviewers. Many of them were commissioned by Bedford/St. Martin's and are listed here in alphabetical order, with my great thanks: Maria S. Arbelaez, University of Nebraska-Omaha; Veronica L. Bale, Mira Costa College; Christopher Bellitto, Kean University; Monica Bord-Lamberty, Northwood High School; Ralph Croizier, University of Victoria; Edward Dandrow, University of Central Florida; Peter L. de Rosa, Bridgewater State University; Amy Forss, Metropolitan Community College; Denis Gainty, Georgia State University; Steven A. Glazer, Graceland University; Sue Gronewald, Kean University; Andrew Hamilton, Viterbo University; J. Laurence Hare, University of Arkansas; Michael Hinckley, Northern Kentucky University; Bram Hubbell, Friends Seminary; Ronald Huch, Eastern Kentucky University; Elizabeth Hyde, Kean University; Mark Lentz, University of Louisiana-Lafayette; Kate McGrath, Central Connecticut State University; C. Brid Nicholson, Kean University; Donna Patch, Westside High School; Jonathan T. Reynolds, Northern Kentucky University; James Sabathne, Hononegah High School; Christopher Sleeper, Mira Costa College; Ira Spar, Ramapo College and Metropolitan Museum of Art; Kristen Strobel, Lexington High School; Michael Vann, Sacramento State University; Peter Winn, Tufts University; and Judith Zinsser, Miami University of Ohio.

A special note of thanks to Eric Nelson of Missouri State University who has offered no end of useful suggestions while preparing the wonderful *Instructor's Resource Manual*. Eric also provided content for the LearningCurve adaptive quizzes and for new special features in the *x-Book for Ways of the World*. I also extend a special thanks to Stanley Burstein, emeritus at California State University-Los Angeles who has been my wonderfully helpful mentor on all matters ancient. Contributors to the supplements also include Phyllis G. Jestice, University of Southern Mississippi; Lisa Tran, California State University-Fullerton; and Michael Vann, Sacramento State University.

The "Bedford village" has been a second community sustaining this enterprise and the one most directly responsible for the book's second edition. It would be difficult for any author to imagine a more supportive and professional publishing team. My chief point of contact with the Bedford village has been Kathryn Abbott, the development editor who also guided much of the first edition. As an experienced professor of history herself, she has masterfully summarized and analyzed numerous reviews of the manuscript and has read and reread every word, perused every map, and examined every image with great care, offering both reassurance and useful criticism. She has brought to this delicate task the sensitivity of a fine historian, the skills of an outstanding editor, and a much appreciated understanding of the author's sensibilities. Photo researcher Carole Frohlich identified and acquired the many images that grace *Ways of the World* and did so with efficiency and courtesy.

Others on the team have also exhibited that lovely combination of personal kindness and professional competence that is so characteristic of the Bedford way. Company president Denise Wydra, co-president of Macmillan Higher Education Joan

Feinberg, and publisher Mary Dougherty have all kept an eye on the project amid many duties. More immediately responsible for the second edition was Traci Crowell, executive editor for history, and Jane Knetzger, director of development, who provided overall guidance as well as the necessary resources. Operating more behind the scenes in the Bedford village, a series of highly competent and always supportive people have shepherded this revised edition along its way. Associate editor Robin Soule and editorial assistant Emily DiPietro provided invaluable assistance in handling the manuscript, contacting reviewers, and keeping on top of the endless details that such an enterprise demands. Bridget Leahy has again served as production editor during the book's production and, again, did so with both grace and efficiency. Copy editor Lisa Wehrle polished the prose and sorted out my inconsistent usages with a seasoned and perceptive eye. Jenna Bookin Barry and Katherine Bates have overseen the marketing process, while Bedford's history specialists John Hunger and Sean Blest and a cadre of humanities specialists and sales representatives have reintroduced the book to the academic world. Jack Cashman supervised the development of ancillary materials to support the book, and Donna Dennison ably coordinated research for the lovely covers that mark *Ways of the World*.

Yet another "village" that contributed much to *Ways of the World* consists in that group of distinguished scholars and teachers who worked with me on an earlier world history text, *The Making of the Modern World*, published by St. Martin's Press (1988, 1995). They include Sandria Freitag, Edwin Hirschmann, Donald Holsinger, James Horn, Robert Marks, Joe Moore, Lynn Parsons, and Robert Smith. That collective effort resembled participation in an extended seminar, from which I benefitted immensely. Their ideas and insights have shaped my own understanding of world history in many ways and greatly enriched *Ways of the World*.

A final and much smaller community sustained this project and its author. It is that most intimate of villages that we know as a marriage. Sharing that village with me is my wife, Suzanne Sturn. It is her work to bring ideas and people to life on stage, even as I try to do between these covers. She knows how I feel about her love and support, and no one else needs to.

To all of my fellow villagers, I offer deep thanks for an immensely rewarding experience. I am grateful beyond measure.

Robert Strayer
La Selva Beach, CA
Summer 2012

Versions and Supplements

Adopters of *Ways of the World* and their students have access to abundant resources, including documents, presentation and testing materials, volumes in the acclaimed Bedford Series in History and Culture, and much more.

To Learn More

For more information on the offerings described below, visit the book's catalog site at bedfordstmartins.com/strayer/catalog, or contact your local Bedford/St. Martin's sales representative.

Get the Right Version for Your Class

To accommodate different course lengths and course budgets, *Ways of the World* is available in several different formats, including three-hole punched loose-leaf Budget books versions and e-books, which are available at a substantial discount.

- Combined edition (Chapters 1–23) — available in paperback, loose-leaf, and e-book formats
- Volume 1: Through the Fifteenth Century (Chapters 1–12) — available in paperback, loose-leaf, and e-book formats
- Volume 2: Since the Fifteenth Century (Chapters 12–23) — available in paperback, loose-leaf, and e-book formats

NEW Assign the online, interactive Bedford x-Book. With all the content of the print book — plus integrated LearningCurve, structured reading exercises, chapter video previews, and extra primary sources — the *x-Book for Ways of the World* goes well beyond the print book in both content and pedagogy. Bob Strayer narrates the short video chapter previews, and in collaboration with Eric Nelson at Southwest Missouri State, offers a structured reading exercise for each chapter based on the book's chapter-opening "Seeking the Main Point" focus question. Designed to help students read actively for key concepts and major developments, the exercise provides a tailored note-taking structure that allows them to associate relevant details and evidence with the chapter's main points as they go along. At the end of the chapter, students are prompted to answer the question in essay form. The x-Book also lets students easily search, highlight, and bookmark. Instructors can easily assign and add pages, hide and rearrange chapters, and link to quizzes and activities.

Let students choose their e-book format. Students can purchase the download-able *Bedford e-Book to Go for Ways of the World* from our Web site or find other PDF versions of the e-book at our publishing partners' sites: CourseSmart, Barnes & Noble NookStudy, Kno, CafeScribe, or Chegg.

NEW Assign LearningCurve So Your Students Come to Class Prepared

As described in the Preface and on the inside front cover, students purchasing new books receive access to LearningCurve for *Ways of the World*, an online learning tool designed to help students rehearse content at their own pace in a non-threatening, game-like environment. The feedback for wrong answers provides instructional coach-ing and sends students back to the book for review. Students answer as many ques-tions as necessary to reach a target score, with repeated chances to revisit material they haven't mastered. Assigning LearningCurve is easy for instructors, and the report-ing features help instructors track overall class trends and spot topics that are giving students trouble. Like the book it serves, LearningCurve for *Ways of the World* empha-sizes major concepts, comparisons, and big-picture developments.

Send Students to Free Online Resources

The book's companion site at bedfordstmartins.com/strayer gives students a way to read, write, and study by providing plentiful quizzes and activities, study aids, and his-tory research and writing help.

FREE Online Study Guide. Available at the companion site, this popular resource provides students with quizzes and activities for each chapter, including multiple-choice self-tests that focus on important concepts; flashcards that test students' knowl-edge of key terms; timeline activities that emphasize causal relationships; and map quizzes intended to strengthen students' geography skills. Instructors can monitor students' progress through an online Quiz Gradebook or receive email updates.

FREE Research, Writing, and Anti-plagiarism Advice. Available at the com-panion site, Bedford's **History Research and Writing Help** includes **History Re-search and Reference Sources**, with links to history-related databases, indexes, and journals; **More Sources and How to Format a History Paper**, with clear advice on how to integrate primary and secondary sources into research papers and how to cite and format sources correctly; **Build a Bibliography**, a simple Web-based tool known as The Bedford Bibliographer that generates bibliographies in four commonly used documentation styles; and **Tips on Avoiding Plagiarism**, an online tutorial that reviews the consequences of plagiarism and features exercises to help students practice integrating sources and recognize acceptable summaries.

Take Advantage of Instructor Resources

Bedford/St. Martin's has developed a rich array of teaching resources for this book and for this course. They range from lecture and presentation materials and assessment tools to course management options. Most can be downloaded or ordered at bedfordstmartins.com/strayer/catalog.

NEW *HistoryClass for Ways of the World.* HistoryClass, a Bedford/St. Martin's Online Course Space, puts the online resources available with this textbook in one convenient and completely customizable course space. There you and your students can access the interactive x-Book; maps, images, documents, and links; chapter review quizzes; and research and writing help. In HistoryClass you can get all our premium content and tools, which you can assign, rearrange, and mix with your own resources. HistoryClass also includes LearningCurve, Bedford/St. Martin's adaptive online learning tool. For more information, visit yourhistoryclass.com.

Bedford Coursepack for Blackboard, Canvas, Desire2Learn, Angel, Sakai, or Moodle. We have free content to help you integrate our rich materials into your course management system. Registered instructors can download coursepacks easily and with no strings attached. The coursepack for *Ways of the World* includes book-specific content as well as our most popular free resources. Visit bedfordstmartins.com/coursepacks to see a demo, find your version, or download your coursepack.

Instructor's Resource Manual. The instructor's manual offers both experienced and first-time instructors tools for preparing lectures and running discussions. It includes chapter-review material, teaching strategies, and a guide to chapter-specific supplements available for the text, plus suggestions on how to get the most out of LearningCurve.

Guide to Changing Editions. Designed to facilitate an instructor's transition from the previous edition of *Ways of the World* to the current edition, this guide presents an overview of major changes as well as changes in each chapter.

Computerized Test Bank. The test bank includes a mix of fresh, carefully crafted multiple-choice, short-answer, and essay questions for each chapter. It also contains the Big Picture, Seeking the Main Point, Margin Review, Portrait, document and visual source headnotes, and Using the Evidence questions from the textbook and model answers for each. Finally, each chapter includes a section of multiple-choice questions focused exclusively on the chapter's documents and visual sources. All questions appear in Microsoft Word format and in easy-to-use test bank software that allows instructors to add, edit, re-sequence, and print questions and answers. Instructors can also export questions into a variety of formats, including WebCT and Blackboard.

NEW *The Bedford Lecture Kit:* **PowerPoint Maps, Images, Lecture Outlines, and i>clicker Content.** Look good and save time with *The Bedford Lecture Kit.* These presentation materials are downloadable individually from the Instructor Resources tab at bedfordstmartins.com/strayer/catalog and are available on *The Bedford Lecture Kit* **Instructor's Resource CD-ROM.** They provide ready-made and fully customizable PowerPoint multimedia presentations that include lecture outlines with embedded maps, figures, and selected images from the textbook and extra background for instructors. Also available are maps and selected images in JPEG and PowerPoint formats; content for i>clicker, a classroom response system, in Microsoft Word and PowerPoint formats; the Instructor's Resource Manual in Microsoft Word format; and outline maps in PDF format for quizzing or handing out. All files are suitable for copying onto transparency acetates.

Make History — **Free Documents, Maps, Images, and Web Sites.** *Make History* combines the best Web resources with hundreds of maps and images, to make it simple to find the source material you need. Browse the collection of thousands of resources by course or by topic, date, and type. Each item has been carefully chosen and helpfully annotated to make it easy to find exactly what you need. Available at bedfordstmartins.com/makehistory.

Videos and Multimedia. A wide assortment of videos and multimedia CD-ROMs on various topics in world history is available to qualified adopters through your Bedford/St. Martin's sales representative.

Package and Save Your Students Money

For information on free packages and discounts up to 50%, visit bedfordstmartins.com/strayer/catalog or contact your local Bedford/St. Martin's sales representative.

Worlds of History: A Comparative Reader. Compiled by Kevin Reilly, a widely respected world historian and community college teacher, *Worlds of History* fosters historical thinking through thematic comparisons of primary and secondary sources from around the world. Each chapter takes up a major theme — such as patriarchy, love and marriage, or globalization — as experienced by two or more cultures. "Thinking Historically" exercises build students' capacity to analyze and interpret sources one skill at a time. This flexible framework accommodates a variety of approaches to teaching world history. Package discounts are available.

The Bedford Series in History and Culture. More than one hundred fifty titles in this highly praised series combine first-rate scholarship, historical narrative, and important primary documents for undergraduate courses. Each book is brief, inexpensive, and focused on a specific topic or period. For a complete list of titles, visit bedfordstmartins.com/history/series. Package discounts are available.

Rand McNally Historical Atlas of the World. This collection of more than seventy full-color maps illustrates the eras and civilizations of world history from the emergence of human societies to the present. Available for $3.00 when packaged with the print text.

The Bedford Glossary for World History. This handy supplement for the survey course gives students historically contextualized definitions for hundreds of terms—from *abolitionism* to *Zoroastrianism*—that they will encounter in lectures, reading, and exams. Available free when packaged with the print text.

World History Matters: A Student Guide to World History Online. Based on the popular "World History Matters" Web site produced by the Center for History and New Media, this unique resource, edited by Kristin Lehner (The Johns Hopkins University), Kelly Schrum (George Mason University), and T. Mills Kelly (George Mason University), combines reviews of 150 of the most useful and reliable world history Web sites with an introduction that guides students in locating, evaluating, and correctly citing online sources. Available free when packaged with the print text.

Trade Books. Titles published by sister companies Hill and Wang; Farrar, Straus and Giroux; Henry Holt and Company; St. Martin's Press; Picador; and Palgrave Macmillan are available at a 50% discount when packaged with Bedford/St. Martin's textbooks. For more information, visit bedfordstmartins.com/tradeup.

A Pocket Guide to Writing in History. This portable and affordable reference tool by Mary Lynn Rampolla, now also available as a searchable e-book, provides reading, writing, and research advice useful to students in all history courses. Concise yet comprehensive advice on approaching typical history assignments, developing critical reading skills, writing effective history papers, conducting research, using and documenting sources, and avoiding plagiarism—enhanced with practical tips and examples throughout—have made this slim reference a best-seller. Package discounts are available.

A Student's Guide to History. This complete guide to success in any history course provides the practical help students need to be effective. In addition to introducing students to the nature of the discipline, author Jules Benjamin teaches a wide range of skills from preparing for exams to approaching common writing assignments, and he explains the research and documentation process with plentiful examples. Package discounts are available.

Brief Contents

Preface   v

Prologue: From Cosmic History to Human History   xxxii

PART ONE   First Things First: Beginnings in History,
to 500 B.C.E.   2

     THE BIG PICTURE Turning Points in Early World History   3

1. First Peoples; First Farmers: Most of History in a Single Chapter,
To 4000 B.C.E.   11

2. First Civilizations: Cities, States, and Unequal Societies,
3500 B.C.E.–500 B.C.E.   47

PART TWO   Second-Wave Civilizations in World
History, 500 B.C.E.–500 C.E.   78

     THE BIG PICTURE After the First Civilizations: What Changed and
What Didn't?   79

3. State and Empire in Eurasia/North Africa, 500 B.C.E.–500 C.E.   87

4. Culture and Religion in Eurasia/North Africa, 500 B.C.E.–500 C.E.   117

5. Society and Inequality in Eurasia/North Africa, 500 B.C.E.–500 C.E.   151

6. Commonalities and Variations: Africa and the Americas,
500 B.C.E.–1200 C.E.   179

PART THREE   An Age of Accelerating Connections,
500–1500   210

     THE BIG PICTURE Defining a Millennium   211

7. Commerce and Culture, 500–1500   219

8. China and the World: East Asian Connections, 500–1300   249

9. The Worlds of Islam: Afro-Eurasian Connections, 600–1500   281

10. The Worlds of Christendom: Contraction, Expansion,
and Division, 500–1300   315

11. Pastoral Peoples on the Global Stage: The Mongol Moment,
1200–1500   353

12. The Worlds of the Fifteenth Century   383

Notes   417
Index   429

Contents

Preface   v

Versions and Supplements   xiii

Maps   xxix

Features   xxxi

Prologue: From Cosmic History to Human History   xxxii

The History of the Universe • The History of a Planet • The History
of the Human Species . . . in a Single Paragraph • Why World
History? • Change, Comparison, and Connection: The Three Cs
of World History

Snapshot: A History of the Universe as a Cosmic Calendar   xxxiii

PART ONE   First Things First: Beginnings in History, to 500 B.C.E.   2

THE BIG PICTURE   Turning Points in Early World History   3

The Emergence of Humankind • The Globalization of Humankind
• The Revolution of Farming and Herding • The Turning Point of
Civilization • A Note on Dates

Mapping Part One   8

1.   First Peoples; First Farmers: Most of History in a Single Chapter, To 4000 B.C.E.   11

Out of Africa to the Ends of the Earth: First Migrations   12
Into Eurasia • Into Australia • Into the Americas • Into the Pacific

The Ways We Were   20
*The First Human Societies • Economy and the Environment • The Realm
of the Spirit • Settling Down: The Great Transition*

Breakthroughs to Agriculture   26
Common Patterns • Variations

The Globalization of Agriculture   34
Triumph and Resistance • The Culture of Agriculture

Social Variation in the Age of Agriculture   39
Pastoral Societies • Agricultural Village Societies • Chiefdoms

Reflections: The Uses of the Paleolithic   43

Second Thoughts   44

 What's the Significance? • *Big Picture Questions* • *Next Steps: For
 Further Study*

Snapshot: Paleolithic Era in Perspective   24

Portrait: Ishi, The Last of His People   36

✔ LearningCurve **bedfordstmartins.com/strayer/LC**

2. **First Civilizations: Cities, States, and Unequal
    Societies, 3500 B.C.E.–500 B.C.E.**   47

Something New: The Emergence of Civilizations   48

 Introducing the First Civilizations • *The Question of Origins* • *An Urban
 Revolution*

The Erosion of Equality   57

 Hierarchies of Class • *Hierarchies of Gender* • *Patriarchy in Practice*

The Rise of the State   61

 Coercion and Consent • *Writing and Accounting* • *The Grandeur of Kings*

Comparing Mesopotamia and Egypt   66

 Environment and Culture • *Cities and States* • *Interaction and Exchange*

Reflections: "Civilization": What's in a Word?   75

Second Thoughts   76

 What's the Significance? • *Big Picture Questions* • *Next Steps: For
 Further Study*

Snapshot: Writing in Ancient Civilizations   65

Portrait: Paneb, An Egyptian Criminal   70

✔ LearningCurve **bedfordstmartins.com/strayer/LC**

PART TWO   Second Wave Civilizations in
World History, 500 B.C.E.–500 C.E.   78

THE BIG PICTURE   After the First Civilizations: What Changed and
What Didn't?   79

Continuities in Civilization • Changes in Civilization

Snapshot: World Population during the Age of Agricultural Civilization   81

Mapping Part Two   84

3. State and Empire in Eurasia/North Africa, 500 B.C.E.–500 C.E.   87

Empires and Civilizations in Collision: The Persians and the Greeks   89
The Persian Empire • The Greeks • Collision: The Greco-Persian Wars • Collision: Alexander and the Hellenistic Era

Comparing Empires: Roman and Chinese   99
Rome: From City-State to Empire • China: From Warring States to Empire • Consolidating the Roman and Chinese Empires • The Collapse of Empires

Intermittent Empire: The Case of India   111
Reflections: Enduring Legacies of Second-Wave Empires   113
Second Thoughts   114
What's the Significance? • Big Picture Questions • Next Steps: For Further Study

Snapshot: Distinctive Features of Second-Wave Eurasian Civilizations   90
Portrait: Trung Trac: Resisting the Chinese Empire   104

✓ LearningCurve   **bedfordstmartins.com/strayer/LC**

4. Culture and Religion in Eurasia/North Africa, 500 B.C.E.–500 C.E.   117

China and the Search for Order   119
The Legalist Answer • The Confucian Answer • The Daoist Answer

Cultural Traditions of Classical India   126
South Asian Religion: From Ritual Sacrifice to Philosophical Speculation • The Buddhist Challenge • Hinduism as a Religion of Duty and Devotion

Toward Monotheism: The Search for God in the Middle East   132
Zoroastrianism • Judaism

The Cultural Tradition of Classical Greece: The Search for a Rational Order   135
The Greek Way of Knowing • The Greek Legacy

The Birth of Christianity . . . with Buddhist Comparisons   139
The Lives of the Founders • The Spread of New Religions • Institutions, Controversies, and Divisions

Reflections: Religion and Historians   147
Second Thoughts   148
What's the Significance? • Big Picture Questions • Next Steps: For Further Study

Snapshot: Thinkers and Philosophies of the Second-Wave Era   120
Portrait: Perpetua, Christian Martyr   144

✓ LearningCurve   **bedfordstmartins.com/strayer/LC**

5.   Society and Inequality in Eurasia/North Africa, 500 B.C.E.–500 C.E   151

Society and the State in China   152
   An Elite of Officials • The Landlord Class • Peasants • Merchants
Class and Caste in India   158
   Caste as Varna • Caste as Jati • The Functions of Caste
Slavery: The Case of the Roman Empire   163
   Slavery and Civilization • The Making of Roman Slavery • Resistance and Rebellion
Comparing Patriarchies   167
   A Changing Patriarchy: The Case of China • Contrasting Patriarchies: Athens and Sparta
Reflections: Arguing with Solomon and the Buddha   174
Second Thoughts   175
   What's the Significance? • Big Picture Questions • Next Steps: For Further Study
Snapshot: Social Life and Duty in Classical India   160
Portrait: Ge Hong, A Chinese Scholar in Troubled Times   156

✓ LearningCurve   **bedfordstmartins.com/strayer/LC**

6.   Commonalities and Variations: Africa and the Americas, 500 B.C.E.–1200 C.E.   179

Continental Comparisons   180
Civilizations of Africa   183
   Meroë: Continuing a Nile Valley Civilization • Axum: The Making of a Christian Kingdom • Along the Niger River: Cities without States
Civilizations of Mesoamerica   190
   The Maya: Writing and Warfare • Teotihuacán: The Americas' Greatest City
Civilizations of the Andes   195
   Chavín: A Pan-Andean Religious Movement • Moche: A Civilization of the Coast • Wari and Tiwanaku: Empires of the Interior
Alternatives to Civilization: Bantu Africa   200
   Cultural Encounters • Society and Religion
Alternatives to Civilization: North America   203
   The Ancestral Pueblo: Pit Houses and Great Houses • Peoples of the Eastern Woodlands: The Mound Builders
Reflections: Deciding What's Important: Balance in World History   207
Second Thoughts   208
   What's the Significance? • Big Picture Questions • Next Steps: For Further Study

Snapshot: Continental Population in the Second-Wave Era   182

Portrait: Piye, Kushite Conqueror of Egypt   186

✓ LearningCurve bedfordstmartins.com/strayer/LC

PART THREE   An Age of Accelerating Connections, 500–1500

210

THE BIG PICTURE Defining a Millennium   211

Third-Wave Civilizations: Something New, Something Old, Something
    Blended • The Ties That Bind: Transregional Interaction in the
    Third-Wave Era

Mapping Part Three   216

7.   Commerce and Culture, 500–1500

219

Silk Roads: Exchange across Eurasia   222
    *The Growth of the Silk Roads • Goods in Transit • Cultures in Transit
    • Disease in Transit*

Sea Roads: Exchange across the Indian Ocean   228
    *Weaving the Web of an Indian Ocean World • Sea Roads as a Catalyst for
    Change: Southeast Asia • Sea Roads as a Catalyst for Change: East Africa*

Sand Roads: Exchange across the Sahara   238
    *Commercial Beginnings in West Africa • Gold, Salt, and Slaves: Trade and
    Empire in West Africa*

An American Network: Commerce and Connection in the
    Western Hemisphere   241

Reflections: Economic Globalization—Ancient and Modern   245

Second Thoughts   246
    *What's the Significance? • Big Picture Questions • Next Steps: For
    Further Study*

Snapshot: Economic Exchange along the Silk Roads   224

Snapshot: Economic Exchange in the Indian Ocean Basin   231

Portrait: Thorfinn Karlsfeni, Viking Voyager   242

✓ LearningCurve bedfordstmartins.com/strayer/LC

8.   China and the World: East Asian Connections, 500–1300

249

Together Again: The Reemergence of a Unified China   250
    A "Golden Age" of Chinese Achievement • Women in the Song Dynasty

China and the Northern Nomads: A Chinese World Order in the Making   257
The Tribute System in Theory • The Tribute System in Practice • Cultural Influence across an Ecological Frontier

Coping with China: Comparing Korea, Vietnam, and Japan   261
Korea and China • Vietnam and China • Japan and China

China and the Eurasian World Economy   268
Spillovers: China's Impact on Eurasia • On the Receiving End: China as Economic Beneficiary

China and Buddhism   272
Making Buddhism Chinese • Losing State Support: The Crisis of Chinese Buddhism

Reflections: Why Do Things Change?   276
Second Thoughts   277
What's the Significance? • Big Picture Questions • Next Steps: For Further Study

Snapshot: Chinese Technological Achievements   270
Portrait: Izumi Shikibu, Japanese Poet and Lover   268

✓ LearningCurve   **bedfordstmartins.com/strayer/LC**

9.   The Worlds of Islam: Afro–Eurasian Connections, 600–1500

281

The Birth of a New Religion   282
The Homeland of Islam • The Messenger and the Message • The Transformation of Arabia

The Making of an Arab Empire   288
War, Conquest, and Tolerance • Conversion • Divisions and Controversies • Women and Men in Early Islam

Islam and Cultural Encounter: A Four-Way Comparison   298
The Case of India • The Case of Anatolia • The Case of West Africa • The Case of Spain

The World of Islam as a New Civilization   306
Networks of Faith • Networks of Exchange

Reflections: Past and Present: Choosing Our History   311
Second Thoughts   312
What's the Significance? • Big Picture Questions • Next Steps: For Further Study

Snapshot: Key Achievements in Islamic Science and Scholarship   310
Portrait: Mansa Musa, West African Monarch and Muslim Pilgrim   304

✓ LearningCurve   **bedfordstmartins.com/strayer/LC**

10. The Worlds of Christendom: Contraction, Expansion, and Division, 500–1300   315

Christian Contraction in Asia and Africa   317
Asian Christianity • African Christianity

Byzantine Christendom: Building on the Roman Past   321
The Byzantine State • The Byzantine Church and Christian Divergence • Byzantium and the World • The Conversion of Russia

Western Christendom: Rebuilding in the Wake of Roman Collapse   328
Political Life in Western Europe • Society and the Church • Accelerating Change in the West • Europe Outward Bound: The Crusading Tradition

The West in Comparative Perspective   340
Catching Up • Pluralism in Politics • Reason and Faith

Reflections: Remembering and Forgetting: Continuity and Surprise in the Worlds of Christendom   348

Second Thoughts   349
What's the Significance? • Big Picture Questions • Next Steps: For Further Study

Snapshot: European Borrowing   342

Portrait: Cecilia Penifader, An English Peasant and Unmarried Woman   336

☑ LearningCurve bedfordstmartins.com/strayer/LC

11. Pastoral Peoples on the Global Stage: The Mongol Moment, 1200–1500   353

Looking Back and Looking Around: The Long History of Pastoral Nomads   354
The World of Pastoral Societies • Before the Mongols: Pastoralists in History

Breakout: The Mongol Empire   361
From Temujin to Chinggis Khan: The Rise of the Mongol Empire • Explaining the Mongol Moment

Encountering the Mongols: Comparing Three Cases   367
China and the Mongols • Persia and the Mongols • Russia and the Mongols

The Mongol Empire as a Eurasian Network   374
Toward a World Economy • Diplomacy on a Eurasian Scale • Cultural Exchange in the Mongol Realm • The Plague: An Afro-Eurasian Pandemic

Reflections: Changing Images of Pastoral Peoples   379

Second Thoughts   380
What's the Significance? • Big Picture Questions • Next Steps: For Further Study

Snapshot: Varieties of Pastoral Societies   356

Portrait: Khutulun, A Mongol Wrestler Princess   370

☑ LearningCurve bedfordstmartins.com/strayer/LC

12. The Worlds of the Fifteenth Century   383

The Shapes of Human Communities   384
*Paleolithic Persistence: Australia and North America • Agricultural Village
Societies: The Igbo and the Iroquois • Pastoral Peoples: Central Asia and
West Africa*

Civilizations of the Fifteenth Century: Comparing China and Europe   390
*Ming Dynasty China • European Comparisons: State Building and Cultural
Renewal • European Comparisons: Maritime Voyaging*

Civilizations of the Fifteenth Century: The Islamic World   400
*In the Islamic Heartland: The Ottoman and Safavid Empires • On the
Frontiers of Islam: The Songhay and Mughal Empires*

Civilizations of the Fifteenth Century: The Americas   404
The Aztec Empire • The Inca Empire

Webs of Connection   410
A Preview of Coming Attractions: Looking Ahead to the Modern Era,
 1500–2012   412
Reflections: What If? Chance and Contingency in World History   415
Second Thoughts   416
*What's the Significance? • Big Picture Questions • Next Steps: For
Further Study*

Snapshot: Major Developments around the World in the Fifteenth Century   386
Snapshot: World Population Growth, 1000–2000   414
Portrait: Zheng He, China's Non-Chinese Admiral   396

 ✓ LearningCurve **bedfordstmartins.com/strayer/LC**

Notes   417
Acknowledgments   427
Index   429
About the Author   last book page

Maps

Big Picture Maps

Mapping Part One   8
Mapping Part Two   84
Mapping Part Three   216

Chapter Maps

MAP 1.1   The Global Dispersion of Humankind   16
MAP 1.2   Migration of Austronesian-Speaking People   19
MAP 1.3   The Global Spread of Agriculture and Pastoralism   28
MAP 1.4   The Fertile Crescent   31
SPOT MAP   Bantu Migrations   35

MAP 2.1   First Civilizations   50
MAP 2.2   Mesopotamia   67
MAP 2.3   An Egyptian Empire   74

MAP 3.1   The Persian Empire   91
MAP 3.2   Classical Greece   93
MAP 3.3   Alexander's Empire and Successor States   97
MAP 3.4   The Roman Empire   101
MAP 3.5   Classical China   105
MAP 3.6   Empire in South Asia   112

SPOT MAP   Ancient Israel   134
MAP 4.1   The Spread of Early Christianity and Buddhism   143

SPOT MAP   Yellow Turban Rebellion   158
SPOT MAP   The Rebellion of Spartacus   167

MAP 6.1   Africa in the Second-Wave Era   184
MAP 6.2   Civilizations of Mesoamerica   191
MAP 6.3   Civilizations of the Andes   196
MAP 6.4   North America in the Second-Wave Era   204

MAP 7.1   The Silk Roads   223
MAP 7.2   The Sea Roads   229

MAP 7.3   Southeast Asia, ca. 1200 C.E.   233
SPOT MAP   The Swahili Coast of East Africa   237
MAP 7.4   The Sand Roads   240
MAP 7.5   The American Web   244

MAP 8.1   Tang and Song Dynasty China   252
MAP 8.2   Korean Kingdoms about 500 C.E.   262
MAP 8.3   Vietnam   263
MAP 8.4   Japan   265
MAP 8.5   The World of Asian Buddhism   273

MAP 9.1   Arabia at the Time of Muhammad   284
MAP 9.2   The Arab Empire and the Initial Expansion of Islam, 622–900 C.E.   290
MAP 9.3   The Growing World of Islam, 900–1500   299
MAP 9.4   The Sultanate of Delhi   300
MAP 9.5   The Ottoman Empire by the Mid-fifteenth Century   301
MAP 9.6   West Africa and the World of Islam   302

MAP 10.1   The Byzantine Empire   323
MAP 10.2   Western Europe in the Ninth Century   330
MAP 10.3   Europe in the High Middle Ages   333
MAP 10.4   The Crusades   339

SPOT MAP   The Xiongnu Confederacy   358
SPOT MAP   The Almoravid Empire   361
MAP 11.1   The Mongol Empire   362
MAP 11.2   Trade and Disease in the Fourteenth Century   375

MAP 12.1   Asia in the Fifteenth Century   391
MAP 12.2   Europe in 1500   394
MAP 12.3   Africa in the Fifteenth Century   398
MAP 12.4   Empires of the Islamic World   401
MAP 12.5   The Americas in the Fifteenth Century   405
MAP 12.6   Religion and Commerce in the Afro-Eurasian World   412

Features

Portraits

Ishi, The Last of His People   36
Paneb, An Egyptian Criminal   70
Trung Trac: Resisting the Chinese Empire   104
Perpetua, Christian Martyr   144
Ge Hong, A Chinese Scholar in Troubled Times   156
Piye, Kushite Conqueror of Egypt   186
Thorfinn Karlsfeni, Viking Voyager   242
Izumi Shikibu, Japanese Poet and Lover   268
Mansa Musa, West African Monarch and Muslim Pilgrim   304
Cecilia Penifader, An English Peasant and Unmarried Woman   336
Khutulun, A Mongol Wrestler Princess   370
Zheng He, China's Non-Chinese Admiral   396

Snapshots

The History of the Universe as a Cosmic Calendar   00
Paleolithic Era in Perspective   24
Writing in Ancient Civilizations   65
World Population during the Age of Agricultural Civilization   81
Distinctive Features of Second-Wave Eurasian Civilizations   90
Thinkers and Philosophies of the Second-Wave Era   120
Social Life and Duty in Classical India   160
Continental Population in the Second-Wave Era   182
Economic Exchange along the Silk Roads   224
Economic Exchange in the Indian Ocean Basin   231
Chinese Technological Achievements   270
Key Achievements in Islamic Science and Scholarship   310
European Borrowing   342
Varieties of Pastoral Societies   356
Major Developments around the World in the Fifteenth Century   386
World Population Growth, 1000–2000   414

Prologue

From Cosmic History to Human History

HISTORY BOOKS IN GENERAL, AND WORLD HISTORY TEXTBOOKS IN PARTICULAR, share something in common with those Russian nested dolls in which a series of carved figures fit inside one another. In much the same fashion, all historical accounts take place within some larger context, as stories within stories unfold. Individual biographies and histories of local communities, particularly modern ones, occur within the context of one nation or another. Nations often find a place in some more encompassing civilization, such as the Islamic world or the West, or in a regional or continental context such as Southeast Asia, Latin America, or Africa. And those civilizational or regional histories in turn take on richer meaning when they are understood within the even broader story of world history, which embraces humankind as a whole.

■ **Change**
What have been the major turning points in the pre-human phases of "big history"?

In recent decades, some world historians have begun to situate that remarkable story of the human journey in the much larger framework of both cosmic and planetary history, an approach which has come to be called "big history." It is really the "history of everything" from the big bang to the present, and it extends over the enormous, almost unimaginable time-scale of some 13.7 billion years, the current rough estimate of the age of the universe.[1]

The History of the Universe

To make this vast expanse of time even remotely comprehensible, some scholars have depicted the history of the cosmos as if it were a single calendar year (see the Snapshot). On that cosmic calendar, most of the action took place in the first few milliseconds of January 1. As astronomers, physicists, and chemists tell it, the universe that we know began in an eruption of inconceivable power and heat. Out of that explosion of creation emerged matter, energy, gravity, electromagnetism, and the "strong and "weak" forces that govern the behavior of atomic nuclei. As gravity pulled the rapidly expanding cosmic gases into increasingly dense masses, stars formed, with the first ones lighting up around 1 to 2 billion years after the big bang, or the end of January to mid-February on the cosmic calendar.

Hundreds of billions of stars followed, each with its own history, though following common patterns. They emerge, flourish for a time, and then collapse and die. In their final stages, they sometimes generate supernova, black holes, and pulsars—phenomena at least as fantastic as the most exotic of earlier creation stories. Within the stars, enormous nuclear reactions gave rise to the elements that are reflected in the periodic table known to all students of chemistry. Over eons, these stars came together

$\mathcal{S}$napshot   **The History of the Universe as a Cosmic Calendar[2]**

Big bang	January 1	13.7 billion years ago
Stars and galaxies begin to form	End of January/ mid-February	12 billion years ago
Milky Way galaxy forms	March/early April	10 billion years ago
Origin of the solar system	September 9	4.7 billion years ago
Formation of the earth	September 15	4.5 billion years ago
Earliest life on earth	Late September/ early October	4 billion years ago
Oxygen forms on earth	December 1	1.3 billion years ago
First worms	December 16	658 million years ago
First fish, first vertebrates	December 19	534 million years ago
First reptiles, first trees	December 23	370 million years ago
Age of dinosaurs	December 24–28	329–164 million years ago
First humanlike creatures	December 31 (late evening)	2.7 million years ago
First agriculture	December 31: 11:59:35	12,000 years ago
Birth of the Buddha/ Greek civilization	December 31: 11:59:55	2,500 years ago
Birth of Jesus	December 31: 11:59:56	2,000 years ago
Aztec and Inca empires	December 31: 11:59:59	500 years ago

in galaxies, such as our own Milky Way, which probably emerged in March or early April, and in even larger structures called groups, clusters, and superclusters. Adding to the strangeness of our picture of the cosmos is the recent and controversial notion that perhaps 90 percent or more of the total mass of the universe is invisible to us, consisting of a mysterious and mathematically predicted substance known to scholars only as "dark matter."

The contemplation of cosmic history has prompted profound religious or philosophical questions about the meaning of human life. For some, it has engendered a sense of great insignificance in the face of cosmic vastness. In disputing the earth- and human-centered view of the cosmos, long held by the Catholic Church, the eighteenth-century French thinker Voltaire wrote: "This little globe, nothing more than a point, rolls in space like so many other globes; we are lost in this immensity."[3]

Nonetheless, human consciousness and our awareness of the mystery of this immeasurable universe render us unique and generate for many people feelings of awe and humility that are almost religious. As tiny but knowing observers of this majestic cosmos, we have found ourselves living in a grander home than ever we knew before.

The History of a Planet

For most of us, one star, our own sun, is far more important than all the others, despite its quite ordinary standing among the billions of stars in the universe and its somewhat remote location on the outer edge of the Milky Way galaxy. Circling that star is a series of planets, formed of leftover materials from the sun's birth. One of those planets, the third from the sun and the fifth largest, is home to all of us. Human history — our history — takes place not only on the earth but also as part of the planet's history.

That history began with the emergence of the entire solar system about two-thirds of the way through cosmic history, some 4.7 billion years ago, or early September on the cosmic calendar. Geologists have learned a great deal about the history of the earth: the formation of its rocks and atmosphere; the movement of its continents; the collision of the tectonic plates that make up its crust; and the constant changes of its landscape as mountains formed, volcanoes erupted, and erosion transformed the surface of the planet. All of this has been happening for more than 4 billion years and continues still.

The most remarkable feature of the earth's history — and so far as we know unrepeated elsewhere — was the emergence of life from the chemical soup of the early planet. It happened rather quickly, only about 600 million years after the earth itself took shape, or late September on the cosmic calendar. Then for some 3 billion years, life remained at the level of microscopic single-celled organisms. According to biologists, the many species of larger multicelled creatures — all of the flowers, shrubs, and trees as well as all of the animals of land, sea, and air — have evolved in an explosive proliferation of life-forms, punctuated by massive die-offs as well, over the past 600 million years, or since mid-December on the cosmic calendar.

Each of these life forms or species has also had a history as its members struggled to find resources, cope with changing environments, and deal with competitors. The history of dinosaurs, for example, from their rise to their extinction, occupied about 165 million years, or about five days in late December on the cosmic calendar. Egocentric creatures that we are, however, human beings have usually focused their history books and history courses entirely on a single species — our own, *Homo sapiens*, humankind. On the cosmic calendar, *Homo sapiens* is an upstart primate whose entire history occurred in the last few minutes of December 31. Almost all of what we normally study in history courses — agriculture, writing, civilizations, empires, industrialization — took place in the very last minute of that cosmic year. The entire history of the United States occurred in the last second.

Yet during that very brief time, humankind has had a career more remarkable and arguably more consequential for the planet than any other species. At the heart of human uniqueness lies our amazing capacity for accumulating knowledge and skills. Other animals learn, of course, but for the most part they learn the same things over and over again. Twenty-first-century chimpanzees in the wild master the same skills as their ancestors did a million years ago. But the exceptional communication abilities provided by human language allow us to learn from one another, to express that learning in abstract symbols, and then to pass it on, cumulatively, to future generations. Thus we have moved from stone axes to lasers, from spears to nuclear weapons, from "talking drums" to the Internet, from grass huts to the pyramids of Egypt and Taj Mahal of India.

This extraordinary ability has translated into a human impact on the earth that is unprecedented among all living species.[4] Human populations have multiplied far more extensively and have come to occupy a far greater range of environments than has any other large animal. Through our ingenious technologies, we have appropriated for ourselves, according to recent calculations, some 25 to 40 percent of the solar energy that enters the food chain. We have recently gained access to the stored solar energy of coal, gas, and oil, all of which have been many millions of years in the making, and we have the capacity to deplete these resources in a few hundred or a few thousand years. Other forms of life have felt the impact of human activity, as numerous extinct or threatened species testify. Human beings have even affected the atmosphere itself as carbon dioxide and other emissions of the industrial age have warmed the climate of the planet. Thus human history has been, and remains, of great significance, not for ourselves alone, but also for the earth itself and for the many other living creatures with which we share it.

The History of the Human Species . . . in a Single Paragraph

The history of our species has occupied roughly the last 250,000 years, conventionally divided into three major phases, based on the kind of technology that was most widely practiced. The enormously long Paleolithic age, with its gathering and hunting way of life, accounts for 95 percent or more of the time that humans have occupied the planet. People utilizing a stone-age Paleolithic technology initially settled every major landmass on the earth and constructed the first human societies (see Chapter 1). Then beginning about 12,000 years ago with the first Agricultural Revolution, the domestication of plants and animals increasingly became the primary means of sustaining human life and societies. In giving rise to agricultural villages and chiefdoms, to pastoral communities depending on their herds of animals, and to state- and city-based civilizations, this agrarian way of life changed virtually everything and fundamentally reshaped human societies and their relationship to the natural order. Finally, around 1750 a quite sudden spurt in the rate of technological change, which we know as the Industrial Revolution, began to take hold. That vast increase in productivity, wealth, and human control over nature once again transformed almost every aspect of human life and gave rise to new kinds of societies that we call "modern."

Here then, in a single paragraph, is the history of humankind — the Paleolithic era, the agricultural era, and, most recently and briefly, the modern industrial era. Clearly this is a big picture perspective, based on the notion that the human species as a whole has a history that transcends any of its particular and distinctive cultures. That perspective — known variously as planetary, global, or world history — has become increasingly prominent among those who study the past. Why should this be so?

Why World History?

Not long ago — in the mid-twentieth century, for example — virtually all college-level history courses were organized in terms of particular civilizations or nations. In the United States, courses such as Western Civilization or some version of American History served to introduce students to the study of the past. Since then, however, a set of profound changes has pushed much of the historical profession in a different direction.

■ **Change**
Why has world history achieved an increasingly prominent place in American education in recent decades?

The world wars of the twentieth century, revealing as they did the horrendous consequences of unchecked nationalism, persuaded some historians that a broader view of the past might contribute to a sense of global citizenship. Economic and cultural globalization has highlighted both the interdependence of the world's peoples and their very unequal positions within that world. Moreover, we are aware as never before that our problems — whether they involve economic well-being, environmental deterioration, disease, or terrorism — respect no national boundaries. To many thoughtful people, a global present seemed to call for a global past. Furthermore, as colonial empires shrank and new nations asserted themselves on the world stage, these peoples also insisted that their histories be accorded equivalent treatment with those of Europe. An explosion of new knowledge about the histories of Asia, Africa, and pre-Columbian America erupted from the research of scholars around the world. All of this has generated a "world history movement," reflected in college and high school curricula, in numerous conferences and specialized studies, and in a proliferation of textbooks, of which this is one.

This world history movement has attempted to create a global understanding of the human past that highlights broad patterns cutting across particular civilizations and countries, while acknowledging in an inclusive fashion the distinctive histories of its many peoples. This is, to put it mildly, a tall order. How is it possible to encompass within a single book or course the separate stories of the world's various peoples? Surely it must be something more than just recounting the history of one civilization or culture after another. How can we distill a common history of humankind as a whole from the distinct trajectories of particular peoples? Because no world history book or course can cover everything, what criteria should we use for deciding what to include and what to leave out? Such questions have ensured no end of controversy among students, teachers, and scholars of world history, making it one of the most exciting fields of historical inquiry.

Change, Comparison, and Connection: The Three Cs of World History

Despite much debate and argument, one thing is reasonably clear: in world history, nothing stands alone. Every event, every historical figure, every culture, society, or civilization gains significance from its inclusion in some larger context. Most world historians would probably agree on three such contexts that define their field of study. Each of those contexts confronts a particular problem in our understanding of the past.

An initial context in which the particulars of world history can be situated is that of time and **change**. In world history, it is the "big picture" changes—those that impact large segments of humankind—that are of greatest interest. How did the transition from a gathering and hunting economy to one based on agriculture take place? How did cities, empires, and civilizations take shape in various parts of the world? What lay behind the emergence of a new balance of global power after 1500, one that featured the growing prominence of Europe on the world stage? What generated the amazing transformations of the "revolution of modernity" in recent centuries? How did the lives of women change as a result of industrialization?

A focus on change provides an antidote to a persistent tendency of human thinking that historians call "essentialism." A more common term is "stereotyping." It refers to our inclination to define particular groups of people with an unchanging or essential set of characteristics. Women are nurturing; peasants are conservative; Americans are aggressive; Hindus are religious. Serious students of history soon become aware that every significant category of people contains endless divisions and conflicts and that those human communities are constantly in flux. Peasants may often accept the status quo, except of course when they rebel, as they frequently have. Americans have experienced periods of isolationism and withdrawal from the world as well as times of aggressive engagement with it. Things change.

But some things persist, even if they also change. We should not allow an emphasis on change to blind us to the continuities of human experience. A recognizably Chinese state has operated for more than 2,000 years. Slavery and patriarchy persisted as human institutions for thousands of years until they were challenged in recent centuries, and in various forms they exist still. The teachings of Buddhism, Christianity, and Islam have endured for centuries, though with endless variations and transformations.

A second major context that operates constantly in world history books and courses is that of **comparison**. Whatever else it may be, world history is a comparative discipline, seeking to identify similarities and differences in the experience of the world's peoples. What is the difference between the development of agriculture in the Middle East and in Mesoamerica? Was the experience of women largely the same in all patriarchal societies? What did the Roman Empire and Han dynasty China have in common? Why did the Industrial Revolution and a modern way of life evolve first in Western Europe rather than somewhere else? What distinguished the French, Russian, and Chinese revolutions from one another? What different postures toward modernity emerged within the Islamic world? Describing and, if possible, explaining such similarities and differences are among the major tasks of world history. Comparison, then, is a recurring theme in this book, with expressions in every chapter.

Comparison has proven an effective tool in the struggle against Eurocentrism, the notion that Europeans or people of European descent have long been the primary movers and shakers of the historical process. That notion arose in recent centuries when Europeans were in fact the major source of innovation in the world and did for a time exercise something close to world domination. This temporary preeminence decisively shaped the way Europeans thought and wrote about their own histories and those of other people. In their own eyes, Europeans alone were progressive people, thanks to some cultural or racial superiority. Everyone else was to some degree stagnant, backward, savage, or barbarian. The unusual power of Europeans allowed them for a time to act on those beliefs and to convey such ways of thinking to much of the world. But comparative world history sets European achievements in a global and historical context, helping us to sort out what was distinctive about its development and what similarities it bore to other major regions of the world. Puncturing the pretensions of Eurocentrism has been high on the agenda of world history.

The art of comparison is a learned skill, entailing several steps. It requires, first of all, asking explicitly comparative questions and determining what particular cases will be involved. If you want to compare revolutions, for example, you would need to decide which ones you are considering—American, French, Russian, Chinese, Cuban. Defining categories of comparison is a further step. Precisely which characteristics of these revolutions will you compare—their origins, their ideologies, the social classes involved, their outcomes? Finally, how will you present your comparison? You might choose a case-by-case analysis in which you would describe, say, the American Revolution first, followed by an account of the Cuban Revolution, which makes explicit comparisons with the former. Or you might choose a thematic approach in which you would consider first the origins of both revolutions, followed by a comparison of their ideologies, and so on. You will find examples of both approaches in this book.

A third context that informs world history involves the interactions, encounters, and **connections** among different and often distant peoples. World history is often less about what happened within particular civilizations or cultures than about the processes and outcomes of their meetings with one another. Focusing on cross-cultural connections—whether those of conflict or more peaceful exchange—represents an effort to counteract a habit of thinking about particular peoples, states, or cultures as self-contained or isolated communities. Despite the historical emergence of many separate and distinct societies, none of them developed alone. Each was embedded in a network of relationships with both near and more distant peoples.

Moreover, these cross-cultural connections did not begin with Columbus. The Chinese, for example, interacted continuously with the nomadic peoples on their northern border; generated technologies that diffused across all of Eurasia; transmitted elements of their culture to Japan, Korea, and Vietnam; and assimilated a foreign religious tradition, Buddhism, which had originated in India. Though clearly distinctive, China was not a self-contained or isolated civilization.

The growing depth and significance of such cross-cultural relationships, known now as globalization, has been a distinguishing feature of the modern era. The voyages of Columbus brought the peoples of the Eastern and Western hemispheres into sustained contact for the first time with enormous global consequences. Several centuries later Europeans took advantage of their industrial power to bring much of the world temporarily under their control. The new technologies of the twentieth century have intertwined the economies, societies, and cultures of the world's peoples more tightly than ever before. During the past five centuries, the encounter with strangers, or at least with their ideas and practices, was everywhere among the most powerful motors of change in human societies. Thus world history remains always alert to the networks, webs, and cross-cultural encounters in which particular civilizations or peoples were enmeshed.

Changes, comparisons, and connections — all of them operating on a global scale — represent three contexts or frameworks that can help us bring some coherence to the multiple and complex stories of world history. They will recur repeatedly in the pages that follow.

Second Thoughts

What's the Significance?

big history, xxxii

cosmic calendar, xxxii

comparative history, xxxvii

the three Cs, xxxvii

Online Study Guide
bedfordstmartins.com/strayer

Big Picture Questions

1. How do modern notions of the immense size and age of the universe affect your understanding of human history?
2. What examples of comparison, connection, and change in world history would you like to explore further as your course unfolds?
3. In what larger contexts might you place your own life history?

Next Steps: For Further Study

David Christian, *Maps of Time* (2004). A brilliant survey of "big history" by a leading world historian.

Ross Dunn, ed., *The New World History* (2000). A collection of articles dealing with the teaching of world history.

Patrick Manning, *Navigating World History* (2003). An up-to-date overview of the growth of world history, the field's achievements, and the debates within it.

For Web sites and documents
related to this prologue,
see **Make History** at
bedfordstmartins.com/strayer.

PART ONE

First Things First

Beginnings in History

TO 500 B.C.E.

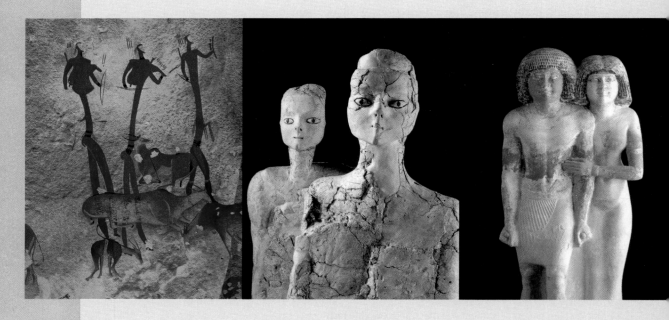

Contents

Chapter 1. First Peoples; First Farmers: Most of History in a Single Chapter, to 4000 B.C.E.
Chapter 2. First Civilizations: Cities, States, and Unequal Societies, 3500 B.C.E.–500 B.C.E.

Turning Points in Early World History

Human beings have long been inveterate storytellers. Our myths, legends, "fairy tales," oral traditions, family sagas, and more have sought to distill meaning from experience, while providing guidance for the living. Much the same might be said of modern historians, although they must operate within accepted rules of evidence. But all tellers of stories—ancient and modern alike—have to decide at what point to begin their accounts and what major turning points in those narratives to highlight. For world historians seeking to tell the story of humankind as a whole, four major "beginnings," each of them an extended historical process, have charted the initial stages of the human journey.

The Emergence of Humankind

Ever since Charles Darwin, most scholars have come to view human beginnings in the context of biological change on the planet. In considering this enormous process, we operate on a timescale quite different from the billions of years that mark the history of the universe and of the earth. According to archeologists and anthropologists, the evolutionary line of descent leading to *Homo sapiens* diverged from that leading to chimpanzees, our closest primate relatives, some 5 million to 6 million years ago, and it happened in eastern and southern Africa. There, perhaps twenty or thirty different species emerged, all of them members of the Homininae (or hominid) family of human-like creatures. What they all shared was bipedalism, the ability to walk upright on two legs. In 1976, the archeologist Mary Leakey uncovered in what is now Tanzania a series of footprints of three such hominid individuals, preserved in cooling volcanic ash about 3.5 million years ago. Two of them walked side by side, perhaps holding hands.

Over time, these hominid species changed. Their brains grew larger, as evidenced by the size of their skulls. About 2.3 million years ago, a hominid creature known as *Homo habilis* began to make and use simple stone tools. Others started to eat meat, at least occasionally. By 1 million years ago, some hominid species, especially *Homo erectus*, began to migrate out of Africa, and their remains have been found in various parts of Eurasia. This species is also associated with the first controlled use of fire.

Eventually all of these earlier hominid species died out, except one: *Homo sapiens*, ourselves. With a remarkable capacity for symbolic language that permitted the accumulation and transmission of learning, we too emerged first in Africa and quite recently, probably no more than 250,000 years ago (although specialists constantly debate these matters). For a long time, all of the small number of *Homo sapiens* lived in Africa,

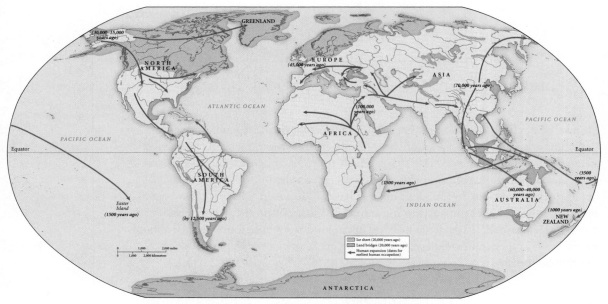

Map 1.1   The Global Dispersion of Humankind (pp. 16–17)

but sometime after 100,000 years ago, they too began to migrate out of Africa onto the Eurasian landmass, then to Australia, and ultimately into the Western Hemisphere and the Pacific islands. The great experiment of human history had begun.

The Globalization of Humankind

Today, every significant landmass on earth is occupied by human beings, but it was not always so. A mere half million years ago our species did not exist, and only 100,000 years ago that species was limited to Africa and numbered, some scholars believe, fewer than 10,000 individuals. These ancient ancestors of ours, rather small in stature and not fast on foot, were armed with a very limited technology of stone tools with which to confront the multiple dangers of the natural world. But then, in perhaps the most amazing tale in all of human history, they moved from this very modest and geographically limited role in the scheme of things to a worldwide and increasingly dominant presence. What kinds of societies, technologies, and understandings of the world accompanied, and perhaps facilitated, this globalization of humankind?

The phase of human history during which these initial migrations took place is known to scholars as the Paleolithic era. The word "Paleolithic" literally means the "old stone age," but it refers more generally to a food-collecting or gathering and hunting way of life, before agriculture allowed people to grow food or raise animals deliberately. Lasting until roughly 11,000 years ago, the Paleolithic era represents over 95 percent of the time that human beings have inhabited the earth, although it accounts for only about 12 percent of the total number of people who have lived on the planet. It was during this time that *Homo sapiens* colonized the world, making themselves at home in every environmental niche, from the frigid Arctic to the rain forests of Central Africa and Brazil, in mountains, deserts, and plains. It was an amazing achievement, accomplished by no other large species. Accompanying this global migration were slow changes in the technological tool kits of early humankind as well as early attempts to impose meaning on the world through art, ritual, religion, and stories. Although often neglected by historians and history textbooks, this long period of the human experience merits greater attention and is the focus of the initial sections of Chapter 1.

The Revolution of Farming and Herding

In 2012, almost all of the world's 7 billion people lived from the food grown on farms and gardens and from domesticated animals raised for their meat, milk, or eggs. But before 11,000 years ago, no one survived in this fashion. Then, repeatedly and fairly rapidly, at least in world history terms, human communities in parts of the Middle East, Asia, Africa, and the Americas began the laborious process of domesticating animals and selecting seeds to be planted. This momentous accomplishment represents another "first" in the human story. After countless millennia of relying on the gathering of wild foods and the hunting of wild animals, why and how did human societies begin to practice farming and animal husbandry? What changes to human life did this new technology bring with it?

This food-producing revolution, also considered in Chapter 1, surely marks the single most significant and enduring transformation of the human condition. The entire period from the beginning of agriculture to the Industrial Revolution around 1750 might be considered a single phase of the human story — the age of agriculture — calculated now on a timescale of millennia or centuries rather than the more extended periods of earlier eras. Although the age of agriculture was far shorter than the immense Paleolithic era that preceded it, farming and raising animals allowed for a substantial increase in human numbers.

In the various beginnings of food production lay the foundations for some of the most enduring divisions within the larger human community. Much depended on the luck of the draw — on the climate and soils, on the various wild plants and animals that were available for domestication. Many agricultural peoples lived in small settled villages, independent of larger political structures, while drawing their food supply from their own gardens and farms. Some depended on root crops, such as potatoes in the Andes; others relied on tree crops, such as the banana; in the most favored areas, highly nutritious wild grains such as rice, wheat, or corn could be domesticated. In more arid regions where farming was difficult, some peoples, known as pastoralists, came to depend heavily on their herds of domesticated animals. Because they moved frequently and in regular patterns to search for pasturelands, they are often referred to as nomads. With regard to animal husbandry, the Americas were at a distinct disadvantage, for there were few large animals that could be tamed — no goats, sheep,

Mohenjo Daro (p. 56)

pigs, horses, camels, or cattle. In the Afro-Eurasian world, conflicts between settled agricultural peoples and more mobile pastoral peoples represented an enduring pattern of interaction across the region.

The Turning Point of Civilization

The most prominent and powerful human communities to emerge from the Agricultural Revolution were those often designated as "civilizations," more complex societies that were based in bustling cities and governed by formal states. Virtually all of the world's people now live in such societies, so that states and cities have come to seem almost natural. In world history terms, however, their appearance is a rather recent phenomenon. Not until several thousand years *after* the beginning of agriculture did the first cities and states emerge, around 3500 B.C.E. Well after 1000 C.E., substantial numbers of people still lived in communities without any state or urban structures. Nonetheless, people living in state- and city-based societies or civilizations have long constituted the most powerful and innovative human communities on the planet. They gave rise to empires of increasing size, to enduring cultural and religious traditions, to new technologies, to sharper class and gender inequalities, to new conceptions of masculinity and femininity, and to large-scale warfare.

For all of these reasons, civilizations have featured prominently in accounts of world history, sometimes crowding out the stories of other kinds of human communities. The earliest civilizations, which emerged in at least seven separate locations between 3500 and 500 B.C.E., have long fascinated professional historians and lovers of history everywhere. What was their relationship to the Agricultural Revolution? What new ways of living did they bring to the experience of humankind? These are the questions that inform Chapter 2.

A Note on Dates

Recently it has become standard in the Western world to refer to dates prior to the birth of Christ as B.C.E. (before the Common Era), replacing the earlier B.C. (before Christ) usage. This convention is an effort to become less Christian-centered and Eurocentric in our use of language, although the chronology remains linked to the birth of Jesus. Similarly, the time following the birth of Christ is referred to as C.E. (the Common Era) rather than A.D. (*Anno Domini*, Latin for "year of the Lord"). Dates in the more distant past are designated in this book as BP (before the present) or simply as so many "years ago." Of course, these conventions are only some of the many ways that human societies have reckoned time. The Chinese frequently dated important events in terms of the reign of particular emperors, while Muslims created a new calendar beginning with Year 1, marking Muhammad's forced relocation from Mecca to Medina in 622 C.E. As with so much else, the maps of time that we construct reflect the cultures in which we have been born and the historical experience of our societies.

Mapping Part One

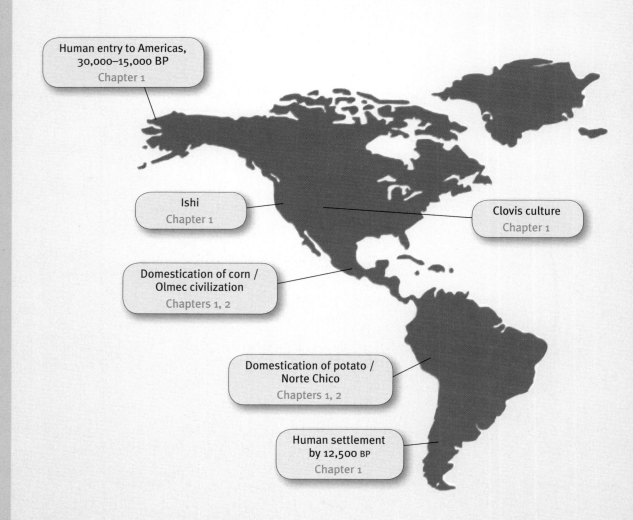

Human entry to Americas,
30,000–15,000 BP
Chapter 1

Ishi
Chapter 1

Clovis culture
Chapter 1

Domestication of corn /
Olmec civilization
Chapters 1, 2

Domestication of potato /
Norte Chico
Chapters 1, 2

Human settlement
by 12,500 BP
Chapter 1

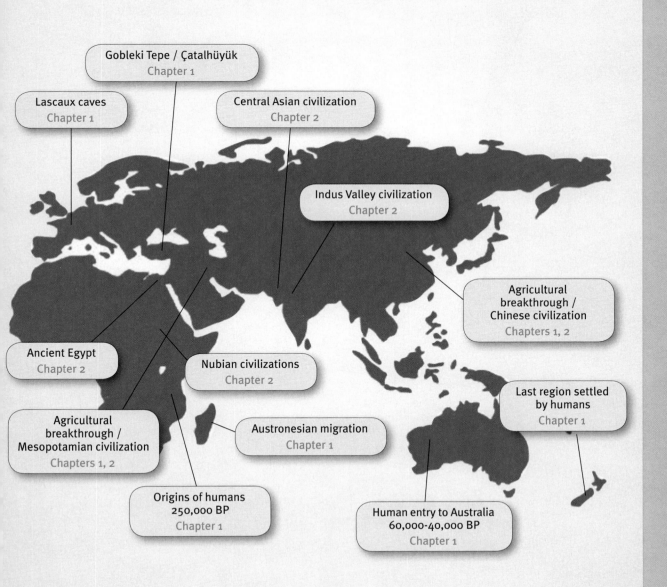

Gobleki Tepe / Çatalhüyük
Chapter 1

Lascaux caves
Chapter 1

Central Asian civilization
Chapter 2

Indus Valley civilization
Chapter 2

Agricultural breakthrough / Chinese civilization
Chapters 1, 2

Ancient Egypt
Chapter 2

Nubian civilizations
Chapter 2

Last region settled by humans
Chapter 1

Agricultural breakthrough / Mesopotamian civilization
Chapters 1, 2

Austronesian migration
Chapter 1

Origins of humans
250,000 BP
Chapter 1

Human entry to Australia
60,000-40,000 BP
Chapter 1

CHAPTER ONE

First Peoples; First Farmers

Most of History in a Single Chapter

TO 4000 B.C.E.

Out of Africa to the Ends of the
  Earth: First Migrations
  Into Eurasia
  Into Australia
  Into the Americas
  Into the Pacific
The Ways We Were
  The First Human Societies
  Economy and the Environment
  The Realm of the Spirit
  Settling Down: The Great Transition
Breakthroughs to Agriculture
  Common Patterns
  Variations
The Globalization of Agriculture
  Triumph and Resistance
  The Culture of Agriculture
Social Variation in the Age of
  Agriculture
  Pastoral Societies
  Agricultural Village Societies
  Chiefdoms
Reflections: The Uses of the
  Paleolithic
Portrait: Ishi, The Last of His People

"We do not want cattle, just wild animals to hunt and water that we can drink."[1] That was the view of Gudo Mahiya, a prominent member of the Hadza people of northern Tanzania, when he was questioned in 1997 about his interest in a settled life of farming and cattle raising. The Hadza then represented one of the very last peoples on earth to continue a way of life that was universal among humankind until 10,000 to 12,000 years ago. At the beginning of the twenty-first century, several hundred Hadza still made a living by hunting game, collecting honey, digging up roots, and gathering berries and fruit. They lived in quickly assembled grass huts located in small mobile camps averaging eighteen people and moved frequently around their remote region. Almost certainly their way of life is doomed, as farmers, governments, missionaries, and now tourists descend on them. The likely disappearance of their culture parallels the experience of many other such societies, which have been on the defensive against more numerous and powerful neighbors for 10,000 years.

NONETHELESS, THAT WAY OF LIFE SUSTAINED HUMANKIND for more than 95 percent of the time that our species has inhabited the earth. During countless centuries, human beings successfully adapted to a wide variety of environments without benefit of deliberate farming or animal husbandry. Instead, our early ancestors wrested a livelihood by gathering wild foods such as berries, nuts, roots, and grain; by scavenging dead animals; by hunting live animals; and by fishing. Known to scholars as "gathering and hunting" peoples, they were foragers

---

Paleolithic Art: The rock art of gathering and hunting peoples has been found in Africa, Europe, Australia, and elsewhere. This image from the San people of southern Africa represents aspects of their outer life in the form of wild animals and hunters with bows as well as the inner life of their shamans during a trance, reflected in the elongated figures with both human and animal features. (Image courtesy of S. A. Tourism)

or food collectors rather than food producers. Because they used stone rather than metal tools, they also have been labeled "Paleolithic," or "Old Stone Age," peoples.

And then, around 12,000 ago years an enormous transformation began to unfold as a few human societies—in Eurasia, Africa, and the Americas alike—started to practice the deliberate cultivation of plants and the domestication of animals. This Agricultural or Neolithic (New Stone Age) Revolution marked a technological breakthrough of immense significance, with implications for every aspect of human life. This chapter, then, dealing with the long Paleolithic era and the initial transition to an agricultural way of life, represents most of human history—everything in fact before the advent of urban-based civilizations, which began around 5,500 years ago.

And yet, history courses and history books often neglect this long phase of the human journey and instead choose to begin the story with the early civilizations of Egypt, Mesopotamia, China, and elsewhere. Some historians identify "real history" with writing and so dismiss the Paleolithic and Neolithic eras as largely unknowable because their peoples did not write. Others, impressed with the rapid pace of change in human affairs in more recent times, assume that nothing much of real significance happened during the long Paleolithic era—and no change meant no history.

But does it make sense to ignore the first 200,000 years or more of human experience? Although written records are absent, scholars have learned a great deal about Paleolithic and Neolithic peoples through their material remains: stones and bones, fossilized seeds, rock paintings and engravings, and much more. Archeologists, biologists, botanists, demographers, linguists, and anthropologists have contributed much to our growing understanding of gathering and hunting peoples and early agricultural societies. Furthermore, the achievements of Paleolithic peoples—the initial settlement of the planet, the creation of the earliest human societies, the beginning of reflection on the great questions of life and death—deserve our attention. And the breakthrough to agriculture arguably represents the single most profound transformation of human life in all of history. The changes wrought by our early ancestors, though far slower than those of more recent times, were extraordinarily rapid in comparison to the transformation experienced by any other species. Those changes were almost entirely cultural or learned, rather than the product of biological evolution, and they provided the foundation on which all subsequent human history was constructed. Our grasp of the human past is incomplete—massively so—if we choose to disregard the Paleolithic and Neolithic eras.

SEEKING THE MAIN POINT

What arguments does this chapter make for paying serious attention to human history before the coming of "civilization"?

Out of Africa to the Ends of the Earth: First Migrations

The first 150,000 years or more of human experience was an exclusively African story. Around 200,000 to 250,000 years ago, in the grasslands of eastern and southern Africa, *Homo sapiens* first emerged, following in the footsteps of many other hominid

A Map of Time   (All dates BP: Before the Present)

250,000–200,000	Earliest *Homo sapiens* in Africa
100,000–60,000	Beginnings of migration out of Africa
70,000	Human entry into eastern Asia
60,000–40,000	Human entry into Australia (first use of boats)
45,000	Human entry into Europe
30,000	Extinction of large mammals in Australia
30,000–15,000	Human entry into the Americas
30,000–17,000	Cave art in Europe
25,000	Extinction of Neanderthals
16,000–10,000	End of last Ice Age (global warming)
12,000–10,000	Earliest agricultural revolutions
11,000	Extinction of large mammals in North America
After 6,000	First chiefdoms in Mesopotamia
6,000–5,000	Beginning of domestication of corn in southern Mexico
3,500–1,000	Austronesian migration to Pacific islands and Madagascar
700–1,000	Human entry into New Zealand (last major region to receive human settlers)

or human-like species before it. Time and climate have erased much of the record of these early people, and Africa has witnessed much less archeological research than have other parts of the world. Nonetheless, scholars have turned up evidence of distinctly human behavior in Africa long before its appearance elsewhere. Africa, almost certainly, was the place where the "human revolution" occurred, where "culture," defined as learned or invented ways of living, became more important than biology in shaping behavior.

What kinds of uniquely human activity show up in the early African record?[2] In the first place, human beings began to inhabit new environments within Africa — forests and deserts — where no hominids had lived before. Accompanying these movements of people were technological innovations of various kinds: stone blades and points fastened to shafts replaced the earlier hand axes; tools made from bones appeared, and so did grindstones. Evidence of hunting and fishing, not just the scavenging of dead animals, marks a new phase in human food collection. Settlements were planned around the seasonal movement of game and fish. Patterns of exchange over a distance of almost 200 miles indicate larger networks of human communication. The use of body ornaments, beads, and pigments such as ochre as well as possible planned burials suggest the kind of social and symbolic behavior that has characterized human activity ever since. The earliest evidence for this kind of human activity comes from the Blombos Cave in South Africa, where excavations in 2008 uncovered a workshop for the processing of ochre dating to around 100,000 years ago, well before such behavior surfaced elsewhere in the world.

Then, sometime between 100,000 and 60,000 years ago, human beings began their long trek out of Africa and into Eurasia, Australia, the Americas, and, much later, the islands of the Pacific (see Map 1.1). In occupying the planet, members of our species accomplished the remarkable feat of learning to live in virtually every environmental niche on earth, something that no other large animal had done; and they did it with only stone tools and a gathering and hunting technology to aid them. Furthermore, much of this long journey occurred during the difficult climatic conditions of the last Ice Age (at its peak around 20,000 years ago), when thick ice sheets covered much of the Northern Hemisphere. The Ice Age did give these outward-bound human beings one advantage, however: the amount of water frozen in northern glaciers lowered sea levels around the planet, creating land bridges among various regions that were separated after the glaciers melted. Britain was then joined to Europe; eastern Siberia was connected to Alaska; and parts of what is now Indonesia were linked to mainland Southeast Asia.

Into Eurasia

■ **Change**

What was the sequence of human migration across the planet?

Human migration out of Africa led first to the Middle East and from there westward into Europe about 45,000 years ago and eastward into Asia. Among the most carefully researched areas of early human settlement in Eurasia are those in southern France and northern Spain. Colder Ice Age climates around 20,000 years ago apparently pushed more northerly European peoples southward into warmer regions. There they altered their hunting habits, focusing on reindeer and horses, and developed new technologies such as spear throwers and perhaps the bow and arrow as well as many different kinds of stone tools. Most remarkably, they also left a record of their world in hundreds of cave paintings, depicting bulls, horses, and other animals, brilliantly portrayed in colors of red, yellow, brown, and black. Images of human beings, impressions of human hands, and various abstract designs sometimes accompanied the cave paintings.

Farther east, archeologists have uncovered still other remarkable Paleolithic adaptations to Ice Age conditions. Across the vast plains of Central Europe, Ukraine, and Russia, new technologies emerged, including bone needles, multilayered clothing, weaving, nets, storage pits, baskets, and pottery. Partially underground dwellings constructed from the bones and tusks of mammoths compensated for the absence of caves and rock shelters. All of this suggests that some of these people had lived in more permanent settlements, at least temporarily abandoning their nomadic journeys. Associated with these Eastern European peoples were numerous female figurines, the earliest of which was uncovered in 2008 in Germany and dated to at least 35,000 years ago. Carved from stone, antlers, mammoth tusks, or, occasionally, baked clay, these so-called Venus figurines depict the female form, often with exaggerated breasts, buttocks, hips, and stomachs. Similar figurines have been found all across Eurasia, raising any number of controversial questions. Does their widespread distribution suggest a network of human communication and cultural diffusion over a wide area? If so, did they move from west to east or vice versa? What do they mean in terms of women's roles and status in Paleolithic societies?

Into Australia

Early human migration to Australia, perhaps 60,000 years ago, came from Indonesia and involved another first in human affairs—the use of boats. Over time, people settled in most regions of this huge continent, though quite sparsely. Scholars estimate the population of Australia at about 300,000 in 1788, when the first Europeans arrived. Over tens of thousands of years, they had developed perhaps 250 languages; collected a wide variety of bulbs, tubers, roots, seeds, and cereal grasses; and hunted large and small animals, as well as birds, fish, and other marine life. A relatively simple technology, appropriate to a gathering and hunting economy, sustained Australia's Aboriginal people into modern times. When outsiders arrived in the late eighteenth century, Aboriginals still practiced that ancient way of life, despite the presence of agriculture in nearby New Guinea.

Australian Rock Art
This Australian rock painting utilized the distinctive Aboriginal X-ray style, showing the internal bones and organs. The largest and main figure at the top is a Creation Ancestor known as Namondjok. To the right is Namarrgon, or Lightning Man, who generates the tremendous lightning storms that occur during the rainy season. The arc around his body represents the lightning, while the axes on his head, elbow, and feet are used to split the dark clouds, creating thunder and lightning. The female figure beneath Namondjok is Barrginj, the wife of Lightning Man, while the people below her, elaborately dressed, are perhaps on their way to a ceremony. (J. Marshall/Visual Connection Archive)

Accompanying their technological simplicity and traditionalism was the development of an elaborate and complex outlook on the world, known as the Dreamtime. Expressed in endless stories, in extended ceremonies, and in the evocative rock art of the continent's peoples, the Dreamtime recounted the beginning of things: how ancestral beings crisscrossed the land, creating its rivers, hills, rocks, and waterholes; how various peoples came to inhabit the land; and how they related to animals and to one another. In this view of the world, everything in the natural order was a vibration, an echo, a footprint of these ancient happenings, which link the current inhabitants intimately to particular places and to timeless events in the past.

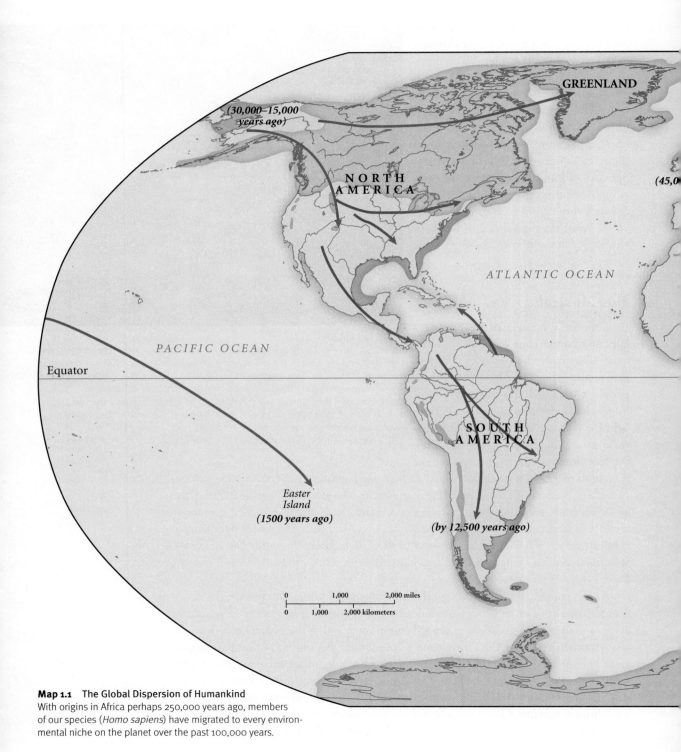

Map 1.1 The Global Dispersion of Humankind
With origins in Africa perhaps 250,000 years ago, members
of our species (*Homo sapiens*) have migrated to every environmental niche on the planet over the past 100,000 years.

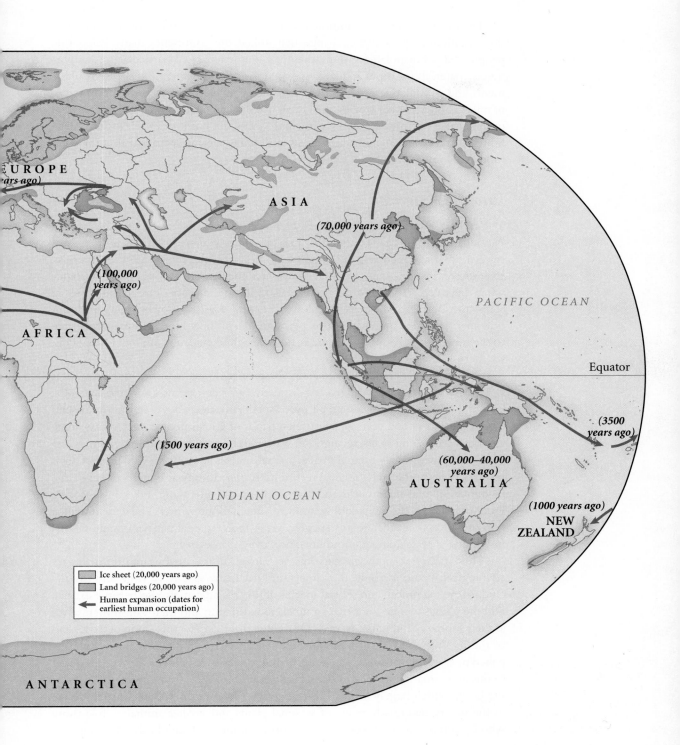

The journeys of the Dreamtime's ancestral beings reflect the networks of migration, communication, and exchange that linked the continent's many Paleolithic peoples. Far from isolated groups, they had long exchanged particular stones, pigments, materials for ropes and baskets, wood for spears, feathers and shells for ornaments, and an addictive psychoactive drug known as *pituri* over distances of hundreds of miles.[3] Songs, dances, stories, and rituals likewise circulated. Precisely how far back in time these networks extend is difficult to pinpoint, but it seems clear that Paleolithic Australia, like ancient Europe, was both many separate worlds and, at the same time, one loosely connected world.

Into the Americas

The earliest settlement of the Western Hemisphere occurred much later than that of Australia, for it took some time for human beings to penetrate the frigid lands of eastern Siberia, which was the jumping-off point for the move into the Americas. Experts continue to argue about precisely when the first migrations occurred (somewhere between 30,000 and 15,000 years ago), about the route of migration (by land across the Bering Strait or by sea down the west coast of North America), about how many separate migrations took place, and about how long it took to penetrate to the tip of South America.[4] There is, however, good evidence of human activity in southern Chile by 12,500 years ago.

One of the first clearly defined and widespread cultural traditions in the Americas is associated with people who made a distinctive projectile point, known to archeologists as a Clovis point. Scattered all over North America, Clovis culture flourished briefly around 13,000 years ago. Scattered bands of Clovis people ranged over huge areas, camping along rivers, springs, and waterholes, where large animals congregated. Although they certainly hunted smaller animals and gathered many wild plants, Clovis men show up in the archeological record most dramatically as hunters of very large mammals, such as mammoths and bison. Killing a single mammoth could provide food for many weeks or, in cold weather, for much of the winter. The wide distribution of Clovis point technology suggests yet again a regional pattern of cultural diffusion and at least indirect communication over a large area.

Then, rather abruptly, all trace of the Clovis culture disappeared from the archeological record at about the same time that many species of large animals, including the mammoth and several species of horses and camels, also became extinct. Did the Clovis people hunt these animals to extinction and then vanish themselves as their source of food disappeared? Or did the drier climate that came with the end of the Ice Age cause this megafaunal extinction? Experts disagree, but what happened next was the creation of a much greater diversity of cultures as people adapted to this new situation in various ways. Hunters on the Great Plains continued to pursue bison, which largely avoided the fate of the mammoths. Others learned to live in the desert, taking advantage of seasonal plants and smaller animals, while those who lived near the sea, lakes, or streams drew on local fish and birds. Many peoples retained their gathering and hunting way of life into modern times, while others became farmers and, in a few favored regions, later developed cities and large-scale states.[5]

Into the Pacific

The last phase of the great human migration to the ends of the earth took place in the Pacific Ocean and was distinctive in many ways. In the first place, it occurred quite recently, jumping off only about 3,500 years ago from the Bismarck and Solomon Islands near New Guinea as well as from the islands of the Philippines. It was everywhere a waterborne migration, making use of oceangoing canoes and remarkable navigational skills, and it happened very quickly and over a huge area of the planet. Speaking Austronesian languages that trace back to southern China, these oceanic voyagers had settled every habitable piece of land in the Pacific basin within about 2,500 years. Other Austronesians had sailed west from Indonesia across the Indian Ocean to settle the island of Madagascar off the coast of eastern Africa. This extraordinary process of expansion made the Austronesian family of languages the most geographically widespread in the world and their trading networks, reaching some 5,000 miles from western Indonesia to the mid-Pacific, the most extensive. With the occupation of Aotearoa (New Zealand) around 1000 to 1300 C.E., the initial human settlement of the planet was finally complete (see Map 1.2).

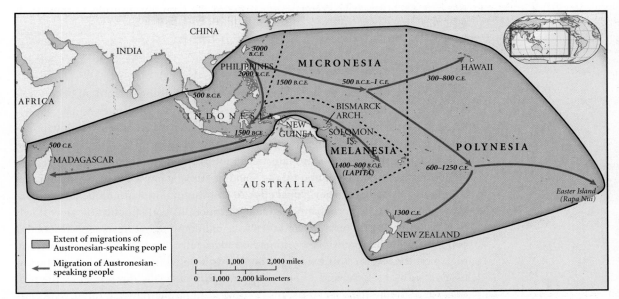

Map 1.2 Migration of Austronesian-Speaking People
People speaking Austronesian languages completed the human settlement of the earth quite recently as they settled the islands of the vast Pacific and penetrated the Indian Ocean to Madagascar, off the coast of southeast Africa.

■ **Comparison**

How did Austronesian migrations differ from other early patterns of human movement?

In contrast with all of the other initial migrations, these Pacific voyages were undertaken by agricultural people who carried both domesticated plants and animals in their canoes. Both men and women made these journeys, suggesting a deliberate intention to colonize new lands. Virtually everywhere they went, two developments followed. One was the creation of highly stratified societies or chiefdoms, of which ancient Hawaiian society is a prime example. In Hawaii, an elite class of chiefs with political and military power ruled over a mass of commoners. The other development involved the quick extinction of many species of animals, especially large flightless birds such as the *moa* of New Zealand, which largely vanished within a century of human arrival. On Rapa Nui (Easter Island) between the fifteenth and seventeenth centuries C.E., deforestation accompanied famine, violent conflict, and a sharp population decline in this small island society, while the elimination of large trees ensured that no one could leave the island, for they could no longer build the canoes that had brought them there.[6]

LearningCurve
bedfordstmartins.com
/strayer/LC

The Ways We Were

During their long journeys across the earth, Paleolithic people created a multitude of separate and distinct societies, each with its own history, culture, language, identity, stories, and rituals, but the limitations of a gathering and hunting technology using stone tools imposed some commonalities on these ancient people. Based on the archeological record and on gathering and hunting societies that still exist in modern times, scholars have sketched out some of the common features of these early societies.

The First Human Societies

Above all else, these Paleolithic societies were small, consisting of bands of twenty-five to fifty people, in which all relationships were intensely personal and normally understood in terms of kinship. The available technology permitted only a very low population density and ensured an extremely slow rate of population growth. Some scholars speculate that this growth was dramatically interrupted around 70,000 years ago by an enormous volcanic eruption on the island of Sumatra in present-day Indonesia, resulting in a cooler and drier global climate and causing human numbers to drop to some 10,000 or less. From that point of near extinction, world population grew slowly to 500,000 by 30,000 years ago and then to 6 million by 10,000 years ago.[7] Paleolithic bands were seasonally mobile or nomadic, moving frequently and in regular patterns to exploit the resources of wild plants and animals on which they depended. The low productivity of a gathering and hunting economy normally did not allow the production of much surplus, and because people were on the move so often, transporting an accumulation of goods was out of the question.

All of this resulted in highly egalitarian societies, lacking the many inequalities of wealth and power that came later with agricultural and urban life. With no formal chiefs, kings, bureaucrats, soldiers, nobles, or priests, Paleolithic men and women were perhaps freer of tyranny and oppression than any subsequent kind of human society, even if they were more constrained by the forces of nature. Without specialists, most people possessed the same set of skills, although male and female tasks often differed sharply. The male role as hunter, especially of big game, perhaps gave rise to one of the first criteria of masculine identity: success in killing large animals.

Relationships between women and men usually were far more equal than in later societies. As the primary food gatherers, women provided the bulk of the family income. One study of the San people, a surviving gathering and hunting society in southern Africa, found that plants, normally gathered by women, provided 70 percent of the diet, while meat, hunted by men, accounted for just 30 percent. This division of labor underpinned what anthropologist Richard Lee called "relative equality between the sexes with no-one having the upper hand." Among the San, teenagers engaged quite freely in sex play, and the concept of female virginity was apparently unknown, as were rape, wife beating, and the sexual double standard. Although polygamy was permitted, most marriages were in fact monogamous because women strongly resisted sharing a husband with another wife. Frequent divorce among very young couples allowed women to leave unsatisfactory marriages easily. Lee found that longer-term marriages seemed to be generally fulfilling and stable. Both men and women expected a satisfying sexual relationship, and both occasionally took lovers, although discreetly.[8]

■ Change
In what ways did a gathering and hunting economy shape other aspects of Paleolithic societies?

When the British navigator and explorer Captain James Cook first encountered the gathering and hunting peoples of Australia in 1770, he described them, perhaps a little enviously, in this way:

> They live in a Tranquillity which is not disturb'd by the Inequality of Conditions: The Earth and sea of their own accord furnishes them with all things necessary for life, they covet not Magnificient houses, Household-stuff. . . . In short they seem'd to set no value upon any thing we gave them. . . . They think themselves provided with all the necessarys of Life.[9]

The Europeans who settled permanently among such people some twenty years later, however, found a society in which physical competition among men was expressed in frequent one-on-one combat and in formalized but bloody battles. It also meant recurrent, public, and quite brutal beatings of wives by their husbands.[10] And some

Native Australians
A small number of Aboriginal Australians maintained their gathering and hunting way of life well into the twentieth century. Here an older woman shows two young boys how to dig for honey ants, a popular food. (Bill Bachman/Alamy)

Aboriginal myths sought to explain how men achieved power over women. Among the San, frequent arguments about the distribution of meat or the laziness or stinginess of particular people generated conflict, as did rivalries among men over women. Richard Lee identified twenty-two murders that had occurred between 1920 and 1955 and several cases in which the community came together to conduct an execution of particularly disruptive individuals. More generally, recent studies have found that in Paleolithic societies some 15 percent of deaths occurred through violence at the hands of other people, a rate far higher than in later civilizations, where violence was largely monopolized by the state.[11] Although sometimes romanticized by outsiders, the relative equality of Paleolithic societies did not always ensure a utopia of social harmony.

Like all other human cultures, Paleolithic societies had rules and structures. A gender-based division of labor usually cast men as hunters and women as gatherers. Values emphasizing reciprocal sharing of goods resulted in clearly defined rules about distributing the meat from an animal kill. Various rules about incest and adultery governed sexual behavior, while understandings about who could hunt or gather in particular territories regulated economic activity. Leaders arose as needed to organize a task such as a hunt, but without conferring permanent power on individuals.

Economy and the Environment

For a long time, modern people viewed their gathering and hunting ancestors as primitive and impoverished, barely eking out a living from the land. In more recent decades, anthropologists studying contemporary Paleolithic societies—those that survived into the twentieth century—began to paint a different picture. They noted that gathering and hunting people frequently worked fewer hours to meet their material needs than did people in agricultural or industrial societies and so had more leisure time. One scholar referred to them as "the original affluent society," not because they had so much but because they wanted or needed so little.[12] Nonetheless, life expectancy was low, probably little more than thirty-five years on average. Life in the wild was surely dangerous, and dependency on the vagaries of nature rendered it insecure as well.

But Paleolithic people also acted to alter the natural environment substantially. The use of deliberately set fires to encourage the growth of particular plants certainly changed the landscape and in Australia led to the proliferation of fire-resistant eucalyptus trees at the expense of other plant species. In many parts of the world—Australia, North America, Siberia, Madagascar, Pacific islands—the extinction of various large animals followed fairly quickly after the arrival of human beings, leading scholars to suggest that Paleolithic humankind played a major role, coupled perhaps with changing climates, in the disappearance of these animals. Other hominid, or humanlike, species, such as the Neanderthals in Europe or "Flores man," discovered in 2003 in Indonesia, also perished after living side by side with *Homo sapiens* for millennia.

Whether their disappearance occurred through massacre, interbreeding, or peaceful competition, they were among the casualties of the rise of humankind. Thus the biological environment inhabited by gathering and hunting peoples was not wholly natural but was shaped in part by their own hands.

The Realm of the Spirit

The religious or spiritual dimension of Paleolithic culture has been hard to pin down because bones and stones tell us little about what people thought, art is subject to many interpretations, and the experience of contemporary gathering and hunting peoples may not reflect the distant past. Clear evidence exists, however, for a rich interior life. The presence of rock art deep inside caves and far from living spaces suggests a "ceremonial space" separate from ordinary life. The extended rituals of contemporary Australian Aboriginals, which sometimes last for weeks, confirm this impression, as do numerous and elaborate burial sites found throughout the world. No full-time religious specialists or priests led these ceremonies, but part-time shamans (people believed to be especially skilled at dealing with the spirit world) emerged as the need arose. Such people often entered an altered state of consciousness or a trance while performing the ceremonies, often with the aid of psychoactive drugs.

Precisely how Paleolithic people understood the nonmaterial world is hard to reconstruct, and speculation abounds. Linguistic evidence from ancient Africa suggests a variety of understandings: some Paleolithic societies were apparently monotheistic; others saw several levels of supernatural beings, including a Creator Deity, various territorial spirits, and the spirits of dead ancestors; still others believed in an impersonal force suffused throughout the natural order that could be accessed by shamans during a trance dance.[13] The prevalence of Venus figurines and other symbols all across Europe has convinced some, but not all, scholars that Paleolithic religious thought had a strongly feminine dimension, embodied in a Great Goddess and concerned with the regeneration and renewal of life.[14] Many gathering and hunting peoples likely developed a cyclical view of time that drew on the changing phases of the moon and on the cycles of female fertility — birth, menstruation, pregnancy, new birth, and death. These understandings of the cosmos, which saw endlessly repeated patterns of regeneration and disintegration, differed from later Western views, which saw time moving in a straight line toward some predetermined goal.[15] Nor did Paleolithic people make sharp distinctions between the material and spiritual worlds, for they understood that animals, rocks, trees, mountains, and much more were animated by spirit or possessed souls of their own. Earlier scholars sometimes dubbed such views as "animistic" and regarded them as "primitive" or "simple" in comparison to later literate religions. More recent accounts generally avoid the term, preferring to focus on the specifics of particular religious traditions rather than some overall evolutionary scheme.

The Willendorf Venus Less than four and a half inches in height and dating to about 25,000 years ago, this female figure, which was found near the town of Willendorf in Austria, has become the most famous of the many Venus figurines. Certain features — the absence of both face and feet, the coils of hair around her head, the prominence of her breasts and sexual organs — have prompted much speculation among scholars about the significance of these intriguing carvings. (Naturhistorisches Museum, Vienna, Austria/The Bridgeman Art Library)

Snapshot   **Paleolithic Era in Perspective**[16]

	Paleolithic Era (from 250,000 to 10,000 years ago)	Agricultural Era (from 10,000 to 200 years ago)	Modern Industrial Era (since 1800)
Duration of each era, as a percentage of 250,000 years	96%	4%	0.08%
Percent of people who lived, out of 80 billion total	12%	68%	20%
Percent of years lived in each era (reflects changing life expectancies)	9%	62%	29%

Settling Down: The Great Transition

■ **Change**

Why did some Paleolithic peoples abandon earlier, more nomadic ways and begin to live a more settled life?

Though glacially slow by contemporary standards, changes in Paleolithic cultures occurred over time as people moved into new environments, as populations grew, as climates altered, and as different human groups interacted with one another. For example, all over the Afro-Eurasian world after 25,000 years ago, a tendency toward the miniaturization of stone tools is evident, analogous perhaps to the miniaturization of electronic components in the twentieth century. Known as micro-blades, these smaller and more refined spear points, arrowheads, knives, and scrapers were carefully struck from larger cores and often mounted in antler, bone, or wooden handles.[17] Another important change in the strategies of Paleolithic people involved the collection of wild grains, which represented a major addition to the food supply beyond the use of roots, berries, and nuts. This innovation originated in northeastern Africa around 16,000 years ago.

But the most striking and significant change in the lives of Paleolithic peoples occurred as the last Ice Age came to an end between 16,000 and 10,000 years ago. What followed was a general global warming, though one with periodic fluctuations and cold snaps. Unlike the contemporary global warming, generated by human activity and especially the burning of fossil fuels, this ancient warming phase was a wholly natural phenomenon, part of a long cycle of repeated heating and cooling characteristic of the earth's climatic history. Plants and animals unable to survive in the Ice Age climate now flourished and increased their range, providing a much richer and more diverse environment for many human societies. Under these improved conditions, human populations grew, and some previously nomadic gathering and hunting communities, but not all of them, found it possible to settle down and live in more permanent settlements or villages. These societies were becoming both larger and more complex, and it was less possible to simply move away if trouble struck. Settlement also meant that households could store and accumulate goods to a greater degree than previously. Because some people were more energetic, more talented, or luckier than others, the thin edge of inequality gradually began to wear away the egalitarianism of Paleolithic communities.

Changes along these lines emerged in many places. Paleolithic societies in Japan, known as Jomon, settled down in villages by the sea, where they greatly expanded the number of animals, both land and marine, that they consumed. They also created some of the world's first pottery, along with dugout canoes, paddles, bows, bowls, and tool handles, all made from wood. A similar pattern of permanent settlement, a broader range of food sources, and specialized technologies is evident in parts of Scandinavia, Southeast Asia, North America, and the Middle East between 12,000 and 4,000 years ago. In Labrador, longhouses accommodating 100 people appear in the archeological record. Far more elaborate burial sites in many places testify to the growing complexity of human communities and the kinship systems that bound them together. Separate cemeteries for dogs suggest that humankind's best friend was also our first domesticated animal friend.

Among the most stunning and unexpected achievements of such sedentary Paleolithic people comes from the archeological complex of Göbekli Tepe (goh–BEHK-lee TEH–peh) in southeastern Turkey, under excavation since 1994. Dating to 11,600

Göbekli Tepe
This monumental ceremonial site in southern Turkey, constructed by gathering and hunting people around 11,600 years ago, has surprised scholars, who have normally regarded such structures as the product of agricultural peoples. (Vincent J. Musi/National Geographic Stock)

years ago, it consists of massive limestone pillars, some weighing as much as sixteen tons, which were carved in a T shape and arranged in a set of some twenty circles or rings. Gracefully carved animals—gazelles, snakes, boars, foxes—decorate the pillars. Göbekli Tepe was probably a ceremonial site, for little evidence of human habitation has been found. Those who constructed or staffed the complex dined on animals hunted at a distance. Dubbed the "world's oldest temple," Göbekli Tepe was the product of people practicing a gathering and hunting way of life though living at least part of the year in settled villages. It represents a kind of monumental construction long associated only with agricultural societies and civilizations.[18]

Studies of more recent gathering and hunting societies, which were able to settle permanently in particular resource-rich areas, show marked differences from their more nomadic counterparts. Among the Chumash of southern California, for example, early Spanish settlers found peoples who had developed substantial and permanent structures accommodating up to seventy persons, hereditary political elites, elements of a market economy including the use of money and private ownership of some property, and the beginnings of class distinctions.

LearningCurve
bedfordstmartins.com
/strayer/LC

This process of settling down among gathering and hunting peoples—and the changes that followed from it—marked a major turn in human history, away from countless millennia of nomadic journeys by very small communities. It also provided the setting within which the next great transition would occur. Growing numbers of men and women, living in settled communities, placed a much greater demand on the environment than did small bands of wandering people. Therefore, it is perhaps not surprising that among the innovations that emerged in these more complex gathering and hunting societies was yet another way for increasing the food supply—agriculture.

SUMMING UP SO FAR

How do you understand the significance of the long Paleolithic era in the larger context of world history?

Breakthroughs to Agriculture

The chief feature of the long Paleolithic era—and the first human process to operate on a global scale—was the initial settlement of the earth. Then, beginning around 12,000 years ago, a second global pattern began to unfold—agriculture. The terms "Neolithic (New Stone Age) Revolution" or "Agricultural Revolution" refer to the deliberate cultivation of particular plants as well as the taming and breeding of particular animals. Thus a whole new way of life gradually replaced the earlier practices of gathering and hunting in most parts of the world. Although it took place over centuries and millennia, the coming of agriculture represented a genuinely revolutionary transformation of human life all across the planet and provided the foundation for almost everything that followed: growing populations, settled villages, animal-borne diseases, horse-drawn chariot warfare, cities, states, empires, civilizations, writing, literature, and much more.

Among the most revolutionary aspects of the age of agriculture was a new relationship between humankind and other living things, for now men and women were not simply using what they found in nature but were actively changing nature as well. They were consciously "directing" the process of evolution. The actions of farmers in the Americas, for example, transformed corn from a plant with a cob of an inch or so to one measuring about six inches by 1500. Later efforts more than doubled that length. Farmers everywhere stamped the landscape with a human imprint in the form of fields with boundaries, terraced hillsides, irrigation ditches, and canals. Animals too were transformed as selective breeding produced sheep that grew more wool, cows that gave more milk, and chickens that laid more eggs than their wild counterparts.

This was "domestication"—the taming, and the changing, of nature for the bene-fit of humankind—but it created a new kind of mutual dependence. Many domes-ticated plants and animals could no longer survive in the wild and relied on human action or protection to reproduce successfully. Similarly, human beings in the agricul-tural era lost the skills of their gathering and hunting ancestors, and in any event there were now too many people to live in that older fashion. As a consequence, farmers and herders became dependent on their domesticated plants and animals. From an outside point of view, it might well seem that corn and cows had tamed human be-ings, using people to ensure their own survival and growth as a species, as much as the other way around.

A further revolutionary aspect of the agricultural age is summed up in the term "intensification." It means getting more for less, in this case more food and resources— far more—from a much smaller area of land than was possible with a gathering and hunting technology. More food meant more people. Growing populations in turn required an even greater need for the intensive exploitation of the environment. And so was launched the continuing human effort to "subdue the earth" and to "have dominion over it," as the biblical story in Genesis recorded God's command to Adam and Eve.

Common Patterns

Perhaps the most extraordinary feature of the Neolithic or Agricultural Revolution was that it occurred, separately and independently, in many widely scattered parts of the world: the Fertile Crescent of Southwest Asia, several places in sub-Saharan Af-rica, China, New Guinea, Mesoamerica, the Andes, and eastern North America (see Map 1.3). Even more remarkably, all of this took place at roughly the same time (at least as measured by the 250,000-year span of human history on the planet)—between 12,000 and 4,000 years ago. These facts have generated many questions with which historians have long struggled. Why was the Agricultural Revolution so late in the history of humankind? What was unique about the period after 10,000 B.C.E. that may have triggered or facilitated this vast upheaval? In what different ways did the Agri-cultural Revolution take shape in its various locations? How did it spread from its several points of origin to the rest of the earth? And what impact did it have on the making of human societies?

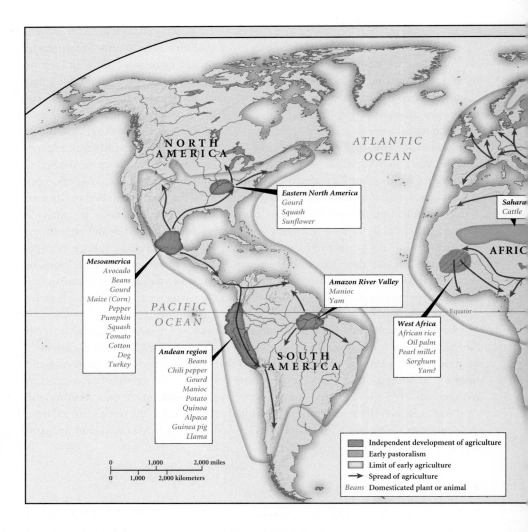

Map 1.3 The Global Spread of Agriculture and Pastoralism
From ten or more separate points of origin, agriculture spread to adjacent areas, eventually encompassing almost all of the world's peoples.

Map labels:

NORTH AMERICA

ATLANTIC OCEAN

Eastern North America
Gourd
Squash
Sunflower

Sahara
Cattle

AFRIC

Mesoamerica
Avocado
Beans
Gourd
Maize (Corn)
Pepper
Pumpkin
Squash
Tomato
Cotton
Dog
Turkey

PACIFIC OCEAN

Amazon River Valley
Manioc
Yam

Equator

West Africa
African rice
Oil palm
Pearl millet
Sorghum
Yam?

Andean region
Beans
Chili pepper
Gourd
Manioc
Potato
Quinoa
Alpaca
Guinea pig
Llama

SOUTH AMERICA

0   1,000   2,000 miles
0   1,000   2,000 kilometers

Independent development of agriculture
Early pastoralism
Limit of early agriculture
→ Spread of agriculture
Beans Domesticated plant or animal

■ **Change**
What accounts for the emergence of agriculture after countless millennia of human life without it?

It is no accident that the Agricultural Revolution coincided with the end of the last Ice Age, a process of global warming that began some 16,000 years ago. By about 11,000 years ago, the Ice Age was over, and climatic conditions similar to those of our own time generally prevailed. This was but the latest of some twenty-five periods of glaciation and warming that have occurred over the past several million years of the earth's history and that are caused by minor periodic changes in the earth's orbit around the sun. The end of the last Ice Age, however, coincided with the migration of *Homo sapiens* across the planet and created new conditions that made agriculture more possible. Combined with active hunting by human societies, climate change in some areas helped to push into extinction various species of large mammals on which Paleolithic people had depended, thus adding to the pressure to find new food sources. The warmer, wetter, and more stable conditions, particularly in the tropical and tem-

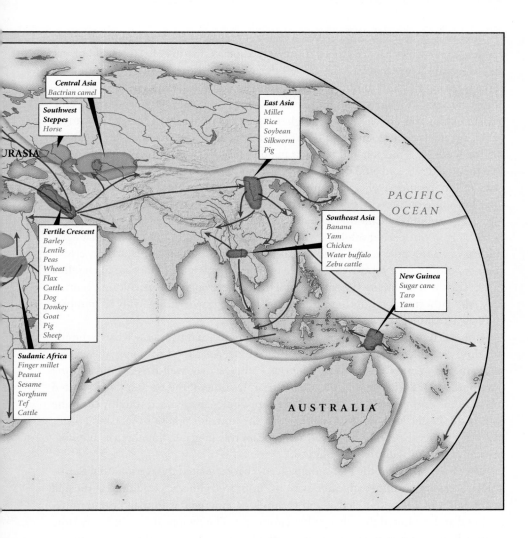

perate regions of the earth, also permitted the flourishing of more wild plants, especially cereal grasses, which were the ancestors of many domesticated crops. What climate change took away with one hand, it apparently gave back with the other.

Over their long history, gathering and hunting peoples had already developed a deep knowledge of the natural world and, in some cases, the ability to manage it actively. They had learned to make use of a large number of plants and to hunt and eat both small and large animals, creating what archeologists call a "broad-spectrum diet." In the Middle East, people had developed sickles for cutting newly available wild grain, baskets to carry it, mortars and pestles to remove the husk, and storage pits to preserve it. Peoples of the Amazon and elsewhere had learned to cut back some plants to encourage the growth of their favorites. Native Australians had built elaborate traps in which they could capture, store, and harvest large numbers of eels.

In hindsight, much of this looks like a kind of preparation for agriculture. Because women in particular had long been intimately associated with collecting wild plants, they were the likely innovators who led the way to deliberate farming, with men perhaps taking the lead in domesticating animals. Clearly the knowledge and technology necessary for agriculture were part of a longer process involving more intense human exploitation of the earth. Nowhere was agriculture an overnight invention.

Using such technologies, and benefiting from the global warming at the end of the last Ice Age, gathering and hunting peoples in various resource-rich areas were able to settle down and establish more permanent villages, abandoning their nomadic ways and more intensively exploiting the local area. In settling down, however, they soon lost some of the skills of their ancestors and found themselves now required to support growing populations. Evidence for increasing human numbers around the world during this period of global warming has persuaded some scholars that agriculture was a response to the need for additional food, perhaps even a "food crisis." Such conditions surely motivated people to experiment and to innovate in an effort to increase the food supply. Clearly, many of the breakthroughs to agriculture occurred only *after* gathering and hunting peoples had already grown substantially in numbers and had established a sedentary way of life.

Göbekli Tepe in Turkey provides a possible example of the process. Klaus Schmidt, the chief archeologist at the site, argues that the need for food to supply those who built and maintained this massive religious complex may well have stimulated the development of agriculture in the area. Certainly, some of the earliest domesticated wheat in the region has been located just twenty miles away and at roughly the same date. If this connection holds, it suggests that the human impulse to worship collectively in a village-based setting played a significant role in generating the epic transformation of the Agricultural Revolution.

These were some of the common patterns that facilitated the Agricultural Revolution. New opportunities appeared with the improved climatic conditions at the end of the Ice Age. New knowledge and technology emerged as human communities explored and exploited that changed environment. The disappearance of many large mammals, growing populations, newly settled ways of life, and fluctuations in the process of global warming—all of these represented pressures or incentives to increase food production and thus to minimize the risks of life in a new era.[19] From some combination of these opportunities and incentives emerged the profoundly transforming process of the Agricultural Revolution.

Variations

This new way of life initially operated everywhere with a simple technology—the digging stick or hoe. Plows were developed much later. But the several transitions to this hoe-based agriculture, commonly known as horticulture, varied considerably, depending on what plants and animals were available locally. For example, potatoes were found in the Andes region, but not in Africa or Asia; wheat and wild pigs existed in the Fertile Crescent, but not in the Americas. Furthermore, of the world's 200,000 plant species, only several hundred have been domesticated, and just five of these — wheat, corn, rice, barley, and sorghum — supply more than half of the calories that sustain human life. Only fourteen species of large mammals have been successfully domesticated, of which sheep, pigs, goats, cattle, and horses have been the most important. Because they are stubborn, nervous, solitary, or finicky, many animals simply cannot be readily domesticated.[20] In short, the kind of Agricultural Revolution that unfolded in particular places depended very much on what happened to be available locally, and that in turn depended on sheer luck.

Among the most favored areas — and the first to experience a full Agricultural Revolution — was the Fertile Crescent, an area sometimes known as Southwest Asia, consisting of present-day Iraq, Syria, Israel/Palestine, Jordan, and southern Turkey (see Map 1.4). In this region, an extraordinary variety of wild plants and animals

■ **Comparison**

In what different ways did the Agricultural Revolution take shape in various parts of the world?

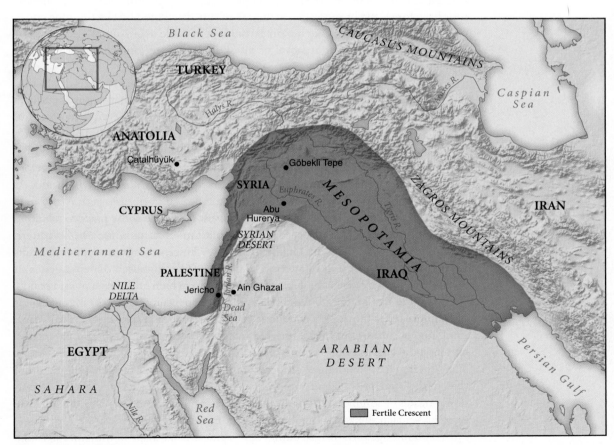

Map 1.4 The Fertile Crescent
Located in what is now called the Middle East, the Fertile Crescent was the site of many significant processes in early world history, including the first breakthrough to agriculture and later the development of some of the First Civilizations.

capable of domestication provided a rich array of species on which the now largely settled gathering and hunting people could draw. What triggered the transition to agriculture, it seems, was a cold and dry spell between 11,000 and 9500 B.C.E., a temporary interruption in the general process of global warming. Larger settled populations were now threatened with the loss of the wild plants and animals on which they had come to depend. Their solution was domestication. Figs were apparently the first cultivated crop, dating to about 9400 B.C.E. In the millennium or so that followed, wheat, barley, rye, peas, lentils, sheep, goats, pigs, and cattle all came under human control, providing the foundation for the world's first, and most productive, agricultural societies.

Archeological evidence suggests that the transition to a fully agricultural way of life in parts of this region took place quite quickly, within as few as 500 years. Signs of that transformation included large increases in the size of settlements, which now housed as many as several thousand people. In these agricultural settings, archeologists have found major innovations: the use of sun-dried mud bricks; the appearance of monuments or shrine-like buildings; displays of cattle skulls; more elaborate human burials, including the removal of the skull; and more sophisticated tools, such as sickles, polished axes, and awls.[21]

At roughly the same time, perhaps a bit later, another process of domestication was unfolding on the African continent in the eastern part of what is now the Sahara in present-day Sudan. Between 10,000 and 5,000 years ago, however, scholars tell us that there was no desert in this region, which received more rainfall than currently, had extensive grassland vegetation, and was "relatively hospitable to human life."[22] It seems likely that cattle were domesticated in this region about 1,000 years before they were separately brought under human control in the Middle East and India. At about the same time, the donkey also was domesticated in northeastern Africa near the Red Sea and spread from there into Southwest Asia, even as the practice of raising sheep and goats moved in the other direction. In terms of farming, the African pattern again was somewhat different. Unlike the Fertile Crescent, where a number of plants were domesticated in a small area, sub-Saharan Africa witnessed the emergence of several widely scattered farming practices. Sorghum, which grows well in arid conditions, was the first grain to be "tamed" in the eastern Sahara region. In the highlands of Ethiopia, teff, a tiny, highly nutritious grain, as well as enset, a relative of the banana, came under cultivation. In the forested region of West Africa, yams, oil palm trees, okra, and the kola nut (used as a flavoring for cola drinks) emerged as important crops. The scattered location of these domestications generated a less productive agriculture than in the more favored and compact Fertile Crescent, but a number of the African domesticates—sorghum, castor beans, gourds, millet, the donkey—subsequently spread to enrich the agricultural practices of Eurasian peoples.

Yet another pattern of agricultural development took shape in the Americas. Like the Agricultural Revolution in Africa, the domestication of plants in the Americas occurred separately in a number of locations—in the coastal Andean regions of western South America, in Mesoamerica, in the Mississippi River valley, and perhaps in the Amazon basin—but surely its most distinctive feature lay in the absence of animals that could be domesticated. Of the fourteen major species of large mammals that have been brought under human control, only one, the llama/alpaca, existed in the Western Hemisphere. Without goats, sheep, pigs, cattle, or horses, the peoples of the Americas lacked sources of protein, manure (for fertilizer), and power (to draw plows or pull carts, for example) that were widely available to societies in the Afro-Eurasian world. Because they could not depend on domesticated animals for meat, agricultural peoples in the Americas relied more on hunting and fishing than did peoples in the Eastern Hemisphere.

Furthermore, the Americas lacked the rich cereal grains that were widely available in Afro-Eurasia. Instead they had maize or corn, first domesticated in southern Mexico by 4000 to 3000 B.C.E. Unlike the cereal grains of the Fertile Crescent, which closely resemble their wild predecessors, the ancestor of corn, a mountain grass called teosinte (tee-uh-SIHN-tee), looks nothing like what we now know as corn or maize.

The Statues of Ain Ghazal
Among the largest of the early agricultural settlements investigated by archeologists is that of Ain Ghazal, located in the modern state of Jordan. Inhabited from about 7200 to 5000 B.C.E., in its prime it was home to some 3,000 people, who lived in multiroomed stone houses; cultivated barley, wheat, peas, beans, and lentils; and herded domesticated goats. These remarkable statues, around three feet tall and made of limestone plaster applied to a core of bundled reeds, were among the most startling finds at that site. Did they represent heroes, gods, goddesses, or ordinary people? No one really knows. (Courtesy, Department of Antiquities of Jordan [DoA]. Photo: Freer Gallery of Art and Arthur M. Sackler Gallery, Washington, DC)

Thousands of years of selective adaptation were required to develop a sufficiently large cob and number of kernels to sustain a productive agriculture, an achievement that one geneticist has called "arguably man's first, and perhaps his greatest, feat of genetic engineering."[23] Even then, corn was nutritionally poorer than the protein-rich cereals of the Fertile Crescent. To provide sufficient dietary protein, corn had to be supplemented with squash and beans, which were also domesticated in the Americas. Thus while Middle Eastern societies quite rapidly replaced their gathering and hunting economy with agriculture, that process took 3,500 years in Mesoamerica.

Another difference in the unfolding of the Agricultural Revolution lay in the north/south orientation of the Americas, which required agricultural practices to move through, and adapt to, quite distinct climatic and vegetation zones if they were to spread. The east/west axis of North Africa/Eurasia meant that agricultural innovations could spread more rapidly because they were entering roughly similar environments. Thus corn, beans, and squash, which were first domesticated in Mesoamerica, took several thousand years to travel the few hundred miles from their Mexican homeland to the southwestern United States and another thousand years or more to arrive in eastern North America. The llama, guinea pig, and potato, which were domesticated in the Andean highlands, never reached Mesoamerica.

LearningCurve
bedfordstmartins.com
/strayer/LC

The Globalization of Agriculture

■ Connection

In what ways did agriculture spread? Where and why was it sometimes resisted?

From the various places where it originated, agriculture spread gradually to much of the rest of the earth, although for a long time it coexisted with gathering and hunting ways of life. Broadly speaking, this extension of farming occurred in two ways. The first, known as diffusion, refers to the gradual spread of agricultural techniques, and perhaps of the plants and animals themselves, but without the extensive movement of agricultural people. Neighboring groups exchanged ideas and products in a down-the-line pattern of communication. A second process involved the slow colonization or migration of agricultural peoples as growing populations pushed them outward. Often this meant the conquest, absorption, or displacement of the earlier gatherers and hunters, along with the spread of the languages and cultures of the migrating farmers. In many places, both processes took place.

Triumph and Resistance

Some combination of diffusion and migration took the original agricultural package of Southwest Asia and spread it widely into Europe, Central Asia, Egypt, and North Africa between 6500 and 4000 B.C.E. Languages originating in the core region accompanied this movement of people and farming practices. Thus Indo-European languages, which originated probably in Turkey and are widely spoken even today from India to Europe, reflect this movement of culture associated with the spread of agriculture. In a similar process, the Chinese farming system moved into Southeast Asia and elsewhere, and with it a number of related language families developed. India

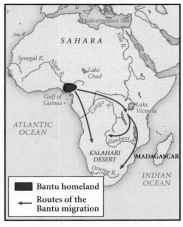

Bantu Migrations

received agricultural influences from the Middle East, Africa, and China alike.

Within Africa, the development of agricultural societies in the southern half of the continent is associated with the migration of peoples speaking one or another of the some 400 Bantu languages. Beginning from what is now southern Nigeria or Cameroon around 3000 B.C.E., Bantu-speaking people moved east and south over the next several millennia, taking with them their agricultural, cattle-raising, and, later, ironworking skills, as well as their languages. The Bantus generally absorbed, killed, or drove away the indigenous Paleolithic peoples or exposed them to animal-borne diseases to which they had no immunities. A similar process brought agricultural Austronesian-speaking people, who originated in southern China, to the Philippine and Indonesian islands, with similar consequences for their earlier inhabitants. Later, Austronesian speakers carried agriculture to the uninhabited islands of the Pacific and to Madagascar off the coast of southeastern Africa (see Map 1.2, p. 19).

The globalization of agriculture was a prolonged process, lasting 10,000 years or more after its first emergence in the Fertile Crescent, but it did not take hold everywhere. The Agricultural Revolution in New Guinea, for example, did not spread much beyond its core region. In particular, it did not pass to the nearby peoples of Australia, who remained steadfastly committed to gathering and hunting ways of life. The people of the west coast of North America, arctic regions, and southwestern Africa also maintained their gathering and hunting economies into the modern era. A very few, such as the Hadza, described at the beginning of this chapter, practice it still.

Some of those who resisted the swelling tide of agriculture lived in areas unsuitable to farming, such as harsh desert or arctic environments; others lived in regions of particular natural abundance, so they felt little need for agriculture. Such societies found it easier to resist agriculture if they were not in the direct line of advancing, more powerful farming people. But many of the remaining gathering and hunting peoples knew about agricultural practices from nearby neighbors, suggesting that they quite deliberately chose to resist it in favor of the freer life of their Paleolithic ancestors.

Nonetheless, by the beginning of the Common Era, the global spread of agriculture had reduced gathering and hunting peoples to a small and dwindling minority of humankind. If that process meant "progress" in certain ways, it also claimed many victims as the relentlessly expanding agricultural frontier slowly destroyed gathering and hunting societies. Whether this process occurred through the peaceful diffusion of new technologies, through intermarriage, through disease, or through the violent displacement of earlier peoples, the steady erosion of this ancient way of life has been a persistent thread of the human story over the past 10,000 years. The final chapters of

■ **Change**
What changes did the Agricultural Revolution bring in its wake?

Ishi, The Last of His People

In late August of 1911, an emaciated and nearly naked man, about fifty years old, staggered into the corral of a slaughterhouse in northern California. As it turned out, he was the last member of his people, a gathering and hunting group known as the Yahi, pushed into extinction by the intrusion of more powerful farming, herding, and "civilized" societies. It was a very old story, played out for over 10,000 years since the Agricultural Revolution placed Paleolithic cultures on the defensive, inexorably eroding their presence on the earth. The tragic story of this individual allows us to put a human face on that enormous and largely unrecorded process.

Within a few days, this bedraggled and no doubt bewildered man was taken into the care of several anthropologists from the University of California, who brought him to a museum in San Francisco, where he

Ishi (Courtesy of The Bancroft Library, University of California, Berkeley)

lived until his death from tuberculosis in 1916. They called him Ishi, which means "person" in his native language, because he was unwilling to provide them with his own given name. In his culture, it was highly impolite to reveal one's name, especially to strangers.

In the mid-nineteenth century, the Yahi consisted of about 300 to 400 people living in a rugged and mountainous area of northern California. There they hunted, fished, gathered acorns, and otherwise provided for themselves in a fashion familiar to gathering and hunting peoples the world over. But the 1849 California gold rush brought a massive influx of American settlers, miners, and farmers that quickly pushed the Yahi to the edge of extinction. Yahi raiding and resistance was met by massacres at the hands of local militias and vigilantes, only too glad to "clean up the In-

that long story are being written in our own times. (See the Portrait of Ishi, above, for a recent example of this process.) After the Agricultural Revolution, the future, almost everywhere, lay with the farmers and herders and with the distinctive societies that they created.

The Culture of Agriculture

What did that future look like? In what ways did societies based on the domestication of plants and animals differ from those rooted in a gathering and hunting economy? In the first place, the Agricultural Revolution led to an increase in human population, as the greater productivity of agriculture was able to support much larger numbers. An early agricultural settlement uncovered near Jericho in present-day Israel probably had 2,000 people, a vast increase in the size of human communities compared to much smaller Paleolithic bands. On a global level, scholars estimate that the world's population was about 6 million around 10,000 years ago, before the Agricultural Revolution got underway, and shot up to some 50 million by 5,000 years ago and

dians," killing and scalping hundreds. One such massacre in 1865 likely killed Ishi's father, while the young Ishi, his mother, and a few others escaped.

By 1870, Ishi's community had dwindled to fifteen or sixteen people, living in an even more inaccessible region of their homeland. In these desperate circumstances, traditional gender roles blurred, even as they undertook great efforts to conceal their presence. To avoid making footprints when traveling, they jumped from rock to rock; they ground acorns on smooth stones rather than on more obvious hollowed out rocks and carefully camouflaged their thatched dwellings and campfires. By 1894, this tiny Yahi community numbered only five people: Ishi, his mother, his sister or cousin, and an older man and woman.

Then in 1908, a group of American surveyors came across a naked Ishi harpooning fish in the river, and a few days later they found the tiny settlement that sheltered the remaining Yahi. Only Ishi's aged mother was present, hidden under a pile of skins and rags. They did not harm her, but they took away every moveable item—tools, food, baskets, bows and arrows—as souvenirs. Ishi returned to carry his mother away and she soon died. He never saw his sister/cousin or the others again. For some time, then,

Ishi lived absolutely alone until he stumbled into the slaughterhouse on August 29, 1911, his hair burned short in a Yahi sign of mourning.

In his new home in the museum, Ishi became something of a media sensation, willingly demonstrating his skills for visitors—fashioning tools and weapons of stone and bone, starting a fire, but refusing to make baskets, because it was women's work. Actively cooperating with anthropologists who sought to document the culture of his people, he took them on a hunt one summer, teaching them how to track and kill deer and to process the meat on the spot. All who met him remarked on his gentleness and kindness, his love of company, his delight in children, his fondness for laughing and joking. According to Alfred Kroeber, the primary anthropologist involved with Ishi: "He was the most patient man I ever knew . . . without trace of self-pity or of bitterness to dull the purity of his cheerful enduringness."[24]

Questions: What accounts for the ability of Ishi's people to survive into the twentieth century? What emotional or moral posture toward Ishi's life seems most appropriate? What perspective does it lend to the larger story of the gradual erosion of gathering and hunting societies the world over?

250 million by the beginning of the Common Era. Here was the real beginning of the human dominance over other forms of life on the planet.

That dominance was reflected in major environmental transformations. In a growing number of places, forests and grasslands became cultivated fields and grazing lands. Human selection modified the genetic composition of numerous plants and animals. In parts of the Middle East within a thousand years after the beginning of settled agricultural life, some villages were abandoned when soil erosion and deforestation led to declining crop yields, which could not support mounting populations.[25] The advent of more intensive agriculture associated with city-based civilizations only heightened this human impact on the landscape.

Human life too changed dramatically in farming communities, and not necessarily for the better. Farming involved hard work and more of it than in many earlier gathering and hunting societies. The remains of early agricultural people show some deterioration in health—more tooth decay, malnutrition, and anemia, a shorter physical stature, and diminished life expectancy. Living close to animals subjected humans to new diseases—smallpox, flu, measles, chicken pox, malaria, tuberculosis, rabies—while

Nok Culture
The agricultural and iron-using Nok culture of northern Nigeria in West Africa generated a remarkable artistic tradition of terracotta or fired clay figures depicting animals and especially people. This one dates to somewhere between 600 B.C.E. and 600 C.E. Some scholars have dubbed this and many similar Nok sculptures as "thinkers." Does it seem more likely that this notion reflects a present-day sensibility or that it might be an insight into the mentality of the ancient artist who created the image? (Musée du Quai Branly/Scala/Art Resource, NY)

living in larger communities generated epidemics for the first time in human history. Furthermore, relying on a small number of plants or animals rendered early agricultural societies vulnerable to famine, in case of crop failure, drought, or other catastrophes. The advent of agriculture bore costs as well as benefits.

Agriculture also imposed constraints on human communities. Some Paleolithic people had settled in permanent villages, but all agricultural people did so, as farming required a settled life. A good example of an early agricultural settlement comes from northern China, one of the original independent sources of agriculture, where the domestication of rice, millet, pigs, and chickens gave rise to settled communities by about 7,000 years ago. In 1953, workers digging the foundation for a factory uncovered the remains of an ancient village, now called Banpo, near the present-day city of Xian. Millet, pigs, and dogs had been domesticated, but diets were supplemented with wild plants, animals, and fish. Some forty-five houses covered with thatch laid over wooden beams provided homes to perhaps 500 people. More than 200 storage pits permitted the accumulation of grain, and six kilns and pottery wheels enabled the production of various pots, vases, and dishes, many decorated with geometric designs and human and animal images. A large central space suggests an area for public religious or political activity, and a trench surrounding the village indicates some common effort to defend the community.

Early agricultural villages such as Banpo reveal another feature of the age of agriculture—an explosion of technological innovation. Mobile Paleolithic peoples had little use for pots, but such vessels were essential for settled societies, and their creation and elaboration accompanied agriculture everywhere. So too did the weaving of textiles, made possible by collecting the fibers of domesticated plants (cotton and flax, for example) and raising animals such as sheep. Evidence for the invention of looms of several kinds dates back to 7,000 years ago, and textiles, some elaborately decorated, show up in Peru, Switzerland, China, and Egypt. Like agriculture itself, weaving was a technology in which women were probably the primary innovators. It was a task that was compatible with child-rearing responsibilities, which virtually all human societies assigned primarily to women.[26] Another technology associated with the Agricultural Revolution was metallurgy. The working of gold and copper, then bronze, and, later, iron became part of the jewelry-, tool-, and weapon-making skill set of humankind. The long "stone age" of human technological history was coming to an end, and the age of metals was beginning.

A further set of technological changes, beginning around 4000 B.C.E., has been labeled the "secondary products revolution."[27] These technological innovations involved new uses for domesticated animals, beyond their meat and hides. Agricultural people in parts of Europe, Asia, and Africa learned to milk their animals, to harvest their wool, and to enrich the soil with their manure. Even more important, they learned to ride horses and camels and to hitch various animals to plows and carts. Because these animals did not exist in the Americas, this revolutionary new source of power and transportation was available only in the Eastern Hemisphere.

Finally the Agricultural Revolution presented to humankind the gift of wine and beer, often a blessing, sometimes a curse. As barley, wheat, rice, and grapes were domesticated, their potential for generating alcoholic beverages was soon discovered. Evidence for wine making in the mountains of present-day northwestern Iran dates to around 5400 B.C.E., though its expense rendered it an elite beverage for millennia. Chinese wine making can be traced to around 4000 B.C.E. Drunken debauchery and carousing among the aristocracy prompted an unsuccessful effort by one Chinese ruler around 1046 B.C.E. to outlaw the beverage. The precise origins of beer are unclear, but its use was already quite widespread in the Middle East by 4000 B.C.E., when a pictogram on a seal from Mesopotamia showed two figures using straws to drink beer from a large pottery jar. Regarded as a gift from the gods, beer, like bread, was understood in Mesopotamia as something that could turn a savage into a fully human and civilized person.[28]

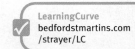

LearningCurve
bedfordstmartins.com
/strayer/LC

Social Variation in the Age of Agriculture

The resources generated by the Agricultural Revolution opened up vast new possibilities for the construction of human societies, but they led to no single or common outcome. Differences in the natural environment, the encounter with strangers, and sometimes deliberate choices gave rise to several distinct kinds of societies early on in the age of agriculture, all of which have endured into modern times.

■ **Comparison**

What different kinds of societies emerged out of the Agricultural Revolution?

Pastoral Societies

One variation of great significance grew out of the difference between the domestication of plants and the domestication of animals. Many societies made use of both, but in regions where farming was difficult or impossible — arctic tundra, certain grasslands, and deserts — some people came to depend far more extensively on their animals, such as sheep, goats, cattle, horses, camels, or reindeer. Animal husbandry was a "distinct form of food-producing economy," relying on the milk, meat, and blood of animals.[29] Known as herders, pastoralists, or nomads, such people emerged in Central Asia, the Arabian Peninsula, the Sahara, and parts of eastern and southern Africa. What they had in common was mobility, for they moved seasonally as they followed the changing patterns of vegetation necessary as pasture for their animals.

The particular animals central to pastoral economies differed from region to region. The domestication of horses by 4000 B.C.E. and several thousand years later the mastery of horseback-riding skills enabled the growth of pastoral peoples all across the steppes of Central Asia by the first millennium B.C.E. Although organized primarily in kinship-based clans or tribes, these nomads periodically created powerful military confederations, which played a major role in the history of Eurasia for thousands of years. In the Inner Asian, Arabian, and Saharan deserts, domesticated camels made possible the human occupation of forbidding environments. The grasslands

The Domestication of Animals

Although farming often gets top billing in discussions of the Neolithic Revolution, the raising of animals was equally important, for they provided meat, pulling power, transportation (in the case of horses and camels), and manure. Animal husbandry also made possible pastoral societies, which were largely dependent on their domesticated animals. This rock art painting from the Sahara (now southeastern Algeria) dates to somewhere around 4000 B.C.E. and depicts an early pastoral community. (Henri Lhote)

south of the Sahara and in parts of eastern Africa supported cattle-raising pastoralists. The absence of large animals capable of domestication meant that no pastoral societies emerged in the Americas.

The relationship between nomadic herders and their farming neighbors has been one of the enduring themes of Afro-Eurasian history. Frequently, it was a relationship of conflict as pastoral peoples, unable to produce their own agricultural products, were attracted to the wealth and sophistication of agrarian societies and sought access to their richer grazing lands as well as their food crops and manufactured products. The biblical story of the deadly rivalry between two brothers — Cain, a "tiller of the ground," and Abel, a "keeper of sheep" — reflects this ancient conflict, which persisted well into modern times. But not all was conflict between pastoral and agricultural peoples. The more peaceful exchange of technologies, ideas, products, and people across the ecological frontier of pastoral and agricultural societies also served to enrich and to change both sides. In the chapters that follow, we will encounter pastoral societies repeatedly, particularly as they interact with neighboring agricultural and "civilized" peoples.

Within pastoral communities the relative equality of men and women, characteristic of most Paleolithic societies, persisted, perhaps because their work was so essential. Women were centrally involved in milking animals, in processing that milk, and in producing textiles such as felt, so widely used in Central Asia for tents, beds, rugs, and clothing. Among the Saka pastoralists in what is now Azerbaijan, women rode horses and participated in battles along with men. A number of archeological sites around the Black Sea have revealed high-status women buried with armor, swords, daggers, and arrows. In the Xinjiang region of western China, still other women were buried with the apparatus of healers and shamans, strongly suggesting an important female role in religious life.

Agricultural Village Societies

The most characteristic early agricultural societies were those of settled village-based horticultural farmers, such as those living in Banpo or Jericho. Many such societies also retained much of the social and gender equality of gathering and hunting communities, as they continued to do without kings, chiefs, bureaucrats, or aristocracies.

An example of this type of social order can be found at Çatalhüyük (cha-TAHL-hoo-YOOK), a very early agricultural village in southern Turkey. A careful excavation of the site revealed a population of several thousand people who buried their dead under their houses and then filled the houses with dirt and built new ones on top, layer upon layer. No streets divided the houses, which were constructed adjacent to one another. People moved about the village on adjoining rooftops, from which they entered their homes. Despite the presence of many specialized crafts, few signs of inherited social inequality have surfaced. Nor is there any indication of male or female dominance, although men were more closely associated with hunting wild animals and women with plants and agriculture. "Both men and women," concludes one scholar, "could carry out a series of roles and enjoy a range of positions, from making tools to grinding grain and baking to heading a household."[30]

In many horticultural villages, women's critical role as farmers as well as their work in the spinning and weaving of textiles no doubt contributed to a social position of relative equality with men. Some such societies traced their descent through the female line and practiced marriage patterns in which men left their homes to live with their wives' families. Archeologist Marija Gimbutas has highlighted the prevalence of female imagery in the art of early agricultural societies in Europe and Anatolia, suggesting to her a widespread cult of the Goddess, focused on "the mystery of birth, death and the renewal of life."[31] But early agriculture did not produce identical gender systems everywhere. Some practiced patrilineal descent and required a woman to live in the household of her husband. Grave sites in early eastern European farming communities reveal fewer adult females than males, indicating perhaps the practice of female infanticide. Some early written evidence from China suggests a long-term preference for male children.

In all of their diversity, many village-based agricultural societies flourished well into the modern era, usually organizing themselves in terms of kinship groups or lineages, which incorporated large numbers of people well beyond the immediate or extended family. Such a system provided the framework within which large numbers of people could make and enforce rules, maintain order, and settle disputes without going to war. In short, the lineage system performed the functions of government, but without the formal apparatus of government, and thus did not require kings or queens, chiefs, or permanent officials associated with a state organization. Despite their democratic qualities and the absence of centralized authority, village-based lineage societies sometimes developed modest social and economic inequalities. Elders could exploit the labor of junior members of the community and sought particularly to control women's reproductive powers, which were essential for the growth of the lineage. Among the Igbo of southern Nigeria well into the twentieth century, "title societies" enabled men and women of wealth and character to earn a series of increasingly prestigious "titles" that set them apart from other members of their community, although these honors could not be inherited. Lineages also sought to expand their numbers, and hence their prestige and power, by incorporating war captives or migrants in subordinate positions, sometimes as slaves.

Given the frequent oppressiveness of organized political power in human history, agricultural village societies represent an intriguing alternative to states, kingdoms, and empires, so often highlighted in the historical record. They pioneered the human settlement of vast areas; adapted to a variety of environments; maintained a substantial degree of social and gender equality; created numerous cultural, artistic, and religious traditions; and interacted continuously with their neighbors.

Chiefdoms

In other places, agricultural village societies came to be organized politically as chiefdoms, in which inherited positions of power and privilege introduced a more distinct element of inequality, but unlike later kings, chiefs could seldom use force to compel the obedience of their subjects. Instead chiefs relied on their generosity or gift giving, their ritual status, or their personal charisma to persuade their followers. The earliest such chiefdoms seem to have emerged in the Tigris-Euphrates river valley called Mesopotamia (present-day Iraq), sometime after 6000 B.C.E., when temple priests may have organized irrigation systems and controlled trade with nearby societies.

Many chiefdoms followed in all parts of the world, and the more recent ones have been much studied by anthropologists. For example, chiefdoms emerged everywhere in the Pacific islands, which had been colonized by agricultural Polynesian peoples. Chiefs usually derived from a senior lineage, tracing their descent to the first son of an imagined ancestor. With both religious and secular functions, chiefs led important rituals and ceremonies, organized the community for warfare, directed its economic life, and sought to resolve internal conflicts. They collected tribute from commoners in the form of food, manufactured goods, and raw materials. These items in turn were redistributed to warriors, craftsmen, religious specialists, and other subordinates, while chiefs kept enough to maintain their prestigious positions and imposing lifestyle.[32] In North America as well, a remarkable series of chiefdoms emerged in the eastern woodlands, where an extensive array of large earthen mounds testify to the organizational capacity of these early societies. The largest of them, known as Cahokia, flourished around 1100 C.E.

Thus the Agricultural Revolution radically transformed both the trajectory of the human journey and the evolution of life on the planet. This epic process granted to one species, *Homo sapiens*, a growing power over many other species of plants and animals and made possible an increase in human numbers far beyond what a gathering and hunting economy could support.

But if agriculture provided humankind with the power to dominate nature, it also, increasingly, enabled some people to dominate others. This was not immediately apparent, and for several thousand years, and much longer in some places, agricultural villages and pastoral communities retained much of the social equality that had characterized Paleolithic life. Slowly, though, many of the resources released by the Agricultural Revolution accumulated in the hands of a few. Rich and poor, chiefs and commoners, landowners and dependent peasants, rulers and subjects, dominant

LearningCurve
bedfordstmartins.com
/strayer/LC

Cahokia
Pictured here in an artist's reconstruction, Cahokia (near St. Louis, Missouri) was the center of an important agricultural chiefdom around 1100 C.E. See Chapter 6 for details. (Cahokia Mounds State Historic Site, Illinois. Painting by Lloyd K. Townsend)

men and subordinate women, slaves and free people—these distinctions, so common in the record of world history, took shape most extensively in highly productive agricultural settings, which generated a substantial economic surplus. There the endless elaboration of such differences, for better or worse, became a major feature of those distinctive agricultural societies known to us as "civilizations."

SUMMING UP SO FAR

What was revolutionary about the Agricultural Revolution?

Reflections: The Uses of the Paleolithic

Even when it is about the distant past, history is also about those who tell it in the present. We search the past, always, for our own purposes. For example, modern people have long been inclined to view their Paleolithic or gathering and hunting ancestors as primitive or superstitious, unable to exercise control over nature, and ignorant of its workings. Such a view was, of course, a kind of self-congratulation, designed to highlight the "progress" of modern humankind. It was a way of saying, "Look how far we have come."

In more recent decades, however, growing numbers of people, disillusioned with modernity, have looked to the Paleolithic era for material with which to criticize, rather than celebrate, contemporary life. Feminists have found in gathering and hunting peoples a much more gender-equal society and religious thinking that featured the divine feminine, qualities that encouragingly suggested that patriarchy was neither inevitable nor eternal. Environmentalists have sometimes identified peoples in the distant past who were uniquely in tune with the natural environment rather than seeking to dominate it. Some nutritionists have advocated a "Paleolithic diet" of wild plants and animals as well suited to our physiology. Critics of modern materialism and competitive capitalism have been delighted to discover societies in which values of sharing and equality predominated over those of accumulation and hierarchy. Still others have asked, in light of the long Paleolithic era, whether the explosive population and economic growth of recent centuries should be considered normal or natural. Perhaps they are better seen as extraordinary, possibly even pathological. All of these uses of the Paleolithic have been a way of asking, "What have we lost in the mad rush to modernity, and how can we recover it?"

Both those who look with disdain on Paleolithic "backwardness" and those who praise, often quite romantically, its simplicity and equality seek to use these ancient people for their own purposes. In our efforts to puzzle out the past, all of us — historians and students of history very much included — stand somewhere. None of us can be entirely detached when we view the past, but this is not necessarily a matter for regret. What we may lose in objectivity, we gain in passionate involvement with the historical record and the many men and women who have inhabited it. Despite its remoteness from us in time and manner of living, the Paleolithic era resonates still in the twenty-first century, reminding us of our kinship with these distant people and the significance of that kinship to finding our own way in a very different world.

Second Thoughts

What's the Significance?

Venus figurines, 14–15; 23

Dreamtime, 15

Clovis culture, 18–19

megafaunal extinction, 18–19

Austronesian migrations, 19–20

"the original affluent society," 22

shamans, 23

trance dance, 23

Paleolithic settling down, 24–26

Göbekli Tepe, 25–26; 30

Fertile Crescent, 27; 30–32

teosinte, 33–34

diffusion, 34

Bantu migration, 35

Ishi, 36–37

Banpo, 38

"secondary products revolution," 38–39

pastoral societies, 39–40

Çatalhüyük, 40–41

chiefdoms, 42–43

Big Picture Questions

1. In what ways did various Paleolithic societies differ from one another, and how did they change over time?

2. The Agricultural Revolution marked a decisive turning point in human history. What evidence might you offer to support this claim, and how might you argue against it?

3. How did early agricultural societies differ from those of the Paleolithic era?

4. Was the Agricultural Revolution inevitable? Why did it occur so late in the story of humankind?

5. "The Agricultural Revolution provides evidence for 'progress' in human affairs." How would you evaluate this statement?

Next Steps: For Further Study

For Web sites and additional documents related to this chapter, see **Make History** at bedfordstmartins.com/strayer.

Elizabeth Wayland Barber, *Women's Work: The First 20,000 Years* (1994). Explores the role of women in early technological development, particularly textile making.

Peter Bellwood, *First Farmers: The Origins of Agricultural Societies* (2005). An up-to-date account of the Agricultural Revolution, considered on a global basis.

David Christian, *This Fleeting World: A Short History of Humanity* (2008). A lovely essay by a leading world historian, which condenses parts of his earlier *Maps of Time* (2004).

Steven Mithen, *After the Ice: A Global Human History, 20,000–5000 B.C.* (2004). An imaginative tour of world archeological sites during the Agricultural Revolution.

Lauren Ristvet, *In the Beginning* (2007). A brief account of human evolution, Paleolithic life, the origins of agriculture, and the first civilizations, informed by recent archeological discoveries.

Andrew Shryock and Daniel Lord Smail, *Deep History* (2011). An interdisciplinary mapping of the human past with a focus on very long periods of time.

Fred Spier, *Big History and the Future of Humanity* (2011). An effort to place human history in the context of cosmic, geological, and biological history with a focus on the growth of complexity.

"The Agricultural Revolution," http://www.public.wsu.edu/gened/learn-modules/top_agrev/agrev-index.html. A Web-based tutorial from Washington State University.

"Prehistoric Art," http://witcombe.sbc.edu/ARTHprehistoric.html#general. An art history Web site with a wealth of links to Paleolithic art around the world.

CHAPTER TWO

First Civilizations

Cities, States, and Unequal Societies

(3500 B.C.E. – 500 B.C.E.)

Something New: The Emergence of Civilizations
Introducing the First Civilizations
The Question of Origins
An Urban Revolution
The Erosion of Equality
Hierarchies of Class
Hierarchies of Gender
Patriarchy in Practice
The Rise of the State
Coercion and Consent
Writing and Accounting
The Grandeur of Kings
Comparing Mesopotamia and Egypt
Environment and Culture
Cities and States
Interaction and Exchange
Reflections: "Civilization": What's in a Word?
Portrait: Paneb, An Egyptian Criminal

"Where could one go if one wanted to escape civilization?" So read an inquiry from a Colorado woman on an Internet forum about "personal development" in 2007. In reply, another subscriber to the forum wrote: "Are you just tired of urban sprawl or are you fed up with people in general? I have lived 'off the land' in Kentucky, with no car, power lines, running water, phones etc. and I survived to tell the tale."[1] This ironic online conversation—using the Internet to express an interest in abandoning civilization—refers to the "back-to-the-land" movement that began in the mid-1960s as an alternative to the pervasive materialism of modern life. Growing numbers of urban dwellers, perhaps as many as a million in North America, exchanged their busy city lives for a few acres of rural land and a very different way of living.

This urge to "escape from civilization" has long been a central feature in modern life. It is a major theme in Mark Twain's famous novel *The Adventures of Huckleberry Finn*, in which the restless and rebellious Huck resists all efforts to "sivilize" him by fleeing to the freedom of life on the river. It is a large part of the "cowboy" image in American culture, and it permeates environmentalist efforts to protect the remaining wilderness areas of the country. Nor has this impulse been limited to modern societies and the Western world. The ancient Chinese teachers of Daoism likewise urged their followers to abandon the structured and demanding world of urban and civilized life and to immerse themselves in the eternal patterns of the natural order. It is a strange paradox that we count the creation of civilizations among the major achievements of humankind and yet people within

Raherka and Mersankh: Writing was among the defining features of civilizations almost everywhere. In ancient Egyptian civilization, the scribes who possessed this skill enjoyed both social prestige and political influence. This famous statue shows Raherka, an "inspector of the scribes" during Egypt's Fifth Dynasty (about 2350 B.C.E.), in an affectionate pose with his wife, Mersankh. (Réunion des Musées Nationaux/Art Resource, NY)

them have often sought to escape the constraints, artificiality, hierarchies, and other discontents of civilized living.

SO WHAT EXACTLY ARE THESE CIVILIZATIONS that have generated such ambivalent responses among their inhabitants? When, where, and how did they first arise in human history? What changes did they bring to the people who lived within them? Why might some people criticize or seek to escape from them?

As historians commonly use the term, "civilization" represents a new and particular type of human society, made possible by the immense productivity of the Agricultural Revolution. Such societies encompassed far larger populations than any earlier form of human community and for the first time concentrated some of those people in sizable cities, numbering in the many tens of thousands. Both within and beyond these cities, people were organized and controlled by states whose leaders could use force to compel obedience. Profound differences in economic function, skill, wealth, and status sharply divided the people of civilizations, making them far less equal and subject to much greater oppression than had been the case in earlier Paleolithic communities, agricultural villages, pastoral societies, or chiefdoms. Pyramids, temples, palaces, elaborate sculptures, written literature, complex calendars, as well as more elaborate class and gender hierarchies, slavery, and large-scale warfare—all of these have been among the cultural products of civilization.

SEEKING THE MAIN POINT

What distinguished "civilizations" from earlier Paleolithic and Neolithic societies?

Something New: The Emergence of Civilizations

■ Change
When and where did the first civilizations emerge?

Like agriculture, civilization was a global phenomenon, showing up independently in seven major locations scattered around the world during the several millennia after 3500 B.C.E. and in a number of other smaller expressions as well (see Map 2.1). In the long run of human history, these civilizations—small breakthroughs to a new way of life—gradually absorbed, overran, or displaced people practicing other ways of living. Over the next 5,000 years, civilization, as a unique kind of human community, gradually encompassed ever-larger numbers of people and extended over ever-larger territories, even as particular civilizations rose, fell, revived, and changed.

Introducing the First Civilizations

The earliest of these civilizations emerged around 3500 B.C.E. to 3000 B.C.E. in three places. One was the "cradle" of Middle Eastern civilization, expressed in the many and competing city-states of Sumer in southern Mesopotamia (located in present-day Iraq). Much studied by archeologists and historians, Sumerian civilization likely gave rise to the world's earliest written language, which was used initially by officials to record the goods received by various temples. Almost simultaneously, the Nile River valley in northeastern Africa witnessed the emergence of Egyptian civilization, famous for its pharaohs and pyramids, as well as a separate civilization known

A Map of Time   (All dates B.C.E.)

3500–3000	Beginnings of Mesopotamian, Egyptian, and Norte Chico civilizations
3400–3200	Nubian kingdom of Ta-Seti
3200–2350	Period of independent Sumerian city-states
2663–2195	Old Kingdom Egypt (high point of pharaoh's power and pyramid building)
2200–2000	Beginnings of Chinese, Indus Valley, and Central Asian (Oxus) civilizations
2070–1600	Xia dynasty in China (traditionally seen as first dynasty of Chinese history)
After 2000	*Epic of Gilgamesh* compiled
1900–1500	Babylonian Empire
1792–1750	Reign of Hammurabi
1700	Abandonment of Indus Valley cities
1550–1064	New Kingdom Egypt
1200	Beginnings of Olmec civilization
760–660	Kush conquest of Egypt
586	Babylonian conquest of Judah
By 500	Egypt and Mesopotamia incorporated into Persian Empire

as Nubia, farther south along the Nile. Unlike the city-states of Sumer, Egyptian civilization took shape as a unified territorial state in which cities were rather less prominent. Later in this chapter, we will compare these two First Civilizations in greater detail.

Less well known and only recently investigated by scholars was a third early civilization that was developing along the central coast of Peru from roughly 3000 B.C.E. to 1800 B.C.E., at about the same time as the civilizations of Egypt and Sumer. This desert region received very little rainfall, but it was punctuated by dozens of rivers that brought the snowmelt of the adjacent Andes Mountains to the Pacific Ocean. Along a thirty-mile stretch of that coast and in the nearby interior, a series of some twenty-five urban centers emerged in an area known as Norte Chico, the largest of which was Caral, in the Supe River valley. In Norte Chico, archeologists have found monumental architecture in the form of earthen platform mounds, one of them measuring 60 feet tall and 500 feet long, as well as large public ceremonial structures, stone buildings with residential apartments, and other signs of urban life.

Norte Chico was a distinctive civilization in many ways. Its cities were smaller than those of Mesopotamia and show less evidence of economic specialization. The economy was based to an unusual degree on an extremely rich fishing industry in anchovies and sardines along the coast. These items apparently were exchanged for

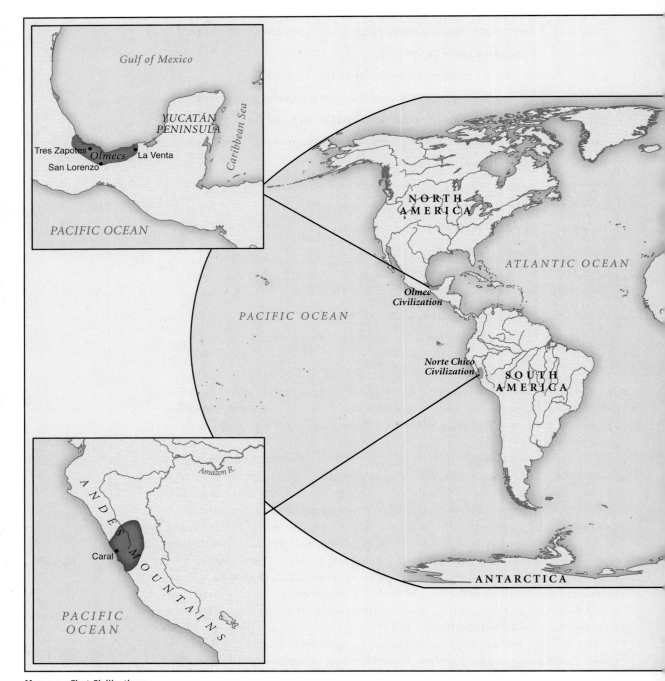

Map 2.1   First Civilizations

Seven First Civilizations emerged independently in locations scattered across the planet, all within a few thousand years, from 3500 to 1000 B.C.E.

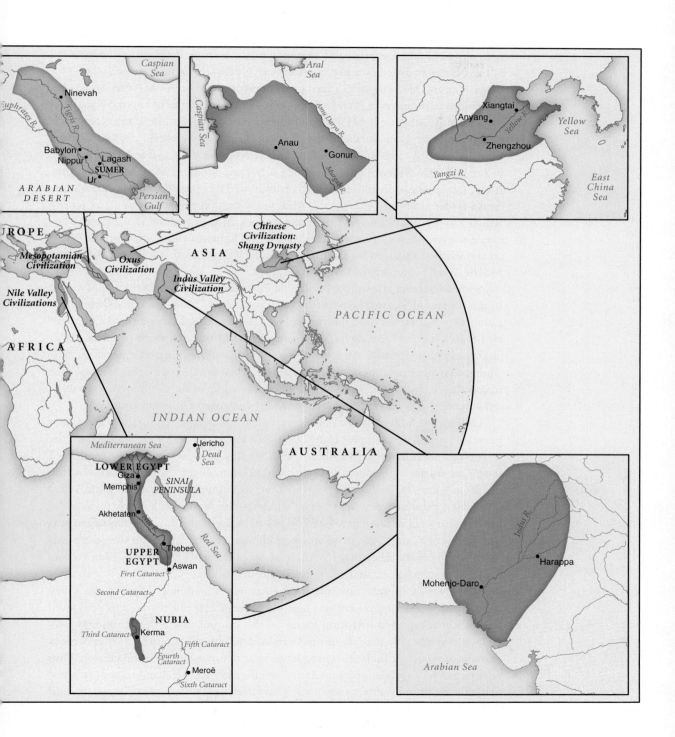

Ninevah

Caspian Sea

Euphrates R.

Tigris R.

Babylon
Nippur
Lagash
SUMER
Ur

ARABIAN DESERT

Persian Gulf

Aral Sea

Caspian Sea

Amu Darya R.

Anau

Gonur

Murghab R.

Xiangtai
Anyang
Zhengzhou

Yellow R.

Yellow Sea

Yangzi R.

East China Sea

EUROPE

Mesopotamian Civilization

Oxus Civilization

ASIA

Chinese Civilization: Shang Dynasty

Nile Valley Civilizations

Indus Valley Civilization

AFRICA

PACIFIC OCEAN

INDIAN OCEAN

AUSTRALIA

Mediterranean Sea

Jericho
Dead Sea

LOWER EGYPT
Giza
Memphis

SINAI PENINSULA

Akhetaten

Nile R.

Red Sea

UPPER EGYPT
Thebes
Aswan
First Cataract

Second Cataract

NUBIA

Third Cataract
Kerma

Fifth Cataract
Fourth Cataract

Meroë

Sixth Cataract

Indus R.

Harappa

Mohenjo-Daro

Arabian Sea

cotton, essential for fishing nets, as well as food crops such as squash, beans, and guava, all of which were grown by inland people in the river valleys using irrigation agriculture. Unlike Egyptian and Mesopotamian societies, Peruvian civilization did not rest on grain-based farming; the people of Norte Chico did not develop pottery or writing; and few sculptures, carvings, or drawings have been uncovered so far. Archeologists have, however, found a 5,000-year-old *quipu* (a series of knotted cords, later used extensively by the Inca for accounting purposes), which some scholars have suggested may have been an alternative form of writing or symbolic communication. Furthermore, the cities of Norte Chico lacked defensive walls, and archeologists have discovered little evidence of warfare, such as burned buildings and mutilated corpses. It was also an unusually self-contained civilization. The only import from the outside world evident in Norte Chico, or in Andean civilization generally, was maize (corn), which was derived ultimately from Mesoamerica, though without direct contact between the two regions. Norte Chico apparently "lighted a cultural fire" in the Andes and established a pattern for the many Andean civilizations that followed—Chavín, Moche, Wari, Tiwanaku, and, much later, Inca.[2]

Somewhat later, at least four additional First Civilizations made their appearance. In the Indus and Saraswati river valleys of what is now Pakistan, a remarkable civilization arose during the third millennium B.C.E. By 2000 B.C.E., it embraced a far larger area than Mesopotamia, Egypt, or coastal Peru and was expressed primarily in its elaborately planned cities. All across this huge area, common patterns prevailed: standardized weights, measures, architectural styles, even the size of bricks. As elsewhere, irrigated agriculture provided the economic foundation for the civilization, and a written language, thus far undeciphered, provides evidence of a literate culture.

Unlike its Middle Eastern counterparts, the Indus Valley civilization apparently generated no palaces, temples, elaborate graves, kings, or warrior classes. In short, the archeological evidence provides little indication of a political hierarchy or centralized state. This absence of evidence has sent scholars scrambling to provide an explanation for the obvious specialization, coordination, and complexity that the Indus Valley civilization exhibited. A series of small republics, rule by priests, an early form of the caste system—all of these have been suggested as alternative mechanisms of integration in this first South Asian civilization. Although no one knows for sure, the possibility that the Indus Valley may have housed a sophisticated civilization without a corresponding state has excited the imagination of scholars.

Whatever its organization, the local environmental impact of the Indus Valley civilization, as in many others, was heavy and eventually undermined its ecological foundations. Repeated irrigation increased the amount of salt in the soil and lowered crop yields. The making of mud bricks, dried in ovens, required an enormous amount of wood for fuel, generating large-scale deforestation and soil erosion. Thus environmental degradation contributed significantly to the abandonment of these magnificent cities by about 1700 B.C.E. Thereafter, they were largely forgotten, until their rediscovery by archeologists in the twentieth century. Nonetheless, many features of this early civilization—ceremonial bathing, ritual burning, yoga positions, bulls

and elephants as religious symbols, styles of clothing and jewelry—continued to nourish the later
civilization of the Indian subcontinent. In fact
they persist into the present.[3]

The early civilization of China, dating to perhaps 2200 B.C.E., was very different from that of the
Indus Valley. The ideal—if not always the reality—
of a centralized state was evident from the days of
the Xia (shyah) dynasty (2070–1600 B.C.E.), whose
legendary monarch Wu organized flood control
projects that "mastered the waters and made them
to flow in great channels." Subsequent dynasties—
the Shang (1600–1046 B.C.E.) and the Zhou (JOH)
(1046–771 B.C.E.)—substantially enlarged the Chinese state, erected lavish tombs for their rulers,
and buried thousands of human sacrificial victims
to accompany them in the next world. By the
Zhou dynasty, a distinctive Chinese political ideology had emerged, featuring a ruler, known as the
Son of Heaven. This monarch served as an intermediary between heaven and earth
and ruled by the Mandate of Heaven only so long as he governed with benevolence
and maintained social harmony among his people. An early form of written Chinese
has been discovered on numerous oracle bones, which were intended to predict the
future and to assist China's rulers in the task of governing. Chinese civilization, more
than any other, has experienced an impressive cultural continuity from its earliest expression into modern times.

Shang Dynasty Bronze
This bronze tiger, created around 1100 B.C.E., illustrates Chinese skill in
working with bronze and the mythological or religious significance of the
tiger as a messenger between heaven and the human world. (Jianxi Provincial
Museum, Nanchang/Cultural Relics Press)

Central Asia was the site of yet another First Civilization. In the Oxus or Amu
Darya river valley and nearby desert oases (what is now northern Afghanistan and
southern Turkmenistan), a quite distinctive and separate civilization took shape very
quickly after 2200 B.C.E. Within two centuries, a number of substantial fortified centers had emerged, containing residential compounds, artisan workshops, and temples,
all surrounded by impressive walls and gates. Economically based on irrigation agriculture and stock raising, this Central Asian or Oxus civilization had a distinctive cultural style, expressed in its architecture, ceramics, burial techniques, seals, and more,
though it did not develop a literate culture. Evidence for an aristocratic social hierarchy comes from depictions of gods and men in widely differing dress performing
various functions from eating at a banquet to driving chariots to carrying heavy bur-
dens. Visitors to this civilization would have found occasional goods from China,
India, and Mesopotamia, as well as products from pastoral nomads of the steppe land
and the forest dwellers of Siberia. According to a leading historian, this Central Asian
civilization was the focal point of a "Eurasian-wide system of intellectual and commercial exchange."[4] Compared to Egypt or Mesopotamia, however, it had a relatively brief history, for by 1700 B.C.E., it had faded away as a civilization, at about the

same time as a similar fate befell its Indus Valley counterpart. Its cities were abandoned and apparently forgotten until their resurrection by archeologists in the twentieth century. And yet its influence persisted as elements of this civilization's cultural style show up much later in Iran, India, and the eastern Mediterranean world.

A final First Civilization, known as the Olmec, took shape around 1200 B.C.E. along the coast of the Gulf of Mexico near present-day Veracruz in southern Mexico. Based on an agricultural economy of maize, beans, and squash, Olmec cities arose from a series of competing chiefdoms and became ceremonial centers filled with elaborately decorated temples, altars, pyramids, and tombs of rulers. The most famous artistic legacy of the Olmecs lay in some seventeen colossal basalt heads, weighing twenty tons or more. Recent discoveries suggest that the Olmecs may well have created the first written language in the Americas by about 900 B.C.E. Sometimes regarded as the "mother civilization" of Mesoamerica, Olmec cultural patterns—mound building, artistic styles, urban planning, a game played with a rubber ball, ritual sacrifice, and bloodletting by rulers—spread widely throughout the region and influenced subsequent civilizations, such as the Maya and Teotihuacán.

Beyond these seven First Civilizations, other, smaller civilizations also flourished. Lying south of Egypt in the Nile Valley, an early Nubian civilization known as Ta-Seti was clearly distinctive and independent of its northern neighbor, although Nubia was later involved in a long and often contentious relationship with Egypt. Likewise in China, a large city known as Sanxingdui, rich in bronze sculptures and much else, arose separately but at the same time as the more well-known Shang dynasty. As a new form of human society, civilization was beginning its long march toward encompassing almost all of humankind by the twentieth century. At the time, however, these breakthroughs to new forms of culture and society were small islands of innovation in a sea of people living in much older ways.

The Question of Origins

■ **Change**
What accounts for the initial breakthroughs to civilization?

The first question that historians ask about almost everything is "How did it get started?" Scholars of all kinds—archeologists, anthropologists, sociologists, and historians—have been arguing about the origins of civilization for a very long time, with no end in sight.[5] Amid all the controversy, one thing seems reasonably clear: civilizations had their roots in the Agricultural Revolution. That is the reason they appeared so late in the human story, for only an agricultural technology permitted human communities to produce sufficient surplus to support large populations and the specialized or elite minorities who did not themselves produce food. But not all agricultural societies or chiefdoms developed into civilizations, so something else must have been involved. It is the search for this "something else" that has provoked such great debate among scholars.

Some historians have emphasized the need to organize large-scale irrigation projects as a stimulus for the earliest civilizations, but archeologists have found that the more complex water control systems appeared long after states and civilizations had already been established. Alternatively, perhaps states responded to the human need for order as larger and more diverse populations grew up in particular localities. Others have suggested that states were useful in protecting the privileges of favored groups. Warfare and trade have figured in still other explanations for the rise of civilizations. Anthropologist Robert Carneiro combined several of these factors in a thoughtful approach to the question.[6] He argued that a growing density of population, producing more congested and competitive societies, was a fundamental motor of change, and especially in areas where rich agricultural land was limited, either by geography (oceans, deserts, mountains) or by powerful neighboring societies. Such settings provided incentives for innovations, such as irrigation or plows that could produce more food, because opportunities for territorial expansion were not readily available. But circumscribed environments with dense populations also generated intense competition among rival groups, which led to repeated warfare. A strong and highly organized state was a decided advantage in such competition. Because losers could not easily flee to new lands, they were absorbed into the winner's society as a lower class. Successful leaders of the winning side emerged as elites with an enlarged base of land, a class of subordinated workers, and a powerful state at their disposal—in short, a civilization.

Although such a process was relatively rapid by world history standards, it took many generations, centuries, or perhaps millennia to evolve. It was, of course, an unconscious undertaking in which the participants had little sense of the long-term outcome as they coped with the practical problems of survival on a day-to-day basis. What is surprising, though, is the rough similarity of the outcome in many widely separated places from about 3500 B.C.E. to the beginning of the Common Era.

However they got started (and much about this is still guesswork), the First Civilizations, once established, represented a very different kind of human society than anything that came before. All of them were based on highly productive agricultural economies. Various forms of irrigation, drainage, terracing, and flood control enabled these early civilizations to tap the food-producing potential of their regions more intensively. All across the Afro-Eurasian hemisphere, though not in the Americas, animal-drawn plows and metalworking greatly enhanced the productivity of farming. Ritual sacrifice, sometimes including people, accompanied the growth of civilization, and the new rulers normally served as high priests, their right to rule legitimated by association with the sacred.

An Urban Revolution

It was the resources from agriculture that made possible one of the most distinctive features of the First Civilizations—cities. What would an agricultural villager have made of Uruk, ancient Mesopotamia's largest city? Uruk had walls more than twenty feet tall and a population around 50,000 in the third millennium B.C.E. The city's center, visible for miles around, was a stepped pyramid, or ziggurat, topped with a temple (see the photo on p. 63). Inside the city, our village visitor would have found

■ **Change**
What was the role of cities in the early civilizations?

other temples as well, serving as centers of ritual performance and as places for the redistribution of stored food. Numerous craftspeople labored as masons, copper workers, weavers, and in many other specialties, while bureaucrats helped administer the city. It was, surely, a "vibrant, noisy, smelly, sometimes bewildering and dangerous, but also exciting place."[7] Here is how the *Epic of Gilgamesh*, Mesopotamia's ancient epic poem, describes the city:

> Come then, Enkidu, to ramparted Uruk,
> Where fellows are resplendent in holiday clothing,
> Where every day is set for celebration,
> Where harps and drums are played.
> And the harlots too, they are fairest of form,
> Rich in beauty, full of delights,
> Even the great gods are kept from sleeping at night.[8]

Equally impressive to a village visitor would have been the city of Mohenjo Daro (moe-hen-joe DAHR-oh), which flourished along the banks of the Indus River around 2000 B.C.E. With a population of perhaps 40,000, Mohenjo Daro and its sister city of Harappa featured large, richly built houses of two or three stories, complete with indoor plumbing, luxurious bathrooms, and private wells. Streets were laid out in a grid-like pattern, and beneath the streets ran a complex sewage system. Workers lived in row upon row of standardized two-room houses. Grand public buildings, including what seems to be a huge public bath, graced the city, while an enormous citadel was surrounded by a brick wall some forty-five feet high.

Mohenjo Daro
Flourishing around 2000 B.C.E., Mohenjo Daro was by far the largest city of the Indus Valley civilization, covering more than 600 acres. This photograph shows a small part of that city as it has been uncovered by archeologists during the past century. The large water-tight tank or pool, shown in the foreground, probably offered bathers an opportunity for ritual purification. (J. Mark Kenoyer/Harappa Images)

Even larger, though considerably later, was the Mesoamerican city of Teotihuacán (tay-uh-tee-wah-KAHN), located in the central valley of Mexico. It housed perhaps 200,000 people in the middle of the first millennium C.E. Broad avenues, dozens of temples, two huge pyramids, endless stone carvings and many bright frescoes, small apartments for the ordinary, palatial homes for the wealthy—all of this must have seemed another world for a new visitor from a distant village. In shopping for obsidian blades, how was she to decide among the 350 workshops in the city? In seeking relatives, how could she find her way among many different compounds, each surrounded by a wall and housing a different lineage? And what would she make of a neighborhood composed entirely of Mayan merchants from the distant coastal lowlands?

Cities, then, were central to most of the First Civilizations, though to varying degrees. They were political/administrative capitals; they functioned as centers for the production of culture, including art, architecture, literature, ritual, and ceremony; they served as marketplaces for both local and long-distance exchange; and they housed most manufacturing activity. Everywhere they generated a unique kind of society, compared to earlier agricultural villages or Paleolithic camps. Urban society was impersonal, for it was no longer possible to know everyone. Relationships of class and occupation were at least as important as those of kinship and village loyalty. Most notably, the degree of specialization and inequality far surpassed that of all preceding human communities.

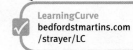

LearningCurve
bedfordstmartins.com
/strayer/LC

The Erosion of Equality

Among the most novel features of early urban life, at least to our imaginary village visitor, was the amazing specialization of work outside of agriculture—scholars, officials, merchants, priests, and artisans of all kinds. In ancient Mesopotamia, even scribes were subdivided into many categories: junior and senior scribes, temple scribes and royal scribes, scribes for particular administrative or official functions.[9] None of these people, of course, grew their own food; they were supported by the highly productive agriculture of farmers.

Hierarchies of Class

Alongside the occupational specialization of the First Civilizations lay their vast inequalities—in wealth, status, and power. Here we confront a remarkable and persistent feature of the human journey. As ingenuity and technology created more productive economies, the greater wealth now available was everywhere piled up rather than spread out. Early signs of this erosion of equality were evident in the more settled and complex gathering and hunting societies and in agricultural chiefdoms, but the advent of urban-based civilizations multiplied and magnified these inequalities many times over, as the more egalitarian values of earlier cultures were everywhere displaced. This transition represents one of the major turning points in the social history of humankind.

■ **Change**
In what ways was social inequality expressed in early civilizations?

As the First Civilizations took shape, inequality and hierarchy soon came to be regarded as normal and natural. Upper classes everywhere enjoyed great wealth in land or salaries, were able to avoid physical labor, had the finest of everything, and occupied the top positions in political, military, and religious life. Frequently, they were distinguished by the clothing they wore, the houses they lived in, and the manner of their burial. Early Chinese monarchs bestowed special clothing, banners, chariots, weapons, and ornaments on their regional officials, and all of these items were graded according to the officials' precise location in the hierarchy. In Mesopotamia, the punishments prescribed in the famous Code of Hammurabi (hahm-moo-RAH-bee) depended on social status. A free-born commoner who struck a person of equal rank had to pay a small fine, but if he struck "a man who is his superior, he shall

War and Slavery
This Mesopotamian victory monument, dating to about 2200 B.C.E., shows the Akkadian ruler Naram-Sin crushing his enemies. Prisoners taken in such wars were a major source of slaves in the ancient world. (Louvre, Paris/The Bridgeman Art Library)

receive 60 strokes with an oxtail whip in public." Clearly, class had consequences.

In all of the First Civilizations, free commoners represented the vast majority of the population and included artisans of all kinds, lower-level officials, soldiers and police, servants, and, most numerous of all, farmers. It was their surplus production—appropriated through a variety of taxes, rents, required labor, and tribute payments—that supported the upper classes. At least some of these people were aware of, and resented, these forced extractions and their position in the social hierarchy. Most Chinese peasants, for example, owned little land of their own and worked on plots granted to them by royal or aristocratic landowners. An ancient poem compared the exploiting landlords to rats and expressed the farmers' vision of a better life:

> Large rats! Large rats!
> Do not eat our spring grain!
> Three years have we had to do with you.
> And you have not been willing to think of our toil.
> We will leave you,
> And go to those happy borders.
> Happy borders, happy borders!
> Who will there make us always to groan?[10]

At the bottom of social hierarchies everywhere were slaves. Slavery and civilization, in fact, seem to have emerged together. Female slaves, captured in the many wars among rival Mesopotamian cities, were put to work in large-scale semi-industrial weaving enterprises, while males helped to maintain irrigation canals and construct ziggurats. Others worked as domestic servants in the households of their owners. In all of the First Civilizations, slaves—derived from prisoners of war, criminals, and debtors—were available for sale; for work in the fields, mines, homes, and shops of their owners; or on occasion for sacrifice. From the days of the earliest civilizations until the nineteenth century, the practice of "people owning people" was an enduring feature of state-based societies everywhere.

The practice of slavery in ancient times varied considerably from place to place. Egypt and the Indus Valley civilizations initially had far fewer slaves than did Mesopotamia, which was highly militarized. Later, the Greeks of Athens and the Romans employed slaves far more extensively than did the Chinese or Indians (see Chapter 5). Furthermore, most ancient slavery differed from the type of slavery practiced in the Americas during recent centuries: in the early civilizations, slaves were not a primary agricultural labor force; many children of slaves could become free people; and slavery was not associated primarily with "blackness" or with Africa.

Hierarchies of Gender

No division of human society has held greater significance for the lives of individuals than those of sex and gender. Sex describes the obvious biological differences between males and females. More important to historians, however, has been gender, which refers to the many and varied ways that cultures have assigned meaning to those sexual differences. To be gendered as masculine or feminine defines the roles and behavior considered appropriate for men and women in every human community. At least since the emergence of the First Civilizations, gender systems have been patriarchal, meaning that women have been subordinate to men in the family and in society generally. The inequalities of gender, like those of class, decisively shaped the character of the First Civilizations and those that followed.

The patriarchal ideal regarded men as superior to women and sons preferable to daughters. Men had legal and property rights unknown to most women. Public life in general was associated with masculinity, which defined men as rulers, warriors, scholars, and heads of households. Women's roles—both productive and reproductive—took place in the home, mostly within a heterosexual family, where women were defined largely by their relationship to a man: as a daughter, wife, mother, or widow. Frequently men could marry more than one woman and claim the right to regulate the social and sexual lives of the wives, daughters, and sisters in their families. Widely seen as weak but feared as potentially disruptive, women required both the protection and control of men.

But the reality of the lives of men and women did not always correspond to these ideals. Most men, of course, were far from prominent and exercised little power, except perhaps over the women and children of their own families. Gender often interacted with class to produce a more restricted but privileged life for upper-class women, who were largely limited to the home and the management of servants. By contrast, the vast majority of women always had to be out in public, working in the fields, tending livestock, buying and selling in the streets, or serving in the homes of their social superiors. A few women also operated in roles defined as masculine, acting as rulers, priests, and scholars, while others pushed against the limits and restrictions assigned to women. But most women no doubt accepted their assigned roles, unable to imagine anything approaching gender equality, even as most men genuinely believed that they were protecting and providing for their women.

The big question for historians lies in trying to explain the origins of this kind of patriarchy. Clearly it was neither natural nor of long standing. For millennia beyond measure, gathering and hunting societies had developed gender systems without the sharp restrictions and vast inequalities that characterized civilizations. Even early horticultural societies, those using a hoe or digging stick for farming, continued the relative gender equality that had characterized Paleolithic peoples. What was it, then, about civilization that seemed to generate a more explicit and restrictive patriarchy? One approach to answering this question highlights the role of a new and more intensive form of agriculture, involving the use of animal-drawn plows and the keeping and milking of large herds of animals. Unlike earlier farming practices that relied on a hoe

■ **Change**

In what ways have historians tried to explain the origins of patriarchy?

or digging stick, plow-based agriculture meant heavier work, which men were better able to perform. Taking place at a distance from the village, this new form of agriculture was perhaps less compatible with women's primary responsibility for child rearing. Furthermore, the growing population of civilizations meant that women were more often pregnant and thus more deeply involved in child care than before. Hence, in plow-based communities, men took over most of the farming work, and the status of women declined correspondingly, even though their other productive activities—weaving and food preparation, for example—continued. "As women were increasingly relegated to secondary tasks," writes archeologist Margaret Ehrenberg, "they had fewer personal resources with which to assert their status."[11]

Women have long been identified not only with the home but also with nature, for they are intimately involved in the primordial natural process of reproduction. But civilization seemed to highlight culture, or the human mastery of nature, through agriculture, monumental art and architecture, and creation of large-scale cities and states. Did this mean, as some scholars have suggested, that women were now associated with an inferior dimension of human life (nature), while men assumed responsibility for the higher order of culture?[12]

A further aspect of civilization that surely contributed to patriarchy was warfare. While earlier forms of human society certainly experienced violent conflict, large-scale military clashes with professionally led armies were a novel feature of almost all of the First Civilizations, and female prisoners of war often were the first slaves. With military service largely restricted to men, its growing prominence in the affairs of civilizations enhanced the values, power, and prestige of a male warrior class and cemented the association of masculinity with organized violence and with the protection of society and especially of its women.

Private property and commerce, central elements of the First Civilizations, may also have helped to shape early patriarchies. Without sharp restrictions on women's sexual activity, how could a father be certain that family property would be inherited by his offspring? In addition, the buying and selling associated with commerce were soon applied to male rights over women, as female slaves, concubines, and wives were exchanged among men.

Patriarchy in Practice

■ **Comparison**

How did Mesopotamian and Egyptian patriarchy differ from each other?

Whatever the precise origins of patriarchy, women's subordination permeated the First Civilizations, marking a gradual change from the more equal relationships of men and women within agricultural villages or Paleolithic bands. By the second millennium B.C.E. in Mesopotamia, various written laws codified and sought to enforce a patriarchal family life that offered women a measure of paternalistic protection while insisting on their submission to the unquestioned authority of men. Central to these laws was the regulation of female sexuality. A wife caught sleeping with another man might be drowned at her husband's discretion, whereas he was permitted to enjoy sexual relations with his female servants, though not with another man's wife. Divorce was far easier for the husband than for the wife. Rape was a serious offense, but the injured party was primarily the father or the husband of the victim, rather than the violated woman herself. While wealthy women might own and operate their own businesses or act on behalf of their powerful husbands, they too saw themselves as dependent. "Let all be well with [my husband]," prayed one such wife, "that I may prosper under his protection."[13]

Furthermore, women in Mesopotamian civilization were sometimes divided into two sharply distinguished categories. Under an Assyrian law code that was in effect between the fifteenth and eleventh centuries B.C.E., respectable women, those under the protection and sexual control of one man, were required to be veiled when outside the home, whereas nonrespectable women, such as slaves and prostitutes, were forbidden to wear veils and were subject to severe punishment if they presumed to cover their heads.

Finally, in some places, the powerful goddesses of earlier times were gradually relegated to the home and hearth. They were replaced in the public arena by dominant male deities, who now were credited with the power of creation and fertility and viewed as the patrons of wisdom and learning. This "demotion of the goddess," argues historian Gerda Lerner, culminated in the Hebrew Scriptures, in which a single male deity, Yahweh (YAH-way), alone undertakes the act of creation without any participation of a female counterpart. Yet this demotion did not occur always or everywhere; in Mesopotamia, for example, the prominent goddess Inanna or Istar long held her own against male gods and was regarded as a goddess of love and sexuality as well as a war deity. In a hymn to Inanna dating to around 2250 B.C.E., the poet and priestess Enheduanna declared: "It is her game to speed conflict and battle, untiring, strapping on her sandals."

Thus expressions of patriarchy varied among the first civilizations. Egypt, while clearly patriarchal, afforded its women greater opportunities than did most other First Civilizations. In Egypt, women were recognized as legal equals to men, able to own property and slaves, to administer and sell land, to make their own wills, to sign their own marriage contracts, and to initiate divorce. Moreover, married women in Egypt were not veiled as they were at times in Mesopotamia. Royal women occasionally exercised significant political power, acting as regents for their young sons or, more rarely, as queens in their own right. Clearly, though, this was seen as abnormal, for Egypt's most famous queen, Hatshepsut (r. 1472–1457 B.C.E.), was sometimes portrayed in statues as a man, dressed in male clothing and sporting the traditional false beard of the pharaoh.

LearningCurve
bedfordstmartins.com
/strayer/LC

The Rise of the State

What, we might reasonably ask, held ancient civilizations together despite the many tensions and complexities of urban living and the vast inequalities of civilized societies? Why did they not fly apart amid the resentments born of class and gender hierarchies? The answer, in large part, lay in yet another distinctive feature of the First

Civilizations—states. Organized around particular cities or larger territories, early states were headed almost everywhere by kings, who employed a variety of ranked officials, exercised a measure of control over society, and defended against external enemies. To modern people, the state is such a familiar reality that we find it difficult to imagine life without it. Nonetheless, it is a quite recent invention in human history, with the state replacing, or at least supplementing, kinship as the basic organizing principle of society and exercising far greater power than earlier chiefdoms. But the power of central states in the First Civilizations was limited and certainly not "totalitarian" in the modern sense of that term. The temple and the private economy rivaled and checked the power of rulers, and most authority was local rather than directed from the capital.

Coercion and Consent

■ **Change**

What were the sources of state authority in the First Civilizations?

Yet early states in Mesopotamia, Egypt, China, Mesoamerica, and elsewhere were influential, drawing their power from various sources, all of which assisted in providing cohesion for the First Civilizations. One basis of authority lay in the recognition that the complexity of life in cities or densely populated territories required some authority to coordinate and regulate the community. Someone had to organize the irrigation systems of river valley civilizations. Someone had to direct efforts to defend the city or territory against aggressive outsiders. Someone had to adjudicate conflicts among the many different peoples, unrelated to one another, who rubbed elbows in the early cities. The state, in short, solved certain widely shared problems and therefore had a measure of voluntary support among the population. For many people, it was surely useful.

The state, however, was more useful for some people than for others, for it also served to protect the privileges of the upper classes, to require farmers to give up a portion of their product to support city-dwellers, and to demand work on large public projects such as pyramids and fortifications. If necessary, state authorities had the ability, and the willingness, to use force to compel obedience. An Egyptian document described what happens to a peasant unable to pay his tax in grain:

> Now the scribe lands on the shore. He surveys the harvest. Attendants are behind him with staffs, Nubians with clubs. One says [to the peasant], "Give grain." There is none. He is beaten savagely. He is bound, thrown into a well, submerged head down. His wife is bound in his presence. His children are in fetters. His neighbors abandon them and flee.[14]

Such was the power of the state, as rulers accumulated the resources to pay for officials, soldiers, police, and attendants. This capacity for violence and coercion marked off the states of the First Civilizations from earlier chiefdoms, whose leaders had only persuasion, prestige, and gifts to back up their authority. But as states increasingly monopolized the legitimate right to use violence, rates of death from interpersonal violence declined as compared to earlier nonstate communities.[15]

Force, however, was not always necessary, for the First Civilizations soon generated ideas suggesting that state authority as well as class and gender inequalities were normal, natural, and ordained by the gods. Kingship everywhere was associated with the sacred. Ancient Chinese kings were known as the Son of Heaven, and only they or their authorized priests could perform the rituals and sacrifices necessary to keep the cosmos in balance. Mesopotamian rulers were thought to be the stewards of their city's patron gods. Their symbols of kingship—crown, throne, scepter, mace—were said to be of divine origin, sent to earth when the gods established monarchy. Egyptians, most of all, invested their pharaohs with divine qualities. Rulers claimed to embody all the major gods of Egypt, and their supernatural power ensured the regular flooding of the Nile and the defeat of the country's enemies.

A Mesopotamian Ziggurat This massive ziggurat/temple to the Mesopotamian moon god Nanna was built around 2100 B.C.E. in the city of Ur. The solitary figure standing atop the staircase illustrates the size of this huge structure. (© Richard Ashworth/ Robert Harding World Imagery/ Corbis)

But if religion served most often to justify unequal power and privilege, it might also on occasion be used to restrain, or even undermine, the established order. Hammurabi claimed that his law code was inspired by Marduk, the chief god of Babylon, and was intended to "bring about the rule of righteousness in the land, to destroy the wicked and the evil-doers; so that the strong should not harm the weak."[16] Another Mesopotamian monarch, Urukagina from the city of Lagash, claimed authority from the city's patron god for reforms aimed at ending the corruption and tyranny of a previous ruler. In China during the Western Zhou dynasty (1046–771 B.C.E.), emperors ruled by the Mandate of Heaven, but their bad behavior could result in the removal of that mandate and their overthrow.

Writing and Accounting

A further support for state authority lay in the remarkable invention of writing. It was a powerful and transforming innovation, regarded almost everywhere as a gift from the gods, while people without writing often saw it as something magical or supernatural. Distinctive forms of writing emerged in most of the First Civilizations (see Snapshot, p. 65), sustaining them and their successors in many ways. Literacy defined elite status and conveyed enormous prestige to those who possessed it. Because it can be learned, writing also provided a means for some commoners to join the charmed circle of the literate. Writing as propaganda, celebrating the great deeds of the kings, was prominent, especially among the Egyptians and later among the Maya. A hymn to the pharaoh, dating to about 1850 B.C.E., extravagantly praised the ruler:

> He has come unto us ... and has given peace to the two Riverbanks
> and has made Egypt to live; he hath banished its suffering;
> he has caused the throat of the subjects to breathe
> and has trodden down foreign countries
> he has delivered them that were robbed he has come unto us, that we may
>   [nurture up?] our children and bury our aged ones.[17]

In Mesopotamia and elsewhere, writing served an accounting function, recording who had paid their taxes, who owed what to the temple, and how much workers had earned. Thus it immensely strengthened bureaucracy. Complex calendars indicated precisely when certain rituals should be performed. Writing also gave weight and specificity to orders, regulations, and laws. Hammurabi's famous law code, while correcting certain abuses, made crystal clear that fundamental distinctions divided men and women and separated slaves, commoners, and people of higher rank.

Once it had been developed, writing, like religion, proved hard to control and operated as a wild card in human affairs. It gave rise to literature and philosophy, to astronomy and mathematics, and, in some places, to history, often recording what had long been oral traditions. On occasion, the written word proved threatening, rather than supportive, to rulers. China's so-called First Emperor, Qin Shihuangdi (r. 221–210 B.C.E.), allegedly buried alive some 460 scholars and burned their books when they challenged his brutal efforts to unify China's many warring states, or so his later critics claimed (see Chapter 3). Thus writing became a major arena for social and political conflict, and rulers always have sought to control it.

LearningCurve
bedfordstmartins.com
/strayer/LC

Olmec Head
This colossal statue, some six feet high and five feet wide, is one of seventeen such carvings, dating to the first millennium B.C.E., that were discovered in the territory of the ancient Olmec civilization. Thought to represent individual rulers, each of the statues has a distinct and realistically portrayed face. (© Danny Lehman/Corbis)

The Grandeur of Kings

Yet another source of state authority derived from the lavish lifestyle of elites, the impressive rituals they arranged, and the imposing structures they created. Everywhere, kings, high officials, and their families lived in luxurious palaces, dressed in splendid clothing, bedecked themselves with the loveliest jewelry, and were attended by endless servants. Their deaths triggered elaborate burials, of which the pyramids of the Egyptian pharaohs were perhaps the most ostentatious. Monumental palaces, temples, ziggurats, pyramids, and statues conveyed the imposing power of the state and its elite rulers. The Olmec civilization of Mesoamerica (1200–400 B.C.E.) erected enormous

Snapshot   Writing in Ancient Civilizations

Most of the early writing systems were "logophonetic," using symbols to designate both whole words and particular sounds or syllables. Chinese characters, which indicated only words, were an exception. None of the early writing systems employed alphabets.

Location	Type	Initial Use	Example	Comment
Sumer	Cuneiform: wedge-shaped symbols on clay tablets representing objects, abstract ideas, sounds, and syllables	Records of economic transactions, such as temple payments and taxes	bird	Regarded as the world's first written language; other languages such as Babylonian and Assryian were written with Sumerian script
Egypt	Hieroglyphs ("sacred carvings"): a series of signs that denote words and consonants (but not vowels or syllables)	Business and administrative purposes; later used for religious inscriptions, stories, poetry, hymns, and mathematics	rain, dew, storm	For everyday use, less formal systems of cursive writing (known as "hieratic" and "demotic") were developed
Andes	Quipu: a complex system of knotted cords in which the color, length, type, and location of knots conveyed mostly numerical meaning	Various accounting functions; perhaps also used to express words	numerical data (possibly in codes), words, and ideas	Widely used in the Inca Empire; recent discoveries place quipus in Caral some 5,000 years ago
Indus River Valley	Some 400 pictographic symbols representing sounds and words, probably expressing a Dravidian language currently spoken in southern India	Found on thousands of clay seals and pottery; probably used to mark merchandise	6 fish	As yet undeciphered
China	Oracle bone script: pictographs (stylized drawings) with no phonetic meaning	Inscribed on turtle shells or animal bones; used for divination (predicting the future) in the royal court of Shang dynasty rulers	horse	Direct ancestor of contemporary Chinese characters
Olmec	Signs that represent sounds (syllables) and words; numbering system using bars and dots	Used to record the names and deeds of rulers and shamans, as well as battles and astronomical data	jaguar	Structurally similar to later Mayan script; Olmec calendars were highly accurate and the basis for later Mesoamerican calendars

SUMMING UP SO FAR

In what ways might the advent of "civilization" have marked a revolutionary change in the human condition? And in what ways did it carry on earlier patterns from the past?

human heads, more than ten feet tall and weighing at least twenty tons, carved from blocks of basalt and probably representing particular rulers. Somewhat later the Maya Temple of the Giant Jaguar, towering 154 feet tall, was the most impressive among many temples, pyramids, and palaces that graced the city of Tikal. All of this must have seemed overwhelming to common people in the cities and villages of the First Civilizations.

Comparing Mesopotamia and Egypt

■ **Comparison**

In what ways did Mesopotamian and Egyptian civilizations differ from each other?

A productive agricultural technology, city living, distinct class and gender inequalities, the emerging power of states — all of these were common features of First Civilizations across the world and also of those that followed. Still, these civilizations were not everywhere the same, for differences in political organization, religious beliefs and practices, the role of women, and much more gave rise to distinctive traditions. Nor were they static. Like all human communities, they changed over the centuries. Finally, these civilizations did not exist in complete isolation, for they participated in networks of interactions with near and sometimes more distant neighbors. In looking more closely at two of these First Civilizations — Mesopotamia and Egypt — we can catch a glimpse of the differences, changes, and connections that characterized early civilizations.

Environment and Culture

The civilizations of both Mesopotamia and Egypt grew up in river valleys and depended on their rivers to sustain a productive agriculture in otherwise arid lands. Those rivers, however, were radically different. At the heart of Egyptian life was the Nile, "that green gash of teeming life," which rose predictably every year to bring the soil and water that nurtured a rich Egyptian agriculture. The Tigris and Euphrates rivers, which gave life to Mesopotamian civilization, also rose annually, but "unpredictably and fitfully, breaking man's dikes and submerging his crops."[18] (See Map 2.2.) Furthermore, an open environment without serious obstacles to travel made Mesopotamia far more vulnerable to invasion than the much more protected space of Egypt, which was surrounded by deserts, mountains, seas, and cataracts. For long periods of its history, Egypt enjoyed a kind of "free security" from external attack that Mesopotamians clearly lacked.

But does the physical environment shape the human cultures that develop within it? Most historians are reluctant to endorse any kind of determinism, especially one suggesting that "geography is destiny," but in the case of Mesopotamia and Egypt, it is hard to deny some relationship between the physical setting and culture.

In at least some of its literature, the Mesopotamian outlook on life, which developed within a precarious, unpredictable, and often violent environment, viewed humankind as caught in an inherently disorderly world, subject to the whims of ca-

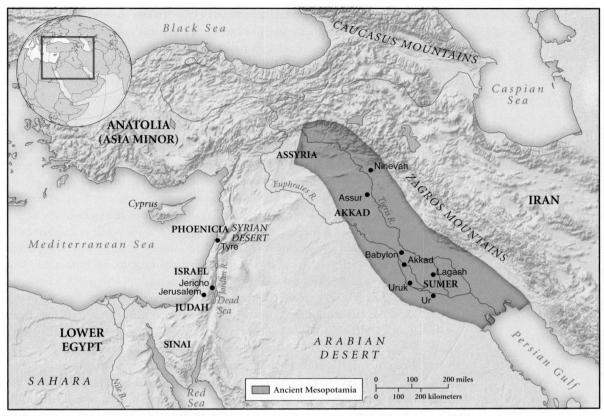

Map 2.2 **Mesopotamia**
After about 1,000 years of independent and competitive existence, the city-states of Sumer were incorporated into a number of larger imperial states based in Akkad, Babylon, and then Assyria.

pricious and quarreling gods, and facing death without much hope of a blessed life beyond. A Mesopotamian poet complained: "I have prayed to the gods and sacrificed, but who can understand the gods in heaven? Who knows what they plan for us? Who has ever been able to understand a god's conduct?"[19] The famous Mesopotamian *Epic of Gilgamesh* likewise depicted a rather pessimistic view of the gods and of the possibility for eternal life.

By contrast, elite literate culture in Egypt, developing in a more stable, predictable, and beneficent environment, produced a rather more cheerful and hopeful outlook on the world. The rebirth of the sun every day and of the river every year seemed to assure Egyptians that life would prevail over death. The amazing pyramids, constructed during Egypt's Old Kingdom (2663–2195 B.C.E.), reflected the firm belief that at least the pharaohs and other high-ranking people could successfully make the journey to eternal life in the Land of the West. Incantations for the dead describe an afterlife of abundance and tranquility that Gilgamesh could only have envied. Over time, larger groups of people, beyond the pharaoh and his entourage, came to believe that they too could gain access to the afterlife if they followed proper procedures and lived a morally upright life. Thus Egyptian civilization not only affirmed the possibility of eternal life but also expanded access to it.

If the different environments of Mesopotamia and Egypt shaped their societies and cultures, those civilizations, with their mounting populations and growing demand for resources, likewise had an impact on the environment.[20] The *Epic of Gilgamesh* inscribed in mythology the deforestation of Mesopotamia. When the ruler Gilgamesh sought to make for himself "a name that endures" by building walls, ramparts, and temples, he required much timber. But to acquire it, he had first to kill Humbaba, appointed by the gods to guard the forests. The epic describes what happened next: "Then there followed confusion. . . . Now the mountains were moved and all the hills, for the guardian of the forest was killed. They attacked the cedars. . . . So they pressed on into the forest . . . and while Gilgamesh felled the first of the trees of the forest, Enkidu [the friend of Gilgamesh] cleared their roots as far as the banks of Euphrates."[21]

In Sumer (southern Mesopotamia), such deforestation and the soil erosion that followed from it sharply decreased crop yields between 2400 and 1700 B.C.E. Also contributing to this disaster was the increasing salinization of the soil, a long-term outcome of intensive irrigation. By 2000 B.C.E., there were reports that "the earth turned white" as salt accumulated in the soil. As a result, wheat was largely replaced by barley, which is far more tolerant of salty conditions. This ecological deterioration clearly weakened Sumerian city-states, facilitated their conquest by foreigners, and shifted the center of Mesopotamian civilization permanently to the north.

Egypt, by contrast, created a more sustainable agricultural system, which lasted for thousands of years and contributed to the remarkable continuity of its civilization. Whereas Sumerian irrigation involved a complex and artificial network of canals and dikes that led to the salinization of the soil, its Egyptian counterpart was much less intrusive, simply regulating the natural flow of the Nile. Such a system avoided the problem of salty soils, allowing Egyptian agriculture to emphasize wheat production, but it depended on the general regularity and relative gentleness of the Nile's annual flooding. On occasion, that pattern was interrupted, with serious consequences for Egyptian society. An extended period of low floods between 2250 and 1950 B.C.E. led to sharply reduced agricultural output, large-scale starvation, the loss of livestock, and, consequently, social upheaval and political disruption. Nonetheless, Egypt's ability to work *with* its more favorable natural environment enabled a degree of stability and continuity that proved impossible in Sumer, where human action intruded more heavily into a less benevolent natural setting.

Cities and States

Politically as well as culturally and environmentally, Mesopotamian and Egyptian civilizations differed sharply. For its first thousand years (3200–2350 B.C.E.), Mesopotamian civilization, located in the southern Tigris-Euphrates region known as Sumer, was organized in a dozen or more separate and independent city-states. Each city-state was ruled by a king, who claimed to represent the city's patron deity and who controlled the affairs of the walled city and surrounding rural area. Quite remarkably, some 80 percent of the population of Sumer lived in one or another of these city-states, making Mesopotamia the most thoroughly urbanized society of ancient times. The chief reason for this massive urbanization, however, lay in the great flaw of this system, for frequent warfare among these Sumerian city-states caused people living in rural areas to flee to the walled cities for protection. With no overarching authority, rivalry over land and water often led to violent conflict.

These conflicts, together with environmental devastation, eventually left Sumerian cities vulnerable to outside forces, and after about 2350 B.C.E., stronger peoples from northern Mesopotamia conquered Sumer's warring cities, bringing an end to the Sumerian phase of Mesopotamian civilization. First the Akkadians (2350–2000 B.C.E.) and later the Babylonians (1900–1500 B.C.E.) and the Assyrians (900–612 B.C.E.) created larger territorial states or bureaucratic empires that encompassed all or most of Mesopotamia. Periods of political unity now descended upon this First Civilization, but it was unity imposed from outside.

Egyptian civilization, by contrast, began its history around 3100 B.C.E., with the merger of several earlier states or chiefdoms into a unified territory that stretched some 1,000 miles along the Nile. For an amazing 3,000 years, Egypt maintained that unity and independence, though with occasional interruptions. A combination of wind patterns that made it easy to sail south along the Nile and a current flowing north facilitated communication, exchange, unity, and stability within the Nile Valley. Here was a record of political longevity and continuity that the Mesopotamians and many other ancient peoples could not replicate.

Cities in Egypt were less important than in Mesopotamia, although political capitals, market centers, and major burial sites gave Egypt an urban presence as well. Most people lived in agricultural villages along the river rather than in urban centers, perhaps because Egypt's greater security made it less necessary for people to gather in fortified towns. The focus of the Egyptian state resided in the pharaoh, believed to be a god in human form. He alone ensured the daily rising of the sun and the annual flooding of the Nile. All of the country's many officials served at his pleasure, and access to the afterlife lay in proximity to him and burial in or near his towering pyramids.

This image of the pharaoh and his role as an enduring symbol of Egyptian civilization persisted over the course of three millennia, but the realities of Egyptian political life did not always match the ideal, as the Portrait of Paneb so vividly illustrates (see pp. 70–71). By 2400 B.C.E., the power of the pharaoh had diminished, as local officials and nobles, who had been awarded their own land and were able to pass their positions on to their sons, assumed greater authority. When changes in the weather resulted in the Nile's repeated failure to flood properly around 2200 B.C.E., the authority of the pharaoh was severely discredited, and Egypt dissolved for several centuries into a series of local principalities.

Even when centralized rule was restored around 2000 B.C.E., the pharaohs never regained their old power and prestige. Kings were now warned that they too would

PORTRAIT

Paneb, An Egyptian Criminal

The life of Paneb (ca. thirteenth century B.C.E.) illuminates an underside of Egyptian life rather different from the images of order and harmony portrayed in much of ancient Egyptian art and literature.[22] Paneb was born into a family and a village of tomb workers—people who quarried, sculpted, and painted the final resting places of the pharaohs at a time when royal pyramids were no longer being constructed. Granted generous allowances of grain, beer, fish, vegetables, firewood, and clothing, tomb workers represented a prestigious occupation in ancient Egypt.

Paneb was apparently orphaned as a youngster and raised by another tomb-working family, that of the childless Neferhotep, a foreman of the tomb workers' crew who brought his adopted son into the profession. But Paneb quarreled violently with Neferhotep, on one occasion smashing the door to his house and threatening to kill him.

As an adult, Paneb married and sired a large family of eight or nine children. He also indulged in numerous

Paneb worshipping a coiled cobra representing the goddess Meretseger, patron deity of the burial grounds in Thebes where Paneb worked. (© The Trustees of the British Museum)

affairs with married women and was involved in at least one rape. One of his lovers was the wife of a man with whom Paneb had grown up in Neferhotep's home; the couple subsequently divorced, a frequent occurrence in ancient Egypt. In another case, Paneb seduced both a married woman and her daughter and shared the sexual favors of the daughter with his son Aapehty. It is not difficult to imagine the tensions that such behavior created in a small close-knit village.

When Paneb's adoptive father Neferhotep died—he was perhaps murdered—Paneb succeeded him as workplace foreman, thus incurring the lifelong hostility of Neferhotep's brother, Amennakht, who felt he had better claim to the job. What turned the tide in Paneb's favor was his "gift" of five servants, made to the vizier, the pharaoh's highest official, who was responsible for such appointments. To add insult to Amennakht's injury, those servants had belonged to Neferhotep himself.

have to account for their actions at the Day of Judgment. Nobles no longer sought to be buried near the pharaoh's pyramid but instead created their own more modest tombs in their own areas. Osiris, the god of the dead, became increasingly prominent, and all worthy men, not only those who had been close to the pharaoh in life, could aspire to immortality in his realm.[23]

Interaction and Exchange

■ **Connection**
In what ways were Mesopotamian and Egyptian civilizations shaped by their interactions with near and distant neighbors?

Although Mesopotamia and Egypt represented separate and distinct civilizations, they interacted frequently with each other and with both near and more distant neighbors. Even in these ancient times, the First Civilizations were embedded in larger networks of commerce, culture, and power. None of them stood alone.

While such bribes were common practice in obtaining promotions, it was Paneb's use of his position as foreman of the tomb workers' crew that got him into ever deeper trouble. He actively harassed his rival Amennakht, preventing him and his family from using the small chapel in which workers celebrated the festivals of their gods. He quarreled with the foreman of another work crew saying: "I'll attack you on the mountain and I'll kill you." Such angry outbursts led to frequent fighting and gained Paneb a reputation for brutality.

Paneb also exploited his position as foreman to his own advantage. He used—or stole—expensive tools given to the work crew for his own purposes. He ordered members of his work crew to do personal work for him—making a bed which he then sold to a high official, feeding his oxen, weaving baskets for his personal use, and preparing and decorating his own tomb, using materials pilfered from the royal tombs he was charged with constructing. On one occasion he stole the covering of a royal chariot and another time he entered a royal tomb, drank the wine intended for the pharaoh's afterlife, and in an act of enormous disrespect . . . even blasphemy . . . actually sat on the sarcophagus containing the embalmed body of the ruler.

Although rebuked from time to time by high officials, Paneb's bad behavior continued. "He could not stop his clamor," according to an official document. At some point, Paneb's son publicly denounced his father's sexual escapades. But the final straw that broke his career came from Amennakht, Paneb's long-time rival. He apparently had had enough and drew up a long list of particulars detailing Paneb's crimes. That document, from which our knowledge of Paneb largely derives, has survived. It concluded in this fashion:

> He is thus not worthy of this position. For truly, he seems well, [but] he is like a crazy person. And he kills people to prevent them from carrying out a mission of the Pharaoh. See, I wish to convey knowledge of his condition to the vizier.

The outcome of this complaint is unclear, for Paneb subsequently disappears from the historical record, and a new foreman was appointed in his place. It was not, however, Amennakht.

Questions: Since most of the evidence against Paneb comes from his archrival, how much weight should historians grant to that account? How might the story appear if written from Paneb's viewpoint? What perspectives on the Egypt of his time does Paneb's career disclose? How do those perspectives differ from more conventional and perhaps idealized understandings?

The early beginnings of Egyptian civilization illustrate the point. Its agriculture drew upon wheat and barley, which likely reached Egypt from Mesopotamia, as well as gourds, watermelon, domesticated donkeys, and cattle, which came from the Sudan to the south. The practice of "divine kingship" probably derived from the central or eastern Sudan, where small-scale agricultural communities had long viewed their rulers as sacred and buried them with various servants and officials. From this complex of influences, the Egyptians created something distinct and unique, but that civilization had roots in both Africa and Southwest Asia.[24]

Furthermore, once they were established, both Mesopotamia and Egypt carried on long-distance trade, mostly in luxury goods destined for the elite. Sumerian merchants had established seaborne contact with the Indus Valley civilization as early as 2300 B.C.E., while Indus Valley traders and their interpreters had taken up residence

Egypt and Nubia
By the fourteenth century B.C.E., Nubia was a part of an Egyptian empire. This wall painting shows Nubian princes bringing gifts or tribute, including rings and bags of gold, to Huy, the Egyptian viceroy of Nubia. The mural comes from Huy's tomb. (© The Trustees of the British Museum)

in Mesopotamia. Other trade routes connected it to Anatolia (present-day Turkey), Egypt, Iran, and Afghanistan. During Akkadian rule over Mesopotamia, a Sumerian poet described its capital of Agade:

> In those days the dwellings of Agade were filled with gold,
> its bright-shining houses were filled with silver,
> into its granaries were brought copper, tin, slabs of
> lapis lazuli [a blue gemstone], its silos bulged at the sides . . .
> its quay where the boats docked were all bustle. . . .[25]

All of this and more came from far away.

Egyptian trade likewise extended far afield. Beyond its involvement with the Mediterranean and the Middle East, Egyptian trading journeys extended deep into Africa, including Nubia, south of Egypt in the Nile Valley, and Punt, along the East African coast of Ethiopia and Somalia. One Egyptian official described his return from an expedition to Nubia: "I came down with three hundred donkeys laden with incense, ebony, . . . panther skins, elephant tusks, throw sticks, and all sorts of good products."[26] What most intrigued the very young pharaoh who sent him, however, was a dancing dwarf that accompanied the expedition back to Egypt.

Along with trade goods went cultural influence from the civilizations of Mesopotamia and Egypt. Among the smaller societies of the region to feel this influence were the Hebrews. Their sacred writings, recorded in the Old Testament, showed the influence of Mesopotamia in the "eye for an eye" principle of their legal system and in the story of a flood that destroyed the world. The Phoenicians, who were commercially active in the Mediterranean basin from their homeland in present-day Lebanon, also were influenced by Mesopotamian civilization. They venerated Asarte, a local form of the Mesopotamian fertility goddess Istar. They also adapted the Sumerian cuneiform method of writing to a much easier alphabetic system, which later became the basis for Greek and Latin writing. Various Indo-European peoples, dispersing probably from north-central Anatolia, also incorporated Sumerian deities into their own religions as well as bronze metallurgy and the wheel into their economies. When their widespread migrations carried them across much of Eurasia, they took these Sumerian cultural artifacts with them.

Egyptian cultural influence likewise spread in several directions. Nubia, located to the south of Egypt in the Nile Valley, not only traded with its more powerful neighbor but also was subject to periodic military intervention and political control from Egypt. Skilled Nubian archers were actively recruited for service as mercenaries in Egyptian armies. They often married Egyptian women and were buried in Egyptian style. All of this led to the diffusion of Egyptian culture in Nubia, expressed in building Egyptian-style pyramids, worshipping Egyptian gods and goddesses, and making use of Egyptian hieroglyphic writing. Despite this cultural borrowing, Nubia remained a distinct civilization, developing its own alphabetic script, retaining many of its own gods, developing a major ironworking industry by 500 B.C.E., and asserting its political independence whenever possible. The Nubian kingdom of Kush, in fact, invaded Egypt in 760 B.C.E. and ruled it for about 100 years. (See the Portrait of Piye, pp. 186–87.)

In the Mediterranean basin, clear Egyptian influence is visible in the art of Minoan civilization, which emerged on the island of Crete about 2500 B.C.E. More controversial has been the claim by historian Martin Bernal in a much-publicized book, *Black Athena* (1987), that ancient Greek culture—its art, religion, philosophy, and language—drew heavily upon Egyptian as well as Mesopotamian precedents. His book lit up a passionate debate among scholars. To some of his critics, Bernal seemed to undermine the originality of Greek civilization by suggesting that it had Afro-Asian origins. His supporters accused the critics of Eurocentrism. Whatever its outcome, the controversy surrounding Bernal's book served to focus attention on Egypt's relationship to black Africa and to the world of the Mediterranean basin.

Influence was not a one-way street, however, as Egypt and Mesopotamia likewise felt the impact of neighboring peoples. Pastoral peoples, speaking Indo-European languages and living in what is now southern Russia, had domesticated the horse by perhaps 4000 B.C.E. and later learned to tie that powerful animal to wheeled carts and chariots. This new technology provided a fearsome military potential that enabled various chariot-driving peoples, such as the Hittites, to threaten ancient civilizations. Based in Anatolia, the Hittites sacked the city of Babylon in 1595 B.C.E. Several centuries later, conflict between the Hittites and Egypt over control of Syria resulted in the world's first written peace treaty. But chariot technology was portable, and soon both the Egyptians and the Mesopotamians incorporated it into their own military forces. In fact, this powerful military innovation, together with the knowledge of bronze metallurgy, spread quickly and widely, reaching China by 1200 B.C.E. There it enabled the creation of a strong Chinese state ruled by the Shang dynasty. All of

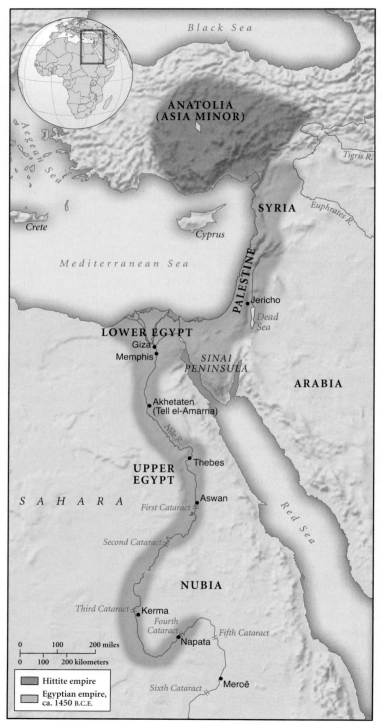

Map 2.3   An Egyptian Empire
During the New Kingdom period after 1550 B.C.E., Egypt became for several centuries an empire, extending its political control southward into Nubia and northward into Palestine.

these developments provide evidence of at least indirect connections across parts of the Afro-Eurasian landmass in ancient times. Even then, no civilization was wholly isolated from larger patterns of interaction.

In Egypt, the centuries following 1650 B.C.E. witnessed the migration of foreigners from surrounding regions and conflict with neighboring peoples, shaking the sense of security that this Nile Valley civilization had long enjoyed. It also stimulated the normally complacent Egyptians to adopt a number of technologies pioneered earlier in Asia, including the horse-drawn chariot; new kinds of armor, bows, daggers, and swords; improved methods of spinning and weaving; new musical instruments; and olive and pomegranate trees. Absorbing these foreign innovations, Egyptians went on to create their own empire, both in Nubia and in the eastern Mediterranean regions of Syria and Palestine. By 1500 B.C.E., the previously self-contained Egypt became for several centuries an imperial state bridging Africa and Asia, ruling over substantial numbers of non-Egyptian peoples (see Map 2.3). It also became part of an international political system that included the Babylonian and later Assyrian empires of Mesopotamia as well as many other peoples of the region. Egyptian and Babylonian rulers engaged in regular diplomatic correspondence, referred to one another as "brother," exchanged gifts, and married their daughters into one another's families. Or at least they tried to. While Babylonian rulers were willing to send their daughters to Egypt, the Egyptians were exceedingly reluctant to return the favor, claiming that "from ancient times the daughter of the king of Egypt has not been given to anyone." To this rebuff, the disappointed Babylonian monarch replied: "You are a king and you can do as pleases you. . . . Send me [any] beautiful woman as if she were your daughter. Who is to say this woman is not the daughter of the king."[27]

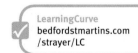

LearningCurve
bedfordstmartins.com
/strayer/LC

Reflections: "Civilization": What's in a Word?

In examining the cultures of ancient Mesopotamia and Egypt, we are worlds away from life in agricultural villages or Paleolithic camps. Much the same holds for those of the Indus Valley, Central Asia, China, Mesoamerica, and the Andes. Strangely enough, historians have been somewhat uncertain as to how to refer to these new forms of human community. Following common practice, I have called them "civilizations," but scholars have reservations about the term for two reasons. The first is its implication of superiority. In popular usage, "civilization" suggests refined behavior, a "higher" form of society, something unreservedly positive. The opposite of "civilized"—"barbarian," "savage," or "uncivilized"—is normally understood as an insult implying inferiority. That, of course, is precisely how the inhabitants of many civilizations have viewed those outside their own societies, particularly those neighboring peoples living without the alleged benefit of cities and states.

Modern assessments of the First Civilizations reveal a profound ambiguity about these new, larger, and more complex societies. On the one hand, these civilizations have given us inspiring art, profound reflections on the meaning of life, more productive technologies, increased control over nature, and the art of writing—all of which have been cause for celebration. On the other hand, as anthropologist Marvin Harris noted, "human beings learned for the first time how to bow, grovel, kneel, and kowtow."[28] Massive inequalities, state oppression, slavery, large-scale warfare, the subordination of women, and epidemic disease also accompanied the rise of civilization, generating discontent, rebellion, and sometimes the urge to escape. This ambiguity about the character of civilizations has led some historians to avoid the word, referring to early Egypt, Mesopotamia, and other regions instead as complex societies, urban-based societies, state-organized societies, or some other more neutral term.

A second reservation about using the term "civilization" derives from its implication of solidity—the idea that civilizations represent distinct and widely shared identities with clear boundaries that mark them off from other such units. It is unlikely, however, that many people living in Mesopotamia, Norte Chico, or ancient China felt themselves part of a shared culture. Local identities defined by occupation, clan affiliation, village, city, or region were surely more important for most people than those of some larger civilization. At best, members of an educated upper class who shared a common literary tradition may have felt themselves part of some more inclusive civilization, but that left out most of the population. Moreover, unlike modern nations, none of the earlier civilizations had definite borders. Any identification with that civilization surely faded as distance from its core region increased. Finally, the line between civilizations and other kinds of societies is not always clear. Just when does a village or town become a city? At what point does a chiefdom become a state? Scholars continue to argue about these distinctions.

Given these reservations, should historians discard the notion of civilization? Maybe so, but this book continues to use it both because it is so deeply embedded in our way of thinking about the world and because no alternative concept has achieved widespread acceptance for making distinctions among different kinds of human communities. When the term appears in the text, keep in mind two points. First, as used by historians, "civilization" is a purely descriptive term, designating a particular and distinctive type of human society—one with cities and states—and does not imply any judgment or assessment, any sense of superiority or inferiority. Second, it is used to define broad cultural patterns in particular geographic regions—Mesopotamia, the Peruvian coast, or China, for example—even though many people living in those regions may have been more aware of differences and conflicts than of those commonalities.

Second Thoughts

What's the Significance?

Norte Chico/Caral, 49; 52

Indus Valley civilization, 52

Central Asian/Oxus civilization, 53–54

Olmec civilization, 54

Uruk, 55–56

Mohenjo Daro/Harappa, 56

Epic of Gilgamesh, 56; 67

Code of Hammurabi, 57–58

patriarchy, 59–61

rise of the state, 61–66

Egypt: "the gift of the Nile," 66–75

Paneb, 70–71

Nubia, 72

Big Picture Questions

1. How does the use of the term "civilization" by historians differ from that of popular usage? How do you use the term?

2. "Civilizations were held together largely by force." Do you agree with this assessment, or were there other mechanisms of integration as well?

3. How did the various First Civilizations differ from one another?

4. **Looking Back:** To what extent did civilizations represent "progress" in comparison with earlier Paleolithic and Neolithic societies? And in what ways did they constitute a setback for humankind?

Next Steps: For Further Study

Cyril Aldred, *The Egyptians* (1998). A brief and up-to-date account from a widely recognized expert.

Jonathan M. Kenoyer, *Ancient Cities of the Indus Valley Civilization* (1998). A thorough and beautifully illustrated study by a leading archeologist of the area.

Samuel Noah Kramer, *History Begins at Sumer* (1981). A classic account of Sumerian civilization, filled with wonderful stories and anecdotes.

David B. O'Connor, *Ancient Nubia: Egypt's Rival in Africa* (1994). An overview of this ancient African civilization, with lovely illustrations based on a museum exhibit.

Christopher A. Pool, *Olmec Archeology and Early Mesoamerica* (2007). A scholarly and up-to-date account of the earliest civilization in Mesoamerica.

Robert Thorp, *China in the Early Bronze Age: Shang Civilization* (2006). An accessible and scholarly account of early Chinese civilization informed by recent archeological discoveries.

"The Indus Civilization," http://www.harappa.com/har/haro.html. Hundreds of vivid pictures and several brief essays on the Indus Valley civilization.

The British Museum, "Ancient Egypt," http://www.ancientegypt.co.uk/menu.html. An interactive exploration of Egyptian civilization.

For Web sites and additional documents related to this chapter, see **Make History** at bedfordstmartins.com/strayer.

PART TWO

Second-Wave Civilizations in World History

500 B.C.E.–500 C.E.

Contents

Chapter 3. State and Empire in Eurasia/North Africa, 500 B.C.E.–500 C.E.

Chapter 4. Culture and Religion in Eurasia/North Africa, 500 B.C.E.–500 C.E.

Chapter 5. Society and Inequality in Eurasia/North Africa, 500 B.C.E.–500 C.E.

Chapter 6. Commonalities and Variations: Africa and the Americas, 500 B.C.E.–1200 C.E.

After the First Civilizations: What Changed and What Didn't?

Studying world history has much in common with using the zoom lens of a camera. Sometimes, we pull the lens back to get a picture of the broadest possible panorama. At other times, we zoom in a bit for a middle-range shot, or even farther for a close-up of some particular feature of the historical landscape. Students of world history soon become comfortable with moving back and forth among these several perspectives.

As we bid farewell to the First Civilizations, we will take the opportunity to pull back the lens and look broadly, and briefly, at the entire age of agricultural civilizations, a period from about 3500 B.C.E., when the earliest of the First Civilizations arose, to about 1750 C.E., when the first Industrial Revolution launched a new and distinctively modern phase of world history. During these more than 5,000 years, the most prominent large-scale trend was the globalization of civilization as this new form of human community increasingly spread across the planet, encompassing more people and larger territories.

The first wave of that process, addressed in Chapter 2, was already global in scope, with expressions in Asia, Africa, and the Americas. Those First Civilizations generated the most impressive and powerful human societies created thus far, but they proved fragile and vulnerable as well. The always-quarreling city-states of ancient Mesopotamia had long ago been absorbed into the larger empires of Babylon and Assyria. By the middle of the second millennium B.C.E., the Indus Valley, Central Asian, and Norte Chico civilizations had collapsed or faded away. Egypt too fell victim to a series of foreign invaders during the first millennium B.C.E., including the forces of Nubia, Assyria, Alexander the Great, and the Roman Empire. The end of Olmec civilization around 400 B.C.E. has long puzzled historians, for it seems that the Olmecs themselves razed and then abandoned their major cities even as their civilizational style spread to neighboring peoples. About the same time, China's Zhou dynasty kingdom fragmented into a series of warring states.

Even though these First Civilizations broke down, there was no going back. Civilization as a form of human community proved durable and resilient as well as periodically fragile. Thus, in the thousand years between 500 B.C.E. and 500 C.E., new or enlarged urban-centered and state-based societies emerged to replace the First Civilizations in the Mediterranean basin, the Middle East, India, China, Mesoamerica, and the Andes. Furthermore, smaller expressions of civilization began to take shape elsewhere — in Ethiopia and West Africa, in Japan and Indonesia, in Vietnam and Cambodia. In short, the development of civilization was becoming a global process.

Many of these second-wave civilizations likewise perished, as the collapse of the Roman Empire, Han dynasty China, and the Mayan cities remind us. They were followed by yet a third wave of civilizations (roughly 500 to 1500 C.E.; see Part Three). Some of them represented the persistence or renewal of older patterns, as in the case of China, for example, while elsewhere — such as in Western Europe, Russia, Japan, and West Africa — newer civilizations emerged, all of which borrowed heavily from their more-established neighbors. The largest of these, Islamic civilization, incorporated a number of older centers of civilization, Egypt and Mesopotamia, for example, under the umbrella of a new religion. Thus, the globalization of civilization continued apace. So too did the interaction of civilizations with one another and with gathering and hunting peoples, agricultural village societies, and pastoral communities.

Continuities in Civilization

As this account of the human journey moves into the second and third waves of civilization, the question arises as to how they differed from the first ones. From a panoramic perspective, the answer is "not much." States and empires rose, expanded, and collapsed with a tiresome regularity. It is arguable, however, that little fundamental change occurred amid these constant fluctuations. Monarchs continued to rule most of the new civilizations; women remained subordinate to men in all of them; a sharp divide between the elite and everyone else persisted almost everywhere, as did the practice of slavery.[1]

Furthermore, no technological or economic breakthrough occurred to create new kinds of human societies as the Agricultural Revolution had done earlier or as the Industrial Revolution would do much later. Landowning elites had little incentive to innovate, for they benefited enormously from simply expropriating the surplus that peasant farmers produced. Nor would peasants have any reason to invest much effort in creating new forms of production when they knew full well that any gains they might generate would be seized by their social superiors. Merchants, who often were risk takers, might have spawned innovations, but they usually were dominated by powerful states and were viewed with suspicion and condescension by more prestigious social groups.

Many fluctuations, repetitive cycles, and minor changes characterize this long era of agricultural civilization, but no fundamental or revolutionary transformation of social or economic life took place. The major turning points in human history had occurred earlier with the emergence of agriculture and the birth of the First Civilizations and would occur later with the breakthrough of industrialization.

Changes in Civilization

While this panoramic perspective allows us to see the broadest outlines of the human journey, it also obscures much of great importance that took place during the second and third waves of the age of agrarian civilization. If we zoom in a bit more closely, significant changes emerge, even if they did not result in a thorough transformation of human life. Population, for example, grew more rapidly than ever before during this period, as the Snapshot illustrates. Even though the overall trend was up, important fluctuations interrupted the pattern, especially during the first millennium C.E., when no overall growth took place. Moreover, the rate of growth, though rapid in comparison with Paleolithic times, was quite slow if we measure it against the explosive expansion of recent centuries, when human numbers quadrupled in the twentieth century alone. This modest and interrupted pattern of population growth during the age of agrarian civilization reflected the absence of any fundamental economic breakthrough, which could have supported much larger numbers.

Another change lies in the growing size of the states or empires that structured civilizations. The Roman, Persian, Indian, and Chinese empires of second-wave civilizations, as well as the Arab, Mongol, and Inca empires of the third wave, all dwarfed the city-states of Mesopotamia and the Egypt of the pharaohs. Each of these empires brought together in a single political system a vast diversity of peoples. Even so, just to keep things in perspective, as late as the seventeenth century C.E., only one-third of the world's landmass was under the control of any state-based system, although these societies now encompassed a considerable majority of the world's people.

The rise and fall of these empires likewise represented very consequential changes to the people who experienced them. In the course of its growth, the Roman Empire

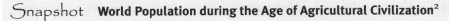

Snapshot   **World Population during the Age of Agricultural Civilization[2]**

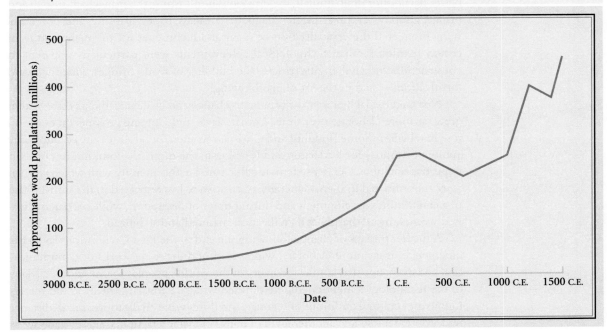

utterly destroyed the city of Carthage in North Africa, with the conquerors allegedly sowing the ground with salt so that nothing would ever grow there again. Similar bloodshed and destruction accompanied the creation of other much-celebrated states. Their collapse also had a dramatic impact on the lives of their people. Scholars have estimated that the large population of Mayan civilization shrank by some 85 percent in less than a century as that society dissolved around 840 c.e. It is difficult to imagine the sense of trauma and bewilderment associated with a collapse of this magnitude.

Second- and third-wave civilizations also generated important innovations in many spheres. Those in the cultural realm have been perhaps the most widespread and enduring. Distinctive "wisdom traditions"—the great philosophical/religious systems of Confucianism and Daoism in China; Hinduism and Buddhism in India; Greek rationalism in the Mediterranean; and Judaism, Zoroastrianism, Christianity, and Islam in the Middle East—have provided the moral and spiritual framework within which most of the world's peoples have sought to order their lives and define their relationship to the mysteries of life and death. All of these philosophical and religious systems are the product of second- and third-wave civilizations.

Although no technological breakthrough equivalent to the Agricultural or Industrial Revolution took place during this time, more modest innovations considerably enhanced human potential for manipulating the environment. China was a primary source of such technological change, though by no means the only one. "Chinese inventions and discoveries," wrote one prominent historian, "passed in a continuous flood from East to West for twenty centuries before the scientific revolution."[3] They included piston bellows, the draw-loom, silk-handling machinery, the wheelbarrow, a better harness for draft animals, the crossbow, iron casting, the iron-chain suspension bridge, gunpowder, firearms, the magnetic compass, paper, printing, and porcelain. India pioneered the crystallization of sugar and techniques for the manufacture of cotton textiles. Roman technological achievements were particularly apparent in construction and civil engineering—the building of roads, bridges, aqueducts, and fortifications—and in the art of glassblowing.

Nor were social hierarchies immune to change and challenge. India's caste system grew far more elaborate over time. Roman slaves and Chinese peasants on occasion rose in rebellion. Some Buddhist and Christian women found a measure of autonomy and opportunities for leadership and learning in the monastic communities of their respective traditions. Gender systems too fluctuated in the intensity with which women were subordinated to men. Generally women were less restricted in the initial phase of a civilization's development and during times of disruption, while patriarchy limited women more sharply as a civilization matured and stabilized.

A further process of change following the end of the First Civilizations lay in the emergence of far more elaborate, widespread, and dense networks of communication and exchange that connected many of the world's peoples to one another. Many of the technologies mentioned here diffused widely across large areas, as did the religious and cultural traditions of second- and third-wave civilizations. Long-distance trade routes represented another form of transregional interaction. Caravan trade across northern Eurasia, seaborne commerce within the Indian Ocean basin, the exchange of goods across the Sahara, river-based commerce in the eastern woodlands of North America, various trading networks radiating from Mesoamerica—all of these carried goods, and sometimes culture and religions as well. In the early centuries of the Common Era, for example, Southeast Asia attracted distant merchants and some settlers from both China and India, bringing Confucianism, Hinduism, and Buddhism to various parts of that vast region. Disease also increasingly linked distant human communities. According to the famous Greek historian Thucydides, a mysterious plague "from parts of Ethiopia above Egypt" descended on Athens in 430 B.C.E., decimating the city.[4]

In all of these ways, the world became quite different from what it had been in the age of the First Civilizations, even though fundamental economic and social patterns had not substantially changed.

The first three chapters of Part Two focus in a thematic fashion on the Eurasian/North African civilizations of the second-wave era (500 B.C.E.–500 C.E.), which hosted the vast majority of the world's population, some 80 percent or more. Chapter 3 introduces them by examining and comparing their political frameworks and especially the empires (great or terrible, depending on your point of view) that took shape in most of them. Far more enduring than their empires were the cultural or religious traditions that second-wave civilizations generated. These are examined, also comparatively, in Chapter 4. The social life of these civilizations, expressed in class, caste, slavery, and gender relationships, also varied considerably, as Chapter 5 spells out. In Chapter 6, the historical spotlight turns to inner Africa and the Americas during the second-wave era, asking whether their histories paralleled Eurasian patterns or explored alternative possibilities.

In recalling this second-wave phase of the human journey, we will have occasion to compare the experiences of its various peoples, to note their remarkable achievements, to lament the tragedies that befell them and the suffering to which they gave rise, and to ponder their continuing power to fascinate us still.

Mapping Part Two

Ancestral Pueblo
Chapter 6

Mound builders
Chapter 6

Maya / Teotihuacán
Chapter 6

Chavín / Moche
Chapter 6

Wari / Tiwanaku
Chapter 6

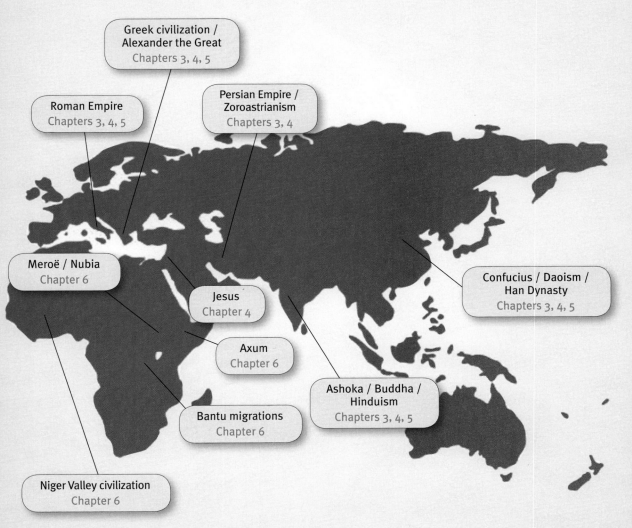

Greek civilization /
Alexander the Great
Chapters 3, 4, 5

Persian Empire /
Zoroastrianism
Chapters 3, 4

Roman Empire
Chapters 3, 4, 5

Meroë / Nubia
Chapter 6

Jesus
Chapter 4

Confucius / Daoism /
Han Dynasty
Chapters 3, 4, 5

Axum
Chapter 6

Bantu migrations
Chapter 6

Ashoka / Buddha /
Hinduism
Chapters 3, 4, 5

Niger Valley civilization
Chapter 6

CHAPTER THREE

State and Empire in Eurasia/North Africa

500 B.C.E.–500 C.E.

Empires and Civilizations in Collision:
  The Persians and the Greeks
  The Persian Empire
  The Greeks
  Collision: The Greco-Persian Wars
  Collision: Alexander and the
    Hellenistic Era
Comparing Empires: Roman and
  Chinese
  Rome: From City-State to Empire
  China: From Warring States to Empire
  Consolidating the Roman and
    Chinese Empires
  The Collapse of Empires
Intermittent Empire: The Case of
  India
Reflections: Enduring Legacies of
  Second-Wave Empires
Portrait: Trung Trac, Resisting the
  Chinese Empire

Are We Rome? It was the title of a thoughtful book, published in 2007, asking what had become a familiar question in the early twenty-first century: "Is the United States the new Roman Empire?"[1] With the collapse of the Soviet Union by 1991 and the subsequent U.S. invasions of Afghanistan and Iraq, some commentators began to make the comparison. The United States' enormous multicultural society, its technological achievements, its economically draining and over-stretched armed forces, its sense of itself as unique and endowed with a global mission, its concern about foreigners penetrating its borders, its apparent determination to maintain military superiority — all of this invited comparison with the Roman Empire. Supporters of a dominant role for the United States argued that Americans must face up to their responsibilities as "the undisputed master of the world" as the Romans did in their time. Critics warned that the Roman Empire became overextended abroad and corrupt and dictatorial at home and then collapsed, suggesting that a similar fate may await the U.S. empire. Either way, the point of reference was an empire that had passed into history some 1,500 years earlier, a continuing reminder of the significance of the distant past to our contemporary world. In fact, for at least several centuries, that empire has been a source of metaphors and "lessons" about personal morality, corruption, political life, military expansion, and much more.

Even in a world largely critical of empires, they still excite the imagination of historians and readers of history. The earliest ones show up in the era of the First Civilizations when Akkadian, Babylonian, and Assyrian empires encompassed the city-states of Mesopotamia

---

Terra-Cotta Archer: Part of the immense funerary complex constructed for the Chinese ruler Qin Shihuangdi, this kneeling archer represents the military power that reunified a divided China under the Qin dynasty in 221 B.C.E. (Museum of the Terra Cotta Army, Xian/Visual Connection Archive)

and established an enduring imperial tradition in the Middle East. Egypt became an imperial state when it temporarily ruled Nubia and the lands of the eastern Mediterranean. Following in their wake were many more empires, whose rise and fall have been central features of world history for the past 4,000 years.

BUT WHAT EXACTLY IS AN EMPIRE? At one level, empires are simply states, political systems that exercise coercive power. The term, however, is normally reserved for larger and more aggressive states, those that conquer, rule, and extract resources from other states and peoples. Thus empires have generally encompassed a considerable variety of peoples and cultures within a single political system, and they have often been associated with political or cultural oppression. Frequently, empires have given political expression to a civilization or culture, as in the Chinese and Persian empires. Civilizations have also flourished without a single all-encompassing state or empire, as in the competing city-states of Mesopotamia, Greece, and Mesoamerica or the many rival states of post-Roman Europe. In such cases, civilizations were expressed in elements of a common culture rather than in a unified political system.

The Eurasian empires of the second-wave era—those of Persia, Greece under Alexander the Great, Rome, China during the Qin (chihn) and Han dynasties, India during the Mauryan (MORE-yuhn) and Gupta dynasties—shared a set of common problems. Would they seek to impose the culture of the imperial heartland on their varied subjects? Would they rule conquered people directly or through established local authorities? How could they extract the wealth of empire in the form of taxes, tribute, and labor while maintaining order in conquered territories? And, no matter how impressive they were at their peak, they all sooner or later collapsed, providing a useful reminder to their descendants of the fleeting nature of all human creation.

Why have these and other empires been of such lasting fascination to both ancient and modern people? Perhaps in part because they were so big, creating a looming presence in their respective regions. Their armies and their tax collectors were hard to avoid. Maybe also because they were so bloody. The violence of conquest easily grabs our attention, and certainly, all of these empires were founded and sustained at a great cost in human life. The collapse of these once-powerful states is likewise intriguing, for the fall of the mighty seems somehow satisfying, perhaps even a delayed form of justice. The study of empires also sets off by contrast those times and places in which civilizations have prospered without an enduring imperial state.

But empires have also commanded attention simply because they were important. While the political values of recent times have almost universally condemned empire building, very large numbers of people—probably the majority of humankind before the twentieth century—have lived out their lives in empires, where they were often governed by rulers culturally different from themselves. These imperial states brought together people of quite different traditions and religions and so stimulated the exchange of ideas, cultures, and values. Despite their violence, exploitation, and oppression, empires also imposed substantial periods of peace

A Map of Time

750–336 B.C.E.	Era of Greek city-states
553–330 B.C.E.	Persian Achaemenid Empire
509 B.C.E.	Founding of the Roman Republic
500–221 B.C.E.	Chinese age of warring states
490–479 B.C.E.	Greco-Persian Wars
479–429 B.C.E.	Golden Age of Athens
431–404 B.C.E.	Peloponnesian War
336–323 B.C.E.	Reign of Alexander the Great
321–185 B.C.E.	India's Mauryan dynasty empire
221–206 B.C.E.	China's Qin dynasty empire
206 B.C.E.–220 C.E.	China's Han dynasty empire
200 B.C.E.–200 C.E.	High point of Roman Empire
First century B.C.E.	Transition from republic to empire in Rome
184 C.E.	Yellow Turban revolt in China
220 C.E.	Collapse of Chinese Han dynasty
320–550 C.E.	India's Gupta dynasty empire
Fifth century C.E.	Collapse of western Roman Empire

and security, which fostered economic and artistic development, commercial exchange, and cultural mixing. In many places, empire also played an important role in defining masculinity as conquest generated a warrior culture that gave particular prominence to the men who created and ruled those imperial states.

SEEKING THE MAIN POINT

How might you assess — both positively and negatively — the role of empires in the history of the second-wave era?

Empires and Civilizations in Collision: The Persians and the Greeks

The millennium between 500 B.C.E. and 500 C.E. in North Africa and Eurasia witnessed the flowering of second-wave civilizations in the Mediterranean world, the Middle East, India, and China. For the most part, these distant civilizations did not directly encounter one another, as each established its own political system, cultural values, and ways of organizing society. A great exception to that rule lay in the Mediterranean world and in the Middle East, where the emerging Persian Empire and Greek civilization, physically adjacent to each other, experienced a centuries-long interaction and clash. It was one of the most consequential cultural encounters of the ancient world.

Snapshot   **Distinctive Features of Second-Wave Eurasian Civilizations**

Civilization	Chinese	South Asian	Middle Eastern	Mediterranean
Political features	Unified empire under Qin and Han dynasties; "Mandate of Heaven" concept; examinations for official positions	Mauryan and Gupta empires; frequent political fragmentation	Persian Empire; royal absolutism; conquest by Alexander the Great	Greek city-states; Athenian democracy; Roman Empire; unification of Mediterranean basin
Cultural features	Confucianism/ Daoism	Hinduism/Buddhism	Zoroastrianism; Judaism; Christianity	Greek rationalism; spread of Christianity
Social features	Class hierarchy; dominance of bureaucratic and landholding elites; peasant rebellions	Caste system; purity and pollution; social position as indicator of spiritual development	Benevolent posture toward minorities in Persian Empire; Jews returned to homeland; tension between Greek and non-Greeks in Hellenistic era	Unusually prominent role of slavery in Greek and Roman society

The Persian Empire

In 500 B.C.E., the largest and most impressive of the world's empires was that of the Persians, an Indo-European people whose homeland lay on the Iranian plateau just north of the Persian Gulf. Living on the margins of the earlier Mesopotamian civilization, the Persians under the Achaemenid (ah-KEE-muh-nid) dynasty (553–330 B.C.E.) constructed an imperial system that drew on previous examples, such as the Babylonian and Assyrian empires, but far surpassed them all in size and splendor. Under the leadership of the famous monarchs Cyrus (r. 557–530 B.C.E.) and Darius (r. 522–486 B.C.E.), Persian conquests quickly reached from Egypt to India, encompassing in a single state some 35 to 50 million people, an immensely diverse realm containing dozens of peoples, states, languages, and cultural traditions (see Map 3.1).

■ **Comparison**

How did Persian and Greek civilizations differ in their political organization and values?

The Persian Empire centered on an elaborate cult of kingship in which the monarch, secluded in royal magnificence, could be approached only through an elaborate ritual. When the king died, sacred fires all across the land were extinguished, Persians were expected to shave their hair in mourning, and the manes of horses were cut short. Ruling by the will of the great Persian god Ahura Mazda (uh-HOORE-uh MAHZ-duh), kings were absolute monarchs, more than willing to crush rebellious regions or officials. Interrupted on one occasion while he was with his wife, Darius ordered the offender, a high-ranking nobleman, killed, along with his entire clan. In the eyes of many, Persian monarchs fully deserved their effusive title —"Great king, King of kings, King of countries containing all kinds of men, King in this great

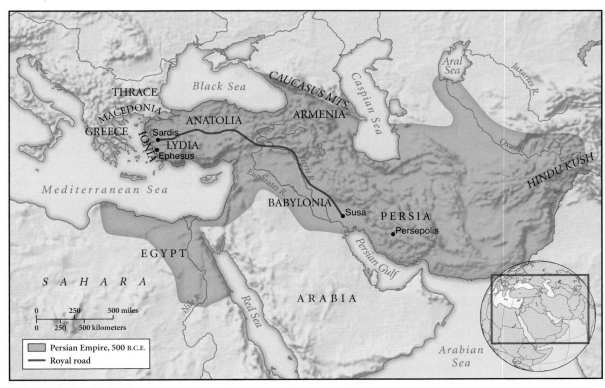

Map 3.1 The Persian Empire
At its height, the Persian Empire was the largest in the world. It dominated the lands of the First Civilizations in the Middle East and was commercially connected to neighboring regions.

earth far and wide." Darius himself best expressed the authority of the Persian ruler when he observed, "what was said to them by me, night and day, it was done."[2]

But more than conquest and royal decree held the empire together. An effective administrative system placed Persian governors, called *satraps* (SAY-traps), in each of the empire's twenty-three provinces, while lower-level officials were drawn from local authorities. A system of imperial spies, known as the "eyes and ears of the King," represented a further imperial presence in the far reaches of the empire. A general policy of respect for the empire's many non-Persian cultural traditions also cemented the state's authority. Cyrus won the gratitude of the Jews when in 539 B.C.E. he allowed those exiled in Babylon to return to their homeland and rebuild their temple in Jerusalem (see Chapter 4, pp. 134–35). In Egypt and Babylon, Persian kings took care to uphold local religious cults in an effort to gain the support of their followers and officials. The Greek historian Herodotus commented that "there is no nation which so readily adopts foreign customs. They have taken the dress of the Medes and in war they wear the Egyptian breastplate. As soon as they hear of any luxury, they instantly make it their own."[3] For the next 1,000 years or more, Persian imperial bureaucracy and court life, replete with administrators, tax collectors, record keepers,

Persepolis
The largest palace in Persepolis, the Persian Empire's ancient capital, was the Audience Hall. The emperor officially greeted visiting dignitaries at this palace, which was constructed around 500 B.C.E. This relief, which shows a lion attacking a bull and Persian guards at attention, adorns a staircase leading to the Audience Hall. (© Gianni Dagli Orti/Corbis)

and translators, provided a model for all subsequent regimes in the region, including, later, those of the Islamic world.

The infrastructure of empire included a system of standardized coinage, predictable taxes levied on each province, and a newly dug canal linking the Nile with the Red Sea, which greatly expanded commerce and enriched Egypt. A "royal road," some 1,700 miles in length, facilitated communication and commerce across this vast empire. Caravans of merchants could traverse this highway in three months, but agents of the imperial courier service, using a fresh supply of horses every twenty-five to thirty miles, could carry a message from one end of the road to another in a week or two. Herodotus was impressed. "Neither snow, nor rain, nor heat, nor darkness of night," he wrote, "prevents them from accomplishing the task proposed to them with utmost speed." And an elaborate underground irrigation system sustained a rich agricultural economy in the semi-arid conditions of the Iranian plateau and spread from there throughout the Middle East and beyond.

The elaborate imperial centers, particularly Susa and Persepolis, reflected the immense wealth and power of the Persian Empire. Palaces, audience halls, quarters for the harem, monuments, and carvings made these cities into powerful symbols of imperial authority. Materials and workers alike were drawn from all corners of the empire and beyond. Inscribed in the foundation of Persepolis was Darius's commentary on what he had set in motion: "And Ahura Mazda was of such a mind, together with all the other gods, that this fortress [should] be built. And [so] I built it. And I built it secure and beautiful and adequate, just as I was intending to."[4]

The Greeks

It would be hard to imagine a sharper contrast than that between the huge and centralized Persian Empire, governed by an absolute and almost unapproachable monarch, and the small competing city-states of classical Greece, which allowed varying degrees of popular participation in political life. Like the Persians, the Greeks were an Indo-European people whose early history drew on the legacy of the First Civilizations. The classical Greece of historical fame emerged around 750 B.C.E. as a new civilization and flourished for about 400 years before it was incorporated into a succession of foreign empires. During that relatively short period, the civilization of Athens and Sparta, of Plato and Aristotle, of Zeus and Apollo took shape and collided with its giant neighbor to the east.

Calling themselves Hellenes, the Greeks created a civilization that was distinctive in many ways, particularly in comparison with the Persians. The total population of Greece and the Aegean basin was just 2 million to 3 million, a fraction of that of the Persian Empire. Furthermore, Greek civilization took shape on a small peninsula, deeply divided by steep mountains and valleys. Its geography certainly contributed to the political shape of that civilization, which found expression not in a Persian-style empire, but in hundreds of city-states or small settlements (see Map 3.2). Most were quite modest in size, with between 500 and 5,000 male citizens. But Greek civilization, like its counterparts elsewhere, also left a decisive environmental mark on the lands it encompassed. Smelting metals such as silver, lead, copper, bronze, and iron required enormous supplies of wood, leading to deforestation and soil erosion. Plato declared

Map 3.2 Classical Greece
The classical civilization of Greece was centered on a small peninsula of south-eastern Europe, but Greek settlers planted elements of that civilization along the coasts of the Mediterranean and Black seas.

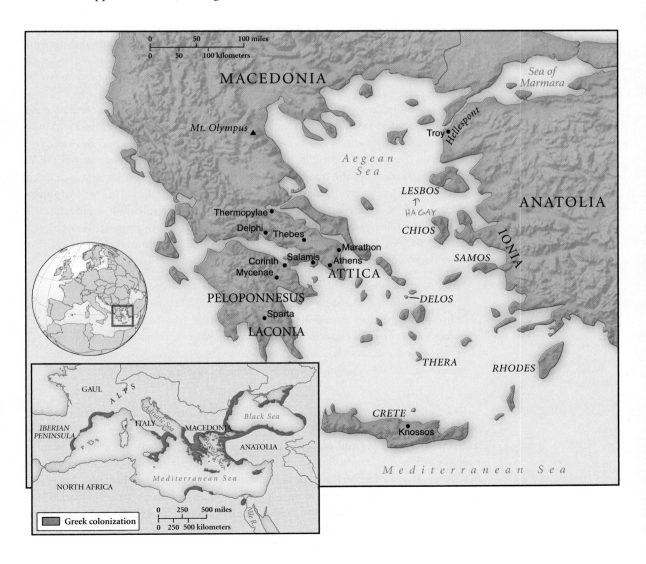

that the area around Athens had become "a mere relic of the original country. . . . All the rich soil has melted away, leaving a country of skin and bone."[5]

■ **Change**
How did semidemocratic governments emerge in some of the Greek city-states?

Each of these city-states was fiercely independent and in frequent conflict with its neighbors, yet they had much in common, speaking the same language and worshipping the same gods. Every four years they temporarily suspended their continual conflicts to participate together in the Olympic Games, which had begun in 776 B.C.E. But this emerging sense of Greek cultural identity did little to overcome the endemic political rivalries of the larger city-states, including Athens, Sparta, Thebes, and Corinth, among many others.

Like the Persians, the Greeks were an expansive people, but their expansion took the form of settlement in distant places rather than conquest and empire. Pushed by a growing population, Greek traders in search of iron and impoverished Greek farmers in search of land stimulated a remarkable emigration. Between 750 and 500 B.C.E., the Greeks established settlements all around the Mediterranean basin and the rim of the Black Sea. Settlers brought Greek culture, language, and building styles to these new lands, even as they fought, traded, and intermarried with their non-Greek neighbors.

The most distinctive feature of Greek civilization, and the greatest contrast with Persia, lay in the extent of popular participation in political life that occurred within at least some of the city-states. It was the idea of "citizenship," of free people managing the affairs of state, of equality for all citizens before the law, that was so unique. A foreign king, observing the operation of the public assembly in Athens, was amazed that male citizens as a whole actually voted on matters of policy: "I find it astonishing," he noted, "that here wise men speak on public affairs, while fools decide them."[6] Compared to the rigid hierarchies, inequalities, and absolute monarchies of Persia and other ancient civilizations, the Athenian experiment was remarkable. This is how one modern scholar defined it:

> Among the Greeks the question of who should reign arose in a new way. Previously the most that had been asked was whether one man or another should govern and whether one alone or several together. But now the question was whether all the citizens, including the poor, might govern and whether it would be possible for them to govern as citizens, without specializing in politics. In other words, should the governed themselves actively participate in politics on a regular basis?[7]

The extent of participation and the role of "citizens" varied considerably, both over time and from city to city. Early in Greek history, only wealthy and well-born men had the rights of full citizenship, such as speaking and voting in the assembly, holding public office, and fighting in the army. Gradually, men of the lower classes, mostly small-scale farmers, also obtained these rights. At least in part, this broadening of political rights was associated with the growing number of men able to afford the armor and weapons that would allow them to serve as hoplites, or infantrymen, in the armies of the city-states. In many places, strong but benevolent rulers known as tyrants emerged for a time, usually with the support of the poorer classes, to challenge the prerogatives of the wealthy. Sparta—famous for its extreme forms of military discipline and its large population of helots, conquered people who lived in slave-like conditions—vested most political authority in its Council of Elders. The council was composed of twenty-eight men over the age of sixty, derived from the wealthier and more influential segment of society, who served for life and provided political leadership for Sparta.

It was in Athens that the Greek experiment in political participation achieved its most distinctive expression. Early steps in this direction were the product of intense class conflict, leading almost to civil war. A reforming leader named Solon emerged in 594 B.C.E. to push Athenian politics in a more democratic direction, breaking the hold of a small group of aristocratic families. Debt slavery was abolished, access to public office was opened to a wider group of men, and all citizens were allowed to take part in the Assembly. Later reformers such as Cleisthenes (KLEYE-sthuh-nees) and Pericles extended the rights of citizens even further. By 450 B.C.E., all holders of public office were chosen by lot and were paid, so that even the poorest could serve. The Assembly, where all citizens could participate, became the center of political life.

Athenian democracy, however, was different from modern democracy. It was direct, rather than representative, democracy, and it was distinctly limited. Women, slaves, and foreigners, together far more than half of the population, were wholly excluded from political participation. Nonetheless, political life in Athens was a world away from that of the Persian Empire and even from that of many other Greek cities.

Collision: The Greco-Persian Wars

In recent centuries, many writers and scholars have claimed classical Greece as the foundation of Western or European civilization. But the ancient Greeks themselves looked primarily to the East—to Egypt and the Persian Empire. In Egypt, Greek scholars found impressive mathematical and astronomical traditions on which they built. And Persia represented both an immense threat and later, under Alexander the Great, an opportunity for Greek empire building.

If ever there was an unequal conflict between civilizations, surely it was the collision of the Greeks and the Persians. The confrontation between the small and divided Greek cities and Persia, the world's largest empire, grew out of their respective patterns of expansion. A number of Greek settlements on the Anatolian seacoast, known to the Greeks as Ionia, came under Persian control as that empire extended its domination to the west. In 499 B.C.E., some of these Ionian Greek cities revolted against Persian domination and found support from Athens on the Greek mainland. Outraged by this assault from the remote and upstart Greeks, the Persians, twice in ten years (490 and 480 B.C.E.), launched major military expeditions to punish the Greeks in general and Athens in particular. Against all odds and all expectations, the Greeks held them off, defeating the Persians on both land and sea.

■ **Connection**

What were the consequences for both sides of the encounter between the Persians and the Greeks?

Though no doubt embarrassing, their defeat on the far western fringes of the empire had little effect on the Persians. However, it had a profound impact on the Greeks and especially on Athens, whose forces had led the way to victory. Beating the Persians in battle was a source of enormous pride for Greece. Years later, elderly Athenian men asked one another how old they had been when the Greeks triumphed in the momentous Battle of Marathon in 490 B.C.E. In their view, this victory was the product of Greek freedoms because those freedoms had motivated men to fight with extraordinary courage for what they valued so highly. It led to a western worldview in which Persia represented Asia and despotism, whereas Greece signified Europe and freedom. Thus was born the notion of an East/West divide, which has shaped European and North American thinking about the world into the twenty-first century.

The Greek victory also radicalized Athenian democracy, for it had been men of the poorer classes who had rowed their ships to victory and who were now in a position to insist on full citizenship. The fifty years or so after the Greco-Persian Wars were not only the high point of Athenian democracy but also the Golden Age of Greek culture. During this period, the Parthenon, that marvelous temple to the Greek goddess Athena, was built; Greek theater was born from the work of Aeschylus, Sophocles, and Euripides; and Socrates was beginning his career as a philosopher and an irritant in Athens.

But Athens's Golden Age was also an era of incipient empire. In the Greco-Persian Wars, Athens had led a coalition of more than thirty Greek city-states on the basis of its naval power, but Athenian leadership in the struggle against Persian aggression had spawned an imperialism of its own. After the war, Athenian efforts to solidify Athens's dominant position among the allies led to intense resentment and finally to a bitter civil war (431–404 B.C.E.), with Sparta taking the lead in defending the traditional independence of Greek city-states. In this bloody conflict, known as the Peloponnesian War, Athens was defeated, while the Greeks exhausted themselves and magnified their distrust of one another. Thus the way was open to their eventual takeover by the growing forces of Macedonia, a frontier kingdom on the northern fringes of the Greek world. The glory days of the Greek experiment were over, but the spread of Greek culture was just beginning.

Collision: Alexander and the Hellenistic Era

■ **Connection**
What changes did Alexander's conquests bring in their wake?

The Macedonian takeover of Greece, led by its king, Philip II, finally accomplished by 338 B.C.E. what the Greeks themselves had been unable to achieve—the political unification of Greece, but at the cost of much of the prized independence of its various city-states. It also set in motion a second round in the collision of Greece and Persia as Philip's son, Alexander, prepared to lead a massive Greek expedition against the Persian Empire. Such a project appealed to those who sought vengeance for the earlier Persian assault on Greece, but it also served to unify the fractious Greeks in a war against their common enemy.

The story of this ten-year expedition (333–323 B.C.E.), accomplished while Alexander was still in his twenties, has become the stuff of legend (see Map 3.3). Surely it was among the greatest military feats of the ancient world in that it created a Greek empire from Egypt and Anatolia in the west to Afghanistan and India in the east. In the process, the great Persian Empire was thoroughly defeated; its capital, Persepolis (per-SEP-uh-lis), was looted and burned; and Alexander was hailed as the "king of Asia." In Egypt, Alexander, then just twenty-four years old, was celebrated as a liberator from Persian domination, was anointed as pharaoh, and was declared by Egyptian priests to be the "son of the gods." Arrian, a later Greek historian, described Alexander in this way:

> His passion was for glory only, and in that he was insatiable. . . . Noble indeed was his power of inspiring his men, of filling them with confidence, and in the moment of danger, of sweeping away their fear by the spectacle of his own fearlessness.[8]

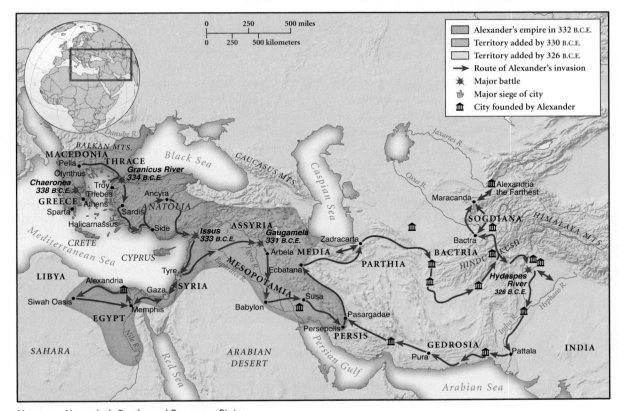

Map 3.3   Alexander's Empire and Successor States
Alexander's conquests, though enormous, did not long remain within a single empire, for his generals divided them into three successor states shortly after his death. This was the Hellenistic world within which Greek culture spread.

Alexander the Great
This mosaic of Alexander on horseback comes from the Roman city of Pompeii. It depicts the Battle of Issus (333 B.C.E.), in which Greek forces, although considerably outnumbered, defeated the Persian army, led personally by Emperor Darius III. (Erich Lessing/Art Resource, NY)

Alexander died in 323 B.C.E., without returning to Greece, and his empire was soon divided into three kingdoms, ruled by leading Macedonian generals.

From the viewpoint of world history, the chief significance of Alexander's amazing conquests lay in the widespread dissemination of Greek culture during what historians call the Hellenistic era (323–30 B.C.E.). Elements of that culture, generated in a small and remote Mediterranean peninsula, now penetrated the lands of the First Civilizations—Egypt, Mesopotamia, and India—resulting in one of the great cultural encounters of the ancient world.

The major avenue for the spread of Greek culture lay in the many cities that Alexander and later Hellenistic rulers established throughout the empire. Complete with Greek monuments, sculptures, theaters, markets, councils, and assemblies, these cities attracted many thousands of Greek settlers serving as state officials, soldiers, or traders. Alexandria in Egypt—the largest of these cities, with half a million people—was an enormous cosmopolitan center where Egyptians, Greeks, Jews, Babylonians, Syrians, Persians, and many others rubbed elbows. A harbor with space for 1,200 ships facilitated long-distance commerce. Greek learning flourished thanks to a library of some 700,000 volumes and the Museum, which sponsored scholars and writers of all kinds.

From cities such as these, Greek culture spread. From the Mediterranean to India, Greek became the language of power and elite culture. The Indian monarch Ashoka published some of his decrees in Greek, while an independent Greek state was established in Bactria in what is now northern Afghanistan. The attraction of many young Jews to Greek culture prompted the Pharisees to develop their own school system, as this highly conservative Jewish sect feared for the very survival of Judaism.

Cities such as Alexandria were very different from the original city-states of Greece, both in their cultural diversity and in the absence of the independence so valued by Athens and Sparta. Now they were part of large conquest states ruled by Greeks: the Ptolemaic (TOL-uh-MAY-ik) empire in Egypt and the Seleucid empire in Persia. These were imperial states, which, in their determination to preserve order, raise taxes, and maintain the authority of the monarch, resembled the much older empires of Mesopotamia, Egypt, Assyria, and Persia. Macedonians and Greeks, representing perhaps 10 percent of the population in these Hellenistic kingdoms, were clearly the elite and sought to keep themselves separate from non-Greeks. In Egypt, different legal systems for Greeks and native Egyptians maintained this separation. An Egyptian agricultural worker complained that "because I am an Egyptian," his supervisors despised him and refused to pay him.[9] Periodic rebellions expressed resentment at Greek arrogance, condescension, and exploitation.

But the separation between the Greeks and native populations was by no means complete, and a fair amount of cultural interaction and blending occurred. Alexander himself had taken several Persian princesses as his wives and actively encouraged intermarriage between his troops and Asian women. In both Egypt and Mesopotamia, Greek rulers patronized the building of temples to local gods and actively supported their priests. A growing number of native peoples were able to become Greek citizens by obtaining a Greek education, speaking the language, dressing appropriately, and assuming Greek names. In India, Greeks were assimilated into the hierarchy of the caste system as members of the Kshatriya (warrior) caste, while in Bactria a substantial number of Greeks converted to Buddhism, including one of their kings, Menander. A school of Buddhist art that emerged in the early centuries of the Common Era depicted the Buddha in human form for the first time, but in Greek-like garb with a face resembling the god Apollo. Clearly, not all was conflict between the Greeks and the peoples of the East.

In the long run, much of this Greek cultural influence faded as the Hellenistic kingdoms that had promoted it weakened and vanished by the first century B.C.E. While it lasted, however, it represented a remarkable cultural encounter, born of the collision of two empires and two second-wave civilizations. In the western part of that Hellenistic world, Greek rule was replaced by that of the Romans, whose empire, like Alexander's, also served as a vehicle for the continued spread of Greek culture and ideas.

LearningCurve
bedfordstmartins.com
/strayer/LC

Comparing Empires: Roman and Chinese

While the adjacent civilizations of the Greeks and the Persians collided, two other empires were taking shape—the Roman Empire on the far western side of Eurasia and China's imperial state on the far eastern end. They flourished at roughly the same time (200 B.C.E.–200 C.E.); they occupied a similar area (about 1.5 million square miles); and they encompassed populations of a similar size (50 to 60 million). They were the giant empires of their time, shaping the lives of close to half of the world's population. Unlike the Greeks and the Persians, the Romans and the Chinese were only dimly aware of each other and had almost no direct contact. Historians, however, have seen them as fascinating variations on an imperial theme and have long explored their similarities and differences.

Rome: From City-State to Empire

The rise of empires is among the perennial questions that historians tackle. Like the Persian Empire, that of the Romans took shape initially on the margins of the civilized world and was an unlikely rags-to-riches story. Rome began as a small and impoverished city-state on the western side of central Italy in the eighth century B.C.E., so weak, according to legend, that Romans were reduced to kidnapping neighboring women to maintain their city's population. In a transformation of epic proportions, Rome subsequently became the center of an enormous imperial state that encompassed the Mediterranean basin and included parts of continental Europe, Britain, North Africa, and the Middle East.

Originally ruled by a king, around 509 B.C.E. Roman aristocrats threw off the monarchy and established a republic in which the men of a wealthy class, known as patricians, dominated. Executive authority was exercised by two consuls, who were advised by a patrician assembly, the Senate. Deepening conflict with the poorer classes, called plebeians (plih-BEE-uhns), led to important changes in Roman political life. A written code of law offered plebeians some protection from abuse; a system of public assemblies provided an opportunity for lower classes to shape public policy; and a new office of tribune, who represented plebeians, allowed them to block unfavorable legislation. Romans took great pride in this political system, believing that they enjoyed greater freedom than did many of their more autocratic neighbors. The values of the republic — rule of law, the rights of citizens, the absence of pretension, upright moral behavior, keeping one's word — were later idealized as "the way of the ancestors."

With this political system and these values, the Romans launched their empire-building enterprise, a prolonged process that took more than 500 years (see Map 3.4). It began in the 490s B.C.E. with Roman control over its Latin neighbors in central Italy and over the next several hundred years encompassed most of the Italian peninsula. Between 264 and 146 B.C.E., victory in the Punic Wars with Carthage, a powerful empire with its capital in North Africa, extended Roman control over the western Mediterranean, including Spain, and made Rome a naval power. Subsequent expansion in the eastern Mediterranean brought the ancient civilizations of Greece, Egypt, and Mesopotamia under Roman domination. Rome also expanded into territories in Southern and Western Europe, including present-day France and Britain. By early in the second century C.E., the Roman Empire had reached its maximum extent. Like classical Greece, that empire has been associated with Europe. But in its own time, elites in North Africa and southwest Asia likewise claimed Roman identity, and the empire's richest provinces were in the east.

■ Change
How did Rome grow from a single city to the center of a huge empire?

No overall design or blueprint drove the building of empire, nor were there any precedents to guide the Romans. What they created was something wholly new — an empire that encompassed the entire Mediterranean basin and beyond. It was a piecemeal process, which the Romans invariably saw as defensive. Each addition of territory created new vulnerabilities, which could be assuaged only by more conquests. For some, the growth of empire represented opportunity. Poor soldiers hoped for land, loot, or salaries that might lift their families out of poverty. The well-to-do or well-connected gained great estates, earned promotions, and sometimes achieved public acclaim and high political office. The wealth of long-established societies in the eastern Mediterranean (Greece and Egypt, for example) beckoned,

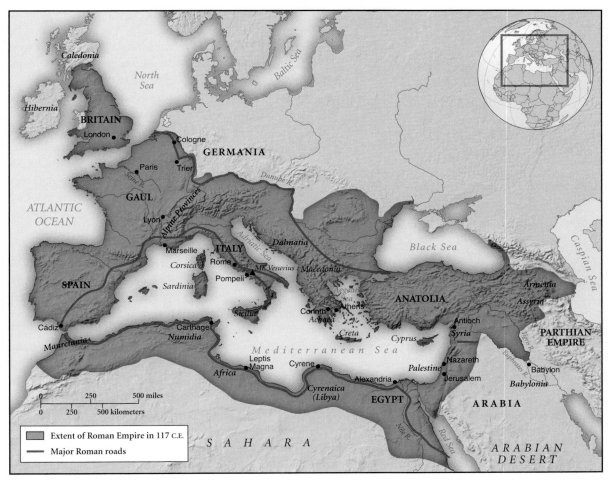

Map 3.4   The Roman Empire
At its height in the second century C.E., the Roman Empire incorporated the entire Mediterranean basin, including the lands of the Carthaginian Empire, the less-developed region of Western Europe, the heartland of Greek civilization, and the ancient civilizations of Egypt and Mesopotamia.

as did the resources and food supplies of the less developed regions, such as Western Europe. There was no shortage of motivation for the creation of the Roman Empire.

Although Rome's central location in the Mediterranean basin provided a convenient launching pad for empire, it was the army, "well-trained, well-fed, and well-rewarded," that built the empire.[10] Drawing on the growing population of Italy, that army was often brutal in war. Carthage, for example, was utterly destroyed; the city was razed to the ground, and its inhabitants were either killed or sold into slavery. Nonetheless, Roman authorities could be generous to former enemies. Some were granted Roman citizenship; others were treated as allies and allowed to maintain

Queen Boudica
This statue in London commemorates the resistance of the Celtic people of eastern Britain against Roman rule during a revolt in 60–61 C.E., led by Queen Boudica. A later Roman historian lamented that "all this ruin was brought upon the Romans by a woman, a fact which in itself caused them the greatest shame." (Daniel Boulet, photographer)

their local rulers. As the empire grew, so too did political forces in Rome that favored its continued expansion and were willing to commit the necessary manpower and resources.

Centuries of empire building and the warfare that made it possible had an impact on Roman society and values. That vast process, for example, shaped Roman understandings of gender and the appropriate roles of men and women. Rome was becoming a warrior society in which the masculinity of upper-class male citizens was defined in part by a man's role as a soldier and a property owner. In private life this translated into absolute control over his wife, children, and slaves, including the theoretical right to kill them without interference from the state. This ability of a free man and a Roman citizen to act decisively in both public and private life lay at the heart of ideal male identity. A Roman woman could participate proudly in this warrior culture by bearing brave sons and inculcating these values in her offspring.

Strangely enough, by the early centuries of the Common Era the wealth of empire, the authority of the imperial state, and the breakdown of older Roman social patterns combined to offer women in the elite classes a less restricted life than they had known in the early centuries of the republic. Upper-class Roman women had never been as secluded in the home as were their Greek counterparts, and now the legal authority of their husbands was curtailed by the intrusion of the state into what had been private life. The head of household, or pater familias, lost his earlier power of life and death over his family. Furthermore, such women could now marry without transferring legal control to their husbands and were increasingly able to manage their own finances and take part in the growing commercial economy of the empire. According to one scholar, Roman women of the wealthier classes gained "almost complete liberty in matters of property and marriage."[11] At the other end of the social spectrum, Roman conquests brought many thousands of women as well as men into the empire as slaves, often brutally treated and subject to the whims of their masters (see Chapter 5, pp. 163–67).

The relentless expansion of empire raised yet another profound question for Rome: could republican government and values survive the acquisition of a huge empire? The wealth of empire enriched a few, enabling them to acquire large estates and many slaves, while pushing growing numbers of free farmers into the cities and poverty. Imperial riches also empowered a small group of military leaders—Marius, Sulla, Pompey, Julius Caesar—who recruited their troops directly from the ranks of the poor and whose fierce rivalries brought civil war to Rome during the first century B.C.E. Traditionalists lamented the apparent decline of republican values—simplicity, service, free farmers as the backbone of the army, the authority of the Senate—amid the self-seeking ambition of the newly rich and powerful. When the dust settled from the civil war, Rome was clearly changing, for authority was now vested primarily in an emperor, the first of whom was Octavian, later granted the title of Augustus (r. 27 B.C.E.–14 C.E.), which implied a divine status for the ruler. The republic was history; Rome had become an empire and its ruler an emperor.

But it was an empire with an uneasy conscience, for many felt that in acquiring an empire, Rome had betrayed and abandoned its republican origins. Augustus was careful to maintain the forms of the republic—the Senate, consuls, public assemblies—and referred to himself as "first man" rather than "king" or "emperor," even as he accumulated enormous personal power. And in a bow to republican values, he spoke of the empire's conquests as reflecting the "power of the Roman people" rather than of the Roman state. Despite this rhetoric, he was emperor in practice, if not in name, for he was able to exercise sole authority, backed up by his command of a professional army. Later emperors were less reluctant to flaunt their imperial prerogatives. During the first two centuries C.E., this empire in disguise provided security, grandeur, and relative prosperity for the Mediterranean world. This was the *pax Romana*, the Roman peace, the era of imperial Rome's greatest extent and greatest authority.

China: From Warring States to Empire

About the same time, on the other side of Eurasia, another huge imperial state was in the making—China. Here, however, the task was understood differently. It was not a matter of creating something new, as in the case of the Roman Empire, but of restoring something old. As one of the First Civilizations, a Chinese state had emerged as early as 2200 B.C.E. and under the Xia, Shang, and Zhou dynasties had grown progressively larger. By 500 B.C.E., however, this Chinese state was in shambles. Any earlier unity vanished in an age of warring states, featuring the endless rivalries of seven competing kingdoms.

To many Chinese, this was a wholly unnatural and unacceptable condition, and rulers in various states vied to reunify China. One of them, known to history as Qin Shihuangdi (chihn shee-HUANG-dee) (i.e., Shihuangdi from the state of Qin), succeeded brilliantly. The state of Qin had already developed an effective bureaucracy, subordinated its aristocracy, equipped its army with iron weapons, and enjoyed rapidly rising agricultural output and a growing population. It also had adopted a political philosophy called Legalism, which advocated clear rules and harsh punishments as a means of enforcing the authority of the state. With these resources, Shihuangdi (r. 221–210 B.C.E.) launched a military campaign to reunify China and in just ten years soundly defeated the other warring states. Believing that he had created a universal and eternal empire, he grandly named himself Shihuangdi, which means the

■ **Comparison**

Why was the Chinese empire able to take shape so quickly, while that of the Romans took centuries?

PORTRAIT

Trung Trac: Resisting the Chinese Empire

Trung Trac and Trung Nhi
(CPA Media)

Empires have long faced resistance from people they conquer and never more fiercely than in Vietnam, which was incorporated into an expanding Chinese empire for over a thousand years (111 B.C.E.–939 C.E.). Among the earliest examples of Vietnamese resistance to this occupation was that led around 40 C.E. by Trung Trac and her younger sister Trung Nhi, daughters in an aristocratic, military family. Trung Trac married a prominent local lord Thi Sach, who was a vocal opponent of offensive Chinese policies — high taxes, even on the right to fish in local rivers; required payoffs to Chinese officials; and the imposition of Chinese culture on the Vietnamese. In response to this opposition, the Chinese governor of the region ordered Thi Sach's execution.

This personal tragedy provoked Trung Trac to take up arms against the Chinese occupiers, quickly gaining a substantial following among peasants and aristocrats alike. Famously addressing some 30,000 soldiers, while dressed in full military regalia rather than the expected mourning clothes, she declared to the assembled crowd:

Foremost I will avenge my country.
Second I will restore the Hung lineage.
Third I will avenge the death of my husband.
Lastly I vow that these goals will be accomplished.

Within months, her forces had captured sixty-five towns, and, for two years, they held the Chinese at bay, while Trung Trac and Trung Nhi ruled a briefly independent state as co-queens. Chinese sources referred to Trung Trac as a "ferocious warrior." During their rule, the sisters eliminated the hated tribute taxes imposed by the Chinese and sought to restore the authority of Vietnamese aristocrats. A large military force, said to number some 80,000, counted among its leaders thirty-six female "generals," including the Trung sisters' mother.

Soon, however, Chinese forces overwhelmed the rebellion and Trung Trac's support faded. Later Vietnamese records explained the failure of the revolt as a consequence of its female leadership. In traditional Vietnamese accounts, the Trung sisters committed suicide, jumping into a nearby river as did a number of their followers.

Although the revolt failed, it lived on in stories and legends to inspire later Vietnamese resistance to invaders — Chinese, French, Japanese, and American alike. Men were reminded that women had led this rebellion. "What a pity," wrote a thirteenth-century Vietnamese historian, "that for a thousand years after this, the men of our land bowed their heads, folded their arms, and served the northerners [Chinese]."[12] To this day, temples, streets, and neighborhoods bear the name of the Trung sisters, and a yearly celebration in their honor coincides with International Women's Day. Usually depicted riding on war elephants and wielding swords, these two women also represent the more fluid gender roles then available to some Vietnamese women in comparison to the stricter patriarchy prevalent in China.

Question: How might you imagine the reactions to the Trung sisters' revolt from Chinese officials, Vietnamese aristocrats, Vietnamese peasants both male and female, and later generations of Vietnamese men and women?

"first emperor." Unlike Augustus, he showed little ambivalence about empire. Subsequent conquests extended China's boundaries far to the south into the northern part of Vietnam, to the northeast into Korea, and to the northwest, where the Chinese pushed back the nomadic pastoral people of the steppes. (See the Portrait of Trung

Trac, opposite, for an example of resistance to Chinese expansion.) Although the boundaries fluctuated over time, Shihuangdi laid the foundations for a unified Chinese state, which has endured, with periodic interruptions, to the present (Map 3.5).

Building on earlier precedents, the Chinese process of empire formation was far more compressed than the centuries-long Roman effort, but it was no less dependent on military force and no less brutal. Scholars who opposed Shihuangdi's policies were executed and their books burned. Aristocrats who might oppose his centralizing policies were moved physically to the capital. Hundreds of thousands of laborers were recruited to construct the Great Wall of China, designed to keep out northern "barbarians," and to erect a monumental mausoleum as the emperor's final resting place. More positively, Shihuangdi imposed a uniform system of weights, measures, and currency and standardized the length of axles for carts and the written form of the Chinese language.

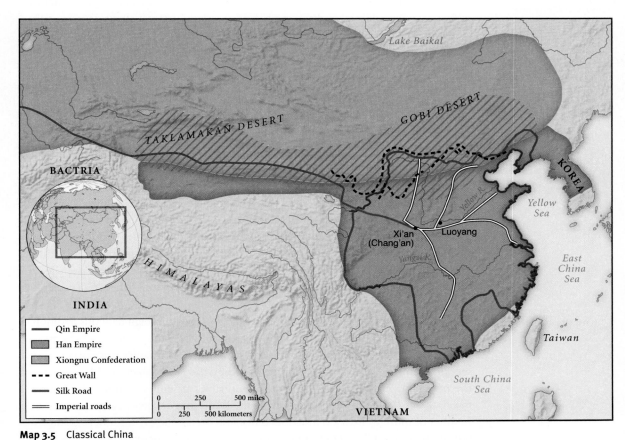

Map 3.5   Classical China

The brief Qin dynasty brought unity to the heartland of Chinese civilization, and the much longer Han dynasty extended its territorial reach south toward Vietnam, east to Korea, and west into Central Asia. To the north lay the military confederacy of the nomadic Xiongnu.

As in Rome, the creation of the Chinese empire had domestic repercussions, but they were brief and superficial compared to Rome's transition from republic to empire. The speed and brutality of Shihuangdi's policies ensured that his own Qin dynasty did not last long, and it collapsed unmourned in 206 B.C.E. The Han dynasty that followed (206 B.C.E.–220 C.E.) retained the centralized features of Shihuangdi's creation, although it moderated the harshness of his policies, adopting a milder and moralistic Confucianism in place of Legalism as the governing philosophy of the states. It was Han dynasty rulers who consolidated China's imperial state and established the political patterns that lasted into the twentieth century.

Consolidating the Roman and Chinese Empires

■ **Explanation**
Why were the Roman and Chinese empires able to enjoy long periods of relative stability and prosperity?

Once established, these two huge imperial systems shared a number of common features. Both, for example, defined themselves in universal terms. The Roman writer Polybius spoke of bringing "almost the entire world" under the control of Rome, while the Chinese state was said to encompass "all under heaven." Both of them invested heavily in public works — roads, bridges, aqueducts, canals, protective walls — all designed to integrate their respective domains militarily and commercially.

Furthermore, Roman and Chinese authorities both invoked supernatural sanctions to support their rule. By the first century C.E., Romans began to regard their deceased emperors as gods and established a religious cult to bolster the authority of living rulers. It was the refusal of early Christians to take part in this cult that provoked their periodic persecution by Roman authorities.

In China, a much older tradition had long linked events on earth with the invisible realm called "heaven." In this conception, heaven was neither a place nor a supreme being, but rather an impersonal moral force that regulated the universe. Emperors were called the Son of Heaven and were said to govern by the Mandate of Heaven so long as they ruled morally and with benevolence. Peasant rebellions, "barbarian" invasions, or disastrous floods were viewed as signs that the emperor had ruled badly and thus had lost the Mandate of Heaven. Among the chief duties of the emperor was the performance of various rituals thought to maintain the appropriate relationship between heaven and earth. What moral government meant in practice was spelled out in the writings of Confucius and his followers, which became the official ideology of the empire (see Chapter 4).

Both of these second-wave civilizations also absorbed a foreign religious tradition — Christianity in the Roman world and Buddhism in China — although the process unfolded somewhat differently. In the case of Rome, Christianity was born as a small sect in a remote corner of the empire. Aided by the *pax Romana* and Roman roads, the new faith spread slowly for several centuries, particularly among the poor and lower classes. Women were prominent in the leadership of the early church, as were a number of more well-to-do individuals from urban families. After suffering intermittent persecution, Christianity in the fourth century C.E. obtained state support from emperors who hoped to shore up a tottering empire with a common religion, and thereafter the religion spread quite rapidly.

In the case of China, by contrast, Buddhism came from India, far beyond the Chinese world. It was introduced to China by Central Asian traders and received little support from Han dynasty rulers. In fact, the religion spread only modestly among Chinese until after the Han dynasty collapsed (220 C.E.), when it appealed to people who felt bewildered by the loss of a predictable and stable society. Not until the Sui (sway) dynasty emperor Wendi (r. 581–604 C.E.) reunified China did the new religion gain state support, and then only temporarily. Buddhism thus became one of several alternative cultural traditions in a complex Chinese mix, while Christianity, though divided internally, ultimately became the dominant religious tradition throughout Europe (see Chapters 8 and 10).

The Roman and Chinese empires also had a different relationship to the societies they governed. Rome's beginnings as a small city-state meant that Romans, and even Italians, were always a distinct minority within the empire. The Chinese empire, by contrast, grew out of a much larger cultural heartland, already ethnically Chinese. Furthermore, as the Chinese state expanded, especially to the south, it actively assimilated the non-Chinese or "barbarian" people. In short, they became Chinese, culturally, linguistically, and through intermarriage in physical appearance as well. Many Chinese in modern times are in fact descended from people who at one point or another were not Chinese at all.

The Roman Empire also offered a kind of assimilation to its subject peoples. Gradually and somewhat reluctantly, the empire granted Roman citizenship to various individuals, families, or whole communities for their service to the empire or in recognition of their adoption of Roman culture. In 212 C.E., Roman citizenship was bestowed on almost all free people of the empire. Citizenship offered clear advantages—the right to hold public office, to serve in the Roman military units known as legions, to wear a toga, and more—but it conveyed a legal status, rather than cultural assimilation, and certainly did not erase other identities, such as being Greek, Egyptian, or a citizen of a particular city.

Various elements of Roman culture—its public buildings, its religious rituals, its Latin language, its style of city life—were attractive, especially in Western Europe, where urban civilization was something new. In the eastern half of the empire, however, things Greek retained tremendous prestige. Many elite Romans in fact regarded Greek culture—its literature, philosophy, and art—as superior to their own and proudly sent their sons to Athens for a Greek education. To some extent, the two blended into a mixed Greco-Roman tradition, which the empire served to disseminate throughout the realm. Other non-Roman cultural traditions—such as the cult of the Persian god Mithra or the compassionate Egyptian goddess Isis, and, most extensively, the Jewish-derived religion of Christianity—also spread throughout the empire. Nothing similar occurred in Han dynasty China, except for Buddhism, which established a modest presence, largely among foreigners. Chinese culture, widely recognized as the model to which others should conform, experienced little competition from older, venerated, or foreign traditions.

Language served these two empires in important but contrasting ways. Latin, an alphabetic language depicting sounds, gave rise to various distinct languages—Spanish, Portuguese, French, Italian, Romanian—whereas Chinese did not. Chinese characters, which represented words or ideas more than sounds, were not easily transferable to other languages. Written Chinese, however, could be understood by all literate people, no matter which spoken dialect of the language they used. Thus Chinese, more than Latin, served as an instrument of elite assimilation. For all of these reasons, the various peoples of the Roman Empire were able to maintain their separate cultural identities far more than was the case in China.

Politically, both empires established effective centralized control over vast regions and huge populations, but the Chinese, far more than the Romans, developed an elaborate bureaucracy to hold the empire together. The Han emperor Wudi (r. 141–87 B.C.E.) established an imperial academy for training officials for an emerging bureaucracy with a curriculum based on the writings of Confucius. This was the beginning of a civil service system, complete with examinations and selection by merit, which did much to integrate the Chinese empire and lasted into the early twentieth century. Roman administration was a somewhat ramshackle affair, relying more on regional aristocratic elites and the army to provide cohesion. Unlike the Chinese, however, the Romans developed an elaborate body of law, applicable equally to all people of the realm, dealing with matters of justice, property, commerce, and family life. Chinese and Roman political development thus generated different answers to the question of what made for good government. For those who inherited the Roman tradition, it was good laws, whereas for those in the Chinese tradition, it was good men.

Finally both Roman and Chinese civilizations had marked effects on the environment. The Roman poet Horace complained of the noise and smoke of the city and objected to the urban sprawl that extended into the adjacent fertile lands. Roman mining operations and the smelting of metals led to extensive deforestation and unprecedented levels of lead in the atmosphere. Large-scale Chinese ironworking during the Han dynasty contributed to substantial urban air pollution, while the growth of intensive agriculture and logging stripped the land of its grass and forest cover, causing sufficient soil erosion to turn the Hwang-ho River its characteristic yellow-brown color. What had been known simply as "the River" now became the Yellow River.

The Collapse of Empires

Empires rise, and then, with some apparent regularity, they fall, and in doing so, they provide historians with one of their most intriguing questions: what causes the collapse of these once-mighty structures? In China, the Han dynasty empire came to an end in 220 C.E.; the traditional date for the final disintegration of the Roman Empire is 476 C.E., although a process of decline had been under way for several centuries. In the Roman case, however, only the western half of the empire collapsed, while the eastern part, subsequently known as the Byzantine Empire, maintained the tradition of imperial Rome for another thousand years.

Despite these differences, a number of common factors have been associated with the end of these imperial states. At one level, they both simply got too big, too overextended, and too expensive to be sustained by the available resources, and no fundamental technological breakthrough was available to enlarge these resources. Furthermore, the growth of large landowning families with huge estates and political clout enabled them to avoid paying taxes, turned free peasants into impoverished tenant farmers, and diminished the authority of the central government. In China, such conditions led to a major peasant revolt, known as the Yellow Turban Rebellion, in 184 C.E. (see pp. 157–58).

Rivalry among elite factions created instability in both empires and eroded imperial authority. In China, persistent tension between castrated court officials (eunuchs) loyal to the emperor and Confucian-educated scholar-bureaucrats weakened the state. In the Roman Empire between 235 and 284 C.E., some twenty-six individuals claimed the title of Roman emperor, only one of whom died of natural causes. In addition, epidemic disease ravaged both societies. The population of the Roman Empire declined by 25 percent in the two centuries following 250 C.E., a demographic disaster that meant diminished production, less revenue for the state, and fewer men available for the defense of the empire's long frontiers.

To these mounting internal problems was added a growing threat from nomadic or semi-agricultural peoples occupying the frontier regions of both empires. The Chinese had long developed various ways of dealing with the Xiongnu and other nomadic people to the north—building the Great Wall to keep them out, offering them trading opportunities at border markets, buying them off with lavish gifts, contracting marriage alliances with nomadic leaders, and conducting periodic military campaigns against them. But as the Han dynasty weakened in the second and third centuries C.E., such peoples more easily breached the frontier defenses and set up a succession of "barbarian states" in north China. Culturally, however, many of these foreign rulers gradually became Chinese, encouraging intermarriage, adopting Chinese dress, and setting up their courts in Chinese fashion.

A weakening Roman Empire likewise faced serious problems from Germanic-speaking peoples living on its northern frontier. Growing numbers of these people began to enter the empire in the fourth century C.E.—some as mercenaries in Roman armies and others as refugees fleeing the invasions of the ferocious Huns, who were penetrating Europe from Central Asia. Once inside the declining empire, various Germanic groups established their own kingdoms, at first controlling Roman emperors and then displacing them altogether by 476 C.E. Unlike the nomadic groups in China, who largely assimilated Chinese culture, Germanic kingdoms in Europe developed their own ethnic identities—Visigoths, Franks, Anglo-Saxons, and others—even as they drew on Roman law and adopted Roman Christianity. Far more than

■ **Change**
What internal and external factors contributed to the collapse of the Roman and Chinese empires?

Meeting of Attila and Pope Leo I
Among the "barbarian" invaders of the Roman Empire, none were more feared than the Huns, led by the infamous Attila. In a celebrated meeting in 452 C.E., Pope Leo I persuaded Attila to spare the city of Rome and to withdraw from Italy. This painting from about 1360 C.E. records that remarkable meeting. (National Szechenyi Library, Budapest)

in China, the fall of the Roman Empire produced a new culture, blending Latin and Germanic elements, which provided the foundation for the hybrid civilization that would arise in Western Europe.

The collapse of empire meant more than the disappearance of centralized government and endemic conflict. In post-Han China and post-Roman Europe, it also meant the decline of urban life, a contracting population, less area under cultivation, diminishing international trade, and vast insecurity for ordinary people. It must have seemed that civilization itself was unraveling.

The most significant difference between the collapse of empire in China and that in the western Roman Empire lay in what happened next. In China, after about 350 years of disunion, disorder, frequent warfare, and political chaos, a Chinese imperial state, similar to that of the Han dynasty, was reassembled under the Sui (589–618 C.E.), Tang (618–907), and Song (960–1279) dynasties. Once again, a single emperor ruled; a bureaucracy selected by examinations governed; and the ideas of Confucius informed the political system. Such a Chinese empire persisted into the early twentieth century, establishing one of the most continuous political traditions of any civilization in world history.

The story line of European history following the end of the western Roman Empire was very different indeed. No large-scale, centralized, imperial authority encompassing all of Western Europe has ever been successfully reestablished there for any length of time. The memory of Roman imperial unity certainly persisted, and many subsequently tried unsuccessfully to re-create it. But most of Western Europe dissolved into highly decentralized political systems involving nobles, knights and vassals, kings with little authority, various city-states in Italy, and small territories ruled by princes, bishops, or the pope. From this point on, Europe would be a civilization without an encompassing imperial state.

From a Chinese point of view, Western Europe's post-Roman history must seem an enormous failure. Why were Europeans unable to reconstruct something of the unity of their classical empire, while the Chinese clearly did? Surely the greater cultural homogeneity of Chinese civilization made that task easier than it was amid the vast ethnic and linguistic diversity of Europe. The absence in the Roman legacy of a strong bureaucratic tradition also contributed to European difficulties, whereas in China the bureaucracy provided some stability even as dynasties came and went. The Chinese also had in Confucianism a largely secular ideology that placed great value on political matters in the here and now. The Roman Catholic Church in Europe, however, was frequently at odds with state authorities, and its "otherworldli-

LearningCurve
bedfordstmartins.com
/strayer/LC

ness" did little to support the creation of large-scale empires. Finally, Chinese agriculture was much more productive than that of Europe, and for a long time its metallurgy was more advanced.[13] These conditions gave Chinese state builders more resources to work with than were available to their European counterparts.

> **SUMMING UP SO FAR**
>
> In comparing the Roman and Chinese empires, which do you find more striking — their similarities or their differences?

Intermittent Empire: The Case of India

Among the second-wave civilizations of Eurasia, empire loomed large in Persian, Mediterranean, and Chinese history, but it played a rather less prominent role in Indian history. In the Indus River valley flourished the largest of the First Civilizations, embodied in exquisitely planned cities such as Harappa but with little evidence of any central political authority (see Chapter 2). The demise of this early civilization by 1500 B.C.E. was followed over the next thousand years by the creation of a new civilization based farther east, along the Ganges River on India's northern plain. That process has occasioned considerable debate, which has focused on the role of the Aryans, a pastoral Indo-European people long thought to have invaded and destroyed the Indus Valley civilization and then created the new one along the Ganges. More recent research questions this interpretation. Did the Aryans invade suddenly, or did they migrate slowly into the Indus River valley? Were they already there as a part of the Indus Valley population? Was the new civilization largely the work of Aryans, or did it evolve gradually from Indus Valley culture? Scholars have yet to reach agreement on any of these questions.[14]

> ■ **Comparison**
>
> Why were centralized empires so much less prominent in India than in China?

However it occurred, by 600 B.C.E. what would become the second-wave civilization of South Asia had begun to take shape across northern India. Politically, that civilization emerged as a fragmented collection of towns and cities, some small republics governed by public assemblies, and a number of regional states ruled by kings. An astonishing range of ethnic, cultural, and linguistic diversity also characterized this civilization, as an endless variety of peoples migrated into India from Central Asia across the mountain passes in the northwest. These features of Indian civilization — political fragmentation and vast cultural diversity — have informed much of South Asian history throughout many centuries, offering a sharp contrast to the pattern of development in China. What gave Indian civilization a recognizable identity and character was neither an imperial tradition nor ethno-linguistic commonality, but rather a distinctive religious tradition, known later to outsiders as Hinduism, and a unique social organization, the caste system. These features of Indian life are explored further in Chapters 4 and 5.

Nonetheless, empires and emperors were not entirely unknown in India's long history. Northwestern India had been briefly ruled by the Persian Empire and then conquered by Alexander the Great. These Persian and Greek influences helped stimulate the first and largest of India's short experiments with a large-scale political system,

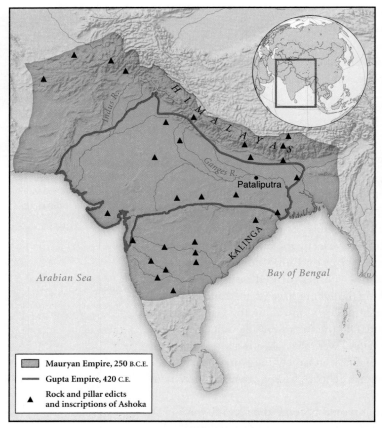

Map 3.6   Empire in South Asia

Large-scale empires in the Indian subcontinent were less frequent and less enduring than in China. Two of the largest efforts were those of the Mauryan and Gupta dynasties.

the Mauryan Empire (326–184 B.C.E.), which encompassed all but the southern tip of the subcontinent (see Map 3.6).

The Mauryan Empire was an impressive political structure, equivalent to the Persian, Chinese, and Roman empires, though not nearly as long-lasting. With a population of perhaps 50 million, the Mauryan Empire boasted a large military force, reported to include 600,000 infantry soldiers, 30,000 cavalry, 8,000 chariots, and 9,000 elephants. A civilian bureaucracy featured various ministries and a large contingent of spies to provide the rulers with local information. A famous treatise called the *Arthashastra* (*The Science of Worldly Wealth*) articulated a pragmatic, even amoral, political philosophy for Mauryan rulers. It was, according to one scholar, a book that showed "how the political world does work and not very often stating how it ought to work, a book that frequently discloses to a king what calculating and sometimes brutal measures he must carry out to preserve the state and the common good."[15] The state also operated many industries—spinning, weaving, mining, shipbuilding, and armaments. This complex apparatus was financed by taxes on trade, on herds of animals, and especially on land, from which the monarch claimed a quarter or more of the crop.

Mauryan India is perhaps best known for one of its emperors, Ashoka (r. 268–232 B.C.E.), who left a record of his activities and his thinking in a series of edicts carved on rocks and pillars throughout the kingdom. Ashoka's conversion to Buddhism and his moralistic approach to governance gave his reign a different tone than that of China's Shihuangdi or Greece's Alexander the Great, who, according to legend, wept because he had no more worlds to conquer. Ashoka's legacy to modern India has been that of an enlightened ruler, who sought to govern in accord with the religious values and moral teachings of Hinduism and Buddhism.

Despite their good intentions, these policies did not long preserve the empire, which broke apart soon after Ashoka's death. About 600 years later, a second brief imperial experiment, known as the Gupta Empire (320–550 C.E.) took shape. Faxian, a Chinese Buddhist traveler in India at the time, noted a generally peaceful, tolerant, and prosperous land, commenting that the ruler "governs without decapitation or corporal punishment." Free hospitals, he reported, were available to "the destitute, crippled and diseased," but he also noticed "untouchables" carrying bells to warn upper-caste people of their polluting presence.[16] Culturally, the Gupta era witnessed a flourishing of art, literature, temple building, science, mathematics, and medicine, much of it patronized by rulers. Indian trade with China also thrived, and elements of Buddhist and Hindu culture took root in Southeast Asia (see Chapter 7). Indian commerce reached as far as the Roman world. A Germanic leader named Alaric laid siege to Rome in 410 C.E., while demanding 3,000 pounds of Indian pepper to spare the city.

Thus, India's political history resembled that of Western Europe after the collapse of the Roman Empire far more than that of China or Persia. Neither imperial nor regional states commanded the kind of loyalty or exercised the degree of influence that they did in other second-wave civilizations. India's unparalleled cultural diversity surely was one reason, as was the frequency of invasions from Central Asia, which repeatedly smashed emerging states that might have provided the nucleus for an all-India empire. Finally, India's social structure, embodied in a caste system linked to occupational groups, made for intensely local loyalties at the expense of wider identities (see Chapter 5).

Ashoka of India
This twelfth-century stone relief provides a visual image of the Mauryan dynasty's best-known ruler. (Philip Baird/www.anthroarcheart.org)

Nonetheless, a frequently vibrant economy fostered a lively internal commerce and made India the focal point of an extensive network of trade in the Indian Ocean basin. In particular, its cotton textile industry long supplied cloth throughout the Afro-Eurasian world. Strong guilds of merchants and artisans provided political leadership in major towns and cities, and their wealth supported lavish temples, public buildings, and religious festivals. Great creativity in religious matters generated Hindu and Buddhist traditions that later penetrated much of Asia. Indian mathematics and science, especially astronomy, also were impressive; Indian scientists plotted the movements of stars and planets and recognized quite early that the earth was round. Clearly, the absence of consistent imperial unity did not prevent the evolution of a lasting civilization.

LearningCurve
bedfordstmartins.com
/strayer/LC

Reflections: Enduring Legacies of Second-Wave Empires

The second-wave empires discussed in this chapter have long ago passed into history, but their descendants have kept them alive in memory, for they have proved useful, even in the twentieth and early twenty-first centuries. Those empires have provided legitimacy for contemporary states, inspiration for new imperial ventures, and abundant warnings and cautions for those seeking to criticize more recent empires. For example, in bringing communism to China in the twentieth century, the

Chinese leader Mao Zedong compared himself to Shihuangdi, the unifier of China and the brutal founder of its Qin dynasty. Reflecting on his campaign against intellectuals in general and Confucianism in particular, Mao declared to a Communist Party conference: "Emperor Qin Shihuang was not that outstanding. He only buried alive 460 Confucian scholars. We buried 460 thousand Confucian scholars. . . . To the charge of being like Emperor Qin, of being a dictator, we plead guilty."[17]

In contrast, modern-day Indians, who have sought to present their country as a model of cultural tolerance and nonviolence, have been quick to link themselves to Ashoka and his policies of inclusiveness. When the country became independent from British colonial rule in 1947, India soon placed an image of Ashoka's Pillar on the new nation's currency.

In the West, it has been the Roman Empire that has provided a template for thinking about political life. Many in Great Britain celebrated their own global empire as a modern version of the Roman Empire. If the British had been "civilized" by Roman rule, then surely Africans and Asians would benefit from falling under the control of the "superior" British. Likewise, to the Italian fascist dictator Benito Mussolini, his country's territorial expansion during the 1930s and World War II represented the creation of a new Roman Empire. Most recently, the United States' dominant role in the world has prompted the question: are the Americans the new Romans?

Historians frequently cringe as politicians and students use (and perhaps misuse) historical analogies to make their case for particular points of view in the present. But we have little else to go on except history in making our way through the complexities of contemporary life, and historians themselves seldom agree on the "lessons" of the past. Lively debate about the continuing relevance of these ancient empires shows that although the past may be gone, it surely is not dead.

Second Thoughts

LearningCurve
Check what you know.
bedfordstmartins.com/strayer/LC

Online Study Guide
bedfordstmartins.com/strayer

What's the Significance?

Persian Empire, 90–92

Athenian democracy, 94–98

Greco-Persian Wars, 95–96

Hellenistic era, 96–99

Alexander the Great, 96–99

Augustus, 103

pax Romana, 103

Qin Shihuangdi, 103–105

Trung Trac, 104

Han dynasty, 106–108

Mauryan Empire, 111–112

Ashoka, 112

Big Picture Questions

1. What common features can you identify in the empires described in this chapter? In what ways did they differ from one another? What accounts for those differences?
2. Are you more impressed with the "greatness" of empires or with their destructive and oppressive features? Why?

3. Do you think that these second-wave empires hold "lessons" for the present, or are contemporary circumstances sufficiently unique as to render the distant past irrelevant?

4. **Looking Back:** How do these empires of the second-wave civilizations differ from the political systems of the First Civilizations?

Next Steps: For Further Study

For Web sites and additional documents related to this chapter, see **Make History** at bedfordstmartins.com/strayer.

Jane Burbank and Frederick Cooper, *Empires in World History* (2010). A fascinating account by two major scholars of the imperial theme across the world. Chapter 2 compares the Roman and Chinese empires.

Arthur Cotterell, *The First Emperor of China* (1988). A biography of Shihuangdi.

Christopher Kelley, *The Roman Empire: A Very Short Introduction* (2006). A brief, up-to-date, and accessible account of the Roman achievement.

Cullen Murphy, *Are We Rome? The Fall of an Empire and the Fate of America* (2007). A reflection on the usefulness and the dangers of comparing the Roman Empire to the present-day United States.

Sarah Pomeroy et al., *Ancient Greece* (1999). A highly readable survey of Greek history by a team of distinguished scholars.

Romila Thapar, *Ashoka and the Decline of the Mauryas* (1961). A classic study of India's early empire builder.

Illustrated History of the Roman Empire, http://www.roman-empire.net. An interactive Web site with maps, pictures, and much information about the Roman Empire.

Culture and Religion in Eurasia/North Africa

500 B.C.E.–500 C.E.

China and the Search for Order
  The Legalist Answer
  The Confucian Answer
  The Daoist Answer
Cultural Traditions of Classical India
  South Asian Religion: From Ritual
    Sacrifice to Philosophical Speculation
  The Buddhist Challenge
  Hinduism as a Religion of Duty and
    Devotion
Toward Monotheism: The Search for
  God in the Middle East
  Zoroastrianism
  Judaism
The Cultural Tradition of Classical
  Greece: The Search for a Rational
  Order
  The Greek Way of Knowing
  The Greek Legacy
The Birth of Christianity . . . with
  Buddhist Comparisons
  The Lives of the Founders
  The Spread of New Religions
  Institutions, Controversies, and
    Divisions
Reflections: Religion and Historians
Portrait: Perpetua, Christian Martyr

In September of 2009, Kong Dejun returned to China from her home in Great Britain. The occasion was a birthday celebration for her ancient ancestor Kong Fuzi, or Confucius, born 2560 years earlier. Together with some 10,000 other people—descendants, scholars, government officials, and foreign representatives—Kong Dejun attended ceremonies at the Confucian Temple in Qufu, the hometown of China's famous sage. "I was touched to see my ancestor being revered by people from different countries and nations," she said.[1] What made this celebration remarkable was that it took place in a country still ruled by the Communist Party, which had long devoted enormous efforts to discrediting Confucius and his teachings. In the view of communist China's revolutionary leader, Mao Zedong, Confucianism was associated with class inequality, patriarchy, feudalism, superstition, and all things old and backward. But the country's ancient teacher and philosopher had apparently outlasted its revolutionary hero, for now the Communist Party claims Confucius as a national treasure and has established over 300 Confucian Institutes to study his writings. He appears in TV shows and movies, even as many anxious parents offer prayers at Confucian temples when their children are taking the national college entrance exams.

Buddhism and Daoism (DOW-i'zm) have also experienced something of a revival in China, as thousands of temples, destroyed during the heyday of communism, have been repaired and reopened. Christianity too has grown rapidly since the death of Mao in 1976. Here are reminders, in a Chinese context, of the continuing appeal of cultural traditions forged long ago. Those traditions are among the

China's Cultural Traditions: In this idealized painting, attributed to the Chinese artist Wang Shugu (1649–1730), the Chinese teacher Confucius presents a baby Buddha to the Daoist master Laozi. The image illustrates the assimilation of a major Indian religion into China as well as the generally peaceful coexistence of these three traditions. (The Art Archive at Art Resource, NY)

most enduring legacies that second-wave civilizations have bequeathed to the modern world.

IN THE SEVERAL CENTURIES SURROUNDING 500 B.C.E., something quite remarkable happened all across Eurasia. More or less simultaneously, in China, India, the Middle East, and Greece, there emerged cultural traditions that spread widely, have persisted in various forms into the twenty-first century, and have shaped the values and outlooks of most people who have inhabited the planet over the past 2,500 years.

In China, it was the time of Confucius and Laozi (low-ZUH), whose teachings gave rise to Confucianism and Daoism, respectively. In India, a series of religious writings known as the Upanishads gave expression to the classical philosophy of Hinduism, while a religious reformer, Siddhartha Gautama (sih-DHAR-tuh GOW-tau-mah), set in motion a separate religion known later as Buddhism. In the Middle East, a distinctively monotheistic religious tradition appeared. It was expressed in Zoroastrianism, derived from the teachings of the Persian prophet Zarathustra (zar-uh-THOO-struh), and in Judaism, articulated in Israel by a number of Jewish prophets such as Amos, Jeremiah, and Isaiah. Later, this Jewish religious outlook became the basis for both Christianity and Islam. Finally, in Greece, a rational and humanistic tradition found expression in the writings of Socrates, Plato, Aristotle, and many others.

These cultural traditions differed greatly. Chinese and Greek thinkers focused more on the affairs of this world and credited human rationality with the power to understand that reality. Indian, Persian, and Jewish intellectuals, by contrast, explored the unseen realm of the divine and the relationship of God or the gods to human life. All these traditions sought an alternative to an earlier polytheism, in which the activities of various gods and spirits explained what happened in this world. These gods and spirits had generally been seen as similar to human beings, though much more powerful. Through ritual and sacrifice, men and women might placate the gods or persuade them to do human bidding. In contrast, the new cultural traditions of the Second Wave era sought to define a single source of order and meaning in the universe, some moral or religious realm, sharply different from and higher than the sphere of human life. The task of humankind, according to these new ways of thinking, was personal moral or spiritual transformation—often expressed as the development of compassion—by aligning with that higher order.[2] These enormously rich and varied traditions have collectively posed the great questions of human life and society that have haunted and inspired much of humankind ever since. They also defined and legitimated the hierarchies of class and gender that distinguished the various second-wave civilizations from one another.

Why did these traditions all emerge at roughly the same time? Here we encounter an enduring issue of historical analysis: What is the relationship between ideas and the circumstances in which they arise? Are ideas generated by particular political, social, and economic conditions? Or are they the product of creative human imagination independent of the material environment? Or do they derive from some combi-

A Map of Time

800–400 B.C.E.	Upanishads composed
8th century B.C.E.	Hebrew prophets (Amos, Hosea, Micah, Isaiah)
ca. 7th–6th centuries B.C.E.	Life of Zarathustra
600–300 B.C.E.	Emergence of Greek rationalism
6th century B.C.E.	Life of Buddha, Confucius, Laozi
586–539 B.C.E.	Jewish exile in Bablyon
558–330 B.C.E.	Achaemenid dynasty in Persia; state support for Zoroastrianism
469–399 B.C.E.	Life of Socrates
403–221 B.C.E.	Age of warring states in China
221–206 B.C.E.	Qin dynasty in China
Early 1st century C.E.	Life of Jesus
10–65 C.E.	Life of Paul
4th century C.E.	Christianity becomes state religion of Roman Empire, Armenia, Axum

nation of the two? In the case of these cultural traditions, many historians have noted the tumultuous social changes that accompanied their emergence. An iron-age technology, available since roughly 1000 B.C.E., made possible more productive economies and more deadly warfare. Growing cities, increased trade, the prominence of merchant classes, the emergence of new states and empires, new contacts among civilizations—all of these disruptions, occurring in already-literate societies, led thinkers to question older outlooks and to come up with new solutions to fundamental questions: What is the purpose of life? How should human society be ordered? What is the relationship between human life in this world and the moral or spiritual realms that lie beyond? But precisely why various societies developed their own distinctive answers to these questions remains elusive—a tribute, perhaps, to the unpredictable genius of human imagination.

> **SEEKING THE MAIN POINT**
>
> Fundamentally, religions are basically alike. Does the material of this chapter support or challenge this idea?

China and the Search for Order

As one of the First Civilizations, China had a tradition of state building that historians have traced back to around 2000 B.C.E. or before. When the Zhou dynasty took power in 1122 B.C.E., the notion of the Mandate of Heaven had taken root, as had the idea that the normal and appropriate condition of China was one of political unity.

Snapshot   **Thinkers and Philosophies of the Second-Wave Era**

Person	Date	Location	Religion/Philosophy	Key Ideas
Zoroaster	7th century B.C.E. (?)	Persia (present-day Iran)	Zoroastrianism	Single High God; cosmic conflict of good and evil
Hebrew prophets (Isaiah, Amos, Jeremiah)	9th–6th centuries B.C.E.	Eastern Mediterranean/ Palestine/Israel	Judaism	Transcendent High God; covenant with chosen people; social justice
Anonymous writers of Upanishads	800–400 B.C.E.	India	Brahmanism/ Hinduism	Brahma (the single impersonal divine reality); karma; rebirth; goal of liberation (moksha)
Confucius	6th century B.C.E.	China	Confucianism	Social harmony through moral example; secular outlook; importance of education; family as model of the state
Mahavira	6th century B.C.E.	India	Jainism	All creatures have souls; purification through nonviolence; opposed to caste
Siddhartha Gautama	6th century B.C.E.	India	Buddhism	Suffering caused by desire/ attachment; end of suffering through modest and moral living and meditation practice
Laozi, Zhuangzi	6th–3rd centuries B.C.E.	China	Daoism	Withdrawal from the world into contemplation of nature; simple living; end of striving
Socrates, Plato, Aristotle	5th–4th centuries B.C.E.	Greece	Greek rationalism	Style of persistent questioning; secular explanation of nature and human life
Jesus	early 1st century C.E.	Palestine/Israel	Christianity	Supreme importance of love based on intimate relationship with God; at odds with established authorities
Saint Paul	1st century C.E.	Palestine/Israel/ eastern Roman Empire	Christianity	Christianity as a religion for all; salvation through faith in Jesus Christ

By the eighth century B.C.E., the authority of the Zhou dynasty and its royal court had substantially weakened, and by 500 B.C.E. any unity that China had earlier enjoyed was long gone. What followed was a period (403–221 B.C.E.) of chaos, growing violence, and disharmony that became known as the "age of warring states" (see pp. 103–06). During these dreadful centuries of disorder and turmoil, a number of Chinese thinkers began to consider how order might be restored, how the apparent tranquility of an earlier time could be realized again. From their reflections emerged classical cultural traditions of Chinese civilization.

The Legalist Answer

One answer to the problem of disorder—though not the first to emerge—was a hardheaded and practical philosophy known as Legalism. To Legalist thinkers, the solution to China's problems lay in rules or laws, clearly spelled out and strictly enforced through a system of rewards and punishments. "If rewards are high," wrote Han Fei, one of the most prominent Legalist philosophers, "then what the ruler wants will be quickly effected; if punishments are heavy, what he does not want will be swiftly prevented."[3] Legalists generally entertained a rather pessimistic view of human nature. Most people were stupid and shortsighted. Only the state and its rulers could act in their long-term interests. Doing so meant promoting farmers and soldiers, the only two groups in society who performed essential functions, while suppressing merchants, aristocrats, scholars, and other classes regarded as useless.

■ **Comparison**
What different answers to the problem of disorder arose in classical China?

Legalist thinking provided inspiration and methods for the harsh reunification of China under Shihuangdi and the Qin dynasty (221–206 B.C.E.), but the brutality of that short dynasty thoroughly discredited Legalism (see pp. 103–06). Although its techniques and practices played a role in subsequent Chinese statecraft, few philosophers or rulers ever again openly advocated its ideas as the sole guide for Chinese political life. The Han and all subsequent dynasties drew instead on the teachings of China's greatest sage—Confucius.

The Confucian Answer

Born to an aristocratic family in the state of Lu in northern China, Confucius (551–479 B.C.E.) was both learned and ambitious. Believing that he had found the key to solving China's problem of disorder, he spent much of his adult life seeking a political position from which he might put his ideas into action. But no such opportunity came his way. Perhaps it was just as well, for it was as a thinker and a teacher that Confucius left a profound imprint on Chinese history and culture and also on other East Asian societies, such as Korea's and Japan's. After his death, his students collected his teachings in a short book called the *Analects*, and later scholars elaborated and commented endlessly on his ideas, creating a body of thought known as Confucianism.

■ **Description**
Why has Confucianism been defined as a "humanistic philosophy" rather than a supernatural religion?

The Confucian answer to the problem of China's disorder was very different from that of the Legalists. Not laws and punishments, but the moral example of superiors was the Confucian key to a restored social harmony. For Confucius, human society consisted primarily of unequal relationships: the father was superior to the son; the husband to the wife; the older brother to the younger brother; and, of course, the ruler to the subject. If the superior party in each of these relationships behaved with sincerity, benevolence, and genuine concern for others, then the inferior party would be motivated to respond with deference and obedience. Harmony then would prevail. As Confucius put it, "The relation between superiors and inferiors is like that between the wind and the grass. The grass must bend when the wind blows across it." Thus, in both family life and in political life, the cultivation of *ren*—translated as human-heartedness, benevolence, goodness, nobility of heart—was the essential ingredient of a tranquil society.

But how were these humane virtues to be nurtured? Believing that people have a capacity for improvement, Confucius emphasized education as the key to moral betterment. He prescribed a broad liberal arts education emphasizing language, literature, history, philosophy, and ethics, all applied to the practical problems of government. Ritual and ceremonies were also important, for they conveyed the rules of appropriate behavior in the many and varying circumstances of life. For the "superior person," or "gentleman" in Confucian terms, this process of improvement involved serious personal reflection and a willingness to strive continuously to perfect his moral character.

Such ideas left a deep mark on Chinese culture. The discrediting of Legalism during the Qin dynasty opened the door to the adoption of Confucianism as the official ideology of the Chinese state, to such an extent that Confucianism became almost synonymous with Chinese culture. As China's bureaucracy took shape during the Han dynasty and after, Confucianism became the central element of the educational system, which prepared students for the examinations required to gain official positions. In those examinations, candidates were required to apply the principles of Confucianism to specific situations that they might encounter in office. Thus generation after generation of China's male elite was steeped in the ideas and values of Confucianism.

Family life had long been central to Chinese popular culture, expressed in the

Filial Piety
This Song dynasty painting served as an illustration of an ancient Confucian text called the "Classic of Filial Piety," originally composed sometime around the fourth century B.C.E. and subsequently reissued many times. Here, a son kneels submissively in front of his parents. The long-enduring social order that Confucius advocated began at home with unquestioning obedience and the utmost respect for parents and other senior members of the family. (National Palace Museum, Taipei, Taiwan, Republic of China/Cultural Relics Press)

practice of ancestor veneration, including visiting the graves of the deceased, presenting them with offerings, and erecting commemorative tablets and shrines in their honor. In Confucian thinking, the family became a model for political life, a kind of miniature state. Filial piety, the honoring of one's ancestors and parents, was both an end in itself and a training ground for the reverence due to the emperor and state officials.

Confucian views of the family were rigidly patriarchal and set the tone for defining the lives of women and men alike. Those views were linked to a hierarchical understanding of the cosmos in which an inferior and receptive Earth was in balance with the superior and creative principle of Heaven. But these were gendered concepts with Heaven associated with things male and Earth with those female. Thus the subordinate and deferential position of women in relation to men was rooted in the structure of the cosmos itself. What this meant for women was spelled out by a somewhat later woman writer, Ban Zhao (bahn jow) (45–116 C.E.) in a famous work called *Lessons for Women*.

> Let a woman modestly yield to others. . . . Always let her seem to tremble and to fear. . . . Then she may be said to humble herself before others. . . . To guard carefully her chastity . . . to choose her words with care . . . , to wash and scrub filth away . . . , with whole-hearted devotion to sew and to weave, to love not gossip and silly laughter, in cleanliness and order to prepare the wine and food for serving guests: [these] may be called the characteristics of womanly work.[4]

Ban Zhao called for greater attention to education for young girls, not because they were equal to boys, but so that a young woman might be better prepared to serve her husband. Education for boys, on the other hand, enabled them to more effectively control their wives.

Corresponding Confucian virtues for ideal men were contained in the paired concepts of *wen* and *wu*, both limited largely to males. The superior principle of *wen* referred to the refined qualities of rationality, scholarship, and literary and artistic abilities, while *wu* focused attention on physical and martial achievements. Thus men alone, and superior men at that, were eligible for the civil service exams that led to political office and high prestige, while military men and merchants occupied a distinctly lower position in male social hierarchy.[5]

Beyond defining gender expectations, Confucianism also placed great importance on history, for the ideal good society lay in the past. Confucian ideas were reformist, perhaps even revolutionary, but they were consistently presented as an effort to restore a past golden age. Those ideas also injected a certain democratic element into Chinese elite culture, for the great sage had emphasized that "superior men" and potential government officials were those of outstanding moral character and intellectual achievement, not simply those of aristocratic background. Usually only young men from wealthy families could afford the education necessary for passing examinations, but on occasion villagers could find the resources to sponsor one of their

Chinese Landscape Paintings
Focused largely on mountains and water, Chinese landscape paintings were much influenced by the Daoist search for harmony with nature. Thus human figures and buildings were usually eclipsed by towering peaks, waterfalls, clouds, and trees. This seventeenth-century painting entitled *Temple on a Mountain Ledge* shows a Buddhist monastery in such a setting, while the poem in the upper right refers to the artist's earlier wanderings, a metaphor for the Buddhist quest for enlightenment. (Mr. and Mrs. John D. Rockefeller 3rd Collection of Asian Art/Asia Society 179.124)

bright sons, potentially propelling him into the stratosphere of the Chinese elite while bringing honor and benefit to themselves.

Confucian values clearly justified the many inequalities of Chinese society, but they also established certain expectations for the superior parties in China's social hierarchy. Thus emperors should keep taxes low, administer justice, and provide for the material needs of the people. Those who failed to govern by the moral norms of Confucian values forfeited the Mandate of Heaven and invited upheaval and their replacement by another dynasty. Likewise husbands should deal kindly with their wives and children, lest they invite conflict and disharmony in the family.

Finally, Confucianism marked Chinese elite culture by its secular, or nonreligious, character. Confucius did not deny the reality of gods and spirits. In fact, he advised people to participate in family and state rituals "as if the spirits were present," and he believed that the universe had a moral character with which human beings should align themselves. But the thrust of Confucian teaching was distinctly this-worldly and practical, concerned with human relationships, effective government, and social harmony. Asked on one occasion about his view of death and the spirits, Confucius replied that because we do not fully understand this life, we cannot possibly know anything about the life beyond. Members of the Chinese elite generally acknowledged that magic, the gods, and spirits were perhaps necessary for the lower orders of society, but educated people, they argued, would find them of little help in striving for moral improvement and in establishing a harmonious society.

The Daoist Answer

No civilization has ever painted its cultural outlook in a single color. As Confucian thinking became generally known in China, a quite different school of thought also took shape. Known as Daoism, it was associated with the legendary figure Laozi, who, according to tradition, was a sixth-century B.C.E. archivist. He is said to have penned a short poetic volume, the *Daodejing* (DOW-DAY-JIHNG) (*The Way and Its Power*), before vanishing in the wilderness to the west of China on his water buffalo. Daoist ideas were later expressed in a more explicit fashion by the philosopher Zhuangzi (369–286 B.C.E.).

In many ways, Daoist thinking ran counter to that of Confucius, who had emphasized the importance of education and earnest striving for moral improvement and good government. The Daoists ridiculed such efforts as artificial and useless, generally making things worse. In the face of China's disorder and chaos, they urged withdrawal into the world of nature and encouraged behavior that was spontaneous, individualistic, and natural. Whereas Confucius focused on the world of human relationships, the Daoists turned the spotlight on the immense realm of nature and its mysterious unfolding patterns. "Confucius roams within society," the Chinese have often said. "Laozi wanders beyond."

■ **Comparison**
How did the Daoist outlook differ from that of Confucianism?

The central concept of Daoist thinking is *dao*, an elusive notion that refers to the way of nature, the underlying and unchanging principle that governs all natural phenomena. According to the *Daodejing*, the dao "moves around and around, but does not on this account suffer. All life comes from it. It wraps everything with its love as in a garment, and yet it claims no honor, for it does not demand to be lord. I do not know its name and so I call it the Dao, the Way, and I rejoice in its power."[6]

Applied to human life, Daoism invited people to withdraw from the world of political and social activism, to disengage from the public life so important to Confucius, and to align themselves with the way of nature. It meant simplicity in living, small self-sufficient communities, limited government, and the abandonment of education and active efforts at self-improvement. "Give up learning," declares the *Daodejing*, "and put an end to your troubles." The flavor of the Daoist approach to life is evident in this passage from the *Daodejing*:

A small country has few people.
Though there are machines that can work ten to a hundred times faster
    than man, they are not needed. . . .
Though they have boats and carriages, no one uses them. . . .
Men return to the knotting of ropes in place of writing.
Their food is plain and good, their clothes fine but simple. . . .
They are happy in their ways.
Though they live within sight of their neighbors,
And crowing cocks and barking dogs are heard across the way,
Yet they leave each other in peace while they grow old and die.[7]

Like Confucianism, the Daoist perspective viewed family life as central to Chinese society, though the element of male/female hierarchy was downplayed in favor of complementarity and balance between the sexes.

Despite its various differences with the ideas of Confucianism, the Daoist perspective was widely regarded by elite Chinese as complementing rather than contradicting Confucian values (see the chapter-opening image on p. 116). Such an outlook was facilitated by the ancient Chinese concept of *yin* and *yang*, which expressed a belief in the unity of opposites (see figure).

The Yin Yang Symbol

Thus a scholar-official might pursue the Confucian project of "government by goodness" during the day, but upon returning home in the evening or following his retirement, he might well behave in a more Daoist fashion—pursuing the simple life, reading Daoist philosophy, practicing Daoist meditation and breathing exercises, or enjoying landscape paintings in which tiny human figures are dwarfed by the vast peaks and valleys of the natural world (see image on p. 124). Daoism also shaped the culture of ordinary people as it entered popular religion. This kind of Daoism sought to tap the power of the dao for practical uses and came to include magic, fortune telling, and the search for immortality. It also on occasion provided an ideology for peasant uprisings, such as the Yellow Turban Rebellion (184–204 C.E.), which imagined a utopian society without the oppression of governments and landlords (see pp. 157–58). In its many and varied forms, Daoism, like Confucianism, became an enduring element of the Chinese cultural tradition.

LearningCurve
bedfordstmartins.com
/strayer/LC

Cultural Traditions of Classical India

The cultural development of Indian civilization was far different from that of China. Whereas Confucianism paid little attention to the gods, spirits, and speculation about religious matters, Indian elite culture embraced the divine and all things spiritual with enthusiasm and generated elaborate philosophical visions about the nature of ultimate reality. But the Indian religious tradition—later called Hinduism—differed from other world religions as well. Unlike Buddhism, Christianity, or Islam, Hinduism had no historical founder; rather, it grew up over many centuries along with Indian civilization. Although it later spread into Southeast Asia, Hinduism was not a missionary religion seeking converts, but was, like Judaism, associated with a particular people and territory.

In fact, "Hinduism" was never a single tradition at all, and the term itself derived from outsiders—Greeks, Muslims, and later the British—who sought to reduce the infinite variety of Indian cultural patterns into a recognizable system. From the inside, however, Hinduism dissolved into a vast diversity of gods, spirits, beliefs, practices, rituals, and philosophies. This endlessly variegated Hinduism served to incorporate into Indian civilization the many diverse peoples who migrated into or invaded the South Asian peninsula over many centuries and several millennia. Its ability to accommodate this diversity gave India's cultural development a distinctive quality.

South Asian Religion: From Ritual Sacrifice to Philosophical Speculation

■ **Change**
In what ways did the religious traditions of South Asia change over the centuries?

Despite the fragmentation and variety of Indian cultural and religious patterns, an evolving set of widely recognized sacred texts provided some commonality. The earliest of these texts, known as the Vedas (VAY-duhs), were collections of poems, hymns, prayers, and rituals. Compiled by priests called Brahmins, the Vedas were for centuries transmitted orally and were reduced to writing in Sanskrit around 600 B.C.E.

In the Vedas, historians have caught fleeting glimpses of Indian civilization in its formative centuries (1500–600 B.C.E.). Those sacred writings tell of small competing chiefdoms or kingdoms, of sacred sounds and fires, of numerous gods, rising and falling in importance over the centuries. They also suggest a clearly patriarchal society, but one that afforded upper-class women somewhat greater opportunities than they later enjoyed. Vedic women participated in religious sacrifices, sometimes engaged in scholarship and religious debate, were allowed to wear the sacred thread that symbolized ritual purity in the higher castes, and could on occasion marry a man of their own choosing. The Vedas described as well the elaborate ritual sacrifices that Brahmin priests required. Performing these sacrifices and rituals with great precision enabled the Brahmins to acquire enormous power and wealth, sometimes exceeding even that of kings and warriors. But Brahmins also generated growing criticism, as ritual became mechanical and formal and as Brahmins required heavy fees to perform them.

From this dissatisfaction arose another body of sacred texts, the Upanishads (oo-PAHN-ee-shahds). Composed by largely anonymous thinkers between 800 and 400 B.C.E., these were mystical and highly philosophical works that sought to probe the inner meaning of the sacrifices prescribed in the Vedas. In the Upanishads, external ritual gave way to introspective thinking, which expressed in many and varied formulations the central concepts of philosophical Hinduism that have persisted into modern times. Chief among them was the idea of Brahman, the World Soul, the final and ultimate reality. Beyond the multiplicity of material objects and individual persons and beyond even the various gods themselves lay this primal unitary energy or divine reality infusing all things, similar in some ways to the Chinese notion of the dao. This alone was real; the immense diversity of existence that human beings perceived with their senses was but an illusion.

The fundamental assertion of philosophical Hinduism was that the individual human soul, or *atman*, was in fact a part of Brahman. Beyond the quest for pleasure, wealth, power, and social position, all of which were perfectly normal and quite legitimate, lay the effort to achieve the final goal of humankind — union with Brahman, an end to our illusory perception of a separate existence. This was *moksha* (MOHK-shuh), or liberation, compared sometimes to a bubble in a glass of water breaking through the surface and becoming one with the surrounding atmosphere.

Achieving this exalted state was held to involve many lifetimes, as the notion of *samsara*, or rebirth/reincarnation, became a central feature of Hindu thinking. Human souls migrated from body to body over many lifetimes, depending on one's actions. This was the law of *karma*. Pure actions, appropriate to one's station in life, resulted in rebirth in a higher social position or caste. Thus the caste system of distinct and ranked groups, each with its own duties, became a register of spiritual progress. Birth in a higher caste was evidence of "good karma," based on actions in a previous life, and offered a better chance to achieve moksha, which brought with it an end to the painful cycle of rebirth.

If Hinduism underpinned caste, it also legitimated and expressed India's gender system. As South Asian civilization crystalized during the second-wave era, its

Hindu Ascetics
Hinduism called for men in the final stage of life to leave ordinary ways of living and withdraw into the forests to seek spiritual liberation, or moksha. Here, in an illustration from an early thirteenth-century Indian manuscript, a holy man explores a text with three disciples in a secluded rural setting. (Réunion des Musées Nationaux/Art Resource, NY)

patriarchal features tightened. Women were increasingly seen as "unclean below the navel," forbidden to learn the Vedas, and excluded from public religious rituals. The Laws of Manu, composed probably in the early C.E. centuries, described a divinely ordained social order and articulated a gender system whose ideals endured for a millennium or more. It taught that all embryos were basically male and that only weak semen generated female babies. It advocated child marriage for girls to men far older than themselves. "A virtuous wife," the Laws proclaimed, "should constantly serve her husband like a god" and should never remarry after his death. In a famous prescription similar to that of Chinese and other patriarchal societies, the Laws declared: "In childhood a female must be subject to her father; in youth to her husband; when her lord is dead to her sons; a woman must never be independent."[8]

And yet some aspects of Hinduism served to empower women. Sexual pleasure was considered a legitimate goal for both men and women, and its techniques were detailed in the *Kamasutra*. Many Hindu deities were female, some life-giving and faithful, others like Kali fiercely destructive. Women were particularly prominent in the growing devotional cults dedicated to particular deities, where neither gender nor caste were obstacles to spiritual fulfillment.

A further feature of Hindu religious thought lay in its provision of different paths to the ultimate goal of liberation or moksha. Various ways to this final release, appropriate to people of different temperaments, were spelled out in Hindu teachings. Some might achieve moksha through knowledge or study; others by means of detached action in the world, doing one's work without regard to consequences; still others through passionate devotion to some deity or through extended meditation practice. Such ideas—carried by Brahmin priests and even more by wandering ascetics, who had withdrawn from ordinary life to pursue their spiritual development—became widely known throughout India.

The Buddhist Challenge

About the same time as philosophical Hinduism was emerging, another movement took shape that soon became a distinct and separate religious tradition—Buddhism. Unlike Hinduism, this new faith had a historical founder, Siddhartha Gautama (ca. 566–ca. 486 B.C.E.), a prince from a small north Indian state. According to Buddhist tradition, the prince had enjoyed a sheltered and delightful youth but was shocked to his core upon encountering old age, sickness, and death. Leaving family and fortune behind, he then set out on a six-year spiritual quest, finally achieving insight, or "enlightenment," at the age of thirty-five. For the rest of his life, he taught what he had learned and gathered a small but growing community whose members came to see him as the Buddha, the Enlightened One, a human being who had awakened.

"I teach but one thing," the Buddha said, "suffering and the end of suffering." To the Buddha, suffering or sorrow—experiencing life as imperfect, impermanent, and unsatisfactory—was the central and universal feature of human life. Its cause was desire or craving for individual fulfillment, attachment to that which inevitably changes, particularly to the notion of a core self or ego that is uniquely and solidly "me." The cure for this "dis-ease" lay in living a modest and moral life combined with meditation practice. Those who followed the Buddhist path most fully could expect to achieve enlightenment, or *nirvana*, a virtually indescribable state in which individual identity would be "extinguished" along with all greed, hatred, and delusion. With the pain of unnecessary suffering finally ended, the enlightened person would experience an overwhelming serenity, even in the midst of difficulty, as well as an immense loving-kindness, or compassion, for all beings. It was a simple message, elaborated endlessly and in various forms by those who followed him.

Much of the Buddha's teaching reflected the Hindu traditions from which it sprang. The idea that ordinary life is an illusion, the concepts of karma and rebirth, the goal of overcoming the incessant demands of the ego, the practice of meditation, the hope for final release from the cycle of rebirth—all of these Hindu elements found their way into Buddhist teaching. In this respect, Buddhism was a simplified and more accessible version of Hinduism.

Other elements of Buddhist teaching, however, sharply challenged prevailing Hindu thinking. Rejecting the religious authority of the Brahmins, the Buddha ridiculed their rituals and sacrifices as irrelevant to the hard work of dealing with one's suffering. Nor was he much interested in abstract speculation about the creation of the world or the existence of God, for such questions, he declared, "are not useful in the quest for holiness; they do not lead to peace and

■ **Comparison**
In what ways did Buddhism reflect Hindu traditions, and in what ways did it challenge them?

Classic Indian Buddha
This sixth-century C.E. image of the Buddha from eastern India shows a classical representation of the great teacher. The Buddha's right hand with palm facing the viewer indicates reassurance, or "have no fear." The partially webbed fingers are among the *lakshanas*, or signs of a Buddha image, that denote the Buddha's unique status. So too is the knot on the top of his head, symbolizing enlightenment. The elongated ear lobes reminds the viewer that earlier in his life the Buddha had worn heavy and luxurious earrings, while his partially closed and downcast eyes and his bare feet indicate detachment from the world. (Image copyright © The Metropolitan Museum of Art/Art Resource, NY)

to the direct knowledge of *nirvana*." Individuals had to take responsibility for their own spiritual development with no help from human authorities or supernatural beings. It was a religion of intense self-effort, based on personal experience. The Buddha also challenged the inequalities of a Hindu-based caste system, arguing that neither caste position nor gender was a barrier to enlightenment. The possibility of "awakening" was available to all.

But when it came to establishing a formal organization of the Buddha's most devoted followers, the prevailing patriarchy of Indian society made itself felt. Buddhist texts recount that the Buddha's foster mother, Prajapati Gotami, sought to enter the newly created order of monks but was repeatedly refused admission by the Buddha himself. Only after the intervention of the Buddha's attendant, Ananda, did he relent and allow women to join a separate order of nuns. Even then, these nuns were subjected to a series of rules that clearly subordinated them to men. Male monks, for example, could officially admonish the nuns, but the reverse was forbidden. Here is a reflection of a particular strain of Buddhist thinking that viewed women as a distracting obstacle to male enlightenment.

Nonetheless, thousands of women flocked to join the Buddhist order of nuns, where they found a degree of freedom and independence unavailable elsewhere in Indian society. Buddhist nuns delighted in the relative freedom of their order, where they largely ran their own affairs, were forbidden to do household chores, and devoted themselves wholly to the search for "awakening," which many apparently achieved. A nun named Mutta declared: "I am free from the three crooked things: mortar, pestle, and my crooked husband. I am free from birth and death and all that dragged me back."[9]

■ **Comparison**
What is the difference between the Theravada and Mahayana expressions of Buddhism?

Gradually, Buddhist teachings found an audience in India. Buddhism's egalitarian message appealed especially to lower-caste groups and to women. The availability of its teaching in the local language of Pali, rather than the classical Sanskrit, made it accessible. Establishing monasteries and stupas containing relics of the Buddha on the site of neighborhood shrines to earth spirits or near a sacred tree linked the new religion to local traditions. The most dedicated followers joined monasteries, devoting their lives to religious practice and spreading the message among nearby people. State support during the reign of Ashoka (268–232 B.C.E.) (see p. 112) likewise helped the new religion gain a foothold in India as a distinct tradition separate from Hinduism.

As Buddhism spread, both within and beyond India, differences in understanding soon emerged, particularly as to how nirvana could be achieved or, in a common Buddhist metaphor, how to cross the river to the far shore of enlightenment. The Buddha had taught a rather austere doctrine of intense self-effort, undertaken most actively by monks and nuns who withdrew from society to devote themselves fully to the quest. This early version of the new religion, known as Theravada (Teaching of the Elders), portrayed the Buddha as an immensely wise teacher and model, but certainly not divine. It was more psychological than religious, a set of practices rather than a set of beliefs. The gods, though never completely denied, played little role in assisting believers in their search for enlightenment. In short, individuals were on their own in crossing the river. Clearly this was not for everyone.

By the early centuries of the Common Era, a modified form of Buddhism called Mahayana (mah-huh-YAH-nah) (Great Vehicle) had taken root in parts of India, proclaiming that help was available for the strenuous voyage. Buddhist thinkers developed the idea of *bodhisattvas* (BOH-dih-SAT-vuhs), spiritually developed people who postponed their own entry into nirvana to assist those who were still suffering. The Buddha himself became something of a god, and both earlier and future Buddhas were available to offer help. Elaborate descriptions of these supernatural beings, together with various levels of heavens and hells, transformed Buddhism into a popular religion of salvation. Furthermore, religious merit, leading to salvation, might now be earned by acts of piety and devotion, such as contributing to the support of a monastery, and that merit might be transferred to others. This was the Great Vehicle, allowing far more people to make the voyage across the river.

Hinduism as a Religion of Duty and Devotion

Strangely enough, Buddhism as a distinct religious practice ultimately died out in the land of its birth as it was reincorporated into a broader Hindu tradition, but it spread widely and flourished, particularly in its Mahayana form, in other parts of Asia. Buddhism declined in India perhaps in part because the mounting wealth of monasteries and the economic interests of their leading figures separated them from ordinary people. Competition from Islam after 1000 C.E. also played a role. But the most important reason for the waning of Buddhism in India was the growth during the first millennium C.E. of a new kind of popular Hinduism, which the masses found more accessible than the elaborate sacrifices of the Brahmins or the philosophical speculations of intellectuals. Expressed in the widely known epic poems known as the *Mahabharata* (mah-hah-BAH-rah-tah) and the *Ramayana*, this revived Hinduism indicated more clearly that action in the world and the detached performance of caste duties might also provide a path to liberation. It was perhaps a response to the challenge of Buddhism.

In the much-beloved Hindu text known as the Bhagavad Gita (BUH-guh-vahd GEE-tuh), the troubled warrior-hero Arjuna is in anguish over the necessity of killing his kinsmen as a decisive battle approaches. But he is assured by his charioteer Lord Krishna, an incarnation of the god Vishnu, that performing his duty as a warrior, and doing so selflessly without regard to consequences, is an act of devotion that would lead to "release from the shackles of repeated rebirth." This was not an invitation to militarism, but rather an affirmation that ordinary people, not just Brahmins, could also find spiritual fulfillment by selflessly performing the ordinary duties of their lives: "The man who, casting off all desires, lives free from attachments, who is free from egoism, and from the feeling that this or that is

■ **Change**
What new emphases characterized Hinduism as it responded to the challenge of Buddhism?

mine, obtains tranquility." Withdrawal and asceticism were not the only ways to moksha.

Also becoming increasingly prominent was yet another religious path—the way of devotion to one or another of India's many gods and goddesses. Beginning in south India and moving northward, this *bhakti* (BAHK-tee) (worship) movement involved the intense adoration of and identification with a particular deity through songs, prayers, and rituals. By far the most popular deities were Vishnu, the protector and preserver of creation and associated with mercy and goodness, and Shiva, representing the divine in its destructive aspect, but many others also had their followers. This form of Hindu expression sometimes pushed against the rigid caste and gender hierarchies of Indian society by inviting all to an adoration of the Divine. After all, Krishna in the Bhagavad Gita had declared that "those who take shelter in Me, though they be of lower birth—women, vaishyas [merchants] and shudras [workers]—can attain the supreme destination."

The proliferation of gods and goddesses, and of their bhakti cults, occasioned very little friction or serious religious conflict. "Hinduism," writes a leading scholar, "is essentially tolerant, and would rather assimilate than rigidly exclude."[10] This capacity for assimilation extended to an already-declining Buddhism, which for many people had become yet another cult worshipping yet another god. The Buddha in fact was incorporated into the Hindu pantheon as the ninth incarnation of Vishnu. By 1000 C.E., Buddhism had largely disappeared as a separate religious tradition within India. Thus a constantly evolving and enormously varied South Asian religious tradition had been substantially transformed. An early emphasis on ritual sacrifice gave way to that of philosophical speculation, devotional worship, and detached action in the world. In the process, that tradition had generated Buddhism, which became the first of the great universal religions of world history, and then had absorbed that new religion back into the fold of an emerging popular Hinduism.

LearningCurve
bedfordstmartins.com
/strayer/LC

SUMMING UP SO FAR

How did the evolution of cultural traditions in India and China differ during the era of second-wave civilizations?

Toward Monotheism: The Search for God in the Middle East

Paralleling the evolution of Chinese and Indian cultural traditions was the movement toward a distinctive monotheistic religious tradition in the Middle East, which found expression in Persian Zoroastrianism and in Judaism. Neither of these religions themselves spread very widely, but the monotheism that they nurtured became the basis for both Christianity and Islam, which have shaped so much of world history over the past 2,000 years. Amid the proliferation of gods and spirits that had long characterized religious life throughout the ancient world, monotheism—the idea of a single supreme deity, the sole source of all life and being—was a radical cultural innovation. That conception created the possibility of a universal religion, open to all of humankind, but it could also mean an exclusive and intolerant faith.

Zoroastrianism

During the glory years of the powerful Persian Empire, a new religion arose to challenge the polytheism of earlier times. Tradition dates its Persian prophet, Zarathustra (Zoroaster to the Greeks), to the sixth or seventh century B.C.E., although some scholars place him hundreds of years earlier. Whenever he actually lived, his ideas took hold in Persia and received a degree of state support during the Achaemenid dynasty (558–330 B.C.E.). Appalled by the endemic violence of recurring cattle raids, Zarathustra recast the traditional Persian polytheism into a vision of a single unique god, Ahura Mazda, who ruled the world and was the source of all truth, light, and goodness. This benevolent deity was engaged in a cosmic struggle with the forces of evil, embodied in an equivalent supernatural figure, Angra Mainyu. Ultimately this struggle would be decided in favor of Ahura Mazda, aided by the arrival of a final savior who would restore the world to its earlier purity and peace. At a day of judgment, those who had aligned with Ahura Mazda would be granted new resurrected bodies and rewarded with eternal life in Paradise. Those who had sided with evil and the "Lie" were condemned to everlasting punishment. Zoroastrian (zohr-oh-ASS-tree-ahn) teaching thus placed great emphasis on the free will of humankind and the necessity for each individual to choose between good and evil.

The Zoroastrian faith achieved widespread support within the Persian heartland, although it also found adherents in other parts of the empire, such as Egypt, Mesopotamia, and Anatolia. But it never became an active missionary religion and did not spread widely beyond the region. Alexander the Great's invasion of the Persian Empire and the subsequent Greek-ruled Seleucid dynasty (330–155 B.C.E.) were disastrous for Zoroastrianism, as temples were plundered, priests slaughtered, and sacred writings burned. But the new faith managed to survive this onslaught and flourished again during the Parthian (247 B.C.E.–224 C.E.) and Sassanid (224–651 C.E.) dynasties. It was the arrival of Islam and an Arab empire that occasioned the final decline of Zoroastrianism in Persia, although a few believers fled to India, where they became known as Parsis ("Persians"). The Parsis have continued their faith into present times.

Like Buddhism, the Zoroastrian faith vanished from its place of origin, but unlike Buddhism, it did not spread beyond Persia in a recognizable form. Some elements of the Zoroastrian belief system, however, did become incorporated into other religious traditions. The presence of many Jews in the Persian Empire meant that they surely became aware of Zoroastrian ideas. Many of those ideas—including the conflict of God and an evil counterpart (Satan); the notion of a last judgment and resurrected bodies; and a belief in the final defeat of evil, the arrival of a savior (Messiah), and the remaking of the world at the end of time—found a place in an evolving Judaism. Some of these teachings, especially the concepts of heaven and

■ **Connection**
What aspects of Zoroastrianism and Judaism subsequently found a place in Christianity and Islam?

Zoroastrian Fire Altar
Representing the energy of the Creator God Ahura Mazda, the fire altar became an important symbol of Zoroastrianism and was often depicted on Persian coins in association with images of Persian rulers. This particular coin dates from the third century C.E. (©AAAC/Topham/The Image Works)

hell, later became prominent in those enormously influential successors to Judaism—Christianity and Islam.[11] Thus the Persian tradition of Zoroastrianism continued to echo well beyond its disappearance in the land of its birth.

Judaism

■ Description

What was distinctive about the Jewish religious tradition?

While Zoroastrianism emerged in the greatest empire of its time, Judaism, the Middle East's other ancient monotheistic tradition, was born among one of the region's smaller and, at the time, less significant peoples—the Hebrews. Their traditions, recorded in the Hebrew scriptures, tell of an early migration from Mesopotamia to Canaan under the leadership of Abraham. Those same traditions report that a portion of these people later fled to Egypt, where they were first enslaved and then miraculously escaped to rejoin their kinfolk in Palestine. There, around 1000 B.C.E., they established a small state, which soon split into two parts—a northern kingdom called Israel and a southern state called Judah.

In a region politically dominated by the large empires of Assyria, Babylon, and Persia, these tiny Hebrew communities lived a precarious existence. Israel was conquered by Assyria in 722 B.C.E., and many of its inhabitants were deported to distant regions, where they assimilated into the local culture. In 586 B.C.E., the kingdom of Judah likewise came under Babylonian control, and its elite class was shipped off to exile. "By the rivers of Babylon," wrote one of their poets, "there we sat down, yea, we wept, when we remembered Zion [Jerusalem]." It was in Babylonian exile that these people, now calling themselves Jews, retained and renewed their cultural identity and later a small number were able to return to their homeland. A large part of that identity lay in their unique religious ideas. It was in creating that religious tradition, rather than in building a powerful empire, that this small people cast a long shadow in world history.

Ancient Israel

From their unique historical memory of exodus from Egypt and exile in Babylon, the Hebrew people evolved over many centuries a distinctive conception of God. Unlike the peoples of Mesopotamia, India, Greece, and elsewhere—all of whom populated the invisible realm with numerous gods and goddesses—Jews found in their God, whom they called Yahweh (YAH-way), a powerful and jealous deity, who demanded their exclusive loyalty. "Thou shalt have no other gods before me"—this was the first of the Ten Commandments. It was a difficult requirement, for as the Hebrews turned from a pastoral life to agriculture, many of them were attracted by the fertility gods of neighboring peoples. Their neighbors' goddesses also were attractive, offering a kind of spiritual support that the primarily masculine Yahweh could not. Foreign deities also entered Hebrew culture through royal treaty obligations with nearby states. Thus the emerging Hebrew conception of the Divine was not quite monotheism, for the repeated demands of the Hebrew prophets to turn away from other gods show that those deities remained real for many Jews. Over time, however, the priesthood that supported the one-god theory triumphed. The Jews came to understand their relationship to Yahweh as a contract or a covenant. In return for their sole devotion and obedience to God's laws, Yahweh would consider the Jews his chosen people, favoring them in battle, causing them to grow in numbers, and bringing them prosperity and blessing.

Unlike the bickering, arbitrary, polytheistic gods of Mesopotamia or ancient Greece, which were associated with the forces of nature and behaved in quite human fashion, Yahweh was increasingly seen as a lofty, transcendent deity of utter holiness and purity, set far above the world of nature, which he had created. But unlike the impersonal conceptions of ultimate reality found in Daoism and Hinduism, Yahweh was encountered as a divine person with whom people could actively communicate. He also acted within the historical process, bringing the Jews out of Egypt or using foreign empires to punish them for their disobedience.

Furthermore, for some, Yahweh was transformed from a god of war, who ordered his people to "utterly destroy" the original inhabitants of the Promised Land, to a god of social justice and compassion for the poor and the marginalized, especially in the passionate pronouncements of Jewish prophets such as Amos and Isaiah. The prophet Isaiah describes Yahweh as rejecting the empty rituals of his chosen but sinful people: "What to me is the multitude of your sacrifices, says the Lord. . . . Wash yourselves, make yourselves clean, . . . cease to do evil, learn to do good; seek justice; correct oppression; defend the fatherless; plead for the widow."[12]

Here was a distinctive conception of the divine—singular, transcendent, personal, ruling over the natural order, engaged in history, and demanding social justice and moral righteousness above sacrifices and rituals. This set of ideas sustained a separate Jewish identity in both ancient and modern times, and it was this understanding of God that provided the foundation on which both Christianity and Islam were built.

LearningCurve
bedfordstmartins.com
/strayer/LC

The Cultural Tradition of Classical Greece: The Search for a Rational Order

Unlike the Jews, the Persians, or the civilization of India, Greek thinkers of the second-wave era generated no lasting religious tradition of world historical importance. The religion of these city-states brought together the unpredictable, quarreling, and lustful gods of Mount Olympus, secret fertility cults, oracles predicting the future, and the ecstatic worship of Dionysus, the god of wine. The distinctive feature of the classical Greek cultural tradition was the willingness of many Greek intellectuals to abandon this mythological framework, to affirm that the world was a physical reality governed by natural laws, and to assert that human rationality could both understand these laws and work out a system of moral and ethical life as well. In separating science and philosophy from conventional religion, the Greeks developed a way of thinking that bore some similarity to the secularism of Confucian thought in China.

Precisely why Greek thought evolved in this direction is hard to say. Perhaps the diversity and incoherence of Greek religious mythology presented its intellectuals

■ **Description**

What are the distinctive features of the Greek intellectual tradition?

with a challenge to bring some order to their understanding of the world. Greece's geographic position on the margins of the great civilizations of Mesopotamia, Egypt, and Persia certainly provided intellectual stimulation. Furthermore, the growing role of law in the political life of Athens possibly suggested that a similar regularity also underlay the natural order.

The Greek Way of Knowing

The foundations of this Greek rationalism emerged in the three centuries between 600 and 300 B.C.E., coinciding with the flourishing of Greek city-states, especially Athens, and with the growth of its artistic, literary, and theatrical traditions. The enduring significance of Greek thinking lay not so much in the answers it provided to life's great issues, for the Greeks seldom agreed with one another, but rather in its way of asking questions. Its emphasis on argument, logic, and the relentless questioning of received wisdom; its confidence in human reason; its enthusiasm for puzzling out the world without much reference to the gods — these were the defining characteristics of the Greek cultural tradition.

The great exemplar of this approach to knowledge was Socrates (469–399 B.C.E.), an Athenian philosopher who walked about the city engaging others in conversation about the good life. He wrote nothing, and his preferred manner of teaching was not the lecture or exposition of his own ideas but rather a constant questioning of the assumptions and logic of his students' thinking. Concerned always to puncture the pretentious, he challenged conventional ideas about the importance of wealth and power in living well, urging instead the pursuit of wisdom and virtue. He was critical of Athenian democracy and on occasion had positive things to say about Sparta, the great enemy of his own city. Such behavior brought him into conflict with city authorities, who accused him of corrupting the youth of Athens and sentenced him to death. At his trial, he defended himself as the "gadfly" of Athens, stinging its citizens into awareness. To any and all, he declared, "I shall question, and examine and cross-examine him, and if I find that he does not possess virtue, but says he does, I shall rebuke him for scorning the things that are most important and caring more for what is of less worth."[13]

The earliest of the classical Greek thinkers, many of them living on the Ionian coast of Anatolia, applied this rational and questioning way of knowing to the world of nature. For example, Thales, drawing on Babylonian astronomy, predicted an eclipse of the sun and argued that the moon simply reflected the sun's light. He also was one of the first Greeks to ask about the fundamental nature of the universe and came up with the idea that water was the basic stuff from which all else derived, for it existed as solid, liquid, and gas. Others argued in favor of air or fire or some combination. Democritus suggested that atoms, tiny "uncuttable" particles, collided in various configurations to form visible matter. Pythagoras believed that beneath the chaos and complexity of the visible world lay a simple, unchanging mathematical order.

The Death of Socrates
Condemned to death by an Athenian jury, Socrates declined to go into exile, voluntarily drank a cup of poison hemlock, and died in 399 B.C.E. in the presence of his friends. The dramatic scene was famously described by Plato and much later was immortalized on canvas by the French painter Jacques-Louis David in 1787. (Image copyright © The Metropolitan Museum of Art/Art Resource, NY)

What these thinkers had in common was a commitment to a rational and nonreligious explanation for the material world.

Such thinking also served to explain the functioning of the human body and its diseases. Hippocrates and his followers came to believe that the body was composed of four fluids, or "humors," which caused various ailments when out of proper balance. He also traced the origins of epilepsy, known to the Greeks as "the sacred disease," to simple heredity: "it appears to me to be nowise more divine nor more sacred than other diseases, but has a natural cause . . . like other afflictions."[14] A similar approach informed Greek thinking about the ways of humankind. Herodotus, who wrote about the Greco-Persian Wars, explained his project as an effort to discover "the reason why they fought one another." This assumption that human reasons lay behind the conflict, not simply the whims of the gods, was what made Herodotus a historian in the modern sense of that word. Ethics and government also figured importantly in Greek thinking. Plato (429–348 B.C.E.) famously sketched out in *The*

Republic a design for a good society. It would be ruled by a class of highly educated "guardians" led by a "philosopher-king." Such people would be able to penetrate the many illusions of the material world and to grasp the "world of forms," in which ideas such as goodness, beauty, and justice lived a real and unchanging existence. Only such people, he argued, were fit to rule.

Aristotle (384–322 B.C.E.), a student of Plato and a teacher of Alexander the Great, represents the most complete expression of the Greek way of knowing, for he wrote or commented on practically everything. With an emphasis on empirical observation, he cataloged the constitutions of 158 Greek city-states, identified hundreds of species of animals, and wrote about logic, physics, astronomy, the weather, and much else besides. Famous for his reflections on ethics, he argued that "virtue" was a product of rational training and cultivated habit and could be learned. As to government, he urged a mixed system, combining the principles of monarchy, aristocracy, and democracy.

The Greek Legacy

The rationalism of the Greek tradition was clearly not the whole of Greek culture. The gods of Mount Olympus continued to be a reality for many people, and the ecstatic songs and dances that celebrated Dionysus, the god of wine, were anything but rational and reflective. The death of Socrates at the hands of an Athenian jury showed that philosophy could be a threat as well as an engaging pastime. Nonetheless, Greek rationalism, together with Greek art, literature, and theater, persisted long after the glory days of Athens were over. Alexander's empire and that of the Romans facilitated the spread of Greek culture within the Mediterranean basin and beyond, and not a few leading Roman figures sent their children to be educated in Athens at the Academy, which Plato had founded. An emerging Christian theology was expressed in terms of Greek philosophical concepts, especially those of Plato. Even after the western Roman Empire collapsed, classical Greek texts were preserved in the eastern half, known as the Byzantine Empire or Byzantium (see pp. 321–28 and Chapter 10).

In the West, however, direct access to Greek texts was far more difficult in the chaotic conditions of post-Roman Europe, and for centuries Greek scholarship was neglected in favor of Christian writers. Much of that legacy was subsequently rediscovered after the twelfth century C.E. as European scholars gained access to classical Greek texts. From that point on, the Greek legacy has been viewed as a central element of an emerging "Western" civilization. It played a role in formulating an updated Christian theology, in fostering Europe's Scientific Revolution, and in providing a point of departure for much of European philosophy.

Long before this European rediscovery, the Greek legacy had also entered the Islamic world. Systematic translations of Greek works of science and philosophy into Arabic, together with Indian and Persian learning, stimulated Muslim thinkers and scientists, especially in the fields of medicine, astronomy, mathematics, geography, and chemistry. It was in fact largely from Arabic translations of Greek writers that Euro-peans became reacquainted with the legacy of classical Greece, especially during the twelfth and thirteenth centuries. Despite the many centuries that have passed since the flourishing of ancient Greek culture, that tradition has remained, especially in the West, an inspiration for those who celebrate the powers of the human mind to probe the mysteries of the universe and to explore the equally challenging domain of human life.

LearningCurve
bedfordstmartins.com
/strayer/LC

The Birth of Christianity . . . with Buddhist Comparisons

About 500 years after the time of Confucius, the Buddha, Zarathustra, and Socrates, a young Jewish peasant/carpenter in the remote province of Judaea in the Roman Empire began a brief three-year career of teaching and miracle working before he got in trouble with local authorities and was executed. In one of history's most un-likely stories, the teachings of that obscure man, barely noted in the historical records of the time, became the basis of the world's second great universal religion, after that of Buddhism. This man, Jesus of Nazareth, and the religion of Christianity that grew out of his life and teaching, had a dramatic impact on world history, similar to and often compared with that of India's Siddhartha Gautama, the Buddha.

■ **Comparison**

How would you compare the lives and teachings of Jesus and the Buddha? In what different ways did the two religions evolve after the deaths of their founders?

The Lives of the Founders

The family background of the two teachers could hardly have been more different. Gautama was born to royalty and luxury, whereas Jesus was a rural or small-town worker from a distinctly lower-class family. But both became spiritual seekers, mys-tics in their respective traditions, who claimed to have personally experienced another and unseen level of reality. Those powerful religious experiences provided the moti-vation for their life's work and the personal authenticity that attracted their growing band of followers.

Both were "wisdom teachers," challenging the conventional values of their time, urging the renunciation of wealth, and emphasizing the supreme importance of love or compassion as the basis for a moral life. The Buddha had instructed his follow-ers in the practice of *metta*, or loving-kindness: "Just as a mother would protect her only child at the risk of her own life, even so, let [my followers] cultivate a boundless heart towards all beings."[15] In a similar vein during his famous Sermon on the Mount, Jesus told his followers: "You have heard that it was said 'Love your neigh-bor and hate your enemy,' but I tell you 'Love your enemies and pray for those who persecute you.'"[16] Both Jesus and the Buddha called for the personal transformation of their followers, through "letting go" of the grasping that causes suffering, in the Buddha's teaching, or "losing one's life in order to save it," in the language of Jesus.[17]

Despite these similarities, there were also some differences in their teachings and their life stories. Jesus inherited from his Jewish tradition an intense devotion to a single personal deity with whom he was on intimate terms, referring to him as Abba ("papa" or "daddy"). According to the New Testament, the miracles he performed reflected the power of God available to him as a result of that relationship. The Buddha's original message, by contrast, largely ignored the supernatural, involved no miracles, and taught a path of intense self-effort aimed at ethical living and mindfulness as a means of ending suffering. Furthermore, Jesus' teachings had a sharper social and political edge than did those of the Buddha. Jesus spoke more clearly on behalf of the poor and the oppressed, directly criticized the hypocrisies of the powerful, and deliberately associated with lepers, adulterous women, and tax collectors, all of whom were regarded as "impure." These actions reflected his lower-class background, the Jewish tradition of social criticism, and the reality of Roman imperial rule over his people, none of which corresponded to the Buddha's experience. Finally, Jesus' public life was very brief, probably less than three years, compared to more than forty years for the Buddha. His teachings had so antagonized both Jewish and Roman authorities that he was crucified as a common criminal. The Buddha's message was apparently less threatening to the politically powerful, and he died a natural death at age eighty.

The Spread of New Religions

■ **Change**

In what ways was Christianity transformed in the five centuries following the death of Jesus?

Neither Jesus nor the Buddha had any intention of founding a new religion; rather, they sought to revitalize the traditions from which they had come. Nonetheless, Christianity and Buddhism soon emerged as separate religions, distinct from Judaism and Hinduism, proclaiming their messages to a much wider and more inclusive audience. In the process, both teachers were transformed by their followers into gods. According to many scholars, Jesus never claimed divine status, seeing himself as a teacher or a prophet, whose close relationship to God could be replicated by anyone.[18] The Buddha likewise viewed himself as an enlightened but fully human person, an example of what was possible for all who followed the path. But in Mahayana Buddhism, the Buddha became a supernatural being who could be worshipped and prayed to and was spiritually available to his followers. Jesus also soon became divine in the eyes of his early followers, such as Saint Paul and Saint John. According to one of the first creeds of the Church, he was "the Son of God, Very God of Very God," while his death and resurrection made possible the forgiveness of sins and the eternal salvation of those who believed.

The transformation of Christianity from a small Jewish sect to a world religion began with Saint Paul (10–65 C.E.), an early convert whose missionary journeys in the eastern Roman Empire led to the founding of small Christian communities that included non-Jews. The Good News of Jesus, Paul argued, was for everyone, and Gentile (non-Jewish) converts need not follow Jewish laws or rituals such as circumcision. In one of his many letters to these new communities, later collected as part of the New Testament, Paul wrote, "There is neither Jew nor Greek . . . neither slave nor free . . . neither male nor female, for you are all one in Christ Jesus."[19]

Despite Paul's egalitarian pronouncement, early Christianity, like Buddhism, offered a mix of opportunities and restrictions for women. Jesus himself had interacted easily with a wide range of women, and they had figured prominently among his followers. Some scholars have argued that Mary Magdalene was a part of his inner circle.[20] And women played leadership roles in the "house churches" of the first century C.E. Nonetheless, Paul counseled women to "be subject to your husbands" and declared that "it is shameful for a woman to speak in church." Men were identified with the role of Christ himself when Paul argued that "the husband is head of the wife as Christ is head of the Church."[21] It was not long before male spokesmen for the faith had fully assimilated older and highly negative views of women. As daughters of Eve, they were responsible for the introduction of sin and evil into the world and were the source of temptation for men. On the other hand, Jesus' mother Mary soon became the focus of a devotional cult; women were among the martyrs of the early church; and growing numbers of Christian women, like their Buddhist counterparts, found a more independent space in the monasteries, even as the official hierarchy of the Church became wholly male.

Nonetheless, the inclusive message of early Christianity was one of the attractions of the new faith as it spread very gradually within the Roman Empire during the several centuries after Jesus' death. The earliest converts were usually lower-stratum people—artisans, traders, and a considerable number of women—mostly from towns and cities, while a scattering of wealthier, more prominent, and better-educated people subsequently joined the ranks of Christians.[22] The spread of the faith was often accompanied by reports of miracles, healings, and the casting out of demons—all of which were impressive to people thoroughly accustomed to seeing the supernatural behind the events of ordinary life. Christian communities also attracted converts by the way their members cared for one another. In the middle of the third century C.E., the Church in Rome supported 154 priests (of whom 52 were exorcists) and some 1,500 widows, orphans, and destitute people.[23] By 300 C.E., perhaps 10 percent of the Roman Empire's population (some 5 million people) identified themselves as Christians.

Although Christians in the West often think of their faith as a European-centered religion, during the first six centuries of the Christian era, most followers of Jesus lived in the non-European regions of the Roman Empire—North Africa, Egypt, Anatolia, Syria—or outside of the empire altogether in Arabia, Persia, Ethiopia, India, and China. Saint Paul's missionary journeys had established various Christian communities in the Roman province of Asia—what is now Turkey—and also in Syria, where the earliest recorded Christian church building was located. The Syrian church also developed a unique liturgy with strong Jewish influences and a distinctive musical tradition of chants and hymns. The language of that liturgy was neither Greek nor Latin, but Syriac, a Semitic tongue closely related to Aramaic, which Jesus spoke.

From Syria, the faith spread eastward into Persia, where it attracted a substantial number of converts, many of them well educated in the sciences and medicine, by the third century C.E. Those converts also encountered periodic persecution from the Zoroastrian rulers of Persia and were sometimes suspected of political loyalty to the Roman Empire, Persia's longtime enemy and rival. To the north of Syria on the slopes of the Caucasus Mountains, the Kingdom of Armenia became the first place where rulers adopted Christianity as a state religion. In time, Christianity became—and remains to this day—a central element of Armenian national identity. A distinctive feature of Armenian Christianity involved the ritual killing of animals at the end of the worship service, probably a continuation of earlier pre-Christian practices.

Syria and Persia represented the core region of the Church of the East, distinct both theologically and organizationally from the Latin church focused on Rome and an emerging Eastern Orthodox church based in Constantinople. Its missionaries took Christianity even farther to the east. By the fourth century, and perhaps much earlier, a well-organized church had taken root in southern India, which later gained tax privileges and special rights from local rulers. In the early seventh century a Persian monk named Alopen initiated a small but remarkable Christian experiment in China, described more fully in Chapter 10. A modest Christian presence in Central Asia was also an outgrowth of this Church of the East.

In other directions as well, Christianity spread from its Palestinian place of origin. By the time Muhammad was born in 570, a number of Arabs had become Christians. One of them, in fact, was among the first to affirm Muhammad as an authentic prophet. A particularly vibrant center of Christianity developed in Egypt, where tradition holds that Jesus's family fled to escape persecution of King Herod. Egyptian priests soon translated the Bible into the Egyptian language known as Coptic, and Egyptian Christians pioneered various forms of monasticism. By 400 C.E., hundreds of monasteries, cells, and caves dotted the desert, inhabited by reclusive monks dedicated to their spiritual practices. Increasingly, the language, theology, and practice of Egyptian Christianity diverged from that of Rome and Constantinople, giving expression to Egyptian resistance against Roman or Byzantine oppression.

To the west of Egypt, a Church of North Africa furnished a number of the intellectuals of the early Church including Saint Augustine as well as many Christian martyrs to Roman persecution (see Portrait of Perpetua, pp. 144–45). Here and elsewhere the coming of Christianity not only provoked hostility from Roman political authorities but also tensions within families. The North African Carthaginian writer Tertullian (160–220 C.E.), known as the "father of Latin Christianity," described the kind of difficulties that might arise between a Christian wife and her "pagan" husband:

> She is engaged in a fast; her husband has arranged a banquet. It is her Christian duty to visit the streets and the homes of the poor; her husband insists on family business. She celebrates the Easter Vigil throughout the night; her husband expects her in his bed. . . . She who has taken a cup at Eucharist will be required to take of a cup with her husband in the tavern. She who has foresworn idolatry must inhale the smoke arising from the incense on the altars of the idols in her husband's home.[24]

Further south in Africa, Christianity became during the fourth century the state religion of Axum, an emerging kingdom in what is now Eritrea and Ethiopia (see Chapter 6). This occurred at about the same time as both Armenia and the Roman Empire officially endorsed Christianity. In Axum, a distinctively African expression of Christianity took root with open-air services, the use of drums and stringed instruments in worship, and colorful umbrellas covering priests and musicians from the elements. Linked theologically and organizationally to Coptic Christianity in Egypt, the Ethiopian church used Ge'ez, a local Semitic language and script, for its liturgy and literature.

In the Roman world, the strangest and most offensive feature of the new faith was its exclusive monotheism and its antagonism to all other supernatural powers, particularly the cult of the emperors. Christians' denial of these other gods caused them to be tagged as "atheists" and was one reason behind the empire's intermittent persecution of Christians during the first three centuries of the Common Era. All of that ended with Emperor Constantine's conversion in the early fourth century C.E. and with growing levels of state support for the new religion in the decades that followed.

Roman rulers sought to use an increasingly popular Christianity as glue to hold together a very diverse population in a weakening imperial state. Constantine and his successors thus provided Christians with newfound security and opportunities. The emperor Theodosius (r. 379–395 C.E.) enforced a ban on all polytheistic ritual

Map 4.1 The Spread of Early Christianity and Buddhism
In the five centuries after the birth of Jesus, Christianity found converts from Spain to northeast Africa, the Middle East, Central Asia, and India. In the Roman Empire, Axum, and Armenia, the new religion enjoyed state support as well. Subsequently, Christianity took root solidly in Europe and after 1000 C.E. in Russia as well. Meanwhile, Buddhism was spreading from its South Asian homeland to various parts of Asia, even as it was weakening in India itself.

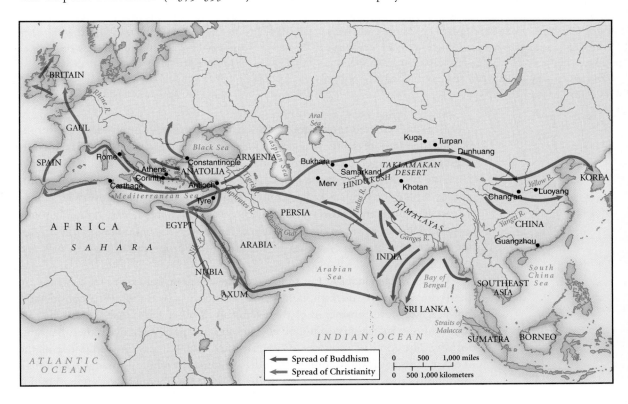

Perpetua, Christian Martyr

"The blood of the martyrs," declared the Christian writer Tertullian, "is the seed of the church." Few of those martyrs, whose stories so inspired the persecuted converts of the early Christian centuries, could match that of Perpetua, a young woman whose prison diary provides a highly personal account of her arrest and trial.[25]

Born in 181 C.E. in the North African city of Carthage, Perpetua hailed from an upper-class Roman family and was quite well educated, literate in Latin and probably Greek, and acquainted with Roman philosophical writings. By the time she enters the historical record at age twenty-two, she had given birth to a son, had lost her husband either to death or abandonment, and had recently begun to study Christianity, one of a small but growing group of educated people who were turning toward the new faith. Coinciding with her conversion was a wave of persecutions ordered by the Roman emperor Septimus Severus,

Perpetua (Vladimir Bugarin/5d012)

also of North African descent and a devotee of the Egyptian cult of Isis and Osiris. Severus sought to forbid new conversions rather than punish long-established Christians. In line with this policy, in 203 C.E., the hard-line governor of the region ordered the arrest of Perpetua along with four others — two slaves, one of them a woman named Felicitas who was eight months pregnant, and two free men. Before she was taken to the prison, however, Perpetua decisively confirmed her commitment to Christianity by accepting baptism.

Once in the "dark hole" of the prison, Perpetua was terrified. It was crowded and stiflingly hot, and she was consumed with anxiety for her child. Several fellow Christians managed to bribe the prison guards to permit Perpetua to nurse her baby son. Reunited with her child, she found that "my prison had suddenly become a palace, so that I wanted to be there rather than anywhere else."

sacrifices and ordered their temples closed. Christians by contrast received patronage for their buildings, official approval for their doctrines, suppression of their rivals, prestige from imperial recognition, and, during the late fourth century, the proclamation of Christianity as the official state religion. All of this set in motion a process by which the Roman Empire, and later all of Europe, became overwhelmingly Christian. At the time, however, Christianity was expanding at least as rapidly to the east and south as it was to the west. In 500, few observers could have predicted that the future of Christianity would lie primarily in Europe rather than in Asia and Africa.

The spread of Buddhism in India was quite different from that of Christianity in the Roman Empire. Even though Ashoka's support gave Buddhism a considerable boost, it was never promoted to the exclusion of other faiths. Ashoka sought harmony among India's diverse population through religious tolerance rather than uniformity. The kind of monotheistic intolerance that Christianity exhibited in the Roman world was quite foreign to Indian patterns of religious practice. Although Buddhism subsequently died out in India as it was absorbed into a reviving Hindu-

A few days later, Perpetua's deeply distressed non-Christian father arrived for a visit, hoping to persuade his only daughter to recant her faith and save her life and the family's honor. It was a heart-breaking encounter. "Daughter," he said, "have pity on my grey head. . . . Do not abandon me to be the reproach of men. Think of your brothers, think of your mother and your aunt, think of your child, who will not be able to live once you are gone. Give up your pride! You will destroy all of us! None of us will ever be able to speak freely again if anything happens to you." Firm in her faith, Perpetua refused his entreaties and she reported that "he left me in great sorrow."

On the day of her trial, with her distraught father in attendance, the governor Hilarianus also begged Perpetua to consider her family and renounce her faith by offering a sacrifice to the emperor. Again she refused and together with her four companions was "condemned to the beasts," a humiliating form of execution normally reserved for the lower classes. Although she was now permanently separated from her child, she wrote that "we returned to the prison in high spirits." During her last days in the prison, Perpetua and the others were treated "more humanely,"

allowed to visit with family and friends, as the head of the jail was himself a Christian.

But then, on the birthday of the emperor, this small band of Christians was marched to the amphitheater, "joyfully as though they were going to heaven," according to an eyewitness account. After the prisoners strenuously and successfully resisted dressing in the robes of pagan priests, the three men were sent into the arena to contend with a boar, a bear, and a leopard. Then it was the turn of the women, Perpetua and the slave Felicitas, who had given birth only two days earlier. When a mad cow failed to kill them, a soldier was sent to finish the work. As he approached Perpetua, he apparently hesitated, but as an eyewitness account put it, "she took the trembling hand of the young gladiator and guided it to her throat." Appended to her diary was this comment from an unknown observer: "It was as though so great a woman, feared as she was by the unclean spirit, could not be dispatched unless she herself were willing."

Questions: How might you understand the actions and attitudes of Perpetua? Is her experience accessible to people living in a largely secular modern society?

ism, no renewal of Roman polytheism occurred, and Christianity became an enduring element of European civilization. Nonetheless, Christianity did adopt some elements of religious practice from the Roman world, including perhaps the cult of saints and the dating of the birth of Jesus to the winter solstice. In both cases, however, these new religions spread widely beyond their places of origin. Buddhism provided a network of cultural connections across much of Asia, while Christianity during its early centuries established an Afro-Eurasian presence.

Institutions, Controversies, and Divisions

As Christianity spread within the Roman Empire and beyond, it developed a hierarchical organization, with patriarchs, bishops, and priests—all men—replacing the house churches of the early years, in which women played a more prominent part. At least in some places, however, women continued to exercise leadership and even priestly roles, prompting Pope Gelasius in 494 to speak out sharply against those who encouraged women "to officiate at the sacred altars, and to take part in all matters imputed to the offices of the male sex, to which they do not belong."[26] In general, though, the exclusion of women from the priesthood established a male-dominated clergy and a patriarchal church, which has lasted into the twenty-first century.

The emerging Christian movement was, however, anything but unified. Its immense geographical reach, accompanied by inevitable differences in language, culture, and political regime, ensured that a single focus for Christian belief and practice was difficult to achieve. Doctrinal differences also tore at the unity of Christianity and embroiled church authorities in frequent controversy about the nature of Jesus (was he human, divine, or both?), his relationship to God (equal or inferior?), and the always-perplexing concept of the Trinity (God as Father, Son, and Holy Spirit). There was debate as well about what writings belonged in the Bible. A series of church councils — at Nicaea (325 C.E.), Chalcedon (451 C.E.), and Constantinople (553 C.E.), for example — sought to define an orthodox, or correct, position on these and other issues, declaring those who disagreed as *anathema* and expelling them from the Church. Thus Egyptian Christians, for example, held to the unorthodox position called Monophysite. This view, that Jesus had a single divine nature simply occupying a human body, expressed resistance to domination from Rome or Constantinople, which held that Jesus was both fully human and fully divine. Likewise the Church of the East adopted Nestorianism, another unorthodox view that emphasized the human side of Jesus' nature and distinguished its theology from the Latin and Eastern Orthodox churches.

Beyond these theological debates, political and cultural differences generated division even among the orthodox. The bishop of Rome gradually emerged as the dominant leader, or pope, of the Church in the western half of the empire, but his authority was sharply contested in the east. This division contributed to the later split between the Latin or Roman Catholic and the Greek or Eastern Orthodox branches of Christendom, a division that continues to the present (see Chapter 10). Thus the Christian world of 500 C.E. was not only geographically extensive but also politically and theologically very diverse and highly fragmented.

Buddhists too clashed over various interpretations of the Buddha's teachings, and a series of councils failed to prevent the division between Theravada, Mahayana, and other approaches. A considerable proliferation of different sects, practices, teachings, and meditation techniques subsequently emerged within the Buddhist world, but these divisions generally lacked the "clear-cut distinction between 'right' and 'wrong' ideas" that characterized conflicts within the Christian world.[27] Although Buddhist states and warrior classes (such as the famous samurai of Japan) sometimes engaged in warfare, religious differences among Buddhists seldom provided the basis for the bitterness and violence that often accompanied religious conflict within Christendom. Nor did Buddhists develop the kind of overall religious hierarchy that characterized Christianity, although communities of monks and nuns, organized in monasteries, created elaborate rules to govern their internal affairs.

LearningCurve
bedfordstmartins.com
/strayer/LC

SUMMING UP SO FAR

How might you understand the appeal of Buddhism and Christianity as opposed to the more rationalist approaches of Greek and Confucian philosophy?

Reflections: Religion and Historians

To put it mildly, religion has always been a sensitive subject, and no less so for historians than for anyone else. Throughout human history the vast majority of people have simply assumed the existence of an Unseen Realm, that of the sacred or the divine, with which human beings should align themselves. More recently, as an outgrowth of the Scientific Revolution and the European Enlightenment, some have challenged that assumption, arguing that the only realities worth considering are those that can be accessed with the techniques of science. Modern secular historians, whatever their personal beliefs, feel compelled to rely on evidence available in this world. This situation has generated various tensions or misunderstandings between historians and religious practitioners.

One of these tensions involves the question of change. Most religions present themselves as timeless, partaking of eternity or at least reflecting ancient practice. In the eyes of historians, however, the religious aspect of human life changes as much as any other. The Hindu tradition changed from a religion of ritual and sacrifice to one of devotion and worship. Buddhism became more conventionally religious, with an emphasis on the supernatural, as it evolved from Theravada to Mahayana forms. A male-dominated hierarchical Christian Church, with its pope, bishops, priests, and state support, was very different from the small house churches that suffered persecution by imperial authorities in the early Christian centuries. The implication—that religions are at least in part a human phenomenon—has been troublesome to some believers.

Historians, on the other hand, have sometimes been uncomfortable in the face of claims by believers that they have actually experienced a divine reality. How could such experiences be verified, when even the biographical details of the lives of the Buddha and Jesus are difficult to prove by the standards of historians? Certainly, modern historians are in no position to validate or refute the spiritual claims of these teachers, but we need to take them seriously. Although we will never know precisely what happened to the Buddha as he sat in meditation in northern India or what transpired when Jesus spent forty days in the wilderness, clearly those experiences changed the two men and motivated their subsequent actions. Later, Muhammad likewise claimed to have received revelations from God in the caves outside Mecca. Millions of the followers of these religious leaders have also acted on the basis of what they perceived to be an encounter with the Divine or the Unseen. This interior dimension of human experience, though difficult to grasp with any precision, has been a significant mover and shaper of the historical process.

Yet a third problem arises from debates within particular religious traditions about which group most accurately represents the "real" or authentic version of the faith. Historians usually refuse to take sides in such disputes. They simply notice with interest that most human cultural traditions generate conflicting views, some of which become the basis for serious conflict in their societies.

Reconciling personal religious convictions with the perspectives of modern historical scholarship is no easy task. At the very least, all of us can appreciate the immense human effort that has gone into the making of religious traditions, and we can acknowledge the enormous significance of these traditions in the unfolding of the human story. They have shaped the meanings that billions of people over thousands of years have attached to the world they inhabit. These religious traditions have justified the vast social inequalities and oppressive states of human civilizations, but they also have enabled human beings to endure the multiple sufferings that attend human life and on occasion they have stimulated reform and rebellion. And the religions born in second-wave civilizations have guided much of humankind in our endless efforts to penetrate the mysteries of the world beyond and of the world within.

Second Thoughts

What's the Significance?

LearningCurve
Check what you know.
**bedfordstmartins.com
/strayer/LC**

Online Study Guide
bedfordstmartins.com/strayer

Legalism, 121
Confucianism, 121–24
Ban Zhao, 123
Daoism, 124–26
Vedas, 126–27
Upanishads, 127
Siddhartha Gautama
   (the Buddha), 128–29
Theravada/Mahayana, 130–31

Bhagavad Gita, 131–32
Zoroastrianism, 133–34
Judaism, 134–35
Greek rationalism, 135
Socrates, Plato, Aristotle, 136–38
Jesus of Nazareth, 139–40
Saint Paul, 140–41
Church of the East, 142
Perpetua, 144–45

Big Picture Questions

1. Is a secular outlook on the world an essentially modern phenomenon, or does it have precedents in the second-wave era?

2. "Religion is a double-edged sword, both supporting and undermining political authority and social elites." How would you support both sides of this statement?

3. How would you define the appeal of the religious/cultural traditions discussed in this chapter? To what groups were they attractive, and why?

4. In what different ways did these religious or cultural traditions define the purposes of human life?

5. **Looking Back:** What relationships can you see between the political dimensions of second-wave civilizations described in Chapter 3 and their cultural or religious aspects discussed in this chapter?

Next Steps: For Further Study

For Web sites and additional documents related to this chapter, see **Make History** at bedfordstmartins.com/strayer.

Karen Armstrong, *The Great Transformation* (2006). A comparative and historical study of the major religions by a well-known scholar.

Robert N. Bellah, *Religion in Human Evolution: From the Paleolithic to the Axial Age* (2011). An impressive but controversial account of the origins of religion in general and those of second-wave civilizations in particular.

Peter Brown, *The Rise of Western Christendom* (2003). A history of the first 1,000 years of Christianity, cast in a global framework.

Huston Smith, *An Illustrated World's Religions* (1994). A sympathetic account of major world religions, beautifully illustrated, by a prominent scholar of comparative religion.

Arthur Waley, *Three Ways of Thought in Ancient China* (1983). A classic work, first published more than half a century ago, about the major philosophies of old China.

Jonathan S. Walters, *Finding Buddhists in Global History* (1998). A brief account that situates Buddhism in a world history framework.

BBC, "Religions," http://www.bbc.co.uk/religion/religions/. A succinct introduction to the history, beliefs, and practices of many of the world's religious traditions.

CHAPTER FIVE

Society and Inequality in Eurasia/North Africa

500 B.C.E.–500 C.E.

Society and the State in China
  An Elite of Officials
  The Landlord Class
  Peasants
  Merchants
Class and Caste in India
  Caste as Varna
  Caste as Jati
  The Functions of Caste
Slavery: The Case of the Roman Empire
  Slavery and Civilization
  The Making of Roman Slavery
  Resistance and Rebellion
Comparing Patriarchies
  A Changing Patriarchy: The Case of China
  Contrasting Patriarchies: Athens and Sparta
Reflections: Arguing with Solomon and the Buddha
Portrait: Ge Hong, A Chinese Scholar in Troubled Times

"Caste has no impact on life today," declared Chezi K. Ganesan in 2010.[1] Certainly Mr. Ganesan's low-caste background as a Nadar, ranking just above the "untouchables," has had little impact on the career of this prosperous high-tech businessman, who shuttles between California's Silicon Valley and the city of Chennai in southern India. Yet his grandfather could not enter Hindu temples, and until the mid-nineteenth century, the women of his caste, as a sign of their low status, were forbidden to cover their breasts in the presence of Brahmin men. But if caste has proven no barrier to Mr. Ganesan, it remains significant for many others in contemporary India. Personal ads for those seeking a marriage partner in many online services often indicate an individual's caste as well as other personal data. Affirmative action programs benefiting low-caste Indians have provoked great controversy and resentment among some upper-caste groups. The brutal murder of an entire Dalit or "untouchable" family in 2006 sparked much soul searching in the India media. So while caste has changed in modern India, it has also persisted. Both the changes and the persistence have a long history.

THE MOST RECENT 250 YEARS OF WORLD HISTORY have called into question social patterns long assumed to be natural and permanent. The French, Russian, and Chinese revolutions challenged and destroyed ancient monarchies and class hierarchies; the abolitionist movement of the nineteenth century attacked slavery, largely unquestioned for millennia; the women's movement has confronted long and deeply

Mother and Child: Mothers and their children have been at the core of social life everywhere and a prominent theme of many artistic traditions. This lovely statue comes from the Sunga dynasty, which flourished in northeastern India from about 185–73 B.C.E. after the collapse of the Mauryan Empire. (Réunion des Musées Nationaux/Art Resource, NY)

held patriarchal assumptions about the proper relationship between the sexes; and Mahatma Gandhi, during India's struggle for independence in the twentieth century, sought to raise the status of "untouchables," referring to them as Harijan, or "children of God." Nevertheless, caste, class, patriarchy, and even slavery have certainly not vanished from human society, even now. During the era of second-wave civilizations in Eurasia, these patterns of inequality found expressions and generated social tensions that endured well beyond that era.

As Chapter 3 pointed out, millions of individual men and women inhabiting the civilizations of Eurasia and North Africa lived within a political framework of states or empires. They also occupied a world of ideas, religions, and values that derived both from local folkways and from the teaching of the great religious or cultural traditions of these civilizations, as described in Chapter 4. In this chapter, we explore the social arrangements of these civilizations—relationships between rich and poor, powerful and powerless, slaves and free people, and men and women. Those relationships shaped the daily lives and the life chances of everyone and provided the foundation for political authority as well as challenges to it.

Like the First Civilizations, those of the second-wave era were sharply divided along class lines, and they too were patriarchal, with women clearly subordinated to men in most domains of life. In constructing their societies, however, these second-wave civilizations differed substantially from one another. Chinese, Indian, and Mediterranean civilizations provide numerous illustrations of the many and varied ways in which these peoples organized their social lives. The assumptions, tensions, and conflicts accompanying these social patterns provided much of the distinctive character and texture that distinguished these diverse civilizations from one another.

> **SEEKING THE MAIN POINT**
>
> To what extent were the massive inequalities of second-wave civilizations generally accepted, and in what ways were they resisted or challenged?

Society and the State in China

■ **Description**
How would you characterize the social hierarchy of China during the second-wave era?

Chinese society was unique in the ancient world in the extent to which it was shaped by the actions of the state. Nowhere was this more apparent than in the political power and immense social prestige of Chinese state officials, all of them male. For more than 2,000 years, these officials, bureaucrats acting in the name of the emperor both in the capital and in the provinces, represented the cultural and social elite of Chinese civilization. This class had its origins in the efforts of early Chinese rulers to find administrators loyal to the central state rather than to their own families or regions. Philosophers such as Confucius had long advocated selecting such officials on the basis of merit and personal morality rather than birth or wealth. As the Han dynasty established its authority in China around 200 B.C.E., its rulers required each province to send men of promise to the capital, where they were examined and chosen for official positions on the basis of their performance.

A Map of Time

470–400 B.C.E.	Life of Aspasia in Athens
200 B.C.E.–200 C.E.	Laws of Manu prescribing proper social behavior in India
124 B.C.E.	Imperial academy for training Chinese officials established
1st century B.C.E.	Poetry of Buddhist nuns set to writing
73 B.C.E.	Spartacus slave rebellion in Italy
Early 1st century C.E.	Reforming emperor Wang Mang in power in China
45–116 C.E.	Life of Ban Zhou in China
79 C.E.	Eruption of Mt. Vesuvius destroys Pompeii
184 C.E.	Yellow Turban Rebellion in China
After 221 C.E.	Loosening of restrictions on elite Chinese women as Han dynasty collapsed
After 500 C.E.	Slavery replaced by serfdom in Roman world
690–705 C.E.	Empress Wu reigned in China

An Elite of Officials

Over time, this system of selecting administrators evolved into the world's first professional civil service. In 124 B.C.E., Emperor Wu Di established an imperial academy where potential officials were trained as scholars and immersed in texts dealing with history, literature, art, and mathematics, with an emphasis on Confucian teachings. By the end of the Han dynasty, it enrolled some 30,000 students, who were by then subjected to a series of written examinations to select officials of various grades. Private schools in the provinces funneled still more aspiring candidates into this examination system, which persisted until the early twentieth century. In theory open to all men, this system in practice favored those whose families were wealthy enough to provide the years of education required to pass even the lower-level exams. Proximity to the capital and family connections to the imperial court also helped in gaining a position in this highest of Chinese elites. Nonetheless, village communities or a local landowner might sponsor the education of a bright young man from a commoner family, enabling him to enter the charmed circle of officialdom. One rags-to-riches story told of a pig farmer who became an adviser to the emperor himself. Thus the examination system provided a modest measure of social mobility in an otherwise quite hierarchical society.

In later dynasties, that system grew even more elaborate and became an enduring and distinguishing feature of Chinese civilization. During the Tang dynasty, the famous poet and official Po Chu-I (772–846 C.E.) wrote a poem entitled "After Passing the Examination," which shows something of the fame and fortune that awaited an accomplished student as well as the continuing loyalty to family and home that ideally marked those who succeeded:

> For ten years I never left my books,
> I went up . . . and won unmerited praise.
> My high place I do not much prize;
> The joy of my parents will first make me proud.
> Fellow students, six or seven men,
> See me off as I leave the City gate.
> My covered coach is ready to drive away;
> Flutes and strings blend their parting tune.
> Hopes achieved dull the pains of parting;
> Fumes of wine shorten the long road. . . .
> Shod with wings is the horse of him who rides
> On a Spring day the road that leads to home.[2]

Those who made it into the bureaucracy entered a realm of high privilege and great prestige. Senior officials moved about in carriages and were bedecked with robes, ribbons, seals, and headdresses appropriate to their rank. Even lower officials who served in the provinces rather than the capital were distinguished by their polished speech, their cultural sophistication, and their urban manners as well as their political authority. Proud of their learning, they were the bearers, and often the makers, of Chinese culture. "Officials are the leaders of the populace," stated an imperial edict of 144 B.C.E., "and it is right and proper that the carriages they ride in and the robes that they wear should correspond to the degrees of their dignity."[3] Some of these men, particularly in times of political turmoil, experienced tension between their official duties and their personal inclination toward a more withdrawn life of reflective scholarship. (See the Portrait of Ge Hong, pp. 156–57.)

The Landlord Class

Most officials came from wealthy families, and in China wealth meant land. When the Qin dynasty unified China by 210 B.C.E., most land was held by small-scale peasant farmers. But by the first century B.C.E., the pressures of population growth, taxation, and indebtedness had generated a class of large landowners as impoverished peasants found it necessary to sell their lands to more prosperous neighbors. This accumulation of land in sizeable estates was a persistent theme in Chinese history, and one that was frequently, though not very successfully, opposed by state authorities. Landlords of such large estates often were able to avoid paying taxes, thus decreasing state revenues and increasing the tax burden for the remaining peasants. In some cases, they could also mount their own military forces that might challenge the authority of the emperor.

One of the most dramatic state efforts to counteract the growing power of large landowners is associated with Wang Mang, a high court official of the Han dynasty who usurped the emperor's throne in 8 C.E. and immediately launched a series of startling reforms. A firm believer in Confucian good government, Wang Mang saw his reforms as re-creating a golden age of long ago in which small-scale peasant farmers represented the backbone of Chinese society. Accordingly, he ordered the great private estates to be nationalized and divided up among the landless. Government loans to peasant families, limits on the amount of land a family might own, and an end to private slavery were all part of his reform program, but these measures proved impossible to enforce. Opposition from wealthy landowners, nomadic invasions, poor harvests, floods, and famines led to the collapse of Wang Mang's reforms and his assassination in 23 C.E.

Large landowning families, therefore, remained a central feature of Chinese society, although the fate of individual families rose and fell as the wheel of fortune raised them to great prominence or plunged them into poverty and disgrace. As a class, they benefited both from the wealth that their estates generated and from the power and prestige that accompanied their education and their membership in the official elite. The term "scholar-gentry" reflected their twin sources of privilege. With homes in both urban and rural areas, members of the scholar-gentry class lived luxuriously. Multistoried houses, the finest of silk clothing, gleaming carriages, private orchestras, high-stakes gambling—all of this was part of the life of China's scholar-gentry class.

Peasants

Throughout the long course of China's civilization, the vast majority of its population consisted of peasants, living in small households representing two or three generations. Some owned enough land to support their families and perhaps even sell something on the local market. Many others could barely survive. Nature, the state, and landlords combined to make the life of most peasants extremely vulnerable. Famines, floods, droughts, hail, and pests could wreak havoc without warning. State authorities required the payment of taxes, demanded about a month's labor every year on various public projects, and conscripted young men for military service. During the Han dynasty, growing numbers of impoverished and desperate peasants had to sell out to large landlords and work as tenants or sharecroppers on their estates, where rents could run as high as

Chinese Peasants
For many centuries, the normal activities of Chinese peasant farmers included plowing, planting, and threshing grain, as shown in this painting from China's Song dynasty (960–1279 C.E.). (Mogao Caves, Dunhuang/The Bridgeman Art Library)

PORTRAIT

Ge Hong, A Chinese Scholar in Troubled Times

Had Ge Hong lived at a different time, he might have pursued the life of a Confucian scholar and civil servant, for he was born to a well-established aristocratic family in southern China. But when he entered the world in 283 C.E., the times were clearly out of joint. The Han dynasty, which had given China four centuries of relative peace and prosperity, had fragmented into a number of competing states. Nomadic peoples invaded and ruled the northern parts of the country. Coups and rebellions were frequent. Many northern Chinese fled south to escape the chaos. The life of Ge Hong illustrates how these larger historical circumstances shaped the life of a single individual.[4]

Ge Hong's family directly experienced the disorder when the family library was destroyed during the repeated wars of the time. Furthermore the family patriarch, Ge Hong's father, died when the young boy was only thirteen years old, an event that brought hardship and a degree of impoverishment to the family. Ge Hong reported later in his autobiography that he had to "walk

A solitary scholar in China, such as Ge Hong sought to become. (National Palace Museum, Taipei, Taiwan / Cultural Relics Press)

long distances to borrow books" and that he cut and sold firewood to buy paper and brushes. Nonetheless, like other young men of his class, he received a solid education, reading the classic texts of Confucianism along with history and philosophy.

At about the age of fourteen or fifteen, Ge Hong began to study with the aged Daoist master Zheng Yin. He had to sweep the floor and perform other menial chores for the master while gaining access to rare and precious texts of the esoteric and alchemical arts aimed at creating the "gold elixir" that could promote longevity and transcendence. Withdrawal into an interior life, reflected in both Daoist and Buddhist thought, had a growing appeal to the elite classes of China in response to the political disturbances and disorder of public life. It was the beginning of a life-long quest for Ge Hong.

And yet the Confucian emphasis on office holding, public service, and moral behavior in society persisted, sending Ge Hong into a series of military positions. Here too was a reflection of the disordered times of his life, for

■ **Change**

What class conflicts disrupted Chinese society?

one-half to two-thirds of the crop. Other peasants fled, taking to a life of begging or joining gangs of bandits in remote areas.

An eighth-century C.E. Chinese poem by Li Shen reflects poignantly on the enduring hardships of peasant life:

> The cob of corn in springtime sown
> In autumn yields a hundredfold.
> No fields are seen that fallow lie:
> And yet of hunger peasants die.
> As at noontide they hoe their crops,
> Sweat on the grain to earth down drops.
> How many tears, how many a groan,
> Each morsel on thy dish did mould![5]

in more settled circumstances, young elite men would have disdained military service, favoring a career in the civil bureaucracy. Thus in 303, at the age of twenty, he organized and led a small group of soldiers to crush a local rebellion, later reporting that he alone among military leaders prevented his troops from looting the valuables of the enemy. For his service he received the title of "wave conquering general" and 100 bolts of cloth. "I was the only one," he wrote "to distribute it among my officers, soldiers, and needy friends." At several other points in his life as well, Ge Hong accepted official appointments, some of them honorary and others more substantive.

But his heart lay elsewhere as he yearned for a more solitary and interior life. "Honor, high posts, power, and profit are like sojourning guests," he wrote in his memoir. "They are not worth all the regret and blame, worry and anxiety they cause." Thus he spent long periods of his life in relative seclusion, refusing a variety of official positions. "Unless I abandon worldly affairs," he asked, "how can I practice the tranquil Way?" To Ge Hong, withdrawal was primarily for the purpose of seeking immortality, "to live as long as heaven and earth," a quest given added urgency no doubt by the chaotic world of his own time. In his writings, he explored various techniques for enhancing qi, the vital energy that sustains all life, including breathing exercises, calisthenics, sexual practices, diet, and herbs. But it was the search for alchemically generated elixirs, especially those containing liquid gold and cinnabar (derived from mercury), that proved most compelling to Ge Hong. Much to his regret, he lacked the resources to obtain and process these rare ingredients.

However, Ge Hong did not totally abandon the Confucian tradition and its search for social order, for he argued in his writings that the moral virtues advocated by China's ancient sage were a necessary prerequisite for attaining immortality. And he found a place in his thinking also for the rewards and punishments of Legalist thinking. Thus he sought to reconcile the three major strands of Chinese thought—Confucianism, Daoism, and Legalism—even as he acknowledged that "my practices are always ill-suited to the times."

Ge Hong spent the last years of his life on the sacred mountain of Luofu in the far south of China, continuing his immortality research until he died in 343 at the age of sixty. When his body was lifted into its coffin, contemporaries reported that it was "exceedingly light as if one were lifting empty clothing."[6] They concluded from this that Ge Hong had in fact achieved transcendence, joining the immortals in everlasting life, as he had so fervently hoped.

Question: In what ways did the larger conditions of China shape the life of Ge Hong?

Such conditions provoked periodic peasant rebellions, which have punctuated Chinese history for over 2,000 years. Toward the end of the second century C.E., wandering bands of peasants began to join together as floods along the Yellow River and resulting epidemics compounded the misery of landlessness and poverty. What emerged was a massive peasant uprising known as the Yellow Turban Rebellion because of the yellow scarves the peasants wore around their heads. (See spot map, p. 158.) That movement, which swelled to about 360,000 armed followers by 184 C.E., found leaders, organization, and a unifying ideology in a popular form of Daoism. Featuring supernatural healings, collective trances, and public confessions of sin, the Yellow Turban movement looked forward to the "Great Peace"—a golden age of equality, social harmony, and common ownership of property. Although the rebellion was suppressed by the military forces of the Han dynasty, the Yellow Turban and other peasant upheavals devastated the economy, weakened the state, and contributed to

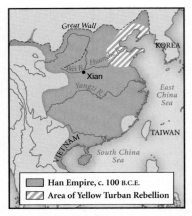

Han Empire, c. 100 B.C.E.
Area of Yellow Turban Rebellion

Yellow Turban Rebellion

the overthrow of the dynasty a few decades later. Repeatedly in Chinese history, such peasant movements, often expressed in religious terms, registered the sharp class antagonisms of Chinese society and led to the collapse of more than one ruling dynasty.

Merchants

Peasants were oppressed in China and certainly exploited, but they were also honored and celebrated in the official ideology of the state. In the eyes of the scholar-gentry, peasants were the solid productive backbone of the country, and their hard work and endurance in the face of difficulties were worthy of praise. Merchants, however, did not enjoy such a favorable reputation in the eyes of China's cultural elite. They were widely viewed as unproductive, making a shameful profit from selling the work of others. Stereotyped as greedy, luxury-loving, and materialistic, merchants stood in contrast to the alleged frugality, altruism, and cultured tastes of the scholar-gentry. They were also seen as a social threat, as their ill-gained wealth impoverished others, deprived the state of needed revenues, and fostered resentments.

Such views lay behind periodic efforts by state authorities to rein in merchant activity and to keep them under control. Early in the Han dynasty, merchants were forbidden to wear silk clothing, ride horses, or carry arms. Nor were they permitted to sit for civil service examinations or hold public office. State monopolies on profitable industries such as salt, iron, and alcohol limited merchant opportunities. Later dynasties sometimes forced merchants to loan large sums of money to the state. Despite this active discrimination, merchants frequently became quite wealthy. Some tried to achieve a more respectable elite status by purchasing landed estates or educating their sons for the civil service examinations. Many had backdoor relationships with state officials and landlords who found them useful and were not averse to profiting from business connections with merchants, despite their unsavory reputation.

LearningCurve
bedfordstmartins.com
/strayer/LC

Class and Caste in India

■ Description
What set of ideas underlies India's caste-based society?

India's social organization shared certain broad features with that of China. In both civilizations, birth determined social status for most people; little social mobility was available for the vast majority; sharp distinctions and great inequalities characterized social life; and religious or cultural traditions defined these inequalities as natural, eternal, and ordained by the gods. Despite these similarities, the organization, flavor, and texture of ancient Indian society were distinctive compared to almost all other civilizations. These unique aspects of Indian society have long been embodied in what we now call the caste system, a term that comes from the Portuguese word *casta*, which means "race" or "purity of blood." That social organization emerged over thousands of years and in some respects has endured into modern times.

Caste as Varna

The origins of the caste system are at best hazy. An earlier idea — that caste evolved from a racially defined encounter between light-skinned Aryan invaders and the darker-hued native peoples — has been challenged in recent years, but no clear alternative theory has emerged. Perhaps the best we can say at this point is that the distinctive social system of India grew out of the interactions among South Asia's immensely varied cultures together with the development of economic and social differences among these peoples as the inequalities of "civilization" spread throughout the Ganges River valley and beyond. Notions of race, however, seem less central to the growth of the caste system than those of economic specialization and of culture.

Whatever the precise origins of the caste system, by around 500 B.C.E., the idea that society was forever divided into four ranked classes, or *varnas*, was deeply embedded in Indian thinking. Everyone was born into and remained within one of these classes for life. At the top of this hierarchical system were the Brahmins, priests whose rituals and sacrifices alone could ensure the proper functioning of the world. They were followed by the Kshatriya class, warriors and rulers charged with protecting and governing society. Next was the Vaisya class, originally commoners who cultivated the land. These three classes came to be regarded as pure Aryans and were called the "twice-born," for they experienced not only a physical birth but also formal initiation into their respective varnas and status as people of Aryan descent. Far below these twice-born in the hierarchy of varna groups were the Sudras, native peoples incorporated into the margins of Aryan society in very subordinate positions. Regarded as servants of their social betters, they were not allowed to hear or repeat the Vedas or to take part in Aryan rituals. So little were they valued that a Brahmin who killed a Sudra was penalized as if he had killed a cat or a dog.

According to varna theory, these four classes were formed from the body of the god Purusha and were therefore eternal and changeless. Although these divisions are widely recognized in India even today, historians have noted considerable social flux in ancient Indian history. Members of the Brahmin and Kshatriya groups, for example, were frequently in conflict over which ranked highest in the

Caste in India

This 1947 photograph from *Life* magazine illustrates the "purity and pollution" thinking that has long been central to the ideology of caste. It shows a high-caste landowner carefully dropping wages wrapped in a leaf into the outstretched hands of his low-caste workers. By avoiding direct physical contact with them, he escapes the ritual pollution that would otherwise ensue. (Margaret Bourke-White/Time Life Pictures/Getty Images)

Snapshot   **Social Life and Duty in Classical India**

Much personal behavior in classical India, at least ideally, was regulated according to caste. Each caste was associated with a particular color, with a part of the body of the god Purusha, and with a set of duties.

Caste (Varna)	Color/Symbolism	Part of Purusha	Duties
Brahmin	white/spirituality	head	priests, teachers
Kshatriya	red/courage	shoulders	warriors, rulers
Vaisya	yellow/wealth	thighs	farmers, merchants, artisans
Sudra	black/ignorance	feet	labor
Untouchables (outside of the varna system; thus no color and not associated with Purusha)	—	—	polluted labor

Beyond caste, behavior was ideally defined in terms of four stages of life, at least for the first three varna groups. Each new stage was marked by a *samskara*, a ritual initiating the person into this new phase of life.

Stage of Life	Duties
Student	Boys live with a teacher (guru); learn Sanskrit, rituals, Vedas; practice obedience, respect, celibacy, nonviolence.
Householder	Marriage and family; men practice caste-based career/occupation; women serve as wives and mothers, perform household rituals and sacrifices, actively support children and elders.
Retirement	Both husband and wife withdraw to the forests following birth of grandchildren; diminished household duties; greater focus on spiritual practice; sex permitted once a month.
Wandering ascetic	Only for men (women return to household); total rejection of ordinary existence; life as wandering hermit without shelter or possessions; caste becomes irrelevant; focus on achieving moksha and avoiding future rebirth.

varna hierarchy, and only slowly did the Brahmins emerge clearly in the top position. Although theoretically purely Aryan, both groups absorbed various tribal peoples as Indian civilization expanded. Tribal medicine men or sorcerers found a place as Brahmins, while warrior groups entered the Kshatriya varna. The Vaisya varna, originally defined as cultivators, evolved into a business class with a prominent place for merchants, while the Sudra varna became the domain of peasant farmers. Finally a whole new category, ranking lower even than the Sudras, emerged in the so-called untouchables, men and women who did the work considered most unclean and polluting, such as cremating corpses, dealing with the skins of dead animals, and serving as executioners.

Caste as Jati

As the varna system took shape in India, another set of social distinctions also arose, based largely on occupations. In India as elsewhere, urban-based civilization gave rise to specialized occupations, many organized in guilds that regulated their own affairs in a particular region. Over time, these occupationally based groups, known as *jatis*, blended with the varna system to create India's unique caste-based society.

■ **Comparison**
What is the difference between varna and jati as expressions of caste?

The many thousands of jatis became the primary cell of India's social life beyond the family or household, but each of them was associated with one of the great classes (varnas). Thus Brahmins were divided into many separate jatis, or subcastes, as were each of the other varnas as well as the untouchables. In a particular region or village, each jati was ranked in a hierarchy known to all, from the highest of the Brahmins to the lowest of the untouchables. Marriage and eating together were permitted only within an individual's own jati. Each jati was associated with a particular set of duties, rules, and obligations, which defined its members' unique and separate place in the larger society. Brahmins, for example, were forbidden to eat meat, while Kshatriyas were permitted to do so. Upper-caste women covered their breasts, while some lower-caste women were forbidden this privilege as a sign of their subordination. "It is better to do one's own duty badly than another's well"—this frequently quoted saying summed up the underlying idea of Indian society.

With its many separate, distinct, and hierarchically ranked social groups, Indian society was quite different from that of China or the Greco-Roman world. It was also unique in the set of ideas that explained and justified that social system. Foremost among them was the notion of ritual purity and pollution applied to caste groups. Brahmins or other high-caste people who came in contact with members of lower castes, especially those who cleaned latrines, handled corpses, or butchered and skinned dead animals, were in great danger of being polluted, or made ritually unclean. Thus untouchables were forbidden to use the same wells or to enter the temples designated for higher-caste people. Sometimes they were required to wear a wooden clapper to warn others of their approach. A great body of Indian religious writing defined various forms of impurity and the ritual means of purification.

A further support for this idea of inherent inequality and permanent difference derived from emerging Hindu notions of *karma*, *dharma*, and rebirth. Being born into a particular caste was generally regarded as reflecting the good or bad deeds (karma) of a previous life. Thus an individual's prior actions were responsible for his or her current status. Any hope for rebirth in a higher caste rested on the faithful and selfless performance of one's present caste duties (dharma) in this life. Doing so contributed to spiritual progress by subduing the relentless demands of the ego. Such teachings, like that of permanent impurity, provided powerful sanctions for the inequalities of Indian society. So too did the threat of social ostracism because each jati had the authority to expel members who violated its rules. No greater catastrophe could befall a person than this, for it meant the end of any recognized social life and the loss of all social support.

As caste restrictions tightened, it became increasingly difficult—virtually impossible—for individuals to raise their social status during their lifetimes. However, another kind of upward mobility enabled entire jatis, over several generations, to raise their standing in the local hierarchy of caste groups. By acquiring land or wealth, by adopting the behaviors of higher-caste groups, by finding some previously overlooked "ancestor" of a higher caste, a particular jati might slowly be redefined in a higher category. India's caste system was in practice rather more fluid and changing than the theory of caste might suggest.

India's social system thus differed from that of China in several ways. It gave priority to religious status and ritual purity (the Brahmins), whereas China elevated political officials to the highest of elite positions. The caste system divided Indian society into vast numbers of distinct social groups; China had fewer, but broader, categories of society—scholar-gentry, landlords, peasants, merchants. Finally, India's caste society defined these social groups far more rigidly and with even less opportunity for social mobility than in China.

The Functions of Caste

This caste-based social structure shaped India's emerging civilization in various ways. Because caste (jati) was a very local phenomenon, rooted in particular regions or villages, it focused the loyalties of most people on a quite restricted territory and weakened the appeal or authority of larger all-Indian states. This localization is one reason that India, unlike China, seldom experienced an empire that encompassed the entire subcontinent (see Chapter 3, pp. 111–13). Caste, together with the shared culture of a diverse Hinduism, provided a substitute for the state as an integrative mechanism for Indian civilization. It offered a distinct and socially recognized place for almost everyone. In looking after widows, orphans, and the destitute, jatis provided a modest measure of social security and support. Even the lowest-ranking jatis had the right to certain payments from the social superiors whom they served.

Furthermore, caste represented a means of accommodating the many migrating or invading peoples who entered the subcontinent. The cellular, or honeycomb, structure of caste society allowed various peoples, cultures, and traditions to find a place within a larger Indian civilization while retaining something of their unique identity. The process of assimilation was quite different in China where it meant becoming Chinese ethnically, linguistically, and culturally. Finally, India's caste system facilitated the exploitation of the poor by the wealthy and powerful. The multitude of separate groups into which it divided the impoverished and oppressed majority of the population made class consciousness and organized resistance across caste lines much more difficult to achieve.

LearningCurve
bedfordstmartins.com
/strayer/LC

SUMMING UP SO FAR

How did India's caste system differ from China's class system?

Slavery: The Case of the Roman Empire

Beyond the inequalities of class and caste lay those of slavery, a social institution with deep roots in human history. Some have suggested that the early domestication of animals provided the model for enslaving people.[7] Certainly slave owners have everywhere compared their slaves to tamed animals. Aristotle, for example, observed that the ox is "the poor man's slave." War, patriarchy, and the notion of private property, all of which accompanied the First Civilizations, also contributed to the growth of slavery. Large-scale warfare generated numerous prisoners, and everywhere in the ancient world capture in war meant the possibility of enslavement. Early records suggest that women captives were the first slaves, usually raped and then enslaved as concubines, whereas male captives were killed. Patriarchal societies, in which men sharply controlled and perhaps even "owned" women, may have suggested the possibility of using other people, men as well as women, as slaves. The class inequalities of early civilizations, which were based on great differences in privately owned property, also made it possible to imagine people owning other people.

Slavery and Civilization

Whatever its precise origins, slavery generally meant ownership by a master, the possibility of being sold, working without pay, and the status of an "outsider" at the bottom of the social hierarchy. For most, it was a kind of "social death,"[8] for slaves usually lacked any rights or independent personal identity recognized by the larger society. By the time Hammurabi's law code casually referred to Mesopotamian slavery (around 1750 B.C.E.), it was already a long-established tradition in the region and in all of the First Civilizations. Likewise, virtually all subsequent civilizations—in the Americas, Africa, and Eurasia—practiced some form of slavery.

■ **Comparison**

How did the inequalities of slavery differ from those of caste?

Slave systems throughout history have varied considerably. In some times and places, such as ancient Greece and Rome, a fair number of slaves might be emancipated in their own lifetimes, through the generosity or religious convictions of their owners, or to avoid caring for them in old age, or by allowing slaves to purchase their freedom with their own funds. In some societies, the children of slaves inherited the status of their parents, while in others, such as the Aztec Empire, they were considered free people. Slaves likewise varied considerably in the labor they were required to do, with some working for the state in high positions, others performing domestic duties in their owner's household, and still others toiling in fields or mines in large work gangs.

The second-wave civilizations of Eurasia differed considerably in the prominence and extent of slavery in their societies. In China, it was a minor element, amounting to perhaps 1 percent of the population. Convicted criminals and their families, confiscated by the government and sometimes sold to wealthy private individuals, were among the earliest slaves in Han dynasty China. In desperate circumstances, impoverished or indebted peasants might sell their children into slavery. In southern China, teenage boys of poor families could be purchased by the wealthy, for whom they served as status symbols. Chinese slavery, however, was never very widespread and did not become a major source of labor for agriculture or manufacturing.

In India as well, people could fall into slavery as criminals, debtors, or prisoners of war and served their masters largely in domestic settings, but religious writings and secular law offered, at least in theory, some protection for slaves. Owners were required to provide adequately for their slaves and were forbidden to abandon them in old age. According to one ancient text, "a man may go short himself or stint his wife and children, but never his slave who does his dirty work for him."[9] Slaves in India could inherit and own property and earn money in their spare time. A master who raped a slave woman was required to set her free and pay compensation. The law encouraged owners to free their slaves and allowed slaves to buy their freedom. All of this suggests that Indian slavery was more restrained than that of other ancient civilizations. Nor did Indian civilization depend economically on slavery, for most work was performed by lower-caste, though free, men and women.

The Making of Roman Slavery

■ **Comparison**
How did Greco-Roman slavery differ from that of other classical civilizations?

In sharp contrast to other second-wave civilizations, slavery played an immense role in the Mediterranean, or Western, world. Although slavery was practiced in Chinese, Indian, and Persian civilizations, in the Greco-Roman world society was based on slavery. By a conservative estimate, classical Athens alone was home to perhaps 60,000 slaves, or about one-third of the total population. In Athens, ironically, the growth of democracy and status as a free person were defined and accompanied by the simultaneous growth of slavery on a mass scale. The greatest of the Greek philosophers, Aristotle, developed the notion that some people were "slaves by nature" and should be enslaved for their own good and for that of the larger society.

"The ancient Greek attitude toward slavery was simple," writes one modern scholar. "It was a terrible thing to become a slave, but a good thing to own a slave."[10] Even poor households usually had at least one or two female slaves, providing domestic work and sexual services for their owners. Although substantial numbers of Greek slaves were granted freedom by their owners, they usually did not become citizens or gain political rights. Nor could they own land or marry

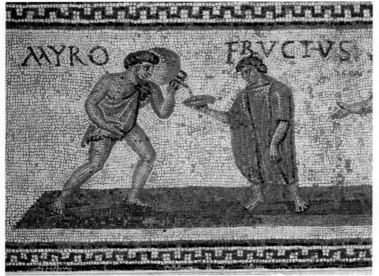

Roman Slavery
This Roman mosaic from the third century C.E. shows the slave Myro serving a drink to his master, Fructus. (The Art Archive at Art Resource, NY)

citizens, and particularly in Athens they had to pay a special tax. Their status remained "halfway between slavery and freedom."[11]

Practiced on an even larger scale, slavery was a defining element of Roman society. By the time of Christ, the Italian heartland of the Roman Empire had some 2 to 3 million slaves, representing 33 to 40 percent of the population.[12] Not until the modern slave societies of the Caribbean, Brazil, and the southern United States was slavery practiced again on such an enormous scale. Wealthy Romans could own many hundreds or even thousands of slaves. One woman in the fifth century C.E. freed 8,000 slaves when she withdrew into a life of Christian monastic practice. Even people of modest means frequently owned two or three slaves. In doing so, they confirmed their own position as free people, demonstrated their social status, and expressed their ability to exercise power. Slaves and former slaves also might be slave owners. One freedman during the reign of Augustus owned 4,116 slaves at the time of his death.

The vast majority of Roman slaves had been prisoners captured in the many wars that accompanied the creation of the empire. In 146 B.C.E., following the destruction of the North African city of Carthage, some 55,000 people were enslaved en masse. From all over the Mediterranean basin, men and women were funneled into the major slave-owning regions of Italy and Sicily. Pirates also furnished slaves, kidnapping tens of thousands and selling them to Roman slave traders on the island of Delos. Roman merchants purchased still other slaves through networks of long-distance commerce extending to the Black Sea, the East African coast, and northwestern Europe. The supply of slaves also occurred through natural reproduction, as the children of slave mothers were regarded as slaves themselves. Such "home-born" slaves had a certain prestige and were thought to be less troublesome than those who had known freedom earlier in their lives. Finally, abandoned or exposed children could legally become the slave of anyone who rescued them.

Unlike American slavery of later times, Roman practice was not identified with a particular racial or ethnic group. Egyptians, Syrians, Jews, Greeks, Gauls, North Africans, and many other people found themselves alike enslaved. From within the empire and its adjacent regions, an enormous diversity of people were bought and sold at Roman slave markets.

Like slave owners everywhere, Romans regarded their slaves as "barbarians"—lazy, unreliable, immoral, prone to thieving—and came to think of certain peoples, such as Asiatic Greeks, Syrians, and Jews, as slaves by nature. Nor was there any serious criticism of slavery in principle, although on occasion owners were urged to treat their slaves in a more benevolent way. Even the triumph of Christianity within the Roman Empire did little to undermine slavery, for Christian teaching held that slaves should be "submissive to [their] masters with all fear, not only to the good and gentle, but also to the harsh."[13] In fact, Saint Paul used the metaphor of slavery to describe the relationship of believers to God, styling them as "slaves of Christ," while Saint Augustine (354–430 C.E.) described slavery as God's punishment for sin. Thus slavery was deeply embedded in the religious thinking and social outlook of elite Romans.

Similarly, slavery was entrenched throughout the Roman economy. No occupation was off-limits to slaves except military service, and no distinction existed between jobs for slaves and those for free people. Frequently they labored side by side. In rural areas, slaves provided much of the labor force on the huge estates, or *latifundia*, which produced grain, olive oil, and wine, mostly for export, much like the later plantations in the Americas. There they often worked chained together. In the cities, slaves worked in their owners' households, but also as skilled artisans, teachers, doctors, business agents, entertainers, and actors. In the empire's many mines and quarries, slaves and criminals labored under brutal conditions. Slaves in the service of the emperor provided manpower for the state bureaucracy, maintained temples and shrines, and kept Rome's water supply system functioning. Trained in special schools, they also served as gladiators in the violent spectacles of Roman public life. Female slaves usually served as domestic servants but were also put to work in brothels, served as actresses and entertainers, and could be used sexually by their male owners. Thus slaves were represented among the highest and most prestigious occupations and in the lowest and most degraded.

Slave owners in the Roman Empire were supposed to provide the necessities of life to their slaves. When this occurred, slaves may have had a more secure life than was available to impoverished free people, who had to fend for themselves, but the price of this security was absolute subjection to the will of the master. Beatings, sexual abuse, and sale to another owner were constant possibilities. Lacking all rights in the law, slaves could not legally marry, although many contracted unofficial unions. Slaves often accumulated money or possessions, but such property legally belonged to their masters and could be seized at any time. If a slave murdered his master, Roman law demanded the lives of all of the victim's slaves. When one Roman official was killed by a slave in 61 C.E., every one of his 400 slaves was condemned to death. For an individual slave, the quality of life depended almost entirely on the character of the master. Brutal owners made it a living hell. Benevolent owners made life tolerable and might even grant favored slaves their freedom or permit them to buy that freedom. As in Greece, manumission of slaves was a widespread practice, and in the Roman Empire, unlike Greece, freedom was accompanied by citizenship.

Resistance and Rebellion

Roman slaves, like their counterparts in other societies, responded to enslavement in many ways. Most, no doubt, did what was necessary to survive, but there are recorded cases of Roman prisoners of war who chose to commit mass suicide rather than face the horrors of slavery. Others, once enslaved, resorted to the "weapons of the weak"—small-scale theft, sabotage, pretending illness, working poorly, and placing curses on their masters. Fleeing to the anonymous crowds of the city or to remote rural areas prompted owners to post notices in public places, asking for information about their runaways. Catching runaway slaves became an organized private business. Occasional murders of slave owners made masters conscious of the dangers they faced. "Every slave we own is an enemy we harbor" ran one Roman saying.[14]

On several notable occasions, the slaves themselves rose in rebellion. The most famous uprising occurred in 73 B.C.E. when a slave gladiator named Spartacus led seventy other slaves from a school for gladiators in a desperate bid for freedom. The surprising initial success of their revolt attracted a growing following of rebellious slaves, numbering perhaps 120,000 men, women, and children at the height of the uprising. For two years, they set Italy ablaze. In a dramatic reversal of roles, they crucified some captured slave owners and set others to fighting one another in the style of gladiators. Following a series of remarkable military victories, the movement split and eventually succumbed to the vastly superior numbers of the Roman legions. A terrible vengeance followed as some 6,000 rebel slaves were nailed to crosses along the Appian Way from Rome to Capua, where the revolt had begun.

Nothing on the scale of the Spartacus rebellion occurred again in the Western world of slavery until the Haitian Revolution of the 1790s. But Haitian rebels sought the creation of a new society free of slavery altogether. None of the Roman slave rebellions, including that of Spartacus, had any such overall plan or goal. They simply wanted to escape Roman slavery themselves. Although rebellions created a perpetual fear in the minds of slave owners, slavery itself was hardly affected.

LearningCurve
bedfordstmartins.com
/strayer/LC

The Rebellion of Spartacus

Comparing Patriarchies

Social inequality was embedded not only in the structures of class, caste, and slavery, but also in the gender systems of second-wave civilizations, as the patriarchies of the First Civilizations (see Chapter 2, pp. 48–54) were replicated and elaborated in those that followed. Until quite recently, women's subordination in all civilizations has been so widespread and pervasive that historians have been slow to recognize that gender systems had a history, changing over time. New agricultural technologies, the rise or decline of powerful states, the incorporation of world religions, interaction with culturally different peoples—all of these developments and more generated significant change in understandings of what was appropriate masculine and feminine behavior. Most often, patriarchies were lighter and less restrictive for women in the early years of a civilization's development and during times of upheaval, when established patterns of male dominance were disrupted.

Furthermore, women were often active agents in the histories of their societies, even while largely accepting their overall subordination. As the central figures in family life, they served as repositories and transmitters of their peoples' culture. Some were able to occupy unorthodox and occasionally prominent positions outside the home as scholars, religious functionaries, managers of property and participants in commerce, and even as rulers or military leaders. In Britain, Egypt, and Vietnam, for example, women led efforts to resist their countries' incorporation into the Roman or Chinese empires. (See, for example, the Portrait of Trung Trac, p. 104 and the statue of Boudica, p. 102.) Both Buddhist and Christian nuns carved out small domains of relative freedom from male control. But these changes or challenges to male dominance occurred within a patriarchal framework, and nowhere did they evolve out of or beyond that framework. Thus a kind of "patriarchal equilibrium" ensured the long-term persistence of women's subordination despite fluctuations and notwithstanding various efforts to redefine gender roles or push against gendered expectations.[15]

Nor was patriarchy everywhere the same. Restrictions on women were far sharper in urban-based civilizations than in those pastoral or agricultural societies that lay beyond the reach of cities and empires. The degree and expression of patriarchy also varied from one civilization to another, as the discussion of Mesopotamia and Egypt in Chapter 2 illustrated. And within particular civilizations, elite women both enjoyed privileges and suffered the restrictions of seclusion in the home to a much greater extent than their lower-class counterparts whose economic circumstances required them to operate in the larger social arena. China provides a fascinating example of how patriarchy changed over time, while the contrasting patriarchies of Athens and Sparta illustrate clear variations even within the much smaller world of Greek civilization.

A Changing Patriarchy: The Case of China

■ Change

In what ways did the expression of Chinese patriarchy change over time, and why did it change?

As Chinese civilization took shape during the Han dynasty, elite thinking about gender issues became more explicitly patriarchal, more clearly defined, and linked to an emerging Confucian ideology. Long-established patterns of thinking in terms of pairs of opposites were now described in gendered and unequal terms. The superior principle of *yang* was viewed as masculine and related to heaven, rulers, strength, rationality, and light, whereas *yin*, the lower feminine principle, was associated with the earth, subjects, weakness, emotion, and darkness. Thus female inferiority was permanent and embedded in the workings of the universe.

What this meant more practically was spelled out repeatedly over the centuries in various Confucian texts. Two notions in particular summarized the ideal position of women, at least in the eyes of elite male writers. The adage "Men go out, women stay in" emphasized the public and political roles of men in contrast to the domestic and private domain of women. A second idea, known as the "three obediences," emphasized a woman's subordination first to her father, then to her husband, and finally to her son. "Why is it," asked one text, "that according to the rites the man takes his wife, whereas the woman leaves her house [to join her husband's family]? It is because the *yin* is lowly, and should not have the initiative; it proceeds to the *yang* in order to be completed."[16]

The Chinese woman writer and court official Ban Zhao (45–116 C.E.) (see p. 123) observed that the ancients had practiced three customs when a baby girl was born. She was placed below the bed to show that she was "lowly and weak," required always to "humble herself before others." Then she was given a piece of broken pottery to play with, signifying that "her primary duty [was] to be industrious." Finally, her birth was announced to the ancestors with an offering to indicate that she was responsible for "the continuation of [ancestor] worship in the home."[17]

Yet such notions of passivity, inferiority, and subordination were not the whole story of women's lives in ancient China. A few women, particularly the wives, concubines, or widows of emperors, were able on occasion to exercise considerable political authority. Several others led peasant rebellions. In doing so, they provoked much anti-female hostility on the part of male officials, who understood governance as a masculine task and often blamed the collapse of a dynasty or natural disasters on the "unnatural" and "disruptive" influence of women in political affairs. Others, however, praised women of virtue as wise counselors to their fathers, husbands, and rulers and depicted them positively as active agents.[18]

Chinese Women Musicians
This tenth-century rendering by the painter Gu Hongzhong shows these upper-class women serving as musicians for a high official of a Tang dynasty emperor. It was titled *The Night Revels of Han Xizai.* The painter was apparently sent by the emperor to spy on the suspicious behavior of the minister, who in various tellings was suspected of either rebellion or undignified activity. (Werner Forman/Art Resource, NY)

Within her husband's family, a young woman was clearly subordinate as a wife and daughter-in-law, but as a mother of sons, she was accorded considerable honor for her role in producing the next generation of male heirs to carry on her husband's lineage. When her sons married, she was able to exercise the significant authority of a mother-in-law. Furthermore, a woman, at least in the upper classes, often brought with her a considerable dowry, which was regarded as her own property and gave her some leverage within her marriage. Women's roles in the production of textiles, often used to pay taxes or to sell commercially, made her labor quite valuable to the family economy. And a man's wife was sharply distinguished from his concubines, for she was legally mother to all her husband's children. Furthermore, peasant women could hardly follow the Confucian ideal of seclusion in the home as their labor was required in the fields. Thus women's lives were more complex and varied than the prescriptions of Confucian orthodoxy might suggest.

Much changed in China following the collapse of the Han dynasty in the third century C.E. Centralized government vanished amid much political fragmentation

Chinese Women at Work
For a long time, the spinning and weaving of cloth were part of women's domestic work in China. So too was fishing, as illustrated by the woman at the bottom right of this Chinese painting. (Palace Museum, Beijing/Cultural Relics Press)

and conflict. Confucianism, the main ideology of Han China, was discredited, while Daoism and Buddhism attracted a growing following. Pastoral and nomadic peoples invaded northern China and ruled a number of the small states that had replaced the Han government. These new conditions resulted in some loosening of the strict patriarchy of Han dynasty China over the next five or six centuries.

The cultural influence of nomadic peoples, whose women were far less restricted than those of China, was noticed, and criticized, by more Confucian-minded male observers. One of them lamented the sad deterioration of gender roles under the influence of nomadic peoples:

In the north of the Yellow river it is usually the wife who runs the household. She will not dispense with good clothing or expensive jewelry. The husband has to settle for old horses and sickly servants. The traditional niceties between husband and wife are seldom observed, and from time to time he even has to put up with her insults.[19]

Others criticized the adoption of nomadic styles of dress, makeup, and music. By the time of the Tang dynasty (618–907), writers and artists depicted elite women as capable of handling legal and business affairs on their own and on occasion riding horses and playing polo, bareheaded and wearing men's clothing. Tang legal codes even recognized a married daughter's right to inherit property from her family of birth. Such images of women were quite different from those of Han dynasty China.

A further sign of a weakening patriarchy and the cause of great distress to advocates of Confucian orthodoxy lay in the unusual reign of Empress Wu (r. 690–705 C.E.), a former high-ranking concubine in the imperial court, who came to power amid much palace intrigue and was the only woman ever to rule China with the title of emperor. With the support of China's growing Buddhist establishment, Empress Wu governed despotically, but she also consolidated China's civil service examination system for the selection of public officials and actively patronized scholarship and the arts. Some of her actions seem deliberately designed to elevate the position of women. She commissioned the biographies of famous women, decreed that the mourning period for mothers be made equal to that for fathers, and ordered the creation of a Chinese character for "human being" that suggested the process of birth flowing from one woman without a prominent male role. Her reign was brief and unrepeated.

The growing popularity of Daoism provided new images of the feminine and new roles for women. Daoist texts referred to the *dao* as "mother" and urged the traditionally feminine virtues of yielding and passive acceptance rather than the male-oriented striving of Confucianism. Daoist sects often featured women as priests, nuns, or reclusive meditators, able to receive cosmic truth and to use it for the benefit of others. A variety of female deities from Daoist or Buddhist traditions found a place in Chinese village religion,[20] while growing numbers of women found an alternative to family life in Buddhist monasteries. None of this meant an end to patriarchy, but it does suggest some change in the tone and expression of that patriarchy. However, during the Song dynasty that followed, a more restrictive patriarchy re-emerged. (See Chapter 8.)

Contrasting Patriarchies: Athens and Sparta

The patriarchies of second-wave civilizations not only fluctuated over time but also varied considerably from place to place. Nowhere is this variation more apparent than in the contrasting cases of Athens and Sparta, two of the leading city-states of Greek civilization (see Map 3.2, p. 93). Even within this small area, the opportunities available to women and the restrictions imposed on them differed substantially. Although Athens has been celebrated as a major expression of democracy and rationalism, its posture toward women was far more restrictive than that of the highly militaristic and much less democratic Sparta.

■ **Comparison**

How did the patriarchies of Athens and Sparta differ from each other?

In the several centuries between about 700 and 400 B.C.E., as the free male citizens of Athens moved toward unprecedented participation in political life, the city's women experienced growing limitations. They had no role whatsoever in the assembly, the councils, or the juries of Athens, which were increasingly the focus of life for free men. In legal matters, women had to be represented by a guardian, and court proceedings did not even refer to them by name, but only as someone's wife or mother.

Greek thinkers, especially Aristotle, provided a set of ideas that justified women's exclusion from public life and their general subordination to men. According to Aristotle, "a woman is, as it were, an infertile male. She is female in fact on account of a kind of inadequacy." That inadequacy lay in her inability to generate sperm, which contained the "form" or the "soul" of a new human being. Her role in the reproductive process was passive, providing a receptacle for the vital male contribution. Compared often to children or domesticated animals, women were associated with instinct and passion and lacked the rationality to take part in public life. "It is the best for all tame animals to be ruled by human beings," wrote Aristotle. "In the same way, the relationship between the male and the female is by nature such that the male is higher, the female lower, that the male rules and the female is ruled."[21]

As in China, elite Athenian women were expected to remain inside the home, except perhaps for religious festivals or funerals. Even within the home, women's space was quite separate from that of men. Although poorer women, courtesans, and prostitutes had to leave their homes to earn money, collect water, or shop, ideal behavior for upper-class women assigned these tasks to slaves or to men and involved a radical segregation of male and female space. "What causes women a bad reputation," wrote

A Woman of Athens
This grave stele from about 400 B.C.E. marked the final resting place of Hegeso, a wealthy Athenian woman, shown in the women's quarter of a Greek home examining her jewelry, perhaps for the last time, while attended by her slave. The domestic setting of this grave marker contrasts with that common for men, which usually showed them as warriors in a public space. (Marie Mauzy/Art Resource, NY)

the Greek playwright Euripides in *The Trojan Women*, "is not remaining inside."

Within the domestic realm, Athenian women were generally married in their mid-teens to men ten to fifteen years older than themselves. Their main function was the management of domestic affairs and the production of sons who would become active citizens. These sons were expected to acquire a literate education, while their sisters were normally limited to learning spinning, weaving, and other household tasks. The Greek writer Menander exclaimed: "Teaching a woman to read and write? What a terrible thing to do! Like feeding a vile snake on more poison." Nor did women have much economic power. Although they could own personal property obtained through dowry, gifts, or inheritance, land was usually passed through male heirs. By law, women were forbidden to buy or sell land and could negotiate contracts only if the sum involved was valued at less than a bushel of barley.

There were exceptions, although rare, to the restricted lives of upper-class Athenian women, the most notable of which was Aspasia (ca. 470–400 B.C.E.). She was born in the Greek city of Miletus, on the western coast of Anatolia, to a wealthy family that believed in educating its daughters. As a young woman, Aspasia found her way to Athens, where her foreign birth gave her somewhat more freedom than was normally available to the women of that city. She soon attracted the attention of Pericles, Athens's leading political figure. The two lived together as husband and wife until Pericles' death in 429 B.C.E., although they were not officially married. Treated as an equal partner by Pericles, Aspasia proved to be a learned and witty conversationalist who moved freely in the cultured circles of Athens. Her foreign birth and her apparent influence on Pericles provoked critics to suggest that she was a *hetaera*, a professional, educated, high-class entertainer and sexual companion, similar to a Japanese geisha. Although little is known about Aspasia, a number of major Athenian writers commented about her, both positively and negatively. She was, by all accounts, a rare and remarkable woman in a city that offered little opportunity for individuality or achievement to its female population.

The evolution of Sparta differed in many ways from that of Athens. Early on, Sparta solved the problem of feeding a growing population not by creating overseas colonies as did many Greek city-states, but by conquering their immediate neighbors and reducing them to a status of permanent servitude, not far removed from slavery. Called helots, these dependents far outnumbered the free citizens of Sparta and represented a permanent threat of rebellion. Solving this problem shaped Spartan society decisively. Sparta's answer was a militaristic regime, constantly ready for war to keep the helots in their place. To maintain such a system, all boys were removed from their families at the age of seven to be trained by the state in military camps, where they learned the ways of war. There they remained until the age of thirty. The ideal Spartan male was a warrior, skilled in battle, able to endure hardship, and willing to die for his city. Mothers are said to have told their sons departing for battle to "come back with your shield . . . or on it." Although economic equality for men was the ideal, it was never completely realized in practice. And unlike Athens, political power was exercised primarily by a small group of wealthy men.

This militaristic and far-from-democratic system had implications for women that, strangely enough, offered them greater freedoms and fewer restrictions. As in many warrior societies, their central task was reproduction—bearing warrior sons for Sparta. To strengthen their bodies for childbearing, girls were encouraged to take part in sporting events—running, wrestling, throwing the discus and javelin, even driving chariots. At times, women and men alike competed in the nude before mixed audiences. Their education, like that of boys, was prescribed by the state, which also insisted that newly married women cut their hair short, unlike adult Greek women elsewhere. Thus Spartan women were not secluded or segregated, as were their Athenian counterparts.

Furthermore, Spartan young women, unlike those of Athens, usually married men of their own age, about eighteen years old, thus putting the new couple on a more equal basis. Marriage often began with a trial period to make sure the new couple could produce children, with divorce and remarriage readily available if they could not. Because men were so often away at war or preparing for it, women exercised much more authority in the household than was the case in Athens.

It is little wonder that the freedom of Spartan women appalled other Greeks, who believed that it undermined good order and state authority. Aristotle complained that the more egalitarian inheritance practices of Spartans led to their women controlling some 40 percent of landed estates. In Sparta, he declared, women "live in every sort of intemperance and luxury" and "the [male] rulers are ruled by women." Plutarch, a Greek writer during the heyday of the Roman Empire, observed critically that "the men of Sparta always obeyed their wives." The clothing worn by Spartan women to give them greater freedom of movement seemed immodest to other Greeks.

Nonetheless, in another way, Sparta may have been more restrictive than Athens and other Greek city-states, particularly in its apparent prohibition of homosexuality. At least this was the assertion of the

A Girl of Sparta
This figurine portrays a young female Spartan athlete or runner. Compare her clothing with that worn by Hegeso on page 172. (British Museum, London/The Bridgeman Art Library)

Athenian writer Xenophon (427–355 B.C.E.), who stated that Sparta's legendary founder Lycurgus "caused lovers to abstain from sexual intercourse with boys."[22] Elsewhere, however, homoerotic relationships were culturally approved and fairly common for both men and women, although this did not prevent their participants from entering heterosexual marriages as well. The ideal homosexual relationship — between an older man and a young adolescent boy — was viewed as limited in time, for it was supposed to end when the boy's beard began to grow. Unlike contemporary Western societies where sexuality is largely seen as an identity, the ancient Greeks viewed sexual choice more casually and as a matter of taste.

Sparta clearly was a patriarchy, with women serving as breeding machines for its military system and lacking any formal role in public life, but it was a lighter patriarchy than that of Athens. The joint efforts of men and women seemed necessary to maintain a huge class of helots in permanent subjugation. Death in childbirth was considered the equivalent of death in battle, for both contributed to the defense of Sparta, and both were honored alike. In Athens, on the other hand, growing freedom and democracy were associated with the strengthening of the male-dominated, property-owning household, and within that household, the cornerstone of Athenian society, men were expected to exercise authority. Doing so required increasingly severe limitations and restrictions on the lives of women. Together, the cases of Athens and Sparta illustrate how the historical record appears in a different light when viewed through the lens of gender. Athens, so celebrated for its democracy and philosophical rationalism, offered little to its women, whereas Sparta, often condemned for its militarism and virtual enslavement of the helots, provided a somewhat wider scope for the free women of the city.

LearningCurve
bedfordstmartins.com
/strayer/LC

⊔ Reflections: Arguing with Solomon and the Buddha

"What has been will be again . . . there is nothing new under the sun." Recorded in the Old Testament book of Ecclesiastes and generally attributed to King Solomon, this was a despairing view about the essential changelessness and futility of human life. In contrast, central to Buddhist teachings has been the concept of "impermanence" — the notion that "everything changes; nothing remains without change." These observations were intended to point to other levels of reality that lay beyond the dreary constancy or the endless changeability of this world. For students of history, however, these comments from Solomon and the Buddha serve to focus attention on issues of change and continuity in the historical record of second-wave Eurasian civilizations. What is more impressive — the innovations and changes or the enduring patterns and lasting features of these civilizations?

Clearly there were some new things under the sun, even if they had roots in earlier times. The Greek conquest of the Persian Empire under the leadership of Alexander the Great was both novel and unexpected. The Roman Empire encompassed the entire Mediterranean basin in a single political system for the first time. Buddhism and Christianity emerged as new, distinct, and universal religious traditions, although both bore the marks of their origin in Hindu and Jewish religious thinking respectively. The collapse of dynasties, empires, and civilizations long thought to be solidly entrenched—the Chinese and Roman, for example—must surely have seemed to people of the time as something new. Historians therefore might take issue with Solomon's dictum, should we seek to apply it to the history of the second-wave era.

Students of the past might also argue a little with the Buddha and his insistence on the "impermanence" of everything. Much that was created in the second-wave era—particularly its social and cultural patterns—has demonstrated an impressive continuity over many centuries, even if it also changed in particular ways over time. China's scholar-gentry class retained its prominence throughout the ups and downs of changing dynasties into the twentieth century. India's caste-based social structure still endures as a way of thinking and behaving for hundreds of millions of men and women on the South Asian peninsula. Although slavery gave way to serfdom in the post-Roman world, it was massively revived in Europe's American colonies after 1500 and remained an important and largely unquestioned feature of all civilizations until the nineteenth century. Patriarchy, with its assumptions of male superiority and dominance, has surely been the most fundamental, long-lasting, and taken-for-granted feature of all civilizations. Not until recent centuries were those assumptions effectively challenged, but even then patriarchy has continued to shape the lives and the thinking of the vast majority of humankind. And many hundreds of millions of people in the twenty-first century still honor or practice religious and cultural traditions begun during the second-wave era.

Neither the insight of Solomon nor that of the Buddha, taken alone, offers an effective guide to the study of history, for continuity and change alike have long provided the inextricable warp and woof of historical analysis. Untangling their elusive relationship has figured prominently in the task of historians and has contributed much to the enduring fascination of historical study.

Second Thoughts

What's the Significance?

China's scholar-gentry class, 154–55
Wang Mang, 155
Ge Hong, 156–57
Yellow Turban Rebellion, 157–58
caste as varna and jati, 159–62
"ritual purity" in Indian social practice, 162
Greek and Roman slavery, 163–67

Spartacus, 167
the "three obediences," 168–69
patriarchy, 168–74
Empress Wu, 170
Aspasia and Pericles, 172
Helots, 172–73

LearningCurve
Check what you know.
**bedfordstmartins.com
/strayer/LC**

Online Study Guide
bedfordstmartins.com/strayer

Big Picture Questions

1. What is the difference between class and caste?
2. Why was slavery so much more prominent in Greco-Roman civilization than in India or China?
3. What philosophical, religious, or cultural ideas served to legitimate the class and gender inequalities of second-wave civilizations?
4. What changes in the patterns of social life in second-wave civilizations can you identify? What accounts for these changes?
5. **Looking Back:** Cultural and social patterns of civilizations seem to endure longer than the political framework of states and empires. What evidence from Chapters 3, 4, and 5 might support this statement? How might you account for this phenomenon? Is there evidence that could support a contrary position?

Next Steps: For Further Study

For Web sites and additional documents related to this chapter, see **Make History** at bedfordstmartins.com/strayer.

Jeannine Auboyer, *Daily Life in Ancient India* (2002). A social history of ancient India, with a focus on caste, ritual, religion, and art.

Sue Blundell, *Women in Ancient Greece* (1999). A well-written academic study, with occasional humorous stories and anecdotes.

Keith Bradley, *Slavery and Society at Rome* (1994). A scholarly but very readable account of slavery in the Roman Empire.

Michael Lowe, *Everyday Life in Early Imperial China* (1968). A vivid description of social life during the Han dynasty.

Merry Weisner-Hanks, *Gender in History* (2001). A thoughtful overview by a leading scholar in both women's history and world history.

"Women in World History," http://chnm.gmu.edu/wwh/index.html. Documents, reviews, and lesson plans for learning and teaching about women's history in a global context.

CHAPTER SIX

Commonalities and Variations

Africa and the Americas

500 B.C.E.—1200 C.E.

Continental Comparisons
Civilizations of Africa
  Meroë: Continuing a Nile Valley
  Civilization
  Axum: The Making of a Christian
  Kingdom
  Along the Niger River: Cities without
  States
Civilizations of Mesoamerica
  The Maya: Writing and Warfare
  Teotihuacán: The Americas'
  Greatest City
Civilizations of the Andes
  Chavín: A Pan-Andean Religious
  Movement
  Moche: A Civilization of the Coast
  Wari and Tiwanaku: Empires of the
  Interior
Alternatives to Civilization: Bantu Africa
  Cultural Encounters
  Society and Religion
Alternatives to Civilization:
  North America
  The Ancestral Pueblo: Pit Houses
  and Great Houses
  Peoples of the Eastern Woodlands:
  The Mound Builders
Reflections: Deciding What's Impor-
  tant: Balance in World History
Portrait: Piye, Kushite Conqueror
  of Egypt

In early 2010, Bolivian President Evo Morales was inaugurated for his second term in office, the only person from the country's Native American population ever elected to that post since independence from Spain in 1825. The day before the official ceremony in the capital of La Paz, Morales traveled to Tiwanaku (tee-wah-NAH-coo), the center of an impressive empire that had flourished in the Andean highlands between 400 and 1000 C.E., long before either the Inca or the Spanish ruled the area. There he sought to link himself and his administration to this ancient culture, a symbol of Bolivian nationalism and indigenous pride. On his arrival, Morales was ritually cleansed with holy water and herbs and dressed in a llama wool robe. After offerings were made to Pachamama, an Andean earth goddess and to Tata Inti, the Inca sun god, Morales was invested with symbols of both kingship and spiritual leadership, thus joining political and religious sources of authority. Proclaiming a new multinational state, Morales declared: "Gone forever is the colonial state, which allowed the looting of our natural resources, and gone also is the discriminatory [against native peoples] colonial state."[1] This recent ceremony provides a reminder that memories of American second-wave civilizations remained alive and were available for mobilizing political support and legitimating political authority in the very different circumstances of the early twenty-first century.

FOR MANY PEOPLE, THE SECOND-WAVE ERA EVOKES most vividly the civilizations of Eurasia — the Greeks and the Romans, the Persians and the Chinese, and the Indians of South Asia — yet those were not the only civilizations of that era. During this period, the Mesoamerican

---

The Maya Temple of the Great Jaguar in Tikal: Located in the Maya city of Tikal in present-day Guatemala, this temple was constructed in the eighth century C.E. and excavated by archeologists in the late nineteenth century. It served as the tomb of the Tikal ruler Jasaw Chan K'awiil I (682–734). Some 144 feet tall, it was topped by a three-room temple complex and a huge roofcomb showing the ruler on his throne. Carved on a wooden beam inside the temple is an image of the ruler protected by a huge jaguar along with illustrations of his military victories. (Peter M. Wilson/Alamy)

Maya and the Andean Tiwanaku thrived, as did several civilizations in sub-Saharan Africa, including Meroë (MER-oh-ee), Axum (AHK-soom), and the Niger River valley. Furthermore, those peoples who did not organize themselves around cities or states likewise had histories of note and alternative ways of constructing their societies, although they are often neglected in favor of civilizations. This chapter explores the histories of the varied peoples of Africa and the Americas during this phase of world history. On occasion, those histories will extend some centuries beyond the chronological boundaries of the second-wave era in Eurasia because patterns of historical development around the world did not always coincide precisely.

SEEKING THE MAIN POINT

To what extent did the histories of Africa and the Americas parallel those of Eurasia? In what ways did they forge new or different paths?

Continental Comparisons

■ **Comparison**
What similarities and differences are noticeable among the three major continents of the world?

At the broadest level human cultures evolved in quite similar fashion around the world. All, of course, were part of that grand process of human migration that initially peopled the planet. Beginning in Africa, that vast movement of humankind subsequently encompassed Eurasia, Australia, the Americas, and Pacific Oceania. Almost everywhere, gathering and hunting long remained the sole basis for sustaining life and society. Then, on the three supercontinents — Eurasia, Africa, and the Americas — the momentous turn of the Agricultural Revolution took place independently and in several distinct areas of each landmass (see Chapter 1). That revolutionary transformation of human life subsequently generated, in particularly rich agricultural environments of all three regions, those more complex societies that we know as civilizations, featuring cities, states, monumental architecture, and great social inequality (see Chapter 2). In these ways, the historical trajectory of the human journey has a certain unity and similarity across quite distinct continental regions. This commonality provides the foundation for a genuinely global history of humankind. At the beginning of the Common Era, that trajectory had generated a total world population of about 250 million people, substantially less than the current population of the United States alone. By contemporary standards, it was still a sparsely populated planet.

The world's human population was then distributed very unevenly across the three giant continents, as the Snapshot on page 182 indicates. If these estimates are even reasonably accurate, then during the second-wave era Eurasia was home to more than 80 percent of the world's people, Africa about 11 percent, and the Americas between 5 and 7 percent. That unevenness in population distribution is part of the reason why world historians focus more attention on Eurasia than on Africa or the Americas. Here lies one of the major differences among the continents.

There were others as well. The absence of most animals capable of domestication meant that no pastoral societies developed in the Americas, and apart from llamas and alpacas in the Andes, no draft animals were available to pull plows or carts or to carry heavy loads for long distances. Africa too lacked wild sheep, goats, chickens,

A Map of Time

750–200 B.C.E.	Chavín religious movement in Peruvian Andes
730 B.C.E.	Nubian conquest of Egypt
300 B.C.E.–100 C.E.	Kingdom of Meroë in upper Nile valley
300 B.C.E.–900 C.E.	Niger Valley civilization in West Africa
200 B.C.E.–400 C.E.	Hopewell "mound-building" culture in U.S. eastern woodlands
1st to 7th century C.E.	Flourishing of Axum (East Africa) and Moche (coastal Peru) civilizations; spread of Bantu-speaking people in eastern and southern Africa
250–900 C.E.	Classical Maya civilization
300–600 C.E.	Flourishing of Teotihuacán
4th century C.E.	Introduction of Christianity to Axum
400–1000 C.E.	Tiwanaku and Wari in the Andes
860–1130 C.E.	Chaco culture in U.S. Southwest
900–1250 C.E.	Cahokia

horses, and camels, but its proximity to Eurasia meant that these animals, once domesticated, became widely available to African peoples. Metallurgy in the Americas was likewise far less developed than in Eurasia and Africa, where iron tools and weapons played such an important role in economic and military life. In the Americas, writing was limited to the Mesoamerican region and was most highly developed among the Maya, whereas in Africa it was confined to the northern and northeastern parts of the continent. In Eurasia, by contrast, writing emerged elaborately in many regions. Furthermore, civilizations in Africa and the Americas were fewer in number and generally smaller than those of Eurasia, and larger numbers of their people lived in communities that did not feature cities and states.

A final continental comparison distinguishes the history of Africa from that of the Americas. Geography placed Africa adjacent to Eurasia, while it separated the Americas from both Africa and Eurasia. This has meant that parts of Africa frequently interacted with Eurasian civilizations. In fact, Mediterranean North Africa was long part of a larger zone of Afro-Eurasian interaction. Ancient Egyptian civilization was certainly in contact with Crete, Syria, and Mesopotamia and provided inspiration for the Greeks. The entire North African coastal region was incorporated into the Roman Empire and used to produce wheat and olives on large estates with slave labor. Christianity spread widely across North Africa, giving rise to some of the early Church's most famous martyrs and theologians. The Christian faith found an even more permanent foothold in the lands now known as Ethiopia.

Snapshot   Continental Population in the Second-Wave Era[2]

(Note: Population figures for such early times are merely estimates and are often controversial among scholars. Percentages do not always total 100 percent due to rounding.)

	Eurasia	Africa	North America	Central/South America	Australia/ Oceania	Total World
Area (in square miles and as percentage of world total)						
	21,049,000 (41%)	11,608,000 (22%)	9,365,000 (18%)	6,880,000 (13%)	2,968,000 (6%)	51,870,000
Population (in millions and as percentage of world total)						
400 B.C.E.	127 (83%)	17 (11%)	1 (0.7%)	7 (5%)	1 (0.7%)	153
10 C.E.	213 (85%)	26 (10%)	2 (0.8%)	10 (4%)	1 (0.4%)	252
200 C.E.	215 (84%)	30 (12%)	2 (0.8%)	9 (4%)	1 (0.4%)	257
600 C.E.	167 (80%)	24 (12%)	2 (1%)	14 (7%)	1 (0.5%)	208
1000 C.E.	195 (77%)	39 (15%)	2 (0.8%)	16 (6%)	1 (0.4%)	253

Arabia was another point of contact with Eurasia for African peoples. The arrival of the domesticated camel, probably from Arabia, generated a nomadic pastoral way of life among some of the Berber peoples of the western Sahara during the first three centuries C.E. A little later, camels also made possible trans-Saharan commerce, which linked interior West Africa to the world of Mediterranean civilization. Over many centuries, the East African coast was a port of call for Egyptian, Roman, and Arab merchants, and that region subsequently became an integral part of Indian Ocean trading networks. The transoceanic voyages of Austronesian-speaking sailors from Southeast Asia brought various food crops of that region, bananas for example, to Madagascar and from there to the East African mainland. The Americas, by contrast, developed almost wholly apart from this Afro-Eurasian network until that separation was breeched by the voyages of Columbus in 1492.

To illustrate the historical developments of the second-wave era beyond Eurasia/ North Africa, this chapter examines first the civilizations that emerged in sub-Saharan Africa and the Americas. Then our historical spotlight turns to several regions on both continents that remained outside the zone of civilization, reminding us that the histories of many peoples took shape without the cities, states, and empires that were so prominent within that zone.

LearningCurve
bedfordstmartins.com
/strayer/LC

Civilizations of Africa

When historians refer to Africa in premodern times, they are speaking generally of a geographic concept, a continental landmass, and not a cultural identity. Certainly few, if any, people living on the continent at that time thought of themselves as Africans. Like Eurasia or the Americas, Africa hosted numerous separate societies, cultures, and civilizations with vast differences among them as well as some interaction between them.

Many of these differences grew out of the continent's environmental variations. Small regions of Mediterranean climate in the northern and southern extremes, large deserts (the Sahara and the Kalahari), even larger regions of savanna grasslands, tropical rain forest in the continent's center, highlands and mountains in eastern Africa—all of these features, combined with the continent's enormous size, ensured endless variation among Africa's many peoples. Africa did, however, have one distinctive environmental feature: bisected by the equator, it was the most tropical of the world's three supercontinents. Persistent warm temperatures caused the rapid decomposition of vegetable matter called humus, resulting in poorer and less fertile soils and a less productive agriculture than in the more temperate Eurasia. Those climatic conditions also spawned numero us disease-carrying insects and parasites, which have long created serious health problems in many parts of the continent. It was within these environmental constraints that African peoples made their histories. In several distinct regions of the continent—the upper Nile valley, northern Ethiopia/Eritrea, and the Niger River valley—small civilizations flourished during the second-wave era, while others followed later.

Meroë: Continuing a Nile Valley Civilization

In the Nile Valley south of Egypt lay the lands of Nubian civilization, almost as old as Egypt itself. Over many centuries, Nubians both traded and fought with Egypt, and on one occasion the Nubian Kingdom of Kush conquered Egypt and ruled it for a century (see Portrait of Piye, pp. 186–87). While borrowing heavily from Egypt, Nubia remained a distinct and separate civilization (see Chapter 2). As Egypt fell increasingly under foreign control, Nubian civilization came to center on the southern city of Meroë (MER-oh-ee), where it flourished between 300 B.C.E. and 100 C.E. (see Map 6.1).

Politically, the Kingdom of Meroë was governed by an all-powerful and sacred monarch, a position held on at least ten occasions by women, governing alone or as co-rulers with a male monarch. Unlike the female pharaoh Hatshepsut in Egypt, who was portrayed in male clothing, Meroë queens appeared in sculptures as women and with a prominence and power equivalent to their male counterparts. In accordance with ancient traditions, such rulers were buried along with a number of human sacrificial victims. The city of Meroë and other urban centers housed a wide variety of economic specialties—merchants, weavers, potters, and masons, as well as servants,

■ **Connection**

How did the history of Meroë and Axum reflect interaction with neighboring civilizations?

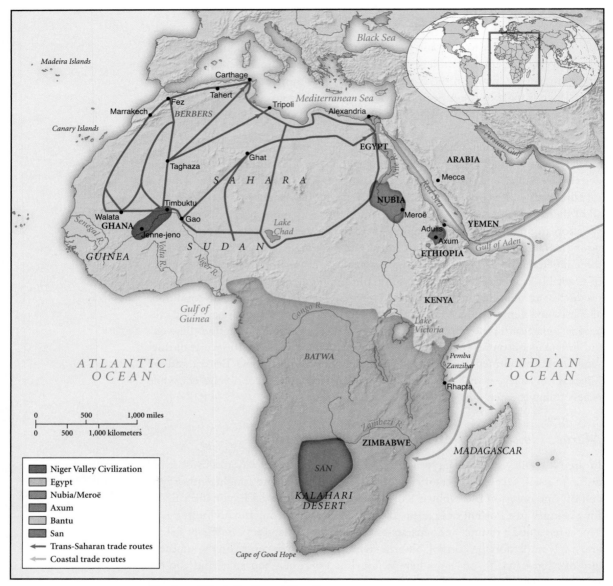

Map 6.1   Africa in the Second-Wave Era

During the second-wave era, older African civilizations such as Egypt and Nubia persisted and changed, while new civilizations emerged in Axum and the Niger River valley. South of the equator, Bantu-speaking peoples spread slowly, creating many new societies and identities.

laborers, and slaves. The smelting of iron and the manufacture of iron tools and weapons were especially prominent industries. The rural areas surrounding Meroë were populated by peoples who practiced some combination of herding and farming and paid periodic tribute to the ruler. Rainfall-based agriculture was possible in Meroë, and consequently farmers were less dependent on irrigation. This meant that the rural population did not need to concentrate so heavily near the Nile and was less directly controlled from the capital than was the case in Egypt, where state authorities were required to supervise an irrigation system serving a dense population along the river.

The wealth and military power of Meroë derived in part from extensive long-distance trading connections, to the north via the Nile and to the east and west by means of camel caravans. Its iron weapons and cotton cloth, as well as its access to gold, ivory, tortoiseshells, and ostrich feathers, gave Meroë a reputation for great riches in the world of northeastern Africa and the Mediterranean. The discovery in Meroë of a statue of the Roman emperor Augustus, probably seized during a raid on Roman Egypt, testifies to contact with the Mediterranean world. Culturally, Meroë seemed to move away from the heavy Egyptian influence of earlier times. A local lion god, Apedemek, grew more prominent than Egyptian deities such as Isis and Osiris, while the use of Egyptian-style writing declined as a new and still undeciphered Meroitic script took its place.

A Bracelet from Meroë
This gold bracelet, dating to about 100 B.C.E., illustrates the skill of Meroë's craftsmen as well as the kingdom's reputation as one of the wealthiest states of the ancient world. (Bracelet with image of Hathor, Nubian, Meroitic Period, about 100 B.C.E. Object Place: Sudan, Nubia, Gebel Barkal, Pyramid 8, Gold, enamel. Museum of Fine Arts, Boston, Harvard University–Boston Museum of Fine Arts Expedition, 20.333. Photograph © 2008 Museum of Fine Arts, Boston)

In the centuries following 100 C.E., the Kingdom of Meroë declined, in part because of deforestation caused by the need for wood to make charcoal for smelting iron. Furthermore as Egyptian trade with the African interior switched from the Nile Valley route to the Red Sea, the resources available to Meroë's rulers diminished and the state weakened. The effective end of the Meroë phase of Nubian civilization came with the kingdom's conquest in the 340s C.E. by the neighboring and rising state of Axum. In the centuries that followed, three separate Nubian states emerged, and Coptic (Egyptian) Christianity penetrated the region. For almost a thousand years, Nubia was a Christian civilization, using Greek as a liturgical language and constructing churches in Coptic or Byzantine fashion. After 1300 or so, political division, Arab immigration, and the penetration of Islam eroded this Christian civilization, and Nubia became part of the growing world of Islam (see Chapter 10).

Axum: The Making of a Christian Kingdom

If Meroë represented the continuation of an old African/Nubian civilization, Axum marked the emergence of a new one. Axum lay in the Horn of Africa, in what is now Eritrea and northern Ethiopia (see Map 6.1). Its economic foundation was a highly productive agriculture that used a plow-based farming system, unlike most of the rest of Africa, which relied on the hoe or digging stick. Axum's agriculture

Piye, Kushite Conqueror of Egypt

During the eighth century B.C.E., a remarkable reversal took place in northeastern Africa. The ancient Kingdom of Kush in the southern Nile Valley, long under the control of Egypt, conquered its former ruler and governed it for a century. The primary agent of that turnabout was Piye, a Kushite ruler (r. 752–721 B.C.E.), who recorded his great victory in a magnificent inscription that provides some hints about his own personality and outlook on the world.[3]

Piye in front of the seated god Amun while to his right and below, defeated rulers prostrate before him. (From James Henry Breasted, The Piankhi Stela, Ancient Records of Egypt *(Chicago, 1906), Part IV, 816ff)*

The very beginning of the inscription discloses Piye's self-image, for he declares himself a "divine emanation, living image of Atum," the Egyptian creator-god closely connected to kingship. Like most of the Kushite elite, Piye had thoroughly assimilated much of Egyptian culture and religion, becoming perhaps "more Egyptian than the Egyptians."[4] Even the inscription was written in hieroglyphic Egyptian and in the style of earlier pharaohs. Who better then to revive an Egypt that, over the past several centuries, had become hopelessly fragmented and

that also had neglected the worship of Amun? Thus Piye's conquest reflected the territorial ambitions of Kush's "Egyptianized" rulers, a sense of divinely inspired mission to set things right in Egypt, and the opportunity presented by the sorry state of Egyptian politics.

If we are to believe the inscription, Piye went to war reluctantly and only in response to requests from various Egyptian "princes, counts, and generals." Furthermore he was careful to pay respect to the gods all along the way. After celebrating the new year in 730 B.C.E., Piye departed from his capital of Napata and made an initial stop in Thebes, a southern Egyptian city already controlled by Kushite forces. There he took part in the annual Opet Festival, honoring Amun, his wife Mut (Egypt's mother goddess), and their offspring Khonsu, associated with the moon. Moving north, Piye then laid siege to Hermopolis, located in middle Egypt. From a high tower, archers poured arrows into the city and "slingers" hurled stones, "slaying people among them

generated substantial amounts of wheat, barley, millet, and teff, a highly nutritious grain unique to that region. By 50 C.E. or so, a substantial state had emerged, stimulated by its participation in the rapidly increasing Red Sea and Indian Ocean commerce, which was itself a product of growing Roman demand for Indian pearls, textiles, and especially pepper. At Adulis, then the largest port on the East African coast, a wide range of merchants sought the products of the African interior—animal hides, rhinoceros horn, ivory, obsidian, tortoiseshells, and slaves. Taxes on this trade provided a major source of revenue for the Axumite state and the complex society that grew up within it. Thus the decline of Meroë and the rise of Axum were both connected to changing patterns of long-distance commerce.[5]

The interior capital city, also known as Axum, was a center of monumental building and royal patronage for the arts. The most famous buildings were huge stone obelisks, which most likely marked royal graves. Some of them were more than 100 feet tall and at the time were the largest structures in the world hewn from a single piece of rock. The language used at court, in the towns, and for commerce was Geez,

daily," according to the inscription. Soon the city had become "foul to the nose," and its ruler, Prince Namlot, prepared for surrender. He sent his wife and daughter, lying on their bellies, to plead with the women in Piye's entourage, begging them to intercede with Piye, which they did. Grandly entering the city, Piye went first to the temple of the chief god, where he offered sacrifices of "bulls, calves and fowl." To establish his authority, he then "entered every chamber of [Namlot's] house, his treasury and his magazines." Piye pointedly ignored the women of Namlot's harem when they greeted him "in the manner of women." Yet in the stable, he was moved by the suffering of the horses. He seized Namlot's possessions for his treasury and assigned his enemy's grain to the temple of Amun.

And so it went as Piye moved northward. Many cities capitulated without resistance, offering their treasure to the Kushites. Presenting himself as a just and generous conqueror, Piye declared that "not a single one has been slain therein, except the enemies who blasphemed against the god, who were dispatched as rebels." However, it was a different story when he arrived outside of the major north Egyptian city of Memphis, then ruled by the Libyan chieftain Tefnakht. There "a multitude of people were

slain" before Tefnakht was induced to surrender, sending an envoy to Piye to deliver an abject and humiliating speech: "Be thou appeased! I have not beheld thy face for shame; I cannot stand before thy flame, I tremble at thy might." The city was ritually cleansed; proper respect was paid to the gods, who confirmed Piye's kingship; and tribute was collected. Soon all resistance collapsed, and Piye, once ruler of a small Kushite kingdom, found himself master of all Egypt.

And then, surprisingly, he departed, leaving his underlings in charge and his sister as the High Priestess and wife of Amun in Thebes. His ships "were laden with silver, gold, copper, clothing, and everything of the Northland, every product of Syria, and all sweet woods of God's Land [Egypt]. His majesty sailed up-stream, with glad heart." Never again did Piye set foot in Egypt, preferring to live out his days in his native country, where he was buried in an Egyptian-style pyramid. But he had laid the foundation for a century of Kushite rule in Egypt, reunifying that ancient country, reinvigorating the cult of Amun, and giving expression to the vitality of an important African civilization.

Questions: How did Piye understand himself and his actions in Egypt? How might modern historians view his conquests?

written in a script derived from South Arabia. The Axumite state exercised a measure of control over the mostly Agaw-speaking people of the country through a loose administrative structure focusing on the collection of tribute payments. To the Romans, Axum was the third major empire within the world they knew, following their own and the Persian Empire.

Through its connections to Red Sea trade and the Roman world, particularly Egypt, Axum was introduced to Christianity in the fourth century C.E. Its monarch at the time, King Ezana, adopted the new religion about the same time as Constantine did in the Roman Empire. Early in his reign, the kingdom's coins featured images of gods derived from southern Arabia, while by the end, they were inscribed with the Christian cross. Supported by royal authority, Christianity took root in Axum, linking that kingdom religiously to Egypt, where a distinctive Christian church known as Coptic was already well established. (See Chapter 4, pp. 142–43, and Chapter 10, pp. 319–21.) Although Egypt subsequently became largely Islamic, reducing its Christian community to a small minority, Christianity maintained a dominant position in

The Columns of Axum
Dating to the time when Axum first encountered Christianity (300–500 C.E.), this column, measuring some seventy-nine feet tall, probably served as a funeral monument for the kingdom's ancient rulers. (Bildagentur RM/TIPS Images)

the mountainous terrain of highland Ethiopia and in the early twenty-first century still represents the faith of perhaps 60 percent of the country's population.

During the fourth through the sixth century C.E., Axum mounted a campaign of imperial expansion that took its forces into the Kingdom of Meroë and across the Red Sea into Yemen in South Arabia. By 571, the traditional date for the birth of Muhammad, an Axumite army, including a number of African war elephants, had reached the gates of Mecca, but it was a fairly short-lived imperial venture. The next several centuries were ones of decline for the Axumite state, owing partly to environmental changes, such as soil exhaustion, erosion, and deforestation, brought about by intensive farming. Equally important was the rise of Islam, which altered trade routes and diminished the revenue available to the Axumite state. Its last coins were struck in the early seventh century. When the state revived several centuries later, it was centered farther south on the Ethiopian plateau. In this new location, there emerged the Christian church and the state that present-day Ethiopia has inherited, but the link to ancient Axum was long remembered and revered.

With their long-distance trading connections, urban centers, centralized states, complex societies, monumental architecture, written languages, and imperial ambitions, both Meroë and Axum paralleled on a smaller scale the major features of the second-wave civilizations of Eurasia. Furthermore, both were in direct contact with the world of Mediterranean civilizations. Across the continent in West Africa, a rather different civilization took shape.

Along the Niger River: Cities without States

■ **Description**
How does the experience of the Niger Valley challenge conventional notions of "civilization"?

The middle stretches of the Niger River in West Africa witnessed the emergence of a remarkable urbanization (see Map 6.1, p. 184). A prolonged dry period during the five centuries after 500 B.C.E. brought growing numbers of people from the southern Sahara into the fertile floodplain of the middle Niger in search of more reliable access to water. Accompanying them were their domesticated cattle, sheep, and goats, their agricultural skills, and their ironworking technology. Over many centuries (roughly 300 B.C.E.–900 C.E.), the peoples of this region created a distinctive city-based civilization. The most fully studied of the urban clusters that grew up along the middle Niger was the city of Jenne-jeno (jihn-AY jihn-OH), which at its high point probably housed more than 40,000 people.

Among the most distinctive features of the Niger Valley civilization was the apparent absence of a corresponding state structure. Unlike the cities of Egypt, China, the Roman Empire, or Axum, these middle Niger urban centers were not encompassed within some larger imperial system. Nor were they like the city-states of ancient Mesopotamia, in which each city had its own centralized political structure, embodied in a monarch and his accompanying bureaucracy. According to a leading historian of the region, they were "cities without citadels," complex urban centers that apparently operated without the coercive authority of a state, for archeologists have found in their remains few signs of despotic power, widespread warfare, or deep social inequalities.[6] In this respect, these urban centers resemble the early cities of the Indus Valley civilization, where likewise little archeological evidence of centralized state structures has been found (see Chapter 2).

In place of such hierarchical organization, Jenne-jeno and other cities of the region emerged as clusters of economically specialized settlements surrounding a larger central town. The earliest and most prestigious of these specialized occupations was iron smithing. Working with fire and earth (ore) to produce this highly useful metal, the smiths of the Niger Valley were both feared and revered. Archeologist Roderick McIntosh, a leading figure in the excavation of Jenne-jeno, argued that "their knowledge of the transforming arts—earth to metal, insubstantial fire to the mass of iron—was the key to a secret, occult realm of immense power and immense danger."[7]

Other specializations followed. Villages of cotton weavers, potters, leather workers, and griots (praise-singers who preserved and recited the oral traditions of their societies) grew up around the central towns. Gradually these urban

Terra-cotta Statue from Jenne-jeno
The artistic tradition of Niger Valley civilization includes a number of terra-cotta couples, reflecting perhaps the emphasis on the separate but complementary roles of men and women in much of African thought. This statue and others like it date to sometime after the twelfth century and may express the resistance of an indigenous tradition to the growing penetration of Islam. (Werner Forman/Art Resource, NY)

artisan communities became occupational castes, whose members passed their jobs and skills to their children and could marry only within their own group. In the surrounding rural areas, as in all urban-based civilizations, farmers tilled the soil and raised their animals, but specialization also occurred in food production as various ethnic groups focused on fishing, rice cultivation, or some other agricultural pursuit. At least for a time, these middle Niger cities represented an African alternative to an oppressive state, which in many parts of the world accompanied an increasingly complex urban economy and society. A series of distinct and specialized economic groups shared authority and voluntarily used the services of one another, while maintaining their own identities through physical separation.

Accompanying this unique urbanization, and no doubt stimulating it, was a growing network of indigenous West African commerce. The middle Niger flood-plain supported a rich agriculture and contained clay for pottery, but it lacked stone, iron ore, salt, and fuel. This scarcity of resources was the basis for a long-distance commerce that operated by boat along the Niger River and overland by donkey to the north and south. Iron ore from more than 50 miles away, copper from mines 200 miles distant, gold from even more distant sources, stones and salt from the Sahara—all of these items have been found in Jenne-jeno, exchanged no doubt for grain, fish, smoked meats, iron implements, and other staples. Jenne-jeno itself was an impor-tant transshipment point in this commerce, in which goods were transferred from boat to donkey or vice versa. By the 500s C.E., there is evidence of an even wider commerce and at least indirect contact, from Mauritania in the west to present-day Mali and Burkina-Faso in the east.

In the second millennium C.E., new historical patterns developed in West Africa (see Chapter 7). A number of large-scale states or empires emerged in the region—Ghana, Mali, and Songhay, among the most well known. At least partially responsible for this development was the flourishing of a camel-borne trans-Saharan commerce, previously but a trickle across the great desert. As West Africa became more firmly connected to North Africa and the Mediterranean, Islam penetrated the region, mark-ing a gradual but major cultural transformation. All of this awaited West Africa in later centuries, submerging, but not completely eliminating, the decentralized city life of the Niger Valley.

LearningCurve
bedfordstmartins.com
/strayer/LC

Civilizations of Mesoamerica

Westward across the Atlantic Ocean lay the altogether separate world of the Ameri-cas. Although geography encouraged some interaction between African and Eur-asian peoples, the Atlantic and Pacific oceans ensured that the cultures and societies of the Western Hemisphere operated in a world apart from their Afro-Eurasian counterparts. Nor were the cultures of the Americas stimulated by the kind of fruit-ful interaction among their own peoples that played such an important role in the Eastern Hemisphere. Nothing similar to the contact between Egypt and Mesopota-mia, or Persia and the Greeks, or the extensive communication along the Silk Road trading network enriched the two major centers of civilization in the Americas—Mesoamerica and the Andes—which had little if any direct contact with each other. Furthermore, the remarkable achievements of early American civilizations and cul-tures occurred without the large domesticated animals or ironworking technologies that were so important throughout the Eastern Hemisphere.

Accounts of pre-Columbian American societies often focus primarily on the Az-tec and Inca empires (see Chapter 12), yet these impressive creations, flourishing in the fifteenth and early sixteenth centuries, were but the latest in a long line of civili-zations that preceded them in Mesoamerica and the Andes respectively. These two regions housed the vast majority of the population of the Americas. Here the historical spotlight focuses on the long period following the First Civilizations of the Olmecs and Norte Chico but preceding the Aztecs and Incas, roughly 500 B.C.E.–1300 C.E.

Stretching from central Mexico to northern Central America, the area known as Mesoamerica was, geographically speaking, one of "extraordinary diversity compressed into a relatively small space."[8] That environment ranged from steamy lowland rain forests to cold and windy highland plateaus, cut by numerous mountains and valleys and generating many microclimates. Such conditions contributed to substantial linguistic and ethnic diversity and to many distinct and competing cities, chiefdoms, and states.

Despite this diversity, Mesoamerica was also a distinct region, bound together by elements of a common culture. Its many peoples shared an intensive agricultural technology devoted to raising maize, beans, chili peppers, and squash. They prepared maize in a distinctive and highly nutritious fashion and based their economies on market exchange. They practiced religions featuring a similar pantheon of male and female deities, understood time as a cosmic cycle of creation and destruction, practiced human sacrifice, and constructed monumental ceremonial centers. Furthermore they employed a common ritual calendar of 260 days and hieroglyphic writing, and they interacted frequently among themselves. During the first millennium B.C.E., for example, the various small states and chiefdoms of the region, particularly the Olmec, exchanged a number of luxury goods used to display social status and for ritual purposes—jade, serpentine, obsidian tools, ceramic pottery, shell ornaments, stingray spines, and turtle shells. As a result, aspects of Olmec culture, such as artistic styles, temple pyramids, the calendar system, and rituals involving human sacrifice, spread widely throughout Mesoamerica and influenced many of the civilizations that followed.

The Maya: Writing and Warfare

Among Mesoamerican civilizations, none has attracted more attention than that of the Maya. Scholars have traced the beginnings of the Maya people to ceremonial centers constructed as early as 2000 B.C.E. in present-day Guatemala and the Yucatán region of Mexico (see Map 6.2). During the first millennium B.C.E., a number of substantial urban centers with concentrated populations and monumental architecture had emerged in the region. In northern Guatemala, for example, the archeological site of El Mirador was home to tens of thousands of people, a pyramid/temple said by some to be the largest in the world, and a stone-carved frieze depicting the Maya creation story known as the Popul Vuh.

But it was during a later phase of Maya civilization, between 250 and 900 C.E., that their most well-known

Map 6.2 Civilizations of Mesoamerica
During the second-wave era, Maya civilization and the large city of Teotihuacán represented the most prominent features of Mesoamerican civilization.

cultural achievements emerged. Intellectuals, probably priests, developed a mathematical system that included the concept of zero and place notation and was capable of complex calculations. They combined this mathematical ability with careful observation of the night skies to plot the cycles of planets, to predict eclipses of the sun and the moon, to construct elaborate calendars, and to calculate accurately the length of the solar year. The distinctive art of the Maya elite was likewise impressive to later observers.

■ **Comparison**

With what Eurasian civilizations might the Maya be compared?

Accompanying these intellectual and artistic achievements was the creation of the most elaborate writing system in the Americas, which used both pictographs and phonetic or syllabic elements. Carved on stone and written on bark paper or deerskin books, Mayan writing recorded historical events, masses of astronomical data, and religious or mythological texts. Temples, pyramids, palaces, and public plazas abounded, graced with painted murals and endless stone carving. It is not surprising that early scholars viewed Maya civilization as a peaceful society led by gentle stargazing priest-kings devoted to temple building and intellectual pursuits.

The economic foundations for these cultural achievements were embedded in an "almost totally engineered landscape."[9] The Maya drained swamps, terraced hillsides, flattened ridgetops, and constructed an elaborate water management system. Much of this underpinned a flourishing agriculture, which supported a very rapidly growing and dense population by 750 C.E. This agriculture sustained substantial elite classes of nobles, priests, merchants, architects, and sculptors, as well as specialized artisans producing pottery, tools, and cotton textiles. And it was sufficiently productive to free a large labor force for work on the many public structures that continue to amaze contemporary visitors.

These many achievements took place within a highly fragmented political system of city-states, local lords, and regional kingdoms with no central authority, with frequent warfare, and with the extensive capture and sacrifice of prisoners. The larger political units of Maya civilization were densely populated urban and ceremonial centers, ruled by powerful kings and on a few occasions queens. They were divine rulers or "state shamans" able to mediate between humankind and the supernatural. One of these cities, Tikal (tee-KAHL), contained perhaps 50,000 people, with another 50,000 or so in the surrounding countryside, by 750 C.E.[10] (See the chapter-opening photo, p. 178, of a temple from Tikal.) Some of these city-states were clearly imperialistic, but none succeeded in creating a unified Maya empire. Various centers of Maya civilization rose and fell; fluctuating alliances among them alternated with periods of sporadic warfare; ruling families intermarried; the elite classes sought luxury goods from far away — jade, gold, shells, feathers from exotic birds, cacao — to bolster their authority and status. In its political dimensions, Maya civilization more closely resembled the competing city-states of ancient Mesopotamia or classical Greece than the imperial structures of Rome, Persia, or China.

But large parts of that imposing civilization collapsed with a completeness and finality rare in world history. Clearly this was not a single or uniform phenomenon, as flourishing centers of Maya civilization persisted in the northern Yucatàn, and many Maya survived to fight the Spanish in the sixteenth century. But in the southern regions where the collapse was most complete, its outcomes were devastating. In less than a century following the onset of a long-term drought in 840, the population of the low-lying southern heartland of the Maya dropped by 85 percent or more as famine, epidemic, and fratricidal warfare reaped a horrific toll. It was a catastrophe from which there was no recovery. Elements of Maya culture survived in scattered settlements, but the great cities were deserted, and large-scale construction and artistic work ceased. The last date inscribed in stone corresponds to 909 C.E. As a complex civilization, the Maya had passed into history.

Explaining this remarkable demise has long kept scholars guessing, with recent accounts focusing on ecological and political factors.[11] Rapid population growth after 600 C.E. pushed total Maya numbers to perhaps 5 million or more and soon outstripped available resources, resulting in deforestation and the erosion of hillsides. Under such conditions, climate change in the form of prolonged droughts in the 800s may well have placed unbearable pressures on Maya society. Political disunity and endemic rivalries, long a prominent feature of Maya civilization, prevented a coordinated and effective response to the emerging catastrophe. Warfare in fact became more frequent as competition for increasingly scarce land for cultivation became sharper. Rulers dependent on ritual splendor for their legitimacy competed to mount ever more elaborate temples, palaces, and pageants, requiring more labor and taxes from their subjects and tribute from their enemies. Whatever the precise explanation, the Maya collapse, like that of the Romans and others, illustrates the fragility of civilizations, whether they are embodied in large empires or organized in a more decentralized fashion.

Teotihuacán: The Americas' Greatest City

At roughly the same time as the Maya flourished in the southern regions of Mesoamerica, the giant city of Teotihuacán (tay-uh-tee-wah-KAHN), was also thriving further north in the Valley of Mexico. Begun around 150 B.C.E. and apparently built to a plan rather than evolving haphazardly, the city came to occupy about eight square miles and by 550 C.E. had a population variously estimated between 100,000 and 200,000. It was by far the largest urban complex in the Americas at the time and one of the six largest in the world. Beyond this, much about Teotihuacán is unknown, such as its original name, the language of its people, the kind of government that ordered its life, and the precise function of its many deities.

Physically, the city was enormously impressive, replete with broad avenues, spacious plazas, huge marketplaces, temples, palaces, apartment complexes, slums, waterways, reservoirs, drainage systems, and colorful murals. Along the main north/south boulevard, now known as the Street of the Dead, were the grand homes of the elite, the headquarters of state authorities, many temples, and two giant pyramids. One of them, the Pyramid of the Sun, had been constructed over an ancient tunnel leading

■ **Connection**
In what ways did Teotihuacán shape the history of Mesoamerica?

Teotihuacán
Taken from the summit of the Pyramid of the Moon, this photograph looks down the famous Avenue of the Dead to the Pyramid of the Sun in the upper left. (Alison Wright/Photo Researchers)

to a cave and may well have been regarded as the site of creation itself, the birthplace of the sun and the moon. At the Temple of the Feathered Serpent, archeologists have found the remains of some 200 people, their hands and arms tied behind them; they were the apparently unwilling sacrificial victims meant to accompany the high-ranking persons buried there into the afterlife.

Off the main avenues in a grid-like pattern of streets lay thousands of residential apartment compounds, home to the city's commoners, each with its own kitchen area, sleeping quarters, courtyards, and shrines. In these compounds, perhaps in groups of related families or lineages, lived many of the farmers who tilled the lands outside the city. Thousands of Maya specialists—masons, leather workers, potters, construction laborers, merchants, civil servants—also made their homes in these apartments. So too did skilled makers of obsidian blades, who plied their trade in hundreds of separate workshops, generating products that were in great demand throughout Mesoamerica. At least two small sections of the city were reserved exclusively for foreigners.

Buildings, both public and private, were decorated with mural paintings, sculptures, and carvings. Many of these works of art display abstract geometric and stylized images. Others depict gods and goddesses, arrayed in various forms—feathered serpents, starfish, jaguars, flowers, and warriors. One set of murals shows happy people cavorting in a paradise of irrigated fields, playing games, singing, and chasing butterflies, which were thought to represent the souls of the dead. Another portrays dancing warriors carrying elaborate curved knives, to which were attached bleeding human hearts.

The art of Teotihuacán, unlike that of the Maya, has revealed few images of self-glorifying rulers or individuals. Nor did the city have a tradition of written public inscriptions as the Maya did, although a number of glyphs or characters indicate at least a limited form of writing. One scholar has suggested that "the rulers of Teotihuacán might have intentionally avoided the personality cult of the dynastic art and writing" so characteristic of the Maya.[12] Perhaps those rulers constituted an oligarchy or council of high-ranking elites rather than a single monarch.

However it was governed, Teotihuacán cast a huge shadow over Mesoamerica, particularly from 300 to 600 C.E. A core region of perhaps 10,000 square miles was administered directly from the city itself, while tribute was no doubt exacted from other areas within its broader sphere of influence. At a greater distance, the power of Teotihuacán's armies gave it a presence in the Maya heartland more than 600 miles to the east. At least one Maya city, Kaminalijuyu in the southern highlands, was completely taken over by the Teotihuacán military and organized as a colony. In Tikal, a major lowland Maya city, in the year 378 C.E., agents of Teotihuacán apparently engineered a coup that placed a collaborator on the throne and turned the city for a time into an ally or a satellite. Elsewhere—in the Zapotec capital of Monte Alban, for example—murals show unarmed persons from Teotihuacán engaged in what seems to be more equal diplomatic relationships.

At least some of this political and military activity was no doubt designed to obtain, either by trade or by tribute, valued commodities from afar—food products, cacao beans, tropical bird feathers, honey, salt, medicinal herbs. The presence in Teotihuacán of foreigners, perhaps merchants, from the Gulf Coast and Maya lowlands, as well as much pottery from those regions, provides further evidence of long-distance trade. Moreover, the sheer size and prestige of Teotihuacán surely persuaded many, all across Mesoamerica, to imitate the architectural and artistic styles of the city. Thus, according to a leading scholar, "Teotihuacán meant something of surpassing importance far beyond its core area."[13] Almost a thousand years after its still-mysterious collapse around 650 C.E., the peoples of the Aztec Empire dubbed the great metropolis as Teotihuacán, the "city of the gods."

LearningCurve
bedfordstmartins.com
/strayer/LC

Civilizations of the Andes

Yet another and quite separate center of civilization in the Americas lay in the dramatic landscape of the Andes. Bleak deserts along the coast supported human habitation only because they were cut by dozens of rivers flowing down from the mountains, offering the possibility of irrigation and cultivation. The offshore waters of the Pacific Ocean also provided an enormously rich marine environment with an endless supply of seabirds and fish. The Andes themselves, a towering mountain chain

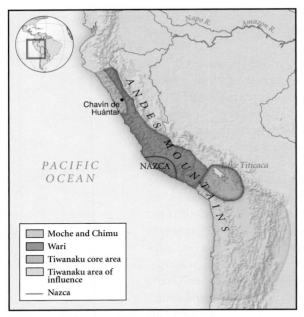

Map 6.3 Civilizations of the Andes

No single civilization dominated the Andes region during the second-wave era. Rather a number of religious movements, states, and empires rose and fell before the entire region was encompassed by the Inca Empire in the fifteenth century.

with many highland valleys, afforded numerous distinct ecological niches, depending on altitude. Andean societies generally sought access to the resources of these various environments through colonization, conquest, or trade—seafood from the coastal regions; maize and cotton from lower-altitude valleys; potatoes, quinoa, and pasture land for their llamas in the high plains; tropical fruits and cocoa leaf from the moist eastern slope of the Andes.

The most well-known of the civilizations to take shape in this environment was that of the Incas, which encompassed practically the entire region, some 2,500 miles in length, in the fifteenth century. Yet the Incas represented only the most recent and the largest in a long history of civilizations in the area.

The coastal region of central Peru had in fact generated one of the world's First Civilizations, known as Norte Chico, dating back to around 3000 B.C.E. (see Chapter 2). During the two millennia between roughly 1000 B.C.E. to 1000 C.E., a number of Andean civilizations rose and passed away. Because none of them had developed writing, historians are largely dependent on archeology for an understanding of these civilizations.

Chavín: A Pan-Andean Religious Movement

■ **Connection**

What kind of influence did Chavín exert in the Andes region?

In both the coastal and highland regions of Peru, archeologists have uncovered numerous local ceremonial centers or temple complexes, dating to between 2000 and 1000 B.C.E. Then around 900 B.C.E., one of them, situated in the Andean highlands at a village called Chavín (cha-BEEN) de Huántar, became the focus of a religious movement that soon swept through both coastal and highland Peru, aided by its strategic location on trade routes to both the coastal region to the west and the Amazon rain forest to the east.

By perhaps 750 B.C.E., this small center had become a town of 2,000 to 3,000 people, with clear distinctions between an elite class, who lived in stone houses, and ordinary people, with adobe dwellings. An elaborate temple complex included numerous galleries, hidden passageways, staircases, ventilation shafts, drainage canals, and distinctive carvings. Chavín artwork suggests influences from both the desert coastal region and the rain forests. Major deities were represented as jaguars, crocodiles, and snakes, all of them native to the Amazon basin. Shamans or priests likely made use of the San Pedro cactus, native to the Andes Mountains, employing its hallucinogenic properties to penetrate the supernatural world. Some of the fantastic artwork of this civilization—its jaguar-human images, for example—may well reflect the visions of these religious leaders.

Over the next several centuries, this blended religious movement proved attractive across much of Peru and beyond, as Chavín-style temple architecture, sculpture, pottery, religious images, and painted textiles were widely imitated within the region. Chavín itself became a pilgrimage site and perhaps a training center for initiates.[14] Although some evidence suggests violence and warfare, no Chavín "empire" emerged. Instead, a widespread religious cult, erected on the back of a trading network, provided for the first time and for several centuries a measure of economic and cultural integration to much of the Peruvian Andes.

Moche: A Civilization of the Coast

By 200 B.C.E., the pan-Andes Chavín cult had faded, replaced by a number of regional civilizations. Among them, Moche (MOH-chee) civilization clearly stands out. Dominating a 250-mile stretch of Peru's northern coast and incorporating thirteen river valleys, the Moche people flourished between about 100 and 800 C.E. Their economy was rooted in a complex irrigation system, requiring constant maintenance, which funneled runoff from the Andes into fields of maize, beans, and squash and acres of cotton, all fertilized by rich bird droppings called guano. Moche fishermen also harvested millions of anchovies from the bountiful Pacific.

■ **Description**
What features of Moche life characterize it as a civilization?

Politically, Moche was governed by warrior-priests, some of whom lived atop huge pyramids, the largest of which was constructed from 143 million sun-dried bricks. There shaman-rulers, often under the influence of hallucinogenic drugs, conducted ancient rituals that mediated between the world of humankind and that of the gods. They also presided over the ritual sacrifice of human victims, drawn from their many prisoners of war, which became central to the politico-religious life of the Moche. Images on Moche pottery show a ruler attired in a magnificent feather headdress and seated on a pyramid, while a parade of naked prisoners marches past him. Other scenes of decapitation and dismemberment indicate the fate that awaited those destined for sacrifice. For these rulers, the Moche world was apparently one of war, ceremony, and diplomacy.

The immense wealth of this warrior-priest elite and the exquisite artistry of Moche craftsmen are reflected in the elaborate burials accorded the rulers. At one site near the town of Sipan, Peruvian archeologists uncovered the final resting place of three such individuals, one of whom they named the Lord of Sipan. Laid in adobe burial chambers, one above the other, each was decked out in his ceremonial regalia— elaborate gold masks, necklaces, and headdresses; turquoise and gold bead bracelets; cotton tunics covered with copper plates; a gold rattle showing a Moche warrior smashing a prisoner with his war club; and a copper knife. In 2005, in another remarkable discovery dating to about 450 C.E., archeologists found the burial place of a high-status woman, who was in her late twenties and heavily tattooed. She had been

The Lord of Sipan
The Moche ruler in the center of the grave, dating to about 290 C.E., was about forty years old when he died and, at five feet five inches, was quite tall for the time. Except for early signs of arthritis, he was in good health and seems to have performed little physical labor during his life. Accompanying him in death were the four individuals shown here, plus three young women, a priest, a guard, a dog, and considerable food and drink. (© Kevin Schafer/Corbis)

laid to rest with hundreds of funeral objects, including gold sewing needles; weaving tools; much gold, silver, and copper jewelry; and a female sacrificial victim lying beside her. Even more suggestive were two elaborate war clubs and twenty-three spear throwers. Was she perhaps a warrior, a priest, or a ruler?

The most accessible aspect of Moche life and much of what scholars know about the Moche world derive from the superb skill of their craftspeople, such as metal workers, potters, weavers, and painters. Face masks, figures of animals, small earrings, and other jewelry items, many plated in gold, display amazing technical abilities and a striking artistic sensibility. Decorating their ceramic pottery are naturalistic portraits of noble lords and rulers and images from the life of common people, including the blind and the sick. Battle scenes show warriors confronting their enemies with raised clubs. Erotic encounters between men and women and gods making love to humans likewise represent common themes, as do grotesque images of their many gods and goddesses. Much of this, of course, reflects the culture of the Moche elite. We know much less about the daily life of the farmers, fishermen, weavers, traders, construction workers, and servants whose labor made that elite culture possible.

These cultural achievements, however, rested on fragile environmental foundations, for the region was subject to drought, earthquakes, and occasional torrential rains associated with El Niño episodes (dramatic changes in weather patterns caused by periodic warming of Pacific Ocean currents). During the sixth century C.E., some combination of these forces caused extended ecological disruption, which seriously undermined Moche civilization. In these circumstances, the Moche were vulnerable to aggressive neighbors and possibly to internal social tensions as well. By the end of the eighth century C.E., that civilization had passed into history.[15]

Wari and Tiwanaku: Empires of the Interior

Far more than the Moche and other coastal civilizations, the interior empires of Wari (wah-ree) and Tiwanaku provided a measure of political integration and cultural commonality for the entire Andean region. Growing out of ancient settlements, these two states flourished between 400 and 1000 C.E., Wari in the northern highlands and Tiwanaku to the south. Both were centered in large urban capitals, marked by monumental architecture and stratified populations numbering in the tens of thousands. Both governments collected surplus food in warehouses as an insurance against times of drought and famine.

But neither state controlled a continuous band of territory. Adapting to their vertical environment, both empires established colonies at lower elevations on the eastern and western slopes of the Andes as well as throughout the highlands, seeking access to resources such as seafood, maize, chili peppers, cocoa, hallucinogenic plants, obsidian, and feathers from tropical birds. Caravans of llamas linked distant centers, allowing the exchange and redistribution of goods, while the religious prestige and ceremonial power of the capital city provided further integration. Cultural influences from the center, such as styles of pottery and textiles, spread well beyond the regions of direct political control. Similar religious symbols and images prevailed in both places, including the ancient Andean Staff God, a deity portrayed with a staff in each hand.

But Wari and Tiwanaku were hardly carbon copies of one another. Wari's agriculture employed an elaborate system of hillside terracing and irrigation, using snow melt from the Andes. A seventeenth-century Jesuit missionary thought the hillsides of the Wari region "were covered with flights of stairs." Tiwanaku's highly productive farming economy, by contrast, utilized a "raised field" system in which artificially elevated planting surfaces in swampy areas were separated by small irrigation canals. Tiwanaku, furthermore, has become famous for its elaborately fitted stone walls and buildings, while Wari's tombs and temples were built of field stone set in mud mortar and covered with smooth plaster. Cities in the Wari region seemed built to a common plan and linked to the capital by a network of highways, which suggests a political system more tightly controlled from the center than in Tiwanaku.[16]

■ **Description**

What was the significance of Wari and Tiwanaku in the history of Andean civilization?

Despite these differences and a 300 mile common border, little overt conflict or warfare occurred between Wari and Tikanaku. In areas where the two peoples lived near one another, they apparently did not mingle much. They each spoke their own language, wore different clothing, furnished their homes with distinctive goods, and looked to their respective capital cities for inspiration.[17]

In the several centuries following 1000 C.E., both civilizations collapsed, their impressive cities permanently abandoned. What followed was a series of smaller kingdoms, one of which evolved into the Inca Empire that gave to Andean civilization a final and spectacular expression before all of the Americas was swallowed up in European empires from across the sea. The Inca themselves clearly drew on the legacy of Wari and Tiwanaku, adopting aspects of their imperial models and systems of statecraft, building on the Wari highway system, and utilizing similar styles of dress and artistic expression. Such was the prestige of Tiwanaku centuries after its collapse that the Inca claimed it as their place of origin.

SUMMING UP SO FAR

What features common to all civilizations can you identify in the civilizations of Africa and the Americas? What distinguishing features give them a distinctive identity?

Alternatives to Civilization: Bantu Africa

World historians are frequently occupied, sometimes almost exclusively, with civilizations, and understandably so, since those urban and state-based communities were clearly the most powerful, expansive, and innovative societies, later embracing almost the entire population of the planet. And yet, it is useful to remind ourselves that other ways of organizing human communities evolved alongside civilizations, and they too made history. Two such regions were Africa south of the equator and North America. They shared environments that featured plenty of land and relatively few people compared to the greater population densities and pressure on the land that characterized many civilizations.

In the vast region of Africa south of the equator, the most significant development during the second-wave era involved the accelerating movement of Bantu-speaking peoples into the enormous subcontinent. It was a process that had begun many centuries earlier, probably around 3000 B.C.E., from a homeland region in what are now southeastern Nigeria and the Cameroons. In the long run, that movement of peoples generated some 400 distinct but closely related languages, known collectively as Bantu. By the first century C.E., agricultural peoples speaking Bantu languages and now bearing an ironworking technology had largely occupied the forest regions of equatorial Africa, and at least a few of them had probably reached the East African coast. In the several centuries that followed, they established themselves quite rapidly in most of eastern and southern Africa (see Map 6.1, p. 184), introducing immense economic and cultural changes to a huge region of the continent.

Bantu expansion was not a conquest or invasion such as that of Alexander the Great; nor was it a massive and self-conscious migration like that of Europeans to the Americas in more recent times. Rather, it was a slow movement of peoples, perhaps a few extended families at a time, but taken as a whole, it brought to Africa south of the equator a measure of cultural and linguistic commonality, marking it as a distinct region of the continent.

Cultural Encounters

That movement of peoples also generated numerous cross-cultural encounters, as the Bantu-speaking newcomers interacted with already established societies, changing both of them in the process. Among those encounters, none was more significant than that between the agricultural Bantu and the gathering and hunting peoples who earlier occupied this region of Africa. Their interaction was part of a long-term global phenomenon in which farmers largely replaced foragers as the dominant people on the planet (see Chapter 1).

In these encounters, Bantu-speaking farmers had various advantages. One was numerical, as agriculture generated a more productive economy, enabling larger numbers to live in a smaller area than was possible with a gathering and hunting way of life. Another advantage was disease, for the farmers brought with them both parasitic and infectious diseases—malaria, for example—to which foraging people had little immunity. A third advantage was iron, so useful for tools and weapons, which Bantu migrants brought to many of their interactions with peoples still operating with stone-age technology. Thus, gathering and hunting peoples were displaced, absorbed, or largely eliminated in most parts of Africa south of the equator—but not everywhere.

In the rain forest region of Central Africa, the foraging Batwa (BAH-twah) (Pygmy) people, at least some of them, became "forest specialists" who produced honey, wild game, elephant products, animal skins, and medicinal barks and plants, all of which entered regional trading networks in exchange for the agricultural products of their Bantu neighbors. They also adopted Bantu languages, while maintaining a nonagricultural lifestyle and a separate identity. For their part, the Bantu farmers regarded their Batwa neighbors as first-comers to the region and therefore closest to the ancestral and territorial spirits that determined the fertility of the land and people. Thus, as forest-dwelling and Bantu-speaking farmers grew in numbers and created chiefdoms, those chiefs appropriated the Batwa title of "owners of the land" for themselves, claimed Batwa ancestry, and portrayed the Batwa as the original "civilizers" of the earth.[18]

In other ways as well, Bantu cultures changed as they encountered different peoples. In the drier environment of East Africa, the yam-based agriculture of the West African Bantu homeland was unable to support their growing numbers, so Bantu farmers increasingly adopted grains as well as domesticated sheep and cattle from the already established people of the region. Their agriculture also was enriched by acquiring a variety of food crops from Southeast Asia—coconuts, sugarcane, and especially bananas—which were brought to East Africa by Indonesian sailors and

■ **Connection**

In what ways did the arrival of Bantu-speaking peoples stimulate cross-cultural interaction?

immigrants early in the first millennium C.E. Bantu farmers then spread this agricultural package and their acquired ironworking technology throughout the vast area of eastern and southern Africa, probably reaching present-day South Africa by 400 C.E. They also brought a common set of cultural and social practices, which diffused widely across Bantu Africa. One prominent historian described these practices as encompassing,

> in religion, the centrality of ancestor observances; in philosophy, the problem of evil understood as the consequence of individual malice or of the failure to honor one's ancestors; in music, an emphasis on polyrhythmic performance with drums as the key instrument; in dance, a new form of expression in which a variety of prescribed body movements took preference over footwork; and in agriculture, the pre-eminence of women as the workers and innovators.[19]

All of this became part of the common culture of Bantu-speaking Africa.

Society and Religion

In the thousand years or so (500–1500 C.E.) that followed their initial colonization of Africa south of the equator, agricultural Bantu-speaking peoples also created a wide variety of quite distinct societies and cultures. Some — in present-day Kenya, for example — organized themselves without any formal political specialists at all. Instead they made decisions, resolved conflicts, and maintained order by using kinship structures or lineage principles supplemented by age grades, which joined men of a particular generation together across various lineages. Elsewhere, lineage heads who acquired a measure of personal wealth or who proved skillful at mediating between the local spirits and the people might evolve into chiefs with a modest political authority. In several areas, such as the region around Lake Victoria or present-day Zimbabwe, larger and more substantial kingdoms evolved. Along the East African coast after 1000 C.E., dozens of rival city-states linked the African interior with the commerce of the Indian Ocean basin (see Chapter 7, pp. 000–00).

Many societies in the Bantu-speaking world developed gender systems that were markedly less patriarchal than those of established urban-based civilizations. Male ironworkers in the Congo River basin, for example, sought to appropriate the power and prestige of female reproductive capacity by decorating their furnaces with clay breasts and speaking of their bellows as impregnating the furnaces. Among the Luba people of Central Africa, male rulers operated in alliance with powerful women, particularly spirit mediums, who were thought to contain the spirit of the king. Only a woman's body was considered sufficiently strong to acquire this potent and dangerous presence. Luba art represented female ancestors as "keepers of secret royal knowledge." And across a wide area of south-central Africa, a system of "gender parallelism" associated female roles with village life (child care, farming, food preparation, making pots, baskets, and mats), while masculine identity revolved around hunting and forest life (fishing, trapping, collecting building materials and medicinal plants). It was a "separate but equal" definition of gender roles.[20]

In terms of religion, Bantu practice in general placed less emphasis on a High or Creator God, who was viewed as remote and largely uninvolved in ordinary life, and focused instead on ancestral or nature spirits. The power of dead ancestors might be accessed through rituals of sacrifice, especially of cattle. Supernatural power deriving from ancient heroes, ancestors, or nature spirits also resided in charms, which could be activated by proper rituals and used to control the rains, defend the village, achieve success in hunting, or identify witches. Belief in witches was widespread, reflecting the idea that evil or misfortune was the work of malicious people. Diviners, skilled in penetrating the world of the supernatural, used dreams, visions, charms, or trances to identify the source of misfortune and to prescribe remedies. Was a particular illness the product of broken taboos, a dishonored ancestor, an unhappy nature spirit, or a witch? Was a remedy to be found in a cleansing ceremony, a sacrifice to an ancestor, the activation of a charm, or the elimination of a witch?[21]

Unlike the major monotheistic religions, with their "once and for all" revelations from God through the Christian Bible or the Muslim Quran, Bantu religious practice was predicated on the notion of "continuous revelation"—the possibility of constantly receiving new messages from the world beyond. Moreover, unlike Buddhism, Christianity, or Islam, Bantu religions were geographically confined, intended to explain, predict, and control local affairs, with no missionary impulse or inclination toward universality.

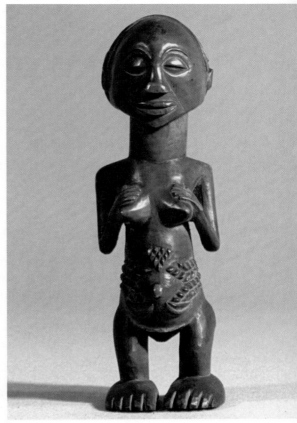

A Female Luba Ancestral Statue
Representations of powerful women, often ancestral figures, were frequent in the wood carvings of the Bantu-speaking Luba people of Central Africa. Many of them showed women touching their breasts, a gesture signifying devotion, respect, and the holding of secret knowledge. (© Photo SCALA, Florence)

Alternatives to Civilization: North America

The peoples of the Americas in the pre-Columbian era might be divided into three large groupings (see Map 12.5, p. 000). The most prominent and well known are those of the Mesoamerican and Andean regions, where cities, states, and dense populations created civilizations recognizably similar to those of Afro-Eurasia. Elsewhere, gathering and hunting peoples carried on the most ancient of human adaptations to the environment. Arctic and subarctic cultures, the bison hunters of the Great Plains, the complex and settled communities of the Pacific coast of North America, nomadic bands living in the arid regions of southern South America—all of these represent the persistence of gathering and hunting ways of living in substantial regions of the Americas.

Even larger areas — the eastern woodlands of the United States, Central America, the Amazon basin, the Caribbean islands — were populated by peoples sometimes defined as "semi-sedentary."[22] These were agricultural societies, although less intensive and productive than those of Mesoamerica or the Andes and supporting usually much smaller populations. Nor did they generate large urban centers or inclusive empires (Map 6.4).

These peoples who lived beyond the direct reach of the major civilizations also made their own histories, changing in response to their unique environments, their interactions with outsiders, and their own visions of the world. The Anasazi of the southwestern United States, now called the Ancestral Pueblo, and the mound-building cultures of the eastern woodlands provide two illustrations from North America.

The Ancestral Pueblo: Pit Houses and Great Houses

■ **Comparison**

In what ways were the histories of the Ancestral Pueblo and the Mound Builders similar to each other, and how did they differ?

The southwestern region of North America, an arid land cut by mountain ranges and large basins, first acquired maize from its place of origin in Mesoamerica during the second millennium B.C.E., but it took roughly 2,000 years for that crop, later supplemented by beans and squash, to become the basis of a settled agricultural way of living. In a desert region, farming was risky, and maize had to be gradually adapted to the local environment. Not until around 600 to 800 C.E. did permanent village life take hold widely. People then lived in pit houses with floors sunk several feet below ground level. Some settlements had only a few such homes, whereas others contained twenty-five or more. By 900 C.E., many of these villages also included kivas, much larger pit structures used for ceremonial purposes, which symbolized the widespread belief that humankind emerged into this world from another world below. Individual settlements were linked to one another in local trading networks and sometimes in wider webs of exchange that brought them buffalo hides, copper, turquoise, seashells, macaw feathers, and coiled baskets from quite distant locations.

These processes of change — growing dependence on agriculture, increasing population, more intensive patterns of exchange — gave rise to larger settlements and adjacent aboveground structures known as pueblos. The most spectacular of these took shape in Chaco canyon in what is now northwestern New Mexico. There, between 860 and 1130 C.E., five major pueblos emerged. This Chaco Phenomenon encompassed 25,000 square miles and linked some seventy outlying settlements to

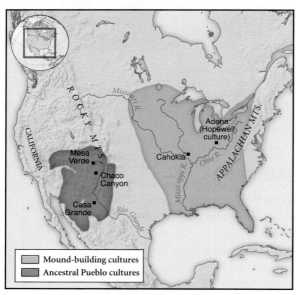

Map 6.4   North America in the Second-Wave Era
A sparsely populated North America hosted a number of semi-sedentary agricultural societies as well as various gathering and hunting peoples rather than the "civilizations" characteristic of Mesoamerica and the Andes.

Pueblo Bonito
Called Pueblo Bonito ("pretty village") by the Spanish, this great house of the Ancestral Pueblo people was at its high point in the eleventh century C.E. The circular structures, known as kivas, were probably ceremonial sites. Their prominence, and the absence of major trash collections, have persuaded some scholars that Pueblo Bonito was more of a ritual center than a residential town. (Courtesy, Chaco Canyon National Historic Park)

the main centers. The population was not large, perhaps as few as 5,000 people, although experts continue to debate the issue. The largest of these towns, or "great houses," Pueblo Bonito, stood five stories high and contained more than 600 rooms and many kivas. Hundreds of miles of roads, up to forty feet wide, radiated out from Chaco, likewise prompting much debate among scholars. Without wheeled carts or large domesticated animals, such an elaborate road system seems unnecessary for ordinary trade or travel. Did the roads represent, as some scholars speculate, a "sacred landscape which gave order to the world," joining its outlying communities to a "Middle Place," an entrance perhaps to the underworld?[23]

Among the Chaco elite were highly skilled astronomers who constructed an observatory of three large rock slabs situated so as to throw a beam of light across a spiral rock carving behind it at the summer solstice. By the eleventh century, Chaco also had become a dominant center for the production of turquoise ornaments, which became a major item of regional commerce, extending as far south as Mesoamerica. Not all was sweetness and light, however. Warfare, internal conflict, and occasional cannibalism (a matter of much controversy among scholars) apparently increased in frequency as an extended period of drought in the half century following 1130 brought this flourishing culture to a rather abrupt end. By 1200, the great houses had been abandoned and their inhabitants scattered in small communities that later became the Pueblo peoples of more recent times.

Peoples of the Eastern Woodlands: The Mound Builders

Unlike the Chaco region in the southwest, the eastern woodlands of North America and especially the Mississippi River valley hosted an independent Agricultural Revolution. By 2000 B.C.E., many of its peoples had domesticated local plant species, including sunflowers, sumpweed, goosefoot, some gourds and squashes, and a form of artichoke. These few plants, however, were not sufficient to support a fully settled agricultural village life; rather they supplemented diets derived from gathering and hunting without fundamentally changing that ancient way of life. Such peoples created societies distinguished by arrays of large earthen mounds, found all over the United States east of the Mississippi, prompting archeologists to dub them the Mound Builders.[24] The earliest of them date to around 2000 B.C.E., but the most elaborate and widespread took shape between 200 B.C.E. and 400 C.E., commonly called the Hopewell culture, after an archeological site in Ohio.

Several features of the Hopewell culture have intrigued archeologists. Particularly significant are the striking burial mounds and geometric earthworks, sometimes covering areas equivalent to several city blocks, and the wide variety of artifacts found within them — smoking pipes, human figurines, mica mirrors, flint blades, fabrics, and jewelry of all kinds. The mounds themselves were no doubt the focus of elaborate burial rituals, but some of them were aligned with the moon with such precision as to allow the prediction of lunar eclipses. Developed most elaborately in the Ohio River valley, Hopewell-style earthworks, artifacts, and ceremonial pottery have also been found throughout the eastern woodlands region of North America. Hopewell centers in Ohio contained mica from the Appalachian Mountains, volcanic glass from Yellowstone, conch shells and sharks' teeth from the Gulf of Mexico, and copper from the Great Lakes. All of this suggests a large "Hopewell Interaction Sphere," linking this entire region in a loose network of exchange, as well as a measure of cultural borrowing of religious ideas and practices.[25]

The next and most spectacular phase in the history of these mound-building peoples took shape as corn-based agriculture, derived ultimately but indirectly from Mexico, gained ground in the Mississippi valley after 800 C.E., allowing larger populations and more complex societies to emerge. The dominant center was Cahokia, near present-day St. Louis, Missouri, which flourished from about 900 to 1250 C.E. Its central mound, a terraced pyramid of four levels, measured 1,000 feet long by 700 feet wide, rose more than 100 feet above the ground, and occupied fifteen acres. It was the largest structure north of Mexico, the focal point of a community numbering 10,000 or more people, and the center of a widespread trading network (see an artist's reconstruction of Cahokia on p. 43).

Cahokia emerged and flourished at about the same time as did the great houses of Chaco canyon, but its settlements were far larger than those of its southwestern counterpart. Both were made possible by the arrival of corn-based agriculture, originating in Mesoamerica, though direct contact with Mexico is much more apparent in Chaco. Finally, Cahokia emerged as the climax of a long history of mound-building cultures in the eastern woodlands, whereas Chaco was more of a "start-up" culture, developing quite quickly "with a relatively shallow history."[26]

Evidence from burials and from later Spanish observers suggests that Cahokia and other centers of this Mississippi culture were stratified societies with a clear elite and with rulers able to mobilize the labor required to build such enormous structures. One high-status male was buried on a platform of 20,000 shell beads, accompanied by 800 arrowheads, sheets of copper and mica, and a number of sacrificed men and women nearby.[27] Well after Cahokia had declined and was abandoned, sixteenth-century Spanish and French explorers encountered another such chiefdom among the Natchez people, located in southwestern Mississippi. Paramount chiefs, known as Great Suns, dressed in knee-length fur coats and lived luxuriously in deerskin-covered homes. An elite class of "principal men" or "honored peoples" clearly occupied a different status from commoners, sometimes referred to as "stinkards." These sharp class distinctions were blunted by the requirement that upper-class people, including the Great Suns, had to marry "stinkards."

The military capacity of these Mississippi chiefdoms greatly impressed European observers, as this Spanish account indicates:

> The next day the cacique [paramount chief] arrived with 200 canoes filled with men, having weapons . . . the warriors standing erect from bow to stern, holding bows and arrows. . . . [F]rom under the canopy where the chief man was, the course was directed and orders issued to the rest. . . . [W]hat with the awnings, the plumes, the shields, the pennons, and the number of people in the fleet, it appeared like a famous armada of galleys.[28]

Here then in the eastern woodlands of North America were peoples who independently generated a modest Agricultural Revolution, assimilated corn and beans from distant sources, developed increasingly complex societies, and created monumental structures, new technologies, and artistic traditions. In doing so, they gave rise to a regional cultural complex that enveloped much of the United States east of the Mississippi in a network of ceremonial, economic, and cultural exchange. But given the presence of two unrelated language families, Algonquin and Iroquoian, the peoples of the eastern woodlands lacked the kind of linguistic commonality that provided the Bantu region of Africa with a measure of cultural unity.

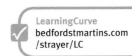

LearningCurve
bedfordstmartins.com
/strayer/LC

Reflections: Deciding What's Important: Balance in World History

Among the perennial problems that teachers and writers of world history confront is sorting through the vast record of times past and choosing what to include and what to leave out. A related issue involves the extent to which particular peoples or civilizations will be treated. Should the Persians get as much space as the Greeks? Does Africa merit equal treatment with Eurasia? Where do the Americas fit in the larger human story? What, in short, are the criteria for deciding what is important in recalling the history of the human venture?

One standard might be duration. Should ways of living that have endured for longer periods of time receive greater attention than those of lesser length? If historians followed only this criterion, then the Paleolithic era of gathering and hunting should occupy 90 percent or more of any world history text. On the other hand, perhaps change is more important than continuity. If so, then something new merits more space than something old. Thus we pay attention to both agriculture and civilizations because they represent significant turning points in human experience. Population provides yet another principle for determining inclusion. That, of course, is the reason that Eurasia/North Africa, with over 80 percent of the world's population, is addressed in three chapters of this section, whereas inner Africa and the Americas together receive just one chapter. There is also the related issue of influence. Buddhism, Christianity, and Islam spread more widely and shaped the lives of more people than did the religions of the Maya or the Bantu-speaking peoples of Africa. Do they therefore deserve more extended treatment? Still another factor involves the availability of evidence. In this respect, Eurasia generated far more written records than either Africa or the Americas did, and therefore its history has been investigated far more thoroughly.

A final possible criterion involves the location of the historian and his or her audience. The recent development of world history as a field of study has sought vigorously to counteract a Eurocentric telling of the human story. Still, is there anything inherently wrong with an account of world history that is centered on one's own people? When I taught history in an Ethiopian high school in the mid-1960s, I was guided by an Afrocentric curriculum, which focused first on Ethiopian history, then on Africa as a whole, and finally on the larger world. Might a world historian from the Middle East, for example, legitimately strike a somewhat different balance in the treatment of various civilizations than someone writing for a largely Western audience or for Chinese readers?

Any account of the world's past will mix and match these criteria in various and contested ways. Among historians, there exists neither a consensus about this question nor any formula to ensure a "proper" balance. You may want to consider whether the balance struck in this chapter, this section, and the book as a whole is appropriate or somehow out of line.

Second Thoughts

What's the Significance?

Meroë, 183–85

Axum, 185–87

Piye, 186–87

Niger Valley civilization, 188–90

Maya civilization, 191–93

Teotihuacán, 193–95

Chavín, 196–97
Moche, 197–99
Wari and Tiwanaku, 199–200

Bantu expansion, 200–05
Chaco Phenomenon, 204–06
Mound Builders/Cahokia, 206–07

Online Study Guide
bedfordstmartins.com/strayer

Big Picture Questions

1. "The particular cultures and societies of Africa and of the Americas discussed in this chapter developed largely in isolation." What evidence would support this statement, and what might challenge it?
2. How do you understand areas of the world, such as Bantu Africa and North America, that did not generate "civilizations"? Do you see them as "backward," as moving slowly toward civilization, or as simply different?
3. How did African proximity to Eurasia shape its history? And how did American separation from the Eastern Hemisphere affect its development?
4. **Looking Back:** "The histories of Africa and the Americas during the second-wave era largely resemble those of Eurasia." Do you agree with this statement? Explain why or why not.

Next Steps: For Further Study

For Web sites and additional documents related to this chapter, see **Make History** at bedfordstmartins.com/strayer.

Richard E. W. Adams, *Ancient Civilizations of the New World* (1997). A broad survey based on current scholarship of the Americas before Columbus.

Christopher Ehret, *The Civilizations of Africa* (2002). A recent overview of African history before 1800 by a prominent scholar.

Brian M. Fagan, *Ancient North America* (2005). A prominent archeologist's account of North American history.

Eric Gilbert and Jonathan T. Reynolds, *Africa in World History* (2004). An accessible account of African history set in a global context.

Guy Gugliotta, "The Maya: Glory and Ruin," *National Geographic* (August 2007). A beautifully illustrated account of the rise and fall of Maya civilization.

Charles Mann, *1491* (2005). A journalist's thoughtful account, delightfully written, of the controversies surrounding the history of the Americas before 1492.

Ancient Africa's Black Kingdoms, http://www.homestead.com/wysinger/ancientafrica.html. A Web site exploring the history of Nubia.

Maya Adventure, http://www.smm.org/sln/ma. A collection of text and pictures about the Maya, past and present.

PART THREE

An Age of Accelerating Connections

500–1500

Contents

Chapter 7. Commerce and Culture, 500–1500

Chapter 8. China and the World: East Asian Connections, 500–1300

Chapter 9. The Worlds of Islam: Afro-Eurasian Connections, 600–1500

Chapter 10. The Worlds of Christendom: Contraction, Expansion, and Division, 500–1300

Chapter 11. Pastoral Peoples on the Global Stage: The Mongol Moment, 1200–1500

Chapter 12. The Worlds of the Fifteenth Century

Defining a Millennium

History seldom turns sharp corners, and historians often have difficulty deciding just when one phase of the human story ends and another begins. Between roughly 200 and 850 C.E., many of the second-wave states and civilizations (Han dynasty China, the Roman Empire, Gupta India, Meroë, Axum, Maya, Teotihuacán, Moche) experienced severe disruption, decline, or collapse. For many historians, this has marked the end of an era and the start of a new period of world history. Furthermore, almost everyone agrees that the transatlantic voyages of Columbus beginning in 1492 represent yet another new departure in world history. This coupling of the Eastern and Western hemispheres set in motion historical processes that transformed most of the world and signaled the beginning of the modern era.

But how are we to understand the thousand years (roughly 500 to 1500) between the end of the second-wave era and the beginning of modern world history? Historians, frankly, have had some difficulty defining a distinct identity for this millennium, a problem reflected in the vague terms used to describe it: a postclassical era, a medieval or "middle" period between the ancient and modern, or, as in this book, an age of third-wave civilizations. At best, these terms indicate where this period falls in the larger time frame of world history, but none of them are very descriptive.

Third-Wave Civilizations: Something New, Something Old, Something Blended

A large part of the problem lies in the rather different trajectories of various regions of the world during this millennium. It is not easy to identify clearly defined features that encompass all major civilizations or human communities during this period and distinguish them from what went before. We can, however, point to several distinct patterns during this third-wave era.

In some areas, for example, wholly new but smaller civilizations arose where none had existed before. Along the East African coast, Swahili civilization emerged in a string of thirty or more city-states, very much engaged in the commercial life of the Indian Ocean basin. The kingdoms of Ghana, Mali, and Songhay, stimulated and sustained by long-distance trade across the Sahara, represented a new West African civilization. In the area now encompassed by Ukraine and western Russia, another new civilization, known as Kievan Rus, likewise took shape with a good deal of cultural borrowing from Mediterranean civilization. East and Southeast Asia also witnessed new centers of civilization. Those in Japan, Korea, and Vietnam were strongly influenced by China, while Srivijaya on the Indonesian island of Sumatra and later the Angkor kingdom, centered in present-day Cambodia, drew on the Hindu and Buddhist traditions of India.

All of these represent a continuation of a well-established pattern in world history — the globalization of civilization. Each of the new third-wave civilizations was, of course, culturally unique, but like their predecessors of the first and second waves, they too featured states, cities, specialized economic roles, sharp class and gender inequalities, and other elements of "civilized" life. As newcomers to the growing number of civilizations, all of them borrowed heavily from larger or more established centers.

The largest, most expansive, and most widely influential of the new third-wave civilizations was surely that of Islam. It began in Arabia in the seventh century C.E., projecting the Arab peoples into a prominent role as builders of an enormous empire while offering a new, vigorous, and attractive religion. Viewed as a new civilization defined by its religion, the world of Islam came to encompass many other centers of civilization — Egypt, Mesopotamia, Persia, India, the interior of West Africa and the coast of East Africa, Spain, southeastern Europe, and more. Here was a uniquely cosmopolitan or "umbrella" civilization that "came closer than any had ever come to uniting all mankind under its ideals."[1]

Yet another, and quite different, historical pattern during the third-wave millennium involved those older civilizations that persisted or were reconstructed. The Byzantine Empire, embracing the eastern half of the old Roman Empire, continued the patterns of Mediterranean Christian civilization and persisted until 1453, when it was overrun by the Ottoman Turks. In China, following almost four centuries of fragmentation, the Sui, Tang, and Song dynasties (589–1279) restored China's imperial unity and reasserted its Confucian tradition. Indian civilization retained its ancient patterns of caste and Hinduism amid vast cultural diversity, even as parts of India fell under the control of Muslim rulers.

Variations on this theme of continuing or renewing older traditions took shape in the Western Hemisphere, where two centers of civilization — in Mesoamerica and in the Andes — had been long established. In Mesoamerica, the collapse of classical Maya civilization and of the great city-state of Teotihuacán by about 900 C.E. opened the way for other peoples to give new shape to this ancient civilization. The most well-known of these efforts was associated with the Mexica or Aztec people, who created a powerful and impressive state in the fifteenth century. About the same time, on the western rim of South America, a Quechua-speaking people, now known as the Inca, incorporated various centers of Andean civilization into a huge bureaucratic empire. Both the Aztecs and the Incas gave a new political expression to much older patterns of civilized life.

Yet another pattern took shape in Western Europe following the collapse of the Roman Empire. There would-be kings and church leaders alike sought to maintain links with the older Greco-Roman-Christian traditions of classical Mediterranean civilization. In the absence of empire, however, new and far more decentralized societies emerged, led now by Germanic peoples and centered in Northern and West-

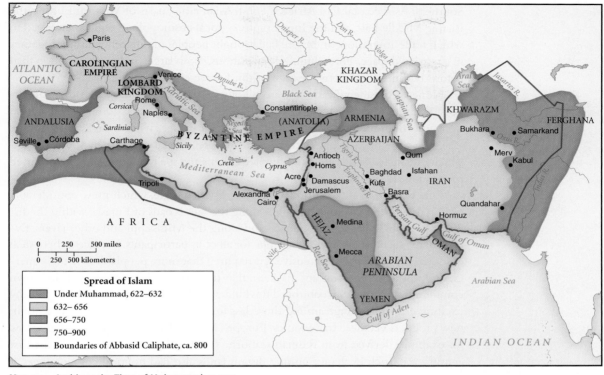

Map 9.1 Arabia at the Time of Muhammad, p. 294

ern Europe, considerably removed from the older centers of Rome and Athens. It was a hybrid civilization, combining old and new, Greco-Roman and Germanic elements, in a distinctive blending. For five centuries or more, this region was a relative back-water, compared to the more vibrant, prosperous, and powerful civilizations of Byzantium, the Islamic world, and China. During the centuries after 1000 C.E., however, Western European civilization emerged as a rapidly growing and expansive set of competitive states, willing, like other new civilizations, to borrow extensively from their more developed neighbors.

The Ties That Bind: Transregional Interaction in the Third-Wave Era

These quite different patterns of development within particular civilizations have made it difficult to define the Third Wave era in a single, all-encompassing fashion. In another way, though, a common theme emerges, for during this time, the world's various regions, cultures, and peoples interacted with one another far more extensively. More than before, change in human societies was the product of contact with strangers, or at least with their ideas, armies, goods, or diseases. In a variety of places — island

Southeast Asia, coastal East Africa, Central Asian cities, parts of Western Europe, the Islamic Middle East, and the Inca Empire—local cosmopolitan regions emerged in which trade, migration, or empire had brought peoples of different cultures together in a restricted space. These "mini-globalizations," both larger and more common than before, became a distinctive feature of third-wave civilizations.

None of these civilizations were wholly isolated or separate from their neighbors, although the range and intensity of cross-cultural interaction certainly varied over time. In limited ways, that had been true for earlier civilizations as well. But the scale and pace of such interaction accelerated considerably between 500 and 1500. Much of Part Three highlights these intersections and spells out their many and varied consequences.

One pattern of interaction lay in long-distance trade, which grew considerably during the third-wave millennium—along the Silk Roads of Eurasia, within the Indian Ocean basin, across the Sahara, and along the Mississippi and other rivers. Everywhere it acted as an agent of change for all of its participants. In places where such commerce was practiced extensively, it required that more people devote their energies to producing for a distant market rather than for the consumption of their own communities. Those who controlled this kind of trade often became extremely wealthy, exciting envy or outrage among those less fortunate. Many societies learned about new products via these trade routes. Europe's knowledge of pepper and other spices, for example, derived from Roman seaborne trade with India beginning in the first century C.E. Such exchange among distant lands also had political consequences as many new states or empires were constructed on the basis of resources derived from long-distance commerce. Furthermore, religious ideas, technologies, and diseases also made their ways along those paths of commerce, disrupting older ways of living and offering new opportunities as well.

Yet another mechanism of cross-cultural interaction lay in large empires. Not only did they incorporate many distinct cultures within a single political system, but their size and stability also provided the security that encouraged travelers and traders to journey long distances from their homelands. Empires, of course, were nothing new in world history, but many of those associated with third-wave civilizations were distinctive. In the first place, they were larger. The Arab Empire, which accompanied the initial spread of Islam, stretched from Spain to India. Even more extensive was the Mongol Empire of the thirteenth and fourteenth centuries. In the Western Hemisphere, the Inca Empire encompassed dozens of distinct peoples in a huge state that ran some 2,500 miles along the spine of the Andes Mountains.

Furthermore, the largest of these empires were the creation of nomadic or pastoral peoples. Earlier empires in the Mediterranean basin, China, India, and Persia had been the work of settled farming societies. But now, in the thousand years between 500 and 1500, peoples with a recent history of a nomadic or herding way of life entered the stage of world history as empire builders—Arabs, Berbers, Turks, Mongols, Aztecs— ruling over agricultural peoples and established civilizations.

Together, large-scale empires and long-distance trade facilitated the spread of ideas, technologies, food crops, and germs far beyond their points of origin. Buddhism spread from India to much of Asia; Christianity encompassed Europe and took root in distant Russia, even as it contracted in the Middle East and North Africa. Hinduism attracted followers in Southeast Asia; and more than any other religion, Islam became an Afro-Eurasian phenomenon with an enormous reach. Beyond the connections born of commerce and conquest, those of culture and religion generated lasting ties among many peoples of the Eastern Hemisphere.

Technologies, too, were diffused widely. Until the sixth century C.E., China maintained a monopoly on the manufacture of raw silk. Then this technology spread beyond East Asia, allowing the development of a silk industry in the eastern Mediterranean and later in Italy. India too contributed much to the larger world — crystallized sugar, a system of numerals and the concept of zero, techniques for making cotton textiles, and many food crops. In the Americas, corn gradually diffused from Mesoamerica, where it was initially domesticated, to North America, where it stimulated population growth and the development of more complex societies. Disease also linked distant communities. The plague, or Black Death, decimated many parts of Eurasia and North Africa as it made its deadly way from east to west in the fourteenth century.

A focus on these accelerating connections across cultural boundaries puts the historical spotlight on merchants, travelers, missionaries, migrants, soldiers, and administrators — people who traveled abroad rather than those who stayed at home. This cross-cultural emphasis in world history raises provocative questions about what happens when cultures interact or when strangers meet. How did external stimuli operate to produce change within particular societies? How did individuals or societies decide what to accept and what to reject when confronted with new ideas or practices? In what ways did they alter foreign customs or traditions to better meet their own needs and correspond to their own values?

Much of the readily visible "action" in third-wave civilizations, as in all earlier civilizations, featured male actors. The vast majority of rulers, traders, soldiers, religious officials, and long-distance travelers were men, as were most heads of households and families. The building of states and empires, so prominent in the third-wave era, meant war and conquest, fostering distinctly masculine warrior values and reinforcing the dominant position of men. Much of what follows in Part Three is, frankly, men's history.

But it is useful to remember that behind all of this lay a vast realm of women's activity, long invisible to historians or simply assumed. Women sustained the family life that was the foundation of all human community; they were the repositories of language, religious ritual, group knowledge, and local history; their labor generated many of the products that entered long-distance trade routes as well those that fed and clothed their communities. The changing roles and relationships of men and women and their understandings of gender also figure in the chapters that follow.

Mapping Part Three

Complex gathering and hunting cultures
Chapter 12

Iroquois Confederacy
Chapters 7, 12

Ancestral Pueblo
Chapter 7

Eastern woodlands
Chapters 7, 12

Aztec Empire
Chapters 7, 12

Amazon River trade
Chapter 12

Maya cities
Chapter 7

Inca Empire
Chapters 7, 12

Byzantine /
Ottoman Empire
Chapter 10

Kievan Russia
Chapter 10

Mongol homeland
Chapter 11

Korean civilization
Chapter 8

Western civilization /
Renaissance
Chapters 10, 12

Silk Roads
Chapter 7

Crusades
Chapter 10

Delhi Sultanate
Chapters 9, 12

Japanese civilization
Chapter 8

Song / Tang Dynasties
Chapter 8

Muhammad / Islam
Chapters 9, 10

Vietnamese civilization
Chapter 8

Trans-Saharan trade
Chapters 7, 9

Swahili civilization
Chapter 7

Songhay Empire
Chapter 12

Great Zimbabwe
Chapter 7

Mali
Chapter 9

Igbo
Chapter 12

Srivijaya
Chapter 7

CHAPTER SEVEN

Commerce and Culture

500–1500

Silk Roads: Exchange across Eurasia
  The Growth of the Silk Roads
  Goods in Transit
  Cultures in Transit
  Disease in Transit
Sea Roads: Exchange across the
  Indian Ocean
  Weaving the Web of an Indian
    Ocean World
  Sea Roads as a Catalyst for Change:
    Southeast Asia
  Sea Roads as a Catalyst for Change:
    East Africa
Sand Roads: Exchange across the
  Sahara
  Commercial Beginnings in West
    Africa
  Gold, Salt, and Slaves: Trade and
    Empire in West Africa
An American Network: Commerce
  and Connection in the Western
  Hemisphere
Reflections: Economic
  Globalization — Ancient and
  Modern

"In the spring of 2004 I was looking for an appropriate college graduation present for my son Ateesh and decided on an Apple iPod music player. . . . I placed my order online. . . . I was astonished by what followed. I received a confirmation e-mail within minutes . . . [and learned that] the product was being shipped not from California but from Shanghai, China. . . . Ateesh's personalized iPod landed on our New Haven [Connecticut] doorstep barely 40 hours after I had clicked "Buy."[1] To Nayan Chanda, a fifty-eight-year-old journalist, born and educated in India and at the time working at Yale University, this was an astonishing transaction. Probably it was less surprising to his son. But both of them, no doubt, understood this kind of commercial exchange as something quite recent in human history.

And in the speed of the transaction, it surely was. But from the perspective of world history, exchange among distant peoples is not altogether new and the roots of economic globalization lie deep in the past. In fact, just three years after purchasing his son's iPod, Nayan Chanda wrote a well-received book titled *Bound Together*, describing how traders, preachers, adventurers, and warriors had long created links among peoples living in widely separated cultures and civilizations. Those early transregional interactions and their capacity for transforming human societies, for better and for worse, played an increasingly significant role in this era of third-wave civilizations, a millennium of accelerating connections.

THE EXCHANGE OF GOODS AMONG COMMUNITIES occupying different ecological zones has long been a prominent feature of human history.

Travels on the Silk Road: This Chinese ceramic figurine from the Tang dynasty (618–907 C.E.) shows a group of musicians riding on a camel along the famous Silk Road commercial network that long linked the civilizations of western and eastern Eurasia. The bearded figures represent Central Asian merchants, while the others depict Chinese. (©Asian Art & Archaeology, Inc./Corbis)

Coastlands and highlands, steppes and farmlands, islands and mainlands, valleys and mountains, deserts and forests—each generates different products. Furthermore, some societies have been able to monopolize, at least temporarily, the production of particular products—such as silk in China, certain spices in Southeast Asia, and incense in southern Arabia—which others have found valuable. This uneven distribution of goods and resources, whether natural or resulting from human activity, has long motivated exchange, not only within particular civilizations or regions but among them as well. In the world of 500–1500, long-distance trade became more important than ever before in linking and shaping distant societies and peoples. For the most part, it was indirect, a chain of separate transactions in which goods traveled farther than individual merchants. Nonetheless, a network of exchange and communication extending all across the Afro-Eurasian world, and separately in parts of the Americas as well, slowly came into being.

Why was trade important? How did it generate change within the societies that it connected? Economically speaking, commerce often altered consumption and shaped daily life. West Africans, for example, imported scarce salt, necessary for human diets and useful for seasoning and preserving food, from distant mines in the Sahara in exchange for the gold of their region. Over several millennia, incense such as frankincense and myrrh, grown in southern Arabia and the adjacent region of northern Somalia, found eager consumers in ancient Egypt and Babylon, India and China, Greece and Rome. Used for medicinal purposes, religious ceremonies, and as an antidote to the odors of unsanitary cities, incense also bore the "aroma of eros." "I have perfumed my bed with myrrh, aloes, and cinnamon," declared a harlot featured in the Old Testament Book of Proverbs. "Come, let us take our fill of love till morning."[2] Trade also affected the working lives of many people, encouraging them to specialize in producing particular products for sale in distant markets rather than for use in their own communities. Trade, in short, diminished the economic self-sufficiency of local societies, even as it altered the structure of those societies as well. Merchants often became a distinct social group, viewed with suspicion by others because of their impulse to accumulate wealth without actually producing anything themselves. In some societies, trade became a means of social mobility, as Chinese merchants, for example, were able to purchase landed estates and establish themselves within the gentry class. Long-distance trade also enabled elite groups in society to distinguish themselves from commoners by acquiring prestigious goods from a distance—silk, tortoiseshell, jade, rhinoceros horn, or particular feathers. The association with faraway or powerful societies, signaled by the possession of their luxury goods, often conveyed status in communities more remote from major civilizations.

Trade also had the capacity to transform political life. The wealth available from controlling and taxing trade motivated the creation of states in various parts of the world and sustained those states once they had been constructed. Furthermore, commerce posed a set of problems to governments everywhere. Should trade be left in private hands, as in the Aztec Empire, or should it be controlled by the state, as in the

A Map of Time

3rd millennium B.C.E.	Beginnings of silk industry in China
200 B.C.E.–200 C.E.	Initial flourishing of Silk Road commerce
By 1st century B.C.E.	Spread of Buddhism to Central Asian cities and northern China
430 B.C.E.	Trade-borne disease enters Greece from Egypt
Early centuries C.E.	Knowledge of monsoons enables expansion of Indian Ocean commerce
300–400 C.E.	Beginning of trans-Saharan trade
350	All-water route opened between India and China
6th century	Chinese monopoly on silk production broken
7th century	Rise of Islam
670–1025	Srivijaya kingdom
800–1300	Khmer kingdom of Angkor
1000–1500	Swahili civilization along East African coast
13th and 14th centuries	Mongol Empire revitalizes Silk Road commerce
1250–1350	Kingdom of Zimbabwe in southeastern Africa
1275–1292	Marco Polo in China
1346–1350	Black Death enters Europe via transcontinental trade routes
1354	Ibn Battuta visits West Africa
15th century	Aztec and Inca empires facilitate commercial exchange in the Americas

Inca Empire? How should state authorities deal with men of commerce, who were both economically useful and potentially disruptive?

Moreover, the saddlebags of camel caravans or the cargo holds of merchant vessels carried more than goods. Trade became the vehicle for the spread of religious ideas, technological innovations, disease-bearing germs, and plants and animals to regions far from their places of origin. In just this fashion, Buddhism made its way from India to Central and East Asia, and Islam crossed the Sahara into West Africa. So did the pathogens that devastated much of Eurasia during the Black Death. These immense cultural and biological transformations were among the most significant outcomes of the increasingly dense network of long-distance commerce during the era of third-wave civilizations.

SEEKING THE MAIN POINT

In what ways did long-distance commerce act as a motor of change in premodern world history?

Silk Roads: Exchange across Eurasia

The Eurasian landmass has long been home to the majority of humankind as well as to the world's most productive agriculture, largest civilizations, and greatest concentration of pastoral peoples. Beyond its many separate societies and cultures, Eurasia also gave rise to one of the world's most extensive and sustained networks of exchange among its diverse peoples. Known as the Silk Roads, a reference to their most famous product, these land-based trade routes linked pastoral and agricultural peoples as well as the large civilizations on the continent's outer rim (see Map 7.1). None of its numerous participants knew the full extent of this network's reach, for it was largely a "relay trade" in which goods were passed down the line, changing hands many times before reaching their final destination. Nonetheless, the Silk Roads provide a certain unity and coherence to Eurasian history alongside the distinct stories of its separate civilizations and peoples.

The Growth of the Silk Roads

■ **Change**

What lay behind the emergence of Silk Road commerce, and what kept it going for so many centuries?

The beginnings of the Silk Roads lay in both geography and history. As a geographic unit, Eurasia is often divided into inner and outer zones that represent quite different environments. Outer Eurasia consists of relatively warm, well-watered areas, suitable for agriculture, which provided the setting for the great civilizations of China, India, the Middle East, and the Mediterranean. Inner Eurasia—the lands of eastern Russia and Central Asia—lies farther north and has a harsher and drier climate, much of it not conducive to agriculture. Herding their animals from horseback, the pastoral people of this region had for centuries traded with and raided their agricultural neighbors to the south. Products of the forest and of semi-arid northern grasslands known as the steppes—such as hides, furs, livestock, wool, and amber—were exchanged for the agricultural products and manufactured goods of adjacent civilizations. The movement of pastoral peoples for thousands of years also served to diffuse Indo-European languages, bronze metallurgy, horse-based technologies, and more all across Eurasia.

The construction of the second-wave civilizations and their imperial states during the last five centuries B.C.E. added another element to these earlier Eurasian connections. From the south, the Persian Empire invaded the territory of pastoral peoples in present-day Turkmenistan and Uzbekistan. From the west, Alexander the Great's empire stretched well into Central Asia. From the east, China's Han dynasty extended its authority westward, seeking to control the nomadic Xiongnu and to gain access to the powerful "heavenly horses" that were so important to Chinese military forces. By the early centuries of the Common Era, indirect trading connections, often brokered by pastoral peoples, linked these Eurasian civilizations in a network of transcontinental exchange.

Silk Road trading networks prospered most when large and powerful states provided security for merchants and travelers. Such conditions prevailed during the second-wave era when the Roman and Chinese empires anchored long-distance

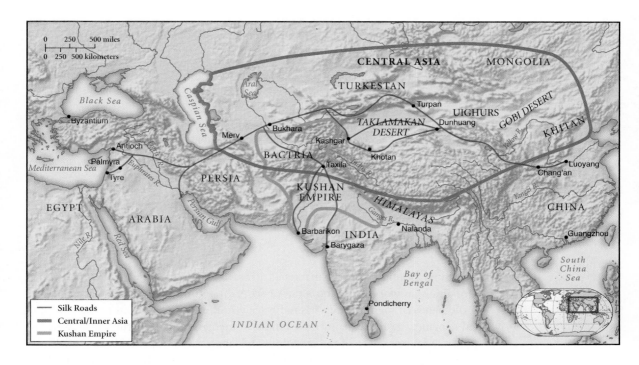

Map 7.1 The Silk Roads
For 2,000 years, goods, ideas, technologies, and diseases made their way across Eurasia on the several routes of the Silk Roads.

commerce at the western and eastern ends of Eurasia. Silk Road trade flourished again during the seventh and eighth centuries C.E. as the Byzantine Empire, the Muslim Abbasid (ah-BAH-sihd) dynasty, and Tang dynasty China created an almost continuous belt of strong states across Eurasia. In the thirteenth and fourteenth centuries, the Mongol Empire briefly encompassed almost the entire route of the Silk Roads in a single state, giving a renewed vitality to long-distance trade. Over many centuries, various technological innovations, such as yokes, saddles, and stirrups, made the use of camels, horses, and oxen more effective means of transportation across the vast distances of the Silk Roads.

Goods in Transit

During prosperous times especially, a vast array of goods (detailed in the Snapshot on p. 224) made its way across the Silk Roads, often carried in large camel caravans that traversed the harsh and dangerous steppes, deserts, and oases of Central Asia. In high demand and hard to find, most of these goods were luxury products, destined for an elite and wealthy market, rather than staple goods, for only readily moved commodities of great value could compensate for the high costs of transportation across such long and forbidding distances.

Of all these luxury goods, it was silk that came to symbolize this Eurasian network of exchange. From its origin in China during the fourth millennium B.C.E., that civilization long held a monopoly on silk production, even as that precious fabric

$Snapshot$ **Economic Exchange along the Silk Roads**

Region	Products Contributed to Silk Road Commerce
China	silk, bamboo, mirrors, gunpowder, paper, rhubarb, ginger, lacquerware, chrysanthemums
Forest lands of Siberia and grasslands of Central Asia	furs, walrus tusks, amber, livestock, horses, falcons, hides, copper vessels, tents, saddles, slaves
India	cotton textiles, herbal medicine, precious stones, spices
Middle East	dates, nuts, almonds, dried fruit, dyes, lapis lazuli, swords
Mediterranean basin	gold coins, glassware, glazes, grapevines, jewelry, artworks, perfume, wool and linen textiles, olive oil

increasingly found a growing market all across the linked commercial network of the Afro-Eurasian world after 300 B.C.E. or so. Although the silk trade itself was largely in the hands of men, women figured hugely in the process both in terms of supply and demand. For many centuries, Chinese women, mostly in the rural areas, were responsible for every step of the ingenious and laborious enterprise of silk production. They tended the mulberry trees on whose leaves silk worms fed; they unwound the cocoons in very hot water to extract the long silk fibers; they turned these fibers into thread and wove them into textiles. Thus Chinese homes became the primary site of textile production with rural women as its main labor force. By the time of the Tang dynasty (618–907 C.E.), women were making a large contribution to the household economy, to technological innovation in the silk industry, and to the state, which depended heavily on peasant taxes, often paid in cloth. Despite these contributions, many rural families persisted in poverty as the thirteenth-century writer Wen-hsiang indicated:

> The silkworms have finished their third sleep and are famished. The family is poor, without cash to buy the mulberry leaves to feed them. What can they do? Hungry silkworms do not produce silk. . . . The daughter is twenty but does not have wedding clothes. Those the government sends to collect taxes are like tigers. If they have no clothes to dress their daughter, they can put the [wedding] off. If they have no silk to turn over to the government, they will go bankrupt.[3]

■ **Significance**
What made silk such a highly desired commodity across Eurasia?

Elite Chinese women, and their men as well, also furnished part of the demand for these luxurious fabrics, which marked their high status. So too did Chinese officials, who required huge quantities of silk to exchange for much needed horses and to buy off "barbarian" invaders from the north. Beyond China, women in many cultures ardently sought Chinese silk for its comfort and its value as a fashion statement. The demand for silk, as well as for cotton textiles from India, was so great in the Roman Empire that various Roman writers were appalled at the drain of resources that it represented. They also were outraged at the moral impact of wearing revealing silk garments. "I can see clothes of silk," lamented Seneca the Younger in the first century C.E., "if materials that do not hide the body, nor even one's decency, can be called clothes. . . . Wretched flocks of maids labour so that the adulteress may be visible through her thin dress, so that her husband has no more acquaintance than any outsider or foreigner with his wife's body."[4]

By the sixth century C.E., the knowledge and technology for producing raw silk had spread beyond China. An old Chinese story attributes it to a Chinese princess who smuggled out silkworms in her turban when she was married off to a Central Asian ruler. In a European version of the tale, Christian monks living in China did the deed by hiding some silkworms in a bamboo cane, an act of industrial espionage that allowed an independent silk-producing and silk-weaving industry to take hold in the Byzantine Empire. However it happened, Koreans, Japanese, Indians, and Persians likewise learned how to produce this precious fabric.

As the supply of silk increased, its many varieties circulated even more extensively across Afro-Eurasian trade routes. In Central Asia, silk was used as currency and as a means of accumulating wealth. In both China and the Byzantine Empire, silk became a symbol of high status, and governments passed laws that restricted silk clothing to members of the elite. Furthermore, silk became associated with the sacred in the expanding world religions of Buddhism and Christianity. Chinese Buddhist pilgrims who made their way to India seeking religious texts and relics took with them large quantities of silk as gifts to the monasteries they visited. Buddhist monks in China received purple silk robes from Tang dynasty emperors as a sign of high honor. In the world of Christendom, silk wall hangings, altar covers, and vestments became highly prestigious signs of devotion and piety. Because no independent silk industry developed in Western Europe until the twelfth century C.E., a considerable market developed for silks imported from the Islamic world. Ironically, the splendor of Christian churches depended in part on Islamic trading networks and on silks manufactured in the Muslim world. Some of those silks were even inscribed with passages in Arabic from the Quran, unbeknownst to their European buyers.[5] By the twelfth century, the West African king of Ghana was wearing silk, and that fabric circulated in Egypt, Ethiopia, and along the East African coast as well.

Compared to contemporary global commerce, the volume of trade on the Silk Roads was modest, and its focus on luxury goods limited its direct impact on most people. Nonetheless, it had important economic and social consequences. Peasants in the Yangzi River delta of southern China sometimes gave up the cultivation of food crops, choosing to focus instead on producing silk, paper, porcelain, lacquer-ware, or iron tools, much of which was destined for the markets of the Silk Roads. In this way, the impact of long-distance trade trickled down to affect the lives of ordinary farmers. Furthermore, favorably placed individuals could benefit immensely from long-distance trade. The twelfth-century Persian merchant Ramisht made a personal fortune from his long-distance trading business and with his profits purchased an enormously expensive silk covering for the Kaaba, the central shrine of Islam in Mecca.[6]

■ **Connection**
What were the major economic, social, and cultural consequences of Silk Road commerce?

Cultures in Transit

■ Change

What accounted for the spread of Buddhism along the Silk Roads?

More important even than the economic impact of the Silk Roads was their role as a conduit of culture. Buddhism in particular, a cultural product of Indian civilization, spread widely throughout Central and East Asia, owing much to the activities of merchants along the Silk Roads. From its beginnings in India during the sixth century B.C.E., Buddhism had appealed to merchants, who preferred its universal message to that of a Brahmin-dominated Hinduism that privileged the higher castes. Indian traders and Buddhist monks, sometimes supported by rulers such as Ashoka, brought the new religion to the trans-Eurasian trade routes. To the west, Persian Zoroastrianism largely blocked the spread of Buddhism, but in the oasis cities of Central Asia, such as Merv, Samarkand, Khotan, and Dunhuang, Buddhism quickly took hold. By the first century B.C.E., many of the inhabitants of these towns had converted to Buddhism, and foreign merchant communities soon introduced it to northern China as well.[7]

Conversion to Buddhism in the oasis cities was a voluntary process, without the pressure of conquest or foreign rule. Dependent on long-distance trade, the inhabitants and rulers of those sophisticated and prosperous cities found in Buddhism a link to the larger, wealthy, and prestigious civilization of India. Well-to-do Buddhist merchants could earn religious merit by building monasteries and supporting monks. The monasteries in turn provided convenient and culturally familiar places of rest and resupply for merchants making the long and arduous trek across Central Asia. Many of these cities became cosmopolitan centers of learning and commerce. Scholars have found thousands of Buddhist texts in the city of Dunhuang, where several branches of the Silk Roads joined to enter western China, together with hundreds of cave temples, lavishly decorated with murals and statues.

Outside of the oasis communities, Buddhism progressed only slowly among pastoral peoples of Central Asia. The absence of a written language was an obstacle to the penetration of a highly literate religion, and their nomadic ways made the founding of monasteries, so important to Buddhism, quite difficult. But as pastoralists became involved in long-distance trade or came to rule settled agricultural peoples, Buddhism seemed more attractive. The nomadic Jie people, who controlled much of northern China after the collapse of the Han dynasty, are a case in point. Their ruler in the early fourth century C.E., Shi Le, became acquainted with a Buddhist monk called Fotudeng, who had traveled

Dunhuang

Located in western China at a critical junction of the Silk Roads trading network, Dunhuang was also a center of Buddhist learning, painting, and sculpture as that religion made its way from India to China and beyond. In some 492 caves, a remarkable gallery of Buddhist art has been preserved. These images of Buddhist deities and heavenly beings date from the sixth century C.E. (© Benoy K. Behl)

widely on the Silk Roads. The monk's reputation as a miracle worker, a rainmaker, and a fortune-teller and his skills as a military strategist cemented a personal relationship with Shi Le and led to the conversions of thousands and the construction of hundreds of Buddhist temples. In China itself, Buddhism remained for many centuries a religion of foreign merchants or foreign rulers. Only slowly did it become popular among the Chinese themselves, a process examined more closely in Chapter 8.

As Buddhism spread across the Silk Roads from India to Central Asia, China, and beyond, it also changed. The original faith had shunned the material world, but Buddhist monasteries in the rich oasis towns of the Silk Roads found themselves very much involved in secular affairs. Some of them became quite wealthy, receiving gifts from well-to-do merchants, artisans, and local rulers. The begging bowls of the monks became a symbol rather than a daily activity. Sculptures and murals in the monasteries depicted musicians and acrobats, women applying makeup, and even drinking parties.[8]

Doctrines changed as well. It was the more devotional Mahayana form of Buddhism (see Chapter 4) — featuring the Buddha as a deity, numerous bodhisattvas, an emphasis on compassion, and the possibility of earning merit — that flourished on the Silk Roads, rather than the more austere psychological teachings of the original Buddha. Moreover, Buddhism picked up elements of other cultures while in transit on the Silk Roads. In the area northwest of India that had been influenced by the invasions of Alexander the Great, statues of the Buddha reveal distinctly Greek influences. The Greco-Roman mythological figure of Herakles, the son of Zeus and associated with great strength, courage, masculinity, and sexual prowess, was used to represent Vajrapani, one of the divine protectors of the Buddha. In a similar way, the gods of many peoples along the Silk Roads were incorporated into Buddhist practice as bodhisattvas.

Disease in Transit

Beyond goods and cultures, diseases too traveled the trade routes of Eurasia, and with devastating consequences.[9] Each of the major population centers of the Afro-Eurasian world had developed characteristic disease patterns, mechanisms for dealing with them, and in some cases immunity to them. But when contact among human communities occurred, people were exposed to unfamiliar diseases for which they had little immunity or few effective methods of coping. An early example involved the Greek city-state of Athens, which in 430–429 B.C.E. was suddenly afflicted by a new and still unidentified infectious disease that had entered Greece via seaborne trade from Egypt, killing perhaps 25 percent of its army and permanently weakening the city-state.

Even more widespread diseases affected the Roman Empire and Han dynasty China as the Silk Roads promoted contact all across Eurasia. Smallpox and measles devastated the populations of both empires, contributing to their political collapse. Paradoxically, these disasters may well have strengthened the appeal of Christianity in Europe and Buddhism in China, for both of them offered compassion in the face of immense suffering.

■ **Connection**

What was the impact of disease along the Silk Roads?

Again in the period between 534 and 750 C.E., intermittent outbreaks of bubonic plague ravaged the coastal areas of the Mediterranean Sea as the black rats that carried the disease arrived via the seaborne trade with India, where they originally lived. What followed was catastrophic. Constantinople, the capital city of the Byzantine Empire, lost thousands of people per day during a forty-day period in 534 C.E., according to a contemporary historian. Disease played an important role in preventing Byzantium from reintegrating Italy into its version of a renewed Roman Empire encompassing the Mediterranean basin. The repeated recurrence of the disease over the next several centuries also weakened the ability of Christendom to resist Muslim armies from Arabia in the seventh century C.E.

The most well-known dissemination of disease was associated with the Mongol Empire, which briefly unified much of the Eurasian landmass during the thirteenth and fourteenth centuries C.E. (see Chapter 11). That era of intensified interaction facilitated the spread of the Black Death — identified variously with the bubonic plague, anthrax, or a package of epidemic diseases — from China to Europe. Its consequences were enormous. Between 1346 and 1348 up to half of the population of Europe perished from the plague. "A dead man," wrote the Italian writer Boccaccio, "was then of no more account than a dead goat."[10] Despite the terrible human toll, some among the living benefited. Tenant farmers and urban workers, now in short supply, could demand higher wages or better terms. Some landowning nobles, on the other hand, were badly hurt as the price of their grains dropped and the demands of their dependents grew.

A similar death toll afflicted China and parts of the Islamic world. The Central Asian steppes, home to many nomadic peoples including the Mongols, also suffered terribly, undermining Mongol rule and permanently altering the balance between pastoral and agricultural peoples to the advantage of settled farmers. In these and many other ways, disease carried by long-distance trade shaped the lives of millions and altered their historical development.

In the long run of world history, the exchange of diseases gave Europeans a certain advantage when they confronted the peoples of the Western Hemisphere after 1500. Exposure over time had provided them with some degree of immunity to Eurasian diseases. In the Americas, however, the absence of domesticated animals, the less intense interaction among major centers of population, and isolation from the Eastern Hemisphere ensured that native peoples had little defense against the diseases of Europe and Africa. Thus, when their societies were suddenly confronted by Europeans and Africans from across the Atlantic, they perished in appalling numbers. Such was the long-term outcome of the very different histories of the two hemispheres.

LearningCurve
bedfordstmartins.com
/strayer/LC

Sea Roads: Exchange across the Indian Ocean

If the Silk Roads linked Eurasian societies by land, sea-based trade routes likewise connected distant peoples all across the Eastern Hemisphere. For example, since the days of the Phoenicians, Greeks, and Romans, the Mediterranean Sea had been an avenue of maritime commerce throughout the region, a pattern that continued during the third-wave era. The Italian city of Venice emerged by 1000 C.E. as a major center of that commercial network, with its ships and merchants active in the Mediterranean and Black seas as well as on the Atlantic coast. Much of its wealth derived from control of expensive and profitable imported goods from Asia, many of which came up the Red Sea through the Egyptian port of Alexandria. There Venetian merchants picked up those goods and resold them throughout the Mediterranean basin. This type of trans-regional exchange linked the maritime commerce of the Mediterranean Sea to the much larger and more extensive network of seaborne trade in the Indian Ocean basin.

Until the creation of a genuinely global oceanic system of trade after 1500, the Indian Ocean represented the world's largest sea-based system of communication and exchange, stretching from southern China to eastern Africa (see Map 7.2). Like the Silk Roads, this trans-oceanic trade—the Sea Roads—also grew out of the vast environmental and cultural diversities of the region. The desire for various goods not available at home—such as porcelain from China, spices from the islands of Southeast Asia, cotton goods and pepper from India, ivory and gold from the East African coast—provided incentives for Indian Ocean commerce. Transportation costs were lower on the Sea Roads than on the Silk Roads because ships could accommodate larger and heavier cargoes than camels. This meant that the Sea Roads could eventually

Map 7.2 The Sea Roads Paralleling the Silk Road trading network, a sea-based commerce in the Indian Ocean basin connected the many peoples between China and East Africa.

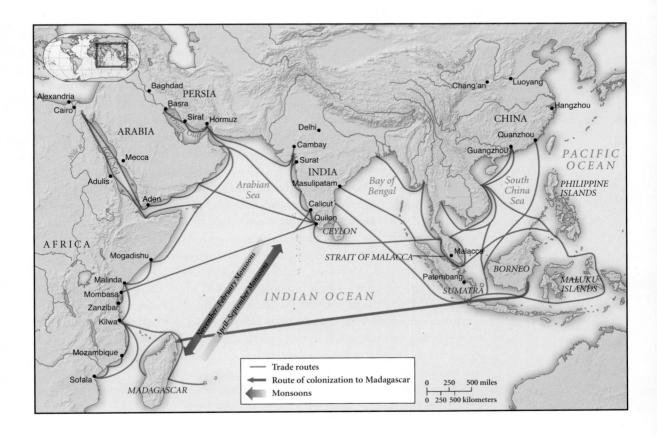

carry more bulk goods and products destined for a mass market—textiles, pepper, timber, rice, sugar, wheat—whereas the Silk Roads were limited largely to luxury goods for the few.

What made Indian Ocean commerce possible were the monsoons, alternating wind currents that blew predictably eastward during the summer months and westward during the winter (see Map 7.2, p. 229). An understanding of monsoons and a gradually accumulating technology of shipbuilding and oceanic navigation drew on the ingenuity of many peoples—Chinese, Malays, Indians, Arabs, Swahilis, and others. Collectively they made "an interlocked human world joined by the common highway of the Indian Ocean."[11]

But this world of Indian Ocean commerce did not occur between entire regions and certainly not between "countries," even though historians sometimes write about India, Indonesia, Southeast Asia, or East Africa as a matter of shorthand or convenience. It operated rather across an "archipelago of towns" whose merchants often had more in common with one another than with the people of their own hinterlands.[12] These urban centers, strung out around the entire Indian Ocean basin, provided the nodes of this widespread commercial network.

Weaving the Web of an Indian Ocean World

The world of Indian Ocean commerce was long in the making, dating back to the time of the First Civilizations. Seaborne trade via the Persian Gulf between ancient Mesopotamia and the Indus Valley civilization is reflected in archeological finds in both places. Perhaps the still-undeciphered Indian writing system was stimulated by Sumerian cuneiform. The ancient Egyptians, and later the Phoenicians, likewise traded down the Red Sea, exchanging their manufactured goods for gold, ivory, frankincense, and slaves from the coasts of Ethiopia, Somalia, and southern Arabia. These ventures mostly hugged the coast and took place over short distances. Malay sailors, however, were an exception to this rule. Speaking Austronesian languages, they jumped off from the islands of present-day Indonesia during the first millennium B.C.E. and made their way in double-outrigger canoes across thousands of miles of open ocean to the East African island of Madagascar. There they introduced their language and their crops—bananas, coconuts, and cocoyams—which soon spread to the mainland, where they greatly enriched the diets of African peoples. Also finding its way to the continent was a Malayo-Polynesian xylophone, which is still played in parts of Africa today.

The tempo of Indian Ocean commerce picked up in the era of second-wave civilizations during the early centuries of the Common Era, as mariners learned how to ride the monsoons. Various technological innovations also facilitated Indian Ocean trade—improvements in sails, new kinds of ships called junks with sternpost rudders and keels for greater stability, new means of calculating latitude such as the astrolabe, and evolving versions of the magnetic needle or compass.

Around the time of Christ, the Greek geographer Strabo reported that "great fleets [from the Roman Empire] are sent as far as India, whence the most valuable

Snapshot   Economic Exchange in the Indian Ocean Basin

Region	Products Contributed to Indian Ocean Commerce
Mediterranean basin	ceramics, glassware, wine, gold, olive oil
East Africa	ivory, gold, iron goods, slaves, tortoiseshells, quartz, leopard skins
Arabia	frankincense, myrrh, perfumes
India	grain, ivory, precious stones, cotton textiles, spices, timber, tortoiseshells
Southeast Asia	tin, sandalwood, cloves, nutmeg, mace
China	silks, porcelain, tea

cargoes are brought back to Egypt and thence exported again to other places."[13] Merchants from the Roman world, mostly Greeks, Syrians, and Jews, established settlements in southern India and along the East African coast. The introduction of Christianity into both Axum and Kerala (in southern India) testifies to the long-term cultural impact of that trade. In the eastern Indian Ocean and the South China Sea, Chinese and Southeast Asian merchants likewise generated a growing commerce, and by 100 C.E. Chinese traders had reached India.

The fulcrum of this growing commercial network lay in India itself. Its ports bulged with goods from both west and east, as illustrated in the Snapshot above. Its merchants were in touch with Southeast Asia by the first century C.E., and settled communities of Indian traders appeared throughout the Indian Ocean basin and as far away as Alexandria in Egypt. Indian cultural practices, such as Hinduism and Buddhism, as well as South Asian political ideas began to take root in Southeast Asia.

In the era of third-wave civilizations between 500 and 1500, two major processes changed the landscape of the Afro-Eurasian world and wove the web of Indian Ocean exchange even more densely than before. One was the economic and political revival of China, some four centuries after the collapse of the Han dynasty. Especially during the Tang and Song dynasties (618–1279), China reestablished an effective and unified state, which actively encouraged maritime trade. Furthermore, the impressive growth of the Chinese economy sent Chinese products pouring into the circuits of Indian Ocean commerce, while providing a vast and attractive market for Indian and Southeast Asian goods. Chinese technological innovations, such as larger ships and the magnetic compass, likewise added to the momentum of commercial growth.

A second transformation in the world of Indian Ocean commerce involved the sudden rise of Islam in the seventh century C.E. and its subsequent spread across much of the Afro-Eurasian world (see Chapter 9). Unlike Confucian culture, which was quite suspicious of merchants, Islam was friendly to commercial life; the Prophet Muhammad himself had been a trader. The creation of an Arab Empire, stretching from the Atlantic Ocean through the Mediterranean basin and all the way to India,

■ **Change**
What lay behind the flourishing of Indian Ocean commerce in the postclassical millennium?

brought together in a single political system an immense range of economies and cultural traditions and provided a vast arena for the energies of Muslim traders.

Those energies greatly intensified commercial activity in the Indian Ocean basin. Middle Eastern gold and silver flowed into southern India to purchase pepper, pearls, textiles, and gemstones. Muslim merchants and sailors, as well as Jews and Christians living within the Islamic world, established communities of traders from East Africa to the south China coast. Efforts to reclaim wasteland in Mesopotamia to produce sugar and dates for export stimulated a slave trade from East Africa, which landed thousands of Africans in southern Iraq to work on plantations and in salt mines under horrendous conditions. A massive fifteen-year revolt (868–883) among these slaves badly disrupted the Islamic Abbasid Empire before that rebellion was brutally crushed.[14]

Beyond these specific outcomes, the expansion of Islam gave rise to an international maritime culture by 1000, shared by individuals living in the widely separated port cities around the Indian Ocean. The immense prestige, power, and prosperity of the Islamic world stimulated widespread conversion, which in turn facilitated commercial transactions. Even those who did not convert to Islam, such as Buddhist rulers in Burma, nonetheless regarded it as commercially useful to assume Muslim names.[15] Thus was created "a maritime Silk Road . . . a commercial and informational network of unparalleled proportions."[16] After 1000, the culture of this network was increasingly Islamic.

Sea Roads as a Catalyst for Change: Southeast Asia

■ **Connection**
In what ways did Indian influence register in Southeast Asia?

Oceanic commerce transformed all of its participants in one way or another, but nowhere more so than in Southeast Asia and East Africa, at opposite ends of the Indian Ocean network. In both regions, trade stimulated political change as ambitious or aspiring rulers used the wealth derived from commerce to construct larger and more centrally governed states or cities. Both areas likewise experienced cultural change as local people were attracted to foreign religious ideas from Confucian, Hindu, Buddhist, or Islamic sources. As on the Silk Roads, trade was a conduit for culture.

Located between the major civilizations of China and India, Southeast Asia was situated by geography to play an important role in the evolving world of Indian Ocean commerce. During the third-wave era, a series of cities and states or kingdoms emerged on both the islands and mainland of Southeast Asia, representing new civilizations in this vast region (Map 7.3). That process paralleled a similar development of new civilizations in East and West Africa, Japan, Russia, and Western Europe in what was an Afro-Eurasian phenomenon. In Southeast Asia, many of those new societies were stimulated and decisively shaped by their interaction with the sea-based trade of Indian Ocean.[17]

The case of Srivijaya (SREE-vih-juh-yuh) illustrates the connection between commerce and state building. When Malay sailors, long active in the waters around Southeast Asia, opened an all-sea route between India and China through the Straits of Malacca around 350 C.E., the many small ports along the Malay Peninsula and the coast of Sumatra began to compete intensely to attract the growing number of traders and travelers making their way through the straits. From this competition emerged the Malay kingdom of Srivijaya, which dominated this critical choke point of Indian Ocean trade from 670 to 1025. A number of factors—Srivijaya's plentiful supply of gold; its access to the source of highly sought-after spices, such as cloves, nutmeg, and mace; and the taxes levied on passing ships—provided resources to attract supporters, to fund an embryonic bureaucracy, and to create the military and naval forces that brought some security to the area.

The inland states on the mainland of Southeast Asia, whose economies were based more on domestically produced rice than international trade, nonetheless participated in commerce of the region. The state of Funan, which flourished during the first six centuries of the Common Era in what is now southern Vietnam and eastern Cambodia, hosted merchants from both India and China. Archeologists have found Roman coins as well as trade goods from Persia, Central Asia, and Arabia in the ruins of its ancient cities. The Khmer kingdom of Angkor (flourished 800–1300) exported exotic forest products, receiving in return Chinese and Indian handicrafts, while welcoming a considerable community of Chinese merchants. Traders from Champa in what is now central and southern Vietnam operated in China, Java, and elsewhere, practicing piracy when trade dried up. Champa's effort to control the trade between China and Southeast Asia provoked warfare with its commercial rivals.

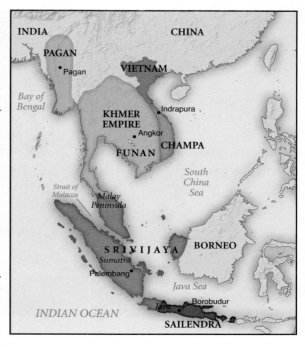

Map 7.3 Southeast Asia ca. 1200 C.E.
Both mainland and island Southeast Asia were centrally involved in the commerce of the Indian Ocean basin, and both were transformed by that experience.

Beyond the exchange of goods, commercial connections served to spread elements of Indian culture across much of Southeast Asia, even as Vietnam was incorporated into the Chinese sphere of influence. (See Chapter 8 for more on Chinese influence in Vietnam.) Indian alphabets such as Sanskrit and Pallava were used to write a number of Southeast Asian languages. Indian artistic forms provided models for Southeast Asian sculpture and architecture, while the Indian epic *Ramayana* became widely popular across the region.

Politically, Southeast Asian rulers and elites found attractive the Indian belief that leaders were god-kings, perhaps reincarnations of a Buddha or the Hindu deity Shiva, while the idea of karma conveyed legitimacy to the rich and powerful based on their moral behavior in earlier lives. Srivijaya monarchs, for example, employed Indians as advisers, clerks, or officials and assigned Sanskrit titles to their subordinates. The capital city of Palembang was a cosmopolitan place, where even the parrots were said to speak four languages. While these rulers drew on indigenous beliefs that chiefs possessed magical powers and were responsible for the prosperity of their people, they also

Borobudur
This huge Buddhist monument, constructed probably in the ninth century C.E., was subsequently abandoned and covered with layers of volcanic ash and vegetation as Java came under Islamic influence. It was rediscovered by British colonial authorities in the early nineteenth century and has undergone several restorations over the past two centuries. Although Indonesia is a largely Muslim country, its small Buddhist minority still celebrates the Buddha's birthday at Borobudur. (Robert Harding World Imagery/Alamy)

made use of imported Indian political ideas and Buddhist religious concepts, which provided a "higher level of magic" for rulers as well as the prestige of association with Indian civilization.[18] They also sponsored the creation of images of the Buddha and various bodhisattvas whose faces resembled those of deceased kings and were inscribed with traditional curses against anyone who would destroy them. Srivijaya grew into a major center of Buddhist observance and teaching, attracting thousands of monks and students from throughout the Buddhist world. The seventh-century Chinese monk Yi Jing was so impressed that he advised Buddhist monks headed for India to study first in Srivijaya for several years.

Elsewhere as well, elements of Indian culture took hold in Southeast Asia. The Sailendra kingdom in central Java, an agriculturally rich region closely allied with Srivijaya, mounted a massive building program between the eighth and tenth centuries featuring Hindu temples and Buddhist monuments. The most famous, known as Borobudur, is an enormous mountain-shaped structure of ten levels, with a three-mile walkway and elaborate carvings illustrating the spiritual journey from ignorance and illusion to full enlightenment. The largest Buddhist monument anywhere in the world, it is nonetheless a distinctly Javanese creation, whose carved figures have Javanese features and whose scenes are clearly set in Java, not India. Its shape resonated with an ancient Southeast Asian veneration of mountains as sacred places and the abode of ancestral spirits. Borobudur represents the process of Buddhism becoming culturally grounded in a new place.

Hinduism too, though not an explicitly missionary religion, found a place in Southeast Asia. It was well rooted in the Champa kingdom, for example, where Shiva was worshipped, cows were honored, and phallic imagery was prominent. But it was in the prosperous and powerful Angkor kingdom of the twelfth century C.E. that Hinduism found its most stunning architectural expression in the temple complex known as Angkor Wat. The largest religious structure in the premodern world, it sought to express a Hindu understanding of the cosmos, centered on a mythical Mt. Meru, the home of the gods in Hindu tradition. Later, it was used by Buddhists as well, with little sense of contradiction. To the west of Angkor, the state of Pagan likewise devoted enormous resources to shrines, temples, and libraries inspired by both Hindu and Buddhist faiths.

This extensive Indian influence in Southeast Asia has led some scholars to speak of the "Indianization" of the region, similar perhaps to the earlier spread of Greek

Angkor Wat
Constructed in the early twelfth century, the Angkor Wat complex was designed as a state temple, dedicated to the Hindu god Vishnu and lavishly decorated with carved bas-reliefs depicting scenes from Hindu mythology. By the late thirteenth century, it was in use by Buddhists as it is to this day. This photo shows a small section of the temple and three Buddhist monks in their saffron robes. (© Jose Fuste Raga/Corbis)

culture within the empires of Alexander the Great and Rome. In the case of Southeast Asia, however, no imperial control accompanied Indian cultural influence. It was a matter of voluntary borrowing by independent societies that found Indian traditions and practices useful and were free to adapt those ideas to their own needs and cultures. Traditional religious practices mixed with the imported faiths or existed alongside them with little conflict. And much that was distinctively Southeast Asian persisted despite influences from afar. In family life, for example, most Southeast Asian societies traced an individual's ancestry from both the mother's and father's line in contrast to India and China where patrilineal descent was practiced. Furthermore, women had fewer restrictions and a greater role in public life than in the more patriarchal civilizations of both East and South Asia. They were generally able to own property together with their husbands and to initiate divorce. According to a Chinese visitor to Angkor, "it is the women who are concerned with commerce." Women in Angkor also served as gladiators, warriors, members of the palace staff, and as poets, artists, and religious teachers. Almost 1800 realistically carved images of women decorate the temple complex of Angkor Wat. In neighboring Pagan, a thirteenth-century Queen Pwa Saw exercised extensive political and religious influence for some forty years amid internal intrigue and external threats, while donating some of her lands and property to a Buddhist temple. Somewhat later, but also via Indian Ocean commerce, Islam too began to penetrate Southeast Asia, as the world of seaborne trade brought yet another cultural tradition to the region.

Sea Roads as a Catalyst for Change: East Africa

■ **Connection**
What was the role of Swahili civilization in the world of Indian Ocean commerce?

On the other side of the Indian Ocean, the transformative processes of long-distance trade were likewise at work, giving rise to an East African civilization known as Swahili. Emerging in the eighth century C.E., this civilization took shape as a set of commercial city-states stretching all along the East African coast, from present-day Somalia to Mozambique.

The earlier ancestors of the Swahili lived in small farming and fishing communities, spoke Bantu languages, and traded with the Arabian, Greek, and Roman merchants who occasionally visited the coast during the second-wave era. But what stimulated the growth of Swahili cities was the far more extensive commercial life of the western Indian Ocean following the rise of Islam. As in Southeast Asia, local people and aspiring rulers found opportunity for wealth and power in the growing demand for East African products associated with an expanding Indian Ocean commerce. Gold, ivory, quartz, leopard skins, and sometimes slaves acquired from interior societies, as well as iron and processed timber manufactured along the coast, found a ready market in Arabia, Persia, India, and beyond. At least one East Africa giraffe found its way to Bengal in northeastern India, and from there was sent on to China. In response to such commercial opportunities, an African merchant class developed, villages turned into sizable towns, and clan chiefs became kings. A new civilization was in the making.

Between 1000 and 1500, that civilization flourished along the coast, and it was a very different kind of society than the farming and pastoral cultures of the East African interior. It was thoroughly urban, centered in cities of 15,000 to 18,000 people, such as Lamu, Mombasa, Kilwa, Sofala, and many others. Like the city-states of ancient Greece, each Swahili city was politically independent, generally governed by its own king, and in sharp competition with other cities. No imperial system or larger territorial states unified the world of Swahili civilization. Nor did any of them control a critical choke point of trade, as Srivijaya did for the Straits of Malacca. Swahili cities were commercial centers that accumulated goods from the interior and exchanged them for the products of distant civilizations, such as Chinese porcelain and silk, Persian rugs, and Indian cottons. While the trans-oceanic journeys occurred largely in Arab vessels, Swahili craft navigated the coastal waterways, concentrating goods for shipment abroad. Swahili cities were class-stratified societies with sharp distinctions between a mercantile elite and commoners.

The Swahili Coast of East Africa

Culturally as well as economically, Swahili civilization participated in the larger Indian Ocean world. Arab, Indian, and Persian merchants were welcome visitors, and some settled permanently. Many ruling families of Swahili cities claimed Arab or Persian origins as a way of bolstering their prestige, even while they dined from Chinese porcelain and dressed in Indian cottons. The Swahili language, widely spoken in East Africa today, was grammatically an African tongue within the larger Bantu family of languages, but it was written in Arabic script and contained a number of Arabic loan words. A small bronze lion found in the Swahili city of Shanga and dating to about 1100 illustrates the distinctly cosmopolitan character of Swahili culture. It depicted a clearly African lion, but it was created in a distinctly Indian artistic style and was made from melted-down Chinese copper coins.[19]

Furthermore, Swahili civilization rapidly became Islamic. Introduced by Arab traders, Islam was voluntarily and widely adopted within the Swahili world. Like Buddhism in Southeast Asia, Islam linked Swahili cities to the larger Indian Ocean world, and these East African cities were soon dotted with substantial mosques. When Ibn Battuta (IH-buhn ba-TOO-tuh), a widely traveled Arab scholar, merchant, and public official, visited the Swahili coast in the early fourteenth century, he found altogether Muslim societies in which religious leaders often spoke Arabic, and all were eager to welcome a learned Islamic visitor. But these were African Muslims, not colonies of transplanted Arabs. "The rulers, scholars, officials, and big merchants as well as the port workers, farmers, craftsmen, and slaves, were dark-skinned people speaking African tongues in everyday life."[20]

Islam sharply divided the Swahili cities from their African neighbors to the west, for neither the new religion nor Swahili culture penetrated much beyond the coast until the nineteenth century. Economically, however, the coastal cities acted as intermediaries between the interior producers of valued goods and the Arab merchants who carried them to distant markets. Particularly in the southern reaches of the Swahili world, this relationship extended the impact of Indian Ocean trade well into the African interior. Hundreds of miles inland, between the Zambezi and Limpopo rivers, lay rich sources of gold, much in demand on the Swahili coast. The emergence of a powerful state, known as Great Zimbabwe, seems clearly connected to the growing trade in gold to the coast as well as to the wealth embodied in its large herds of cattle.

At its peak between 1250 and 1350, Great Zimbabwe had the resources and the labor power to construct huge stone enclosures entirely without mortar, with walls sixteen feet thick and thirty-two feet tall. "[It] must have been an astonishing sight," writes a recent historian, "for the subordinate chiefs and kings who would have come there to seek favors at court."[21] Here in the interior of southeastern Africa lay yet another example of the reach and transforming power of Indian Ocean commerce.

LearningCurve
bedfordstmartins.com
/strayer/LC

SUMMING UP SO FAR

To what extent did the Silk Roads and the Sea Roads operate in a similar fashion? How did they differ?

Sand Roads: Exchange across the Sahara

In addition to the Silk Roads and the Sea Roads, another important pattern of long-distance trade—this one across the vast reaches of the Sahara—linked North Africa and the Mediterranean world with the land and peoples of interior West Africa. Like the others, these Sand Road commercial networks had a transforming impact, stimulating and enriching West African civilization and connecting it to larger patterns of world history during the third-wave era.

Commercial Beginnings in West Africa

Trans-African trade, like the commerce of the Silk Roads and the Sea Roads, was rooted in environmental variation. The North African coastal regions, long part of Roman or later Arab empires, generated cloth, glassware, weapons, books, and other manufactured goods. The great Sahara held deposits of copper and especially salt, while its oases produced sweet and nutritious dates. While the sparse populations of the desert were largely pastoral and nomadic, farther south lived agricultural peoples who grew a variety of crops, produced their own textiles and metal products, and mined a considerable amount of gold. The agricultural regions of sub-Saharan Africa are normally divided into two ecological zones: the savanna grasslands immediately south of the Sahara, which produced grain crops such as millet and sorghum; and the forest areas farther south, where root and tree crops such as yams and kola nuts predominated. These quite varied environments provided the economic incentive for the exchange of goods.

The earliest long-distance trade within this huge region was not across the Sahara at all, but largely among the agricultural peoples themselves in the area later known to Arabs as the Sudan, or "the land of black people." During the first millennium B.C.E., the peoples of Sudanic West Africa began to exchange metal goods, cotton textiles, gold, and various food products across considerable distances using boats along the

Niger River and donkeys overland. On the basis of this trade, a number of independent urban clusters emerged by the early centuries of the Common Era. The most well known was Jenne-jeno, which was located at a crucial point on the Niger River where goods were transshipped from boat to donkey or vice versa.[22] This was the Niger Valley civilization, described in Chapter 6.

Gold, Salt, and Slaves: Trade and Empire in West Africa

A major turning point in African commercial life occurred with the introduction of the camel to North Africa and the Sahara in the early centuries of the Common Era. This remarkable animal, which could go for ten days without water, finally made possible the long trek across the Sahara. It was camel-owning dwellers of desert oases who initiated regular trans-Saharan commerce by 300 to 400 C.E. Several centuries later, North African Arabs, now bearing the new religion of Islam, also organized caravans across the desert.

■ **Connection**

What changes did trans-Saharan trade bring to West Africa?

What they sought, above all else, was gold, which was found in some abundance in the border areas straddling the grasslands and the forests of West Africa. From its source, it was transported by donkey to transshipment points on the southern edge of the Sahara and then transferred to camels for the long journey north across the desert. African ivory, kola nuts, and slaves were likewise in considerable demand in the desert, the Mediterranean basin, and beyond. In return, the peoples of the Sudan received horses, cloth, dates, various manufactured goods, and especially salt from the rich deposits in the Sahara.

Thus the Sahara was no longer simply a barrier to commerce and cross-cultural interaction; it quickly became a major international trade route that fostered new relationships among distant peoples. The caravans that made the desert crossing could be huge, with as many as 5,000 camels and hundreds of people. Traveling mostly at night to avoid the daytime heat, the journey might take up to seventy days, covering fifteen to twenty-five miles per day. For well over 1,000 years, such caravans traversed the desert, linking the interior of West Africa with lands and people far to the north.

As in Southeast Asia and East Africa, this long-distance trade across the Sahara provided both incentives and resources for the construction of new and larger political structures. It was the peoples of the western and central Sudan, living between the forests and the desert, who were in the best position to take advantage of these new opportunities. Between roughly 500 and 1600, they constructed a series of states, empires, and city-states that reached from the Atlantic coast to Lake Chad, including Ghana, Mali, Songhay, Kanem, and the city-states of the Hausa people (see Map 7.4). All of them were monarchies with elaborate court life and varying degrees of administrative complexity and military forces at their disposal. All drew on the wealth of trans-Saharan trade, taxing the merchants who conducted it. In the wider world, these states soon acquired a reputation for great riches. An Arab traveler in the tenth century C.E. described the ruler of Ghana as "the wealthiest king on the face of the earth because of his treasures and stocks of gold."[23] At its high point in the fourteenth

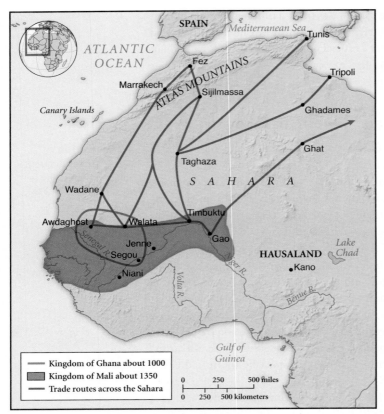

Map 7.4   The Sand Roads

For a thousand years or more, the Sahara was an ocean of sand that linked the interior of West Africa with the world of North Africa and the Mediterranean but separated them as well.

century, Mali's rulers monopolized the import of strategic goods such as horses and metals; levied duties on salt, copper, and other merchandise; and reserved large nuggets of gold for themselves while permitting the free export of gold dust.

This growing integration with the world of international commerce generated the social complexity and hierarchy characteristic of all civilizations. Royal families and elite classes, mercantile and artisan groups, military and religious officials, free peasants and slaves—all of these were represented in this emerging West African civilization. So too were gender hierarchies, although without the rigidity of more established Eurasian civilizations. Rulers, merchants, and public officials were almost always male, and by 1200 earlier matrilineal descent patterns had been largely replaced by those tracing descent through the male line. Male bards, the repositories for their communities' history, often viewed powerful women as dangerous, not to be trusted, and a seductive distraction for men. But ordinary women were central to agricultural production and weaving; royal women played important political roles in many places; and oral traditions and mythologies frequently portrayed a complementary rather than hierarchal relationship between the sexes. According to a recent scholar:

> Men [in West African civilization] derive their power and authority by releasing and accumulating *nyama* [a pervasive vital power] through acts of transforming one thing into another—making a living animal dead in hunting, making a lump of metal into a fine bracelet at the smithy. Women derive their power from similar acts of transformation—turning clay into pots or turning the bodily fluids of sex into a baby.[24]

Certainly the famous Muslim traveler, Ibn Battuta, visiting Mali in the fourteenth century, was surprised, and appalled, at the casual intimacy of unmarried men and women.

As in all civilizations, slavery found a place in West Africa. Early on, most slaves had been women, working as domestic servants and concubines. As West African civilization crystallized, however, male slaves were put to work as state officials, porters, craftsmen, miners harvesting salt from desert deposits, and especially agricultural laborers producing for the royal granaries on large estates or plantations. Most came from non-Islamic and stateless societies farther south, which were raided during the dry season by cavalry-based forces of West African states, though some white slave women from the eastern Mediterranean also made an appearance in Mali. A song in honor of one eleventh-century ruler of Kanem boasted of his slave-raiding achievements.

> The best you took (and sent home) as the first fruits of battle. The children crying on their mothers you snatched away from their mothers. You took the slave wife from a slave, and set them in lands far removed from one another.[25]

Most of these slaves were used within this emerging West African civilization, but a trade in slaves also developed across the Sahara. Between 1100 and 1400, perhaps 5,500 slaves per year made the perilous trek across the desert, where most were put to work in the homes of the wealthy in Islamic North Africa.

Manuscripts of Timbuktu
The West African city of Timbuktu, a terminus of the Sand Roads commercial network, became an intellectual center of Islamic learning—both scientific and religious. Its libraries were stocked with books and manuscripts, often transported across the Sahara from the heartland of Islam. Many of these have been preserved, as this recent photograph shows, and are now being studied once again. (Photo 2000: Alida Jay Boye, Timbuktu Manuscripts Project, University of Oslo)

These states of Sudanic Africa developed substantial urban and commercial centers—such as Koumbi-Saleh, Jenne, Timbuktu, Gao, Gobir, and Kano—where traders congregated and goods were exchanged. Some of these cities also became centers of manufacturing, creating finely wrought beads, iron tools, or cotton textiles, some of which entered the circuits of commerce. Visitors described them as cosmopolitan places where court officials, artisans, scholars, students, and local and foreign merchants all rubbed elbows. As in East Africa, Islam accompanied trade and became an important element in the urban culture of West Africa. (See Chapter 9.) The growth of long-distance trade had stimulated the development of an African civilization, which was linked to the wider networks of exchange in the Eastern Hemisphere.

LearningCurve
bedfordstmartins.com
/strayer/LC

An American Network: Commerce and Connection in the Western Hemisphere

Before the voyages of Columbus, the world of the Americas developed quite separately from that of Afro-Eurasia. Intriguing hints of occasional contacts with Polynesia and other distant lands have been proposed, but the only clearly demonstrated connection was that occasioned by the brief Viking voyages to North America around

Thorfinn Karlsfeni, Viking Voyager

While the peoples of eastern and western hemispheres remained almost completely isolated from one another before Columbus, the Viking journeys to North America, part of a larger age of Viking expansion, represent an exception to that generalization. Between 800 and 1050, Scandinavian Vikings had raided, traded, and sometimes settled across much of Europe, generating a fearful reputation. They also colonized Iceland and Greenland, and from that base sought yet more land in North America. Yet their trans-Atlantic voyages, although impressive feats of oceanic exploration, represented a historical dead-end, for they bore no long-term consequences. Their significance lies in their role as a prelude to Columbus rather than in any immediate outcomes.

Among those voyagers was Thorfinn Karlsefni, who set off from southern Greenland in the spring of 1007 bound for what he called Vinland, what we know as North America. A well-born, wealthy merchant and seaman of Norwegian Viking background, he had come the previous summer from his home in Iceland to the small Viking

A Viking ship similar to that used by Thorfinn Karlsfeni and other Viking explorers.
(Yvette Cardozo/Alamy)

community in Greenland on a trading mission. There he found winter accommodations with Eric the Red, a pioneer of Nordic settlement in Greenland. He also found a wife, Gudrid, the widow of one of Eric's sons. Two of Eric's sons, including Leif Ericsson, had previously made the journey to Vinland. And so, during that long winter, talk turned to another voyage, for that land was reputed to be rich in furs, timber, and other valuable resources. Thus, Thorfinn came to lead 160 people, including his new wife and other women, on three ships heading to a virtually unknown land. The story of that voyage comes to us from two Icelandic sagas, based on oral traditions and committed to writing several hundred years after the events they describe.[26]

Arriving along the coast of what is now Newfoundland, Thorfinn and his people first looked for pasture land for the cattle that had accompanied them. With food in short supply, the first winter was very difficult and provoked a religious controversy. The Christians among the group "made prayers to God for food," but Thorhall, a large, soli-

the year 1000. (See Portrait.) Certainly, no sustained interaction between the peoples of the two hemispheres took place. But if the Silk, Sea, and Sand Roads linked the diverse peoples of the Eastern Hemisphere, did a similar network of interaction join and transform the various societies of the Western Hemisphere?

Clearly, direct connections among the various civilizations and cultures of the Americas were less densely woven than in the Afro-Eurasian region. The llama and the potato, both domesticated in the Andes, never reached Mesoamerica; nor did the writing system of the Maya diffuse to Andean civilizations. The Aztecs and the Incas, contemporary civilizations in the fifteenth century, had little if any direct contact with each other. The limits of these interactions owed something to the absence of horses, donkeys, camels, wheeled vehicles, and large oceangoing vessels, all of which facilitated long-distance trade and travel in Afro-Eurasia.

Geographic or environmental differences added further obstacles. The narrow bottleneck of Panama, largely covered by dense rain forests, surely inhibited contact

■ **Comparison**

In what ways did networks of interaction in the Western Hemisphere differ from those in the Eastern Hemisphere?

tary, and "foul-mouthed" hunter, declared: "Has it not been that the Redbeard [Thor, the Norse god of thunder] has proved a better friend than your Christ?"

The following spring, the small Viking community had its first encounter with native peoples when dozens of canoes described in the sagas as "black, and ill favoured" appeared offshore. What followed was a kind of mutual inspection, as the natives "stayed a while in astonishment" and then rowed away. They returned the following year, this time to barter. The Vikings offered red cloth and milk porridge in exchange for furs and skins. But what began as a peaceful encounter ended badly when a bull from the Norsemen's herd erupted out of the forest bellowing loudly. The surprised and frightened locals quickly departed, and, when they returned three weeks later, violence erupted. Considerably outnumbered and attacked with catapults and a "great shower of missiles," Thorfinn and his company reacted with "great terror."

This encounter and the "fear of hostilities" that it provoked persuaded the Vikings "to depart and return to their own country." As they made their way north along the coast, they came upon a group of five natives sleeping near the sea. Perhaps in revenge, the Vikings simply killed them. In another incident before departing for home, they captured two boys, baptized them as Christians, and taught them the Viking language. After three difficult years in this remote land, Thorfinn and Gudrid returned home, with a son named Snorri, the first European born in the Western Hemisphere.

Although intermittent Viking voyages to North America probably occurred over the next several centuries, they established no permanent presence. Their numbers were small, and they lacked the support of a strong state, such as Columbus and the Spanish conquistadores later enjoyed. For some time, many doubted that those voyages had occurred at all. But in the 1960s, archeological work on the northern tip of the island of Newfoundland uncovered the remains of a Norse settlement dating to the time of Thorfinn's visit. Eight sod dwellings, evidence of iron-working and boat repair, household items such as needles and spindles confirmed the existence of a Viking settlement, consisting of both men and women. The interaction of Thorfinn and the other Vikings with native peoples of North America raised, but did not answer, the question of how the epic encounter of these two continents would turn out. The later voyages of Columbus and other West Europeans provided that answer.

Question: How might these interactions have appeared if they were derived from the sagas of the native peoples?

between South and North America. Furthermore, the north/south orientation of the Americas—which required agricultural practices to move through, and adapt to, quite distinct climatic and vegetation zones—slowed the spread of agricultural products. By contrast, the east/west axis of Eurasia meant that agricultural innovations could diffuse more rapidly because they were entering roughly similar environments. Thus nothing equivalent to the long-distance trade of the Silk, Sea, or Sand Roads of the Eastern Hemisphere arose in the Americas, even though local and regional commerce flourished in many places. Nor did distinct cultural traditions such as Buddhism, Christianity, and Islam spread so widely to integrate distant peoples.

Nonetheless, scholars have discerned "a loosely interactive web stretching from the North American Great Lakes and upper Mississippi south to the Andes."[27] (See Map 7.5, p. 244.) Partly, it was a matter of slowly spreading cultural elements, such as the gradual diffusion of maize from its Mesoamerican place of origin to the southwestern United States and then on to eastern North America as well as to much of South

Map 7.5
The American Web
Transcontinental interactions within the American web were more modest than those of the Afro-Eurasian hemisphere. The most intense areas of exchange and communication occurred within the Mississippi valley, Mesoamerican, and Andean regions.

America in the other direction. A game played with rubber balls on an outdoor court has left traces in the Caribbean, Mexico, and northern South America. Construction in the Tantoc region of northeastern Mexico resembled the earlier building styles of Cahokia, indicating the possibility of some interaction between the two regions.[28] The spread of particular pottery styles and architectural conventions likewise suggests at least indirect contact over wide distances.

Commerce too played an important role in the making of this "American web." A major North American chiefdom at Cahokia, near present-day St. Louis, flourished from about 900 to 1250 at the confluence of the Mississippi, Illinois, and Missouri rivers (see pp. 206–07). Cahokia lay at the center of a widespread trading network that brought it shells from the Atlantic coast, copper from the Lake Superior region, buffalo hides from the Great Plains, obsidian from the Rocky Mountains, and mica from the southern Appalachian Mountains. Sturdy dugout canoes plied the rivers of the eastern woodlands, loosely connecting their diverse societies. Early European explorers and travelers along the Amazon and Orinoco rivers of South America reported active networks of exchange that may well have operated for many centuries. Caribbean peoples using large oceangoing canoes had long conducted an inter-island trade, and the Chincha people undertook ocean-based exchange in copper, beads, and shells along the Pacific coasts of Peru and Ecuador in large seagoing rafts.[29] Another regional commercial network, centered in Mesoamerica, extended north to what is now the southwestern United States and south to Ecuador and Colombia. Many items from Mesoamerica — copper bells, macaw feathers, tons of shells — have been found in the Chaco region of New Mexico. Residents of Chaco also drank liquid chocolate, using jars of Mayan origin and cacao beans imported from Mesoamerica, where the practice began.[30] Turquoise, mined and worked among the Ancestral Pueblo (see pp. 204–06) flowed in the other direction.

But the most active and dense networks of communication and exchange in the Americas lay within, rather than between, the regions that housed the two great civilizations of the Western Hemisphere — Mesoamerica and the Andes. During the flourishing of Mesoamerican civilization (200–900 C.E.), both the Maya cities in the Yucatán area of Mexico and Guatemala and the huge city-state of Teotihuacán in central Mexico maintained commercial relationships with one another and throughout the region. In addition to this land-based trade, the Maya conducted a seaborne commerce, using large dugout canoes holding forty to fifty people, along both the Atlantic and Pacific coasts.[31]

Although most of this trade was in luxury goods rather than basic necessities, it was critical to upholding the position and privileges of royal and noble families. Items such as cotton clothing, precious jewels, and feathers from particular birds marked the status of elite groups and served to attract followers. Controlling access to such high-prestige goods was an important motive for war among Mesoamerican states.[32] Among the Aztecs of the fifteenth century, professional merchants known as pochteca (pohch-TEH-cah) undertook large-scale trading expeditions both within and well beyond the borders of their empire, sometimes as agents for the state or for members of the nobility, but more often acting on their own as private businessmen.

Unlike the Aztec Empire, in which private traders largely handled the distribution of goods, economic exchange in the Andean Inca Empire during the fifteenth century was a state-run operation, and no merchant group similar to the Aztec pochteca emerged there. Instead, great state storehouses bulged with immense quantities of food, clothing, military supplies, blankets, construction materials, and more, all carefully recorded on *quipus* (knotted cords used to record numerical data) by a highly trained class of accountants. From these state centers, goods were transported as needed by caravans of human porters and llamas across the numerous roads and bridges of the empire. Totaling some 20,000 miles, Inca roads traversed the coastal plain and the high Andes in a north/south direction, while lateral roads linked these diverse environments and extended into the eastern rain forests and plains as well. Despite the general absence of private trade, local exchange took place at highland fairs and along the borders of the empire with groups outside the Inca state.

Inca Roads
Used for transporting goods by pack animal or sending messages by foot, the Inca road network included some 2,000 inns where travelers might find food and shelter. Messengers, operating in relay, could cover as many as 150 miles a day. Here a modern-day citizen of Peru walks along an old Inca trail road. (Loren McIntyre/lorenmcintyre.com)

LearningCurve
bedfordstmartins.com/strayer/LC

⊢⊢ Reflections: Economic Globalization— Ancient and Modern

The densely connected world of the modern era, linked by ties of commerce and culture around the planet, certainly has roots in much earlier patterns. Particularly in the era of third-wave civilizations from 500 to 1500, the Silk, Sea, and Sand Roads of the Afro-Eurasian world and the looser networks of the American web linked distant peoples both economically and culturally, prompted the emergence of new states, and sustained elite privileges in many ancient civilizations. In those ways, they resembled the globalized world of modern times.

In other respects, though, the networks and webs of the premodern millennium differed sharply from those of more recent centuries. Most people still produced primarily for their own consumption rather than for the market, and a much smaller range of goods was exchanged in the marketplaces of the world. Far fewer people then were required to sell their own labor for wages, an almost universal practice in modern economies. Because of transportation costs and technological limitations, most trade was in luxury goods rather than in necessities. In addition, the circuits of commerce were rather more limited than the truly global patterns of exchange that emerged after 1500.

Furthermore, the world economy of the modern era increasingly had a single center—industrialized Western European countries—which came to dominate much of the world both economically and politically during the nineteenth century. Though never completely equal, the economic relationships of earlier times occurred among much more equivalent units. For example, no one region dominated the complex pattern of Indian Ocean exchange, although India and China generally offered manufactured goods, while Southeast Asia and East Africa mostly contributed agricultural products or raw materials. And with the exception of the brief Mongol control of the Silk Roads and the Inca domination of the Andes for a century, no single power exercised political control over the other major networks of world commerce.

Economic relationships among third-wave civilizations, in short, were more balanced and multicentered than those of the modern era. Although massive inequalities occurred within particular regions or societies, interaction among the major civilizations operated on a rather more equal basis than in the globalized world of the past several centuries. With the rise of China, India, Turkey, and Brazil, as major players in the world economy of the twenty-first century, are we perhaps witnessing a return to that earlier pattern?

Second Thoughts

LearningCurve
Check what you know.
bedfordstmartins.com
/strayer/LC

Online Study Guide
bedfordstmartins.com/strayer

What's the Significance?

Silk Roads, 222–28

Black Death, 227–28

Indian Ocean trading network, 228–38

Srivijaya, 232–34

Borobudur, 234–35

Angkor Wat, 235

Swahili civilization, 237–38

Great Zimbabwe, 238

Sand Roads, 238–39

Ghana, Mali, Songhay, 239–41

trans-Saharan slave trade, 239–41

American web, 241–45

Thorfinn Karlsfeni, 242–43

pochteca, 245

Big Picture Questions

1. What motivated and sustained the long-distance commerce of the Silk Roads, Sea Roads, and Sand Roads?
2. Why did the peoples of the Eastern Hemisphere develop long-distance trade more extensively than did those of the Western Hemisphere?
3. "Cultural change derived often from commercial exchange in the third-wave era." What evidence from this chapter supports this observation?
4. In what ways was Afro-Eurasia a single interacting zone, and in what respects was it a vast region of separate cultures and civilizations?
5. **Looking Back:** Compared to the cross-cultural interactions of earlier times, what was different about those of the third-wave era?

Next Steps: For Further Study

For Web sites and additional documents related to this chapter, see **Make History** at bedfordstmartins.com/strayer.

Jerry Bentley, *Old World Encounters* (1993). A wonderfully succinct and engaging history of cross-cultural interaction all across Afro-Eurasia before 1500.

William J. Bernstein, *A Splendid Exchange* (2008). A global account of "how trade shaped the world."

E. W. Bovill, *The Golden Trade of the Moors* (1970). A classic account of the trans-Saharan trade.

Nayan Chanda, *Bound Together* (2007). Places contemporary globalization in a rich world historical context.

K. N. Chaudhuri, *Trade and Civilization in the Indian Ocean* (1985). A well-regarded study that treats the Indian Ocean basin as a single region linked by both commerce and culture during the third-wave era.

Philip Curtin, *Cross-Cultural Trade in World History* (1984). Explores long-distance trade as a generator of social change on a global level.

Xinru Liu, *The Silk Road in World History* (2010). A brief, accessible, and up-to-date account by a leading scholar.

Silk Road Seattle, http://depts.washington.edu/silkroad/. A wonderful Web site about the Silk Road with many artistic images and maps as well as extensive narrative description of vast network of exchange.

CHAPTER EIGHT

China and the World

East Asian Connections

500–1300

Together Again: The Reemergence of
 a Unified China
  A "Golden Age" of Chinese
   Achievement
  Women in the Song Dynasty
China and the Northern Nomads:
 A Chinese World Order in the Making
  The Tribute System in Theory
  The Tribute System in Practice
  Cultural Influence across an
   Ecological Frontier
Coping with China: Comparing Korea,
 Vietnam, and Japan
  Korea and China
  Vietnam and China
  Japan and China
China and the Eurasian World Economy
  Spillovers: China's Impact on Eurasia
  On the Receiving End: China as
   Economic Beneficiary
China and Buddhism
  Making Buddhism Chinese
  Losing State Support: The Crisis of
   Chinese Buddhism
Reflections: Why Do Things Change?
Portrait: Izumi Shikibu, Japanese Poet
 and Lover

"China will be the next superpower."[1] That was the frank assertion of an article in the British newspaper the *Guardian* in June 2006. Nor was it alone in that assessment. As the new millennium dawned, headlines with this message appeared with increasing frequency in public lectures, in newspaper and magazine articles, and in book titles all across the world. China's huge population, its booming economy, its massive trade surplus with the United States, its entry into world oil markets, its military potential, and its growing presence in global political affairs—all of this suggested that China was headed for a major role, perhaps even a dominant role, in the world of the twenty-first century. Few of these authors, however, paused to recall that China's prominence on the world stage was hardly something new or that its nineteenth- and twentieth-century position as a "backward," weak, or dependent country was distinctly at odds with its long history. Is China perhaps poised to resume in the twenty-first century a much older and more powerful role in world affairs?

IN THE WORLD OF THIRD-WAVE CIVILIZATIONS, even more than in earlier times, China cast a long shadow. Its massive and powerful civilization, widely imitated by adjacent peoples, gave rise to a China-centered "world order" encompassing most of eastern Asia.[2] China extended its borders deep into Central Asia, while its wealthy and cosmopolitan culture attracted visitors from all over Eurasia. None of its many neighbors—whether nomadic peoples to the north and west or smaller peripheral states such as Tibet, Korea, Japan, and Vietnam—could escape its gravitational pull. All of them had to deal

Chinese Astronomy: The impressive achievements of Chinese astronomy included the observation of sunspots, supernovae, and solar and lunar eclipses as well as the construction of elaborate star maps and astronomical devices such as those shown here. The print itself is of Japanese origin and shows a figure wearing the dragon robes of a Chinese official. It illustrates the immense cultural influence of China on its smaller Japanese neighbor. (© The Trustees of the British Museum)

with China. Far beyond these near neighbors, China's booming economy and many technological innovations had ripple effects all across the Afro-Eurasia world.

Even as China so often influenced the world, it too was changed by its many interactions with non-Chinese peoples. Northern nomads—"barbarians" to the Chinese—frequently posed a military threat and on occasion even conquered and ruled parts of China. The country's growing involvement in international trade stimulated important social, cultural, and economic changes within China itself. Buddhism, a religion of Indian origin, took root in China, and, to a lesser extent, so did Christianity and Islam. In short, China's engagement with the wider world became a very significant element in a global era of accelerating connections.

SEEKING THE MAIN POINT

Chinese history has often been viewed in the West as impressive perhaps, but largely static or changeless and self-contained or isolated. In what ways might the material in this chapter counteract such impressions?

Together Again: The Reemergence of a Unified China

The collapse of the Han dynasty around 220 C.E. ushered in more than three centuries of political fragmentation in China and signaled the rise of powerful and locally entrenched aristocratic families. It also meant the incursion of northern nomads, many of whom learned Chinese, dressed like Chinese, married into Chinese families, and governed northern regions of the country in a Chinese fashion. Such conditions of disunity, unnatural in the eyes of many thoughtful Chinese, discredited Confucianism and opened the door to a greater acceptance of Buddhism and Daoism among the elite. (See Portrait of Ge Hong in Chapter 5, pp. 156–57.)

Those centuries also witnessed substantial Chinese migration southward toward the Yangzi River valley, a movement of people that gave southern China some 60 percent of the country's population by 1000. That movement of Chinese people, accompanied by their intensive agriculture, set in motion a vast environmental transformation, marked by the destruction of the old-growth forests that once covered much of the country and the retreat of the elephants that had inhabited those lands. Around 800 C.E., the Chinese official and writer Liu Zongyuan lamented what was happening.

> A tumbled confusion of lumber as flames on the hillside crackle
> Not even the last remaining shrubs are safeguarded from destruction
> Where once mountain torrents leapt—nothing but rutted gullies.[3]

A "Golden Age" of Chinese Achievement

■ **Change**
Why are the centuries of the Tang and Song dynasties in China sometimes referred to as a "golden age"?

Unlike the fall of the western Roman Empire, where political fragmentation proved to be a permanent condition, China regained its unity under the Sui dynasty (589–618). Its emperors solidified that unity by a vast extension of the country's canal system, stretching some 1,200 miles in length and described by one scholar as "an engineering feat without parallel in the world of its time."[4] Those canals linked northern and

A Map of Time

39	Trung sisters rebellion against China in Vietnam
4th–6th centuries	Early state building in Korea
300–800	Buddhism takes root in China
589–618	Sui dynasty and the reunification of China
604	Seventeen Article Constitution in Japan
618–907	Tang dynasty in China
688	Withdrawal of Chinese military forces from Korea
794–1192	Heian period in Japanese history
845	Suppression of Buddhism in China
868	First printed book in China
939	Vietnam establishes independence from China
960–1279	Song dynasty in China
ca. 1000	Invention of gunpowder in China; beginning of foot binding
1000	*Tale of Genji* (Japan)
1279–1369	Mongol rule in China

southern China economically and contributed much to the prosperity that followed. But the ruthlessness of Sui emperors and a futile military campaign to conquer Korea exhausted the state's resources, alienated many people, and prompted the overthrow of the dynasty.

This dynastic collapse, however, witnessed no prolonged disintegration of the Chinese state. The two dynasties that followed—the Tang (618–907) and the Song (960–1279)—built on the Sui foundations of renewed unity (see Map 8.1, p. 252). Together they established patterns of Chinese life that endured into the twentieth century, despite a fifty-year period of disunity between the two dynasties. Culturally, this era has long been regarded as a "golden age" of arts and literature, setting standards of excellence in poetry, landscape painting, and ceramics. Particularly during the Song dynasty, an explosion of scholarship gave rise to Neo-Confucianism, an effort to revive Confucian thinking while incorporating into it some of the insights of Buddhism and Daoism.

Politically, the Tang and Song dynasties built a state structure that endured for a thousand years. Six major ministries—personnel, finance, rites, army, justice, and public works—were accompanied by the Censorate, an agency that exercised surveillance over the rest of the government, checking on the character and competence of public officials. To staff this bureaucracy, the examination system was revived and made

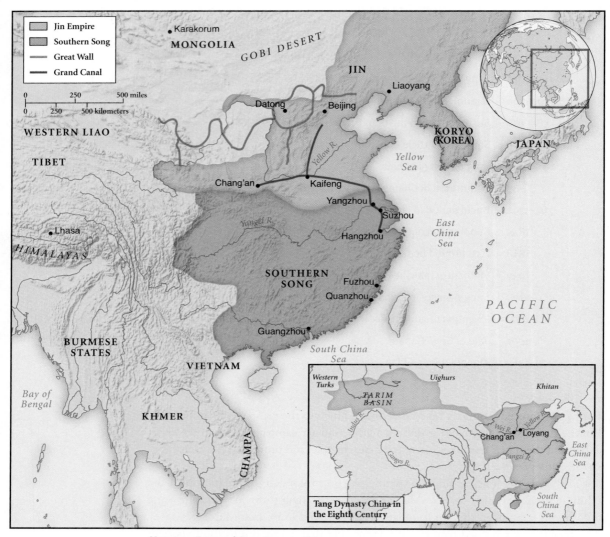

Map 8.1   Tang and Song Dynasty China
During the third-wave millennium, China interacted extensively with its neighbors. The Tang dynasty extended Chinese control deep into Central Asia, while the Song dynasty witnessed incursions by the nomadic Jurchen people, who created the Jin Empire, which ruled parts of northern China.

more elaborate, facilitated by the ability to print books for the first time in world history. Efforts to prevent cheating on the exams included searching candidates entering the examination hall and placing numbers rather than names on their papers. Schools and colleges proliferated to prepare candidates for the rigorous exams, which became a central feature of upper-class life. A leading world historian has described Tang dynasty China as "the best ordered state in the world."[5]

Selecting officials on the basis of merit represented a challenge to established aristocratic families' hold on public office. Still, a substantial percentage of official positions went to the sons of the privileged, even if they had not passed the exams. Moreover, because education and the examination system grew far more rapidly than the number of official positions, many who passed lower-level exams could not be accommodated with a bureaucratic appointment. Often, however, they were able to combine landowning and success in the examination system to maintain an immense cultural prestige and prominence in their local areas. Despite the state's periodic efforts to redistribute land in favor of the peasantry, the great families of large landowners continued to encroach on peasant plots, a recurring pattern in rural China from ancient times to the present.

Underlying these cultural and political achievements was an "economic revolution" that made Song dynasty China "by far the richest, most skilled, and most populous country on earth."[6] The most obvious sign of China's prosperity was its rapid growth in population, which jumped from about 50 million or 60 million during the Tang dynasty to 120 million by 1200. Behind this doubling of the population were remarkable achievements in agricultural production, particularly the adoption of a fast-ripening and drought-resistant strain of rice from Vietnam.

Many people found their way to the cities, making China the most urbanized country in the world. Dozens of Chinese cities numbered over 100,000, while the Song dynasty capital of Hangzhou was home to more than a million people. A Chinese observer in 1235 provided a vivid description of that city.[7] Specialized markets abounded for meat, herbs, vegetables, books, rice, and much more, with troupes of actors performing for the crowds. Restaurants advertised their unique offerings—sweet bean soup, pickled dates, juicy lungs, meat pies, pigs' feet—and some offered vegetarian fare for religious banquets. Inns of various kinds appealed to different groups. Those that served only wine, a practice known as "hitting the cup," were regarded as "unfit for polite company." "Luxuriant inns," marked by red lanterns, featured prostitutes and "wine chambers equipped with beds." Specialized agencies managed elaborate dinner parties for the wealthy, complete with a Perfume and Medicine Office to "help sober up the guests." Schools for musicians offered thirteen different courses. Numerous clubs provided companionship for poets, fishermen, Buddhists, physical fitness enthusiasts, antiques collectors, horse lovers, and many other groups. No wonder the Italian visitor Marco Polo described Hangzhou later in the thirteenth century as "beyond dispute the finest and noblest [city] in the world."[8]

Supplying these cities with food was made possible by an immense network of internal waterways—canals, rivers, and lakes—stretching perhaps 30,000 miles. They provided a cheap transportation system that bound the country together economically and created the "world's most populous trading area."[9]

Industrial production likewise soared. In both large-scale enterprises employing hundreds of workers and in smaller backyard furnaces, China's iron industry increased its output dramatically. By the eleventh century, it was providing the government with

Kaifeng
This detail comes from a huge watercolor scroll, titled *Upper River during Qing Ming Festival*, originally painted during the Song dynasty. It illustrates the urban sophistication of Kaifeng and other Chinese cities at that time and has been frequently imitated and copied since then. (Palace Museum, Beijing/Cultural Relics Press)

32,000 suits of armor and 16 million iron arrowheads annually, in addition to supplying metal for coins, tools, construction, and bells in Buddhist monasteries. Technological innovation in other fields also flourished. Inventions in printing, both woodblock and movable type, generated the world's first printed books, and by 1000 relatively cheap books on religious, agricultural, mathematical, and medical topics became widely available in China. Its navigational and shipbuilding technologies led the world. The Chinese invention of gunpowder created within a few centuries a revolution in military affairs that had global dimensions. (See Snapshot, p. 224.)

Most remarkably, perhaps, all of this occurred within the world's most highly commercialized society, in which producing for the market, rather than for local consumption, became a very widespread phenomenon. Cheap transportation allowed peasants to grow specialized crops for sale, while they purchased rice or other staples on the market. In addition, government demands for taxes paid in cash rather than in kind required peasants to sell something—their products or their labor—in order to meet their obligations. The growing use of paper money as well as financial instruments such as letters of credit and promissory notes further contributed to the commercialization of Chinese society. Two prominent scholars have described the outcome: "Output increased, population grew, skills multiplied, and a burst of inventiveness made Song China far wealthier than ever before—or than any of its contemporaries."[10]

Women in the Song Dynasty

The "golden age" of Song dynasty China was perhaps less than "golden" for many of its women, for that era marked yet another turning point in the history of Chinese patriarchy. Under the influence of steppe nomads, whose women led less restricted lives, elite Chinese women of the Tang dynasty era, at least in the north, had participated in social life with greater freedom than in earlier times. Paintings and statues show aristocratic women riding horses, while the Queen Mother of the West, a Daoist deity, was widely worshipped by female Daoist priests and practitioners. By the Song dynasty, however, a reviving Confucianism and rapid economic growth seemed to tighten patriarchal restrictions on women and to restore some of the earlier Han dynasty notions of female submission and passivity.

Once again Confucian writers highlighted the subordination of women to men and the need to keep males and females separate in every domain of life. The Song dynasty historian and scholar Sima Guang (1019–1086) summed up the prevailing view: "The boy leads the girl, the girl follows the boy; the duty of husbands to be resolute and wives to be docile begins with this."[11] For men, masculinity came to be defined less in terms of horseback riding, athleticism, and the warrior values of northern nomads and more in terms of the refined pursuits of calligraphy, scholarship, painting, and poetry. Corresponding views of feminine qualities emphasized women's weakness, reticence, and delicacy. Women were also frequently viewed as a distraction to men's pursuit of a contemplative and introspective life. The remarriage of widows, though legally permissible, was increasingly condemned, for "to walk through two courtyards is a source of shame for a woman."[12]

The most compelling expression of a tightening patriarchy lay in foot binding. Apparently beginning among dancers and courtesans in the tenth or eleventh century C.E., this practice involved the tight wrapping of young girls' feet, usually breaking the bones of the foot and causing intense pain. During and after the Song dynasty, foot binding spread widely among elite families and later became even more widespread in Chinese society. It was associated with new images of female beauty and eroticism that emphasized small size, frailty, and deference and served to keep women restricted to the "inner quarters," where Confucian tradition asserted that they belonged. Many mothers imposed this painful procedure on their daughters, perhaps to enhance their marriage prospects and to assist them in competing with concubines for the attention of their husbands.[13] For many women it became a rite of passage and source of some pride in their tiny feet and the beautiful slippers that encased them, even the occasion for poetry for some literate women. Foot binding also served to

■ **Change**
In what ways did women's lives change during the Tang and Song dynasties?

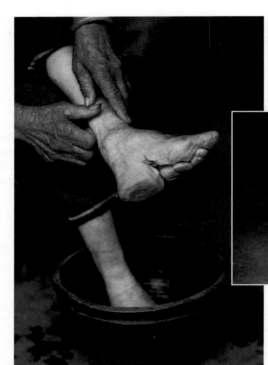

Foot Binding
While the practice of foot binding painfully deformed the feet of young girls and women, it was also associated esthetically with feminine beauty, particularly in the delicate and elaborately decorated shoes that encased their bound feet. (Foot: Jodi Cobb/National Geographic Stock; Shoe: ClassicStock/Masterfile)

distinguish Chinese women from their "barbarian" counterparts and elite women from commoners and peasants.

Furthermore, a rapidly commercializing economy undermined the position of women in the textile industry. Urban workshops and state factories, run by men, increasingly took over the skilled tasks of weaving textiles, especially silk, which had previously been the work of rural women in their homes. Although these women continued to tend silk worms and spin silk thread, they had lost the more lucrative income-generating work of weaving silk fabrics. But as their economic role in textile production declined, other opportunities beckoned in an increasingly prosperous Song China. In the cities, women operated restaurants, sold fish and vegetables, and worked as maids, cooks, and dressmakers. The growing prosperity of elite families funneled increasing numbers of women into roles as concubines, entertainers, courtesans, and prostitutes. Their ready availability surely reduced the ability of wives to negotiate as equals with their husbands, setting women against one another and creating endless household jealousies.

In other ways, the Song dynasty witnessed more positive trends in the lives of women. Their property rights expanded, in terms of controlling their own dowries and inheriting property from their families. "Neither in earlier nor in later periods," writes one scholar, "did as much property pass through women's hands" as during the Song dynasty.[14] Furthermore, lower-ranking but ambitious officials strongly urged the education of women, so that they might more effectively raise their sons and increase the family's fortune. Song dynasty China, in short, offered a mixture of tightening restrictions and new opportunities to its women.

LearningCurve
bedfordstmartins.com
/strayer/LC

China and the Northern Nomads: A Chinese World Order in the Making

From early times to the nineteenth century, China's many interactions with a larger Eurasian world shaped both China's own development and that of world history more generally. The country's most enduring and intense interaction with foreigners lay to the north, involving the many nomadic pastoral or semi-agricultural peoples of the steppes. Living in areas unable to sustain Chinese-style farming, the northern nomads had long focused their economies around the raising of livestock (sheep, cattle, goats) and the mastery of horse riding. Organized locally in small, mobile, kinship-based groups, sometimes called tribes, these peoples also periodically created much larger and powerful states or confederations that could draw on the impressive horsemanship and military skills of virtually the entire male population of their societies. Such specialized pastoral societies needed grain and other agricultural products from China, and their leaders developed a taste for Chinese manufactured and luxury goods—wine and silk, for example—with which they could attract and reward followers. Thus the nomads were drawn like a magnet toward China, trading, raiding, and extorting to obtain the resources so vital to their way of life. For 2,000 years or more, pressure from the steppes and the intrusion of nomadic peoples were constant factors in China's historical development.

From the nomads' point of view, the threat often came from the Chinese, who periodically directed their own military forces deep into the steppes, built the Great Wall to keep the nomads out, and often proved unwilling to allow pastoral peoples easy access to trading opportunities within China.[15] And yet the Chinese needed the nomads. Their lands were the source of horses, so essential for the Chinese military. Other products of the steppes and the forests beyond, such as skins, furs, hides, and amber, were also of value in China. Furthermore, pastoral nomads controlled much of the Silk Road trading network, which funneled goods from the West into China. The continuing interaction between China and the northern nomads brought together peoples occupying different environments, practicing different economies, governing themselves with different institutions, and thinking about the world in quite different ways.

The Tribute System in Theory

An enduring outcome of this cross-cultural encounter was a particular view the Chinese held of themselves and of their neighbors, fully articulated by the time of the Han dynasty (200 B.C.E.–200 C.E.) and lasting for more than two millennia. That understanding cast China as the "middle kingdom," the center of the world, infinitely superior to the "barbarian" peoples beyond its borders. With its long history, great cities, refined tastes, sophisticated intellectual and artistic achievements, bureaucratic state, literate elite, and prosperous economy, China represented "civilization." All of this, in Chinese thinking, was in sharp contrast to the rude cultures and primitive life of the northern nomads, who continually moved about "like beasts and birds," lived in tents,

■ **Connection**

How did the Chinese and their nomadic neighbors to the north view each other?

■ **Connection**

What assumptions underlay the tribute system?

ate mostly meat and milk, and practically lived on their horses, while making war on everyone within reach. Educated Chinese saw their own society as self-sufficient, requiring little from the outside world, while barbarians, quite understandably, sought access to China's wealth and wisdom. Furthermore, China was willing to permit that access under controlled conditions, for its sense of superiority did not preclude the possibility that barbarians could become civilized Chinese. China was a "radiating civilization," graciously shedding its light most fully to nearby barbarians and with diminished intensity to those farther away.[16]

Such was the general understanding of literate Chinese about their own civilization in relation to northern nomads and other non-Chinese peoples. That worldview also took shape as a practical system for managing China's relationship with these people. Known as the "tribute system," it was a set of practices that required non-Chinese authorities to acknowledge Chinese superiority and their own subordinate place in a Chinese-centered world order. Foreigners seeking access to China had to send a delegation to the Chinese court, where they would perform the kowtow, a series of ritual bowings and prostrations, and present their tribute—produce of value from their countries—to the Chinese emperor. In return for these expressions of submission, he would grant permission for foreigners to trade in China's rich markets and would provide them with gifts or "bestowals," often worth far more than the tribute they had offered. This was the mechanism by which successive Chinese dynasties attempted to regulate their relationships with northern nomads; with neighboring states such as Korea, Vietnam, Tibet, and Japan; and, after 1500, with those European barbarians from across the sea.

Often, this system seemed to work. Over the centuries, countless foreign delegations proved willing to present their tribute, say the required words, and perform the necessary rituals required to gain access to the material goods of China. Aspiring non-Chinese rulers also gained prestige as they basked in the reflected glory of even this subordinate association with the great Chinese civilization. The official titles, seals of office, and ceremonial robes they received from China proved useful in their local struggles for power.

The Tribute System in Practice

■ **Connection**

How did the tribute system in practice differ from the ideal Chinese understanding of its operation?

But the tribute system also disguised some realities that contradicted its assumptions. On occasion, China was confronting not separate and small-scale barbarian societies, but large and powerful nomadic empires able to deal with China on at least equal terms. An early nomadic confederacy was that of the Xiongnu, established about the same time as the Han dynasty and eventually reaching from Manchuria to Central Asia (see Map 3.5, p. 105). Devastating Xiongnu raids into northern China persuaded the Chinese emperor to negotiate an arrangement that recognized the nomadic state as a political equal, promised its leader a princess in marriage, and, most important, agreed to supply him annually with large quantities of grain, wine, and silk. Although

The Tribute System
This Qing dynasty painting shows an idealized Chinese version of the tribute system. The Chinese emperor receives barbarian envoys, who perform rituals of subordination and present tribute in the form of a horse. (Réunion des Musées Nationaux/Art Resource, NY)

these goods were officially termed "gifts," granted in accord with the tribute system, they were in fact tribute in reverse or even protection money. In return for these goods, so critical for the functioning of the nomadic state, the Xiongnu agreed to refrain from military incursions into China. The basic realities of the situation were summed up in this warning to the Han dynasty in the first century B.C.E.:

> Just make sure that the silks and grain stuffs you bring the Xiongnu are the right measure and quality, that's all. What's the need for talking? If the goods you deliver are up to measure and good quality, all right. But if there is any deficiency or the quality is no good, then when the autumn harvest comes, we will take our horses and trample all over your crops.[17]

Something similar occurred during the Tang dynasty as a series of Turkic empires arose in Mongolia. Like the Xiongnu, they too extorted large "gifts" from the Chinese. One of these peoples, the Uighurs, actually rescued the Tang dynasty from a serious internal revolt in the 750s. In return, the Uighur leader gained one of the Chinese emperor's daughters as a wife and arranged a highly favorable exchange of poor-quality horses for high-quality silk that brought half a million rolls of the precious fabric annually into the Uighur lands. Despite the rhetoric of the tribute system, the Chinese were not always able to dictate the terms of their relationship with the northern nomads.

Steppe nomads were generally not much interested in actually conquering and ruling China. It was easier and more profitable to extort goods from a functioning Chinese state. On occasion, though, that state broke down, and various nomadic groups moved in to "pick up the pieces," conquering and governing parts of China. Such a process took place following the fall of the Han dynasty and again after the collapse of the Tang dynasty, when the Khitan (kee-THAN) (907–1125) and then the Jin or Jurchen (JER-chihn) (1115–1234) peoples established states that encompassed parts of northern China as well as major areas of the steppes to the north. Both of them required the Chinese Song dynasty, located farther south, to deliver annually huge quantities of silk, silver, and tea, some of which found its way into the Silk Road trading network. The practice of "bestowing gifts on barbarians," long a part of the tribute system, allowed the proud Chinese to imagine that they were still in control of the situation even as they were paying heavily for protection from nomadic incursion. Those gifts, in turn, provided vital economic resources to nomadic states.

Cultural Influence across an Ecological Frontier

■ Connection

In what ways did China and the nomads influence each other?

When nomadic peoples actually ruled parts of China, some of them adopted Chinese ways, employing Chinese advisers, governing according to Chinese practice, and, at least for the elite, immersing themselves in Chinese culture and learning. This process of "becoming Chinese" went furthest among the Jurchen, many of whom lived in northern China and learned to speak Chinese, wore Chinese clothing, married Chinese husbands and wives, and practiced Buddhism or Daoism. On the whole, however, Chinese culture had only a modest impact on the nomadic people of the northern steppes. Unlike the native peoples of southern China, who were gradually absorbed into Chinese culture, the pastoral societies north of the Great Wall generally retained their own cultural patterns. Few of them were incorporated, at least not for long, within a Chinese state, and most lived in areas where Chinese-style agriculture was simply impossible. Under these conditions, there were few incentives for adopting Chinese culture wholesale. But various modes of interaction—peaceful trade, military conflict, political negotiations, economic extortion, some cultural influence—continued across the ecological frontier that divided two quite distinct and separate ways of life. Each was necessary for the other.

On the Chinese side, elements of steppe culture had some influence in those parts of northern China that were periodically conquered and ruled by nomadic peoples. The founders of the Sui and Tang dynasties were in fact of mixed nomad and Chinese ancestry and came from the borderland region where a blended Chinese/Turkic culture had evolved. High-ranking members of the imperial family personally led their troops in battle in the style of Turkic warriors. Furthermore, Tang dynasty China was awash with foreign visitors from all over Asia—delegations bearing tribute, merchants carrying exotic goods, bands of clerics or religious pilgrims bringing new religions such as Christianity, Islam, Buddhism, and Manichaeism. For a time in the Tang dynasty, almost anything associated with "western barbarians"—Central Asians, Persians, Indians, Arabs—had great appeal among northern Chinese elites. Their music, dancing, clothing, foods, games, and artistic styles found favor among the upper classes. The more traditional southern Chinese, feeling themselves heir to the legacy of the Han dynasty, were sharply critical of their northern counterparts for allowing women too much freedom, for drinking yogurt rather than tea, for listening to "western" music, all of which they attributed to barbarian influence. Around 800 C.E., the poet Yuan Chen gave voice to a growing backlash against this too easy acceptance of things "Western":

Ever since the Western horsemen began raising smut and dust,
Fur and fleece, rank and rancid, have filled Hsien and Lo [two Chinese cities].
Women make themselves Western matrons by the study of Western makeup.
Entertainers present Western tunes, in their devotion to Western music.[18]

LearningCurve
bedfordstmartins.com
/strayer/LC

Coping with China: Comparing Korea, Vietnam, and Japan

Also involved in tributary relationships with China were the newly emerging states and civilizations of Korea, Vietnam, and Japan. Unlike the northern nomads, these societies were thoroughly agricultural and sedentary. During the first millennium C.E., they were part of a larger process—the globalization of civilization—which produced new city- and state-based societies in various parts of the world. Proximity to their giant Chinese neighbor decisively shaped the histories of these new East Asian civilizations, for all of them borrowed major elements of Chinese culture. But unlike the native peoples of southern China, who largely became Chinese, the peoples of Korea, Vietnam, and Japan did not. They retained distinctive identities, which have lasted into modern times. While resisting Chinese political domination, they also appreciated Chinese culture and sought the source of Chinese wealth and power. In such ways, these smaller East Asian civilizations resembled the "developing" Afro-Asian societies of the twentieth century, which embraced "modernity" and elements of Western culture, while trying to maintain their political and cultural independence from the European and American centers of that modern way of life. Korea, Vietnam, and Japan, however, encountered China and responded to it in quite different ways.

■ **Connection**

In what ways did China have an influence in Korea, Vietnam, and Japan? In what ways was that influence resisted?

Korea and China

Immediately adjacent to northeastern China, the Korean peninsula and its people have long lived in the shadow of their imposing neighbor (see Map 8.2). Temporary Chinese conquest of northern Korea during the Han dynasty and some colonization by Chinese settlers provided an initial channel for Chinese cultural influence, particularly in the form of Buddhism. Early Korean states, which emerged in the fourth through seventh centuries C.E., all referred to their rulers with the Chinese term *wang* (king). Bitter rivals with one another, these states strenuously resisted Chinese political control, except when they found it advantageous to join with China against a local enemy. In the seventh century, one of these states—the Silla (SHEE-lah) kingdom—allied with Tang dynasty China to bring some political unity to the peninsula for the first time. But Chinese efforts to set up puppet regimes and to assimilate Koreans to Chinese culture provoked sharp military resistance, persuading the Chinese to withdraw their military forces in 688 and to establish a tributary relationship with a largely independent Korea.

Under a succession of dynasties—the Silla (688–900), Koryo (918–1392), and Yi (1392–1910)—Korea generally maintained its political independence while participating in China's tribute system. Its leaders actively embraced the connection with

China and, especially during the Silla dynasty, sought to turn their small state into a miniature version of Tang China.

Tribute missions to China provided legitimacy for Korean rulers and knowledge of Chinese court life and administrative techniques, which they sought to replicate back home. A new capital city of Kumsong was modeled directly on the Chinese capital of Chang'an (chahng-ahn). Tribute missions also enabled both official and private trade, mostly in luxury goods such as ceremonial clothing, silks, fancy teas, Confucian and Buddhist texts, and artwork — all of which enriched the lives of a Korean aristocracy that was becoming increasingly Chinese in culture. Thousands of Korean students were sent to China, where they studied primarily Confucianism but also natural sciences and the arts. Buddhist monks visited centers of learning and pilgrimage in China and brought back popular forms of Chinese Buddhism, which quickly took root in Korea. Schools for the study of Confucianism, using texts in the Chinese language, were established in Korea. In these ways, Korea became a part of the expanding world of Chinese culture, and refugees from the peninsula's many wars carried Chinese culture to Japan as well.

These efforts to plant Confucian values and Chinese culture in Korea had what one scholar has called an "overwhelmingly negative" impact on Korean women, particularly after 1300.[19] Early Chinese observers noticed, and strongly disapproved of, "free choice" marriages in Korea as well as the practice of women singing and dancing together late at night. With the support of the Korean court, Chinese models of family life and female behavior, especially among the elite, gradually replaced the more flexible Korean patterns. Earlier, a Korean woman had generally given birth and raised her young children in her parents' home, where she was often joined by her husband. This was now strongly discouraged, for it was deeply offensive to Confucian orthodoxy, which held that a married woman belonged to her husband's family. Some Korean customs — funeral rites in which a husband was buried in the sacred plot of his wife's family, the remarriage of widowed or divorced women, and female inheritance of property — eroded under the pressure of Confucian orthodoxy. So too did the practice of plural marriages for men. In 1413, a legal distinction between primary and secondary wives required men to identify one of their wives as primary. Because she and her children now had special privileges and status, sharp new tensions emerged within families.

Map 8.2 Korean Kingdoms about 500 C.E. The three early kingdoms of Korea were brought together by the seventh century in a unified state, which was subsequently governed by a series of dynastic regimes.

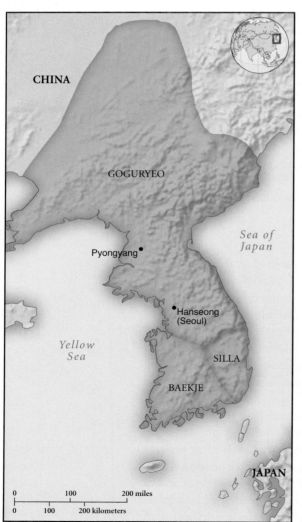

Korean restrictions on elite women, especially widows, came to exceed even those in China itself.

Still, Korea remained Korean. After 688, the country's political independence, though periodically threatened, was largely intact. Chinese cultural influence, except for Buddhism, had little impact beyond the aristocracy and certainly did not penetrate the lives of Korea's serf-like peasants. Nor did it register among Korea's many slaves, amounting to about one-third of the country's population by 1100 C.E. A Chinese-style examination system to recruit government officials, though encouraged by some Korean rulers, never assumed the prominence that it gained in Tang and Song dynasty China. Korea's aristocratic class was able to maintain an even stronger monopoly on bureaucratic office than their Chinese counterparts. And in the 1400s, Korea moved toward greater cultural independence by developing a phonetic alphabet, known as *hangul* (HAHN-gool), for writing the Korean language. Although resisted by conservative male elites, who were long accustomed to using the more prestigious Chinese characters to write Korean, this new form of writing gradually took hold, especially in private correspondence, in popular fiction, and among women. Clearly part of the Chinese world order, Korea nonetheless retained a distinctive culture as well as a separate political existence.

Vietnam and China

At the southern fringe of the Chinese cultural world, the people who eventually came to be called Vietnamese had a broadly similar historical encounter with China (see Map 8.3). As in Korea, the elite culture of Vietnam borrowed heavily from China—adopting Confucianism, Daoism, Buddhism, administrative techniques, the examination system, artistic and literary styles—even as its popular culture remained distinctive. And, like Korea, Vietnam achieved political independence, while participating fully in the tribute system as a vassal state.

But there were differences as well. The cultural heartland of Vietnam in the Red River valley was fully incorporated into the Chinese state for more than a thousand years (111 B.C.E.–939 C.E.), far longer than corresponding parts of Korea. Regarded by the Chinese as "southern barbarians," the Vietnamese were ruled by Chinese officials who expected to fully assimilate this rich rice-growing region into China culturally as well as politically. To these officials, it was simply a further extension of the southward expansion of Chinese civilization.

Map 8.3 Vietnam
As Vietnam threw off Chinese control, it also expanded to the south, while remaining wary of its larger Chinese neighbor to the north.

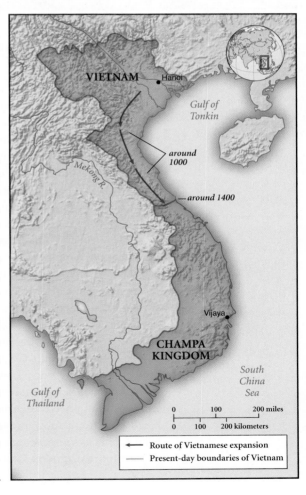

Independence for Vietnam

In 938, Vietnamese forces under the leadership of General Ngo Quyen defeated the Chinese in the Battle of Bach Dang River, thus ending a thousand years of direct Chinese rule. This image is one of many that celebrate that victory. (CPA Media)

Thus Chinese-style irrigated agriculture was introduced; Vietnamese elites were brought into the local bureaucracy and educated in Confucian-based schools; Chinese replaced the local language in official business; Chinese clothing and hairstyles became mandatory; and large numbers of Chinese, some fleeing internal conflicts at home, flooded into the relative security of what they referred to as "the pacified south," while often despising the local people.[20] The heavy pressure of the Chinese presence generated not only a Vietnamese elite thoroughly schooled in Chinese culture but also periodic rebellions, on several occasions led by women. (See the portrait of Trung Trac, p. 104.)

The weakening of the Tang dynasty in the early tenth century C.E. finally enabled a particularly large rebellion to establish Vietnam as a separate state, though one that carefully maintained its tributary role, sending repeated missions to do homage at the Chinese court. Nonetheless, successive Vietnamese dynasties found the Chinese approach to government useful, styling their rulers as emperors, claiming the Mandate of Heaven, and making use of Chinese court rituals, while expanding their state steadily southward. More so than in Korea, a Chinese-based examination system in Vietnam functioned to undermine an established aristocracy, to provide some measure of social mobility for commoners, and to create a merit-based scholar-gentry class to staff the bureaucracy. Furthermore, the Vietnamese elite class remained deeply committed to Chinese culture, viewing their own country less as a separate nation than as a southern extension of a universal civilization, the only one they knew.[21]

Beyond the elite, however, there remained much that was uniquely Vietnamese, such as a distinctive language, a fondness for cockfighting, and the habit of chewing betel nuts. More importantly, Vietnam long retained a greater role for women in social and economic life, despite heavy Chinese influence. In the third century C.E., a woman leader of an anti-Chinese resistance movement declared: "I want to drive away the enemy to save our people. I will not resign myself to the usual lot of women who bow their heads and become concubines." Female nature deities and a "female Buddha" continued to be part of Vietnamese popular religion, even as Confucian-based ideas took root among the elite. In the centuries following independence from China as Vietnam expanded to the south, northern officials tried in vain to impose more orthodox Confucian gender practices in place of local customs that allowed women to choose their own husbands and married men to live in the house-holds of their wives. So persistent were these practices that a seventeenth-century Chinese visitor opined, with disgust, that Vietnamese preferred the birth of a girl to that of a boy. These features of Vietnamese life reflected larger patterns of Southeast Asian culture that distinguished it from China. And like Korea, the Vietnamese developed a variation of Chinese writing called *chu nom* ("southern script"), which provided the basis for an independent national literature and a vehicle for the writing of most educated women.[22]

Japan and China

Unlike Korea and Vietnam, the Japanese islands were physically separated from China by 100 miles or more of ocean and were never successfully invaded or conquered by their giant mainland neighbor (see Map 8.4). Thus Japan's very extensive borrowing from Chinese civilization was wholly voluntary, rather than occurring under conditions of direct military threat or outright occupation. The high point of that borrowing took place during the seventh to the ninth centuries C.E., as the first more or less unified Japanese state began to emerge from dozens of small clan-based aristocratic chiefdoms. That state found much that was useful in Tang dynasty China and set out, deliberately and systematically, to transform Japan into a centralized bureaucratic state on the Chinese model.

The initial leader of this effort was Shotoku Taishi (572–622), a prominent aristocrat from one of the major clans. He launched a series of large-scale missions to China, which took hundreds of Japanese monks, scholars, artists, and students to the mainland, and when they returned, they put into practice what they had learned. He issued the Seventeen Article Constitution, proclaiming the Japanese ruler as a Chinese-style emperor and encouraging both Buddhism and Confucianism. In good Confucian fashion, that document emphasized the moral quality of rulers as a foundation for social harmony. In the decades that followed, Japanese authorities adopted Chinese-style court rituals and a system of court rankings for officials as well as the Chinese calendar. Subsequently, they likewise established Chinese-based taxation systems, law codes, government ministries, and provincial administration, at least on paper. Two capital cities, first Nara and then Heian (Kyoto), arose, both modeled on the Chinese capital of Chang'an.

Map 8.4 Japan

Japan's distance from China enabled it to maintain its political independence and to draw selectively from Chinese culture.

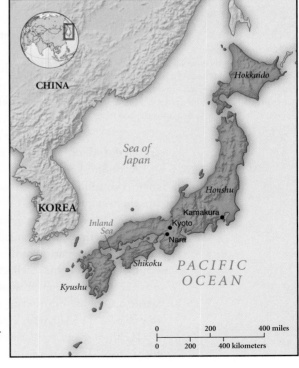

The Samurai of Japan
This late nineteenth-century image shows a samurai warrior on horseback clad in armor and a horned helmet while carrying a sword as well as a bow and arrows. The prominence of martial values in Japanese culture was one of the ways in which Japan differed from its Chinese neighbor, despite much borrowing. (Library of Congress, ID # pd 01046)

Chinese culture, no less than its political practices, also found favor in Japan. Various schools of Chinese Buddhism took root, first among the educated and literate classes and later more broadly in Japanese society, deeply affecting much of Japanese life. Art, architecture, education, medicine, views of the afterlife, attitudes toward suffering and the impermanence of life—all of this and more reflected the influence of Buddhist culture in Japan.[23] The Chinese writing system—and with it an interest in historical writing, calligraphy, and poetry—likewise proved attractive among the elite.

The absence of any compelling threat from China made it possible for the Japanese to be selective in their borrowing. By the tenth century, deliberate efforts to absorb additional elements of Chinese culture diminished, and formal tribute missions to China stopped, although private traders and Buddhist monks continued to make the difficult journey to the mainland. Over many centuries, the Japanese combined what they had assimilated from China with elements of their own tradition into a distinctive Japanese civilization, which differed from Chinese culture in many ways.

In the political realm, for example, the Japanese never succeeded in creating an effective centralized and bureaucratic state to match that of China. Although the court and the emperor retained an important ceremonial and cultural role, their real political authority over the country gradually diminished in favor of competing aristocratic families, both at court and in the provinces. A Chinese-style university trained officials, but rather than serving as a mechanism for recruiting talented commoners into the political elite, it enrolled students who were largely the sons of court aristocrats.

As political power became increasingly decentralized, local authorities developed their own military forces, the famous *samurai* warrior class of Japanese society. Bearing their exquisite curved swords, the samurai developed a distinctive set of values featuring great skill in martial arts, bravery, loyalty, endurance, honor, and a preference for death over surrender. This was *bushido* (boo-shee-doh), the way of the warrior. Japan's celebration of the samurai and of military virtues contrasted sharply with China's emphasis on intellectual achievements and political office holding, which were accorded higher prestige than bearing arms. "The educated men of the land," wrote a Chinese minister in the eleventh century, "regard the carrying of arms as a disgrace."[24] The Japanese, clearly, did not agree.

Religiously as well, Japan remained distinctive. Although Buddhism in many forms took hold in the country, it never completely replaced the native beliefs and practices, which focused attention on numerous *kami*, sacred spirits associated with human ancestors and various natural phenomena. Much later referred to as Shinto, this tradition provided legitimacy to the imperial family, based on claims of descent from the sun goddess. Because veneration of the kami lacked an elaborate philosophy or ritual, it conflicted very little with Buddhism. In fact, numerous kami were assimilated into Japanese Buddhism as local expressions of Buddhist deities or principles.

Japanese literary and artistic culture likewise evolved in distinctive ways, despite much borrowing from China. As in Korea and Vietnam, there emerged a unique writing system that combined Chinese characters with a series of phonetic symbols. A highly stylized Japanese poetic form, known as tanka, developed early and has remained a favored means of expression ever since. (See portrait of Izumi Shikibu, pp. 268–69, for the life of Japan's best-known female tanka poet.) Particularly during the Heian period of Japanese history (794–1192), a highly refined esthetic culture found expression at the imperial court, even as the court's real political authority melted away. Court aristocrats and their ladies lived in splendor, composed poems, arranged flowers, and conducted their love affairs. "What counted," wrote one scholar, "was the proper costume, the right ceremonial act, the successful turn of phrase in a poem, and the appropriate expression of refined taste."[25] Much of our knowledge of this courtly culture comes from the work of women writers, who composed their diaries and novels in the vernacular Japanese script, rather than in the classical Chinese used by elite men. *The Tale of Genji*, a Japanese novel written by the woman author Murasaki Shikibu around 1000, provides an intimate picture of the intrigues and romances of court life.

At this level of society, Japan's women, unlike those in Korea, largely escaped the more oppressive features of Chinese Confucian culture, such as the prohibition of remarriage for widows, seclusion within the home, and foot binding. Perhaps this is because the most powerful Chinese influence on Japan occurred during the Tang dynasty, when Chinese elite women enjoyed considerable freedom. Japanese women continued to inherit property; Japanese married couples often lived apart or with the wife's family; and marriages were made and broken easily. None of this corresponded to Confucian values. When Japanese women did begin to lose status in the twelfth century and later, it had less to do with Confucian pressures than with the rise of a warrior culture. As the personal relationships of samurai warriors to their lords replaced marriage alliances as a political strategy, the influence of women in political life was reduced, but this was an internal Japanese phenomenon, not a reflection of Chinese influence.

Japan's ability to borrow extensively from China while developing its own distinctive civilization perhaps provided a model for its encounter with the West in the nineteenth century. Then, as before, Japan borrowed selectively from a foreign culture without losing either its political independence or its cultural uniqueness.

■ **Comparison**

In what different ways did Japanese and Korean women experience the pressures of Confucian orthodoxy?

LearningCurve
bedfordstmartins.com/strayer/LC

SUMMING UP SO FAR

In what different ways did Korea, Vietnam, Japan, and northern nomads experience and respond to Chinese influence?

Izumi Shikibu, Japanese Poet and Lover

Nowhere in world history has poetry played a more central role than in the imperial court of Japan, located in the capital city of Heian-kyo (now Kyoto) between the ninth and twelfth centuries. There amid the political posturing and the love affairs of aristocratic women and men, almost every event, public or private, called for a poem—the first sighting of spring blossoms or a new moon; births, deaths, and marriages; various official rituals; the morning after a romantic encounter. "It is poetry," wrote one famous Japanese author in the early tenth century, "which . . . awakens the world of invisible spirits . . . , softens the relationship between men and women, and consoles the hearts of fierce warriors."[26] Izumi Shikibu, Japan's most illustrious female poet, was a master of this art, particularly in the lyric five-line, thirty-one-syllable form known as tanka. In her exquisite poetry, we can catch a glimpse of her erotic intensity, expressed in many scandalous love affairs, as well as her engagement in more spiritual pursuits.

Izumi Shikibu
(Courtesy National Diet Library (http://
dl.ndl.go.jp/info:ndljp/pid/1313149/1))

Born around 975 as the daughter of a midlevel official, Izumi grew up in the imperial court where a literary education was essential for girls of her status, for at least in matters of poetry and the arts, women and men operated on an equal basis. At about the age of 20, Izumi married a provincial governor, but she soon began an affair with Prince Tametaka, son of the emperor, shocking court society partly because of the sharp difference in their social positions. Tametaka's death in 1002, widely credited to his sexual excess with Izumi, only deepened the scandal and led to Izumi's divorce from her husband and estrangement from her family. Addressing her parents and sisters in a poem, she declared: "One of you / I was, but am no more."[27]

Less than a year later, she ignited another scandal by taking up with Tametaka's brother, Prince Atsumichi. The first year of this affair became the subject of Izumi's famous *Diary*. When the Prince sent her a sprig of orange blossoms, she responded with a poem: "Rather than recall / in these flowers / the fragrance of the past, / I would like to hear

China and the Eurasian World Economy

Beyond China's central role in East Asia was its economic interaction with the wider world of Eurasia generally. On the one hand, China's remarkable economic growth, taking place during the Tang and Song dynasties, could hardly be contained within China's borders and clearly had a major impact throughout Eurasia. On the other hand, China was recipient as well as donor in the economic interactions of the third-wave era, and its own economic achievements owed something to the stimulus of contact with the larger world.

Spillovers: China's Impact on Eurasia

One of the outcomes of China's economic revolution lay in the diffusion of its many technological innovations to peoples and places far from East Asia as the movements of

this nightingale's voice, / to know if his song is as sweet." What followed was a year of nocturnal visits, frequent absences, rumors and gossip, doubts and longings, and the endless exchange of poems. Finally Izumi took up residence in the Prince's compound, much to the distress of his principal wife. Atsumichi's death in 1007 prompted an outpouring of poetry mourning the loss of her great love. "I long for the sound / of your voice. / The face / I see so clearly / doesn't say a word."[28]

Despite Izumi's behavior, she was subsequently appointed as a lady-in-waiting for the Empress Akiko, for her literary reputation added splendor to the court. But the scandal of her personal life continued to shadow her. A rival literary figure at the court, the renowned Lady Murasaki, author of *The Tale of Genji*, commented: "How interestingly Izumi Shikibu writes. Yet what a disgraceful person she is."[29] A subsequent marriage to a much older provincial governor took Izumi away from the court for the rest of her life. But her affairs continued. "I do not feel in the least disposed to sleep alone," she wrote.[30]

Her poetry gave frequent expression to erotic love and to the anguished yearning that accompanied it. "Lying alone, / my black hair tangled, / uncombed / I long for the one / who touched it first." To a monk who left his fan behind after a visit, she wrote, "I think / you may have briefly forgotten / this fan, / but everyone must know / how it came to be dropped."

Izumi's experiences of love within her social circle gave her an acute sense of the ephemerality of all things. "Come quickly—as soon as / these blossoms open, / they fall. / This world exists / as a sheen of dew on flowers." Her understanding of impermanence was reinforced by her Buddhist faith with its emphasis on the transience of human life. From time to time, she felt the desire to withdraw into a monastery, and she did take periodic retreats in mountain temples. Even there, however, Izumi experienced the pull of the world. "Although I try / to hold the single thought / of Buddha's teaching in my heart, / I cannot help but hear / the many crickets' voices calling as well."[31]

Perhaps Izumi's best-known poem was composed when she was still in her teens, though it has sometimes been viewed as a prayer on her deathbed. Written to a Buddhist cleric, it reveals her early and continuing desire for spiritual enlightenment, symbolized here as the light of the moon. "From utter darkness / I must embark upon an / even darker road / O distant moon, cast your light / from the rim of the mountains."[32]

Question: How do you understand Izumi's involvement in multiple love relationships and her religious sensibilities?

traders, soldiers, slaves, and pilgrims conveyed Chinese achievements abroad. (See the Snapshot, p. 270, for a wider view of Chinese technological achievements.) Chinese techniques for producing salt by solar evaporation spread to the Islamic world and later to Christian Europe. Papermaking, known in China since the Han dynasty, spread to Korea and Vietnam by the fourth century C.E., to Japan and India by the seventh, to the Islamic world by the eighth, to Muslim Spain by 1150, to France and Germany in the 1300s, and to England in the 1490s. Printing, likewise a Chinese invention, rapidly reached Korea, where movable type became a highly developed technique, and Japan as well. Both technologies were heavily influenced by Buddhism, which accorded religious merit to the reproduction of sacred texts. The Islamic world, however, highly valued handwritten calligraphy and generally resisted printing as impious until the nineteenth century. The adoption of printing in Europe was likewise delayed because of the absence of paper until the fourteenth century. Then movable type was reinvented by Johannes Gutenberg in the fifteenth century, although it is unclear whether

■ **Connection**

In what ways did China participate in the world of Eurasian commerce and exchange, and with what outcomes?

$\mathcal{S}$napshot   **Chinese Technological Achievements**[33]

Before the technological explosion of the European Industrial Revolution during the eighteenth and nineteenth centuries, China had long been the major center of global technological innovation. Many of those inventions spread to other civilizations where they stimulated imitation or modification. Since Europe was located at the opposite end of the Eurasian continent from China, it often took considerable time for those innovations to give rise to something similar in the West. That lag is also a measure of the relative technological development of the two civilizations in premodern times.

Innovation	First Used in China (approximate)	Adoption/Recognition in the West: Time lag in years (approximate)
Iron plow	6th–4th century B.C.E.	2000+
Cast iron	4th century B.C.E.	1000–1200
Efficient horse collar	3rd–1st century B.C.E.	1000
Paper	2nd century B.C.E.	1000
Wheelbarrow	1st century B.C.E.	900–1000
Rudder for steering ships	1st century C.E.	1100
Iron chain suspension bridge	1st century C.E.	1000–1300
Porcelain	3rd century C.E.	1500
Magnetic compass for navigation	9th–11th century C.E.	400
Gunpowder	9th century C.E.	400
Chain drive for transmission of power	976 C.E.	800
Moveable type printing	1045 C.E.	400

he was aware of Chinese and Korean precedents. With implications for mass literacy, bureaucracy, scholarship, the spread of religion, and the exchange of information, papermaking and printing were Chinese innovations of revolutionary and global dimensions.

Chinese technologies were seldom simply transferred from one place to another. More often a particular Chinese technique or product stimulated innovations in more distant lands in accordance with local needs.[34] For example, as the Chinese formula for gunpowder, invented around 1000, became available in Europe, together with some early and simple firearms, these innovations triggered the development of cannons in the early fourteenth century. Soon cannons appeared in the Islamic world and by 1356 in China itself, which first used cast iron rather than bronze in their construction. But the highly competitive European state system drove the "gunpowder revolution" much further and more rapidly than in China's imperial state. Chinese textile, metal-lurgical, and naval technologies likewise stimulated imitation and innovation all across Eurasia. An example is the magnetic compass, a Chinese invention eagerly embraced by mariners of many cultural backgrounds as they traversed the Indian Ocean.

In addition to its technological influence, China's prosperity during the Song dynasty greatly stimulated commercial life and market-based behavior all across the Afro-Eurasian trading world. China's products—silk, porcelain, lacquerware—found eager buyers from Japan to East Africa, and everywhere in between. The immense size and wealth of China's domestic economy also provided a ready market for hundreds of commodities from afar. For example, the lives of many thousands of people in the spice-producing islands of what is now Indonesia were transformed as they came to depend on Chinese consumers' demand for their products. "[O]ne hundred million [Chinese] people," wrote historian William McNeill, "increasingly caught up within a commercial network, buying and selling to supplement every day's livelihood, made a significant difference to the way other human beings made their livings throughout a large part of the civilized world."[35] Such was the ripple effect of China's economic revolution.

On the Receiving End: China as Economic Beneficiary

If Chinese economic growth and technological achievements significantly shaped the Eurasian world of the third-wave era, that pattern of interaction was surely not a one-way street, for China too was changed by its engagement with a wider world. During this period, for example, China had learned about the cultivation and processing of both cotton and sugar from India. From Vietnam, around 1000, China gained access to the new, fast-ripening, and drought-resistant strains of rice that made a highly productive rice-based agriculture possible in the drier and more rugged regions of southern China. This marked a major turning point in Chinese history as the frontier region south of the Yangzi River grew rapidly in population, overtaking the traditional centers of Chinese civilization in the north.

Technologically as well, China's extraordinary burst of creativity owed something to the stimulus of cross-cultural contact. Awareness of Persian windmills, for example, spurred the development of a distinct but related device in China. Printing arose from China's growing involvement with the world of Buddhism, which put a spiritual premium on the reproduction of the Buddha's image and of short religious texts that were carried as charms. It was in Buddhist monasteries during the Tang dynasty that the long-established practice of printing with seals was elaborated by Chinese monks into woodblock printing. The first printed book, in 868 C.E., was a famous Buddhist text, the *Diamond Sutra*. Gunpowder too seems to have had an Indian and Buddhist connection. An Indian Buddhist monk traveling in China in 644 C.E. identified soils that contained saltpeter and showed that they produced a purple flame when put into a fire. This was the beginning of Chinese experiments, which finally led to a reliable recipe for gunpowder.

A further transforming impact of China's involvement with a wider world derived from its growing participation in Indian Ocean trade. By the Tang dynasty, thousands of ships annually visited the ports of southern China, and settled communities of foreign merchants—Arabs, Persians, Indians, Southeast Asians—turned some of these cities into cosmopolitan centers. Buddhist temples, Muslim mosques and cemeteries, and Hindu phallic sculptures graced the skyline of Quanzhou, a coastal city in southern China. Occasionally the tensions of cultural diversity erupted in violence, such as the massacre of tens of thousands of foreigners in Canton during the 870s when Chinese rebel forces sacked the city. Indian Ocean commerce also contributed much to the transformation of southern China from a subsistence economy to one more heavily based on producing for export. In the process, merchants achieved a degree of social acceptance not known before, including their frequent appointment to high-ranking bureaucratic positions. Finally, much-beloved stories of the monkey god, widely popular even in contemporary China, derived from Indian sources transmitted by Indian Ocean commerce.[36]

LearningCurve
bedfordstmartins.com
/strayer/LC

China and Buddhism

By far the most important gift that China received from India was neither cotton, nor sugar, nor the knowledge of saltpeter, but a religion, Buddhism. The gradual assimilation of this South Asian religious tradition into Chinese culture illustrates the process of cultural encounter and adaptation and invites comparison with the spread of Christianity into Europe. Until the adoption of Marxism in the twentieth century, Buddhism was the only large-scale cultural borrowing in Chinese history. It also made China into a launching pad for Buddhism's dispersion to Korea and from there to Japan as well. Thus, as Buddhism faded in the land of its birth, it became solidly rooted in much of East Asia, providing an element of cultural commonality for a vast region (see Map 8.5).

Making Buddhism Chinese

■ **Change**
What facilitated the rooting of Buddhism within China?

Buddhism initially entered China via the Silk Road trading network during the first and second centuries C.E. The stability and prosperity of the Han dynasty, then at its height, ensured that the new "barbarian" religion held little appeal for native Chinese. Furthermore, the Indian culture from which Buddhism sprang was at odds with Chinese understandings of the world in many ways. Buddhism's commitment to a secluded and monastic life for monks and nuns seemed to dishonor Chinese family values, and its concern for individual salvation or enlightenment appeared selfish, contradicting the social orientation of Confucian thinking. Its abstract philosophy ran counter to the more concrete, "this-worldly" concerns of Chinese thinkers; and the Buddhist concept of infinite eons of time, endlessly repeating themselves, was quite a stretch for the Chinese, who normally thought in terms of finite family generations or dynastic cycles. No wonder that for the first several centuries C.E., Buddhism was largely the preserve of foreign merchants and monks living in China.

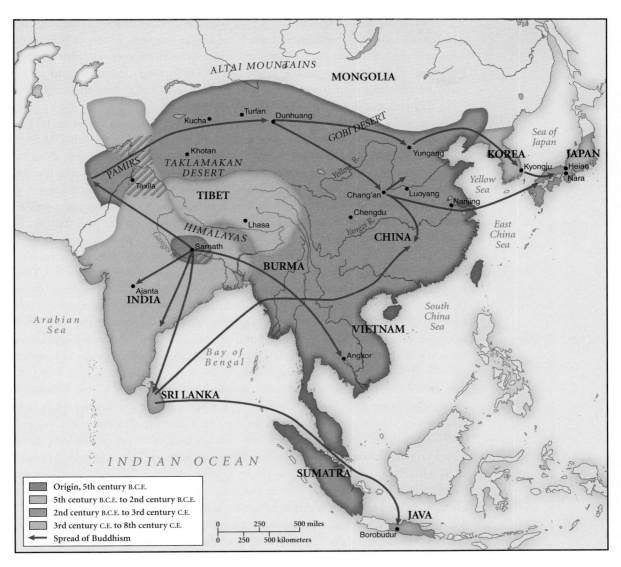

Map 8.5 The World of Asian Buddhism
Born in India, Buddhism later spread widely throughout much of Asia to provide a measure of cultural or religious commonality across this vast region.

In the half millennium between roughly 300 and 800 C.E., however, Buddhism took solid root in China within both elite and popular culture, becoming a permanent, though fluctuating, presence in Chinese life. How did this remarkable transformation unfold? It began, arguably, with the collapse of the Han dynasty around 200 C.E. The chaotic, violent, and politically fragmented centuries that followed seriously discredited Confucianism and opened the door to alternative understandings of the world. Nomadic rulers, now governing much of northern China, found Buddhism useful in part because it was foreign. "We were born out of the marches," declared one of them, "and though we are unworthy, we have complied with our appointed destiny and govern the Chinese as their prince. . . . Buddha being a barbarian god is the very one we should worship."[37] Rulers and elite families provided patronage for Buddhist monasteries, temples, and works of art. In southern China, where many northern aristocrats had fled following the disastrous decline of the Han dynasty, Buddhism provided some comfort in the face of a collapsing society. Its emphasis on ritual, morality, and contemplation represented an intellectually and esthetically satisfying response to times that were so clearly out of joint.

Meanwhile, Buddhist monasteries increasingly provided an array of social services for ordinary people. In them, travelers found accommodation; those fleeing from China's many upheavals discovered a place of refuge; desperate people received charity; farmers borrowed seed for the next planting; the sick were treated; children learned to read. And for many, Buddhism was associated with access to magical powers as reports of miracles abounded. Battles were won, rain descended on drought-ridden areas, diseases were cured, and guilt was relieved—all through the magical ministrations of charismatic monks.

Accompanying all of this was a serious effort by monks, scholars, and translators to present this Indian religion in terms that Chinese could more readily grasp. Thus the Buddhist term *dharma*, referring to the Buddha's teaching, was translated as *dao*, or "the way," a notion long familiar in both Daoist and Confucian thinking (see Chapter 4). The Buddhist notion of "morality" was translated with the Confucian term that referred to "filial submission and obedience." Some Indian concepts were modified in the process of translation. For example, the idea that "husband supports wife," which reflected a considerable respect for women and mothers in early Indian Buddhism, became in translation "husband controls wife."[38]

As Buddhism took hold in China, it was primarily in its broader Mahayana form—complete with numerous deities, the veneration of relics, many heavens and hells, and bodhisattvas to aid the believer—rather than the more psychological and individualistic Theravada Buddhism (see Chapter 4). One of the most popular forms of Buddhism in China was the Pure Land School, in which faithfully repeating the name of an earlier Buddha, the Amitabha, was sufficient to ensure rebirth in a beautifully described heavenly realm, the Pure Land. In its emphasis on salvation by faith, without arduous study or intensive meditation, Pure Land Buddhism became a highly popular and authentically Chinese version of the Indian faith.

China's reunification under the Sui and early Tang dynasties witnessed growing state support for Buddhism. The Sui emperor Wendi (ruled 581–604 C.E.) had monasteries constructed at the base of China's five sacred mountains, further identifying the imported religion with traditional Chinese culture. He even used Buddhism to justify his military campaigns. "With a hundred victories in a hundred battles," he declared, "we promote the practice of the ten Buddhist virtues."[39] With state support and growing popular acceptance, monasteries became centers of great wealth, largely exempt from taxation, owning large estates; running businesses such as oil presses, water mills, and pawn shops; collecting gems, gold, and lavish works of art; and even employing slaves. But Buddhism, while solidly entrenched in Chinese life by the early Tang dynasty, never achieved the independence from state authorities that the Christian church acquired in Europe. The examinations for becoming a monk were supervised by the state, and education in the monasteries included the required study of the Confucian classics. In the mid-ninth century, the state showed quite dramatically just how much control it could exercise over the Buddhist establishment.

Losing State Support: The Crisis of Chinese Buddhism

The impressive growth of Chinese Buddhism was accompanied by a persistent undercurrent of resistance and criticism. Some saw the Buddhist establishment, at least potentially, as a "state within a state" and a challenge to imperial authority. More important was a deepening resentment of its enormous wealth. One fifth-century critic, referring to monks, put the issue squarely: "Why is it that their ideals are noble and far-reaching and their activities still are base and common? [They] become merchants and engage in barter, wrangling with the masses for profit."[40] When state treasuries were short of funds, government officials cast a covetous eye on wealthy and tax-exempt monasteries. Furthermore, Buddhism was clearly of foreign origin and offensive for that reason to some Confucian and Daoist thinkers. The celibacy of the monks and their withdrawal from society, the critics argued, undermined the Confucian-based family system of Chinese tradition.

> ■ **Change**
> What were the major sources of opposition to Buddhism within China?

Such criticisms took on new meaning in the changed environment of China after about 800 C.E. Following centuries of considerable foreign influence in China, a growing resentment against foreign culture, particularly among the literate classes, increasingly took hold. The turning point may well have been the An Lushan rebellion (755–763), in which a general of foreign origin led a major revolt against the Tang dynasty. Whatever its origin, an increasingly xenophobic reaction set in among the upper classes, reflected in a desire to return to an imagined "purity" of earlier times.[41] In this setting, the old criticisms of Buddhism became more sharply focused. In 819, Han Yu, a leading figure in the Confucian counterattack on Buddhism, wrote a scathing memorial to the emperor, criticizing his willingness to honor a relic of the Buddha's finger.

> Now the Buddha was of barbarian origin. His language differed from Chinese speech; his clothes were of a different cut; his mouth did not pronounce the prescribed words of the Former Kings. . . . He did not recognize the relationship between prince and subject, nor the sentiments of father and son. . . . I pray that Your Majesty will turn this bone over to the officials that it may be cast into water or fire.[42]

Several decades later, the Chinese state took direct action against the Buddhist establishment as well as against other foreign religions. A series of imperial decrees between 841 and 845 ordered some 260,000 monks and nuns to return to normal life as tax-paying citizens. Thousands of monasteries, temples, and shrines were either destroyed or turned to public use, while the state confiscated the lands, money, metals, and serfs belonging to monasteries. Buddhists were now forbidden to use gold, silver, copper, iron, and gems in constructing their images. These actions dealt a serious blow to Chinese Buddhism. Its scholars and monks were scattered, its creativity diminished, and its institutions came even more firmly under state control.

Despite this persecution, Buddhism did not vanish from China. At the level of elite culture, its philosophical ideas played a role in the reformulation of Confucian thinking that took place during the Song dynasty. At the village level, Buddhism became one element of Chinese popular religion, which also included the veneration of ancestors, the honoring of Confucius, and Daoist shrines and rituals. Temples frequently included statues of Confucius, Laozi, and the Buddha, with little sense of any incompatibility among them. "Every black-haired son of Han," the Chinese have long said, "wears a Confucian thinking cap, a Daoist robe, and Buddhist sandals." (See photo, p. 116.) Unlike Europe, where an immigrant religion triumphed over and excluded all other faiths, Buddhism in China became assimilated into Chinese culture alongside its other traditions.

LearningCurve
bedfordstmartins.com
/strayer/LC

Reflections: Why Do Things Change?

The rapidity of change in modern societies is among the most distinctive features of recent history, but change and transformation, though at various rates, have been constants in the human story since the very beginning. Explaining how and why human societies change is perhaps the central issue that historians confront, no matter which societies or periods of time they study. Those who specialize in the history of some particular culture or civilization often emphasize sources of change operating within those societies, although there is intense disagreement as to which are most significant. The ideas of great thinkers, the policies of leaders, struggles for power, the conflict of classes, the invention of new technologies, the growth or decline in population, variations in local climate or weather—all of these and more have their advocates as the primary motor of historical transformation.

Of course, it is not necessary to choose among them. The history of China illustrates the range of internal factors that have driven change in that civilization. The political conflicts of the "era of warring states" provided the setting and the motivation for the emergence of Confucianism and Daoism, which in turn have certainly shaped the character and texture of Chinese civilization over many centuries. The personal qualities and brutal policies of Shihuangdi surely played a role in China's unification and in the brief duration of the Qin dynasty. The subsequent creation of a widespread network of canals and waterways as well as the country's technological achievements served to maintain that unity over very long periods of time. But the massive inequalities of Chinese society generated the peasant upheavals, which periodically shattered that unity and led to new ruling dynasties. Sometimes natural events, such as droughts and floods, triggered those rebellions.

World historians, more than those who study particular civilizations or nations, have been inclined to find the primary source of change in contact with strangers, in external connections and interactions, whether direct or indirect. The history of China and East Asia provide plenty of examples for this point of view as well. Conceptions of China as the "middle kingdom," infinitely superior to all surrounding societies, grew out of centuries of involvement with its neighbors. Some of those neighbors became Chinese as China's imperial reach grew, especially to the south. Even those that did not, such as Korea, Vietnam, and Japan, were decisively transformed by proximity to the "radiating civilization" of China. China's own cuisine, so distinctive in recent centuries, may well be a quite recent invention, drawing heavily on Indian and Southeast Asian cooking. Buddhism, of course, is an obvious borrowing from abroad, although its incorporation into Chinese civilization and its ups and downs within China owed much to internal cultural and political realities.

In the end, clear distinctions between internal and external sources of change in China's history—or that of any other society—are perhaps misleading. The boundary between "inside" and "outside" is itself a constantly changing line. Should the borderlands of northern China, where Chinese and Turkic peoples met and mingled, be regarded as internal or external to China itself? And, as the histories of Chinese Buddhism and of Japanese culture so clearly indicate, what comes from beyond is always transformed by what it encounters within.

Second Thoughts

What's the Significance?

Sui dynasty, 250–51

Tang dynasty, 251–52

Song dynasty, 251–56

Hangzhou, 253

economic revolution, 253–55

foot binding, 255–56

tribute system, 257–58

Xiongnu, 258–59

Khitan/Jurchen people, 259–60

Silla dynasty (Korea), 261–63

hangul, 263

chu nom, 265

Shotoku Taishi, 265

bushido, 266

Izumi Shikibu, 268–69

Chinese Buddhism, 272–76

Emperor Wendi, 274

LearningCurve
Check what you know.
**bedfordstmartins.com
/strayer/LC**

Online Study Guide
bedfordstmartins.com/strayer

Big Picture Questions

1. How can you explain the changing fortunes of Buddhism in China?
2. How did China influence the world of the third-wave era? How was China itself transformed by its encounters with a wider world?
3. How might China's posture in the world during the Tang and Song dynasty era compare to its emerging role in global affairs in the twenty-first century?
4. **Looking Back:** In what ways did Tang and Song dynasty China resemble the earlier Han dynasty period, and in what ways had China changed?

For Web sites and additional documents related to this chapter, see **Make History** at bedfordstmartins.com/strayer.

Next Steps: For Further Study

Samuel Adshead, *Tang China: The Rise of the East in World History* (2004). Explores the role of China within the larger world.

Patricia Ebrey, *The Inner Quarters* (1993). A balanced account of the gains and losses experienced by Chinese women during the changes of the Song dynasty.

Mark Elvin, *The Pattern of the Chinese Past* (1973). A classic account of the Chinese economic revolution.

James L. Huffman, *Japan in World History* (2010). The first three chapters of this recent work place Japan's early history in the framework of world history.

Paul S. Ropp, *China in World History* (2010). An up-to-date telling of China's historical development, cast in a global context.

Arthur F. Wright, *Buddhism in Chinese History* (1959). An older account filled with wonderful stories and anecdotes.

Upper River during the Qing Ming Festival, http://www.ibiblio.org/ulysses/gec/painting/qingming/full.htm. A scrolling reproduction of a huge Chinese painting, showing in detail the Song dynasty city of Kaifeng.

وَكَادَ يَنْزِعُ الْجِمَالَ الشَّمَّ وَأَنْشَدَ

مَا الْحَجُّ سِيرُكَ تَأْوِيبًا وَإِدْلَاجًا وَلَا اعْتِيَامَكَ أَجْمَالًا وَأَحْدَاجَا

الْحَجُّ أَنْ تَقْصِدَ الْبَيْتَ الْحَرَامَ عَلَى تَحْرِيرِكَ الْحَجَّ لَا تَبْغِي بِهِ حَاجَا

وَتَنْطَوِي كَامِلَ الْإِنْصَافِ مُتَّخِذًا رَدْعَ الْهَوَى هَادِيًا وَالْحَقَّ مِنْهَاجَا

CHAPTER NINE

The Worlds of Islam

Afro-Eurasian Connections

600–1500

The Birth of a New Religion
  The Homeland of Islam
  The Messenger and the Message
  The Transformation of Arabia
The Making of an Arab Empire
  War, Conquest, and Tolerance
  Conversion
  Divisions and Controversies
  Women and Men in Early Islam
Islam and Cultural Encounter:
  A Four-Way Comparison
  The Case of India
  The Case of Anatolia
  The Case of West Africa
  The Case of Spain
The World of Islam as a New
  Civilization
  Networks of Faith
  Networks of Exchange
Reflections: Past and Present:
  Choosing Our History
Portrait: Mansa Musa, West African
  Monarch and Muslim Pilgrim

"There were tens of thousands of pilgrims, from all over the world. They were of all colors, from blue-eyed blondes to black-skinned Africans. But we were all participating in the same ritual, displaying a spirit of unity and brotherhood that my experiences in America had led me to believe never could exist between the white and non-white. . . . I have never before seen sincere and true brotherhood practiced by all colors together, irrespective of their color."[1] So said Malcolm X, the American black radical leader and convert to Islam, following his participation in the hajj, the Muslim pilgrimage to Mecca, in 1964. That experience persuaded him to abandon his earlier commitment to militant black separatism, for he was now convinced that racial barriers could indeed be overcome within the context of Islam.

As the twenty-first century dawned, Islam had acquired a noticeable presence in the United States, with more than 1,200 mosques and an estimated 8 million Muslims. Here was but one sign of the growing international significance of the Islamic world. Independence from colonial rule, the Iranian Revolution of 1979, repeated wars between Israel and its Arab neighbors, the rising price of oil—all of this focused global attention on the Islamic world in the second half of the twentieth century. Then in the new millennium, the 2001 attacks on the United States, American military action in Afghanistan and Iraq, and in 2011 the popular uprisings in the Middle East known as the Arab Spring as well as the killing of Osama bin Laden likewise signaled the growing role of Islamic civilization in world affairs.

The Hajj: The pilgrimage to Mecca, known as the hajj, has long been a central religious ritual in Islamic practice. It also embodies the cosmopolitan character of Islam as pilgrims from all over the vast Islamic realm assemble in the city where the faith was born. This painting shows a group of joyful pilgrims, led by a band, on their way to Mecca.
(Bibliothèque nationale de France)

AS IN CHINA, MUSLIM SOCIETIES OVER MUCH OF THE PAST CENTURY have been seeking to overcome several hundred years of humiliating European intrusion and to find their place in the modern world. In doing so, many Muslims have found inspiration and encouragement in the early history of their civilization and their faith. For a thousand years (roughly 600–1600), peoples claiming allegiance to Islam represented a highly successful, prosperous, and expansive civilization, encompassing parts of Africa, Europe, the Middle East, and Asia. While Chinese culture and Buddhism provided the cultural anchor for East Asia during the third-wave millennium and Christianity did the same for Europe, the realm of Islam touched on both of them and decisively shaped the history of the entire Afro-Eurasian world.

The significance of a burgeoning Islamic world during the third-wave era was enormous. It thrust the previously marginal and largely nomadic Arabs into a central role in world history, for it was among them and in their language that the newest of the world's major religions was born. The sudden emergence and rapid spread of that religion in the seventh century C.E. was accompanied by the creation of a huge empire that stretched from Spain to India. Both within that empire and beyond it, a new and innovative civilization took shape, drawing on Arab, Persian, Turkish, Greco-Roman, South Asian, and African cultures. It was clearly the largest and most influential of the new third-wave civilizations. Finally, the broad reach of Islam generated many of the great cultural encounters of this age of accelerating connections, as Islamic civilization challenged and provoked Christendom, penetrated and was transformed by African cultures, and also took root in India, Central Asia, and Southeast Asia. The spread of Islam continued in the modern era so that by the beginning of the twenty-first century, some 1.2 billion people, or 22 percent of the world's population, identified as Muslims. It was second only to Christianity as the world's most widely practiced religion, and it extended far beyond the Arab lands where it had originated.

SEEKING THE MAIN POINT

In what ways did the civilization of Islam draw on other civilizations in the Afro-Eurasian world? And in what respects did it shape or transform those civilizations?

The Birth of a New Religion

Most of the major religious or cultural traditions of the second-wave era had emerged from the core of established civilizations—Confucianism and Daoism from China, Hinduism and Buddhism from India, Greek philosophy from the Mediterranean world, and Zoroastrianism from Persia. Christianity and Islam, by contrast, emerged more from the margins of Mediterranean and Middle Eastern civilizations. Christianity, of course, appeared among a small Middle Eastern people, the Jews, in a remote province of the Roman Empire, while Islam took hold in the cities and deserts of the Arabian Peninsula.

The Homeland of Islam

The central region of the Arabian Peninsula had long been inhabited by nomadic Arabs, known as Bedouins, who herded their sheep and camels in seasonal migrations. These peoples lived in fiercely independent clans and tribes, which often engaged

A Map of Time

570–632	Life of Muhammad
632–661	Era of Rightly Guided Caliphs
633–644	Muslim conquest of Persia
650s	Quran compiled
656–661; 680–692	Civil war; emergence of Sunni/Shi'a split
661–750	Umayyad caliphate
750–900	High point of Abbasid caliphate
711–718	Conquest of Spain
751	Battle of Talas River
756	Baghdad established as capital of Abbasid Caliphate
800–1000	Emergence of Sufism
1099	Crusaders seize Jerusalem
1206	Delhi sultanate established in India
1258	Mongols sack Baghdad; formal end of Abbasid caliphate
1324	Mansa Musa pilgrimage to Mecca
1453	Ottoman Empire conquers Constantinople; end of Byzantine Empire
1492	Christian reconquest of Spain complete; end of Muslim Spain
1526	Mughal Empire established in India

■ **Description**

In what ways did the early history of Islam reflect its Arabian origins?

in bitter blood feuds with one another. They recognized a variety of gods, ancestors, and nature spirits; valued personal bravery, group loyalty, and hospitality; and greatly treasured their highly expressive oral poetry. But there was more to Arabia than camel-herding nomads. In scattered oases, the highlands of Yemen, and interior mountain communities, sedentary village-based agriculture was practiced, and in the northern and southern regions of Arabia, small kingdoms had flourished in earlier times. Arabia also sat astride increasingly important trade routes that connected the Indian Ocean world with that of the Mediterranean Sea, a location that gave rise to cosmopolitan commercial cities, whose values and practices were often in conflict with those of traditional Arab tribes (see Map 9.1, p. 284).

One of those cities, Mecca, came to occupy a distinctive role in Arabia. Though somewhat off the major long-distance trade routes, Mecca was the site of the Kaaba, the most prominent religious shrine in Arabia, which housed representations of some 360 deities and was the destination for many pilgrims. Mecca's dominant tribe, the Quraysh (koor-EYE'SH), had come to control access to the Kaaba and grew wealthy by taxing the local trade that accompanied the annual pilgrimage season. By the sixth century, Mecca was home to people from various tribes and clans as well as

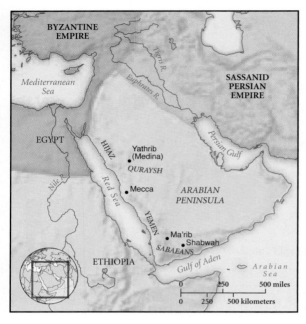

Map 9.1 Arabia at the Time of Muhammad
Located adjacent to the Byzantine and Persian empires, the eastern coast of Arabia was the site of a major trade route between the Indian Ocean and the Mediterranean Sea.

an assortment of individual outlaws, exiles, refugees, and foreign merchants, but much of its growing wealth was concentrated in the hands of a few ruling Quraysh families.

Furthermore, Arabia was located on the periphery of two established and rival civilizations of that time — the Byzantine Empire, heir to the Roman world, and the Sassanid Empire, heir to the imperial traditions of Persia. This location, coupled with long-distance trade, ensured some familiarity with the larger world, particularly in the cities and settled farming regions of the peninsula. Many Jews and Christians as well as some Zoroastrians lived among the Arabs, and their monotheistic ideas became widely known. By the time of Muhammad, most of the settled Arabs had acknowledged the preeminent position of Allah, the supreme god of the Arab pantheon, although they usually found the lesser gods, including the three daughters of Allah, far more accessible. Moreover, they increasingly identified Allah with Yahweh, the Jewish High God, and regarded themselves too as "children of Abraham." A few Arabs were beginning to explore the possibility that Allah/Yahweh was the only God and that the many others, residing in the Kaaba and in shrines across the peninsula, were nothing more than "helpless and harmless idols."[2]

To an outside observer around 600, it might well have seemed that Arabs were moving toward Judaism religiously or that Christianity, the most rapidly growing religion in western Asia, would encompass Arabia as well. Any such expectations, however, were thoroughly confounded by the dramatic events of the seventh century.

The Messenger and the Message

■ **Description**
What did the Quran expect from those who followed its teachings?

The catalyst for those events and for the birth of this new religion was a single individual, Muhammad Ibn Abdullah (570–632 C.E.), who was born in Mecca to a Quraysh family. As a young boy, Muhammad lost his parents, came under the care of an uncle, and worked as a shepherd to pay his keep. Later he became a trader and traveled as far north as Syria. At the age of twenty-five, he married a wealthy widow, Khadija, herself a prosperous merchant, with whom he fathered six children. A highly reflective man deeply troubled by the religious corruption and social inequalities of Mecca, he often undertook periods of withdrawal and meditation in the arid mountains outside the city. There, like the Buddha and Jesus, Muhammad had a powerful, overwhelming religious experience that left him convinced, albeit reluctantly, that he was Allah's messenger to the Arabs, commissioned to bring to them a scripture in their own language.

According to Muslim tradition, the revelations began in 610 and continued periodically over the next twenty-two years. Those revelations, recorded in the Quran, became the sacred scriptures of Islam, which to this day most Muslims regard as the very words of God and the core of their faith. Intended to be recited rather than simply read for information, the Quran, Muslims claim, when heard in its original Arabic, conveys nothing less than the very presence of the Divine. Its unmatched poetic beauty, miraculous to Muslims, convinced many that it was indeed a revelation from God. One of the earliest converts testified to its power: "When I heard the Quran, my heart was softened and I wept and Islam entered into me."[3]

Muslims, Jews, and Christians
The close relationship of three Middle Eastern monotheistic traditions is illustrated in this fifteenth-century Persian painting, which portrays Muhammad leading Moses, Abraham, and Jesus in prayer. The fire surrounding the Prophet's head represents his religious fervor. The painting reflects the Islamic belief that the revelations granted to Muhammad built on and completed those given earlier to Jews and Christians. (Bibliothèque nationale de France)

In its Arabian setting, the Quran's message, delivered through Muhammad, was revolutionary. Religiously, it was radically monotheistic, presenting Allah as the only God, the all-powerful Creator, good, just, and merciful. Allah was the "Lord sustainer of the worlds, the Compassionate, the Caring, master of the day of reckoning" and known to human beings "on the farthest horizon and within their own selves."[4] Here was an exalted conception of Deity that drew heavily on traditions of Jewish and Christian monotheism. As "the Messenger of God," Muhammad presented himself in the line of earlier prophets — Abraham, Moses, Jesus, and many others. He was the last, "the seal of the prophets," bearing God's final revelation to humankind. It was not so much a call to a new faith as an invitation to return to the old and pure religion of Abraham from which Jews, Christians, and Arabs alike had deviated. Jews had wrongly conceived of themselves as a uniquely "chosen people"; Christians had made their prophet into a god; and Arabs had become wildly polytheistic. To all of this, the message of the Quran was a corrective.

Submission to Allah ("Muslim" means "one who submits") was the primary obligation of believers and the means of achieving a God-conscious life in this world and a place in paradise after death. According to the Quran, however, submission was not merely an individual or a spiritual act, for it involved the creation of a whole new society. Over and again, the Quran denounced the prevailing social practices of an increasingly prosperous Mecca: the hoarding of wealth, the exploitation of the poor, the charging of high rates of interest on loans, corrupt business deals, the abuse of women, and the neglect of widows and orphans. Like the Jewish prophets of the Old Testament, the Quran demanded social justice and laid out a prescription for its implementation. It sought a return to the older values of Arab tribal life—solidarity, equality, concern for the poor—which had been undermined, particularly in Mecca, by growing wealth and commercialism.

The message of the Quran challenged not only the ancient polytheism of Arab religion and the social injustices of Mecca but also the entire tribal and clan structure of Arab society, which was so prone to war, feuding, and violence. The just and moral society of Islam was the *umma* (UMH-mah), the community of all believers, replacing tribal, ethnic, or racial identities. Such a society would be a "witness over the nations," for according to the Quran, "You are the best community evolved for mankind, enjoining what is right and forbidding what is wrong."[5] In this community, women too had an honored and spiritually equal place. "The believers, men and women, are protectors of one another," declared the Quran.[6] The umma, then, was to be a new and just community, bound by a common belief rather than by territory, language, or tribe.

The core message of the Quran—the remembrance of God—was effectively summarized as a set of five requirements for believers, known as the Pillars of Islam. The first pillar expressed the heart of the Islamic message: "There is no god but Allah, and Muhammad is the messenger of God." The second pillar was ritual prayer, performed five times a day. Accompanying practices, including cleansing, bowing, kneeling, and prostration, expressed believers' submission to Allah and provided a frequent reminder, amid the busyness of daily life, that they were living in the presence of God. The third pillar, almsgiving, reflected the Quran's repeated demands for social justice by requiring believers to give generously to support the poor and needy of the community. The fourth pillar established a month of fasting during Ramadan, which meant abstaining from food, drink, and sexual relations from the first light of dawn to sundown. It provided an occasion for self-purification and a reminder of the needs of the hungry. The fifth pillar encouraged a pilgrimage to Mecca, known as the hajj (HAHJ), during which believers from all over the Islamic world assembled once a year and put on identical simple white clothing as they reenacted key events in Islamic history. For at least the few days of the hajj, the many worlds of Islam must surely have seemed a single realm.

A further requirement for believers, sometimes called the sixth pillar, was "struggle," or *jihad* in Arabic. Its more general meaning, which Muhammad referred to as the "greater jihad," was an interior personal effort of each believer against greed and selfishness, a spiritual striving toward living a God-conscious life. In its "lesser" form, the "jihad of the sword," the Quran authorized armed struggle against the forces of unbelief and evil as a means of establishing Muslim rule and of defending the umma from the threats of infidel aggressors. The understanding and use of the jihad concept has varied widely over the many centuries of Islamic history and remains a matter of much controversy among Muslims in the twenty-first century.

The Transformation of Arabia

As the revelations granted to Muhammad became known in Mecca, they attracted a small following of some close relatives, a few prominent Meccan leaders, and an assortment of lower-class dependents, freed slaves, and members of poorer clans. Those teachings also soon attracted the vociferous opposition of Mecca's elite families, particularly those of Muhammad's own tribe, the Quraysh. Muhammad's claim to be a "messenger of Allah," his unyielding monotheism, his call for social reform, his condemnation of Mecca's business practices, and his apparent disloyalty to his own tribe enraged the wealthy and ruling families of Mecca. So great had this opposition become that in 622 Muhammad and his small band of followers emigrated to the more welcoming town of Yathrib, soon to be called Medina, the city of the Prophet. This agricultural settlement of mixed Arab and Jewish population had invited Muhammad to serve as an arbitrator of their intractable conflicts. The emigration to Yathrib, known in Arabic as the *hijra* (HIHJ-ruh) (the journey), was a momentous turning point in the early history of Islam and thereafter marked the beginning of a new Islamic calendar.

■ **Change**
How was Arabia transformed by the rise of Islam?

The new community, or umma, that took shape in Medina was a kind of "supertribe," but very different from the traditional tribes of Arab society. Membership was a matter of belief rather than birth, allowing the community to expand rapidly. Furthermore, all authority, both political and religious, was concentrated in the hands of Muhammad, who proceeded to introduce radical changes. Usury was outlawed, tax-free marketplaces were established, and a mandatory payment to support the poor was imposed.

In Medina, Muhammad not only began to create a new society but also declared his movement's independence from its earlier affiliation with Judaism. In the early years, he had anticipated a warm response from Jews and Christians, based on a common monotheism and prophetic tradition, and had directed his followers to pray facing Jerusalem. But when some Jewish groups allied with his enemies, Muhammad acted harshly to suppress them, exiling some and enslaving or killing others. This was not, however, a general suppression of Jews since others among them remained loyal to Muhammad's new state. But the Prophet now redirected his followers' prayer toward Mecca, essentially declaring Islam an Arab religion, though one with a universal message.

From its base in Medina, the Islamic community rapidly extended its reach throughout Arabia. Early military successes against Muhammad's Meccan opponents convinced other Arab tribes that the Muslims and their God were on the rise, and they sought to negotiate alliances with the new power. Growing numbers converted. The religious appeal of the new faith, its promise of material gain, the end of incessant warfare among feuding tribes, periodic military actions skillfully led by Muhammad, and the Prophet's willingness to enter into marriage alliances with leading tribes—all of this contributed to the consolidation of Islamic control throughout Arabia. In 630, Muhammad triumphantly and peacefully entered Mecca itself, purging the Kaaba of its idols and declaring it a shrine to the one God, Allah. By the time Muhammad died in 632, most of Arabia had come under the control of this new Islamic state, and many had embraced the new faith.

Thus the birth of Islam differed sharply from that of Christianity. Jesus' teaching about "giving to Caesar what is Caesar's and to God what is God's" reflected the minority and subordinate status of the Jews within the Roman Empire. Early Christians found themselves periodically persecuted by Roman authorities for more than three centuries, requiring them to work out some means of dealing with an often hostile state. The answer lay in the development of a separate church hierarchy and the concept of two coexisting authorities, one religious and one political, an arrangement that persisted even after the state became Christian.

The young Islamic community, by contrast, found itself constituted as a state, and soon a huge empire, at the very beginning of its history. Muhammad was not only a religious figure but also, unlike Jesus or the Buddha, a political and military leader able to implement his vision of an ideal Islamic society. Nor did Islam give rise to a separate religious organization, although tension between religious and political goals frequently generated conflict. No professional clergy mediating between God and humankind emerged within Islam. Teachers, religious scholars, prayer leaders, and judges within an Islamic legal system did not have the religious role that priests held within Christianity. No distinction between religious law and civil law, so important in the Christian world, existed within the realm of Islam. One law, known as the *sharia* (shah-REE-ah), regulated every aspect of life. The sharia (literally, "a path to water," which is the source of life) evolved over the several centuries following the birth of this new religion and found expression in a number of separate schools of Islamic legal practice.

In little more than twenty years (610–632), a profound transformation had occurred in the Arabian Peninsula. What would subsequently become a new religion had been born, though it was one with roots in earlier Jewish, Christian, and Zoroastrian traditions. A new and vigorous state had emerged, bringing peace to the warring tribes of Arabia. Within that state, a distinctive society had begun to take shape, one that served ever after as a model for Islamic communities everywhere. In his farewell sermon, Muhammad described the outlines of this community:

> All mankind is from Adam and Eve, an Arab has no superiority over a non-Arab nor a non-Arab has any superiority over an Arab; also a white has no superiority over a black nor a black has any superiority over a white — except by piety and good action. Learn that every Muslim is a brother to every Muslim and that the Muslims constitute one brotherhood.[7]

LearningCurve
bedfordstmartins.com
/strayer/LC

The Making of an Arab Empire

It did not take long for the immense transformations occurring in Arabia to have an impact beyond the peninsula. In the centuries that followed, the energies born of those vast changes profoundly transformed much of the Afro-Eurasian world. The new Arab state became a huge empire, encompassing all or part of Egyptian, Roman/Byzantine, Persian, Mesopotamian, and Indian civilizations. The Islamic faith spread widely within and outside that empire. So too did the culture and language of Arabia, as many Arabs migrated far beyond their original homeland and many others found it advantageous to learn Arabic. From the mixing and blending of these many peoples emerged the new and distinctive third-wave civilization of Islam, bound by the ties of a common faith but divided by differences of culture, class, politics, gender, and religious understanding. These enormously consequential processes—the making of a new religion, a new empire, and a new civilization—were central to world history during the third-wave millennium.

War, Conquest, and Tolerance

Within a few years of Muhammad's death in 632, Arab armies engaged the Byzantine and Persian Sassanid empires, the great powers of the region. It was the beginning of a process that rapidly gave rise to an Arab empire that stretched from Spain to India, penetrating both Europe and China and governing most of the lands between them (see Map 9.2). In creating that empire, Arabs were continuing a long pattern of tribal raids into surrounding civilizations, but now these Arabs were newly organized in a state of their own with a central command able to mobilize the military potential of the entire population. The Byzantine and Persian empires, weakened by decades of war with each other and by internal revolts, continued to view the Arabs as a mere nuisance rather than a serious threat. But by 644 the Sassanid Empire had been defeated by Arab forces, while Byzantium, the remaining eastern regions of the old Roman Empire, soon lost the southern half of its territories. Beyond these victories, Muslim forces, operating on both land and sea, swept westward across North Africa, conquered Spain in the early 700s, and attacked southern France. To the east, Arab armies reached the Indus River and seized some of the major oases towns of Central Asia. In 751, they inflicted a crushing defeat on Chinese forces in the Battle of Talas River, which had lasting consequences for the cultural evolution of Asia, for it checked the further expansion of China to the west and made possible the conversion to Islam of Central Asia's Turkic-speaking people. Most of the violence of conquest involved imperial armies, though on occasion civilians too were caught up in the fighting and suffered terribly. In 634, for example, a battle between Byzantine and Arab forces in Palestine resulted in the death of some 4,000 villagers.

> **■ Change**
> Why were Arabs able to construct such a huge empire so quickly?

The motives driving the creation of the Arab Empire were broadly similar to those of other empires. The merchant leaders of the new Islamic community wanted to capture profitable trade routes and wealthy agricultural regions. Individual Arabs found in military expansion a route to wealth and social promotion. The need to harness the immense energies of the Arabian transformation was also important. The fragile unity of the umma threatened to come apart after Muhammad's death, and external expansion provided a common task for the community.

While many among the new conquerors viewed the mission of empire in terms of jihad, bringing righteous government to the peoples they conquered, this did not mean imposing a new religion. In fact for the better part of a century after Muhammad's death, his followers usually referred to themselves as "believers," a term that appears in the Quran far more often than "Muslims" and one that included pious Jews and Christians as well as newly monotheistic Arabs. Such a posture eased the acceptance of the new political order, for many people recently incorporated in the emerging Arab

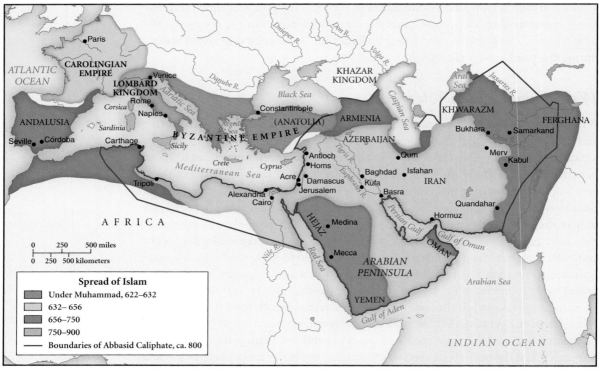

Map 9.2   The Arab Empire and the Initial Expansion of Islam, 622–900 C.E.
Far more so than with Buddhism or Christianity, the initial spread of Islam was both rapid and extensive. And unlike the other two world religions, Islam quickly gave rise to a huge empire, ruled by Muslim Arabs, which encompassed many of the older civilizations of the region.

Empire were already monotheists and familiar with the core ideas and practices of the Believers' Movement—prayer, fasting, pilgrimage, revelation, and prophets. Furthermore, the new rulers were remarkably tolerant of established Jewish and Christian faiths. The first governor of Arab-ruled Jerusalem was a Jew. Many old Christian churches continued to operate and new ones were constructed. A Nestorian Christian patriarch in Iraq wrote to one of his bishops around 647 C.E. observing that the new rulers "not only do not fight Christianity, they even commend our religion, show honor to the priests and monasteries and saints of the Lord, and make gifts to the monasteries and churches."[8] Formal agreements or treaties recognized Jews, Christians, and Zoroastrians as "people of the book," giving them the status of *dhimmis* (dihm-mees), protected but second-class subjects. Such people were permitted to freely practice their own religion, so long as they paid a special tax known as the *jizya*. Theoretically the tax was a substitute for military service, supposedly forbidden to non-Muslims. In practice, many dhimmis served in the highest offices within Muslim kingdoms and in their armies as well.

In other ways too, the Arab rulers of an expanding empire sought to limit the disruptive impact of conquest. To prevent indiscriminate destruction and exploitation of conquered peoples, occupying Arab armies were restricted to garrison towns, segregated from the native population. Local elites and bureaucratic structures were incorporated into the new Arab Empire. Nonetheless, the empire worked many changes on its subjects, the most enduring of which was the mass conversion of Middle Eastern peoples to what became by the eighth century the new and separate religion of Islam.

Conversion

For some people, no doubt, converting to Islam was or subsequently became a matter of profound spiritual or psychological transformation, but far more often, at least initially, it was "social conversion," defined as "movement from one religiously defined social community to another."[9] It happened at various rates and in different ways, but in the four centuries or so after the death of Muhammad, millions of individuals and many whole societies within the Arab Empire found their cultural identity bound up with a belief in Allah and the message of his prophet. They had become Muslims. How had this immense cultural change occurred?

In some ways, perhaps, the change was not so dramatic, as major elements of Islam—monotheism; ritual prayer and cleansing ceremonies; fasting; divine revelation; the ideas of heaven, hell, and final judgment—were quite familiar to Jews, Christians, and Zoroastrians. Furthermore, Islam was from the beginning associated with the sponsorship of a powerful state, quite unlike the experience of early Buddhism or Christianity. Conquest called into question the power of old gods, while the growing prestige of the Arab Empire attracted many to Allah. Although deliberately forced conversion was rare, living in an Islamic-governed state provided a variety of incentives for claiming Muslim identity.[10] Slaves and prisoners of war were among the early converts, particularly in Persia. Converts could also avoid the jizya, the tax imposed on non-Muslims. In Islam, merchants found a religion friendly to commerce, and in the Arab Empire they enjoyed a huge and secure arena for trade. People aspiring to official positions found conversion to Islam an aid to social mobility.

Conversion was not an automatic or easy process. Vigorous resistance delayed conversion for centuries among the Berbers of North Africa; a small group of zealous Spanish Christians in the ninth century provoked their own martyrdom by publicly insulting the Prophet; and some Persian Zoroastrians fled to avoid Muslim rule. More generally, though, a remarkable and lasting religious transformation occurred throughout the Arab Empire.

In Persia, for example, between 750 and 900, about 80 percent of the population had made the transition to a Muslim religious identity. But they did so in a manner quite distinct from the people of Iraq, Syria, Egypt, and North Africa. In these regions, converts to Islam gradually abandoned their native languages, adopted Arabic, and

■ **Explanation**
What accounts for the widespread conversion to Islam?

came to see themselves as Arabs. In Iran or Persia, by contrast, Arab conquest did not involve cultural Arabization, despite some initial efforts to impose the Arabic language. By the tenth century, the vast majority of Persians had become Muslims, but the Persian language, Farsi (still spoken in modern Iran), flourished, enriched now by a number of Arabic loan words and written in an Arabic script. In 1010, that language received its classic literary expression when the Persian poet Ferdowsi completed his epic work, the *Shahnama* (*The Book of Kings*). A huge text of some 60,000 rhyming couplets, it recorded the mythical and pre-Islamic history of Iran and gave an enduring expression to a distinctly Persian cultural identity. Thus, in places where large-scale Arab migration had occurred, such as Egypt, North Africa, and Iraq, Arabic culture and language, as well as the religion of Islam, took hold. Such areas are today both Muslim and Arab, while the peoples of Iran, Turkey, and Pakistan, for example, have "Islamized" without "Arabizing."

The preservation of Persian language and culture had enormous implications for the world of Islam. Many religious ideas of Persian Zoroastrianism — an evil satanic power, final judgment, heaven and hell, paradise — found their way into Islam, often indirectly via Jewish or Christian precedents. In Iran, Central Asia, India, and later in the Ottoman Empire, Islam was accompanied by pervasive Persian influences. Persian administrative and bureaucratic techniques; Persian court practices with their palaces, gardens, and splendid garments; Persian architecture, poetry, music, and painting — all of this decisively shaped the high culture of these eastern Islamic lands. One of the Abbasid caliphs, himself an Arab, observed: "The Persians ruled for a thousand years and did not need us Arabs even for a day. We have been ruling them for one or two centuries and cannot do without them for an hour."[11]

Divisions and Controversies

The ideal of a unified Muslim community, so important to Muhammad, proved difficult to realize as conquest and conversion vastly enlarged the Islamic umma. A central problem was that of leadership and authority in the absence of Muhammad's towering presence. Who should hold the role of caliph (KAY-lihf), the successor to Muhammad as the political leader of the umma, the protector and defender of the faith? That issue crystallized a variety of emerging conflicts within the Islamic world — between early and later converts, among various Arab tribes and factions, between Arabs and non-Arabs, between privileged and wealthy rulers and their far less fortunate subjects. Many of these political and social conflicts found expression in religious terms as various understandings of the Quran and of Muhammad's life and teachings took shape within the growing Islamic community.

■ Comparison
What is the difference between Sunni and Shia Islam?

The first four caliphs, known among most Muslims as the Rightly Guided Caliphs (632–661), were close "companions of the Prophet," selected by the Muslim elders of Medina. Division surfaced almost immediately as a series of Arab tribal rebellions and new "prophets" persuaded the first caliph, Abu Bakr, to suppress them forcibly. The third and fourth caliphs, Uthman and Ali, were both assassinated, and by 656, less than twenty-five years after Muhammad's death, civil war pitted Muslim against Muslim.

Out of that conflict emerged one of the deepest and most enduring rifts within the Islamic world. On one side were the Sunni Muslims (SOON-nee), who held that the caliphs were rightful political and military leaders, selected by the Islamic community. On the other side of this sharp divide was the Shia (SHEE-ah) (an Arabic word meaning "party" or "faction") branch of Islam. Its adherents felt strongly that leadership in the Islamic world should derive from the line of Ali and his son Husayn, blood relatives of Muhammad, both of whom died at the hands of their political or religious enemies.

In the beginning, therefore, this divide was simply a political conflict without serious theological or religious mean-

The Kaaba
Located in Mecca, this stone structure covered with a black cloth and known as the Kaaba, was originally home to the numerous deities of pre-Islamic Arabia. Cleansed by Muhammad, it became the sacred shrine of Islam and the destination of countless pilgrims undertaking the hajj. Part of that ritual involves circling the Kaaba seven times, as shown here in a photograph from 2004. (Dan Mohiuddin/Visual Connection Archive)

ing, but over time the Sunni/Shia split acquired deeper significance. For Sunni Muslims, religious authority in general emerged from the larger community, particularly from the religious scholars known as *ulama* (oo-leh-MAH). Shia Muslims, on the other hand, invested their leaders, known as *imams*, with a religious authority that the caliphs lacked, allowing them to infallibly interpret divine revelation and law. For much of early Islamic history, Shia Muslims saw themselves as the minority opposition within Islam. They felt that history had taken a wrong turn and that they were "the defenders of the oppressed, the critics and opponents of privilege and power," while the Sunnis were the advocates of the established order.[12] Various armed revolts by Shias over the centuries, most of which failed, led to a distinctive conception of martyrdom and to the expectation that their defeated leaders were merely in hiding and not really dead and that they would return in the fullness of time. Thus a messianic element entered Shia Islam. The Sunni/Shia schism became a lasting division in the Islamic world, reflected in conflicts among various Islamic states, and was exacerbated by further splits among the Shia. Those divisions echo still in the twenty-first century.

As the Arab Empire grew, its caliphs were transformed from modest Arab chiefs into absolute monarchs of the Byzantine or Persian variety, complete with elaborate court rituals, a complex bureaucracy, a standing army, and centralized systems of taxation and coinage. They were also subject to the dynastic rivalries and succession disputes common to other empires. The first dynasty, following the era of the Rightly Guided Caliphs, came from the Umayyad (oo-MEYE-ahd) family (ruled 661–750).

Under its leadership, the Arab Empire expanded greatly, caliphs became hereditary rulers, and the capital moved from Medina to the cosmopolitan Roman/Byzantine city of Damascus in Syria. Its ruling class was an Arab military aristocracy, drawn from various tribes. But Umayyad rule provoked growing criticism and unrest. The Shia viewed the Umayyad caliphs as illegitimate usurpers, and non-Arab Muslims resented their second-class citizenship in the empire. Many Arabs protested the luxurious living and impiety of their rulers. The Umayyads, they charged, "made God's servants slaves, God's property something to be taken by turns among the rich, and God's religion a cause of corruption."[13]

Such grievances lay behind the overthrow of the Umayyads in 750 and their replacement by a new Arab dynasty, the Abbasids. With a splendid new capital in Baghdad, the Abbasid caliphs presided over a flourishing and prosperous Islamic civilization in which non–Arabs, especially Persians, now played a prominent role. But the political unity of the Abbasid Empire did not last long. Beginning in the mid-ninth century, many local governors or military commanders effectively asserted the autonomy of their regions, while still giving formal allegiance to the caliph in Baghdad. Long before Mongol conquest put an official end to the Abbasid Empire in 1258, the Islamic world had fractured politically into a series of "sultanates," many ruled by Persian or Turkish military dynasties.

■ **Comparison**

In what ways were Sufi Muslims critical of mainstream Islam?

A further tension within the world of Islam, though one that seldom produced violent conflict, lay in different answers to the central question: What does it mean to be a Muslim, to submit wholly to Allah? That question took on added urgency as the expanding Arab Empire incorporated various peoples and cultures that had been unknown during Muhammad's lifetime. One answer lay in the development of the sharia, the body of Islamic law developed by religious scholars, the ulama, primarily in the eighth and ninth centuries.

Based on the Quran, the life and teachings of Muhammad, deductive reasoning, and the consensus of scholars, the emerging sharia addressed in great detail practically every aspect of life. It was a blueprint for an authentic Islamic society, providing detailed guidance for prayer and ritual cleansing; marriage, divorce, and inheritance; business and commercial relationships; the treatment of slaves; political life; and much more. Debates among the ulama led to the creation of four schools of law among Sunni Muslims and still others in the lands of Shia Islam. To the ulama and their followers, living as a Muslim meant following the sharia and thus participating in the creation of an Islamic society.

A second and quite different understanding of the faith emerged among those who saw the worldly success of Islamic civilization as a distraction and deviation from the purer spirituality of Muhammad's time. Known as Sufis (SOO-fees), they represented Islam's mystical dimension, in that they sought a direct and personal experience of the Divine. Through renunciation of the material world, meditation on the words of the Quran, chanting the names of God, the use of music and dance, the veneration of Muhammad and various "saints," Sufis pursued an interior life, seeking to tame the ego and achieve spiritual union with Allah. To describe that inexpressible experience, they often resorted to metaphors of drunkenness or the embrace of lovers. "Stain your prayer rug with wine," urged the famous Sufi poet Hafiz, referring to the intoxication of the believer with the divine presence.

This mystical tendency in Islamic practice, which became widely popular by the ninth and tenth centuries, was sharply critical of the more scholarly and legalistic practitioners of the sharia. To Sufis, establishment teachings about the law and correct behavior, while useful for daily living, did little to bring the believer into the presence of God. For some, even the Quran had its limits. Why spend time reading a love letter (the Quran), asked one Sufi master, when one might be in the very presence of the Beloved who wrote it?[14] Furthermore, they felt that many of the ulama had been compromised by their association with worldly and corrupt governments. Sufis therefore often charted their own course to God, implicitly challenging the religious authority of the ulama. For these orthodox religious scholars, Sufi ideas and practice verged on heresy, as Sufis on occasion claimed unity with God, received new revelations, or incorporated novel religious practices from outside the Islamic world.

Sufis and Worldly Power This early seventeenth-century painting from India illustrates the tension between Sufis and worldly authorities. Here the Muslim Mughal Emperor Jahangir gives his attention to the white-bearded Sufi holy man rather than to the kings and artists shown in the bottom left. (Freer Gallery of Art, Smithsonian Institution, Washington, D.C. Purchase, F1942.15a)

Despite their differences, the legalistic emphasis of the ulama and Sufi spirituality never became irreconcilable versions of Islam. A major Islamic thinker, al-Ghazali (1058–1111), himself both a legal scholar and a Sufi practitioner, in fact worked out an intellectual accommodation among different strands of Islamic thought. Rational philosophy alone could never enable believers to know Allah, he argued. Nor were revelation and the law sufficient, for Muslims must know God in their hearts, through direct personal encounter with Allah. Thus Sufism entered mainstream Islamic thinking, and Sufi spiritual practices long served as an element of popular Islam. Nonetheless, differences in emphasis remained an element of tension and sometimes discord within the world of Islam.

Women and Men in Early Islam

What did the rise of Islam and the making of the Arab Empire mean for the daily lives of women and their relationship with men? Virtually every aspect of this question has been and remains highly controversial. The debates begin with the Quran itself. Did its teachings release women from earlier restrictions, or did they impose new limitations? At the level of spiritual life, the Quran was quite clear and explicit: men and women were equal.

■ Change
How did the rise of Islam change the lives of women?

Those who surrender themselves to Allah and accept the true faith; who are devout, sincere, patient, humble, charitable, and chaste; who fast and are ever mindful of Allah—on these, both men and women, Allah will bestow forgiveness and rich reward.[15]

But in social terms, and especially within marriage, the Quran, like the written texts of almost all civilizations, viewed women as inferior and subordinate: "Men have authority over women because Allah has made the one superior to the other, and because they spend their wealth to maintain them. Good women are obedient."[16] More specifically, the Quran provided a mix of rights, restrictions, and protections for women. Female infanticide, for example, widely practiced in many cultures as a means of gender selection, was now forbidden for Muslims. Women were given control over their own property, particularly their dowries, and were granted rights of inheritance, but at half the rate of their male counterparts. Marriage was considered a contract between consenting parties, thus making marriage by capture illegitimate. Divorce was possible for both parties, although it was far more readily available for men. The practice of taking multiple husbands, which operated in some pre-Islamic Arab tribes, was prohibited, while polygyny (the practice of having multiple wives) was permitted,

Men and Women at Worship
This sixteenth-century Persian painting of a mosque service shows older men with beards toward the front, younger men behind them, and veiled women and children in a separate area. (Bodleian Library, University of Oxford, Ms. Ouseley. Add 24, fol. 55v)

though more clearly regulated than before. Men were limited to four wives and required to treat each of them equally. The difficulty of doing so has been interpreted by some as virtually requiring monogamy. Men were, however, permitted to have sexual relations with female slaves, but any children born of those unions were free, as was the mother once her owner died. Furthermore, men were strongly encouraged to marry orphans, widows, and slaves.

Such Quranic prescriptions were but one factor shaping the lives of women and men. At least as important were the long-established practices of the societies into which Islam spread and the growing sophistication, prosperity, and urbanization of Islamic civilization. As had been the case in Athens and China during their "golden ages," Muslim women, particularly in the upper classes, experienced growing restrictions as Islamic civilization flourished culturally and economically in the Abbasid era. In early Islamic times, a number of women played visible public roles, particularly Muhammad's youngest wife, Aisha. Women prayed in the mosques, although separately, standing beside the men. Nor were women generally veiled or secluded. As the Arab empire grew in size and splendor, however, the position of women became more limited. The second caliph, Umar, asked women to offer prayers at home. Now veiling and the seclusion of women became standard practice among the upper and ruling classes, removing them from public life. Separate quarters within the homes of the wealthy were the domain of women, from which they could emerge only completely veiled. The caliph Mansur (ruled 754–775) carried this separation of the sexes even further when he ordered a separate bridge for women to be built over the Euphrates River in the new capital of Baghdad. Such seclusion was less possible for lower-class women, who lacked the servants of the rich and had to leave the home for shopping or work.

Such practices derived far more from established traditions of Middle Eastern cultures than from the Quran itself, but they soon gained an Islamic rationale in the writings of Muslim thinkers. The famous philosopher and religious scholar al-Ghazali clearly saw a relationship between Muslim piety and the separation of the sexes:

> It is not permissible for a stranger to hear the sound of a pestle being pounded by a woman he does not know. If he knocks at the door, it is not proper for the woman to answer him softly and easily because men's hearts can be drawn to [women] for the most trifling [reason]. . . . However, if the woman has to answer the knock, she should stick her finger in her mouth so that her voice sounds like that of an old woman.[17]

Other signs of a tightening patriarchy — such as "honor killing" of women by their male relatives for violating sexual taboos and, in some places, clitorectomy (female genital cutting) — likewise derived from local cultures, with no sanction in the Quran or Islamic law. Where they were practiced, such customs often came to be seen as Islamic, but they were certainly not limited to the Islamic world. In many cultures, concern with family honor linked to women's sexuality dictated harsh punishments for women who violated sexual taboos.

Negative views of women, presenting them variously as weak, deficient, and a sexually charged threat to men and social stability, emerged in the *hadiths* (hah-DEETHS), traditions about the sayings or actions of Muhammad, which became an important source of Islamic law. A changing interpretation of the Adam and Eve story illustrates the point. The Quran attaches equal blame to both Adam and Eve for yielding to the temptation of Satan, and both alike ask for and receive God's forgiveness. Nothing suggests that Eve tempted or seduced Adam into sin. In later centuries, however, several hadiths and other writings took up Judeo-Christian versions of the story that blamed Eve, and thus women in general, for Adam's sin and for the punishment that followed, including expulsion from the garden and pain in childbirth.[18]

Even as women faced growing restrictions in society generally, Islam, like Buddhism and Christianity, also offered new outlets for them in religious life. The Sufi practice of mystical union with Allah allowed a greater role for women than did mainstream Islam. Some Sufi orders had parallel groups for women, and a few welcomed women as equal members. Among the earliest of well-known Sufi practitioners was Rabia, an eighth-century woman from Basra, who renounced numerous proposals of marriage and engaged, apparently successfully, in repeated religious debates with men. The greatest of the Sufi scholars, Ibn al-Arabi (1165–1240), sang the praises of divine beauty in an explicitly feminine form. The spiritual equality that the Quran accorded to male and female alike allowed women also to aspire to union with God. But for some male Sufi scholars, such as the twelfth-century mystical poet Attar, doing so meant that "she is a man and one cannot any more call her a woman."[19]

Beyond Sufi practice, within the world of Shia Islam, women teachers of the faith were called mullahs, the same as their male counterparts. Islamic education, either in the home or in Quranic schools, allowed some to become literate and a few to achieve higher levels of learning. Visits to the tombs of major Islamic figures as well as the ritual of the public bath likewise provided some opportunity for women to interact with other women beyond their own family circle.

LearningCurve
bedfordstmartins.com
/strayer/LC

Islam and Cultural Encounter: A Four-Way Comparison

In its earliest centuries, the rapid spread of Islam had been accompanied by the creation of an immense Arab Empire, very much in the tradition of earlier Mediterranean and Middle Eastern empires. By the tenth century, however, little political unity remained, and in 1258 even the powerless symbol of that earlier unity vanished as Mongol forces sacked Baghdad and killed the last Abbasid caliph. But even as the empire disintegrated, the civilization that was born within it grew and flourished. Perhaps the most significant sign of a flourishing Islamic civilization was the continued spread of the religion both within and beyond the boundaries of a vanishing Arab Empire (see Map 9.3), although that process differed considerably from place to place. The examples of India, Anatolia, West Africa, and Spain illustrate the various ways that Islam penetrated these societies as well as the rather different outcomes of these epic cultural encounters.

The Case of India

■ **Comparison**

What similarities and differences can you identify in the spread of Islam to India, Anatolia, West Africa, and Spain?

In South Asia, Islam found a permanent place in a long-established civilization as invasions by Turkic-speaking warrior groups from Central Asia, recently converted to Islam, brought the faith to northern India. Thus the Turks became the third major carrier of Islam, after the Arabs and Persians, as their conquests initiated an enduring encounter between Islam and a Hindu-based Indian civilization. Beginning around 1000, those conquests gave rise to a series of Turkic and Muslim regimes that governed much of India until the British takeover in the eighteenth and nineteenth centuries. The early centuries of this encounter were violent indeed, as the invaders smashed Hindu and Buddhist temples and carried off vast quantities of Indian treasure. With the establishment of the Sultanate of Delhi in 1206 (see Map 9.4), Turkic rule became more systematic, although their small numbers and internal conflicts allowed only a very modest penetration of Indian society.

In the centuries that followed, substantial Muslim communities emerged in India, particularly in regions less tightly integrated into the dominant Hindu culture. Disillusioned Buddhists as well as low-caste Hindus and untouchables found the more egalitarian Islam attractive. So did peoples just beginning to make the transition to

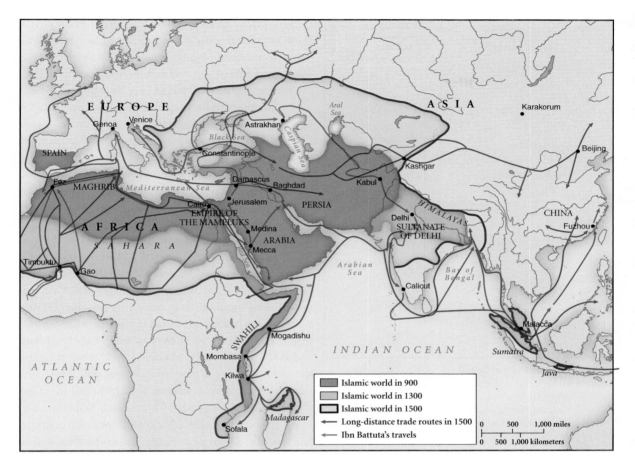

Map 9.3 The Growing World of Islam, 900–1500

Islam as a religion, a civilization, and an arena of commerce continued to grow even as the Arab Empire fragmented.

settled agriculture. Others benefited from converting to Islam by avoiding the tax imposed on non-Muslims. Sufis were particularly important in facilitating conversion, for India had always valued "god-filled men" who were detached from worldly affairs. Sufi holy men, willing to accommodate local gods and religious festivals, helped to develop a "popular Islam" that was not always so sharply distinguished from the more devotional forms of Hinduism.

Unlike the earlier experience of Islam in the Middle East, North Africa, and Persia, where Islam rapidly became the dominant faith, in India it was never able to claim more than 20 to 25 percent of the total population. Furthermore, Muslim communities were especially concentrated in the Punjab and Sind regions of northwestern India and in Bengal to the east. The core regions of Hindu culture in the northern Indian plain were not seriously challenged by the new faith, despite centuries of Muslim rule. One reason perhaps lay in the sharpness of the cultural divide between Islam and Hinduism. Islam was the most radically monotheistic of the world's religions, forbidding any representation of Allah, while Hinduism was surely among the most prolifically polytheistic, generating endless statues and images of the Divine in many forms. The Muslim notion

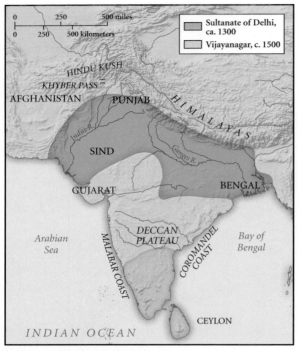

Map 9.4 The Sultanate of Delhi
Between 1206 and 1526 a number of Muslim dynasties ruled northern India as the Delhi sultanate, while an explicitly Hindu kingdom of Vijayanagar arose in the south after 1340. It drew on north Indian Muslim architectural features and made use of Muslim mercenaries for its military forces.

of the equality of all believers contrasted sharply with the hierarchical assumptions of the caste system. The sexual modesty of Muslims was deeply offended by the open eroticism of some Hindu religious art.

Although such differences may have limited the appeal of Islam in India, they also may have prevented it from being absorbed into the tolerant and inclusive embrace of Hinduism as had so many other religious ideas, practices, and communities. The religious exclusivity of Islam, born of its firm monotheistic belief and the idea of a unique revelation, set a boundary that the great sponge of Hinduism could not completely absorb.

Certainly not all was conflict across that boundary. Many prominent Hindus willingly served in the political and military structures of a Muslim-ruled India. Mystical seekers after the divine blurred the distinction between Hindu and Muslim, suggesting that God was to be found "neither in temple nor in mosque." "Look within your heart," wrote the great fifteenth-century mystic poet Kabir, "for there you will find both [Allah] and Ram [a famous Hindu deity]."[20] During the early sixteenth century, a new and distinct religious tradition emerged in India, known as Sikhism (SIHK-iz'm), which blended elements of Islam, such as devotion to one universal God, with Hindu concepts, such as karma and rebirth. "There is no Hindu and no Muslim. All are children of God," declared Guru Nanak (1469–1539), the founder of Sikhism.

Nonetheless, Muslims usually lived quite separately, remaining a distinctive minority within an ancient Indian civilization, which they now largely governed but which they proved unable to completely transform.

The Case of Anatolia

■ **Change**
In what ways was Anatolia changed by its incorporation into the Islamic world?

At the same time as India was being subjected to Turkic invasion, so too was Anatolia (now modern Turkey), where the largely Christian and Greek-speaking population was then governed by the Byzantine Empire (see Map 9.2, p. 290, and Map 9.5). Here, as in India, the invaders initially wreaked havoc as Byzantine authority melted away in the eleventh century. Sufi practitioners likewise played a major role in the process of conversion. The outcome, however, was a far more profound cultural transformation than in India. By 1500, the population was 90 percent Muslim and largely Turkic-speaking, and Anatolia was the heartland of the powerful Turkish Ottoman Empire that had overrun Christian Byzantium. Why did the Turkic intrusion into Anatolia generate a much more thorough Islamization than in India?

One factor clearly lies in a very different demographic balance. The population of Anatolia—perhaps 8 million—was far smaller than India's roughly 48 million people, but far more Turkic-speaking peoples settled in Anatolia, giving them a much greater cultural weight than the smaller colonizing force in India. Furthermore, the disruption of Anatolian society was much more extensive. Massacres, enslavement, famine, and flight led to a sharp drop in the native population. The Byzantine state had been fatally weakened. Church properties were confiscated, and monasteries were destroyed or deserted. Priests and bishops were sometimes unable to serve their congregations. Christians, though seldom forced to convert, suffered many discriminations. They had to wear special clothing and pay special taxes, and they were forbidden to ride saddled horses or carry swords. Not a few Christians came to believe that these disasters represented proof that Islam was the true religion.[21] Thus Byzantine civilization in Anatolia, previously focused on the centralized institutions of church and state, was rendered leaderless and dispirited, whereas India's decentralized civilization, lacking a unified political or religious establishment, was better able to absorb the shock of external invasion while retaining its core values and identity.

The Turkish rulers of Anatolia built a new society that welcomed converts and granted them material rewards and opportunity for high office. Moreover, the cultural barriers to conversion were arguably less severe than in India. The common monotheism of Islam and Christianity, and Muslim respect for Jesus and the Christian scriptures, made conversion easier than crossing the great gulf between Islam and Hinduism. Such similarities lent support to the suggestion of some Sufi teachers that the two religions were but different versions of the same faith. Sufis also established schools, mills, orchards, hospices, and rest places for travelers and thus replaced the destroyed or decaying institutions of Christian Anatolia.[22] All of this contributed to the thorough religious transformation of Anatolia and laid a foundation for the Ottoman Empire, which by 1500 became the most impressive and powerful state within the Islamic world.

But the Islamization of Anatolia occurred within a distinctly Turkish context. A Turkish language, not Arabic, predominated. Some Sufi religious practices, such as ecstatic turning dances, derived from Central Asian Turkic shamanism. And Turkic traditions offering

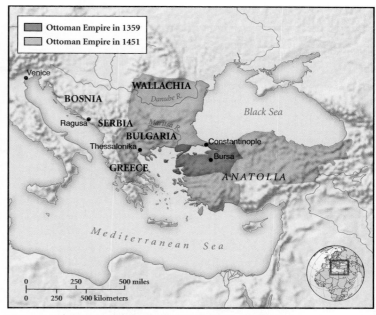

Map 9.5   The Ottoman Empire by the Mid-fifteenth Century

As Turkic-speaking migrants bearing the religion of Islam penetrated Anatolia, the Ottoman Empire took shape, reaching into southeastern Europe and finally displacing the Christian Byzantine Empire. Subsequently, it came to control much of the Middle East and North Africa as well.

a freer, more gender-equal life for women, common among pastoral people, persisted well after conversion to Islam, much to the distress of the Arab Moroccan visitor Ibn Battuta during his travels among them in the fourteenth century: "A remarkable thing that I saw ... was the respect shown to women by the Turks, for they hold a more dignified position than the men. ... The windows of the tent are open and her face is visible, for the Turkish women do not veil themselves."[23] He was not pleased.

The Case of West Africa

Still another pattern of Islamic expansion prevailed in West Africa. Here Islam accompanied Muslim traders across the Sahara rather than being brought by invading Arab or Turkic armies. Its gradual acceptance in the emerging civilization of West African states in the centuries after 1000 was largely peaceful and voluntary, lacking the incentives associated elsewhere with foreign conquest. Introduced by Muslim merchants from an already Islamized North Africa, the new faith was accepted primarily in the urban centers of the West African empires—Ghana, Mali, Songhay, Kanem-Bornu, and others (see Map 9.6 and the portrait of Mansa Musa, pp. 304–05). For African merchant communities, Islam provided an important link to Muslim trading partners, much as Buddhism had done in Southeast Asia. For the monarchs and their courts, it offered a source of literate officials to assist in state administration as well as religious legiti-

Map 9.6   West Africa and the World of Islam
Both trans-Saharan commerce and Islam linked the civilization of West Africa to the larger Muslim world.

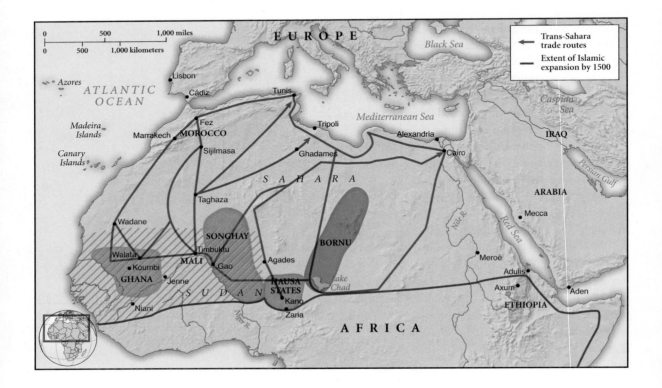

macy, particularly for those who gained the prestige conferred by a pilgrimage to Mecca. Islam was a world religion with a single Creator-God, able to comfort and protect people whose political and economic horizons had expanded well beyond the local realm where ancestral spirits and traditional deities might be effective. It had a religious appeal for societies that were now participating in a wider world.

The Great Mosque at Jenne
This mosque in the city of Jenne, initially constructed in the thirteenth century, illustrates the assimilation of Islam into West African civilization. (Antonello Lanzellotto/TIPS Images)

By the sixteenth century, a number of West African cities had become major centers of Islamic religious and intellectual life, attracting scholars from throughout the Muslim world. Timbuktu boasted more than 150 lower-level Quranic schools and several major centers of higher education with thousands of students from all over West Africa and beyond. Libraries held tens of thousands of books and scholarly manuscripts (see the image on p. 309). Monarchs subsidized the construction of mosques as West Africa became an integral part of a larger Islamic world. Arabic became an important language of religion, education, administration, and trade, but it did not become the dominant language of daily life. Nor did West Africa experience the massive migration of Arab peoples that had promoted the Arabization of North Africa and the Middle East. Moreover, in contrast to India and Anatolia, Sufi holy men played a far more modest role until at least the eighteenth century. Scholars, merchants, and rulers, rather than mystic preachers, initially established Islam in West Africa.

Islam remained the culture of urban elites and spread little into the rural areas of West Africa until the nineteenth century. No thorough religious transformation occurred in West Africa as it had in Anatolia. Although many rulers adopted Islam, they governed people who steadfastly practiced African religions and whose sensibilities they had to respect if social peace were to prevail. Thus they made few efforts to impose the new religion on their rural subjects or to govern in strict accordance with Islamic law. The fourteenth-century Arab visitor Ibn Battuta was appalled that practicing Muslims in Mali permitted their women to appear in public almost naked and to mingle freely with unrelated men. "The association of women with men is agreeable to us," he was told, "and a part of good conduct to which no suspicion attaches. They are not like the women of your country."[24] Ibn Battuta also noted with disapproval a "dance of the masks" on the occasion of an Islamic festival and the traditional practice of sprinkling dust on their heads as a sign of respect for the king. Sonni Ali, a fifteenth-century ruler of Songhay, observed Ramadan and built mosques, but he also consulted traditional diviners and performed customary sacrifices. In such ways, Islam became Africanized even as parts of West Africa became Islamized.

PORTRAIT

Mansa Musa, West African Monarch and Muslim Pilgrim

In 1324, Mansa Musa, the ruler or *mansa* of the Kingdom of Mali, set out on an arduous journey from his West African homeland to the holy city of Mecca. His kingdom stretched from the Atlantic coast a thousand miles or more to the fabled inland city of Timbuktu and beyond, even as his pilgrimage to Mecca reflected the growing penetration of Islam in this emerging West African civilization. Mansa Musa was a pious Muslim, fluent in Arabic, inclined on occasion to free a few slaves, and an avid builder of mosques.

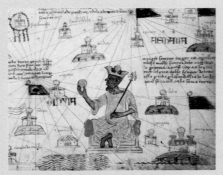

Mansa Musa (Bibliothèque nationale de France)

In the fourteenth century, Mali was an expanding empire. According to Musa, one of his immediate predecessors had launched a substantial maritime expedition "to discover the furthest limits of the Atlantic Ocean."[25] The voyagers never returned, and no other record of it exists, but it is intriguing to consider that Africans and Europeans alike may have been exploring the Atlantic at roughly the same time. Mansa Musa, however, was more inclined to expand on land as he sought access to the gold fields to the south and the trans-Saharan trade network to the north.

Control of this lucrative commercial complex enriched Mansa Musa's empire, enabled a major building program of mosques and palaces, and turned the city of Timbuktu into a thriving center of trade, religion, and intellectual life. Merchants and scholars from across West and North Africa flocked to the city.

Mansa Musa's journey to Mecca has fascinated observers then and now. Such a pilgrimage has long been one of the duties—and privileges—of all Muslims. It also added the prestigious title of *hajji* to their names. For rulers in particular it conveyed a spiritual power known as *baraka*, which helped legitimate their rule.

When Mansa Musa began his journey in 1324, he was accompanied by an enormous entourage, with thousands of fellow pilgrims, some 500 slaves, his wife and other women, hundreds of camels, and a huge quantity of gold. It was the gold that attracted the most attention, as he distributed it lavishly along his journey. Egyptian sources reported that the value of gold in their country was depressed for years after his visit. On his return trip, Mansa

The Case of Spain

The chief site of Islamic encounter with Christian Europe occurred in Spain, called al-Andalus by Muslims, which was conquered by Arab and Berber forces in the early eighth century during the first wave of Islamic expansion. By the tenth century, Muslim Spain was a vibrant civilization, often portrayed as a place of harmony and tolerance between its Muslim rulers and its Christian and Jewish subjects.

Certainly Spain's agricultural economy was the most prosperous in Europe during this time and its capital of Córdoba was among the largest and most splendid cities in the world. Muslims, Christians, and Jews alike contributed to a brilliant high culture in which astronomy, medicine, the arts, architecture, and literature flourished. Furthermore, social relationships among upper-class members of different faiths were easy and frequent. By 1000, perhaps 75 percent of the population had converted to Islam. Many of the remaining Christians learned Arabic, veiled their women, stopped eating pork, appreciated Arabic music and poetry, and sometimes married Muslims. One Chris-

Musa apparently had exhausted his supply and had to borrow money from Egyptian merchants at high interest rates. Those merchants also made a killing on Musa's pilgrims, who, unsophisticated in big-city shopping, were made to pay far more than their purchases were worth. Europeans too now became aware of Mansa Musa, featuring him holding a large nugget of gold in a famous map from 1375 with a caption reading: "This Negro lord is called Musa Mali. . . . So abundant is the gold found in his country that he is the richest and most noble king in all the land."[26]

In Cairo, Mansa Musa displayed both his pride and his ignorance of Islamic law. Invited to see the sultan of Egypt, he was initially reluctant because of a protocol requirement to kiss the ground and the sultan's hand. He consented only when he was persuaded that he was really prostrating before God, not the sultan. And in conversation with learned clerics, Mansa Musa was surprised to learn that Muslim rulers were not allowed to take the beautiful unmarried women of their realm as concubines. "By God, I did not know that," he replied. "I hereby leave it and abandon it utterly."[27]

In Mecca, Mansa Musa completed the requirements of the hajj, dressing in the common garb of all pilgrims, repeatedly circling the Kaaba, performing ritual prayers, and visiting various sites associated with Muhammad's life, including a side trip to the Prophet's tomb in Medina. He also sought to recruit a number of sharifs, prestigious descendants of Muhammad's family, to add Islamic luster to his kingdom. After considerable difficulty and expense, he found four men who were willing to return with him to what Arabs understood to be the remote frontier of the Islamic world. Some reports suggested that they were simply freed slaves, hoping for better lives.

In the end, perhaps Mansa Musa's goals for the pilgrimage were achieved. On a personal level, one source reported that he was so moved by the pilgrimage that he actually considered abandoning his throne altogether and returning to Mecca where he might live as "a dweller near the sanctuary [the Kaaba]."[28] His visit certainly elevated Mali's status in the Islamic world. Some 200 years after that visit, one account of his pilgrimage placed the Sultan of Mali as one of four major rulers in the Islamic world, equal to those of Baghdad and Egypt. Mansa Musa would have been pleased.

Question: What significance did Mansa Musa likely attach to his pilgrimage? How might Egyptians, Arabians, and Europeans have viewed it?

tian bishop complained that Spanish Christians knew the rules of Arabic grammar better than those of Latin. During the reign of Abd al-Rahman III (ruled 912–961), freedom of worship was declared as well as the opportunity for all to rise in the bureaucracy of the state.

But this so-called golden age of Muslim Spain was both limited and brief. Even assimilated or Arabized Christians remained religious infidels and second-class citizens in the eyes of their Muslim counterparts, and by the late tenth century toleration began to erode. The Córdoba-based regime fragmented into numerous rival states. Warfare with the remaining Christian kingdoms in northern Spain picked up in the tenth and eleventh centuries, and more puritanical and rigid forms of Islam entered Spain from North Africa. Under the rule of al-Mansur (ruled 981–1002), an official policy of tolerance turned to one of overt persecution against Christians, which now included the plundering of churches and the seizure of their wealth, although he employed many Christian mercenaries in his armies. Social life also changed. Devout Muslims avoided contact with Christians; Christian homes had to be built lower than those of Muslims; priests were forbidden to carry a cross or a Bible, lest they offend Muslim sensibilities; and Arabized Christians were permitted to live only in particular places. Thus, writes one scholar, "the era of harmonious interaction between Muslim and Christian in Spain came to an end, replaced by intolerance, prejudice, and mutual suspicion."[29]

That intolerance intensified as the Christian reconquest of Spain gained ground after 1200. The end came in 1492, when Ferdinand and Isabella, the Catholic monarchs of a unified Spain, took Granada, the last Muslim stronghold on the Iberian Peninsula. To Christopher Columbus, who witnessed the event before leaving on his first trans-Atlantic voyage, it was a grand Christian triumph. "I saw the royal banners of your Highnesses planted by force of arms upon the towers of the Alhambra," he wrote. To Muslims, it was a catastrophe. Tradition has it that Boabdil, the final ruler of Muslim Granada, wept as he left his beloved city for the last time. Observing his grief, Boabdil's mother famously said to him: "Thou dost weep like a woman for what thou couldst not defend as a man."

After the conquest, many Muslims were forced to emigrate, replaced by Christian settlers. While those who remained under Christian rule were legally guaranteed freedom of worship, they were forbidden to make converts, to give the call to prayer, or to go on pilgrimage. And all Jews, some 200,000 of them, were expelled from the country. In the early seventeenth century, even Muslim converts to Christianity were likewise banished from Spain. And yet cultural interchange persisted for a time. The translation of Arab texts into Latin continued under Christian rule, while Christian churches and palaces were constructed on the sites of older mosques and incorporated Islamic artistic and architectural features.

Thus Spain, unlike most other regions incorporated into the Islamic world, experienced a religious reversal as Christian rule was reestablished and Islam painfully eradicated from the Iberian Peninsula. In world historical terms, perhaps the chief significance of Muslim Spain was its role in making the rich heritage of Islamic learning available to Christian Europe. As a cross-cultural encounter, it was largely a one-way street. European scholars wanted the secular knowledge — Greek as well as Arab — that had accumulated in the Islamic world, and they flocked to Spain to acquire it. That knowledge of philosophy, mathematics, medicine, optics, astronomy, botany, and more played a major role in the making of a new European civilization in the thirteenth century and beyond. Muslim Spain remained only as a memory.

LearningCurve
bedfordstmartins.com
/strayer/LC

SUMMING UP SO FAR

"Islam had a revolutionary impact on every society that it touched." What evidence might support this statement, and what might challenge it?

The World of Islam as a New Civilization

As the religion spread and the Abbasid dynasty declined, the civilization of Islam, unlike that of China but similar to Western Christendom, operated without a dominant political center, bound more by a shared religious culture than by a shared state. Twice that civilization was threatened from outside. The most serious intrusion came during the thirteenth century from the Mongols, whose conquest of Central Asia and Persia proved devastating while incorporating many Muslims within the huge Mongol domains (see Chapter 11). Less serious but more well known, at least in the West, were the Christian crusaders who established in the twelfth and thirteenth centuries several small and temporary outposts along the eastern Mediterranean (see Chapter 10).

Despite these external threats and its various internal conflicts, Islamic civilization flourished and often prospered, embracing at least parts of virtually every other civilization in the Afro-Eurasian hemisphere. It was in that sense "history's first truly global civilization," although the Americas, of course, were not involved.[30] What held the Islamic world together? What enabled many people to feel themselves part of a single civilization despite its political fragmentation, religious controversies, and cultural and regional diversity?

Networks of Faith

At the core of that vast civilization was a common commitment to Islam. No group was more important in the transmission of those beliefs and practices than the ulama. These learned scholars were not "priests" in the Christian sense, for in Islam, at least theoretically, no person could stand between the believer and Allah. Rather they served as judges, interpreters, administrators, prayer leaders, and reciters of the Quran, but especially as preservers and teachers of the sharia. Supported mostly by their local communities, some also received the patronage of sultans, or rulers, and were therefore subject to criticism for corruption and undue submission to state authority. In their homes, mosques, shrines, and Quranic schools, the ulama passed on the core teachings of the faith. Beginning in the eleventh century, formal colleges called *madrassas* offered more advanced instruction in the Quran and the sayings of Muhammad; grammar and rhetoric; sometimes philosophy, theology, mathematics, and medicine; and, above all else, law. Teaching was informal, mostly oral, and involved much memorization of texts. It was also largely conservative, seeking to preserve an established body of Islamic learning.

The ulama were an "international elite," and the system of education they created served to bind together an immense and diverse civilization. Common texts were shared widely across the world of Islam. Students and teachers alike traveled great distances in search of the most learned scholars. From Indonesia to West Africa, educated Muslims inhabited a "shared world of debate and reference."[31]

Paralleling the educational network of the ulama were the emerging religious orders of the Sufis. By the tenth century, particular Sufi *shaykhs* (shakes), or teachers, began to attract groups of disciples who were eager to learn their unique devotional practices and techniques of personal transformation. The disciples usually swore allegiance to their teacher and valued highly the chain of transmission by which those teachings and practices had come down from earlier masters. In the twelfth and thirteenth centuries, Sufis began to organize in a variety of larger associations, some limited to particular regions and others with chapters throughout the Islamic world. The

■ Description
What makes it possible to speak of the Islamic world as a distinct and coherent civilization?

Qadiriya order, for example, began in Baghdad but spread widely throughout the Arab world and into sub-Saharan Africa.

Sufi orders were especially significant in the frontier regions of Islam because they followed conquering armies or traders into Central and Southeast Asia, India, Anatolia, parts of Africa, and elsewhere. Their devotional teachings, modest ways of living, and reputation for supernatural powers gained a hearing for the new faith. Their emphasis on personal experience of the Divine, rather than on the law, allowed the Sufis to accommodate elements of local belief and practice and encouraged the growth of a popular or blended Islam. The veneration of deceased Sufi "saints," or "friends of God," particularly at their tombs, created sacred spaces that enabled Islam to take root in many places despite its foreign origins. But that flexibility also often earned Sufi practitioners the enmity of the ulama, who were sharply critical of any deviations from the sharia.

Like the madrassas and the sharia, Sufi religious ideas and institutions spanned the Islamic world and were yet another thread in the cosmopolitan web of Islamic civilization. Particular devotional teachings and practices spread widely, as did the writings of such famous Sufi poets as Hafiz and Rumi. Devotees made pilgrimages to the distant tombs of famous teachers, who, they often believed, might intercede with God on their behalf. Wandering Sufis, in search of the wisdom of renowned shaykhs, found fellow seekers and welcome shelter in the compounds of these religious orders.

In addition to the networks of the Sufis and the ulama, many thousands of people, from kings to peasants, made the grand pilgrimage to Mecca—the hajj—no doubt gaining some sense of the umma. There men and women together, hailing from all over the Islamic world, joined as one people to rehearse the central elements of their faith. The claims of local identities based on family, clan, tribe, ethnicity, or state never disappeared, but now overarching them all was the inclusive unity of the Muslim community.

Networks of Exchange

■ Connection

In what ways was the world of Islam a "cosmopolitan civilization"?

The world of Islamic civilization cohered not only as a network of faith but also as an immense arena of exchange in which goods, technologies, food products, and ideas circulated widely. It rapidly became a vast trading zone of hemispheric dimensions. In part, this was due to its central location in the Afro-Eurasian world and the breaking down of earlier political barriers between the Byzantine and Persian empires. Furthermore, commerce was valued positively within Islamic teaching, for Muhammad himself had been a trader. The pilgrimage to Mecca, as well as the urbanization that accompanied the growth of Islamic civilization, likewise fostered commerce. Baghdad, established in 756 as the capital of the Abbasid Empire, soon grew into a magnificent city of half a million people. The appetite of urban elites for luxury goods stimulated both craft production and the desire for foreign products.

Thus Muslim merchants, Arabs and Persians in particular, quickly became prominent and sometimes dominant players in all of the major Afro-Eurasian trade routes of the third-wave era—in the Mediterranean Sea, along the revived Silk Roads, across the Sahara, and throughout the Indian Ocean basin (see Chapter 7). By the eighth century, Arab and Persian traders had established a commercial colony in Canton in southern China, thus linking the Islamic heartland with Asia's other giant and flourishing economy. Various forms of banking, partnerships, business contracts, and instruments for granting credit facilitated these long-distance economic relationships and generated a prosperous, sophisticated, and highly commercialized economy that spanned the Old World.[32]

The vast expanses of Islamic civilization also contributed to ecological change as agricultural products and practices spread from one region to another, a process already under way in the earlier Roman and Persian empires. The Muslim conquest of northwestern India opened the Middle East to a veritable treasure trove of crops that had been domesticated long before in South and Southeast Asia, including rice, sugarcane, new strains of sorghum, hard wheat, bananas, lemons, limes, watermelons, coconut palms, spinach, artichokes, and cotton. Some of these subsequently found their way into the Middle East and Africa and by the thirteenth century to Europe as well.[33] Both cotton and sugarcane, associated with complex production processes and slave labor, came to play central roles in the formation of the modern global system after 1500. These new crops, together with the diffusion of Middle Eastern and Indian irrigation systems, contributed to an "Islamic Green Revolution" of increased food production as well as to population growth, urbanization, and industrial development across the Islamic world.

A Muslim Astronomical Observatory
Drawing initially on Greek, Indian, and Persian astronomy, the Islamic world after 1000 developed its own distinctive tradition of astronomical observation and prediction, reflected in this Turkish observatory constructed in 1557. Muslim astronomy subsequently exercised considerable influence in both China and Europe. (University Library, Istanbul, Turkey/The Bridgeman Art Library)

Technology too diffused widely within the realm of Islam. Ancient Persian techniques for obtaining water by drilling into the sides of hills now spread across North Africa as far west as Morocco. Muslim technicians made improvements on rockets, first developed in China, by developing one that carried a small warhead and another used to attack ships.[34] Papermaking techniques entered the Abbasid Empire from China in the eighth century, with paper mills soon operating in Persia, Iraq, and Egypt. This revolutionary technology, which everywhere served to strengthen bureaucratic governments, passed from the Middle East into India and Europe over the following centuries.

Ideas likewise circulated across the Islamic world. The religion itself drew heavily and quite openly on Jewish and Christian precedents. Persia also contributed much in the way of bureaucratic practice, court ritual, and poetry, with Persian becoming a major literary language in elite circles. Scientific, medical, and philosophical texts, especially from ancient Greece, the Hellenistic world, and India, were systematically

$Snapshot$ **Key Achievements in Islamic Science and Scholarship**

Person/Dates	Achievement
al-Khwarazim (790–840)	Mathematician; spread use of Arabic numerals in Islamic world; wrote first book on algebra
al-Razi (865–925)	Discovered sulfuric acid; wrote a vast encyclopedia of medicine drawing on Greek, Syrian, Indian, and Persian work and his own clinical observation
al-Biruni (973–1048)	Mathematician, astronomer, cartographer; calculated the radius of the earth with great accuracy; worked out numerous mathematical innovations; developed a technique for displaying a hemisphere on a plane
Ibn Sina (Avicenna) (980–1037)	Prolific writer in almost all fields of science and philosophy; especially known for *Canon of Medicine*, a fourteen-volume work that set standards for medical practice in Islamic and Christian worlds for centuries
Omar Khayyam (1048–1131)	Mathematician; critic of Euclid's geometry; measured the solar year with great accuracy; Sufi poet; author of *The Rubaiyat*
Ibn Rushd (Averroës) (1126–1198)	Translated and commented widely on Aristotle; rationalist philosopher; made major contributions in law, mathematics, and medicine
Nasir al-Din Tusi (1201–1274)	Founder of the famous Maragha observatory in Persia (data from Maragha probably influenced Copernicus); mapped the motion of stars and planets
Ibn Khaldun (1332–1406)	Greatest Arab historian; identified trends and structures in world history over long periods of time

translated into Arabic, for several centuries providing an enormous boost to Islamic scholarship and science. In 830, the Abbasid caliph al-Mamun, himself a poet and scholar with a passion for foreign learning, established the House of Wisdom in Baghdad as an academic center for this research and translation. Stimulated by Greek texts, a school of Islamic thinkers known as Mutazalites ("those who stand apart") argued that reason, rather than revelation, was the "surest way to truth."[35] In the long run, however, the philosophers' emphasis on logic, rationality, and the laws of nature was subject to increasing criticism by those who held that only the Quran, the sayings of the Prophet, or mystical experience represented a genuine path to God.

But the realm of Islam was much more than a museum of ancient achievements from the civilizations that it encompassed. Those traditions mixed and blended to generate a distinctive Islamic civilization with many new contributions to the world of learning.[36] (See the Snapshot on p. 310.) Using Indian numerical notation, for example, Arab scholars developed algebra as a novel mathematical discipline. They also undertook much original work in astronomy and optics. They built on earlier Greek and Indian practice to create a remarkable tradition in medicine and pharmacology. Arab physicians such as al-Razi and Ibn Sina accurately diagnosed many diseases, such as hay fever, measles, smallpox, diphtheria, rabies, and diabetes. In addition, treatments such as using a mercury ointment for scabies, cataract and hernia operations, and filling teeth with gold emerged from Arab doctors. The first hospitals, traveling clinics, and examinations for physicians and pharmacologists also were developed within the Islamic world. In the eleventh and twelfth centuries, this enormous body of Arab medical scholarship entered Europe via Spain, and it remained at the core of European medical practice for many centuries.[37]

LearningCurve
bedfordstmartins.com
/strayer/LC

Reflections: Past and Present: Choosing Our History

Prominent among the many uses of history is the perspective it provides on the present. Although historians sometimes worry that an excessive "present-mindedness" may distort our perception of the past, all of us look to history, almost instinctively, to comprehend the world we now inhabit. Given the obvious importance of the Islamic world in the international arena of the twenty-first century, how might some grasp of the early development of Islamic civilization assist us in understanding our present circumstances?

Certainly that history reminds us of the central role that Islam played in the Afro-Eurasian world for a thousand years or more. From 600 to 1600 or later, it was a proud, cosmopolitan, often prosperous, and frequently powerful civilization that spanned Africa, Europe, the Middle East, and Asia. What followed were several centuries of European or Western imperialism that many Muslims found humiliating, even if some were attracted by elements of modern Western culture. In their recent efforts to overcome those centuries of subordination and exploitation, Muslims have found encouragement and inspiration in reflecting on the more distant and perhaps more glorious past. But they have not all chosen to emphasize the same past. Those labeled as "fundamentalists" have often viewed the early Islamic community associated with Medina, Mecca, and Muhammad as a model for Islamic renewal in the present. Others, often known as Islamic modernizers, have looked to the somewhat later achievements of Islamic science and scholarship as a foundation for a more open engagement with the West and the modern world.

The history of Islam also reveals to us a world of great diversity and debate. Sharp religious differences between Sunni and Shia understandings of the faith; differences in emphasis between advocates of the sharia and of Sufi spirituality; political conflicts among various groups and regions within the larger Islamic world; different postures toward women in Arab lands and in West Africa—all of this and more divided the umma and divide it still. Recalling that diversity is a useful reminder for any who would tag all Muslims with a single label.

A further dimension of that diversity lies in the many cultural encounters that the spread of Islam has spawned. Sometimes great conflict and violence have accompanied those encounters as in the Crusades and in Turkic invasions of India and Anatolia. At other times and places, Muslims and non-Muslims have lived together in relative tranquility and tolerance—in Spain, in West Africa, in India, and in the Ottoman Empire. Some commentaries on the current interaction of Islam and the West seem to assume an eternal hostility or an inevitable clash of civilizations. The record of the past, however, shows considerable variation in the interaction of Muslims and others. While the past certainly shapes and conditions what happens next, the future, as always, remains open. Within limits, we can choose the history on which we seek to build.

Second Thoughts

LearningCurve
Check what you know.
bedfordstmartins.com
/strayer/LC

Online Study Guide
bedfordstmartins.com/strayer

What's the Significance?

Quran, 285–86
umma, 286
Pillars of Islam, 286
hijra, 287
sharia, 288
jizya, 290
ulama, 293, 307
Umayyad caliphate, 293–94
Abbasid caliphate, 294
Sufism, 294–95

al-Ghazali, 295
Sikhism, 300
Ibn Battuta, 302–03
Timbuktu, 303
Mansa Musa, 304–05
al-Andalus, 304–06
madrassas, 307
House of Wisdom, 310
Ibn Sina, 310–11

Big Picture Questions

1. How might you account for the immense religious and political/military success of Islam in its early centuries?

2. In what ways might Islamic civilization be described as cosmopolitan, international, or global?

3. "Islam was simultaneously a single world of shared meaning and interaction and a series of separate, distinct, and conflicting communities." What evidence could you provide to support both sides of this argument?

4. What changes did Islamic expansion generate in those societies that encountered it, and how was Islam itself transformed by those encounters?

5. **Looking Back:** What distinguished the early centuries of Islamic history from a similar phase in the history of Christianity and Buddhism?

Next Steps: For Further Study

Reza Aslan, *No God but God* (2005). A well-written and popular history of Islam by an Iranian immigrant to the United States.

Fred M. Donner, *Muhammad and the Believers* (2010). An innovative account of the first century of Islam by a leading scholar of that era.

Richard Eaton, *Islamic History as Global History* (1990). A short account by a major scholar that examines Islam in a global framework.

John Esposito, ed., *The Oxford History of Islam* (1999). Up-to-date essays on various periods and themes in Islamic history. Beautifully illustrated.

Francis Robinson, ed., *Cambridge Illustrated History of the Islamic World* (1996). A series of essays by major scholars, with lovely pictures and maps.

Judith Tucker, *Gender and Islamic History* (1994). A brief overview of the changing lives of Islamic women.

"The Travels of Ibn Battuta: A Virtual Tour with the Fourteenth Century Traveler," http://fms-sfusd-ca .schoolloop.com/Battuta. A beautifully illustrated journey across the Islamic world in the early 1300s.

For Web sites and additional documents related to this chapter, see **Make History** at bedfordstmartins.com/strayer.

CHAPTER TEN

The Worlds of Christendom

Contraction, Expansion, and Division

500–1300

Christian Contraction in Asia and Africa
  Asian Christianity
  African Christianity
Byzantine Christendom: Building on
  the Roman Past
  The Byzantine State
  The Byzantine Church and Christian
    Divergence
  Byzantium and the World
  The Conversion of Russia
Western Christendom: Rebuilding in
  the Wake of Roman Collapse
  Political Life in Western Europe
  Society and the Church
  Accelerating Change in the West
  Europe Outward Bound: The
    Crusading Tradition
The West in Comparative Perspective
  Catching Up
  Pluralism in Politics
  Reason and Faith
Reflections: Remembering and
  Forgetting: Continuity and Surprise
  in the Worlds of Christendom
Portrait: Cecilia Penifader, An English
  Peasant and Unmarried Woman

Yao Hong, a Chinese woman, was about twenty years of age, when, distraught at discovering that her husband was having an affair, she became a Christian sometime around 1990. As a migrant from a rural village to Shanghai, Yao Hong found support and a sense of family in a Christian community. Interviewed in 2010, she observed, "Whether they know you or not, they treat you as a brother or sister. If you have troubles, they help out with money or material assistance or spiritual aid." Nor did she find the Christian faith alien to her Chinese culture. To the contrary, she felt conversion to Christianity as a patriotic act, even a way of becoming more fully modern. "God is rising here in China," she declared. "If you look at the United States or England, their gospel is very advanced. Their churches are rich, because God blesses them. So I pray for China."[1]

YAO HONG IS BUT ONE OF MANY MILLIONS who have made Christianity a very rapidly growing faith in China over the past thirty years or so. Other Asian countries—South Korea, Taiwan, Singapore, the Philippines, Vietnam, and parts of India—also host substantial Christian communities. Even more impressively, the non-Muslim regions of Africa have witnessed an explosive advance of Christianity during the twentieth century, while Latin America, long a primarily Catholic region, has experienced a spectacular growth of Pentecostal Protestant Christianity since the 1970s. In the early twenty-first century, over 60 percent of the world's Christians lived in Asia, Africa, or Latin America. Thus Europe and North America, long regarded as the centers of the Christian world, have been increasingly outnumbered in the census of global Christianity.

Charlemagne: This fifteenth-century manuscript painting depicts Charlemagne, King of the Franks, who was crowned Emperor by the pope in 800 C.E. His reign illustrates the close and sometimes conflicted relationship of political and religious authorities in an emerging European civilization. It also represents the futile desire of many in Western Europe to revive the old Roman Empire, even as a substantially new civilization was taking shape in the aftermath of the Roman collapse several centuries earlier. (Victoria & Albert Museum, London, UK/The Bridgeman Art Library)

Interestingly enough, the sixth- and seventh-century world of Christendom revealed a broadly similar pattern. Christianity then enjoyed an Afro-Eurasian reach with flourishing communities in Arabia, Egypt, North Africa, Ethiopia, Nubia, Syria, Armenia, Persia, India, and China, as well as Europe. (See Chapter 4, pp. 140–45.) But during the next thousand years, radical changes reshaped that Christian world. Its African and Asian outposts largely vanished, declined, or were marginalized as Christianity became primarily a European phenomenon for the next thousand years or more.

During this millennium, Christianity came to provide a measure of cultural commonality for the diverse peoples of western Eurasia, much as Chinese civilization and Buddhism did for those of East Asia and Islam did for the Middle East and beyond. By 1300, almost all of these societies—from Ireland and England in the west to Russia in the east—had embraced in some form the teachings of the Jewish carpenter called Jesus. At the same time, that part of the Christian world became deeply divided. Its eastern half, known as the Byzantine Empire or Byzantium (bihz-ANN-tee-uhm), encompassed much of the eastern Mediterranean basin while continuing the traditions of the Greco-Roman world, though on a smaller scale, until its conquest by the Muslim Ottoman Empire in 1453. Centered on the magnificent city of Constantinople, Byzantium gradually evolved a particular form of Christianity known as Eastern Orthodoxy within a distinctive third-wave civilization.

In Western or Latin Christendom, encompassing what we now know as Western Europe, the setting was far different. There the Roman imperial order had largely vanished by 500 C.E., accompanied by the weakening of many features of Roman civilization. Roads fell into disrepair, cities decayed, and long-distance trade shriveled. What replaced the old Roman order was a highly localized society—fragmented, decentralized, and competitive—in sharp contrast to the unified state of Byzantium. Like Byzantium, the Latin West ultimately became thoroughly Christian, but it was a gradual process lasting centuries, and its Roman Catholic version of the faith, increasingly centered on the pope, had an independence from political authorities that the Eastern Orthodox Church did not. Moreover, the Western church in particular and its society in general were far more rural than Byzantium and certainly had nothing to compare to the splendor of Constantinople. However, slowly at first and then with increasing speed after 1000, Western Europe emerged as an especially dynamic, expansive, and innovative third-wave civilization, combining elements of its Greco-Roman past with the culture of Germanic and Celtic peoples to produce a distinctive hybrid, or blended, civilization.

Thus the story of global Christendom in the era of third-wave civilizations is one of contractions and expansions. As a religion, Christianity contracted sharply in Asia and Africa even as it expanded in Western Europe and Russia. As a civilization, Christian Byzantium flourished for a time, then gradually contracted and finally disappeared. The trajectory of civilization in the West traced an opposite path, at first contracting as the Roman Empire collapsed and later expanding as a new and blended civilization took hold in Western Europe.

SEEKING THE MAIN POINT

In what different ways did the history of Christianity unfold in various parts of the Afro-Eurasian world during the third-wave era?

A Map of Time

4th century	Christianity becomes state religion of Armenia, Axum, and Roman Empire
5th–6th centuries	Introduction of Christianity into Nubia
476	Collapse of western Roman Empire
527–565	Justinian rules Byzantine Empire
7th century	Introduction of Christianity into China; initial spread of Islam
726–843	Iconoclasm in Byzantium
800	Charlemagne crowned as new "Roman Emperor"
988	Conversion of Kievan Rus to Christianity
1054	Mutual excommunication of pope and patriarch
1095–1291	Crusaders in the Islamic world
12th–13th centuries	Translations of Greek and Arab works available in Europe
1346–1350	Black Death in Europe
1453	Turks capture Constantinople; end of Byzantine Empire
1492	Christian reconquest of Spain completed; Columbus's first voyage

Christian Contraction in Asia and Africa

How had Christianity become by 1500 a largely European faith, with its earlier and promising Asian and African communities diminished, defeated, or disappeared? The answer, in large measure, was Islam. The wholly unforeseen birth of yet another monotheistic faith in the Middle East, its rapid spread across much of the Afro-Eurasian world, the simultaneous creation of a large and powerful Arab Empire, the emergence of a cosmopolitan and transcontinental Islamic civilization—these were the conditions, described more fully in Chapter 9, that led to the contraction of Christendom in Asia and Africa, leaving Europe as the principal center of the Christian faith.[2]

■ **Comparison**

What variations in the experience of African and Asian Christian communities can you identify?

Asian Christianity

It was in Arabia, the homeland of Islam, that the decimation of earlier Christian communities occurred most completely and most quickly, for within a century or so of Muhammad's death in 632, only a few Christian groups remained. During the eighth century, triumphant Muslims marked the replacement of the old religion by using pillars of a demolished Christian cathedral to construct the Grand Mosque of Sana'a in southern Arabia.

The Dome of the Rock, Jerusalem
To Muslims, the Dome of the Rock was constructed on the site from which Muhammad ascended into the presence of Allah during his Night Journey. It was the first large-scale building in the Islamic world and drew heavily on Roman, Byzantine, and Persian precedents. Its location in Jerusalem marked the arrival of a competing faith to Jews and Christians who had long considered the city sacred. (© Aaron Horowitz/Corbis)

Elsewhere in the Middle East, other Jewish and Christian communities soon felt the impact of Islam. When expanding Muslim forces took control of Jerusalem in 638 and subsequently constructed the Muslim shrine known as the Dome of the Rock (687–691), that precise location had long been regarded as sacred. To Jews, it contained the stone on which Abraham prepared to offer his son Isaac as a sacrifice to God, and it was the site of the first two Jewish temples. To Christians, it was a place that Jesus had visited as a youngster to converse with learned teachers and later to drive out the moneychangers. Thus, when the Umayyad caliph (successor to the prophet) Abd al-Malik ordered a new construction on that site, he was appropriating for Islam both Jewish and Christian legacies. But he was also demonstrating the victorious arrival of a new faith and announcing to Christians and Jews that "the Islamic state was here to stay."[3]

In Syria and Persia with more concentrated populations of Christians, accommodating policies generally prevailed. Certainly Arab conquest of these adjacent areas involved warfare, largely against the military forces of existing Byzantine and Persian authorities, but not to enforce conversion. In both areas, however, the majority of people turned to Islam voluntarily, attracted perhaps by its aura of success. A number of Christian leaders in Syria, Jerusalem, Armenia, and elsewhere negotiated agreements with Muslim authorities whereby remaining Christian communities were guaranteed the right to practice their religion, largely in private, in return for payment of a special tax.

Much depended on the attitudes of local Muslim rulers. On occasion churches were destroyed, villages plundered, fields burned, and Christians forced to wear distinctive clothing. By contrast, a wave of church building took place in Syria under Muslim rule, and Christians were recruited into the administration, schools, translation services, and even the armed forces of the Arab Empire. In 649, only 15 years after Damascus had been conquered by Arab forces, a Nestorian Bishop wrote: "These Arabs fight not against our Christian religion; nay rather they defend our faith, they revere our priests and Saints, and they make gifts to our churches and monasteries."[4]

Thus the Nestorian Christian communities of Syria, Iraq, and Persia, sometimes called the Church of the East, survived the assault of Islam, but they did so as shrinking communities of second-class subjects regulated minorities forbidden from propagating their message to Muslims. They also abandoned their religious paintings and sculptures, fearing to offend Muslims, who generally objected to any artistic representation of the Divine.

But further east, a small and highly creative Nestorian church, initiated in 635 by a Persian missionary monk, had taken root in China with the approval of the country's Tang dynasty rulers. Both its art and literature articulated the Christian message using Buddhist and Daoist concepts. The written texts themselves, known as the Jesus Sutras, refer to Christianity as the "Religion of Light from the West" or the "Luminous Religion." They describe God as the "Cool Wind," sin as "bad karma," and a good life as one of "no desire" and "no action." "People can live only by dwelling in the living breath of God," the Jesus Sutras declare. "All the Buddhas are moved by this wind, which blows everywhere in the world."[5] The contraction of this remarkable experiment owed little to Islam, but derived rather from the vagaries of Chinese politics. In the mid–ninth century the Chinese state turned against all religions of foreign origin, Islam and Buddhism as well as Christianity (see Chapter 8). Wholly dependent on the goodwill of Chinese authorities, this small outpost of Christianity withered.

Later the Mongol conquest of China in the thirteenth century offered a brief opportunity for Christianity's renewal, as the religiously tolerant Mongols welcomed Nestorian Christians as well as various other faiths. A number of prominent Mongols became Christians, including one of the wives of Chinggis Khan. Considering Jesus as a powerful shaman, Mongols also appreciated that Christians, unlike Buddhists, could eat meat and unlike Muslims, could drink alcohol, even including it in their worship.[6] But Mongol rule was short, ending in 1368, and the small number of Chinese Christians ensured that the faith almost completely vanished with the advent of the vigorously Confucian Ming dynasty.

Nestorian Stele

The Nestorian Stele is a large limestone block inscribed with a text detailing the early history of Christianity in China. At the top a Christian cross arising out of a white cloud (a characteristic Daoist symbol) and a lotus flower (an enduring Buddhist image) illustrate the blended character of this Christian experiment in China. (Photographer: Dr Hugh Houghton, © The University of Birmingham, UK. Reproduced with permission)

African Christianity

The churches of Africa, like those of the Middle East, also found themselves on the defensive and declining in the face of an expanding Islam. Across coastal North Africa, widespread conversion to Islam over several centuries reduced to virtual extinction Christian communities that had earlier provided many of the martyrs and intellectuals of the early Church.

In Egypt, however, Christianity had become the religion of the majority by the time of the Muslim conquest around 640, and for the next 500 years or so, large numbers continued to speak Coptic and practice their religion as *dhimmis*, legally inferior but protected people paying a special tax, under relatively tolerant Muslim rulers. Many found Arab government less oppressive than that of their former Byzantine overlords, who considered Egyptian Christians heretics. By the thirteenth century, things changed dramatically as Christian crusaders from Europe and Mongol invaders from the east threatened Egypt. In these circumstances, the country's Muslim rulers came to suspect the political loyalty of their Christian subjects. The mid-fourteenth century witnessed violent anti-Christian pogroms, destruction of churches, and the forced removal of Christians from the best land. Many felt like "exiles in their own country." As a result, most rural Egyptians converted to Islam and moved toward the use of Arabic rather than Coptic, which largely died out. Although Egypt was becoming an Arab and Muslim country, a substantial Christian minority persisted among the literate in urban areas and in monasteries located in remote regions. In the early twenty-first century, Egyptian Christians still numbered about 10 percent of the population.

Even as Egyptian Christianity was contracting, a new center of African Christianity was taking shape during the fifth and sixth centuries in the several kingdoms of Nubia to the south of Egypt, where the faith had been introduced by Egyptian traders and missionaries. Parts of the Bible were translated into the Nubian language, while other writings appeared in Greek, Arabic, and the Ethiopian language of Ge'ez. A great cathedral in the Nubian city of Faras was decorated with magnificent murals, and the earlier practice of burying servants to provide for rulers in the afterlife stopped abruptly. At times, kings served as priests, and Christian bishops held state offices. By the mid-seventh century, both the ruling class and many commoners had become Christian. At the same time, Nubian armies twice defeated Arab incursions, following which an agreement with Muslim Egypt protected this outpost of Christianity for some 600 years. But pressures mounted in the 1200s and 1300s as Egypt adopted a more hostile stance toward Christians, while Islamized tribes from the desert and Arab migrants pushed against Nubia. By 1500 Nubian Christianity, like its counterparts in coastal North Africa, had largely disappeared.

An important exception to these various contractions of Asian and African Christianity lay in Ethiopia. There the rulers of Axum had adopted Christianity in the fourth century, and it subsequently took root among the general population as well. (See Chapter 4, p. 143, and Chapter 6, pp. 185–88.) Over the centuries of Islamic expansion, Ethiopia became a Christian island in a Muslim sea, protected by its mountainous geography and its distance from major centers of Islamic power. Many Muslims also remembered gratefully that Christian Ethiopia had sheltered some of the beleaguered and persecuted followers of Muhammad in Islam's early years. Nonetheless, the spread of Islam largely cut Ethiopia off from other parts of Christendom and rendered its position in northeast Africa precarious.

In its isolated location, Ethiopian Christianity developed some of its most distinctive features. One of these was a fascination with Judaism and Jerusalem, reflected in a much-told story about the visit of an Ethiopian Queen of Sheba to King Solomon. The story includes an episode in which Solomon seduces the Queen, producing a child who becomes the founding monarch of the Ethiopian state. Since

Solomon figures in the line of descent to Jesus, it meant that Ethiopia's Christian rulers could legitimate their position by tracing their ancestry to Jesus himself. Furthermore, Ethiopian monks long maintained a presence in Jerusalem's Church of the Holy Sepulcher, said to mark the site where Jesus was crucified and buried. Then, in the twelfth century, the rulers of a new Ethiopian dynasty constructed a remarkable series of twelve linked underground churches, apparently attempting to create a New Jerusalem on Christian Ethiopian soil, as the original city lay under Muslim control. Those churches are in use to this day in modern Ethiopia, where over 60 percent of the country's population retain their affiliation with this ancient Christian church.

The Church of St. George, Lalibela, Ethiopia
Excavated from solid rock in the twelfth century, the churches of Lalibela were distinctive Christian structures, invisible from a distance and apparent only when looking down on them from ground level. Local legend has it that their construction was aided by angels. This one in the shape of a cross is named for St. George, the patron saint of Ethiopia. (© Heltler/Robert Harding World/Corbis)

Byzantine Christendom: Building on the Roman Past

The contraction of the Christian faith and Christian societies in Asia and Africa left Europe and Anatolia, largely by default, as the centers of Christendom. The initial expansion of Islam and the Arab Empire had quickly stripped away what had been the Middle Eastern and North African provinces of the Roman Empire and had brought Spain under Muslim control. But after the Mediterranean frontier between the Islamic and Christian worlds stabilized somewhat in the early eighth century, the immediate threat of Muslim incursions into the heartland of Christendom lifted, although border conflicts persisted. It was within this space of relative security, unavailable to most African and Asian Christian communities, that the diverging histories of the Byzantine Empire and Western Europe took shape.

Unlike most empires, Byzantium has no clear starting point. Its own leaders, as well as its neighbors and enemies, viewed it as simply a continuation of the Roman Empire. Some historians date its beginning to 330 C.E., when the Roman emperor Constantine, who began to favor Christianity during his reign, established a new capital, Constantinople, on the site of an ancient Greek city called Byzantium. At the end of that century, the Roman Empire was formally divided into eastern and western halves, thus launching a division of Christendom that has lasted into the twenty-first century.

Although the western Roman Empire collapsed during the fifth century, the eastern half persisted for another thousand years. Housing the ancient civilizations of Egypt, Greece, Syria, and Anatolia, the eastern Roman Empire (Byzantium) was far wealthier, more urbanized, and more cosmopolitan than its western counterpart; it possessed a much more defensible capital in the heavily walled city of Constantinople; and it had a shorter frontier to guard. Byzantium also enjoyed access to the Black Sea and command of the eastern Mediterranean. With a stronger army, navy, and merchant marine as well as clever diplomacy, its leaders were able to deflect the Germanic and Hun invaders who had overwhelmed the western Roman Empire.

■ **Continuity
and Change**
In what respects did
Byzantium continue the
patterns of the classical
Roman Empire? In what
ways did it diverge from
those patterns?

Much that was late Roman—its roads, taxation system, military structures, centralized administration, imperial court, laws, Christian church—persisted in the east for many centuries. Like Tang dynasty China seeking to restore the glory of the Han era, Byzantium consciously sought to preserve the legacy of classical Greco-Roman civilization. Constantinople was to be a "New Rome," and people referred to themselves as "Romans." Fearing contamination by "barbarian" customs, emperors forbade the residents of Constantinople from wearing boots, trousers, clothing made from animal skins, and long hairstyles, all of which were associated with Germanic peoples, and insisted instead on Roman-style robes and sandals. But much changed as well over the centuries, marking the Byzantine Empire as the home of a distinctive civilization.

The Byzantine State

Perhaps the most obvious change was one of scale, as the Byzantine Empire never approximated the size of its Roman predecessor (see Map 10.1). The western Roman Empire was permanently lost to Byzantium, despite Emperor Justinian's (r. 527–565) impressive but short-lived attempt to reconquer the Mediterranean basin. The rapid Arab/Islamic expansion in the seventh century resulted in the loss of Syria/Palestine, Egypt, and North Africa. Nonetheless, until roughly 1200, a more compact Byzantine Empire remained a major force in the eastern Mediterranean, controlling Greece, much of the Balkans (southeastern Europe), and Anatolia. A reformed administrative system gave appointed generals civil authority in the empire's provinces and allowed them to raise armies from the landowning peasants of the region. From that territorial base, the empire's naval and merchant vessels were active in both the Mediterranean and Black seas.

In its heyday, the Byzantine state was an impressive creation. Political authority remained tightly centralized in Constantinople, where the emperor claimed to govern all creation as God's worldly representative, styling himself the "peer of the Apostles" and the "sole ruler of the world." The imperial court tried to imitate the awesome grandeur of what they thought was God's heavenly court, but in fact it resembled ancient Persian imperial splendor. Aristocrats trained in Greek rhetoric and literature occupied high positions in the administration, participating in court ceremonies that maintained their elite status. Parades of these silk-clad officials added splendor to the imperial court, which also included mechanical lions that roared, birds that sang, and an immense throne that quickly elevated the emperor high above his presumably awestruck visitors. Nonetheless, this centralized state touched only lightly on the lives of most people, as it focused primarily on collecting taxes, main-

Map 10.1 The Byzantine Empire
The Byzantine Empire reached its greatest extent under Emperor Justinian in the mid-sixth century C.E. It subsequently lost considerable territory to various Christian European powers as well as to Muslim Arab and Turkic invaders.

taining order, and suppressing revolts. "Personal freedom in the provinces was constrained more by neighbors and rival households," concluded one historian, "than by the imperial government."[7]

After 1085, Byzantine territory shrank, owing to incursions by aggressive Western European powers, by Catholic Crusaders, and by Turkic Muslim invaders. The end came in 1453 when the Turkic Ottoman Empire, then known as the "sword of Islam," finally took Constantinople. One eyewitness to the event wrote a moving lament to his fallen city:

> And the entire city was to be seen in the tents of the [Turkish] camp, the city deserted, lying lifeless, naked, soundless, without either form or beauty. O city, head of all cities, center of the four corners of the world, pride of the Romans, civilizer of the barbarians. . . . Where is your beauty, O paradise . . . ? Where are the bodies of the Apostle of my Lord . . . ? Where are the relics of the saints, those of the martyrs? Where are the remains of Constantine the Great and the other emperors? . . . Oh, what a loss![8]

The Byzantine Church and Christian Divergence

■ **Comparison**

How did Eastern Orthodox Christianity differ from Roman Catholicism?

Intimately tied to the state was the Church, a relationship that became known as caesaropapism. Unlike Western Europe, where the Roman Catholic Church maintained some degree of independence from political authorities, in Byzantium the emperor assumed something of the role of both "Caesar," as head of state, and the pope, as head of the Church. Thus he appointed the patriarch, or leader, of the Orthodox Church; sometimes made decisions about doctrine; called church councils into session; and generally treated the Church as a government department. "The [Empire] and the church have a great unity and community," declared a twelfth-century patriarch. "Indeed they cannot be separated."[9] A dense network of bishops and priests brought the message of the Church to every corner of the empire, while numerous monasteries accommodated holy men, whose piety, self-denial, and good works made them highly influential among both elite and ordinary people.

Eastern Orthodox Christianity had a pervasive influence on every aspect of Byzantine life. It legitimated the supreme and absolute rule of the emperor, for he was a God-anointed ruler, a reflection of the glory of God on earth. It also provided a cultural identity for the empire's subjects. Even more than being "Roman," they were orthodox, or "right-thinking," Christians for whom the empire and the Church were equally essential to achieving eternal salvation. Constantinople was filled with churches and the relics of numerous saints. And the churches were filled with icons—religious paintings of Jesus, Mary, and numerous saints—some of them artistic masterpieces, that many believed conveyed Divine Presence to believers. Complex theological issues about the Trinity and especially about the relationship of God and Jesus engaged the attention of ordinary people. One fourth-century bishop complained: "I wish to know the price of bread; one answers 'The Father is greater than the Son.' I inquire whether my bath is ready; one answers 'The Son has been made out of nothing.'"[10] Partisans of competing chariot-racing teams, known as the Greens and the Blues, vigorously debated theological issues as well as the merits of their favorite drivers.

In its early centuries and beyond, the Christian movement was rent by theological controversy and political division. Followers of Arius, an Egyptian priest, held that Jesus had been created by God the Father rather than living eternally with Him. Nestorius, the fifth-century bishop of Constantinople, argued that Mary had given birth only to the human Jesus, who then became the "temple" of God. This view, defined as heretical in the Western Christian world, predominated in a separate Persian church, which spread its views to India, China, and Arabia.

But the most lasting and deepest division within the Christian world occurred as Eastern Orthodoxy came to define itself against an emerging Latin Christianity centered on papal Rome. Both had derived, of course, from the growth of Christianity in the Roman Empire and therefore had much in common—the teachings of Jesus; the Bible; the sacraments; a church hierarchy of patriarchs, bishops, and priests; a missionary impulse; and intolerance toward other religions. Despite these shared features, any sense of a single widespread Christian community was increasingly replaced by an awareness of difference, competition, and outright hostility that even a common fear of Islam could not overcome. In part, this growing religious divergence reflected the political separation and rivalry between the Byzantine Empire and the emerging kingdoms of Western Europe. As the growth of Islam in the seventh century (described more fully in Chapter 9) submerged earlier centers of Christianity in the Middle East and North Africa, Constantinople and Rome alone remained as alternative hubs of the Church. But they were now in different states that competed with each other for territory and for the right to claim the legacy of imperial Rome.

Beyond such political differences were those of language and culture. Although Latin remained the language of the Church and of elite communication in the West, it was abandoned in the Byzantine Empire in favor of Greek, which remained the basis for Byzantine education. More than in the West, Byzantine thinkers sought to formulate Christian doctrine in terms of Greek philosophical concepts.

Differences in theology and church practice likewise widened the gulf between Orthodoxy and Catholicism, despite agreement on fundamental doctrines. Disagreements about the nature of the Trinity, the source of the Holy Spirit, original sin, and the relative importance of faith and reason gave rise to much controversy. So too, for a time, did the Byzantine efforts to prohibit the use of icons, popular paintings of saints and biblical scenes, usually painted on small wooden panels. Other more modest differences also occasioned mutual misunderstanding and disdain. Priests in the West shaved and, after 1050 or so, were supposed to remain celibate, while those in Byzantium allowed their beards to grow long and were permitted to marry. Orthodox ritual called for using bread leavened with yeast in the Communion, but Catholics used unleavened bread. Far more significant was the question of authority. Eastern Orthodox leaders sharply rejected the growing claims of Roman popes to be the sole and final authority for all Christians everywhere.

The rift in the world of Christendom grew gradually from the seventh century on, punctuated by various efforts to bridge the mounting divide between the western

St. Mark's Basilica
Consecrated in 1094, this ornate cathedral, although located in Venice, Italy, is a classic example of Byzantine architecture. Such churches represented perhaps the greatest achievement of Byzantine art and were certainly the most monumental expressions of Byzantine culture. (Erich Lessing/Art Resource, NY)

and eastern branches of the Church. A sign of this continuing deterioration occurred in 1054 when representatives of both churches mutually excommunicated each other, declaring in effect that those in the opposing tradition were not true Christians. The Crusades, launched in 1095 by the Catholic pope against the forces of Islam, made things worse. Western Crusaders, passing through the Byzantine Empire on their way to the Middle East, engaged in frequent conflict with local people and thus deepened the distrust between them. From the western viewpoint, Orthodox practices were "blasphemous, even heretical." One western observer of the Second Crusade noted that the Greeks "were judged not to be Christians and the Franks [French] considered killing them a matter of no importance."[11] During the Fourth Crusade in 1204, western forces seized and looted Constantinople and ruled Byzantium for the next half century. Their brutality only confirmed Byzantine views of their Roman Catholic despoilers as nothing more than barbarians. According to one Byzantine account, "they sacked the sacred places and trampled on divine things . . . they tore children from their mothers . . . and they defiled virgins in the holy chapels, fearing neither God's anger nor man's vengeance."[12] After this, the rupture in the world of Christendom proved irreparable.

Byzantium and the World

■ **Connection**

In what ways was the Byzantine Empire linked to a wider world?

Beyond its tense relationship with Western Europe, the Byzantine Empire, located astride Europe and Asia, also interacted intensively with its other neighbors. On a political and military level, Byzantium continued the long-term Roman struggle with the Persian Empire. That persisting conflict weakened both of them and was one factor in the remarkable success of Arab armies as they poured out of Arabia in the seventh century. Although Persia quickly became part of the Islamic world, Byzantium held out, even as it lost considerable territory to the Arabs. A Byzantine military innovation, known as "Greek fire"—a potent and flammable combination of oil, sulfur, and lime that was launched from bronze tubes—helped to hold off the Arabs. It operated something like a flamethrower and subsequently passed into Arab and Chinese arsenals as well. Byzantium's ability to defend its core regions delayed for many centuries the Islamic advance into southeastern Europe, which finally occurred at the hands of the Turkish Ottoman Empire in the fifteenth and sixteenth centuries.

Economically, the Byzantine Empire was a central player in the long-distance trade of Eurasia, with commercial links to Western Europe, Russia, Central Asia, the Islamic world, and China. Its gold coin, the bezant, was a widely used currency in the Mediterranean basin for more than 500 years, and wearing such coins as pendants was a high-status symbol in the less developed kingdoms of Western Europe.[13] The luxurious products of Byzantine craftspeople—jewelry, gemstones, silver and gold work, linen and woolen textiles, purple dyes—were much in demand. Its silk industry, based on Chinese technology, supplied much of the Mediterranean basin with this precious fabric.

The cultural influence of Byzantium was likewise significant. Preserving much of ancient Greek learning, the Byzantine Empire transmitted this classical heritage to the Islamic world as well as to the Christian West. In both places, it had an immensely stimulating impact among scientists, philosophers, theologians, and other intellectuals. Some saw it as an aid to faith and to an understanding of the world, while others feared it as impious and distracting. (See "Reason and Faith" later in this chapter.)

Byzantine religious culture also spread widely among Slavic-speaking peoples in the Balkans and Russia. As lands to the south and the east were overtaken by Islam, Byzantium looked to the north. By the early eleventh century, steady military pressure had brought many of the Balkan Slavic peoples, especially the Bulgars, under Byzantine control. Christianity and literacy accompanied this Byzantine offensive. Already in the ninth century, two Byzantine missionaries, Cyril and Methodius, had developed an alphabet, based on Greek letters, with which Slavic languages could be written. This Cyrillic script made it possible to translate the Bible and other religious literature into these languages and greatly aided the process of conversion.

The Conversion of Russia

The most significant expansion of Orthodox Christianity occurred among the Slavic peoples of what is now Ukraine and western Russia. In this culturally diverse region, which also included Finnic and Baltic peoples as well as Viking traders, a modest state known as Kievan Rus (KEE-yehv-ihn ROOS) — named after the most prominent city, Kiev — emerged in the ninth century. Like many of the new third-wave civilizations, the development of Rus was stimulated by trade, in this case along the Dnieper River, linking Scandinavia and Byzantium. Loosely led by various princes, especially the prince of Kiev, Rus was a society of slaves and freemen, privileged people and commoners, dominant men and subordinate women. This stratification marked it as a third-wave civilization in the making (see Map 10.3, p. 333).

■ **Connection**

How did links to Byzantium transform the new civilization of Kievan Rus?

Religion reflected the region's cultural diversity, with the gods and practices of many peoples much in evidence. Ancestral spirits, household deities, and various gods related to the forces of nature were in evidence with Perun, the god of thunder, perhaps the most prominent. Small numbers of Christians, Muslims, and Jews were likewise part of the mix. Then, in the late tenth century, a decisive turning point occurred. The growing interaction of Rus with the larger world prompted Prince Vladimir of Kiev to affiliate with one of the major religions of the area. He was searching for a faith that would unify the diverse peoples of his region, while linking Rus into wider networks of communication and exchange. According to ancient chronicles, he actively considered Judaism, Islam, and Roman Catholicism, before finally deciding on Eastern Orthodoxy, the religion of Byzantium. He rejected Islam, the chronicles tell us, because it prohibited alcoholic drink and "drinking is the joy of the Russes." The splendor of Constantinople's Orthodox churches apparently captured the imagination of Rus's envoys, for there, they reported, "We knew not whether we were in heaven or on earth."[14] Political and commercial considerations no doubt also played a role in Vladimir's decision, and he acquired a sister of the Byzantine emperor as his bride, along with numerous Byzantine priests and advisers. Whatever the precise process, it was a freely made decision. Eastern Orthodox Christianity thus came to Rus without the pressure of foreign military defeat or occupation. Eventually, it took deep root among the Russian people.

It was a fateful choice with long-term implications for Russian history, for it brought this fledgling civilization firmly into the world of Orthodox Christianity, separating it from both the realm of Islam and the Roman Catholic West. Like many new civilizations, Rus borrowed extensively from its older and more sophisticated neighbor. Among these borrowings were Byzantine architectural styles, the Cyrillic alphabet, the extensive use of icons, a monastic tradition stressing prayer and service, and political ideals of imperial control of the Church, all of which became part of a transformed Rus. Orthodoxy also provided a more unified identity for this emerging civilization and religious legitimacy for its rulers. Centuries later, when Byzantium had fallen to the Turks, a few Russian church leaders proclaimed the doctrine of a "third Rome." The original Rome had abandoned the true faith, and the second Rome, Constantinople, had succumbed to Muslim infidels. Moscow was now the third Rome, the final protector and defender of Orthodox Christianity. Though not widely proclaimed in Russia itself, such a notion reflected the "Russification" of Eastern Orthodoxy and its growing role as an element of Russian national identity. It was also a reminder of the enduring legacy of a thousand years of Byzantine history, long after the empire itself had vanished.

LearningCurve
bedfordstmartins.com
/strayer/LC

Western Christendom: Rebuilding in the Wake of Roman Collapse

The western half of the European Christian world followed a rather different path than that of the Byzantine Empire. For much of the third-wave millennium, it was distinctly on the margins of world history, partly because of its geographic location at the far western end of the Eurasian landmass. Thus it was at a distance from the growing routes of world trade — by sea in the Indian Ocean and by land across the Silk Roads to China and the Sand Roads to West Africa. Not until the Eastern and Western hemispheres were joined after 1500 did Western Europe occupy a geographically central position in the global network. Internally, Europe's geography made political unity difficult. It was a region in which population centers were divided by mountain ranges and dense forests as well as by five major peninsulas and two large islands (Britain and Ireland). However, its extensive coastlines and interior river systems facilitated exchange within Europe, while a moderate climate, plentiful rainfall, and fertile soils enabled a productive agriculture that could support a growing population.

Political Life in Western Europe

■ **Change**

What replaced the Roman order in Western Europe?

In the early centuries of this era, history must have seemed more significant than geography, for the Roman Empire, long a fixture of the western Mediterranean region, was gone. The traditional date marking the collapse of the empire is 476, when the German general Odoacer overthrew the last Roman emperor in the West. In itself not very important, this event has come to symbolize a major turning point in the West, for much that had characterized Roman civilization also weakened, declined, or disappeared in the several centuries before and after 476. Any semblance of large-scale centralized rule vanished. Disease and warfare reduced Western Europe's population by more than 25 percent. Land under cultivation contracted, while forests, marshland, and wasteland expanded. Urban life too diminished sharply, as Europe reverted to a largely rural existence. Rome at its height was a city of 1 million people, but by the tenth century it numbered perhaps 10,000. Public buildings crumbled from lack of care. Outside Italy, long-distance trade dried up as Roman roads deteriorated, and money exchange gave way to barter in many places. Literacy lost ground as well. Germanic peoples, whom the Romans had viewed as barbarians—Goths, Visigoths, Franks, Lombards, Angles, Saxons—now emerged as the dominant peoples of Western Europe. In the process, Europe's center of gravity moved away from the Mediterranean toward the north and west.

Yet much that was classical or Roman persisted, even as a new order emerged in Europe. On the political front, a series of regional kingdoms—led by Visigoths in Spain, Franks in France, Lombards in Italy, and Angles and Saxons in England—arose to replace Roman authority. But many of these Germanic peoples, originally organized in small kinship-based tribes with strong warrior values, had already been substantially Romanized. Contact with the Roman Empire in the first several centuries C.E. had generated more distinct ethnic identities among them, militarized their societies, and gave greater prominence to Woden, their god of war. As Germanic peoples migrated into or invaded Roman lands, many were deeply influenced by Roman culture, especially if they served in the Roman army. On the funeral monument of one such person was the telling inscription: "I am a Frank by nationality, but a Roman soldier under arms."[15]

The prestige of things Roman remained high, even after the empire itself had collapsed. Now as leaders of their own kingdoms, the Germanic rulers actively embraced written Roman law, using fines and penalties to provide order and justice in their new states in place of feuds and vendettas. One Visigoth ruler named Athaulf (r. 410–415), who had married a Roman noblewoman, gave voice to the continuing attraction of Roman culture and its empire.

> At first I wanted to erase the Roman name and convert all Roman territory into a Gothic empire.... But long experience has taught me that ... without law a state is not a state. Therefore I have more prudently chosen the different glory of reviving the Roman name with Gothic vigour, and I hope to be acknowledged by posterity as the initiator of a Roman restoration.[16]

Several of the larger, though relatively short-lived, Germanic kingdoms also had aspirations to re-create something of the unity of the Roman Empire. Charlemagne (SHAHR-leh-mane) (r. 768–814), ruler of the Carolingian Empire, occupying what is now France, Belgium, the Netherlands, and parts of Germany and Italy, erected

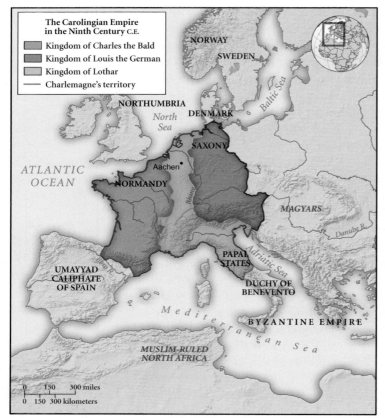

The Carolingian Empire in the Ninth Century C.E.
- Kingdom of Charles the Bald
- Kingdom of Louis the German
- Kingdom of Lothar
- Charlemagne's territory

Map 10.2   Western Europe in the Ninth Century
Charlemagne's Carolingian Empire brought a temporary political unity to parts of Western Europe, but it was subsequently divided among his three sons, who waged war on one another.

an embryonic imperial bureaucracy, standardized weights and measures, and began to act like an imperial ruler. On Christmas Day of the year 800, he was crowned as a new Roman emperor by the pope, although his realm splintered shortly after his death (see Map 10.2). Later Otto I of Saxony (r. 936–973) gathered much of Germany under his control, saw himself as renewing Roman rule, and was likewise invested with the title of emperor by the pope. Otto's realm, subsequently known as the Holy Roman Empire, was largely limited to Germany and soon proved little more than a collection of quarreling principalities. Though unsuccessful in reviving anything approaching Roman imperial authority, these efforts testify to the continuing appeal of the classical world, even as a new political system of rival kingdoms blended Roman and Germanic elements.

Society and the Church

Within these new kingdoms, a highly fragmented and decentralized society widely known as feudalism emerged with great local variation. In thousands of independent, self-sufficient, and largely isolated landed estates or manors, power—political, economic, and social—was exercised by a warrior elite of landowning lords. In the constant competition of these centuries, lesser lords and knights swore allegiance to greater lords or kings and thus became their vassals, frequently receiving lands and plunder in return for military service.

Such reciprocal ties between superior and subordinate were also apparent at the bottom of the social hierarchy, as Roman-style slavery gradually gave way to serfdom. Unlike slaves, serfs were not the personal property of their masters, could not be arbitrarily thrown off their land, and were allowed to live in families. However, they were bound to their masters' estates as peasant laborers and owed various payments and services to the lord of the manor. One family on a manor near Paris in the ninth century owed four silver coins, wine, wood, three hens, and fifteen eggs per year. Women generally were required to weave cloth and make clothing for the lord, while men labored in the lord's fields. In return, the serf family received a small farm and such protection as the lord could provide. In a violent and insecure world adjusting to the absence of Roman authority, the only security available to many individuals or families lay in these communities, where the ties to kin, manor, and lord constituted the primary human loyalties. It was a world apart from the stability of life in imperial Rome or its continuation in Byzantium.

Also filling the vacuum left by the collapse of empire was the Church, later known as Roman Catholic, yet another link to the now defunct Roman world. Its hierarchical organization of popes, bishops, priests, and monasteries was modeled on that of the Roman Empire and took over some of its political, administrative, educational, and welfare functions. Latin continued as the language of the Church even as it gave way to various vernacular languages in common speech. In fact, literacy in the classical languages of Greek and Latin remained the hallmark of educated people in the West well into the twentieth century.

Like the Buddhist establishment in China, the Church subsequently became quite wealthy, with reformers often accusing it of forgetting its central spiritual mission. It also provided a springboard for the conversion of Europe's many "pagan" peoples. Numerous missionaries, commissioned by the pope, monasteries, or already converted rulers, fanned out across Europe, generally pursuing a "top-down" strategy. Frequently it worked, as local kings and warlords found status and legitimacy in association with a literate and "civilized" religion that still bore something of the grandeur of Rome. With "the wealth and protection of the powerful," ordinary people followed their rulers into the fold of the Church.[17]

This process was similar to Buddhism's appeal for the nomadic rulers of northern and western China following the collapse of the Han dynasty. Christianity, like Buddhism, also bore the promise of superior supernatural powers, and its spread was frequently associated with reported miracles of healing, rainfall, fertility, and victory in battle.

But it was not an easy sell. Outright coercion was sometimes part of the process. More often, however, softer methods prevailed. The Church proved willing to accommodate a considerable range of earlier cultural practices, absorbing them into an emerging Christian tradition. For example, amulets and charms to ward off evil became medals with the image of Jesus or the Virgin Mary; traditionally sacred wells and springs became the sites of churches; and festivals honoring ancient gods became Christian holy days. December 25 was selected as the birthday of Jesus, for it was associated with the winter solstice, the coming of more light, and the birth or rebirth of various deities in pre-Christian European traditions. By 1100, most of Europe had embraced Christianity. Even so, for centuries priests and bishops had to warn their congregations against the worship of rivers, trees, and mountains, and for many people, ancient gods, monsters, trolls, and spirits still inhabited the land. The spreading Christian faith, like the new political framework of European civilization, was a blend of many elements.

Church authorities and the nobles/warriors who exercised political influence reinforced each other. Rulers provided protection for the papacy and strong encouragement for the faith. In return, the Church offered religious legitimacy for the powerful and the prosperous. "It is the will of the Creator," declared the teaching of the Church, "that the higher shall always rule over the lower. Each individual and class should stay in its place [and] perform its tasks."[18] But Church and nobility competed as well as cooperated, for they were rival centers of power in post-Roman Europe. Particularly controversial was the right to appoint bishops and the pope himself; this issue, known as the investiture conflict, was especially prominent in the eleventh and twelfth centuries. Was the right to make such appointments the responsibility of the Church alone, or did kings and emperors also have a role? In the compromise that ended the conflict, the Church won the right to appoint its own officials, while secular rulers retained an informal and symbolic role in the process.

Accelerating Change in the West

The pace of change in this emerging civilization picked up considerably in the several centuries after 1000. For the preceding 300 years, Europe had been subject to repeated invasions from every direction. Muslim armies had conquered Spain and threatened the rest of Europe. Magyar (Hungarian) invasions from the east and Viking incursions from the north likewise disrupted and threatened post-Roman Europe (see Map 10.3). But by the year 1000, these invasions had been checked and the invaders absorbed into settled society. The greater security and stability that came with relative peace arguably opened the way to an accelerating tempo of change. The climate also seemed to cooperate. A generally warming trend after 750 reached its peak in the eleventh and twelfth centuries, enhancing agricultural production.

■ **Change**

In what ways was European civilization changing after 1000?

Whatever may have launched this new phase of European civilization, commonly called the High Middle Ages (1000–1300), the signs of expansion and growth were widely evident. The population of Europe grew from perhaps 35 million in 1000 to about 80 million in 1340. With more people, many new lands were opened for cultivation in a process paralleling that of China's expansion to the south at the same time. Great lords, bishops, and religious orders organized new villages on what had recently been forest or wasteland. Marshes were drained; land was reclaimed from the sea in the Netherlands; everywhere trees were felled. By 1300, the forest cover of Europe had been reduced to about 20 percent of the land area. "I believe that the forest . . . covers the land to no purpose," declared a German abbot, "and hold this to be an unbearable harm."[19]

The increased production associated with this agricultural expansion stimulated a considerable growth in long-distance trade, much of which had dried up in the aftermath of the Roman collapse. One center of commercial activity lay in Northern Europe from England to the Baltic coast and involved the exchange of wood, beeswax, furs, rye, wheat, salt, cloth, and wine. The other major trading network centered on northern Italian towns such as Florence, Genoa, and Venice. Their trading part-

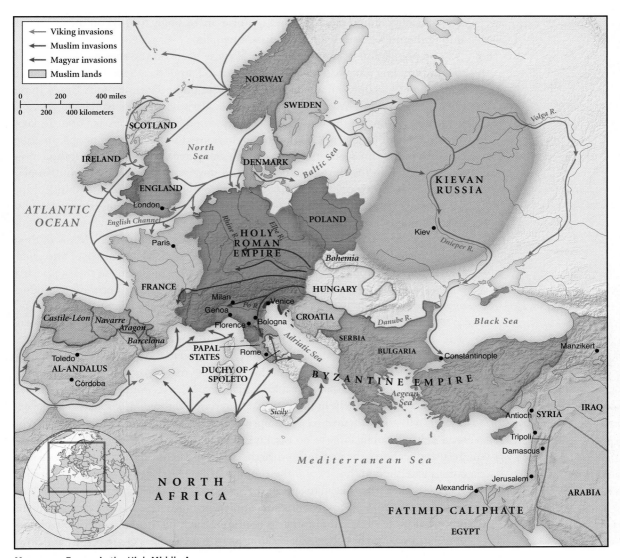

Map 10.3   Europe in the High Middle Ages

By the eleventh century, the national monarchies that would organize European political life—France, Spain, England, Poland, and Germany—had begun to take shape. The earlier external attacks on Europe from Vikings, Magyars, and Muslims had largely ceased, although it was clear that European civilization was developing in the shadow of the Islamic world.

ners were the more established civilizations of Islam and Byzantium, and the primary objects of trade included the silks, drugs, precious stones, and spices from Asia. At great trading fairs, particularly those in the Champagne area of France near Paris, merchants from Northern and Southern Europe met to exchange the products of their respective areas, such as northern woolens for Mediterranean spices. Thus the self-sufficient communities of earlier centuries increasingly forged commercial bonds among themselves and with more distant peoples.

The population of towns and cities likewise grew on the sites of older Roman towns, at trading crossroads and fortifications, and around cathedrals all over Europe. Some towns had only a few hundred people, but others became much larger. In the early 1300s, London had about 40,000 people, Paris had approximately 80,000, and Venice by the end of the fourteenth century could boast perhaps 150,000. To keep these figures in perspective, Constantinople housed some 400,000 people in 1000, Córdoba in Muslim Spain about 500,000, the Song dynasty capital of Hangzhou more than 1 million in the thirteenth century, and the Aztec capital of Tenochtitlán perhaps 200,000 by 1500. Nonetheless, urbanization was proceeding apace in Europe, though never hosting more than 10 percent of the population. These towns gave rise to and attracted new groups of people, particularly merchants, bankers, artisans, and university-trained professionals such as lawyers, doctors, and scholars. Many of these groups, including university professors and students, organized themselves into guilds (associations of people pursuing the same line of work) to regulate their respective professions. Thus from the rural social order of lord and peasant, a new more productive and complex division of labor took shape in European society.

A further sign of accelerating change in the West lay in the growth of territorial states with more effective institutions of government commanding the loyalty, or at least the obedience, of their subjects. Since the disintegration of the Roman Empire, Europeans' loyalties had focused on the family, the manor, or the religious community, but seldom on the state. Great lords may have been recognized as kings, but their authority was extremely limited and was exercised through a complex and decentralized network of feudal relationships with earls, counts, barons, and knights, who often felt little obligation to do the king's bidding. But in the eleventh through the thirteenth century, the nominal monarchs of Europe gradually and painfully began to consolidate their authority, and the outlines of French, English, Spanish, Scandinavian, and other states began to appear, each with its own distinct language and culture (see Map 10.3, p. 333). Royal courts and embryonic bureaucracies were established, and groups of professional administrators appeared. Such territorial kingdoms were not universal, however. In Italy, city-states flourished as urban areas grew wealthy and powerful, whereas the Germans remained divided among a large number of small principalities within the Holy Roman Empire.

These changes, which together represented the making of a new civilization, had implications for the lives of countless women and men. (See the portrait of Cecilia Penifader, pp. 336–37, for an account of a rural unmarried woman's life in England during this time.) Economic growth and urbanization initially offered European women substantial new opportunities. Women were active in a number of urban professions, such as weaving, brewing, milling grain, midwifery, small-scale retailing, laundering, spinning, and prostitution. In twelfth-century Paris, for example, a list of 100 occupations identified 86 as involving women workers, of which 6 were exclusively female. In England, women worked as silk weavers, hatmakers, tailors, brewers, and leather processors and were entitled to train female apprentices in some of these trades. In Frankfurt, about one-third of the crafts and trades were entirely female, another 40 percent were dominated by men, and the rest were open to both. Widows of great merchants sometimes continued their husbands' businesses, and one of them, Rose Burford, lent a large sum of money to the king of England to finance a war against Scotland in 1318.

Much as economic and technological change in China had eroded female silk production, by the fifteenth century, artisan opportunities were declining for European women as well. Most women's guilds were gone, and women were restricted or banned from many others. Even brothels were run by men. In England, guild regulations now outlawed women's participation in manufacturing particular fabrics and forbade their being trained on new and larger weaving machines. Women might still spin thread, but the more lucrative and skilled task of weaving fell increasingly to men. Technological progress may have been one reason for this change. Water- and animal-powered grain mills replaced the hand-grinding previously undertaken by women, and larger looms making heavier cloth replaced the lighter looms that women had worked. Men increasingly took over these professions and trained their sons as apprentices, making it more difficult for women to remain active in these fields.

The Church had long offered some women an alternative to home, marriage, family, and rural life. As in Buddhist lands, substantial numbers of women, particularly from aristocratic families, were attracted to the secluded monastic life of poverty, chastity, and obedience within a convent, in part for the relative freedom from male control that it offered. Here was one of the few places where women might exercise authority as abbesses of their orders and obtain a measure of education. The twelfth-century Abbess Hildegard of Bingen, for example, won wide acclaim for her writings on theology, medicine, botany, and music.

But by 1300, much of the independence that such abbesses and their nuns had enjoyed was curtailed and male control tightened, even as veneration of the Virgin Mary swept across Western Christendom. Restrictions on women hearing confessions, preaching, and chanting the Gospel were now more strictly enforced. The educational activities of monastic centers, where men and women could both participate, now gave way to the new universities where only ordained men could study and teach. Furthermore, older ideas of women's intellectual inferiority, the impurity of menstruation, and her role as a sexual temptress were mobilized to explain why women could never be priests and must operate under male control.

Another religious opportunity for women, operating outside of monastic life and the institutional church, was that of the Beguines. These were groups of laywomen, often from poorer families in Northern Europe, who lived together, practiced celibacy, and devoted themselves to weaving and to working with the sick, the old, and the poor. Though widely respected for their piety and service, their independence from the church hierarchy prompted considerable opposition from both religious and secular authorities suspicious of women operating outside of male control, and the movement gradually faded away. More acceptable to male authorities was the role of

Cecilia Penifader, An English Peasant and Unmarried Woman

Born in 1297 in a small English village, Cecilia Penifader was an illiterate peasant woman, who seldom if ever traveled more than twenty miles beyond her birthplace. She was of no particular historical importance outside of her family and community. Nonetheless, her life, reconstructed from court records by historian Judith Bennett, provides a window into the conditions of ordinary rural people as a new European civilization was taking shape.[20]

From birth to death, Cecilia lived in Brigstock, a royal manor owned by the King of England or a member of the royal family. Free tenants such as Cecilia owed rents and various dues to the lord of the manor. Thus Cecilia occupied a social position above that of serfs, unfree people who owed labor service to the lord, but infinitely below the clergy and nobility to whom the lower orders of society owed constant deference. But within the class of "those who work"—the peasantry—Cecilia was fortunate. She was born the seventh of eight children, six of whom survived to adulthood, an unusual occurrence at

A European peasant woman such as Cecilia Penifader. (V & A Images, London/ Art Resource, NY)

a time when roughly half of village children died. Her family had substantially larger landholdings than most of their neighbors and no doubt lived in a somewhat larger house. Still, it was probably a single-room dwelling about 30 by 15 feet, with a dirt floor, and surely it was smoky, for chimneys were not a part of peasant homes.

Between 1315 and 1322, as Cecilia entered early adulthood, England experienced an immense famine, caused by several years of especially cold and wet weather. During those years, Cecilia first entered the court records of Brigstock. In 1316 another peasant lodged a complaint against Cecilia and her father for ignoring his boundary stones and taking hay from his fields. Such petty quarrels and minor crimes proliferated as neighborliness broke down in the face of bad harvest and desperate circumstances. Furthermore both of Cecilia's parents died during the famine years.

Thus Cecelia was left a single woman in her early twenties, but the relative prosperity of her family allowed her to lead a rather independent life. In 1317 she acquired

anchoress, a woman who withdrew to a locked cell, usually attached to a church, where she devoted herself to prayer and fasting. Some of them gained reputations for great holiness and were much sought after for spiritual guidance. The English mystic and anchoress Julian of Norwich (1342–1416), for example, acquired considerable public prominence and spiritual influence, even as she emphasized the feminine dimension of the Divine and portrayed Jesus as a mother, who "feeds us with Himself."[21]

Thus tightening male control of women took place in Europe as it had in Song dynasty China at about the same time. Accompanying this change was a new understanding of masculinity, at least in the growing towns and cities. No longer able to function as warriors protecting their women, men increasingly defined themselves as "providers," braving the new marketplaces "to win wealth for himself and his children." In one popular tale, a woman praised her husband: "He was a good provider; he knew how to rake in the money and how to save it." By 1450 the English word "husband" had become a verb meaning "to keep" or "to save."[22]

her first piece of land, probably with financial assistance from her father and her own earnings as a day laborer. In fact, Cecilia benefited from the famine as it forced desperate peasants to sell their land at reduced prices. As a result, Cecilia was able to accumulate additional land. By the time of her death in 1344, she was a fairly prosperous woman with a house and farmyard, seventy acres of pasture and two acres of good farming land. She hired servants or day laborers to work her lands and depended considerably on her brothers, who lived nearby.

If class and family shaped Cecilia's life, so did gender. As a woman, she was unable to hold office in the manor; she was paid about one-third less than men when she worked as an unskilled day laborer; and she could not serve as an official ale-taster, responsible for the quality of the beverage, although women brewed the ale. Like all women, she suffered under a sexual double standard. Two of her brothers, one of whom was a priest, produced children out of wedlock, with no apparent damage to their reputations. But should Cecilia have done so, scandal would surely have ensued.

Unlike most women of her time, Cecilia never married. Did her intended perhaps die during the famine? Did she have a socially inappropriate lover? Did she have an intimate relationship with Robert Malin, a man to whom she left one-third of her estate? Or did she consider marriage a disadvantage? Married women and their property were legally under the control of their husbands, but as a free tenant and head of household, Cecilia bought and sold land on her own and participated as a full member in the deliberations of local court, which regulated the legal affairs of the manor.

For a woman, the pros and cons of marriage depended very much on whom she married. As a medieval poem put it: "The good and bad happenstances that some women have had / Stands in the choice of a good husband or bad." So while Cecilia missed out on the social approval and support that marriage offered as well as the pleasures of intimacy and children, she also avoided the potential abuse and certain dependency that married life carried for women.

Cecilia's death in 1344 provoked sharp controversy within her family network over the familiar issues of inheritance, kinship, and land. She left her considerable property to the illegitimate son of her brother, to the daughter of her sister Agnes, and to the mysterious Robert Malin. Aggrieved parties, particularly her sister Christina and a nephew Martin, succeeded in having her will overturned.

Question: In what ways did class, family, gender, and natural catastrophe shape Cecilia's life?

Europe Outward Bound: The Crusading Tradition

■ **Change**
What was the impact of the Crusades in world history?

Accompanying the growth of a new European civilization after 1000 were efforts to engage more actively with both near and more distant neighbors. This "medieval expansion" of Western Christendom took place as the Byzantine world was contracting under pressure from the West, from Arab invasion, and later from Turkish conquest. (See Map 10.1, p. 323.) The western half of Christendom was on the rise, while the eastern part was in decline. It was a sharp reversal of their earlier trajectories.

Expansion, of course, has been characteristic of virtually every civilization and has taken a variety of forms — territorial conquest, empire building, settlement of new lands, vigorous trading initiatives, and missionary activity. European civilization was no exception. As population mounted, settlers cleared new land, much of it on the eastern fringes of Europe. The Vikings of Scandinavia, having raided much of Europe, set off on a maritime transatlantic venture around 1000 that briefly established a colony in Newfoundland in North America, and more durably in Greenland and Iceland. (See Portrait of Thorfinn Karlsfeni in Chapter 7, pp. 242–43.) As Western economies grew, merchants, travelers, diplomats, and missionaries brought European society into more intensive contact with more distant peoples and with Eurasian commercial networks. By the thirteenth and fourteenth centuries, Europeans had direct, though limited, contact with India, China, and Mongolia. Europe clearly was outward bound.

Nothing more dramatically revealed European expansiveness and the religious passions that informed it than the Crusades, a series of "holy wars" that captured the imagination of Western Christendom for several centuries, beginning in 1095. In European thinking and practice, the Crusades were wars undertaken at God's command and authorized by the pope as the Vicar of Christ on earth. They required participants to swear a vow and in return offered an indulgence, which removed the penalties for any confessed sins, as well as various material benefits, such as immunity from lawsuits and a moratorium on the repayment of debts. Any number of political, economic, and social motives underlay the Crusades, but at their core they were religious wars. Within Europe, the amazing support for the Crusades reflected an understanding of them "as providing security against mortal enemies threatening the spiritual health of all Christendom and all Christians."[23] Crusading drew on both Christian piety and the warrior values of the elite, with little sense of contradiction between these impulses.

The most famous Crusades were those aimed at wresting Jerusalem and the holy places associated with the life of Jesus from Islamic control and returning them to Christendom (see Map 10.4). Beginning in 1095, wave after wave of Crusaders from all walks of life and many countries flocked to the eastern Mediterranean, where they temporarily carved out four small Christian states, the last of which was recaptured by Muslim forces in 1291. Led or supported by an assortment of kings, popes, bishops, monks, lords, nobles, and merchants, the Crusades demonstrated a growing European capacity for organization, finance, transportation, and recruitment, made all the more impressive by the absence of any centralized direction for the project. They also demonstrated considerable cruelty. The seizure of Jerusalem in 1099 was accompanied by the slaughter of many Muslims and Jews as the Crusaders made their way, according to perhaps exaggerated reports, through streets littered with corpses and ankle deep in blood to the tomb of Christ.

Crusading was not limited to targets in the Islamic Middle East, however. Those Christians who waged war for centuries to reclaim the Iberian Peninsula from Muslim hands were likewise declared "crusaders," with a similar set of spiritual and material benefits. So too were Scandinavian and German warriors who took part in wars to conquer, settle, and convert lands along the Baltic Sea. The Byzantine Empire and Russia, both of which followed Eastern Orthodox Christianity, were also on the receiving end of Western crusading, as were Christian heretics and various enemies of the pope in Europe itself. Crusading, in short, was a pervasive feature of European expansion, which persisted as Europeans began their oceanic voyages in the fifteenth century and beyond.

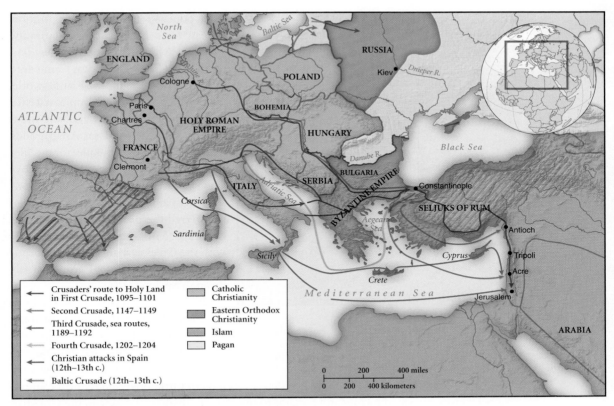

Map 10.4   The Crusades

Western Europe's crusading tradition reflected the expansive energy and religious impulses of an emerging civilization. It was directed against Muslims in the Middle East, Sicily, and Spain as well as the Eastern Orthodox Christians of the Byzantine Empire. The Crusades also involved attacks on Jewish communities, probably the first organized mass pogroms against Jews in Europe's history.

Surprisingly perhaps, the Crusades had little lasting impact, either politically or religiously, in the Middle East. European power was not sufficiently strong or long-lasting to induce much conversion, and the small European footholds there had come under Muslim control by 1300. The penetration of Turkic-speaking peoples from Central Asia and the devastating Mongol invasions of the thirteenth century were far more significant in Islamic history than were the temporary incursions of European Christians. In fact, Muslims largely forgot about the Crusades until the late nineteenth and early twentieth centuries, when their memory was revived in the context of a growing struggle against European imperialism.

In Europe, however, crusading in general and interaction with the Islamic world in particular had very significant long-term consequences. Spain, Sicily, and the Baltic region were brought permanently into the world of Western Christendom, while a declining Byzantium was further weakened by the Crusader sacking of Constantinople in 1204 and left even more vulnerable to Muslim Turkish conquest. In Europe

The Crusades
This fourteenth-century painting illustrates the Christian seizure of Jerusalem during the First Crusade in 1099. The crowned figure in the center is Godefroi de Bouillon, a French knight and nobleman who played a prominent role in the attack and was briefly known as the king of Jerusalem. (Snark/Art Resource, NY)

LearningCurve
bedfordstmartins.com
/strayer/LC

SUMMING UP SO FAR

How did the historical development of the European West differ from that of Byzantium in the third-wave era?

itself, popes strengthened their position, at least for a time, in their continuing struggles with secular authorities. Tens of thousands of Europeans came into personal contact with the Islamic world, from which they picked up a taste for the many luxury goods available there, stimulating a demand for Asian goods. They also learned techniques for producing sugar on large plantations using slave labor, a process that had incalculable consequences in later centuries as Europeans transferred the plantation system to the Americas. Muslim scholarship, together with the Greek learning that it incorporated, also flowed into Europe, largely through Spain and Sicily.

If the cross-cultural contacts born of crusading opened channels of trade, technology transfer, and intellectual exchange, they also hardened cultural barriers between peoples. The rift between Eastern Orthodoxy and Roman Catholicism deepened further and remains to this day a fundamental divide in the Christian world. Christian anti-Semitism was both expressed and exacerbated as Crusaders on their way to Jerusalem found time to massacre Jews, regarded as "Christ-killers," in a number of European cities, particularly in Germany. Such pogroms, however, were not sanctioned by the Church. A leading figure in the second crusade, Bernard of Clairvaux, declared that "it is good that you march against the Muslims, but anyone who touches a Jew to take his life, is as touching Jesus himself."[24] European empire building, especially in the Americas, continued the crusading notion that "God wills it." And more recently, over the past two centuries, as the world of the Christian West and that of Islam collided, both sides found many occasions in which images of the Crusades, however distorted, proved politically popular or ideologically useful.[25]

The West in Comparative Perspective

At one level, the making of Western civilization was unremarkable. Civilizations had risen, fallen, renewed themselves, and evolved at many times and in many places. The European case has received extraordinary scrutiny, not so much because of its special significance at the time, but because of its later role as a globally dominant region. However we might explain Europe's subsequent rise to prominence on the world stage, its development in the several centuries after 1000 made only modest ripples beyond its own region. In some respects, Europe was surely distinctive, but it was not yet a major player in the global arena. Comparisons, particularly with China and the Islamic world, help to place these European developments in a world history context.

Catching Up

As the civilization of the West evolved, it was clearly less developed in comparison to Byzantium, China, India, and the Islamic world. Europe's cities were smaller, its political authorities weaker, its economy less commercialized, and its technology inferior to the more established civilizations. Muslim observers who encountered Europeans saw them as barbarians. An Arab geographer of the tenth century commented on Europeans: "Their bodies are large, their manners harsh, their understanding dull, and their tongues heavy . . . Those of them who are farthest to the north are the most subject to stupidity, grossness and brutishness."[26] Muslim travelers over the next several centuries saw more to be praised in West African kingdoms, where Islam was practiced and gold was plentiful.

Furthermore, thoughtful Europeans who directly encountered other peoples often acknowledged their own comparative backwardness. "In our time," wrote a twelfth-century European scholar, "it is in Toledo [a Spanish city long under Muslim rule] that the teaching of the Arabs . . . is offered to the crowds. I hastened there to listen to the teaching of the wisest philosophers of this world."[27] The Italian traveler Marco Polo in the thirteenth century proclaimed Hangzhou in China "the finest and noblest [city] in the world." In the early sixteenth century, Spanish invaders of Mexico were stunned at the size and wealth of the Aztec capital, especially its huge market, claiming that "we had never seen such a thing before."[28]

Curious about the rest of the world, Europeans proved quite willing to engage with and borrow from the more advanced civilizations to the east. Growing European economies, especially in the northwest, reconnected with the Eurasian trading system, with which they had lost contact after the fall of Rome. Now European elites eagerly sought spices, silks, porcelain, and sugar from afar even as they assimilated various technological, intellectual, and cultural innovations, as the Snapshot demonstrates. When the road to China opened in the thirteenth and fourteenth centuries, many Europeans, including the merchant-traveler Marco Polo, were more than willing to make the long and difficult journey, returning with amazing tales of splendor and abundance far beyond what was available in Europe. When Europeans took to the oceans in the fifteenth and sixteenth centuries, they were seeking out the sources of African and Asian wealth. Thus the accelerating growth of European civilization was accompanied by its reintegration into the larger Afro-Eurasian networks of exchange and communication.

In this willingness to borrow, Europe resembled several other third-wave civilizations of the time. Japan, for example, took much from China; West Africa drew heavily on Islamic civilization; and Russia actively imitated Byzantium. All of them were then

■ **Change**
In what ways did borrowing from abroad shape European civilization after 1000?

Snapshot   **European Borrowing**

Like people in other emerging civilizations of the third-wave era, Europeans borrowed extensively from their near and more distant counterparts. They adapted these imports, both technological and cultural, to their own circumstances and generated distinctive innovations as well.

Borrowing	Source	Significance
Horse collar	China/Central Asia via Tunisia	Enabled heavy plowing and contributed to European agricultural development
Stirrup	India/Afghanistan	Revolutionized warfare by enhancing cavalry forces
Gunpowder	China	Enhanced the destructiveness of warfare
Paper	China	Enabled bureaucracy; fostered literacy; prerequisite for printing
Spinning wheel	India	Sped up production of yarn, usually by women at home
Wheelbarrow	China	Labor saving device for farm and construction work
Aristotle	Byzantium/Islamic Spain	Recovery of classical Greek thought
Medical knowledge/treatments	Islamic world	Sedatives, antiseptics, knowledge of contagious diseases, surgical techniques, optics enriched European medicine
Christian mysticism	Muslim Spain	Mutual influence of Sufi, Jewish, and Christian mysticism
Music/poetry	Muslim Spain	Contributed to tradition of troubadour poetry about chivalry and courtly love
Mathematics	India/Islamic world	Foundation for European algebra
Chess	India/Persia	A game of prestige associated with European nobility

developing civilizations, in a position analogous perhaps to the developing countries of the twentieth century.

Technological borrowing required adaptation to the unique conditions of Europe and was accompanied by considerable independent invention as well. Together these processes generated a significant tradition of technological innovation that allowed Europe by 1500 to catch up with, and in some areas perhaps to surpass, China and the Islamic world. That achievement bears comparison with the economic revolution of Tang and Song dynasty China, although Europe began at a lower level and depended more on borrowing than did its Chinese counterpart (see Chapter 8). But in the several centuries surrounding 1000 at both ends of Eurasia, major processes of technological innovation were under way.

In Europe, technological breakthroughs first became apparent in agriculture as Europeans adapted to the very different environmental conditions north of the Alps in the several centuries following 500 C.E. They developed a heavy wheeled plow that could handle the dense soils of Northern Europe far better than the light or "scratch" plow used in Mediterranean agriculture. To pull the plow, Europeans began to rely increasingly on horses rather than oxen and to use iron horseshoes and a more efficient collar, which probably originated in China or Central Asia and could support much heavier loads. In addition, Europeans developed a new three-field system of crop rotation, which allowed considerably more land to be planted at any one time. These were the technological foundations for a more productive agriculture that could support the growing population of European civilization, and especially its urban centers, far more securely than before.

Beyond agriculture, Europeans began to tap non-animal sources of energy in a major way, particularly after 1000. A new type of windmill, very different from an earlier Persian version, was widely used in Europe by the twelfth and thirteenth centuries. The water-driven mill was even more important. The Romans had used such mills largely to grind grain, but their development was limited, since few streams flowed all year and many slaves were available to do the work. By the ninth century, however, water mills were rapidly becoming more evident in Europe. In the early

European Technology
Europeans' fascination with technology and their religious motivation for investigating the world are apparent in this thirteenth-century portrayal of God as a divine engineer, laying out the world with a huge compass. (Erich Lessing/Art Resource, NY)

fourteenth century, a concentration of sixty-eight mills dotted a one-mile stretch of the Seine River near Paris. In addition to grinding grain, these mills provided power for sieving flour, tanning hides, making beer, sawing wood, manufacturing iron, and making paper. Devices such as cranks, flywheels, camshafts, and complex gearing mechanisms, when combined with water or wind power, enabled Europeans of the High Middle Ages to revolutionize production in a number of industries and to break with the ancient tradition of depending almost wholly on animal or human muscle as sources of energy. So intense was the interest of European artisans and engineers in tapping mechanical sources of energy that a number of them experimented with perpetual-motion machines, an idea borrowed from Indian philosophers.

Technological borrowing also was evident in the arts of war. Gunpowder was invented in China, but Europeans were probably the first to use it in cannons, in the early fourteenth century, and by 1500 they had the most advanced arsenals in the world. In 1517, one Chinese official, on first encountering European ships and weapons, remarked with surprise,

"The westerns are extremely dangerous because of their artillery. No weapon ever made since memorable antiquity is superior to their cannon."[29] Advances in ship-building and navigational techniques — including the magnetic compass and sternpost rudder from China and adaptations of the Mediterranean or Arab lateen sail, which enabled vessels to sail against the wind — provided the foundation for European mastery of the seas.

Europe's passion for technology was reflected in its culture and ideas as well as in its machines. About 1260, the English scholar and Franciscan friar Roger Bacon wrote of the possibilities he foresaw, and in doing so, he expressed the confident spirit of the age:

> Machines of navigation can be constructed, without rowers . . . which are borne under the guidance of one man at a greater speed than if they were full of men. Also a chariot can be constructed, that will move with incalculable speed without any draught animal. . . . Also flying machines may be constructed so that a man may sit in the midst of the machine turning a certain instrument by means of which wings artificially constructed would beat the air after the manner of a bird flying . . . and there are countless other things that can be constructed.[30]

Pluralism in Politics

■ **Comparison**
Why was Europe unable to achieve the kind of political unity that China experienced? What impact did this have on the subsequent history of Europe?

Unlike the large centralized states of Byzantium, the Islamic world, and China, this third-wave European civilization never regained the earlier unity it had under Roman rule. Rather, political life gradually crystallized into a system of competing states (France, Spain, England, Sweden, Prussia, the Netherlands, and Poland, among others) that has persisted into the twenty-first century and that the European Union still confronts. Geographic barriers, ethnic and linguistic diversity, and the shifting balances of power among its many states prevented the emergence of a single European empire, despite periodic efforts to re-create something resembling the still-remembered unity of the Roman Empire.

This multicentered political system shaped the emerging civilization of the West in many ways. It gave rise to frequent wars, enhanced the role and status of military men, and drove the "gunpowder revolution." Thus European society and values were militarized far more than in China, which gave greater prominence to scholars and bureaucrats. Intense interstate rivalry, combined with a willingness to borrow, also stimulated European technological development. By 1500, Europeans had gone a long way toward catching up with their more advanced Asian counterparts in agriculture, industry, war, and sailing.

Thus endemic warfare did not halt European economic growth. Capital, labor, and goods found their way around political barriers, while the common assumptions of Christian culture and the use of Latin and later French by the literate elite fostered communication across political borders. Europe's multistate system thus provided enough competition to be stimulating but also sufficient order and unity to allow economic endeavors to prosper.

The states within this emerging European civilization also differed from those to the east. Their rulers generally were weaker and had to contend with competing sources of power. Unlike the Orthodox Church in Byzantium, with its practice of caesaropapism, the Roman Catholic Church in the West maintained a degree of independence from state authority that served to check the power of kings and lords. European vassals had certain rights in return for loyalty to their lords and kings. By the thirteenth century, this meant that high-ranking nobles, acting through formal councils, had the right to advise their rulers and to approve new taxes.

This three-way struggle for power among kings, warrior aristocrats, and church leaders, all of them from the nobility, enabled urban-based merchants in Europe to achieve an unusual independence from political authority. Many cities, where wealthy merchants exercised local power, won the right to make and enforce their own laws and appoint their own officials. Some of them—Venice, Genoa, Pisa, and Milan, for example—became almost completely independent city-states. Elsewhere, kings granted charters that allowed cities to have their own courts, laws, and governments, while paying their own kind of taxes to the king instead of feudal dues. Powerful, independent cities were a distinctive feature of European life after 1100 or so. By contrast, Chinese cities, which were far larger than those of Europe, were simply part of the empire and enjoyed few special privileges. Although commerce was far more extensive in China than in an emerging European civilization, the powerful Chinese state favored the landowners over merchants, monopolized the salt and iron industries, and actively controlled and limited merchant activity far more than the new and weaker royal authorities of Europe were able to do.

The relative weakness of Europe's rulers allowed urban merchants more leeway and, according to some historians, paved the way to a more thorough development of capitalism in later centuries. It also led to the development of representative institutions or parliaments through which the views and interests of these contending forces could be expressed and accommodated. Intended to strengthen royal authority by consulting with major social groups, these embryonic parliaments did not represent the "people" or the "nation" but instead embodied the three great "estates of the realm"—the clergy (the first estate), the landowning nobility (the second estate), and urban merchants (the third estate).

Reason and Faith

A further feature of this emerging European civilization was a distinctive intellectual tension between the claims of human reason and those of faith. Christianity had developed in a world suffused with Greek rationalism. Some early Christian thinkers sought to maintain a clear separation between the new religion and the ideas of Plato and Aristotle. "What indeed has Athens to do with Jerusalem?" asked Tertullian (150–225 C.E.), an early church leader from North Africa. More common, however, was the notion that Greek philosophy could serve as a "handmaiden" to faith, more fully disclosing the truths of Christianity. In the reduced circumstances of Western Europe after the collapse of the Roman Empire, the Church had little direct access

■ **Comparison**

In what different ways did classical Greek philosophy and science have an impact in the West, in Byzantium, and in the Islamic world?

to the writings of the Greeks, although some Latin translations and commentaries provided a continuing link to the world of classical thought.

But intellectual life in Europe changed dramatically in the several centuries after 1000, amid a rising population, a quickening commercial life, emerging towns and cities, and the Church's growing independence from royal or noble authorities. Moreover, the West was developing a legal system that provided a measure of independence for a variety of institutions—towns and cities, guilds, professional associations, and especially universities. An outgrowth of earlier cathedral schools, these European universities—in Paris, Bologna, Oxford, Cambridge, Salamanca—became "zones of intellectual autonomy" in which scholars could pursue their studies with some freedom from the dictates of religious or political authorities, although that freedom was never complete and was frequently contested.[31]

This was the setting in which European Christian thinkers, a small group of literate churchmen, began to emphasize, quite self-consciously, the ability of human reason to penetrate divine mysteries and to grasp the operation of the natural order. An early indication of this new emphasis occurred in the late eleventh century when students in a monastic school in France asked their teacher, Anselm, to provide them a proof for the existence of God based solely on reason, without using the Bible or other sources of divine revelation.

The new interest in rational thought was applied first and foremost to theology, the "queen of the sciences" to European thinkers. Here was an effort to provide a rational foundation for faith, not to replace faith or to rebel against it. Logic, philosophy, and rationality would operate in service to Christ. Of course, some opposed this new emphasis on human reason. Bernard of Clairvaux, a twelfth-century French abbot, declared, "Faith believes. It does not dispute."[32] His contemporary and intellectual opponent, the French scholar William of Conches, lashed out: "You poor fools. God can make a cow out of a tree, but has he ever done so? Therefore show some reason why a thing is so or cease to hold that it is so."[33]

European intellectuals also applied their newly discovered confidence in human reason to law, medicine, and the world of nature, exploring optics, magnetism, astronomy, and alchemy. Slowly and never completely, the scientific study of nature, known as "natural philosophy," began to separate itself from theology. In European universities, natural philosophy

European University Life in the Middle Ages
This fourteenth-century manuscript painting shows a classroom scene from the University of Bologna in Italy. Note the sleeping and disruptive students. Some things apparently never change. (bpk, Berlin/Kupferstichkabinett, Staatliche Museen, Berlin, Germany/Joerg P. Anders/ Art Resource, NY)

was studied in the faculty of arts, which was separate from the faculty of theology, although many scholars contributed to both fields.

This mounting enthusiasm for rational inquiry stimulated European scholars to seek out original Greek texts, particularly those of Aristotle. They found them in the Greek-speaking world of Byzantium and in the Islamic world, where they had long ago been translated into Arabic. In the twelfth and thirteenth centuries, an explosion of translations from Greek and Arabic into Latin, much of it undertaken in Spain, gave European scholars direct access to the works of ancient Greeks and to the remarkable results of Arab scholarship in astronomy, optics, medicine, pharmacology, and more. Much of this Arab science was now translated into Latin and provided a boost to Europe's changing intellectual life, centered in the new universities. One of these translators, Adelard of Bath (1080–1142), remarked that he had learned, "under the guidance of reason from Arabic teachers," not to trust established authority.[34]

It was the works of the prolific Aristotle, with his logical approach and "scientific temperament," that made the deepest impression. His writings became the basis for university education and largely dominated the thought of Western Europe in the five centuries after 1200. In the work of the thirteenth-century theologian Thomas Aquinas, Aristotle's ideas were thoroughly integrated into a logical and systematic presentation of Christian doctrine. In this growing emphasis on human rationality, at least partially separate from divine revelation, lay one of the foundations of the later Scientific Revolution and the secularization of European intellectual life.

Surprisingly, nothing comparable occurred in the Byzantine Empire, where knowledge of the Greek language was widespread and access to Greek texts was easy. Although Byzantine scholars kept the classical tradition alive, their primary interest lay in the humanities (literature, philosophy, history) and theology rather than in the natural sciences or medicine. Furthermore, both state and church had serious reservations about Greek learning. In 529, the emperor Justinian closed Plato's Academy in Athens, claiming that it was an outpost of paganism. Its scholars dispersed into lands that soon became Islamic, carrying Greek learning into the Islamic world. Church authorities as well were suspicious of Greek thought, sometimes persecuting scholars who were too enamored with the ancients. Even those who did study the Greek writers did so in a conservative spirit, concerned to preserve and transmit the classical heritage rather than using it as a springboard for creating new knowledge. "The great men of the past," declared the fourteenth-century Byzantine scholar and statesman Theodore Metochites, "have said everything so perfectly that they have left nothing for us to say."[35]

In the Islamic world, Greek thought was embraced "with far more enthusiasm and creativity" than in Byzantium.[36] A massive translation project in the ninth and tenth centuries made Aristotle and many other Greek writers available in Arabic. That work contributed to a flowering of Arab scholarship, especially in the sciences and natural philosophy, between roughly 800 and 1200 (see Chapter 9), but it also stimulated a debate about faith and reason among Muslim thinkers, many of whom greatly admired

Greek philosophical, scientific, and medical texts. As in the Christian world, the issue was whether secular Greek thought was an aid or a threat to the faith. Western European church authorities after the thirteenth century had come to regard natural philosophy as a wholly legitimate enterprise and had thoroughly incorporated Aristotle into university education, but learned opinion in the Islamic world swung the other way. Though never completely disappearing from Islamic scholarship, the ideas of Plato and Aristotle receded after the thirteenth century in favor of teachings that drew more directly from the Quran or from mystical experience. Nor was natural philosophy a central concern of Islamic higher education as it was in the West. The integration of political and religious life in the Islamic world, as in Byzantium, contrasted with their separation in the West, where there was more space for the independent pursuit of scientific subjects.

LearningCurve
bedfordstmartins.com
/strayer/LC ✓

Reflections: Remembering and Forgetting: Continuity and Surprise in the Worlds of Christendom

Many of the characteristic features of Christendom, which emerged during the era of third-wave civilizations, have had a long life, extending well into the modern era. The crusading element of European expansion was prominent among the motives of Spanish and Portuguese explorers. Europe's grudging freedom for merchant activity and its eagerness to borrow foreign technology arguably contributed to the growth of capitalism and industrialization in later centuries. The endemic military conflicts of European states, unable to recover the unity of the Roman Empire, found terrible expression in the world wars of the twentieth century. The controversy about reason and faith resonates still, at least in the United States, in debates about the authority of the Bible in secular and scientific matters. The rift between Eastern Orthodoxy and Roman Catholicism remains one of the major divides in the Christian world. Modern universities and the separation of religious and political authority likewise have their origins in the European Middle Ages. Such a perspective, linking the past with what came later, represents one of the great contributions that the study of history makes to human understanding. We are limited and shaped by our histories.

Yet that very strength of historical study can be misleading, particularly if it suggests a kind of inevitability, in which the past determines the future. Knowing the outcome of the stories we tell can be a serious disadvantage, for it may rob the people we study of the freedom and uncertainty that they surely experienced. In 500, few people would have predicted that Europe would become the primary center of Christianity, while the African and Asian expressions of that faith withered away. As late as 1000, the startling reversal of roles between the Eastern and Western wings of Christendom, which the next several centuries witnessed, was hardly on the horizon. At that time, the many small, rural, unsophisticated, and endlessly quarreling warrior-based societies of Western Europe would hardly have borne comparison with the powerful Byzantine Empire and its magnificent capital of Constantinople. Even in 1500, when Europe had begun to catch up with China and the Islamic world in various ways, there was little to predict its remarkable transformation over the next several centuries and the dramatic change in the global balance of power that this transformation produced.

Usually students of history are asked to remember. But forgetting can also be an aid to historical understanding. To recapture the unexpectedness of the historical process and to allow ourselves to be surprised, it may be useful on occasion to forget what we know about what happened next and to see the world as contemporaries viewed it.

Second Thoughts

What's the Significance?

Nubian Christianity, 316; 320
Jesus sutras, 319
Ethiopian Christianity, 320–21
Byzantine Empire, 321–27
Constantinople, 322
Justinian, 322
caesaropapism, 324
Eastern Orthodox Christianity, 324–26
icons, 325

Prince Vladimir of Kiev, 327
Kievan Rus, 327–28
Charlemagne, 329–30
Holy Roman Empire, 330; 333
Roman Catholic Church, 330–32
Western Christendom, 332–37
Cecilia Penifader, 336–37
Crusades, 337–40

LearningCurve
Check what you know.
**bedfordstmartins.com
/strayer/LC**

Online Study Guide
bedfordstmartins.com/strayer

Big Picture Questions

1. What accounts for the different historical trajectories of the Byzantine and West European expressions of Christendom?

2. How did Byzantium and Western Europe interact with each other and with the larger world of the third-wave era?

3. In what respects was the civilization of the Latin West distinctive and unique, and in what ways was it broadly comparable to other third-wave civilizations?

4. **Looking Back:** How does the evolution of the Christian world in the third-wave era compare with that of Tang and Song dynasty China and of the Islamic world?

Next Steps: For Further Study

Bonnie S. Anderson and Judith P. Zinsser, *A History of Their Own* (2000). An overview of European women's history by two prominent scholars.

Edward Grant, *Science and Religion from Aristotle to Copernicus* (2004). Demonstrates the impact of Greek philosophy and science in Europe, with comparisons to Byzantium and the Islamic world.

Barbara A. Hanawalt, *The Middle Ages: An Illustrated History* (1999). A brief and beautifully illustrated introduction to the Middle Ages in European history.

For Web sites and additional documents related to this chapter, see **Make History** at bedfordstmartins.com/strayer.

Rowena Loverance, *Byzantium* (2004). A lavishly illustrated history of the Byzantine Empire, drawing on the rich collection of artifacts in the British Museum.

Diarmaid MacCulloch, *Christianity: The First Three Thousand Years* (2010). A recent and much-praised overview of the history of Christendom.

Christopher Tyerman, *Fighting for Christendom: Holy Wars and the Crusades* (2005). A very well-written, up-to-date history of the Crusades designed for nonspecialists.

"Middle Ages," http://www.learner.org/exhibits/middleages. An interactive Web site with text and images relating to life in Europe after the collapse of the Roman Empire.

CHAPTER ELEVEN

Pastoral Peoples on the Global Stage

The Mongol Moment

1200–1500

Looking Back and Looking Around:
  The Long History of Pastoral
  Nomads
  The World of Pastoral Societies
  Before the Mongols: Pastoralists in
  History
Breakout: The Mongol Empire
  From Temujin to Chinggis Khan:
  The Rise of the Mongol Empire
  Explaining the Mongol Moment
Encountering the Mongols:
  Comparing Three Cases
  China and the Mongols
  Persia and the Mongols
  Russia and the Mongols
The Mongol Empire as a Eurasian
  Network
  Toward a World Economy
  Diplomacy on a Eurasian Scale
  Cultural Exchange in the Mongol
  Realm
  The Plague: An Afro-Eurasian
  Pandemic
Reflections: Changing Images of
  Pastoral Peoples
Portrait: Khutulun, A Mongol
  Wrestler Princess

In 1937, the great Mongol warrior Chinggis Khan (CHEEN-gihs kahn) lost his soul, some seven centuries after his death. According to Mongol tradition, a warrior's soul was contained in his spirit banner, consisting of strands of hair from his best horses attached to a spear. For many centuries, Chinggis Khan's spirit banner had been housed in a Buddhist monastery in central Mongolia, where lamas (religious teachers) had tended it.[1] But in the 1930s, Mongolia, then under communist control and heavily dominated by Stalin's Soviet Union, launched a brutal anti-religious campaign that destroyed many monasteries and executed some 2,000 monks. In the confusion that ensued, Chinggis Khan's spirit banner, and thus his soul, disappeared.

By the end of the twentieth century, as communism faded away, the memory of Chinggis Khan, if not his spirit banner, made a remarkable comeback in the land of his birth. Vodka, cigarettes, a chocolate bar, two brands of beer, the country's best rock band, and the central square of the capital city all bore his name, while his picture appeared on Mongolia's stamps and money. Rural young people on horseback sang songs in his honor, and their counterparts in urban Internet cafés constructed Web sites to celebrate his achievements. The country organized elaborate celebrations in 2006 to mark the 800th anniversary of his founding of the Mongol Empire.

ALL OF THIS IS A REMINDER OF THE ENORMOUS AND SURPRISING role that the Mongols played in the Eurasian world of the thirteenth and fourteenth centuries and of the continuing echoes of that long-vanished empire. More generally, the story of the Mongols serves as a useful corrective to the almost exclusive focus that historians often

---

Chinggis Khan at Prayer: This sixteenth-century Indian painting shows Chinggis Khan at prayer in the midst of battle. He is perhaps praying to Tengri, the great sky god, on whom the Mongol conqueror based his power. (Werner Forman/Art Resource, NY)

devote to agricultural peoples and their civilizations, for the Mongols, and many other such peoples, were pastoral nomads who disdained farming while centering their economic lives around their herds of animals. Normally they did not construct elaborate cities, enduring empires, or monumental works of art, architecture, and written literature. Nonetheless, they left an indelible mark on the historical development of the entire Afro-Eurasian hemisphere, and particularly on the agricultural civilizations with which they so often interacted.

SEEKING THE MAIN POINT

What has been the role in world history of pastoral peoples in general and the Mongols in particular?

Looking Back and Looking Around: The Long History of Pastoral Nomads

The "revolution of domestication," beginning around 11,500 years ago, involved both plants and animals. People living in more favored environments were able to combine farming with animal husbandry and on this economic foundation generated powerful and impressive civilizations with substantial populations. But on the arid margins of agricultural lands, where productive farming was difficult or impossible, an alternative kind of food-producing economy emerged around 4000 B.C.E., focused on the raising of livestock. Peoples practicing such an economy learned to use the milk, blood, wool, hides, and meat of their animals to occupy lands that could not support agricultural societies. Some of those animals also provided new baggage and transportation possibilities. Horses, camels, goats, sheep, cattle, yaks, and reindeer were the primary animals that separately, or in some combination, enabled the construction of pastoral or herding societies. Such societies took shape in the vast grasslands of inner Eurasia and sub-Saharan Africa, in the Arabian and Saharan deserts, in the subarctic regions of the Northern Hemisphere, and in the high plateau of Tibet. Pastoralism emerged only in the Afro-Eurasian world, for in the Americas the absence of large animals that could be domesticated precluded a herding economy. But where such animals existed, their domestication shaped unique societies adapted to diverse environments.

The World of Pastoral Societies

■ Comparison
In what ways did pastoral societies differ from their agricultural counterparts?

Despite their many differences, pastoral societies shared several important features that distinguished them from settled agricultural communities and civilizations. Pastoral societies' generally less productive economies and their need for large grazing areas meant that they supported far smaller populations than did agricultural societies. People generally lived in small and widely scattered encampments of related kinfolk rather than in the villages, towns, and cities characteristic of agrarian civilizations. Beyond the family unit, pastoral peoples organized themselves in kinship-based groups or clans that claimed a common ancestry, usually through the male line. Related clans might on occasion come together as a tribe, which could also absorb unrelated people into the community. Although their values stressed equality and individual achievement, in some pastoral societies clans were ranked as noble or commoner, and con-

A Map of Time

ca. 4000 B.C.E.	Beginning of pastoral economies
ca. 1000 B.C.E.	Beginning of horseback riding
ca. 200 B.C.E.–200 C.E.	Xiongnu Empire
6th–10th centuries	Various Turkic empires
7th–10th centuries	Arab Empire
10th–14th centuries	Conversion of Turkic peoples to Islam
11th–12th centuries	Almoravid Empire
1162–1227	Life of Temujin (Chinggis Khan)
1209–1368	Mongol rule in China
1237–1480	Mongol rule in Russia
1241–1242	Mongol attacks on Eastern Europe
1258	Mongol seizure of Baghdad
1274, 1281	Failed Mongol attacks on Japan
1295	Mongol ruler of Persia converts to Islam
1348–1350	High point of Black Death in Europe

siderable differences emerged between wealthy aristocrats owning large flocks of animals and poor herders. Many pastoral societies held slaves as well.

Furthermore, nomadic societies generally offered women a higher status, fewer restrictions, and a greater role in public life than their counterparts in agricultural civilizations. Everywhere women were involved in productive labor as well as having domestic responsibility for food and children. The care of smaller animals such as sheep and goats usually fell to women, although only rarely did women own or control their own livestock. Among the Mongols, the remarriage of widows carried none of the negative connotations that it did among the Chinese, and women could initiate divorce. Mongol women frequently served as political advisers and were active in military affairs as well. (See Portrait of Khutulun, pp. 370–71.) A thirteenth-century European visitor, the Franciscan friar Giovanni DiPlano Carpini, recorded his impressions of Mongol women:

> Girls and women ride and gallop as skillfully as men. We even saw them carrying quivers and bows, and the women can ride horses for as long as the men; they have shorter stirrups, handle horses very well, and mind all the property. [Mongol] women make everything: skin clothes, shoes, leggings, and everything made of leather. They drive carts and repair them, they load camels, and are quick and vigorous in all their tasks. They all wear trousers, and some of them shoot just like men.[2]

Snapshot   **Varieties of Pastoral Societies**[3]

Region and Peoples	Primary Animals	Features
Inner Eurasian steppes (Xiongnu, Yuezhi, Turks, Uighurs, Mongols, Huns, Kipchaks)	Horses; also sheep, goats, cattle, Bactrian (two-humped) camel	Domestication of horse by 4000 B.C.E.; horseback riding by 1000 B.C.E.; site of largest nomadic empires
Southwestern and Central Asia (Seljuks, Ghaznavids, Mongol Il-khans, Uzbeks, Ottomans)	Sheep and goats; used horses, camels, and donkeys for transport	Close economic relationship with neighboring towns; provided meat, wool, milk products, and hides in exchange for grain and manufactured goods
Arabian and Saharan deserts (Bedouin Arabs, Berbers, Tuareg)	Dromedary (one-humped) camel; sometimes sheep	Camel caravans made possible long-distance trade; camel-mounted warriors central to early Arab/Islamic expansion
Grasslands of sub-Saharan Africa (Fulbe, Nuer, Turkana, Masai)	Cattle; also sheep and goats	Cattle were a chief form of wealth and central to ritual life; little interaction with wider world until nineteenth century
Subarctic Scandinavia, Russia (Sami, Nenets)	Reindeer	Reindeer domesticated only since 1500 C.E.; many also fished
Tibetan plateau (Tibetans)	Yaks; also sheep, cashmere goats, some cattle	Tibetans supplied yaks as baggage animal for overland caravan trade; exchanged wool, skins, and milk with valley villagers and received barley in return

■ **Connection**

In what ways did pastoral societies interact with their agricultural neighbors?

Certainly literate observers from adjacent civilizations noticed and clearly disapproved of the freedom granted to pastoral women. Ancient Greek writers thought that the pastoralists with whom they were familiar were "women governed." To Han Kuan, a Chinese Confucian scholar in the first century B.C.E., China's northern nomadic neighbors "[made] no distinction between men and women."[4]

The most characteristic feature of pastoral societies was their mobility. As people frequently on the move, they are often referred to as nomads because they shifted their herds in regular patterns to systematically follow the seasonal changes in vegetation and water supply. It was a life largely dictated by local environmental conditions and based on turning grass, which people cannot eat, into usable food and energy. Nor were nomads homeless; they took their homes, often elaborate felt tents, with them. According to a prominent scholar of pastoral life, "They know where they are going and why."[5]

Although nomadic pastoralists represented an alternative to the agricultural way of life that they disdained, they were almost always deeply connected to, and often dependent on, their agricultural neighbors. Few nomadic peoples could live solely from the products of their animals, and most of them actively sought access to the foodstuffs, manufactured goods, and luxury items available from the urban workshops and farming communities of nearby civilizations. Particularly among the nomadic peoples of inner Eurasia, this desire for the fruits of

The Scythians

An ancient horse-riding nomadic people during the second-wave era, the Scythians occupied a region in present-day Kazakhstan and southern Russia. Their pastoral way of life is apparent in this detail from an exquisite gold necklace from the fourth century B.C.E. (Private Collection/Photo Boltin Picture Library/The Bridgeman Art Library)

civilization periodically stimulated the creation of tribal confederations or nomadic states that could more effectively deal with the powerful agricultural societies on their borders. The Mongol Empire of the thirteenth century was but the most recent and largest in a long line of such efforts, dating back to the first millennium B.C.E.

Constructing a large state among nomadic pastoralists was no easy task. Such societies generally lacked the surplus wealth needed to pay for the professional armies and bureaucracies that everywhere sustained the states and empires of agricultural civilizations. And the fierce independence of widely dispersed pastoral clans and tribes as well as their internal rivalries made any enduring political unity difficult to achieve. Nonetheless, charismatic leaders, such as Chinggis Khan, were periodically able to weld together a series of tribal alliances that for a time became powerful states. In doing so, they often employed the device of "fictive kinship," designating allies as blood relatives and treating them with a corresponding respect.

Despite their limited populations, such states had certain military advantages in confronting larger and more densely populated civilizations. They could draw on the horseback riding and hunting skills of virtually the entire male population and some women as well. Easily transferred to the role of warrior, these skills, which were practiced from early childhood, were an integral part of pastoral life. But what sustained nomadic states was their ability to extract wealth, through raiding, trading, or extortion, from agricultural civilizations such as China, Persia, and Byzantium. As long as that wealth flowed into pastoral states, rulers could maintain the fragile alliances among fractious clans and tribes. When it was interrupted, however, those states often fragmented.

Pastoral nomads interacted with their agricultural neighbors not only economically and militarily but also culturally as they "became acquainted with and tried on for size all the world and universal religions."[6] At one time or another, Judaism, Buddhism, Islam, and several forms of Christianity all found a home somewhere among the nomadic peoples of inner Eurasia. So did Manichaeism, a religious tradition born in third-century Persia and combining elements of Zoroastrian, Christian, and Buddhist practice. Usually conversion was a top-down process as nomadic elites and rulers adopted a foreign religion for political purposes, sometimes changing religious allegiance as circumstances altered. Nomadic peoples, in short, did not inhabit a world totally apart from their agricultural and civilized neighbors.

Surely the most fundamental contribution of pastoralists to the larger human story was their mastery of environments unsuitable for agriculture. Through the creative use of their animals, they brought a version of the food-producing revolution and a substantial human presence to the arid grasslands and desert regions of Afro-Eurasia. As the pastoral peoples of the Inner Asian steppes learned the art of horseback riding, by roughly 1000 B.C.E., their societies changed dramatically. Now they could accumulate and tend larger herds of horses, sheep, and goats and move more rapidly over a much wider territory. New technologies, invented or adapted by pastoral societies, added to the mastery of their environment and spread widely across the Eurasian steppes, creating something of a common culture in this vast region. These innovations included complex horse harnesses, saddles with iron stirrups, a small compound bow that could be fired from horseback, various forms of armor, and new kinds of swords. Agricultural peoples were amazed at the centrality of the horse in pastoral life. As a Roman historian noted about the Huns, "From their horses, by day and night every one of that nation buys and sells, eats and drinks, and bowed over the narrow neck of the animal relaxes in a sleep so deep as to be accompanied by many dreams."[7]

Before the Mongols: Pastoralists in History

What enabled pastoral peoples to make their most visible entry onto the stage of world history was the military potential of horseback riding, and of camel riding somewhat later. Their mastery of mounted warfare made possible a long but intermittent series of nomadic empires across the steppes of inner Eurasia and parts of Africa. For 2,000 years, those states played a major role in Afro-Eurasian history and represented a standing challenge to and influence upon the agrarian civilizations on their borders.

One early large-scale nomadic empire was associated with the people known as the Xiongnu, who lived in the Mongolian steppes north of China (see Chapter 8). Provoked by Chinese penetration of their territory, the Xiongnu in the third and second centuries B.C.E. created a huge military confederacy that stretched from Manchuria deep into Central Asia. Under the charismatic leadership of Modun (r. 210–174 B.C.E.), the Xiongnu Empire effected a revolution in nomadic life. Earlier fragmented and egalitarian societies were now transformed into a far more centralized

The Xiongnu Confederacy

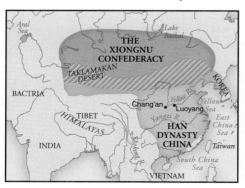

and hierarchical political system in which power was concentrated in a divinely sanc-tioned ruler and differences between "junior" and "senior" clans became more promi-nent. "All the people who draw the bow have now become one family," declared Modun. Tribute, exacted from other nomadic peoples and from China itself, sustained the Xiongnu Empire and forced the Han dynasty emperor Wen to acknowledge, un-happily, the equality of people he regarded as barbarians. "Our two great nations," he declared, no doubt reluctantly, "the Han and the Xiongnu, stand side by side."[8]

Although it subsequently disintegrated under sustained Chinese counterattacks, the Xiongnu Empire created a model that later Turkic and Mongol empires emulated. Even without a powerful state, various nomadic or semi-nomadic peoples played a role in the collapse of the already weakened Chinese and Roman empires and in the subsequent rebuilding of those civilizations (see Chapter 4).

It was during the era of third-wave civilizations (500–1500) that nomadic peoples made their most significant mark on the larger canvas of world history. Arabs, Ber-bers, Turks, and Mongols—all of them of nomadic origin—created the largest and most influential empires of that millennium. The most expansive religious tradition of the era, Islam, derived from a largely nomadic people, the Arabs, and was carried to new regions by another nomadic people, the Turks. In that millennium, most of the great civilizations of outer Eurasia—Byzantium, Persia, India, and China—had come under the control of previously nomadic people, at least for a time. But as pastoral nomads entered and shaped the arena of world history, they too were transformed by the experience.

The first and most dramatic of these nomadic incursions came from Arabs. In the Arabian Peninsula, the development of a reliable camel saddle somewhere be-tween 500 and 100 B.C.E. enabled nomadic Bedouin (desert-dwelling) Arabs to fight effectively from atop their enormous beasts. With this new military advantage, they came to control the rich trade routes in incense running through Arabia. Even more important, these camel nomads served as the shock troops of Islamic expansion, pro-viding many of the new religion's earliest followers and much of the military force that carved out the Arab Empire. Although intellectual and political leadership came from urban merchants and settled farming communities, the Arab Empire was in some respects a nomadic creation that subsequently became the foundation of a new and distinctive civilization.

Even as the pastoral Arabs encroached on the world of Eurasian civilizations from the south, Turkic-speaking nomads were making inroads from the north. Never a single people, various Turkic-speaking clans and tribes migrated from their home-land in Mongolia and southern Siberia generally westward and entered the historical record as creators of a series of nomadic empires between 552 and 965 C.E., most of them lasting little more than a century. Like the Xiongnu Empire, they were fragile alliances of various tribes headed by a supreme ruler known as a *kaghan*, who was sup-ported by a faithful corps of soldiers called "wolves," for the wolf was the mythical an-cestor of Turkic peoples. From their base in the steppes, these Turkic states confronted the great civilizations to their south—China, Persia, Byzantium—alternately raiding

■ Significance
In what ways did the Xiongnu, Arabs, Turks, and Berbers make an impact on world history?

Seljuk Tiles

Among the artistic achievements of Turkic Muslims were lovely ceramic tiles used to decorate mosques, minarets, palaces, and other public spaces. They contained intricate geometric designs, images of trees and birds, and inscriptions from the Quran. This one, dating from the thirteenth century, was used in a Seljuk palace, built as a summer residence for the Sultan in the city of Konya in what is now central Turkey. (© Zater Kizilkaya/Images and Stories)

them, allying with them against common enemies, trading with them, and extorting tribute payments from them. Turkic language and culture spread widely over much of Inner Asia, and elements of that culture entered the agrarian civilizations. In the courts of northern China, for example, yogurt thinned with water, a drink derived from the Turks, replaced for a time the traditional beverage of tea, and at least one Chinese poet wrote joyfully about the delights of snowy evenings in a felt tent.[9]

A major turning point in the history of the Turks occurred with their conversion to Islam between the tenth and fourteenth centuries. This extended process represented a major expansion of the faith and launched the Turks into a new role as the third major carrier of Islam, following the Arabs and the Persians. It also brought the Turks into an increasingly important position within the heartland of an established Islamic civilization as they migrated southward into the Middle East. There they served first as slave soldiers within the Abbasid caliphate, and then, as the caliphate declined, they increasingly took political and military power themselves. In the Seljuk Turkic Empire of the eleventh and twelfth centuries, centered in Persia and present-day Iraq, Turkic rulers began to claim the Muslim title of *sultan* (ruler) rather than the Turkic *kaghan*. Although the Abbasid caliph remained the formal ruler, real power was exercised by Turkic sultans.

Not only did Turkic peoples become Muslims themselves, but they carried Islam to new areas as well. Their invasions of northern India solidly planted Islam in that ancient civilization. In Anatolia, formerly ruled by Christian Byzantium, they brought both Islam and a massive infusion of Turkic culture, language, and people, even as they created the Ottoman Empire, which by 1500 became one of the great powers of Eurasia (see pp. 400–02). In both places, Turkic dynasties governed and would continue to do so well into the modern era. Thus Turkic people, many of them at least, had transformed themselves from pastoral nomads to sedentary farmers, from creators of steppe empires to rulers of agrarian civilizations, and from polytheistic worshippers of their ancestors and various gods to followers and carriers of a monotheistic Islam.

Broadly similar patterns prevailed in Africa as well. All across northern Africa and the Sahara, the introduction of the camel, probably during the first millennium B.C.E., gave rise to pastoral nomadic societies. Much like the Turkic-speaking pastoralists of

Central Asia, many of these peoples later adopted Islam, but at least initially had little formal instruction in the religion. In the eleventh century C.E., a reform movement arose among the Sanhaja Berber pastoralists, living in the western Sahara, only recently converted to Islam, and practicing it rather superficially. It was sparked by a scholar, Ibn Yasin, who returned from a pilgrimage to Mecca around 1039 seeking to purify the practice of the faith among his own people in line with orthodox principles. That religious movement soon became an expansive state, the Almoravid Empire, which incorporated a large part of northwestern Africa and in 1086 crossed into southern Spain, where it offered vigorous opposition to Christian efforts to conquer the region.

For a time, the Almoravid state enjoyed considerable prosperity, based on its control of much of the West African gold trade and the grain-producing Atlantic plains of Morocco. The Almoravids also brought to Morocco the sophisticated Islamic culture of southern Spain, still visible in the splendid architecture of the city of Marrakesh, for a time the capital of the Almoravid Empire. By the mid-twelfth century, that empire had been overrun by its long-time enemies, Berber farming people from the Atlas Mountains. But for roughly a century, the Almoravid movement represented an African pastoral people, who had converted to Islam, came into conflict with their agricultural neighbors, built a short-lived empire, and had a considerable impact on neighboring civilizations in both North Africa and Europe.

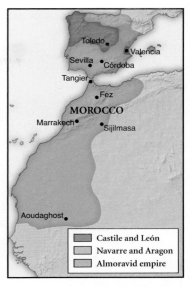

■	Castile and León
■	Navarre and Aragon
■	Almoravid empire

The Almoravid Empire

LearningCurve
bedfordstmartins.com
/strayer/LC

Breakout: The Mongol Empire

Of all the pastoral peoples who took a turn on the stage of world history, the Mongols made the most stunning entry. Their thirteenth-century breakout from Mongolia gave rise to the largest land-based empire in all of human history, stretching from the Pacific coast of Asia to Eastern Europe (see Map 11.1). This empire joined the nomadic peoples of the inner Eurasian steppes with the settled agricultural civilizations of outer Eurasia more extensively and more intimately than ever before. It also brought the major civilizations of Eurasia—Europe, China, and the Islamic world—into far more direct contact than in earlier times. Both the enormous destructiveness of the process and the networks of exchange and communication that it spawned were the work of the Mongols, numbering only about 700,000 people. It was another of history's unlikely twists.

For all of its size and fearsome reputation, the Mongol Empire left a surprisingly modest cultural imprint on the world it had briefly governed. Unlike the Arabs, the Mongols bequeathed to the world no new language, religion, or civilization. Whereas Islam offered a common religious home for all converts—conquerors and conquered alike—the Mongols never tried to spread their own faith among subject peoples. Their religion centered on rituals invoking the ancestors, which were performed around the family hearth. Rulers sometimes consulted religious specialists, known as shamans,

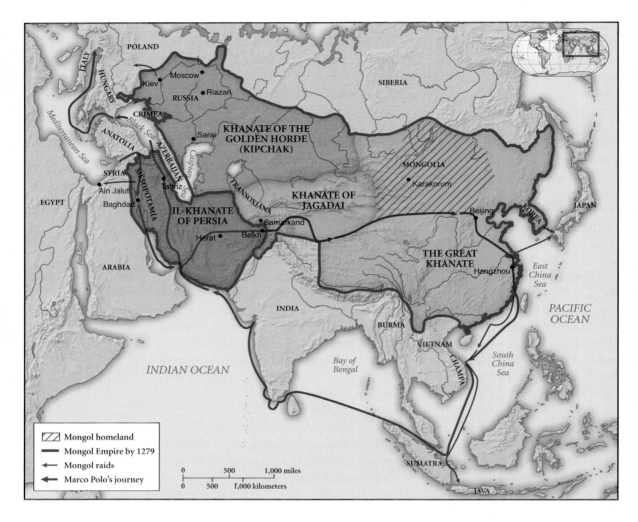

Map 11.1
The Mongol Empire
Encompassing much of
Eurasia, the Mongol Empire
was divided into four khan-
ates after the death of
Chinggis Khan.

who might predict the future, offer sacrifices, and communicate with the spirit world, and particularly with Tengri, the supreme sky god of the Mongols. There was little in this tradition to attract outsiders, and in any event the Mongols proved uninterested in religious imperialism.

The Mongols offered the majority of those they conquered little more than the status of defeated, subordinate, and exploited people, although people with skills were put to work in ways useful to Mongol authorities. Unlike the Turks, whose languages and culture flourish today in many places far from the Turkic homeland, Mongol culture remains confined largely to Mongolia. Furthermore, the Mongol Empire, following in the tradition of Xiongnu and Turkic state building, proved to be "the last, spectacular bloom of pastoral power in Inner Eurasia."[10] Some Mongols themselves became absorbed into the settled societies they conquered. After the decline and disintegration of the Mongol Empire, the tide turned against the pastoralists of inner

Eurasia, who were increasingly swallowed up in the expanding Russian or Chinese empires. Nonetheless, while it lasted and for a few centuries thereafter, the Mongol Empire exercised an enormous impact throughout the entire Eurasian world.

From Temujin to Chinggis Khan: The Rise of the Mongol Empire

World historians are prone to focus attention on large-scale and long-term processes of change in explaining "what happened in history," but in understanding the rise of the Mongol Empire, most scholars have found themselves forced to look closely at the role of a single individual—Temujin (TEM-oo-chin) (1162–1227), later known as Chinggis Khan (universal ruler). The twelfth-century world into which he was born found the Mongols an unstable and fractious collection of tribes and clans, much reduced from a somewhat earlier and more powerful position in the shifting nomadic alliances in what is now Mongolia. "Everyone was feuding," declared a leading Mongol shaman. "Rather than sleep, they robbed each other of their possessions. . . . There was no respite, only battle. There was no affection, only mutual slaughter."[11]

The early life of Temujin showed few signs of a prominent future. The boy's father had been a minor chieftain of a noble clan, but he was murdered by tribal rivals before Temujin turned ten, and the family was soon deserted by other members of the clan. As social outcasts, Temujin's small family, headed by his resourceful mother, was forced to live by hunting, fishing, and gathering wild foods. Without livestock, they had fallen to the lowest level of nomadic life. In these desperate circumstances, Temujin's remarkable character came into play. His personal magnetism and courage and his inclination to rely on trusted friends rather than ties of kinship allowed him to build up a small following and to ally with a more powerful tribal leader. This alliance received a boost from Chinese patrons, who were always eager to keep the nomads divided. Military victory over a rival tribe resulted in Temujin's recognition as a chief in his own right with a growing band of followers.

Temujin's rise to power amid the complex tribal politics of Mongolia was a surprise to everyone. It took place among shifting alliances and betrayals, a mounting string of military victories, the indecisiveness of his enemies, a reputation as a leader generous to friends and ruthless to enemies, and the incorporation of warriors from defeated tribes into his own forces. In 1206, a Mongol tribal assembly recognized Temujin as Chinggis Khan, supreme leader of a now unified Great Mongol Nation. It was a remarkable achievement, but one little noticed beyond the highland steppes of Mongolia. That would soon change.

The unification of the Mongol tribes raised an obvious question: What was Chinggis Khan to do with the powerful army he had assembled? Without a common task, the new and fragile unity of the Mongols would surely dissolve into quarrels and chaos; and without external resources to reward his followers, Chinggis Khan would be hard-pressed to maintain his supreme position. Both considerations pointed in a

■ **Description**
Identify the major steps in the rise of the Mongol Empire.

single direction—expansion, particularly toward China, long a source of great wealth for nomadic peoples.[12]

In 1209, the first major attack on the settled agricultural societies south of Mongolia set in motion half a century of a Mongol world war, a series of military campaigns, massive killing, and empire building without precedent in world history. In the process, Chinggis Khan, followed by his sons and grandsons (Ogodei, Mongke, and Khubilai), constructed an empire that contained China, Korea, Central Asia, Russia, much of the Islamic Middle East, and parts of Eastern Europe (see Map 11.1, p. 362). "In a flash," wrote a recent scholar, "the Mongol warriors would defeat every army, capture every fort, and bring down the walls of every city they encountered. Christians, Muslims, Buddhists, and Hindus would soon kneel before the dusty boots of illiterate young Mongol horsemen."[13]

Various setbacks marked the outer limits of the Mongol Empire—the Mongols' withdrawal from Eastern Europe (1242), their defeat at Ain Jalut in Palestine at the hands of Egyptian forces (1260), the failure of their invasion of Japan owing to two typhoons (1274, 1281), and the difficulty of penetrating the tropical jungles of Southeast Asia. But what an empire it was! How could a Mongol confederation, with a total population of less than 1 million people and few resources beyond their livestock, assemble an imperial structure of such staggering transcontinental dimensions?

Explaining the Mongol Moment

Like the Roman Empire but far more rapidly, the Mongol realm grew of its own momentum without any grand scheme or blueprint for world conquest. Each fresh victory brought new resources for making war and new threats or insecurities that seemed to require further expansion. As the empire took shape and certainly by the end of his life, Chinggis Khan had come to see his career in terms of a universal mission. "I have accomplished a great work," he declared, "uniting the whole world in one empire."[14] Thus the Mongol Empire acquired an ideology in the course of its construction.

What made this "great work" possible? The odds seemed overwhelming, for China alone outnumbered the Mongols 100 to 1 and possessed incomparably greater resources. Nor did the Mongols enjoy any technological superiority over their many adversaries. They did, however, enjoy the luck of good timing, for China was divided, having already lost control of its northern territory to the nomadic Jurchen people, while the decrepit Abbasid caliphate, once the center of the Islamic world, had shrunk to a fraction of its earlier size. But clearly, the key to the Mongols' success lay in their army. According to one scholar, "Mongol armies were simply better led, organized, and disciplined than those of their opponents."[15] In an effort to diminish a divisive tribalism, Chinggis Khan reorganized the entire social structure of the Mongols into military units of 10, 100, 1,000, and 10,000 warriors, an arrangement that allowed for effective command and control. Conquered tribes especially were broken up and their members scattered among these new units, which enrolled virtually all nomadic men and supplied the cavalry forces of Mongol armies. A highly prestigious imperial guard, also recruited across tribal lines, marked the further decline of the old tribalism as a social revolution, imposed from above, reshaped Mongol society.

An impressive discipline and loyalty to their leaders characterized Mongol military forces, and discipline was reinforced by the provision that should any members of a unit desert in battle, all were subject to the death penalty. More positively, loyalty was cemented by the leaders' willingness to share the hardships of their men. "I eat the same food and am dressed in the same rags as my humble herdsmen," wrote Chinggis Khan. "I am always in the forefront, and in battle I am never at the rear."[16] Such discipline and loyalty made possible the elaborate tactics of encirclement, retreat, and deception that proved decisive in many a battle. Furthermore, the enormous flow of wealth from conquered civilizations benefited all Mongols, though not equally. Even ordinary Mongols could now dress in linens and silks rather than hides and felt, could own slaves derived from the many prisoners of war, and had far greater opportunities to improve their social position in a constantly expanding empire.

A Mongol Warrior
Horseback-riding skills, honed in herding animals and adapted to military purposes, were central to Mongol conquests, as illustrated in this Ming-dynasty Chinese painting of a mounted Mongol archer. (© Victoria and Albert Museum, London)

To compensate for their own small population, the Mongols incorporated huge numbers of conquered peoples into their military forces. "People who lived in felt tents"—mostly Mongol and Turkic nomads—were conscripted en masse into the cavalry units of the Mongol army, while settled agricultural peoples supplied the infantry and artillery forces. As the Mongols penetrated major civilizations, with their walled cities and elaborate fortifications, they quickly acquired Chinese techniques and technology of siege warfare. Some 1,000 Chinese artillery crews, for example, took part in the Mongol invasion of distant Persia. Beyond military recruitment, Mongols demanded that their conquered people serve as laborers, building roads and bridges and ferrying supplies over long distances. Artisans, craftsmen, and skilled people generally were carefully identified, spared from massacre, and often sent to distant regions of the empire where their services were required. A French goldsmith, captured by Mongol forces in Hungary, wound up as a slave in the Mongol capital of Karakorum (kah-rah-KOR-um), where he constructed an elaborate silver fountain that dispensed wine and other intoxicating drinks.

A further element in the military effectiveness of Mongol forces lay in a growing reputation for a ruthless brutality and utter destructiveness. Chinggis Khan's policy was clear: "Whoever submits shall be spared, but those who resist, they shall be destroyed with their wives, children and dependents . . . so that the others who hear and see should fear and not act the same."[17] The Central Asian kingdom of Khwarizm, whose ruler had greatly offended Chinggis Khan by murdering and mutilating Mongol envoys and merchants, was among the first, but by no means the last, to feel the full effects of Mongol terror. City after city was utterly destroyed, and enemy soldiers were passed out in lots to Mongol troops for execution, while women and skilled craftsmen were enslaved. Unskilled civilians served as human shields for attacks on the next city or were used as human fill in the moats surrounding those cities.

One scholar explained such policies in this way: "Extremely conscious of their small numbers and fearful of rebellion, Chinggis often chose to annihilate a region's entire population, if it appeared too troublesome to govern."[18] These policies also served as a form of psychological warfare, a practical inducement to surrender for those who knew of the Mongol terror. Historians continue to debate the extent and uniqueness of the Mongols' brutality, but their reputation for unwavering harshness proved a military asset.

Underlying the purely military dimensions of the Mongols' success was an impressive ability to mobilize both the human and material resources of their growing empire. Elaborate census taking allowed Mongol leaders to know what was available to them and made possible the systematic taxation of conquered people. An effective system of relay stations, about a day's ride apart, provided rapid communication across the empire and fostered trade as well. Marco Polo, the Venetian trader who traveled through Mongol domains in the thirteenth century, claimed that the Mongols maintained some 10,000 such stations, together with 200,000 horses available to authorized users. The beginnings of a centralized bureaucracy with various specialized offices took shape in the new capital of Karakorum. There scribes translated official decrees into the various languages of the empire, such as Persian, Uighur, Chinese, and Tibetan.

Other policies appealed to various groups among the conquered peoples of the empire. Interested in fostering commerce, Mongol rulers often offered merchants 10 percent or more above their asking price and allowed them the free use of the relay stations for transporting their goods. In administering the conquered regions, Mongols held the highest decision-making posts, but Chinese and Muslim officials held many advisory and lower-level positions in China and Persia respectively. In religious matters, the Mongols welcomed and supported many religious traditions—Buddhist, Christian, Muslim, Daoist—as long as they did not become the focus of political opposition. This policy of religious toleration allowed Muslims to seek converts among Mongol troops and afforded Christians much greater freedom than they had enjoyed under Muslim rule.[19] Toward the end of his life and apparently feeling his approaching death, Chinggis Khan himself summoned a famous Daoist master from China and begged him to "communicate to me the means of preserving life." One of his successors, Mongke, arranged a debate among representatives of several religious faiths, after which he concluded: "Just as God gave different fingers to the hand, so has He given different ways to men."[20] Such economic, administrative, and religious policies provided some benefits and a place within the empire—albeit subordinate—for many of its conquered peoples.

LearningCurve
bedfordstmartins.com
/strayer/LC

SUMMING UP SO FAR

What accounts for the political and military success of the Mongols?

Encountering the Mongols: Comparing Three Cases

The Mongol moment in world history represented an enormous cultural encounter between nomadic pastoralists and the settled civilizations of Eurasia. Differences among those civilizations—Confucian China, Muslim Persia, Christian Russia—ensured considerable diversity as this encounter unfolded across a vast realm. The process of conquest, the length and nature of Mongol rule, the impact on local people, and the extent of Mongol assimilation into the cultures of the conquered—all this and more varied considerably across the Eurasian domains of the empire. The experiences of China, Persia, and Russia provide brief glimpses into several expressions of this massive clash of cultures.

China and the Mongols

Long the primary target for nomadic steppe dwellers in search of agrarian wealth, China proved the most difficult and extended of the Mongols' many conquests, lasting some seventy years, from 1209 to 1279. The invasion began in northern China, which had been ruled for several centuries by various dynasties of nomadic origin, and was characterized by destruction and plunder on a massive scale. Southern China, under the control of the native Song dynasty, was a different story, for there the Mongols were far less violent and more concerned to accommodate the local population. Landowners, for example, were guaranteed their estates in exchange for their support or at least their neutrality. By whatever methods, the outcome was the unification of a divided China, a treasured ideal among educated Chinese. This achievement persuaded some of them that the Mongols had indeed been granted the Mandate of Heaven and, despite their foreign origins, were legitimate rulers.

> ■ **Change**
> How did Mongol rule change China? In what ways were the Mongols changed by China?

Having acquired China, what were the Mongols to do with it? One possibility, apparently considered by the Great Khan Ogodei (ERG-uh-day) in the 1230s, was to exterminate everyone in northern China and turn the country into pastureland for Mongol herds. That suggestion, fortunately, was rejected in favor of extracting as much wealth as possible from the country's advanced civilization. Doing so meant some accommodation to Chinese culture and ways of governing, for the Mongols had no experience with the operation of a complex agrarian society.

That accommodation took many forms. The Mongols made use of Chinese administrative practices, techniques of taxation, and their postal system. They gave themselves a Chinese dynastic title, the Yuan, suggesting a new beginning in Chinese history. They transferred their capital from Karakorum in Mongolia to what is now Beijing, building a wholly new capital city there known as Khanbalik, the "city of the khan." Thus the Mongols were now rooting themselves solidly on the soil of a highly sophisticated civilization, well removed from their homeland on the steppes. Khubilai Khan (koo-buh-l'eye kahn), the grandson of Chinggis Khan and China's Mongol ruler from 1271 to 1294, ordered a set of Chinese-style ancestral tablets to honor his ancestors and posthumously awarded them Chinese names. Many of his

Marco Polo and Khubilai Khan
In ruling China, the Mongols employed in high positions a number of Muslims and a few Europeans, such as Marco Polo, shown here kneeling before Khubilai Khan in a painting from the fifteenth century. (Bibliothèque nationale de France, Paris, France/The Bridgeman Art Library)

policies evoked the values of a benevolent Chinese emperor as he improved roads, built canals, lowered some taxes, patronized scholars and artists, limited the death penalty and torture, supported peasant agriculture, and prohibited Mongols from grazing their animals on peasants' farmland. Mongol khans also made use of traditional Confucian rituals, supported the building of some Daoist temples, and were particularly attracted to a Tibetan form of Buddhism, which returned the favor with strong political support for the invaders.

Despite these accommodations, Mongol rule was still harsh, exploitative, foreign, and resented. The Mongols did not become Chinese, nor did they accommodate every aspect of Chinese culture. Deep inside the new capital, the royal family and court could continue to experience something of steppe life as their animals roamed freely in large open areas, planted with steppe grass. Many of the Mongol elite much preferred to live, eat, sleep, and give birth in the traditional tents that sprouted everywhere. In administering the country, the Mongols largely ignored the traditional Chinese examination system and relied heavily on foreigners, particularly Muslims from Central Asia and the Middle East, to serve as officials, while keeping the top decision-making posts for themselves. Few Mongols learned Chinese, and Mongol law discriminated against the Chinese, reserving for them the most severe punishments. Furthermore, the Mongols honored and supported merchants and artisans far more than Confucian bureaucrats had been inclined to do.

In social life, the Mongols forbade intermarriage and prohibited Chinese scholars from learning the Mongol script. Mongol women never adopted foot binding and scandalized the Chinese by mixing freely with men at official gatherings and riding to the hunt with their husbands. The Mongol ruler Khubilai Khan retained the Mongol tradition of relying heavily on female advisers, the chief of which was his favorite wife Chabi. Ironically, she urged him to accommodate his Chinese subjects, forcefully and successfully opposing an early plan to turn Chinese farmland into pastureland. Unlike many Mongols, biased as they were against farming, Chabi recognized the advantages of agriculture and its ability to generate tax revenue. With a vision of turning Mongol rule into a lasting dynasty that might rank with the splendor of the Tang, she urged her husband to emulate the best practices of that earlier era of Chinese history.

However one assesses Mongol rule in China, it was brief, lasting little more than a century. By the mid-fourteenth century, intense factionalism among the Mongols, rapidly rising prices, furious epidemics of the plague, and growing peasant rebellions combined to force the Mongols out of China. By 1368, rebel forces had triumphed, and thousands of Mongols returned to their homeland in the steppes. For several centuries, they remained a periodic threat to China, but during the Ming dynasty that followed, the memory of their often brutal and alien rule stimulated a renewed commitment to Confucian values and restrictive gender practices and an effort to wipe out all traces of the Mongols' impact.

Persia and the Mongols

A second great civilization conquered by the Mongols was that of an Islamic Persia. There the Mongol takeover was far more abrupt than the extended process of conquest in China. A first invasion (1219–1221), led by Chinggis Khan himself, was followed thirty years later by a second assault (1251–1258) under his grandson Hulegu (HE-luh-gee), who became the first il-khan (subordinate khan) of Persia. More destructive than the conquest of Song dynasty China, the Mongol offensive against Persia and Iraq had no precedent in their history, although Persia had been repeatedly attacked, from the invasion of Alexander the Great to that of the Arabs. The most recent incursion had featured Turkic peoples, but they had been Muslims, recently converted, small in number, and seeking only acceptance within the Islamic world. The Mongols, however, were infidels in Muslim eyes, and their stunning victory was a profound shock to people accustomed to viewing history as the progressive expansion of Islamic rule. Furthermore, Mongol military victory brought in its wake a degree of ferocity and slaughter that had no parallel in Persian experience. The Persian historian Juwayni described it in fearful terms:

■ **Comparison**

How was Mongol rule in Persia different from that in China?

Khutulun,
A Mongol Wrestler Princess[21]

Born around 1260 into the extended family network of Chinggis Khan, Khutulun was the only girl among fourteen brothers. Even among elite Mongol women, many of whom played important roles in public life, Khutulun was unique. Her father, Qaidu Khan, was the Mongol ruler of Central Asia and a bitter opponent of Khubilai Khan, the Mongol ruler of China who was trying to extend his control over Central Asia. A large and well-built young woman, Khutulun excelled in horse riding, archery, and wrestling, outperforming her brothers. Winning fame as a wrestler in public competitions, she soon joined her father on the battlefield, was awarded a medallion of office normally reserved for men alone,

A Mongol woman riding with Chinggis Khan as Khutulun rode with her father. (National Palace Museum, Taipei, Taiwan / Cultural Relics Press)

and gained a reputation for being blessed of the gods. According to Marco Polo, during battle Khutulun would often seize one of the enemy, "as deftly as a hawk pounces on a bird," and carry him off to her father.

It was when she became of marriageable age that trouble began. She turned down the possibility of marrying a cousin who governed Mongol Persia, for this woman of the steppes had no desire to live as a secluded urban wife. In fact she declared that she would only marry someone who could defeat her in wrestling. Many suitors tried, wagering 10, 100, or in one case 1,000 horses that they could defeat her. All of them failed, and, in the process, Khutulun accumulated a very substantial herd of horses.

> Every town and every village has been several times subjected to pillage and massacre and has suffered this confusion for years so that even though there be generation and increase until the Resurrection the population will not attain to a tenth part of what it was before.[22]

The sacking of Baghdad in 1258, which put an end to the Abbasid caliphate, was accompanied by the massacre of more than 200,000 people, according to Hulegu himself.

Beyond this human catastrophe lay the damage to Persian and Iraqi agriculture and to those who tilled the soil. Heavy taxes, sometimes collected twenty or thirty times a year and often under torture or whipping, pushed large numbers of peasants off their land. Furthermore, the in-migration of nomadic Mongols, together with their immense herds of sheep and goats, turned much agricultural land into pasture and sometimes into desert. As a result, a fragile system of underground water channels that provided irrigation to the fields was neglected, and much good agricultural land was reduced to waste. Some sectors of the Persian economy gained, however. Wine production increased because the Mongols were fond of alcohol, and the Persian silk industry benefited from close contact with a Mongol-ruled China. In general, though, even more so than in China, Mongol rule in Persia represented "disaster on a grand and unparalleled scale."[23]

Khutulun's extraordinary public life and her unwillingness to marry provided an opening for her enemies. Rumors circulated that she refused to marry because she was engaged in an incestuous relationship with her father. To put an end to such stories, Khutulun finally agreed to wed one of her father's followers without any wrestling contest. Still, the decision was hers. As the Mongol chronicles put it: "She chose him herself for her husband."

Even after her marriage, Khutulun continued to campaign with Qaidu Khan and together they protected the steppe lands of Central Asia from incorporation into Mongol-ruled China. In 1301 her father was wounded in battle and, shortly thereafter, died. Some accounts suggest that he tried to name Khutulun as khan in his place, but the resistance of her brothers nixed that plan. "You should mind your scissors and needles," declared her rivals. "What have you to do with kingship?" Khutulun herself supported one of her brothers as khan, while she remained at the head of the army. She died in 1306, though whether in battle or as the result of an assassination remains unclear.

In her public and military life and in her fierce independence about marriage, Khutulun reflected the relative freedom and influence of Mongol women, particularly of the elite class. In her preference for the open life of the steppes and in her resistance to the intrusion of Mongol-ruled China, she aligned with those who saw themselves as "true Mongols" in opposition to those who had come under the softening influence of neighboring Chinese or Persian civilizations. To this day, when Mongolian men wrestle, they wear a vest with an open chest in honor of Khutulun, ensuring that they are wrestling with other men rather than with a woman who might throw them.

Question: What does the life of Khutulun reveal about Mongol gender relationships?

Nonetheless, the Mongols in Persia were themselves transformed far more than their counterparts in China. They made extensive use of the sophisticated Persian bureaucracy, leaving the greater part of government operations in Persian hands. During the reign of Ghazan (haz-ZAHN) (1295–1304), they made some efforts to repair the damage caused by earlier policies of ruthless exploitation by rebuilding damaged cities and repairing neglected irrigation works. Most important, the Mongols who conquered Persia became Muslims, following the lead of Ghazan, who converted to Islam in 1295. No such widespread conversion to the culture of the conquered occurred in China or in Christian Russia. Members of the court and Mongol elites learned at least some Persian, unlike most of their counterparts in China. A number of Mongols also turned to farming, abandoning their nomadic ways, while some married local people.

When the Mongol dynasty of Hulegu's descendants collapsed in the 1330s for lack of a suitable heir, the Mongols were not driven out of Persia as they had been from China. Rather they and their Turkic allies simply disappeared, assimilated into Persian society. From a Persian point of view, the barbarians had been civilized, and Persians had successfully resisted cultural influence from their uncivilized conquerors. When the great Persian historian Rashid al-Din wrote his famous history of the Mongols, he apologized for providing information about women, generally unmentioned in Islamic writing, explaining that Mongols treated their women equally and included

Mongol Rulers and Their Women
The wives of Mongol rulers exercised considerable influence at court. This fourteenth-century painting shows Chinggis Khan's fourth son Tului, the ruler of the Mongol heartland after his father's death, with his Christian wife Sorgaqtani. After her husband's early death from alcoholism, she maneuvered her children, including Khubilai Khan, into powerful positions and strongly encouraged them in the direction of religious toleration. (Bibliothèque nationale de France)

■ **Comparison**

What was distinctive about the Russian experience of Mongol rule?

them in decisions of the court.[24] Now Persian rulers could return to their more patriarchal ways.

Russia and the Mongols

When the Mongol military machine rolled over Russia between 1237 and 1240, it encountered a relatively new third-wave civilization, located on the far eastern fringe of Christendom (see Chapter 10). Whatever political unity this new civilization of Kievan Rus had earlier enjoyed was now gone, and various independent princes proved unable to unite even in the face of the Mongol onslaught. Although they had interacted extensively with nomadic people of the steppes north of the Black Sea, nothing had prepared them for the Mongols.

The devastation wrought by the Mongol assault matched or exceeded anything experienced by the Persians or the Chinese. City after city fell to Mongol forces, which were now armed with the catapults and battering rams adopted from Chinese or Muslim sources. The slaughter that sometimes followed was described in horrific terms by Russian chroniclers, although twentieth-century historians often regard such accounts as exaggerated. From the survivors and the cities that surrendered early, laborers and skilled craftsmen were deported to other Mongol lands or sold into slavery. A number of Russian crafts were so depleted of their workers that they did not recover for a century or more.

If the ferocity of initial conquest bore similarities to the experiences of Persia, Russia's incorporation into the Mongol Empire was very different. To the Mongols, it was the Kipchak (KIP-chahk) Khanate, named after the Kipchak Turkic-speaking peoples north of the Caspian and Black seas, among whom the Mongols had settled. To the Russians, it was the "Khanate of the Golden Horde." By whatever name, the Mongols had conquered Russia, but they did not occupy it as they had China and Persia. Because there were no garrisoned cities, permanently stationed administrators, or Mongol settlers, the Russian experience of Mongol rule was quite different from elsewhere. From the Mongol point of view, Russia had little to offer. Its economy was far less developed than that of more established civilizations; nor was it located on major international trade routes. It was simply not worth the expense of occupying. Furthermore, the availability of extensive steppe lands for pasturing their flocks north of the Black and Caspian seas meant that the Mongols could maintain their preferred nomadic way of life, while remaining in easy reach of Russian cities when the need arose to send further military expeditions. They could dominate and exploit Russia from the steppes.

And exploit they certainly did. Russian princes received appointment from the khan and were required to send substantial tribute to the Mongol capital at Sarai, located on the lower Volga River. A variety of additional taxes created a heavy burden, especially on the peasantry, while continuing border raids sent tens of thousands of Russians into slavery. The Mongol impact was highly uneven, however. Some Russian princes benefited considerably because they were able to manipulate their role as tribute collectors to grow wealthy. The Russian Orthodox Church likewise flourished under the Mongol policy of religious toleration, for it received exemption from many taxes. Nobles who participated in Mongol raids earned a share of the loot. Some cities, such as Kiev, resisted the Mongols and were devastated, while others collaborated and were left undamaged. Moscow in particular emerged as the primary collector of tribute for the Mongols, and its princes parlayed this position into a leading role as the nucleus of a renewed Russian state when Mongol domination receded in the fifteenth century.

Mongol Russia
This sixteenth-century painting depicts the Mongol burning of the Russian city of Ryazan in 1237. Similar destruction awaited many Russian towns that resisted the invaders. (Sovfoto/Eastfoto)

The absence of direct Mongol rule had implications for the Mongols themselves, for they were far less influenced by or assimilated within Russian cultures than their counterparts in China and Persia had been. The Mongols in China had turned themselves into a Chinese dynasty, with the khan as a Chinese emperor. Some learned calligraphy, and a few came to appreciate Chinese poetry. In Persia, the Mongols had converted to Islam, with some becoming farmers. Not so in Russia. There "the Mongols of the Golden Horde were still spending their days in the saddle and their nights in tents."[25] They could dominate Russia from the adjacent steppes without in any way adopting Russian culture. Even though they remained culturally separate from Christian Russians, eventually the Mongols assimilated to the culture and the Islamic faith of the Kipchak people of the steppes, and in the process they lost their distinct identity and became Kipchaks.

Despite this domination from a distance, "the impact of the Mongols on Russia was, if anything, greater than on China and Iran [Persia]," according to a leading scholar.[26]

Russian princes, who were more or less left alone if they paid the required tribute and taxes, found it useful to adopt the Mongols' weapons, diplomatic rituals, court practices, taxation system, and military draft. Mongol policies facilitated, although not intentionally, the rise of Moscow as the core of a new Russian state, and that state made good use of the famous Mongol mounted courier service, which Marco Polo had praised so highly. Mongol policies also strengthened the hold of the Russian Orthodox Church and enabled it to penetrate the rural areas more fully than before. Some Russians, seeking to explain their country's economic backwardness and political autocracy in modern times, have held the Mongols responsible for both conditions, though most historians consider such views vastly exaggerated.

Divisions among the Mongols and the growing strength of the Russian state, centered now on the city of Moscow, enabled the Russians to break the Mongols' hold by the end of the fifteenth century. With the earlier demise of Mongol rule in China and Persia, and now in Russia, the Mongols had retreated from their brief but spectacular incursion into the civilizations of outer Eurasia. Nonetheless, they continued to periodically threaten these civilizations for several centuries, until their homelands were absorbed into the expanding Russian and Chinese empires. But the Mongol moment in world history was over.

LearningCurve
bedfordstmartins.com
/strayer/LC

The Mongol Empire as a Eurasian Network

During the third-wave millennium, Chinese culture and Buddhism provided a measure of integration among the peoples of East Asia; Christianity did the same for Europe, while the realm of Islam connected most of the lands in between. But it was the Mongol Empire, during the thirteenth and fourteenth centuries, that brought all of these regions into a single interacting network. It was a unique moment in world history and an important step toward the global integration of the modern era.

Toward a World Economy

■ **Connection**

What kinds of cross-cultural interactions did the Mongol Empire generate?

The Mongols themselves produced little of value for distant markets, nor were they active traders. Nonetheless, they consistently promoted international commerce, largely so that they could tax it and thus extract wealth from more developed civilizations. The Great Khan Ogodei, for example, often paid well over the asking price to attract merchants to his capital of Karakorum. The Mongols also provided financial backing for caravans, introduced standardized weights and measures, and gave tax breaks to merchants.

In providing a relatively secure environment for merchants making the long and arduous journey across Central Asia between Europe and China, the Mongol Empire brought the two ends of the Eurasian world into closer contact than ever before and launched a new phase in the history of the Silk Roads. Marco Polo was only the most famous of many European merchants, mostly from Italian cities, who made their way to China through the Mongol Empire. So many traders attempted the journey that guidebooks were published with much useful advice about the trip. Merchants returned with tales of rich lands and prosperous commercial opportunities, but what they described were long-established trading networks of which Europeans had been largely ignorant.

The Mongol trading circuit was a central element in an even larger commercial network that linked much of the Afro-Eurasian world in the thirteenth century (see Map 11.2). Mongol-ruled China was the fulcrum of this vast system, connecting the overland route through the Mongol Empire with the oceanic routes through the South China Sea and Indian Ocean.

Diplomacy on a Eurasian Scale

Not only did the Mongol Empire facilitate long-distance commerce, but it also prompted diplomatic relationships from one end of Eurasia to the other. As their invasion of Russia spilled over into Eastern Europe, Mongol armies destroyed Polish, German, and Hungarian forces in 1241–1242 and seemed poised to march on Central and Western Europe. But the death of the Great Khan Ogodei required Mongol leaders to return to Mongolia, and Western Europe lacked adequate pasture for Mongol

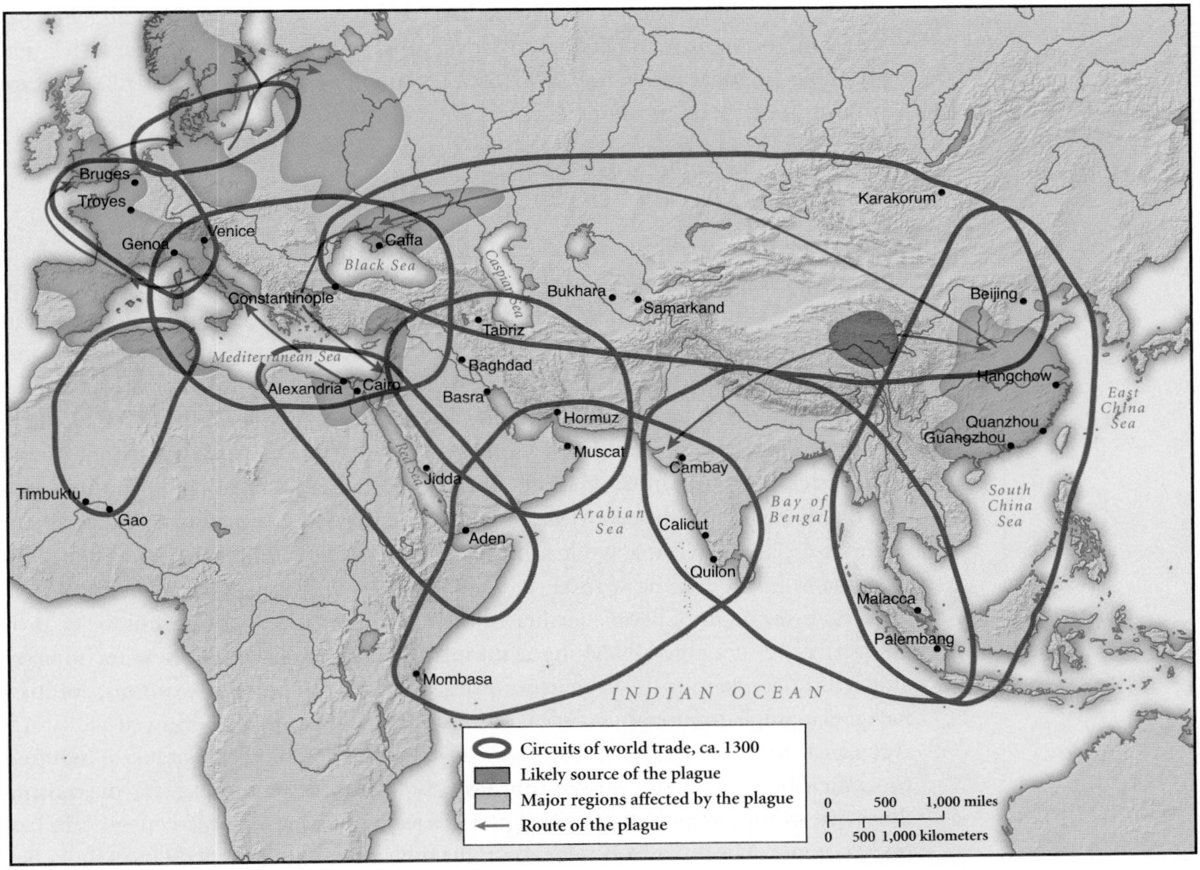

Map 11.2
Trade and Disease in the Fourteenth Century
The Mongol Empire played a major role in the commercial integration of the Eurasian world as well as in the spread of the plague across this vast area.

herds. Thus Western Europe was spared the trauma of conquest, but fearing the possible return of the Mongols, both the pope and European rulers dispatched delegations to the Mongol capital, mostly led by Franciscan friars. They hoped to learn something about Mongol intentions, to secure Mongol aid in the Christian crusade against Islam, and, if possible, to convert Mongols to Christianity.

These efforts were largely in vain, for no alliance or widespread conversion occurred. In fact, one of these missions came back with a letter for the pope from the Great Khan Guyuk, demanding that Europeans submit to him. "But if you should not believe our letters and the command of God nor hearken to our counsel," he warned, "then we shall know for certain that you wish to have war. After that we do not know what will happen."[27] Perhaps the most important outcome of these diplomatic probings was the useful information about lands to the east that European missions brought back. Those reports contributed to a dawning European awareness of a wider world, and they have certainly provided later historians with much useful information about the Mongols. Somewhat later, in 1287, the il-khanate of Persia sought an alliance with European powers to take Jerusalem and crush the forces of Islam, but the Persian Mongols' conversion to Islam soon put an end to any such anti-Muslim coalition.

Within the Mongol Empire itself, close relationships developed between the courts of Persia and China. They regularly exchanged ambassadors, shared intelligence information, fostered trade between their regions, and sent skilled workers back and forth. Thus political authorities all across Eurasia engaged in diplomatic relationships with one another to an unprecedented degree.

Cultural Exchange in the Mongol Realm

Accompanying these transcontinental economic and political relationships was a substantial exchange of peoples and cultures. Mongol policy forcibly transferred many thousands of skilled craftsmen and educated people from their homelands to distant parts of the empire, while the Mongols' religious tolerance and support of merchants drew missionaries and traders from afar. The Mongol capital at Karakorum was a cosmopolitan city with places of worship for Buddhists, Daoists, Muslims, and Christians. Chinggis Khan and several other Mongol rulers married Christian women. Actors and musicians from China, wrestlers from Persia, and a jester from Byzantium provided entertainment for the Mongol court. Persian and Arab doctors and administrators were sent to China, while Chinese physicians and engineers found their skills in demand in the Islamic world.

This movement of people facilitated the exchange of ideas and techniques, a process actively encouraged by Mongol authorities. A great deal of Chinese technology and artistic conventions — such as painting, printing, gunpowder weapons, compass navigation, high-temperature furnaces, and medical techniques — flowed westward. Acupuncture, for example, was poorly received in the Middle East because it required too much bodily contact for Muslim taste, but Chinese techniques for diagnosing illness by taking the pulse of patients proved quite popular, as they involved minimal body contact. Muslim astronomers brought their skills and knowledge to China because Mongol authorities wanted "second opinions on the reading of heavenly signs and portents" and assistance in constructing accurate calendars, so necessary for ritual purposes.[28] Plants and crops likewise circulated within the Mongol domain. Lemons and carrots from the Middle East found a welcome reception in China, while the Persian Il-Khan Ghazan sent envoys to India, China, and elsewhere to seek "seeds of things which are unique in that land."[29]

Europeans arguably gained more than most from these exchanges, for they had long been cut off from the fruitful interchange with Asia, and in comparison to the Islamic and Chinese worlds, they were less technologically developed. Now they could reap the benefits of much new technology, new crops, and new knowledge of a wider world. And almost alone among the peoples of Eurasia, they could do so without having suffered the devastating consequences of Mongol conquest. In these circumstances, some historians have argued, lay the roots of Europe's remarkable rise to global prominence in the centuries that followed.

The Plague: An Afro-Eurasian Pandemic

Any benefits derived from participation in Mongol networks of communication and exchange must be measured alongside the hemispheric catastrophe known as the "plague" or the "pestilence" and later called the Black Death. Originating most likely in China, the bacteria responsible for the disease, known as *Yersinia pestis*, spread across the trade routes of the vast Mongol Empire in the early fourteenth century (see Map 11.2, p. 375). Carried by rodents and transmitted by fleas to humans, the plague erupted initially in 1331 in northeastern China and had reached the Middle East and Western Europe by 1347. One lurid but quite uncertain story has the Mongols using catapults to hurl corpses infected with the plague into the Genoese city of Caffa in the Crimea. In 1409, the plague reached East Africa, probably by way of the famous Chinese maritime expeditions that encompassed the Indian Ocean basin.

The disease itself was associated with swelling of the lymph nodes, most often in the groin; terrible headaches; high fever; and internal bleeding just below the skin. Infected people generally died within a few days. In the densely populated civilizations of China, the Islamic world, and Europe as well as in the steppe lands of the nomads, the plague claimed enormous numbers of human victims, causing a sharp contraction in Eurasian population for a century or more. Chroniclers reported rates of death that ranged from 50 to 90 percent of the affected population, depending on the time and place. A recent study suggests that about half of Europe's people perished during the initial outbreak of 1348–1350.[30] A fifteenth-century Egyptian historian wrote that within a month of the plague's arrival in 1349, "Cairo had become an abandoned desert. . . . Everywhere one heard lamentations and one could not pass by any house without being overwhelmed by the howling."[31] The Middle East generally had lost perhaps one-third of its population by the early fifteenth century.[32] The intense first wave of the plague was followed by periodic visitations over the next several centuries, although India and sub-Saharan Africa were much less affected than other regions of the Eastern Hemisphere.

■ **Change**
Disease changes societies. How might this argument apply to the plague?

The Plague
This illustration depicts a European doctor visiting a patient with the plague. Notice that the doctor and others around the bedside cover their noses to prevent infection. During the Black Death, doctors were often criticized for refusing to treat dying patients, as they feared for their own lives. (The Granger Collection, New York)

But in those places where it struck, the plague left thoughtful people grasping for language with which to describe a horror of such unprecedented dimensions. One Italian man, who had buried all five of his children with his own hands, wrote in 1348 that "so many have died that everyone believes it is the end of the world."[33] Another Italian, the Renaissance scholar Francesco Petrarch, was equally stunned by the impact of the Black Death; he wrote to a friend in 1349:

> When at any time has such a thing been seen or spoken of? Has what happened in these years ever been read about: empty houses, derelict cities, ruined estates, fields strewn with cadavers, a horrible and vast solitude encompassing the whole world? Consult historians, they are silent; ask physicians, they are stupefied; seek the answers from philosophers, they shrug their shoulders, furrow their brows, and with fingers pressed against their lips, bid you be silent. Will posterity believe these things, when we who have seen it can scarcely believe it . . . ?[34]

In the Islamic world, the famous historian Ibn Khaldun, who had lost both of his parents to the plague, also wrote about it in apocalyptic terms:

> Civilization in both the East and the West was visited by a destructive plague which devastated nations and caused populations to vanish. It swallowed up many of the good things of civilization and wiped them out. . . . It was as if the voice of existence had called out for oblivion and restriction, and the world responded to its call.[35]

Beyond its immediate devastation, the Black Death worked longer-term changes in European society, the region where the plague's impact has been most thoroughly studied. Labor shortages following the initial outburst provoked sharp conflict between scarce workers, who sought higher wages or better conditions, and the rich, who resisted those demands. A series of peasant revolts in the fourteenth century reflected this tension, which also undermined the practice of serfdom. That labor shortage also may have fostered a greater interest in technological innovation and created, at least for a time, more employment opportunities for women. Thus a resilient European civilization survived a cataclysm that had the power to destroy it. In a strange way, that catastrophe may have actually fostered its future growth.

Whatever its impact in particular places, the plague also had larger consequences. Ironically, that human disaster, born of the Mongol network, was a primary reason for the demise of that network in the fourteenth and fifteenth centuries. Population contracted, cities declined, and the volume of trade diminished all across the Mongol world. By 1350, the Mongol Empire itself was in disarray, and within a century the Mongols had lost control of Chinese, Persian, and Russian civilizations. The Central Asian trade route, so critical to the entire Afro-Eurasian world economy, largely closed.

This disruption of the Mongol-based land routes to the east, coupled with a desire to avoid Muslim intermediaries, provided incentives for Europeans to take to the sea in their continuing efforts to reach the riches of Asia. Their naval technology gave them military advantages on the seas, much as the Mongols' skill with the bow and their mobility on horseback gave these nomads a decisive edge in land battles. As Europeans penetrated Asian and Atlantic waters in the sixteenth century, they took on, in some ways, the role of the Mongols in organizing and fostering world trade and in creating a network of communication and exchange over an even larger area. Like the Mongols, Europeans were people on the periphery of the major established civilizations; they too were economically less developed in comparison to Chinese and Islamic civilizations; both were prone to forcibly plundering the wealthier civilizations they encountered; and European empire-building in the Americas, like that of the Mongols in Eurasia, brought devastating disease and catastrophic population decline in its wake.[36] Europeans, of course, brought far more of their own culture and many more of their own people to the societies they conquered, as Christianity, European languages, settler societies, and western science and technology took root within their empires. Although their imperial presence lasted far longer and operated on a much larger scale, European actions at the beginning of their global expansion bore some resemblance to those of their Mongol predecessors. They were, as one historian put it, "the Mongols of the seas."[37]

LearningCurve
bedfordstmartins.com
/strayer/LC

Reflections: Changing Images of Pastoral Peoples

Historians frequently change their minds, and long-term consensus on most important matters has been difficult to achieve. For example, until recently, pastoral nomads generally received bad press in history books. Normally they entered the story only when they were threatening or destroying established civilizations. In presenting a largely negative image of pastoral peoples, historians were reflecting the long-held attitudes of literate elites in the civilizations of Eurasia. Fearing and usually despising such peoples, educated observers in China, the Middle East, and Europe often described them as bloodthirsty savages or barbarians, bringing only chaos and destruction in their wake. Han Kuan, a Chinese scholar of the first century B.C.E., described the Xiongnu people as "abandoned by Heaven . . . in foodless desert wastes, without proper houses, clothed in animal hides, eating their meat uncooked and drinking blood."[38] To the Christian Saint Jerome (340–420 C.E.), the nomadic Huns "filled the whole earth with slaughter and panic alike as they flitted hither and thither on their swift horses."[39] Almost a thousand years later, the famous Arab historian Ibn Khaldun described nomads in a very similar fashion: "It is their nature to plunder whatever other people possess."[40]

Because pastoral peoples generally did not have written languages, the sources available to historians came from less-than-unbiased observers in adjacent agricultural civilizations. Furthermore, in the long-running conflict across the farming/pastoral frontier, agricultural civilizations ultimately triumphed. Over the centuries, some nomadic or semi-agricultural peoples, such as the Germanic tribes of Europe and the Arabs, created new civilizations. Others, such as the Turkic and Mongol peoples, took over existing civilizations or were encompassed within established agrarian empires. By the early twentieth century, and in most places much earlier, pastoral peoples everywhere had lost their former independence and had often shed their nomadic life as well. Since "winners" usually write history, the negative views of pastoral nomads held by agrarian civilizations normally prevailed.

Reflecting more inclusive contemporary values, historians in recent decades have sought to present a more balanced picture of pastoralists' role in world history, emphasizing what they created as well as what they destroyed. These historians have highlighted the achievements of herding peoples, such as their adaptation to inhospitable environments; their technological innovations; their development of horse-, camel-, or cattle-based cultures; their role in fostering cross-cultural exchange; and their state-building efforts.

A less critical or judgmental posture toward the Mongols may also owe something to the "total wars" and genocides of the twentieth century, in which the mass slaughter of civilians became a strategy to induce enemy surrender. During the cold war, the United States and the Soviet Union were prepared, apparently, to obliterate each other's entire population with nuclear weapons in response to an attack. In light of this recent history, Mongol massacres may appear a little less unique. Historians living in the glass houses of contemporary societies are perhaps more reluctant to cast stones at the Mongols. In understanding the Mongols, as in so much else, historians are shaped by the times and circumstances of their own lives as much as by "what really happened" in the past.

Second Thoughts

What's the Significance?

LearningCurve
Check what you know.
**bedfordstmartins.com
/strayer/LC**

Online Study Guide
bedfordstmartins.com/strayer

pastoralism, 354–61
Modun, 358
Xiongnu, 358–59
Turks, 359–60
Almoravid Empire, 360–61

Temujin/Chinggis Khan, 363–65
the Mongol world war, 364–66
Yuan dynasty China, 367–68
Khubilai Khan, 367–68
Hulegu, 369

Khutulun, 370–71
Kipchak Khanate/Golden
    Horde, 372–74
Black Death/
    plague, 377–79

Big Picture Questions

1. What accounts for the often negative attitudes of settled societies toward the pastoral peoples living on their borders?

2. Why have historians often neglected pastoral peoples' role in world history? How would you assess the perspective of this chapter toward the Mongols? Does it strike you as negative and critical of the Mongols, as bending over backward to portray them in a positive light, or as a balanced presentation?

3. In what different ways did Mongol rule affect the Islamic world, Russia, China, and Europe? In what respects did it foster Eurasian integration?

4. Why did the Mongol Empire last only a relatively short time?

5. **Looking Back:** In what ways did the Mongol Empire resemble previous empires (Arab, Roman, Chinese, or the Greek empire of Alexander, for example), and in what ways did it differ from them?

Next Steps: For Further Study

John Aberth, *The First Horseman: Disease in Human History* (2007). A global study of the history of disease, with a fine chapter on the Black Death.

Thomas Allsen, *Culture and Conquest in Mongol Eurasia* (2001). A history of cultural exchange within the Mongol realm, particularly between China and the Islamic world.

Thomas J. Barfield, *The Nomadic Alternative* (1993). An anthropological and historical survey of pastoral peoples on a global basis.

Carter Finley, *The Turks in World History* (2005). The evolution of Turkic-speaking people, from their nomadic origins to the twentieth century.

Jack Weatherford, *Genghis Khan and the Making of the Modern World* (2004). A lively, well-written, and balanced account of the world the Mongols made and the legacy they left for the future.

"The Mongols in World History," http://afe.easia.columbia.edu/mongols. A wonderful resource on the Mongols generally, with a particular focus on their impact in China.

For Web sites and additional documents related to this chapter, see **Make History** at bedfordstmartins.com/strayer.

CHAPTER TWELVE

The Worlds of the Fifteenth Century

The Shapes of Human Communities
  Paleolithic Persistence: Australia and
    North America
  Agricultural Village Societies: The Igbo
    and the Iroquois
  Pastoral Peoples: Central Asia and West
    Africa
Civilizations of the Fifteenth Century:
  Comparing China and Europe
  Ming Dynasty China
  European Comparisons: State Building
    and Cultural Renewal
  European Comparisons: Maritime Voyaging
Civilizations of the Fifteenth Century:
  The Islamic World
  In the Islamic Heartland: The Ottoman
    and Safavid Empires
  On the Frontiers of Islam: The Songhay
    and Mughal Empires
Civilizations of the Fifteenth Century:
  The Americas
  The Aztec Empire
  The Inca Empire
Webs of Connection
A Preview of Coming Attractions:
  Looking Ahead to the Modern Era,
  1500–2012
Reflections: What If? Chance and
  Contingency in World History
Portrait: Zheng He, China's Non-Chinese
  Admiral

"Columbus was a perpetrator of genocide . . . , a slave trader, a thief, a pirate, and most certainly not a hero. To celebrate Columbus is to congratulate the process and history of the invasion."[1] This was the view Winona LaDuke, president of the Indigenous Women's Network, on the occasion in 1992 of the 500th anniversary of Columbus's arrival in the Americas. Much of the commentary surrounding the event echoed the same themes, citing the history of death, slavery, racism, and exploitation that followed in the wake Columbus's first voyage to what was for him an altogether New World. A century earlier, in 1892, the tone of celebration had been very different. A presidential proclamation cited Columbus as a brave "pioneer of progress and enlightenment" and instructed Americans to "express honor to the discoverer and their appreciation of the great achievements of four completed centuries of American life." The century that followed witnessed the erosion of Western dominance in the world and the discrediting of racism and imperialism and, with it, the reputation of Columbus.

THIS SHARP REVERSAL OF OPINION ABOUT COLUMBUS provides a reminder that the past is as unpredictable as the future. Few Americans in 1892 could have guessed that their daring hero could emerge so tarnished only a century later. And few people living in 1492 could have imagined the enormous global processes set in motion by the voyage of Columbus's three small ships—the Atlantic slave trade, the decimation of the native peoples of the Americas, the massive growth of world population, the Industrial Revolution, and the growing prominence of Europeans on the world stage. None of these developments were even remotely foreseeable in 1492.

The Meeting of Two Worlds: This famous sixteenth-century engraving by the Flemish artist Theodore de Bry shows Columbus landing in Hispaniola (Haiti), where the Taino people bring him presents, while the Europeans claim the island for God and monarch. In light of its long-range consequences, this voyage represents a major turning point in world history. (bpk, Berlin/Art Resource, NY)

Thus in historical hindsight, that voyage of Columbus was arguably the single most important event of the fifteenth century. But it was not the only significant marker of that century. A Central Asian Turkic warrior named Timur launched the last major nomadic invasion of adjacent civilizations. Russia emerged from two centuries of Mongol rule to begin a huge empire-building project across northern Asia. A new European civilization was taking shape in the Renaissance. In 1405 an enormous Chinese fleet, dwarfing that of Columbus, set out across the entire Indian Ocean basin, only to voluntarily withdraw 28 years later. The Islamic Ottoman Empire put a final end to Christian Byzantium with the conquest of Constantinople in 1453, even as Spanish Christians completed the "reconquest" of the Iberian Peninsula from the Muslims in 1492. And in the Americas, the Aztec and Inca Empires gave a final and spectacular expression to Mesoamerican and Andean civilizations before they were both swallowed up in the burst of European imperialism that followed the arrival of Columbus.

Because the fifteenth century was a hinge of major historical change on many fronts, it provides an occasion for a bird's-eye view of the world through a kind of global tour. This excursion around the world will serve to briefly review the human saga thus far and to establish a baseline from which the enormous transformations of the centuries that followed might be measured. How then might we describe the world, and the worlds, of the fifteenth century?

SEEKING THE MAIN POINT

What predictions about the future might a global traveler in the fifteenth century have reasonably made?

The Shapes of Human Communities

One way to describe the world of the fifteenth century is to identify the various types of societies that it contained. Bands of hunters and gatherers, villages of agricultural peoples, newly emerging chiefdoms or small states, nomadic/pastoral communities, established civilizations and empires—all of these social or political forms would have been apparent to a widely traveled visitor in the fifteenth century. Representing alternative ways of organizing human communities, all of them were long established by the fifteenth century, but the balance among these distinctive kinds of societies in 1500 was quite different than it had been a thousand years earlier.

Paleolithic Persistence: Australia and North America

■ **Comparison**

In what ways did the gathering and hunting people of Australia differ from those of the north-west coast of North America?

Despite millennia of agricultural advance, substantial areas of the world still hosted gathering and hunting societies, known to historians as Paleolithic (old stone age) peoples. All of Australia, much of Siberia, the arctic coastlands, and parts of Africa and the Americas fell into this category. These peoples were not simply relics of a bygone age. They too had changed over time, though more slowly than their agricultural counterparts, and they too interacted with their neighbors. In short, they had a history, although most history books largely ignore them after the age of agriculture arrived.

A Map of Time

1345–1521	Aztec Empire in Mesoamerica
1368–1644	Ming dynasty in China
1370–1406	Conquests of Timur
15th century	Spread of Islam in Southeast Asia Civil war among Japanese warlords Rise of Hindu state of Vijayanagara in southern India European renaissance Flourishing of African states of Ethiopia, Kongo, Benin, Zimbabwe
1405–1433	Chinese maritime voyages
1420	Beginning of Portuguese exploration of West African coast
1438–1533	Inca Empire along the Andes
1453	Ottoman seizure of Constantinople
1464–1591	Songhay Empire in West Africa
1492	Christian reconquest of Spain from Muslims completed; Columbus's first trans-Atlantic voyage
1497–1520s	Portuguese entry into the Indian Ocean world
1501	Founding of Safavid Empire in Persia
1526	Founding of Mughal Empire in India

Nonetheless, this most ancient way of life still had a sizable and variable presence in the world of the fifteenth century.

Consider, for example, Australia. That continent's many separate groups, some 250 of them, still practiced a gathering and hunting way of life in the fifteenth century, a pattern that continued well after Europeans arrived in the late eighteenth century. Over many thousands of years, these people had assimilated various material items or cultural practices from outsiders—outrigger canoes, fish hooks, complex netting techniques, artistic styles, rituals, and mythological ideas—but despite the presence of farmers in nearby New Guinea, no agricultural practices penetrated the Australian mainland. Was it because large areas of Australia were unsuited for the kind of agriculture practiced in New Guinea? Or did the peoples of Australia, enjoying an environment of sufficient resources, simply see no need to change their way of life?

Despite the absence of agriculture, Australia's peoples had mastered and manipulated their environment, in part through the practice of "firestick farming," a pattern of deliberately set fires, which they described as "cleaning up the country."

$\mathcal{S}$napshot	**Major Developments around the World in the Fifteenth Century**
Region	**Major Developments**
Central, East, and Southeast Asia	Ming dynasty China, 1368–1644
	Conquests of Timur, 1370–1406
	Zheng He's maritime voyages, 1405–1433
	Spread of Islam into Southeast Asia
	Rise of Malacca
	Civil war among competing warlords in Japan
South Asia/India	Timur's invasion of India, 1398
	Various Muslim sultanates in northern India
	Rise of Hindu state of Vijayanagar in southern India
	Founding of Mughal Empire, 1526
Middle East	Expansion of Ottoman Empire
	Ottoman seizure of Constantinople, 1453
	Founding of Safavid Empire in Persia, 1501
	Ottoman siege of Vienna, 1529
Christendom/Europe	European Renaissance
	Portuguese voyages of exploration along West African coast
	Completion of reconquest of Spain, ending Muslim control
	End of the Byzantine Empire, 1453
	End of Mongol rule in Russia; reign of Ivan the Great, 1462–1505
Africa	Songhay Empire in West Africa, 1464–1591
	Kingdom of the Kongo in West Central Africa
	Expansion of Ethiopian state in East Africa
	Kingdom of Zimbabwe/Mwene Mutapa in southern Africa
The Americas/Western Hemisphere	Aztec Empire in Mesoamerica, 1345–1521
	Inca Empire along the Andes, 1438–1533
	Iroquois confederacy (New York State)
	"Complex" Paleolithic societies along west coast of North America
Pacific Oceania	Paleolithic persistence in Australia
	Chiefdoms and stratified societies on Pacific islands
	Yap as center of oceanic trading network with Guam and Palau

These controlled burns served to clear the underbrush, thus making hunting easier and encouraging the growth of certain plant and animal species. In addition, native Australians exchanged goods among themselves over distances of hundreds of miles, created elaborate mythologies and ritual practices, and developed sophisticated traditions of sculpture and rock painting. They accomplished all of this on the basis of an economy and technology rooted in the distant Paleolithic past.

A very different kind of gathering and hunting society flourished in the fifteenth century along the northwest coast of North America among the Chinookan, Tulalip, Skagit, and other peoples. With some 300 edible animal species and an abundance of salmon and other fish, this extraordinarily bounteous environment provided the foundation for what scholars sometimes call "complex" or "affluent" gathering and hunting cultures. What distinguished the northwest coast peoples from those of Australia were permanent village settlements with large and sturdy houses, considerable economic specialization, ranked societies that sometimes included slavery, chiefdoms dominated by powerful clan leaders or "big men," and extensive storage of food.

Although these and other gathering and hunting peoples persisted still in the fifteenth century, both their numbers and the area they inhabited had contracted greatly as the Agricultural Revolution unfolded across the planet. That relentless advance of the farming frontier continued in the centuries ahead as the Russian, Chinese, and European empires encompassed the lands of the remaining Paleolithic peoples. By the early twenty-first century, what was once the only human way of life had been reduced to minuscule pockets of people whose cultures seemed doomed to a final extinction.

Agricultural Village Societies: The Igbo and the Iroquois

Far more numerous than gatherers and hunters were those many peoples who, though fully agricultural, had avoided incorporation into larger empires or civilizations and had not developed their own city- or state-based societies. Living usually in small village-based communities and organized in terms of kinship relations, such people predominated during the fifteenth century in much of North America and in parts of the Amazon River basin, Southeast Asia, and Africa south of the equator. They had created societies largely without the oppressive political authority, class inequalities, and seclusion of women that were so common in civilizations. Historians have largely relegated such societies to the periphery of world history, marginal to their overwhelming focus on states, cities, and large-scale civilizations. Viewed from within their own circles, though, these societies were at the center of things, each with its own history of migration, cultural transformation, social conflict, incorporation of new people, political rise and fall, and interaction with strangers. In short, they too changed as their histories took shape.

East of the Niger River in the heavily forested region of West Africa lay the lands of the Igbo (EE-boh) peoples. By the fifteenth century, their neighbors, the Yoruba

■ **Change**
What kinds of changes were transforming the societies of the West African Igbo and the North American Iroquois as the fifteenth century unfolded?

and Bini, had begun to develop small states and urban centers. But the Igbo, whose dense population and extensive trading networks might well have given rise to states, declined to follow suit. The deliberate Igbo preference was to reject the kingship and state-building efforts of their neighbors. They boasted on occasion that "the Igbo have no kings." Instead they relied on other institutions to maintain social cohesion beyond the level of the village: title societies in which wealthy men received a series of prestigious ranks, women's associations, hereditary ritual experts serving as mediators, a balance of power among kinship groups. It was a "stateless society," famously described in Chinua Achebe's *Things Fall Apart*, the most widely read novel to emerge from twentieth-century Africa.

But the Igbo peoples and their neighbors did not live in isolated, self-contained societies. They traded actively among themselves and with more distant peoples, such as the large African kingdom of Songhay (sahn-GEYE) far to the north. Cotton cloth, fish, copper and iron goods, decorative objects, and more drew neighboring peoples into networks of exchange. Common artistic traditions reflected a measure of cultural unity in a politically fragmented region, and all of these peoples seem to have changed from a matrilineal to a patrilineal system of tracing their descent. Little of this registered in the larger civilizations of the Afro-Eurasian world, but to the peoples of the West African forest during the fifteenth century, these processes were central to their history and their daily lives. Soon, however, all of them would be caught up in the transatlantic slave trade and would be changed substantially in the process.

Across the Atlantic in what is now central New York State, other agricultural village societies were also in the process of substantial change during the several centuries preceding their incorporation into European trading networks and empires. The Iroquois-speaking peoples of that region had only recently become fully agricultural, adopting maize- and bean-farming techniques that had originated centuries earlier in Mesoamerica. As this productive agriculture took hold by 1300 or so, the population grew, the size of settlements increased, and distinct peoples emerged. Frequent warfare also erupted among them. Some scholars have speculated that as agriculture, largely seen as women's work, became the primary economic activity, "warfare replaced successful food getting as the avenue to male prestige."[2]

Whatever caused it, this increased level of conflict among Iroquois peoples triggered a remarkable political innovation around the fifteenth century: a loose alliance or confederation among five Iroquois-speaking peoples—the Mohawk, Oneida, Onondaga, Cayuga, and Seneca. Based on an agreement known as the Great Law of Peace (see Map 12.5, p. 405), the Five Nations, as they called themselves, agreed to settle their differences peacefully through a confederation council of clan leaders, some fifty of them altogether, who had the authority to adjudicate disputes and set reparation payments. Operating by consensus, the Iroquois League of Five Nations effectively sup-

Igbo Art

Widely known for their masks, used in a variety of ritual and ceremonial occasions, the Igbo were also among the first to produce bronze castings using the "lost wax" method. This exquisite bronze pendant in the form of a human head derives from the Igbo Ukwu archeological site in eastern Nigeria and dates to the ninth century C.E. (Werner Forman/ Art Resource, NY)

pressed the blood feuds and tribal conflicts that had only recently been so widespread. It also coordinated their peoples' relationship with outsiders, including the Europeans, who arrived in growing numbers in the centuries after 1500.

The Iroquois League gave expression to values of limited government, social equality, and personal freedom, concepts that some European colonists found highly attractive. One British colonial administrator declared in 1749 that the Iroquois had "such absolute Notions of Liberty that they allow no Kind of Superiority of one over another, and banish all Servitude from their Territories."[3] Such equality extended to gender relationships, for among the Iroquois, descent was matrilineal (reckoned through the woman's line), married couples lived with the wife's family, and women controlled agriculture and property. While men were hunters, warriors, and the primary political officeholders, women selected and could depose those leaders.

Wherever they lived in 1500, over the next several centuries independent agricultural peoples such as the Iroquois and Igbo were increasingly encompassed in expanding economic networks and conquest empires based in Western Europe, Russia, China, or India. In this respect, they replicated the experience of many other village-based farming communities that had much earlier found themselves forcibly included in the powerful embrace of Egyptian, Mesopotamian, Roman, Indian, Chinese, and other civilizations.

Pastoral Peoples: Central Asia and West Africa

■ **Significance**
What role did Central Asian and West African pastoralists play in their respective regions?

Nomadic pastoral peoples had long impinged more directly and dramatically on civilizations than did hunting and gathering or agricultural village societies. The Mongol incursion, along with the enormous empire to which it gave rise, was one in a long series of challenges from the steppes, but it was not quite the last. As the Mongol Empire disintegrated, a brief attempt to restore it occurred in the late fourteenth and early fifteenth centuries under the leadership of a Turkic warrior named Timur, born in what is now Uzbekistan and known in the West as Tamerlane (see Map 12.1, p. 391).

With a ferocity that matched or exceeded that of his model, Chinggis Khan, Timur's army of nomads brought immense devastation yet again to Russia, Persia, and India. Timur himself died in 1405, while preparing for an invasion of China. Conflicts among his successors prevented any lasting empire, although his descendants retained control of the area between Persia and Afghanistan for the rest of the fifteenth century. That state hosted a sophisticated elite culture, combining Turkic and Persian elements, particularly at its splendid capital of Samarkand, as its rulers patronized artists, poets, traders, and craftsmen. Timur's conquest proved to be the last great military success of nomadic peoples from Central Asia. In the centuries that followed, their homelands were swallowed up in the expanding Russian and Chinese empires, as the balance of power between steppe nomads of inner Eurasia and the civilizations of outer Eurasia turned decisively in favor of the latter.

In Africa, pastoral peoples stayed independent of established empires several centuries longer than the nomads of Inner Asia, for not until the late nineteenth century were they incorporated into European colonial states. The experience of the Fulbe, West Africa's largest pastoral society, provides an example of an African herding people with a highly significant role in the fifteenth century and beyond. From their homeland in the western fringe of the Sahara along the upper Senegal River, the Fulbe had migrated gradually eastward in the centuries after 1000 C.E. (see Map 12.3, p. 398). Unlike the pastoral peoples of Inner Asia, they generally lived in small communities among agricultural peoples and paid various grazing fees and taxes for the privilege of pasturing their cattle. Relations with their farming hosts often were tense because the Fulbe resented their subordination to agricultural peoples, whose way of life they despised. That sense of cultural superiority became even more pronounced as the Fulbe, in the course of their eastward movement, slowly adopted Islam. Some of them in fact dropped out of a pastoral life and settled in towns, where they became highly respected religious leaders. In the eighteenth and nineteenth centuries, the Fulbe were at the center of a wave of religiously based uprisings, or jihads, which greatly expanded the practice of Islam and gave rise to a series of new states, ruled by the Fulbe themselves.

LearningCurve
bedfordstmartins.com
/strayer/LC

Civilizations of the Fifteenth Century: Comparing China and Europe

Beyond the foraging, farming, and pastoral societies of the fifteenth-century world were its civilizations, those city-centered and state-based societies that were far larger and more densely populated, more powerful and innovative, and much more unequal in terms of class and gender than other forms of human community. Since the First Civilizations had emerged between 3500 and 1000 B.C.E., both the geographic space they encompassed and the number of people they embraced had grown substantially. By the fifteenth century, a considerable majority of the world's population lived within one or another of these civilizations, although most of these people no doubt identified more with local communities than with a larger civilization. What might an imaginary global traveler notice about the world's major civilizations in the fifteenth century?

Ming Dynasty China

■ **Description**
How would you define the major achievements of Ming dynasty China?

Such a traveler might well begin his or her journey in China, heir to a long tradition of effective governance, Confucian and Daoist philosophy, a major Buddhist presence, sophisticated artistic achievements, and a highly productive economy. That civilization, however, had been greatly disrupted by a century of Mongol rule, and its population had been sharply reduced by the plague. During the Ming dynasty (1368–1644), however, China recovered (see Map 12.1). The early decades of that dynasty witnessed an effort to eliminate all signs of foreign rule, discouraging the use of Mon-

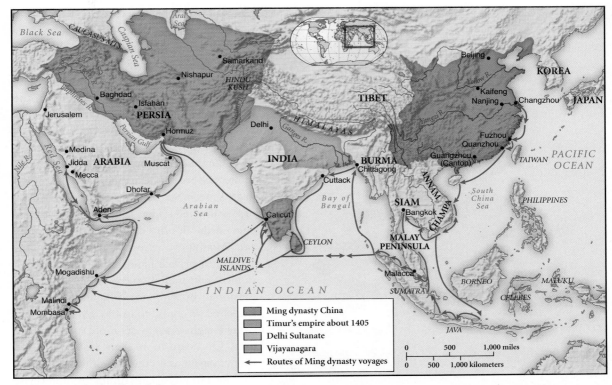

Map 12.1 Asia in the Fifteenth Century
The fifteenth century in Asia witnessed the massive Ming dynasty voyages into the Indian Ocean, the last major eruption of nomadic power in Timur's empire, and the flourishing of the maritime city of Malacca.

gol names and dress, while promoting Confucian learning and orthodox gender roles, based on earlier models from the Han, Tang, and Song dynasties. Emperor Yongle (YAHNG-leh) (r. 1402–1422) sponsored an enormous *Encyclopedia* of some 11,000 volumes. With contributions from more than 2,000 scholars, this work sought to summarize or compile all previous writing on history, geography, philosophy, ethics, government, and more. Yongle also relocated the capital to Beijing, ordered the building of a magnificent imperial residence known as the Forbidden City, and constructed the Temple of Heaven, where subsequent rulers performed Confucian-based rituals to ensure the well-being of Chinese society. Two empresses wrote instructions for female behavior, emphasizing traditional expectations after the disruptions of the previous century. Culturally speaking, China was looking to its past.

Politically, the Ming dynasty reestablished the civil service examination system that had been neglected under Mongol rule and went on to create a highly centralized government. Power was concentrated in the hands of the emperor himself, while a cadre of eunuchs (castrated men) personally loyal to the emperor exercised great authority, much to the dismay of the official bureaucrats. The state acted vigorously to repair the damage of the Mongol years by restoring millions of acres to cultivation;

Temple of Heaven
Set in a forest of more than 650 acres, the Temple of Heaven was constructed in the early fifteenth century. In Chinese thinking it was the primary place where Heaven and Earth met. From his residence in the Forbidden City, the Chinese emperor led a procession of thousands twice a year to this sacred site, where he offered sacrifices, implored the gods for a good harvest, and performed the rituals that maintained the cosmic balance. (Imaginechina for AP Images)

rebuilding canals, reservoirs, and irrigation works; and planting, according to some estimates, a billion trees in an effort to reforest China. As a result, the economy rebounded, both international and domestic trade flourished, and the population grew. During the fifteenth century, China had recovered and was perhaps the best-governed and most prosperous of the world's major civilizations.

China also undertook the largest and most impressive maritime expeditions the world had ever seen. Since the eleventh century, Chinese sailors and traders had been a major presence in the South China Sea and in Southeast Asian port cities, with much of this activity in private hands. But now, after decades of preparation, an enormous fleet, commissioned by Emperor Yongle himself, was launched in 1405, followed over the next twenty-eight years by six more such expeditions. On board more than 300 ships of the first voyage was a crew of some 27,000, including 180 physicians, hundreds of government officials, 5 astrologers, 7 high-ranking or grand eunuchs, carpenters, tailors, accountants, merchants, translators, cooks, and thousands of soldiers and sailors. Visiting many ports in Southeast Asia, Indonesia, India, Arabia, and East Africa, these fleets, captained by the Muslim eunuch Zheng He (JUHNG-huh), sought to enroll distant peoples and states in the Chinese tribute system (see Map 12.1). Dozens of rulers accompanied the fleets back to China, where they presented tribute, performed the required rituals of submission, and received in return abundant gifts, titles, and trading opportunities. Chinese officials were amused by some of the exotic products to be found abroad — ostriches, zebras, and giraffes, for example. Officially described as "bringing order to the world," Zheng He's expeditions served to establish Chinese power and prestige in the Indian Ocean and to exert Chinese control over foreign trade in the region. The Chinese, however, did not seek to conquer new territories, establish Chinese settlements, or spread their culture, though they did intervene in a number of local disputes. (See Portrait of Zheng He, pp. 396–97.)

The most surprising feature of these voyages was how abruptly and deliberately they were ended. After 1433, Chinese authorities simply stopped such expeditions and allowed this enormous and expensive fleet to deteriorate in port. "In less than a hundred years," wrote a recent historian of these voyages, "the greatest navy the world had ever known had ordered itself into extinction."[4] Part of the reason involved the death of the emperor Yongle, who had been the chief patron of the enterprise. Many high-ranking officials had long seen the expeditions as a waste of resources because China, they believed, was the self-sufficient "middle kingdom," requiring little from the outside world. In their eyes, the real danger to China came from the north, where nomadic barbarians constantly threatened. Finally, they viewed the voyages as the project of the court eunuchs, whom these officials despised. Even as these voices of Chinese officialdom prevailed, private Chinese merchants and craftsmen continued to settle and trade in Japan, the Philippines, Taiwan, and Southeast Asia, but they did so without the support of their government. The Chinese state quite deliberately turned its back on what was surely within its reach—a large-scale maritime empire in the Indian Ocean basin.

European Comparisons: State Building and Cultural Renewal

At the other end of the Eurasian continent, similar processes of demographic recovery, political consolidation, cultural flowering, and overseas expansion were under way. Western Europe, having escaped Mongol conquest but devastated by the plague, began to regrow its population during the second half of the fifteenth century. As in China, the infrastructure of civilization proved a durable foundation for demographic and economic revival.

> ■ **Comparison**
>
> What political and cultural differences stand out in the histories of fifteenth-century China and Western Europe? What similarities are apparent?

Politically too Europe joined China in continuing earlier patterns of state building. In China, however, this meant a unitary and centralized government that encompassed almost the whole of its civilization, while in Europe a decidedly fragmented system of many separate, independent, and highly competitive states made for a sharply divided Christendom (see Map 12.2). Many of these states—Spain, Portugal, France, England, the city-states of Italy (Milan, Venice, and Florence), various German principalities—learned to tax their citizens more efficiently, to create more effective administrative structures, and to raise standing armies. A small Russian state centered on the city of Moscow also emerged in the fifteenth century as Mongol rule faded away. Much of this state building was driven by the needs of war, a frequent occurrence in such a fragmented and competitive political environment. England and France, for example, fought intermittently for more than a century in the Hundred Years' War (1337–1453) over rival claims to territory in France. Nothing remotely similar disturbed the internal life of Ming dynasty China.

A renewed cultural blossoming, known in European history as the Renaissance, likewise paralleled the revival of all things Confucian in Ming dynasty China. In Europe, however, that blossoming celebrated and reclaimed a classical Greco-Roman tradition that earlier had been lost or obscured. Beginning in the vibrant commercial cities of Italy between roughly 1350 and 1500, the Renaissance reflected the belief of the wealthy male elite that they were living in a wholly new era, far removed from

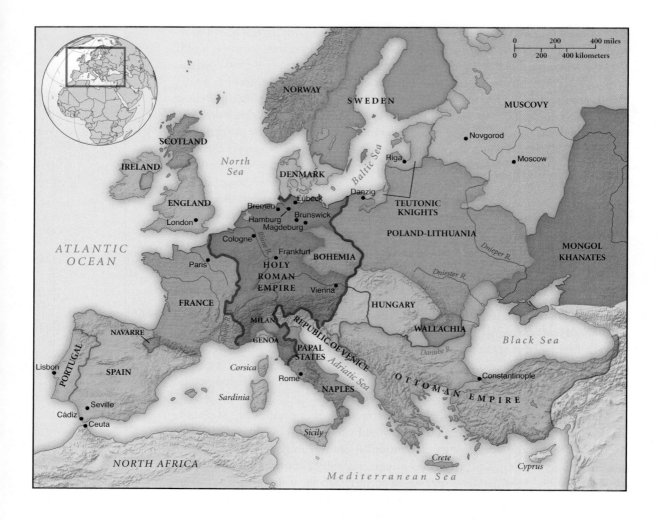

Map 12.2 Europe in 1500
By the end of the fifteenth century, Christian Europe had assumed its early modern political shape as a system of competing states threatened by an expanding Muslim Ottoman Empire.

the confined religious world of feudal Europe. Educated citizens of these cities sought inspiration in the art and literature of ancient Greece and Rome; they were "returning to the sources," as they put it. Their purpose was not so much to reconcile these works with the ideas of Christianity, as the twelfth- and thirteenth-century university scholars had done, but to use them as a cultural standard to imitate and then to surpass. The elite patronized great Renaissance artists such as Leonardo da Vinci, Michelangelo, and Raphael, whose paintings and sculptures were far more naturalistic, particularly in portraying the human body, than those of their medieval counterparts. Some of these artists looked to the Islamic world for standards of excellence, sophistication, and abundance.

Although religious themes remained prominent, Renaissance artists now included portraits and busts of well-known contemporary figures, scenes from ancient mythology, and depictions of Islamic splendor. In the work of scholars, known as human-

The Waldseemüller Map of 1507
Just fifteen years after Columbus landed in the Western Hemisphere, this map, which was created by the German cartographer Martin Waldseemüller, reflected a dawning European awareness of the planet's global dimensions and location of the world's major landmasses. (bpk, Berlin/Staatsbibliothek zu Berlin, Stiftung Preussischer Kulturbesitz, Berlin, Germany/Ruth Schacht, Map Division/Art Resource, NY)

ists, reflections on secular topics such as grammar, history, politics, poetry, rhetoric, and ethics complemented more religious matters. For example, Niccolò Machiavelli's (1469–1527) famous work *The Prince* was a prescription for political success based on the way politics actually operated in a highly competitive Italy of rival city-states rather than on idealistic and religiously based principles. To the question of whether a prince should be feared or loved, Machiavelli replied:

> One ought to be both feared and loved, but as it is difficult for the two to go together, it is much safer to be feared than loved. . . . For it may be said of men in general that they are ungrateful, voluble, dissemblers, anxious to avoid danger, and covetous of gain. . . . Fear is maintained by dread of punishment which never fails. . . . In the actions of men, and especially of princes, from which there is no appeal, the end justifies the means.[5]

While the great majority of Renaissance writers and artists were men, among the remarkable exceptions to that rule was Christine de Pizan (1363–1430), the daughter of a Venetian official, who lived mostly in Paris. Her writings pushed against the misogyny of so many European thinkers of the time. In her *City of Ladies*, she mobilized numerous women from history, Christian and pagan alike, to demonstrate that women too could be active members of society and deserved an education equal to

PORTRAIT

Zheng He, China's Non-Chinese Admiral

At the helm of China's massive maritime expeditions in the early fifteenth century was a most unusual person named Zheng He.[6] Born in 1371 in the frontier region of Yunnan in southwestern China, his family roots were in Central Asia in what is now Uzbekistan. Both his father and grandfather were devout Muslims who had made the pilgrimage to Mecca. The family had also achieved local prominence as high officials serving the Mongol rulers of China for a century. Zheng He would surely have continued in this tradition had not a major turning point in China's history decisively altered the trajectory of his life.

Zheng He's birth, as it happened, coincided with the end of Mongol rule. His own father was killed resisting the forces of the new Ming dynasty that ousted the Mongols from Yunnan in 1382. Eleven-year-old Zheng He was taken prisoner along with hundreds of Mongols and their Muslim supporters. But young Zheng He lost more than his freedom; he also lost

Among the acquisitions of Zheng He's expeditions, none excited more interest in the Chinese court than an African giraffe. (The Philadelphia Museum of Art/Art Resource, NY)

his male sex organs, becoming a eunuch as he underwent castration. The practice had a long history in China as well as in Christian and Islamic civilizations. During the 276 years of the Ming dynasty (1368–1644), some 1 million eunuchs served the Chinese emperor and members of the elite. A small number became powerful officials, especially at the central imperial court, where their utter dependence upon and loyalty to the emperor gained them the enduring hostility of the scholar-bureaucrats of China's civil service. Strangely enough, substantial numbers of Chinese men voluntarily became eunuchs, trading their manhood for the possibility of achieving power, prestige, and wealth.

After his castration, pure chance shaped Zheng He's life as he was assigned to Zhu Di, the fourth son of the reigning emperor, who was then establishing himself in northern Chinese region around Beijing. Zheng He soon won the confidence of his master and eventually the almost seven-foot-tall

that of men. Aiding in the construction of this allegorical city is Lady Reason who offers to assist Christine in dispelling her poor opinion of her own sex. "No matter which way I looked at it," she wrote, "I could find no evidence from my own experience to bear out such a negative view of female nature and habits. Even so . . . I could scarcely find a moral work by any author which didn't devote some chapter or paragraph to attacking the female sex."[7]

Heavily influenced by classical models, Renaissance figures were more interested in capturing the unique qualities of particular individuals and in describing the world as it was than in portraying or exploring eternal religious truths. In its focus on the affairs of this world, Renaissance culture reflected the urban bustle and commercial preoccupations of Italian cities. Its secular elements challenged the otherworldliness of Christian culture, and its individualism signaled the dawning of a more capitalist economy of private entrepreneurs. A new Europe was in the making, one

eunuch proved himself an effective military leader in various skirmishes against the Mongols and in the civil war that brought Zhu Di to power as the Emperor Yongle in 1402. With his master as emperor, Zheng He served first as Grand Director of Palace Servants. Now he could don the prestigious red robe, rather than the blue one assigned to lower-ranking eunuchs. But soon Zheng He found himself with a far more ambitious assignment — commander of China's huge oceangoing fleet.

The seven voyages that Zheng He led between 1405 and 1433 have defined his role in Chinese and world history. But they also revealed something of the man himself. Clearly he was not an explorer in the mold of Columbus, for he sailed in well-traveled waters and usually knew where he was going. While his journeys were largely peaceful with no effort to establish colonies or control trade, on several occasions Zheng He used force to suppress piracy or to punish those who resisted Chinese overtures. Once he personally led 2,000 Chinese soldiers against a hostile ruler in the interior of Ceylon. He also had a keen eye for the kind of exotica that the imperial court found fascinating, returning to China with ostriches, zebras, lions, elephants, and a giraffe.

The voyages also disclose Zheng He's changing religious commitments. Born and raised a Muslim, he had not lived in a primarily Islamic setting since his capture at the age of eleven. Thus, it is hardly surprising that he adopted the more eclectic posture toward religion common in China. During his third voyage in Ceylon, he erected a trilingual tablet recording lavish gifts and praise to the Buddha, to Allah, and to a local form of the Hindu deity Vishnu. He also apparently expressed some interest in a famous relic said to be a tooth of the Buddha. And Zheng He credited the success of his journeys to the Taoist goddess Tianfei, protector of sailors and seafarers.

To Zheng He the voyages surely represented the essential meaning of his own life. In an inscription erected just prior to his last voyage, Zheng He summarized his achievements: "When we arrived at the foreign countries, barbarian kings who resisted transformation [by Chinese civilization] and were not respectful we captured alive, and bandit soldiers who looted and plundered recklessly we exterminated. Because of this, the sea routes became pure and peaceful and the foreign peoples could rely upon them and pursue their occupations in safety." But after his death, Zheng He vanished from the historical record, even as his country largely withdrew from the sea and most Chinese forgot about the unusual man who had led those remarkable voyages.

Questions: How might you describe the arc of Zheng He's life? What were its major turning points? How did Zheng He's castration shape his life?

more different from its own recent past than Ming dynasty China was from its pre-Mongol glory.

European Comparisons: Maritime Voyaging

A global traveler during the fifteenth century might be surprised to find that Europeans, like the Chinese, were also launching outward-bound maritime expeditions. Initiated in 1415 by the small country of Portugal, those voyages sailed ever farther down the west coast of Africa, supported by the state and blessed by the pope (see Map 12.3). As the century ended, two expeditions marked major breakthroughs, although few suspected it at the time. In 1492, Christopher Columbus, funded by Spain, Portugal's neighbor and rival, made his way west across the Atlantic hoping to arrive in the East and, in one of history's most consequential mistakes, ran into the

■ **Comparison**

In what ways did European maritime voyaging in the fifteenth century differ from that of China? What accounts for these differences?

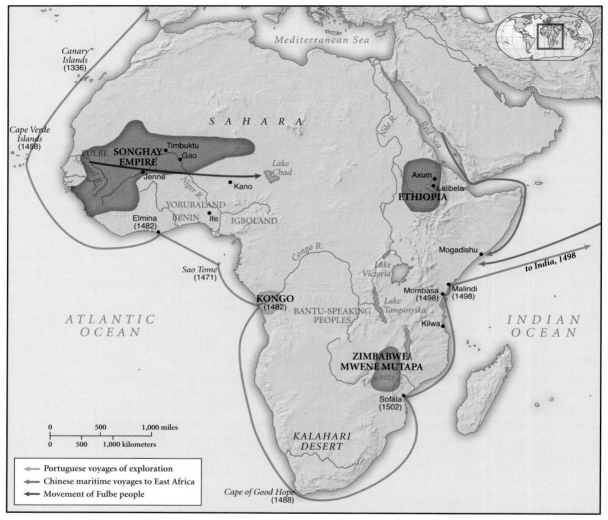

Map 12.3   Africa in the Fifteenth Century
By the 1400s, Africa was a virtual museum of political and cultural diversity, encompassing large empires, such as Songhay; smaller kingdoms, such as Kongo; city-states among the Yoruba, Hausa, and Swahili peoples; village-based societies without states at all, as among the Igbo; and nomadic pastoral peoples, such as the Fulbe. Both European and Chinese maritime expeditions touched on Africa during that century, even as Islam continued to find acceptance in the northern half of the continent.

Americas. Five years later, in 1497, Vasco da Gama launched a voyage that took him around the tip of South Africa, along the East African coast, and, with the help of a Muslim pilot, across the Indian Ocean to Calicut in southern India.

The differences between the Chinese and European oceangoing ventures were striking, most notably perhaps in terms of size. Columbus captained three ships and a crew of about 90, while da Gama had four ships, manned by perhaps 170 sailors.

These were minuscule fleets compared to Zheng He's hundreds of ships and a crew in the many thousands. "All the ships of Columbus and da Gama combined," according to a recent account, "could have been stored on a single deck of a single vessel in the fleet that set sail under Zheng He."[8]

Motivation as well as size differentiated the two ventures. Europeans were seeking the wealth of Africa and Asia—gold, spices, silk, and more. They also were in search of Christian converts and of possible Christian allies with whom to continue their long crusading struggle against threatening Muslim powers. China, by contrast, faced no equivalent power, needed no military allies in the Indian Ocean basin, and required little that these regions produced. Nor did China possess an impulse to convert foreigners to Chinese culture or religion as the Europeans surely did. Furthermore, the confident and overwhelmingly powerful Chinese fleet sought neither conquests nor colonies, while the Europeans soon tried to monopolize by force the commerce of the Indian Ocean and violently carved out huge empires in the Americas.

The most striking difference in these two cases lay in the sharp contrast between China's decisive ending of its voyages and the continuing, indeed escalating, European effort, which soon brought the world's oceans and growing numbers of the world's people under its control. This is why Zheng He's voyages were so long neglected in China's historical memory. They led nowhere, whereas the initial European expeditions, so much smaller and less promising, were but the first steps on a journey to world power. But why did the Europeans continue a process that the Chinese had deliberately abandoned?

In the first place, Europe had no unified political authority with the power to order an end to its maritime outreach. Its system of competing states, so unlike China's single unified empire, ensured that once begun, rivalry alone would drive the Europeans to the ends of the earth. Beyond this, much of Europe's elite had an interest in overseas expansion. Its budding merchant communities saw opportunity for profit; its competing monarchs eyed the revenue from taxing overseas trade or from seizing overseas resources; the Church foresaw the possibility of widespread conversion; impoverished nobles might imagine fame and fortune abroad. In China, by contrast, support for Zheng He's voyages was very shallow in official circles, and when the emperor Yongle passed from the scene, those opposed to the voyages prevailed within the politics of the court.

Finally, the Chinese were very much aware of their own antiquity, believed strongly in the absolute superiority of their culture, and felt with good reason that, should they desire something from abroad, others would bring it to them. Europeans too believed themselves unique, particularly in religious terms as the possessors of Christianity, the "one true religion." In material terms, though, they were seeking out the greater riches of the East, and they were highly conscious that Muslim power blocked easy access to these treasures and posed a military and religious threat to Europe itself. All of this propelled continuing European expansion in the centuries that followed.

The Chinese withdrawal from the Indian Ocean actually facilitated the European entry. It cleared the way for the Portuguese to penetrate the region, where they faced only the eventual naval power of the Ottomans. Had Vasco da Gama encountered Zheng He's massive fleet as his four small ships sailed into Asian waters in 1498, world history may well have taken quite a different turn. As it was, however, China's abandonment of oceanic voyaging and Europe's embrace of the seas marked different responses to a common problem that both civilizations shared—growing populations and land shortage. In the centuries that followed, China's rice-based agriculture was able to expand production internally by more intensive use of the land, while the country's territorial expansion was inland toward Central Asia. By contrast, Europe's agriculture, based on wheat and livestock, expanded primarily by acquiring new lands in overseas possessions, which were gained as a consequence of a commitment to oceanic expansion.

LearningCurve
bedfordstmartins.com
/strayer/LC ✓

Civilizations of the Fifteenth Century: The Islamic World

■ **Comparison**

What differences can you identify among the four major empires in the Islamic world of the fifteenth and sixteenth centuries?

Beyond the domains of Chinese and European civilization, our fifteenth-century global traveler would surely have been impressed with the transformations of the Islamic world. Stretching across much of Afro-Eurasia, the enormous realm of Islam experienced a set of remarkable changes during the fifteenth and early sixteenth centuries, as well as the continuation of earlier patterns. The most notable change lay in the political realm, for an Islamic civilization that had been severely fragmented since at least 900 now crystallized into four major states or empires (see Map 12.4). At the same time, a long-term process of conversion to Islam continued the cultural transformation of Afro-Eurasian societies both within and beyond these new states.

In the Islamic Heartland: The Ottoman and Safavid Empires

The most impressive and enduring of the new Islamic states was the Ottoman Empire, which lasted in one form or another from the fourteenth to the early twentieth century. It was the creation of one of the many Turkic warrior groups that had earlier migrated into Anatolia. By the mid-fifteenth century, these Ottoman Turks had already carved out a state that encompassed much of the Anatolian peninsula and had pushed deep into southeastern Europe (the Balkans), acquiring in the process a substantial Christian population. In the two centuries that followed, the Ottoman Empire extended its control to much of the Middle East, coastal North Africa, the lands surrounding the Black Sea, and even farther into Eastern Europe.

The Ottoman Empire was a state of enormous significance in the world of the fifteenth century and beyond. In its huge territory, long duration, incorporation of many diverse peoples, and economic and cultural sophistication, it was one of the great empires of world history. In the fifteenth century, only Ming dynasty China and the Incas matched it in terms of wealth, power, and splendor. The empire represented the emergence of the Turks as the dominant people of the Islamic world,

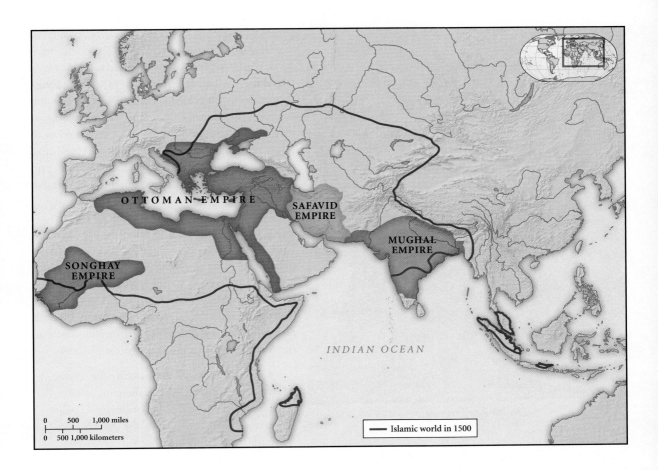

Map 12.4 Empires of the Islamic World
The most prominent political features of the vast Islamic world in the fifteenth and sixteenth centuries were four large states: the Songhay, Ottoman, Safavid, and Mughal empires.

ruling now over many Arabs, who had initiated this new faith more than 800 years before. In adding "caliph" (successor to the Prophet) to their other titles, Ottoman sultans claimed the legacy of the earlier Abbasid Empire. They sought to bring a renewed unity to the Islamic world, while also serving as protector of the faith, the "strong sword of Islam."

The Ottoman Empire also represented a new phase in the long encounter between Christendom and the world of Islam. In the Crusades, Europeans had taken the aggressive initiative in that encounter, but the rise of the Ottoman Empire reversed their roles. The seizure of Constantinople in 1453 marked the final demise of Christian Byzantium and allowed Ottoman rulers to see themselves as successors to the Roman Empire. In 1529, a rapidly expanding Ottoman Empire laid siege to Vienna in the heart of Central Europe. The political and military expansion of Islam, at the expense of Christendom, seemed clearly under way. Many Europeans spoke fearfully of the "terror of the Turk."

In the neighboring Persian lands to the east of the Ottoman Empire, another Islamic state was also taking shape in the late fifteenth and early sixteenth centuries — the

Ottoman Janissaries
Originating in the fourteenth century, the Janissaries became the elite infantry force of the Ottoman Empire. Complete with uniforms, cash salaries, and marching music, they were the first standing army in the region since the days of the Roman Empire. When gunpowder technology became available, Janissary forces soon were armed with muskets, grenades, and hand-held cannon. This image dates from the seventeenth century. (Austrian National Library, picture archive, Vienna: Cod. 8626, fol. 15r)

Safavid (SAH-fah-vihd) Empire. Its leadership was also Turkic, but in this case it had emerged from a Sufi religious order founded several centuries earlier by Safi al-Din (1252–1334). The long-term significance of the Safavid Empire, which was established in the decade following 1500, was its decision to forcibly impose a Shia version of Islam as the official religion of the state. Over time, this form of Islam gained popular support and came to define the unique identity of Persian (Iranian) culture.

This Shia empire also introduced a sharp divide into the political and religious life of heartland Islam, for almost all of Persia's neighbors practiced a Sunni form of the faith. For a century (1534–1639), periodic military conflict erupted between the Ottoman and Safavid empires, reflecting both territorial rivalry and sharp religious differences. In 1514, the Ottoman sultan wrote to the Safavid ruler in the most bitter of terms:

> You have denied the sanctity of divine law ... you have deserted the path of salvation and the sacred commandments ... you have opened to Muslims the gates of tyranny and oppression ... you have raised the standard of irreligion and heresy.... [Therefore] the *ulama* and our doctors have pronounced a sentence of death against you, perjurer and blasphemer.[9]

This Sunni/Shia hostility has continued to divide the Islamic world into the twenty-first century.

On the Frontiers of Islam: The Songhay and Mughal Empires

While the Ottoman and Safavid empires brought both a new political unity and a sharp division to the heartland of Islam, two other states performed a similar role on the expanding African and Asian frontiers of the faith. In the West African savannas, the Songhay Empire rose in the second half of the fifteenth century. It was the most recent and the largest in a series of impressive states that operated at a crucial intersection of the trans-Saharan trade routes and that derived much of their revenue from taxing that commerce. Islam was a growing faith in Songhay but was limited largely to urban elites. This cultural divide within Songhay largely accounts for the religious behavior of its fifteenth-century monarch Sonni Ali (r. 1465–1492), who gave alms and fasted during Ramadan in proper Islamic style but also enjoyed a reputation as a magician and possessed a charm thought to render his soldiers invisible to their enemies. Nonetheless, Songhay had become a major center of Islamic learning and commerce by the early sixteenth century. A North African traveler known as Leo Africanus remarked on the city of Timbuktu:

> Here are great numbers of [Muslim] religious teachers, judges, scholars, and other learned persons who are bountifully maintained at the king's expense. Here too are brought various manuscripts or written books from Barbary [North Africa] which are sold for more money than any other merchandise. . . . Here are very rich merchants and to here journey continually large numbers of negroes who purchase here cloth from Barbary and Europe. . . . It is a wonder to see the quality of merchandise that is daily brought here and how costly and sumptuous everything is.[10]

Sonni Ali's successor made the pilgrimage to Mecca and asked to be given the title "Caliph of the Land of the Blacks." Songhay then represented a substantial Islamic state on the African frontier of a still-expanding Muslim world. (See the photo on p. 241 for manuscripts long preserved in Timbuktu.)

The Mughal (MOO-guhl) Empire in India bore similarities to Songhay, for both governed largely non-Muslim populations. Much as the Ottoman Empire initiated a new phase in the interaction of Islam and Christendom, so too did the Mughal Empire continue an ongoing encounter between Islamic and Hindu civilizations. Established in the early sixteenth century, the Mughal Empire was the creation of yet another Islamized Turkic group, which invaded India in 1526. Over the next century, the Mughals (a Persian term for Mongols) established unified control over most of the Indian peninsula, giving it a rare period of political unity and laying the foundation for subsequent British colonial rule. During its first 150 years, the Mughal Empire, a land of great wealth and imperial splendor, undertook a remarkable effort to blend many Hindu groups and a variety of Muslims into an effective partnership. The inclusive policies of the early Mughal emperors showed that Muslim rulers could accommodate their overwhelmingly Hindu subjects in somewhat the same fashion as Ottoman authorities provided religious autonomy for their Christian peoples. In southernmost India, however, the distinctly Hindu kingdom of Vijayanagara flourished in the fifteenth century, even as it borrowed architectural styles from the Muslim states of northern India and sometimes employed Muslim mercenaries in its military forces.

Together these four Muslim empires—Ottoman, Safavid, Songhay, and Mughal—brought to the Islamic world a greater measure of political coherence, military power, economic prosperity, and cultural brilliance than it had known since the early centuries of Islam. This new energy, sometimes called a "second flowering of Islam," impelled the continuing spread of the faith to yet new regions. The most prominent of these was oceanic Southeast Asia, which for centuries had been intimately bound up in the world of Indian Ocean commerce, while borrowing elements of both Hindu and Buddhist traditions. By the fifteenth century, that trading network was largely in Muslim hands, and the demand for Southeast Asian spices was mounting as the Eurasian world recovered from the devastation of Mongol conquest and the plague. Growing numbers of Muslim traders, many of them from India, settled in Java and Sumatra, bringing their faith with them. Eager to attract those traders to their port cities, a number of Hindu or Buddhist rulers along the Malay Peninsula and in Indonesia converted to Islam, while transforming themselves into Muslim sultans and imposing Islamic law. Thus, unlike the Middle East and India, where Islam was established in the wake of Arab or Turkic conquest, in Southeast Asia, as in West Africa, it was introduced by traveling merchants and solidified through the activities of Sufi holy men.

The rise of Malacca, strategically located on the waterway between Sumatra and Malaya, was a sign of the times (see Map 12.1, p. 391). During the fifteenth century, it was transformed from a small fishing village to a major Muslim port city. A Portuguese visitor in 1512 observed that Malacca had "no equal in the world. . . . Commerce between different nations for a thousand leagues on every hand must come to Malacca."[11] That city also became a springboard for the spread of Islam throughout the region. In the eclectic style of Southeast Asian religious history, the Islam of Malacca demonstrated much blending with local and Hindu/Buddhist traditions, while the city itself, like many port towns, had a reputation for "rough behavior." An Arab Muslim pilot in the 1480s commented critically: "They have no culture at all. . . . You do not know whether they are Muslim or not."[12] Nonetheless, Malacca, like Timbuktu on the West African frontier of an expanding Islamic world, became a center for Islamic learning, and students from elsewhere in Southeast Asia were studying there in the fifteenth century. As the more central regions of Islam were consolidating politically, the frontier of the faith continued to move steadily outward.

LearningCurve
bedfordstmartins.com
/strayer/LC

SUMMING UP SO FAR

In what ways do the civilizations of China, Europe, and the Islamic world in the fifteenth century seem to be moving in the same direction, and in what respects were they diverging from one another?

Civilizations of the Fifteenth Century: The Americas

■ **Comparison**

What distinguished the Aztec and Inca empires from each other?

Across the Atlantic, centers of civilization had long flourished in Mesoamerica and in the Andes. The fifteenth century witnessed new, larger, and more politically unified expressions of those civilizations, embodied in the Aztec and Inca empires. Both were the work of previously marginal peoples who had forcibly taken over and absorbed older cultures, giving them new energy, and both were decimated in the sixteenth century at the hands of Spanish conquistadores and their diseases. To conclude this global tour of world civilizations, we will send our weary traveler to the Western Hemisphere for a brief look at these American civilizations (see Map 12.5).

The Aztec Empire

The empire known to history as the Aztec state was largely the work of the Mexica (Meh-SHEEH-kah) people, a semi-nomadic group from northern Mexico who had migrated southward and by 1325 had established themselves on a small island in Lake

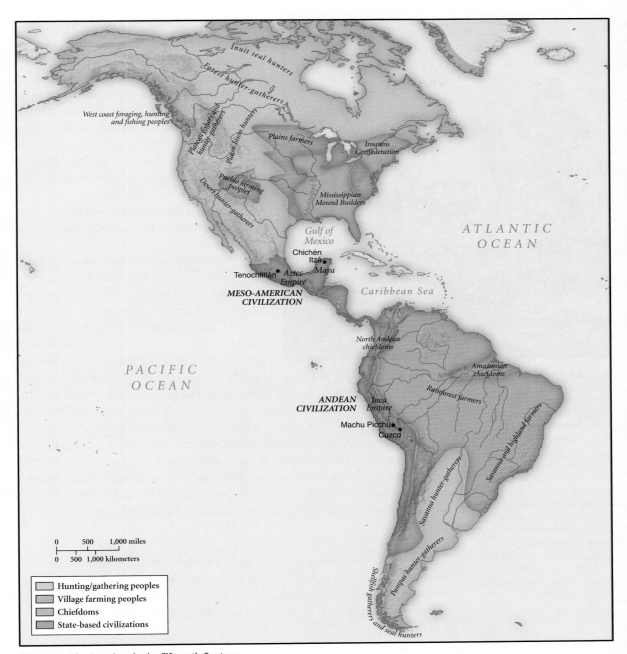

Map 12.5   The Americas in the Fifteenth Century

The Americas before Columbus represented a world almost completely separate from Afro-Eurasia. It featured similar kinds of societies, though with a different balance among them, but it completely lacked the pastoral economies that were so important in the Eastern Hemisphere.

Aztec Women
Within the home, Aztec women cooked, cleaned, spun and wove cloth, raised their children, and undertook ritual activities. Outside the home, they served as officials in palaces, priestesses in temples, traders in markets, teachers in schools, and members of craft workers' organizations. This domestic image comes from the sixteenth-century Florentine Codex, which was compiled by the Spanish but illustrated by Aztec artists. (The Art Archive at Art Resource, NY)

Texcoco. Over the next century, the Mexica developed their military capacity, served as mercenaries for more powerful people, negotiated elite marriage alliances with them, and built up their own capital city of Tenochtitlán. In 1428, a Triple Alliance between the Mexica and two other nearby city-states launched a highly aggressive program of military conquest, which in less than 100 years brought more of Mesoamerica within a single political framework than ever before. Aztec authorities, eager to shed their rather undistinguished past, now claimed descent from earlier Mesoamerican peoples such as the Toltecs and Teotihuacán.

With a core population recently estimated at 5 to 6 million people, the Aztec Empire was a loosely structured and unstable conquest state that witnessed frequent rebellions by its subject peoples. Conquered peoples and cities were required to regularly deliver to their Aztec rulers impressive quantities of textiles and clothing, military supplies, jewelry and other luxuries, various foodstuffs, animal products, building materials, rubber balls, paper, and more. The process was overseen by local imperial tribute collectors, who sent the required goods on to Tenochtitlán, a metropolis of 150,000 to 200,000 people, where they were meticulously recorded.

That city featured numerous canals, dikes, causeways, and bridges. A central walled area of palaces and temples included a pyramid almost 200 feet high. Surrounding the city were "floating gardens," artificial islands created from swamplands that supported a highly productive agriculture. Vast marketplaces reflected the commercialization of the economy. A young Spanish soldier who beheld the city in 1519 described his reaction:

Gazing on such wonderful sights, we did not know what to say, or whether what appeared before us was real, for on one side, on the land there were great cities, and in the lake ever so many more, and the lake was crowded with canoes, and in the causeway were many bridges at intervals, and in front of us stood the great city of Mexico.[13]

Beyond tribute from conquered peoples, ordinary trade, both local and long-distance, permeated Aztec domains. The extent of empire and rapid population growth stimulated the development of markets and the production of craft goods, particularly in the fifteenth century. Virtually every settlement, from the capital city to the smallest village, had a marketplace that hummed with activity during weekly market days.

The largest was that of Tlatelolco, near the capital city, which stunned the Spanish with its huge size, its good order, and the immense range of goods available. Hernán Cortés, the Spanish conquistador who defeated the Aztecs, wrote that "every kind of merchandise such as can be met with in every land is for sale there, whether of food and victuals, or ornaments of gold and silver, or lead, brass, copper, tin, precious stones, bones, shells, snails and feathers."[14] Professional merchants, known as *pochteca*, were legally commoners, but their wealth, often exceeding that of the nobility, allowed them to rise in society and become "magnates of the land."

■ **Description**
How did Aztec religious thinking support the empire?

Among the "goods" that the pochteca obtained were slaves, many of whom were destined for sacrifice in the bloody rituals so central to Aztec religious life. Long a part of Mesoamerican and many other world cultures, human sacrifice assumed an unusually prominent role in Aztec public life and thought during the fifteenth century. Tlacaelel (1398–1480), who was for more than half a century a prominent official of the Aztec Empire, is often credited with crystallizing the ideology of state that gave human sacrifice such great importance.

In that cyclical understanding of the world, the sun, central to all of life and identified with the Aztec patron deity Huitzilopochtli (wee-tsee-loh-pockt-lee), tended to lose its energy in a constant battle against encroaching darkness. Thus the Aztec world hovered always on the edge of catastrophe. To replenish its energy and thus postpone the descent into endless darkness, the sun required the life-giving force found in human blood. Because the gods had shed their blood ages ago in creating humankind, it was wholly proper for people to offer their own blood to nourish the gods in the present. The high calling of the Aztec state was to supply this blood, largely through its wars of expansion and from prisoners of war, who were destined for sacrifice. The victims were "those who have died for the god." The growth of the Aztec Empire therefore became the means for maintaining cosmic order and avoiding utter catastrophe. This ideology also shaped the techniques of Aztec warfare, which put a premium on capturing prisoners rather than on killing the enemy. As the empire grew, priests and rulers became mutually dependent, and "human sacrifices were carried out in the service of politics."[15] Massive sacrificial rituals, together with a display of great wealth, served to impress enemies, allies, and subjects alike with the immense power of the Aztecs and their gods.

Alongside these sacrificial rituals was a philosophical and poetic tradition of great beauty, much of which mused on the fragility and brevity of human life. Such an outlook characterized the work of Nezahualcoyotl (1402–1472), a poet and king of the city-state of Texcoco, which was part of the Aztec Empire:

Truly do we live on Earth?
Not forever on earth; only a little while here.
Although it be jade, it will be broken.
Although it be gold, it is crushed.
Although it be a quetzal feather, it is torn asunder.
Not forever on earth; only a little while here.[16]

The Inca Empire

While the Mexica were constructing an empire in Mesoamerica, a relatively small community of Quechua (KEHTCH-wah)-speaking people, known to us as the Inca, was building the Western Hemisphere's largest imperial state along the entire spine of the Andes Mountains. Much as the Aztecs drew on the traditions of the Toltecs and Teotihuacán, the Incas incorporated the lands and cultures of earlier Andean civilizations: the Chavín, Moche, Wari, and Tiwanaku. The Inca Empire, however, was much larger than the Aztec state; it stretched some 2,500 miles along the Andes and contained perhaps 10 million subjects. Although the Aztec Empire controlled only part of the Mesoamerican cultural region, the Inca state encompassed practically the whole of Andean civilization during its short life in the fifteenth and early sixteenth centuries.

Both the Aztec and Inca empires represent rags-to-riches stories in which quite modest and remotely located people very quickly created by military conquest the largest states ever witnessed in their respective regions, but the empires themselves were quite different. In the Aztec realm, the Mexica rulers largely left their conquered people alone, if the required tribute was forthcoming. No elaborate administrative system arose to integrate the conquered territories or to assimilate their people to Aztec culture.

■ **Description**

In what ways did Inca authorities seek to integrate their vast domains?

The Incas, on the other hand, erected a rather more bureaucratic empire. At the top reigned the emperor, an absolute ruler regarded as divine, a descendant of the creator god Viracocha and the son of the sun god Inti. In theory, the state owned all land and resources, and each of the some eighty provinces in the empire had an Inca governor. At least in the central regions of the empire, subjects were grouped into hierarchical units of 10, 50, 100, 500, 1,000, 5,000, and 10,000 people, each headed by local officials, who were appointed and supervised by an Inca governor or the emperor. A separate set of "inspectors" provided the imperial center with an independent check on provincial officials. Births, deaths, marriages, and other population data were carefully recorded on *quipus*, the knotted cords that served as an accounting device. A resettlement program moved one-quarter or more of the population to new locations, in part to disperse conquered and no doubt resentful people. Efforts at cultural integration required the leaders of conquered peoples to learn Quechua. Their sons were removed to the capital of Cuzco for instruction in Inca culture and language. Even now, millions of people from Ecuador to Chile still speak Quechua, and it is the official second language of Peru after Spanish.

But the sheer human variety of the Inca's enormous empire required great flexibility.[17] In some places Inca rulers encountered bitter resistance; in others local elites were willing to accommodate Incas and thus benefit from their inclusion in the empire. Where centralized political systems already existed, Inca overlords could delegate control to native authorities. Elsewhere they had to construct an administrative system from scratch. Everywhere they sought to incorporate local people into the lower levels of the administrative hierarchy. While the Incas required their subject peoples to acknowledge major Inca deities, these peoples were then largely free to carry on their own religious traditions. The Inca Empire was a fluid system that varied greatly from

Machu Picchu
Machu Picchu, high in the Andes Mountains, was constructed by the Incas in the 1400s on a spot long held sacred by local people. Its 200 buildings stand at some 8,000 feet above sea level, making it a "city in the sky." It was probably a royal retreat or religious center, rather than serving administrative, commercial, or military purposes. The outside world became aware of Machu Picchu only in 1911, when it was discovered by a Yale University archeologist. (fStop/Superstock)

place to place and over time. It depended as much on the posture of conquered peoples as on the Inca's demands and desires.

Like the Aztec Empire, the Inca state represented an especially dense and extended network of economic relationships within the "American web," but these relationships took shape in quite a different fashion. Inca demands on their conquered people were expressed, not so much in terms of tribute, but as labor service, known as *mita*, which was required periodically of every household.[18] What people produced at home usually stayed at home, but almost everyone also had to work for the state. Some labored on large state farms or on "sun farms," which supported temples and religious institutions; others herded, mined, served in the military, or toiled on state-directed construction projects.

Those with particular skills were put to work manufacturing textiles, metal goods, ceramics, and stonework. The most well known of these specialists were the "chosen women," who were removed from their homes as young girls, trained in Inca ideology, and set to producing corn beer and cloth at state centers. Later they were given as wives to men of distinction or sent to serve as priestesses in various temples, where they were known as "wives of the Sun." In return for such labor services, Inca ideology, expressed in terms of family relationships, required the state to provide elaborate feasts at which large quantities of food and drink were consumed. Thus the authority of the state penetrated and directed Inca society and economy far more than did that of the Aztecs.

If the Inca and Aztec civilizations differed sharply in their political and economic arrangements, they resembled each other more closely in their gender systems. Both societies practiced what scholars call "gender parallelism," in which "women and men operate in two separate but equivalent spheres, each gender enjoying autonomy in its own sphere."[19]

In both Mesoamerican and Andean societies, such systems had emerged long before their incorporation into the Aztec and Inca empires. In the Andes, men reckoned their descent from their fathers and women from their mothers, while Mesoamericans had long viewed children as belonging equally to their mothers and fathers. Parallel religious cults for women and men likewise flourished in both societies. Inca men venerated the sun, while women worshipped the moon, with matching religious officials. In Aztec temples, both male and female priests presided over rituals dedicated to deities of both sexes. Particularly among the Incas, parallel hierarchies of male and female political officials governed the empire, while in Aztec society, women officials exercised local authority under a title that meant "female person in charge of people." Social roles were clearly defined and different for men and women, but the domestic concerns of women—childbirth, cooking, weaving, cleaning—were not regarded as inferior to the activities of men. Among the Aztec, for example, sweeping was a powerful and sacred act with symbolic significance as "an act of purification and a preventative against evil elements penetrating the center of the Aztec universe, the home."[20] In the Andes, men broke the ground, women sowed, and both took part in the harvest.

None of this meant gender equality. Men occupied the top positions in both political and religious life, and male infidelity was treated more lightly than was women's unfaithfulness. As the Inca and Aztec empires expanded, military life, limited to men, grew in prestige, perhaps skewing an earlier gender parallelism. In other ways, the new Aztec and Inca rulers adapted to the gender systems of the people they had conquered. Among the Aztecs, the tools of women's work, the broom and the weaving spindle, were ritualized as weapons; sweeping the home was believed to assist men at war; and childbirth for women was regarded as "our kind of war."[21] Inca rulers did not challenge the gender parallelism of their subjects but instead replicated it at a higher level, as the *sapay Inca* (the Inca ruler) and the *coya* (his female consort) governed jointly, claiming descent respectively from the sun and the moon.

LearningCurve
bedfordstmartins.com
/strayer/LC

Webs of Connection

■ Connection

In what different ways did the peoples of the fifteenth century interact with one another?

Few people in the fifteenth century lived in entirely separate and self-contained communities. Almost all were caught up, to one degree or another, in various and overlapping webs of influence, communication, and exchange.[22] Perhaps most obvious were the webs of empire, large-scale political systems that brought together a variety of culturally different people. Christians and Muslims encountered each other directly in the

Ottoman Empire, as did Hindus and Muslims in the Mughal Empire. And no empire tried more diligently to integrate its diverse peoples than the fifteenth-century Incas.

Religion too linked far-flung peoples, and divided them as well. Christianity provided a common religious culture for peoples from England to Russia, although the great divide between Roman Catholicism and Eastern Orthodoxy endured, and in the sixteenth century the Protestant Reformation would shatter permanently the Christian unity of the Latin West. Although Buddhism had largely vanished from its South Asian homeland, it remained a link among China, Korea, Tibet, Japan, and parts of Southeast Asia, even as it splintered into a variety of sects and practices. More than either of these, Islam actively brought together its many peoples. In the hajj, the pilgrimage to Mecca, Africans, Arabs, Persians, Turks, Indians, and many others joined as one people as they rehearsed together the events that gave birth to their common faith. And yet divisions and conflicts persisted within the vast realm of Islam, as the violent hostility between the Sunni Ottoman Empire and the Shia Safavid Empire so vividly illustrates.

Long-established patterns of trade among peoples occupying different environments and producing different goods were certainly much in evidence during the fifteenth century, as they had been for millennia. Hunting societies of Siberia funneled furs and other products of the forest into the Silk Road trading network traversing the civilizations of Eurasia. In the fifteenth century, some of the agricultural peoples in southern Nigeria were receiving horses brought overland from the drier regions of Africa to the north, where those animals flourished better. The Mississippi River in North America and the Orinoco and Amazon rivers in South America facilitated a canoe-borne commerce along those waterways. Coastal shipping in large seagoing canoes operated in the Caribbean and along the Pacific coast between Mexico and Peru. In the Pacific, the Micronesian island of Yap by the fifteenth century was the center of an oceanic trading network, which included the distant islands of Guam and Palau, where large stone disks served as money. Likewise the people of Tonga, Samoa, and Fiji intermarried and exchanged a range of goods, including mats and canoes.

The great long-distance trading patterns of the Afro-Eurasian world, in operation for a thousand years or more, likewise continued in the fifteenth century, although the balance among them was changing (see Map 12.6). The Silk Road overland network, which had flourished under Mongol control in the thirteenth and fourteenth centuries, contracted in the fifteenth century as the Mongol Empire broke up and the devastation of the plague reduced demand for its products. The rise of the Ottoman Empire also blocked direct commercial contact between Europe and China, but oceanic trade from Japan, Korea, and China through the islands of Southeast Asia and across the Indian Ocean picked up considerably. Larger ships made it possible to trade in bulk goods such as grain as well as luxury products, while more sophisticated partnerships and credit mechanisms greased the wheels of commerce. A common Islamic culture over much of this vast region likewise smoothed the passage of goods among very different peoples, as it also did for the trans-Saharan trade.

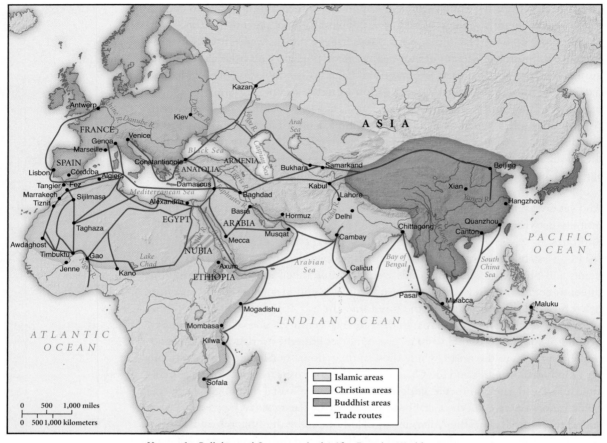

Map 12.6   Religion and Commerce in the Afro-Eurasian World

By the fifteenth century, the many distinct peoples and societies of the Eastern Hemisphere were linked to one another by ties of religion and commerce. Of course, most people were not directly involved in long-distance trade, and many people in areas shown as Buddhist or Islamic on the map practiced other religions. While much of India, for example, was ruled by Muslims, the majority of its people followed some form of Hinduism. And although Islam had spread to West Africa, that religion had not penetrated much beyond the urban centers of the region.

LearningCurve
bedfordstmartins.com
/strayer/LC

A Preview of Coming Attractions: Looking Ahead to the Modern Era, 1500–2012

While ties of empire, culture, and commerce surely linked many of the peoples in the world of the fifteenth century, none of those connections operated on a genuinely global scale. Although the densest webs of connection had been woven within the Afro-Eurasian zone of interaction, this huge region had no sustained ties with the Americas, and neither of them had meaningful contact with the peoples of Pacific

Oceania. That situation was about to change as Europeans in the sixteenth century and beyond forged a set of genuinely global relationships that generated sustained interaction among all of these regions. That huge process and the many outcomes that flowed from it marked the beginning of what world historians commonly call the modern age—the more than five centuries that followed the voyages of Columbus starting in 1492.

Over those five centuries, the previously separate worlds of Afro-Eurasia, the Americas, and Pacific Oceania became inextricably linked, with enormous consequences for everyone involved. Global empires, a global economy, global cultural exchanges, global migrations, global disease, global wars, and global environmental changes have made the past 500 years a unique phase in the human journey. Those webs of communication and exchange have progressively deepened, so much so that by the end of the twentieth century few people in the world lived beyond the cultural influences, economic ties, or political relationships of a globalized world.

Several centuries after the Columbian voyages, and clearly connected to them, a second distinctive feature of the modern era took shape: the emergence of a radically new kind of human society, first in Europe during the nineteenth century and then in various forms elsewhere in the world. The core feature of such societies was industrialization, rooted in a sustained growth of technological innovation. The human ability to create wealth made an enormous leap forward in a very short period of time, at least by world history standards. Accompanying this economic or industrial revolution was an equally distinctive and unprecedented jump in human numbers, a phenomenon that has affected not only human beings but also many other living species and the earth itself (see the Snapshot).

Moreover, these modern societies were far more urbanized and much more commercialized than ever before, as more and more people began to work for wages, to produce for the market, and to buy the requirements of daily life rather than growing or making those products for their own use. These societies gave prominence and power to holders of urban wealth—merchants, bankers, industrialists, educated professionals—at the expense of rural landowning elites, while simultaneously generating a substantial factory working class and diminishing the role of peasants and handicraft artisans.

Modern societies were generally governed by states that were more powerful and intrusive than earlier states and empires had been, and they offered more of their people an opportunity to play an active role in public and political life. Literacy in modern societies was far more widespread than ever before, while new national identities became increasingly prominent, competing with more local loyalties and with those of empire. To the mix of established religious ideas and folk traditions were now added the challenging outlook and values of modern science, with its secular emphasis on the ability of human rationality to know and manipulate the world. Modernity has usually meant a self-conscious awareness of living and thinking in new ways that deliberately departed from tradition.

Snapshot   **World Population Growth, 1000–2000**[23]

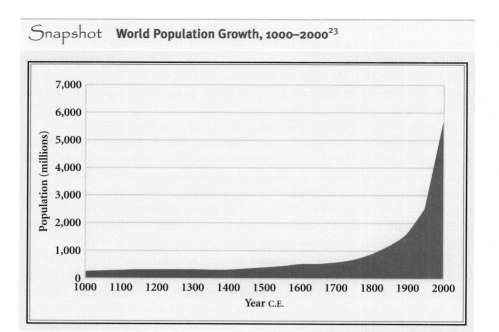

This revolution of modernity, comparable in its pervasive consequences only to the Agricultural Revolution of some 10,000 years ago, introduced new divisions and new conflicts into the experience of humankind. The ancient tensions between rich and poor within particular societies were now paralleled by new economic inequalities among entire regions and civilizations and a much-altered global balance of power. The first societies to experience the modern transformation—those in Western Europe and North America—became both a threat and a source of envy to much of the rest of the world. As modern societies emerged and spread, they were enormously destructive of older patterns of human life, even as they gave rise to many new ways of living. Sorting out what was gained and what was lost during the modern transformation has been a persistent and highly controversial thread of human thought over the past several centuries.

A third defining feature of the last 500 years was the growing prominence of European peoples on the global stage. In ancient times, the European world, focused in the Mediterranean basin of Greek culture and the Roman Empire, was but one of several second-wave civilizations in the Eastern Hemisphere. After 500 C.E., Western Europe was something of a backwater, compared to the more prosperous and powerful civilizations of China and the Islamic world.

In the centuries following 1500, however, this western peninsula of the Eurasian continent became the most innovative, most prosperous, most powerful, most expansive, and most imitated part of the world. European empires spanned the globe. European peoples created new societies all across the Americas and as far away as Australia and New Zealand. Their languages were spoken and their Christian religion was widely practiced throughout the Americas and in parts of Asia and Africa. Their businessmen bought, sold, and produced goods around the world. It was among Europeans that the Scientific and Industrial Revolutions first took shape, with enormously powerful intellectual and economic consequences for the entire planet. The quintessentially modern ideas of liberalism, nationalism, feminism, and socialism all bore the imprint of their European origin. By the beginning of the twentieth century, Europeans or peoples of European descent exercised unprecedented influence and control over the earth's many other peoples, a wholly novel experience in human history.

For the rest of the world, growing European dominance posed a common task. Despite their many differences, the peoples of Asia, Africa, the Middle East, the Americas, and Pacific Oceania all found themselves confronted by powerful and intrusive Europeans. The impact of this intrusion and how various peoples responded to it — resistance, submission, acceptance, imitation, adaptation — represent critically important threads in the world history of the past five centuries.

LearningCurve
bedfordstmartins.com
/strayer/LC

Reflections: What If? Chance and Contingency in World History

Seeking meaning in the stories they tell, historians are inclined to look for deeply rooted or underlying causes for the events they recount. And yet, is it possible that, at least on occasion, historical change derives less from profound and long-term sources than on coincidence, chance, or the decisions of a few that might well have gone another way?

Consider, for example, the problem of explaining the rise of Europe to a position of global power in the modern era. What if the Great Khan Ogodei had not died in 1241, requiring the Mongol forces then poised for an assault on Germany to return to Mongolia? It is surely possible that Central and Western Europe might have been overrun by Mongol armies as so many other civilizations had been, a prospect that could have drastically altered the trajectory of European history. Or what if the Chinese had decided in 1433 to continue their huge maritime expeditions, creating an empire in the Indian Ocean basin and perhaps moving on to "discover" the Americas and Europe? Such a scenario suggests a wholly different future for world history than the one that in fact occurred. Or what if the forces of the Ottoman Empire had taken the besieged city of Vienna in 1529? Might they then have incorporated even larger parts of Europe into their expanding domain, requiring a halt to Europe's overseas empire-building enterprise?

None of this necessarily means that the rise of Europe was merely a fluke or an accident of history, but it does raise the issue of "contingency," the role of unforeseen or small events in the unfolding of the human story. An occasional "what if" approach to history reminds us that alternative possibilities existed in the past and that the only certainty about the future is that we will be surprised.

Second Thoughts

What's the Significance?

Paleolithic persistence, 384
Igbo, 387–88
Iroquois, 388–89
Timur, 389
Fulbe, 390
Ming dynasty China, 390–91

European Renaissance, 393–97
Zheng He, 396–97
Ottoman Empire, 400–08
seizure of Constantinople
    (1453), 401
Safavid Empire, 401–02

Songhay Empire, 402–04
Timbuktu, 403
Mughal Empire, 403–04
Malacca, 404
Aztec Empire, 404–07
Inca Empire, 408–10

Big Picture Questions

1. Assume for the moment that the Chinese had not ended their maritime voyages in 1433. How might the subsequent development of world history have been different? What value is there in asking this kind of "what if" or counterfactual question?

2. How does this chapter distinguish among the various kinds of societies that comprised the world of the fifteenth century? What other ways of categorizing the world's peoples might work as well or better?

3. What common patterns might you notice across the world of the fifteenth century? And what variations in the historical trajectories of various regions can you identify?

4. **Looking Back:** What would surprise a knowledgeable observer from 500 or 1000 C.E., were he or she to make a global tour in the fifteenth century? What features of that earlier world might still be recognizable?

For Web sites and additional documents related to this chapter, see **Make History** at bedfordstmartins.com/strayer.

Next Steps: For Further Study

Terence N. D'Altroy, *The Incas* (2002). A history of the Inca Empire that draws on recent archeological and historical research.

Edward L. Dreyer, *Zheng He: China and the Oceans in the Early Ming Dynasty* (2006). The most recent scholarly account of the Ming dynasty voyages.

Halil Inalcik and Donald Quataert, *An Economic and Social History of the Ottoman Empire, 1300–1914* (1994). A classic study of the Ottoman Empire.

Robin Kirkpatrick, *The European Renaissance, 1400–1600* (2002). A beautifully illustrated history of Renaissance culture as well as the social and economic life of the period.

Charles Mann, *1491: New Revelations of the Americas before Columbus* (2005). A review of Western Hemisphere societies and academic debates about their pre-Columbian history.

J. R. McNeill and William H. McNeill, *The Human Web* (2003). A succinct account of the evolving webs or relationships among human societies in world history.

Michael Smith, *The Aztecs* (2003). A history of the Aztec Empire, with an emphasis on the lives of ordinary people.

"Ming Dynasty," http://www.metmuseum.org/toah/hd/ming/hd_ming.htm. A sample of Chinese art from the Ming dynasty from the collection of the Metropolitan Museum of Art.

"Renaissance Art in Italy," http://witcombe.sbc.edu/ARTHrenaissanceitaly.html. An extensive collection of painting and sculpture from the Italian Renaissance.

Notes

Prologue

1. Adapted from Carl Sagan, *The Dragons of Eden* (New York: Random House, 1977), 13–17.
2. See David Christian, *Maps of Time* (Berkeley: University of California Press, 2004).
3. Voltaire, *Treatise on Toleration*, chap. 22.
4. See David Christian, "World History in Context," *Journal of World History* 14, no. 4 (December 2003), 437–58.

Chapter 1

1. Richard Rainsford, "What Chance, the Survival Prospects of East Africa's Last Hunting and Gathering Tribe the Hadzabe, in a Gameless Environment?," Information about Northern Tanzania, March 1997, http://www.ntz.info/gen/n00757.html.
2. What follows comes from Sally McBreatry and Alison S. Brooks, "The Revolution That Wasn't: A New Interpretation of the Origin of Modern Human Behavior," *Journal of Human Evolution* 39 (2000): 453–563.
3. John Mulvaney and Johan Kaminga, *Prehistory of Australia* (Washington, DC: Smithsonian Institution Press, 1999), 93–102.
4. For a recent summary of this debate, see Charles C. Mann, *1491: New Revelations of the Americas before Columbus* (New York: Alfred Knopf, 2005), chap. 5.
5. Brian M. Fagan, *Ancient North America* (London: Thames and Hudson, 1995), 77–87.
6. Ben Finney, "The Other One-Third of the Globe," *Journal of World History* 5, no. 2 (1994): 273–85.
7. Fred Spier, *Big History and the Future of Humanity* (West Sussex: Wiley-Blackwell, 2011), 132; David Christian, *Maps of Time* (Berkeley: University of California Press, 2004), 143.
8. Richard B. Lee, *The Dobe Ju/'hoansi* (New York: Harcourt Brace, 1993), 58.
9. J. C. Beaglehole, *The Journals of Captain James Cook* (Cambridge: Hakluyt Society, 1968), 1:399.
10. Inga Clendinnen, *Dancing with Strangers* (Cambridge: Cambridge University Press, 2005), 159–67.
11. Steven Pinker, *The Better Angels of Our Nature* (New York: Viking, 2011), 47–52.
12. Marshall Sahlins, *Stone Age Economics* (London: Tavistock, 1972), 1–39.
13. Christopher Ehret, *The Civilizations of Africa* (Charlottesville: University of Virginia Press, 2002), chap. 2.
14. Marija Gimbutas, *The Language of the Goddess* (San Francisco: HarperCollins, 1989), 316–18.
15. D. Bruce Dickson, *The Dawn of Belief* (Tucson: University of Arizona Press, 1990), 210.
16. Derived from Christian, *Maps of Time*, 208.
17. Brian Fagan, *People of the Earth* (New York: HarperCollins, 1992), 200–201.
18. Charles C. Mann, "The Birth of Religion," *National Geographic*, June 2011, 35–59.
19. Bruce Smith, *The Emergence of Agriculture* (New York: Scientific American Library, 1995), 206–14.
20. Jared Diamond, *Guns, Germs, and Steel* (New York: Vintage, 1997), 132, 157–75.
21. Peter Bellwood, *First Farmers: The Origins of Agricultural Societies* (Malden, MA: Blackwell, 2005), 54–55.
22. Neil Roberts, *The Holocene: An Environmental History* (Oxford: Blackwell, 1998), 116.
23. Nina V. Federoff, "Prehistoric GM Corn," *Science* 302 (November 2003): 1158.
24. Theodora Kroeber, *Ishi in Two Worlds* (Berkeley: University of California Press, 1961), 229. See also Karl Kroeber and Clifton Kroeber, *Ishi in Three Centuries* (Lincoln: University of Nebraska Press, 2003).
25. Clive Ponting, *A Green History of the World* (New York: St. Martin's Press, 1991), 69.
26. Elizabeth Wayland Barber, *Women's Work: The First 20,000 Years* (New York: W. W. Norton, 1994), chap. 3.
27. Andrew Sherrat, "The Secondary Exploitation of Animals in the Old World," *World Archeology* 15, no. 1 (1983): 90–104.
28. Tom Standage, *A History of the World in Six Glasses* (New York: Walker and Company, 2005), chaps. 1, 2; Li Zhengping, *Chinese Wine* (Cambridge: Cambridge University Press, 2011), 1–3.
29. Anatoly M. Khazanov, *Nomads and the Outside World* (Madison: University of Wisconsin Press, 1994), 15.
30. Ian Hodder, "Women and Men at Catalhoyuk," *Scientific American* 15, no. 1 (2005): 35–41.
31. Marija Gimbutas, *The Language of the Goddess* (New York: Harper and Row, 1989), xix.

32. Allen W. Johnson and Timothy Earle, *The Evolution of Human Societies* (Stanford, CA: Stanford University Press, 2000), 281–94.

Chapter 2

1. Personal Development for Smart People Forum: Fun and Recreation, "Escaping Civilization," May 30, 2007, http://www.stevepavlina.com/forums/fun-recreation/7504 -escaping-civilization.html.
2. Charles C. Mann, *1491: New Revelations of the Americas before Columbus* (New York: Alfred A. Knopf, 2005), 174–91; Proyecto Arqueológico Norte Chico, "Project Description," Field Museum, 2005, http://archive.fieldmuseum.org/ research_collections/anthropology/anthro_sites/PANC/ proj_desc.htm.
3. Jonathan Mark Kenoyer, *Ancient Cities of the Indus Valley Civilization* (Oxford: Oxford University Press, 1998), 83–84.
4. David Christian, *A History of Russia, Central Asia and Mongolia* (Oxford: Blackwell, 1998), 114.
5. For a summary of many theories, see Stephen K. Sanderson, *Social Transformations* (Oxford: Blackwell, 1995), chap. 3.
6. Robert Carneiro, "A Theory of the Origin of the State," *Science* 169 (1970): 733–38.
7. Susan Pollock, *Ancient Mesopotamia* (Cambridge: Cambridge University Press, 1999), 48.
8. *The Epic of Gilgamesh*, translated and edited by Benjamin R. Foster (New York: W. W. Norton, 2001), 10, tablet 1: 226–32.
9. Samuel Noah Kramer, *History Begins at Sumer* (Philadelphia: University of Pennsylvania Press, 1981), 3–4.
10. James Legge, trans., *The Chinese Classics* (London: Henry Frowde, 1893), 4:171–72.
11. Margaret Ehrenberg, *Women in Prehistory* (London: British Museum, 1989), 107.
12. Sherry Ortner, "Is Female to Male as Nature Is to Culture?" in *Women, Culture, and Society*, edited by Michelle Rosaldo and Louise Lamphere (Stanford, CA: Stanford University Press, 1974), 67–88.
13. Gerda Lerner, *The Creation of Patriarchy* (New York: Oxford University Press, 1986), 70.
14. Marian Lichtheim, *Ancient Egyptian Literature* (Berkeley: University of California Press, 1975), 2:168–75.
15. Steven Pinker, *The Better Angels of our Nature* (New York: Viking, 2011), chaps. 2, 3.
16. Prologue to *The Code of Hammurabi*, http://www .thenagain.info/Classes/Sources/Hammurabi-Prologue.
17. Adolf Erman, *The Literature of the Ancient Egyptians*, translated by Aylward M. Blackman (London: Methuen, 1927), 136–37.
18. Henri Frankfort et al., *Before Philosophy: The Intellectual Adventure of Ancient Man* (Baltimore: Penguin Books, 1963), 39, 138.
19. Quoted in Peter Stearns et al., *World Civilizations* (New York: Longman, 1996), 1:30.
20. See Clive Ponting, *A Green History of the World* (New York: St. Martin's Press, 1991), chap. 5.
21. K. J. W. Oosthoek, "The Role of Wood in World History," Environmental History Resources, 1998, http://www .eh-resources.org/wood.html#_ednref1.
22. Pascal Vernus, *Affairs and Scandals in Ancient Egypt* (Ithaca, NY: Cornell University Press, 2003), 70–86; Toby Wilkinson, *Lives of the Ancient Egyptians* (London: Thames and Hudson, 2007), 259–61.
23. Cyril Aldred, *The Egyptians* (London: Thames and Hudson, 1998), 138.
24. For a summary of a long debate about the relationship of Egypt and Africa, see David O'Connor and Andrew Reid, eds., *Ancient Egypt in Africa* (London: UCL Press, 2003).
25. James B. Pritchard, ed., *Ancient Near Eastern Texts Relating to the Old Testament* (Princeton, NJ: Princeton University Press, 1969), 647–48.
26. Lichtheim, *Ancient Egyptian Literature*, 1:25–27.
27. M. J. Rowlands et al., eds., *Center and Periphery in the Ancient World* (Cambridge: Cambridge University Press, 1987), 59.

Part 2

1. Stephen K. Sanderson, *Social Transformation* (Oxford: Blackwell, 1995), chap. 4.
2. From ibid., 103.
3. Colin Ronan and Joseph Needham, *The Shorter Science and Civilization in China* (Cambridge: Cambridge University Press, 1978), 58.
4. William H. McNeill, *Plagues and Peoples* (New York: Doubleday, 1977), 94.

Chapter 3

1. Cullen Murphy, *Are We Rome? The Fall of an Empire and the Fate of America* (Boston: Houghton Mifflin, 2007).
2. J. M. Cook, *The Persian Empire* (London: J. M. Dent & Sons, 1983), 76.
3. George Rawlinson, trans., *The Histories of Herodotus* (London: Dent, 1910), 1:131–40.
4. Erich F. Schmidt, *Persepolis I: Structures, Reliefs, Inscriptions*, OIP 68 (Chicago: University of Chicago Press, 1953), 63.
5. Quoted in Anthony N. Penna, *The Human Footprint* (Oxford: Wiley-Blackwell, 2010), 151.
6. Quoted in Thomas R. Martin, *Ancient Greece from Prehistoric to Hellenistic Times* (New Haven, CT: Yale University Press, 1996), 86.

7. Christian Meier, *Athens* (New York: Metropolitan Books, 1993), 93.

8. Arrian, *The Campaigns of Alexander*, translated by Aubrey de Selincourt, revised by J. R. Hamilton (London: Penguin, 1971), 395–96.

9. Stanley Burstein, *The Hellenistic Period in World History* (Washington, DC: American Historical Association, 1996), 12.

10. Norman F. Cantor, *Antiquity* (New York: HarperCollins, 2003), 25.

11. Paul Halsall, "Early Western Civilization Under the Sign of Gender," in *A Companion to Gender History*, edited by Teresa A. Meade and Merry E. Wiesner-Hanks (London: Blackwell, 2004), 293–94.

12. Keith W. Taylor, *The Birth of Vietnam* (Berkeley: University of California Press, 1983), 334.

13. S. A. M. Adshead, *China in World History* (London: McMillan Press, 1988), 4–21.

14. See Padma Manian, "Harappans and Aryans: Old and New Perspectives on Ancient Indian History," *History Teacher* 32, no. 1 (1998): 17–32.

15. Roger Boesche, *The First Great Political Realist: Kautilya and His Arthashastra* (Lanham, MD: Lexington Books, 2002), 17.

16. Stanley Wolpert, *A New History of India* (New York: Oxford University Press, 1993), 90.

Chapter 4

1. "Birthday of Confucius . . . ," China View, September 28, 2009. [http://news.xinhuanet.com/english/2009-09/28/content_12123115.html]

2. S. N. Eisenstadt, ed., *The Origins and Diversity of Axial Age Civilizations* (Albany: SUNY Press, 1986), 1–4; Karen Armstrong, *The Great Transformation* (New York: Alfred A. Knopf, 2006).

3. Quoted in Arthur Waley, *Three Ways of Thought in Ancient China* (Garden City, NY: Doubleday, 1956), 159–60.

4. Nancy Lee Swann, trans., *Pan Chao: Foremost Woman Scholar of China* (New York: Century, 1932), 111–14.

5. Kam Louie and Morris Low, *Asian Masculinities* (London: Rutledge, 2003), 3–6.

6. Quoted in Huston Smith, *The Illustrated World's Religions* (San Francisco: HarperCollins, 1994), 123.

7. Lao Tsu, *Tao Te Ching*, translated by Gia-Fu Feng and Jane English (New York: Vintage Books, 1972), 80.

8. Catherine Clay et al., *Envisioning Women in World History* (New York: McGraw-Hill, 2009), 1:67–77.

9. Quoted in Karen Andrews, "Women in Theravada Buddhism," Institute of Buddhist Studies, accessed February 19, 2012, http://www.enabling.org/ia/vipassana/Archive/A/Andrews/womenTheraBudAndrews.html.

10. A. L. Basham, *The Wonder That Was India* (London: Sidgwick and Jackson, 1967), 309.

11. S. A. Nigosian, *The Zoroastrian Faith: Tradition and Modern Research* (Montreal: McGill–Queen's University Press, 1993), 95–97.

12. Isaiah 1:11–17.

13. Plato, *Apologia*, translated by Benjamin Jowett (1891).

14. Hippocrates, *On the Sacred Disease*, translated by Francis Adams, Internet Classics Archive, accessed February 2, 2012, http://classics.mit.edu/Hippocrates/sacred.html.

15. Thanissaro Bhikkhu, trans., "Karaniya Metta Sutta: Good Will," 2004, http://www.accesstoinsight.org/tipitaka/kn/snp/snp.1.08.than.html.

16. Matthew 5:43–44.

17. See Marcus Borg, ed., *Jesus and Buddha: The Parallel Sayings* (Berkeley, CA: Ulysses Press, 1997).

18. For a popular summary of the voluminous scholarship on Jesus, see Stephen Patterson et al., *The Search for Jesus: Modern Scholarship Looks at the Gospels* (Washington, DC: Biblical Archeological Society, 1994).

19. Galatians 3:28.

20. Cynthia Bourgeault, *The Meaning of Mary Magdalene* (Boston: Shambala, 2010).

21. Ephesians 5:22–23; 1 Corinthians 14:35.

22. Ekkehard W. Stegemann and Wolfgang Stegemann, *The Jesus Movement: A History of Its First Century* (Minneapolis: Fortress Press, 1999), 291–96.

23. Peter Brown, *The Rise of Western Christendom* (London: Blackwell, 2003), 69–71.

24. Robert Sider, "Early Christians in North Africa," *Coptic Church Review* 19, no. 3 (1998): 2.

25. "The Martyrdom of Saints Perpetua and Felicitas," *Frontline*, "From Jesus to Christ," PBS, April 1998, http://www.pbs.org/wgbh/pages/frontline/shows/religion/maps/primary/perpetua.html.

26. Mary Ann Rossi, "Priesthood, Precedent, and Prejudice: On Recovering the Women Priests of Early Christianity," *Journal of Feminist Studies* 7, no. 1 (1991): 73–94.

27. Chai-Shin Yu, *Early Buddhism and Christianity* (Delhi: Motilal Banarsidass, 1981), 211.

Chapter 5

1. Lydia Polgreen, "Business Class Rises in Ashes of Caste System," *New York Times*, September 10, 2010.

2. Po Chu-I, "After Passing the Examination," in *More Translations from the Chinese*, by Arthur Waley (New York: Alfred A. Knopf, 1919), 37.

3. Quoted in Michael Lowe, *Everyday Life in Early Imperial China* (New York: Dorset, 1968), 38.

4. "Ge Hong's Autobiography," in *Chinese Civilization*, 2nd ed., edited by Patricia B. Ebrey (New York: Free

Press, 1993), 91–96; Keith Knapp, "Ge Hong," *Internet Encyclopedia of Philosophy*, 2005, http://www.iep.utm.edu/gehong/.

5. Selected Poems from T'ang Dynasty, Li Shen, "Old Style," http://xinshi.org/xlib/lingshidao/hanshi/tang1.htm, accessed February 21, 2012.

6. Robert Ford Campany, *To Live as Long as Heaven and Earth* (Berkeley: University of California Press, 2002), 91–96.

7. Karl Jacoby, "Slaves by Nature: Animals and Human Slaves," *Slavery and Abolition* 15 (1994): 89–97.

8. Orlando Patterson, *Slavery and Social Death* (Cambridge, MA: Harvard University Press, 1982).

9. A. L. Basham, *The Wonder That Was India* (London: Sidgwick and Jackson, 1967), 152.

10. Sarah Pomeroy et al., *Ancient Greece* (New York: Oxford University Press, 1999), 63, 239.

11. R. Zelnick-Abramovitz, *Not Wholly Free* (Leiden: Brill, 2005), 337, 343.

12. Keith Bradley, *Slavery and Society at Rome* (Cambridge: Cambridge University Press, 1994), 30.

13. 1 Peter 2:18.

14. Milton Meltzer, *Slavery: A World History* (New York: Da Capo Press, 1993), 189.

15. Judith Bennett, *History Matters: Patriarchy and the Challenge of Feminism* (Philadelphia: University of Pennsylvania Press, 2006), chap. 4.

16. Quoted in Bret Hinsch, *Women in Early Imperial China* (Oxford: Rowman and Littlefield, 2002), 155.

17. Nancy Lee Swann, trans., *Pan Chao: Foremost Woman Scholar of China* (New York: Century, 1932), 111–14.

18. Lisa Raphals, *Sharing the Light: Representations of Women and Virtue in Early China* (Albany: SUNY Press, 1998).

19. Valerie Hansen, *The Open Empire* (New York: Norton, 2000), 183–84; Thomas Barfield, *The Perilous Frontier* (Cambridge: Blackwell, 1989), 140.

20. Vivian-Lee Nyitray, "Confucian Complexities," in *A Companion to Gender History*, edited by Teresa A. Meade and Merry E. Weisner-Hanks (Oxford: Blackwell, 2004), 278.

21. Aristotle, *Politica*, translated by H. Rackham, Loeb Classical Library No. 264 (Cambridge, MA: Harvard University Press, 1932), 1254b10–14.

22. Quoted in Pomeroy et al., *Ancient Greece*, 146.

Chapter 6

1. "Morales Becomes Head of a Pluri-national State Blessed by Aymara Gods," *MercoPress*, January 22, 2010, http://en.mercopress.com/2010/01/22/morales-becomes-head-of-a-pluri-national-state-blessed-by-aymara-gods.

2. Population figures are taken from Paul Adams et al., *Experiencing World History* (New York: New York University Press, 2000), 334.

3. "The Stela of Piye," accessed February 3, 2012, http://wysinger.homestead.com/piyevictorystela.html.

4. Toby Wilkinson, *Lives of the Ancient Egyptians* (London: Thames and Hudson, 2007), 287.

5. Stanley Burstein, "State Formation in Ancient Northeast Africa and the Indian Ocean Trade," History Cooperative, 2001, http://www.historycooperative.org/proceedings/interactions/burstein.html.

6. Roderick J. McIntosh, *Ancient Middle Niger* (Cambridge: Cambridge University Press, 2005), 10.

7. Roderick J. McIntosh, *The Peoples of the Middle Niger* (Oxford: Blackwell, 1998), 1776.

8. Richard E. W. Adams, *Prehistoric Mesoamerica* (Norman: University of Oklahoma Press, 2005), 16.

9. Richard E. W. Adams, *Ancient Civilizations of the New World* (Boulder, CO: Westview Press, 1997), 53–56; T. Patrick Culbert, "The New Maya," *Archeology* 51, no. 5 (1998): 47–51.

10. William Haviland, "State and Power in Classic Maya Society," *American Anthropologist* 94, no. 4 (1992): 937.

11. Jared Diamond, *Collapse: How Societies Choose to Fail or Succeed* (New York: Viking, 2005), chap. 5.

12. Esther Pasztory, *Teotihuacán: An Experiment in Living* (Norman: University of Oklahoma Press, 1997), 193.

13. George L. Cowgill, "The Central Mexican Highlands . . . ," in *The Cambridge History of the Native Peoples of the Americas*, vol. 2, pt. 1, "Mesoamerica," edited by Richard E. W. Adams and Murdo J. MacLeod (Cambridge: Cambridge University Press, 2000), 289.

14. Karen Olsen Bruhns, *Ancient South America* (Cambridge: Cambridge University Press, 1994), 126–41; Sylvia R. Kembel and John W. Rick, "Building Authority at Chavín de Huántar," in *Andean Archeology*, edited by Helaine Silverman (Oxford: Blackwell, 2004), 59–76.

15. Garth Bawden, *The Moche* (Oxford: Blackwell, 1996), chaps. 9, 10.

16. Gordon F. McEwan, *The Inca: New Perspectives* (New York: W. W. Norton, 2008), 39–41.

17. Charles C. Mann, *1491* (New York: Alfred A. Knopf, 2005), 234.

18. Kairn A. Klieman, *"The Pygmies Were Our Compass": Bantu and Batwa in the History of West Central Africa, Early Times to c. 1900 C.E.* (Portsmouth, NH: Heinemann, 2003), chaps. 4, 5.

19. Christopher Ehret, *The Civilizations of Africa* (Charlottesville: University of Virginia Press, 2002), 175.

20. David Schoenbrun, "Gendered Themes in Early African History" in *A Companion to Gender History*, edited by Teresa

Meade and Merry Wiesner-Hanks (Oxford: Blackwell, 2004), 253–56.

21. See Jan Vansina, *Paths in the Rainforest* (Madison: University of Wisconsin Press, 1990), 95–99.

22. John E. Kicza, *The Peoples and Civilizations of the Americas before Contact* (Washington, DC: American Historical Association, 1998), 43–44.

23. Much of this section draws on Brian M. Fagan, *Ancient North America* (London: Thames and Hudson, 2005), chaps. 14, 15. The quote is on page 345.

24. George R. Milner, *The Moundbuilders: Ancient Peoples of Eastern North America* (London: Thames and Hudson, 2004).

25. David Hurst Thomas, *Exploring Ancient Native America* (New York: Routledge, 1999), 137–42.

26. Stephen H. Lekson and Peter N. Peregrine, "A Continental Perspective for North American Archeology," *SAA Archeological Record* 4, no. 1 (2004): 15–19.

27. Fagan, *Ancient North America*, 475.

28. Quoted in Lynda Norene Shaffer, *Native Americans before 1492* (Armonk, NY: M. E. Sharpe, 1992), 70.

Part Three

1. Marshall G. S. Hodgson, *The Venture of Islam* (Chicago: University of Chicago Press, 1974), 1:71.

Chapter 7

1. Nayan Chanda, *Bound Together* (New Haven, CT: Yale University Press, 2007), 35–36.

2. William J. Bernstein, *A Splendid Exchange* (New York: Grove Press, 2008), 58–66; Proverbs 7:17–18.

3. Patricia B. Ebrey, *The Inner Quarters* (Berkeley: University of California Press, 1993), 150.

4. Seneca the Younger, *Declamations*, vol. 1.

5. Liu Xinru, "Silks and Religion in Eurasia, A.D. 600–1200," *Journal of World History* 6, no. 1 (1995): 25–48.

6. Jerry Bentley, "Hemispheric Integration, 500–1500 C.E.," *Journal of World History* 9, no. 2 (1998): 241–44.

7. See Jerry Bentley, *Old World Encounters* (New York: Oxford University Press, 1993), 42–53, 69–84.

8. Liu Xinru, *The Silk Road* (Washington, DC: American Historical Association, 1998), 10.

9. See William H. McNeill, *Plagues and Peoples* (New York: Doubleday, 1977), chaps. 3, 4.

10. Boccaccio, *The Decameron*, translated by M. Rigg (London: David Campbell, 1921), 1:5–11.

11. Kenneth McPherson, *The Indian Ocean* (Oxford: Oxford University Press, 1993), 15.

12. Janet L. Abu-Lughod, *Before European Hegemony* (Oxford: Oxford University Press, 1989), 269.

13. Stanley Burstein, "State Formation in Ancient Northeast Africa and the Indian Ocean Trade" (paper presented at Interactions: Regional Studies, Global Processes, and Historical Analysis, Library of Congress, Washington, DC, February 28–March 3, 2001), http://www.historycooperative.org/proceedings/interactions/burstein.html.

14. Nigel D. Furlonge, "Revisiting the Zanj and Revisioning Revolt," *Negro History Bulletin* 62 (December 1999), 7–14.

15. Patricia Risso, *Merchants and Faith: Muslim Commerce and Culture in the Indian Ocean* (Boulder, CO: Westview, 1995), 54.

16. McPherson, *Indian Ocean*, 97.

17. This section draws heavily on Craig A. Lockard, *Southeast Asia in World History* (Oxford: Oxford University Press, 2009), chaps. 2, 3. See also Victor Lieberman, *Strange Parallels* (Cambridge: Cambridge University Press, 2009), chaps. 1, 7.

18. Kenneth R. Hall, *Maritime Trade and State Development in Early Southeast Asia* (Honolulu: University of Hawaii Press, 1985), 101.

19. M. C. Horton and T. R. Burton, "Indian Metalwork in East Africa: The Bronze Lion Statuette from Shanga," *Antiquities* 62 (1988): 22.

20. Ross Dunn, *The Adventures of Ibn Battuta* (Berkeley: University of California Press, 1986), 124.

21. Christopher Ehret, *The Civilizations of Africa* (Charlottesville: University of Virginia Press, 2002), 255.

22. Ibid., 227–32.

23. Nehemia Levtzion and Jay Spaulding, eds., *Medieval West Africa: Views from Arab Scholars and Merchants* (Princeton, NJ: Marcus Wiener, 2003), 5.

24. David Schoenbrun, "Gendered Themes in Early African History" in *A Companion to Gender History*, edited by Teresa Meade and Merry Wiesner-Hanks (Oxford: Blackwell, 2004), 263.

25. Quoted in John Iliffe, *Africans: The History of a Continent* (Cambridge: Cambridge University Press, 1995), 75–76.

26. "The Saga of Eric the Red" and "The Saga of Thorsfinn Karlsefni" in *The Norse Discovery of America*, translated by Arthur Reeves et al. (London: Norroena Society, 1906), http://www.sacred-texts.com/neu/nda/index.htm.

27. J. R. McNeill and William McNeill, *The Human Web* (New York: W. W. Norton, 2003), 160.

28. Lauren Ristvet, *In the Beginning* (New York: McGraw-Hill, 2007), 165.

29. Maria Rostworowski de Diez Canseco, *History of the Inca Realm* (Cambridge: Cambridge University Press, 1999), 209–12.

30. Michael Haederle, "Mystery of Ancient Pueblo Jars Is Solved," *New York Times*, February 4, 2009.

31. Anthony Andrews, "America's Ancient Mariners," *Natural History*, October 1991, 72–75.

Chapter 8

1. *Guardian*, June 15, 2006.
2. John K. Fairbank, ed., *The Chinese World Order* (Cambridge, MA: Harvard University Press, 1968).
3. Quoted in Mark Elvin, *The Retreat of the Elephants* (New Haven, CT: Yale University Press, 2004), chap. 1. The quote is on page 19.
4. Mark Elvin, *The Pattern of the Chinese Past* (London: Eyre Methuen, 1973), 55.
5. Samuel Adshead, *Tang China: The Rise of the East in World History* (New York: Palgrave, 2004), 30.
6. Elvin, *Pattern of the Chinese Past*, pt. 2; William McNeill, *The Pursuit of Power* (Chicago: University of Chicago Press, 1984), 50.
7. See "The Attractions of the Capital," in *Chinese Civilization: A Sourcebook*, edited by Patricia B. Ebrey (New York: Free Press, 1993), 178–85.
8. Marco Polo, *The Travels of Marco Polo* (Toronto: General, 1993), 2:185.
9. John K. Fairbank, *China: A New History* (Cambridge, MA: Harvard University Press, 1992), 89.
10. J. R. McNeill and William H. McNeill, *The Human Web* (New York: W. W. Norton, 2003), 123.
11. Francesca Bray, *Technology and Gender: Fabrics of Power in Late Imperial China* (Berkeley: University of California Press, 1997), 116.
12. Patricia Ebrey, *The Inner Quarters* (Berkeley: University of California Press, 1993), 207.
13. Ibid., 37–43.
14. Ibid., 6.
15. See Nicolas DiCosmo, *Ancient China and Its Enemies* (Cambridge: Cambridge University Press, 2002), chap. 6.
16. Ibid., 94.
17. Quoted in Thomas J. Barfield, "Steppe Empires, China, and the Silk Route," in *Nomads in the Sedentary World*, edited by Anatoly M. Khazanov and Andre Wink (Richmond: Kurzon Press, 2001), 237.
18. Quoted in Edward H. Shafer, *The Golden Peaches of Samarkand* (Berkeley: University of California Press, 1963), 28.
19. Susan Mann, "Women in East Asia," in *Women's History in Global Perspective*, edited by Bonnie Smith (Urbana: University of Illinois Press, 2005), 2:53–56.
20. Joseph Buttinger, *A Dragon Defiant: A Short History of Vietnam* (New York: Praeger, 1972), 32–34; Jerry Bentley, *Old World Encounters* (New York: Oxford University Press, 1993), 85–86.
21. Liam C. Kelley, *Beyond the Bronze Pillars: Envoy Poetry and the Sino-Vietnamese Relationship* (Honolulu: University of Hawai'i Press, 2005).

22. Teresa Meade and Merry Wiesner-Hanks (eds.), *A Companion to Gender History* (Oxford: Blackwell, 2004), 188, 281–82, 332–33.
23. H. Paul Varley, "Japan, 550–838," in *Asia in Western and World History*, edited by Ainslee T. Embrey and Carol Gluck (Armonk, NY: M. E. Sharpe, 1997), 353.
24. Quoted in McNeill, *Pursuit of Power*, 40.
25. John K. Fairbank et al., *East Asia: Tradition and Transformation* (Boston: Houghton Mifflin, 1978), 353.
26. Quoted in Jane Hirshfield, trans., *The Ink Dark Moon* (New York: Vintage Books, 1990), xiii.
27. Edwin A. Cranston, trans., *The Izumi Shikibu Diary* (Cambridge, MA: Harvard University Press, 1969), 11.
28. Hirshfield, *Ink Dark Moon*, 94, 148.
29. Quoted in Earl Miner, *Japanese Poetic Diaries* (Berkeley: University of California Press, 1969), 33.
30. Cranston, *Izumi Shikibu Diary*, 18, 206.
31. Hirshfield, *Ink Dark Moon*, 49, 65, 96, 139.
32. Chieko Irie Mulhern, ed., *Japanese Women Writers* (Westport, CT: Greenwood Press, 1994), 155.
33. Compiled from Joseph Needham, *Science and Civilization in China* (Cambridge: Cambridge University Press, 1965), 1:242; and Robert Temple, *The Genius of China* (New York: Simon and Schuster, 1986).
34. Arnold Pacey, *Technology in World Civilization* (Cambridge, MA: MIT Press, 1991), 50–53.
35. McNeill, *Pursuit of Power*, 24–25.
36. Hugh Clark, "Muslims and Hindus in the Culture and Morphology of Quanzhou from the Tenth to the Thirteenth Century," *Journal of World History* 6, no. 1 (1995): 49–74.
37. Quoted in Arthur F. Wright, *Studies in Chinese Buddhism* (New Haven, CT: Yale University Press, 1990), 16.
38. Arthur F. Wright, *Buddhism in Chinese History* (Stanford, CA: Stanford University Press, 1959), 36–39.
39. Quoted in Wright, *Buddhism in Chinese History*, 67.
40. Quoted in Eric Zurcher, *The Buddhist Conquest of China* (Leiden: E. J. Brill, 1959), 1:262.
41. Jacquet Gernet, *A History of Chinese Civilization* (Cambridge: Cambridge University Press, 1996), 291–96.
42. Edwin O. Reischauer, *Ennin's Travels in Tang China* (New York: Ronald Press, 1955), 221–24.

Chapter 9

1. Letter from Malcolm X, April 1964. http://www.malcolm-x.org/docs/let_mecca.htm.
2. Reza Aslan, *No God but God* (New York: Random House, 2005), 14.
3. Quoted in Karen Armstrong, *A History of God* (New York: Ballantine Books, 1993), 146.
4. Quran 1:5 and 41:53.

5. Ibid., 3:110.

6. Ibid., 9:71.

7. "Prophet Muhammad's Farewell Sermon," http://www .islamicity.com/articles/Articles.asp?ref=ic0107-322.

8. Fred M. Donner, *Muhammad and the Believers* (Cambridge. MA: Harvard University Press, 2010), 114. The preceding section draws on chapter 3.

9. Richard Bulliet, *Conversion to Islam in the Medieval Period* (Cambridge, MA: Harvard University Press, 1979), 33.

10. Nehemiah Levtzion, ed., *Conversion to Islam* (New York: Holmes and Meier, 1979), chap. 1.

11. Bertold Spuler. *The Muslim World*, vol. 1, *The Age of the Caliph* (Leiden: E. J. Brill, 1960), 29.

12. Bernard Lewis, *Islam and the West* (New York: Oxford University Press, 1993), 157.

13. Quoted in Patricia Crone, "The Rise of Islam in the World," in *Cambridge Illustrated History of the Islamic World*, edited by Francis Robinson (Cambridge: Cambridge University Press, 1996), 14.

14. Aslan, *No God but God*, 201.

15. Quran 33:35.

16. Ibid., 4:34.

17. Quoted in Judith Tucker, "Gender and Islamic History," in *Islamic and European Expansion*, edited by Michael Adas (Philadelphia: Temple University Press, 1993), 46.

18. Nikki R. Keddie, "Women in the Middle East since the Rise of Islam," in *Women's History in Global Perspective*, edited by Bonnie G. Smith (Urbana: University of Illinois Press, 2005), 74–75.

19. Ria Kloppenborg and Wouter Hanegraaf, eds., *Female Stereotypes in Religious Traditions* (Leiden: E. J. Brill, 1995), 111.

20. Quoted in William T. de Bary, ed., *Sources of Indian Tradition* (New York: Columbia University Press, 1958), 2:355–57.

21. V. L. Menage, "The Islamization of Anatolia," in Levtzion, *Conversion to Islam*, chap. 4.

22. Ira M. Lapidus, *A History of Islamic Societies* (Cambridge: Cambridge University Press, 1988), 304–6.

23. Quoted in Keddie, "Women in the Middle East," 81.

24. Ross Dunn, *The Adventures of Ibn Battuta* (Berkeley: University of California Press, 1986), 300.

25. Al-Umari, "The Kingdoms of the Muslim Sudan," in *Medieval West Africa*, edited by Nehemia Levtzion and Jay Spaulding (Princeton, NJ: Markus Weiner, 2003), 60.

26. Marq de Villieres and Sheila Hirtle, *Timbuktu* (New York: Walker, 2007), 77.

27. Al-Umari, "Kingdoms of the Muslim Sudan," 59.

28. Ibid.

29. Jane I. Smith, "Islam and Christendom," in *The Oxford History of Islam*, edited by John L. Esposito (Oxford: Oxford University Press, 1999), 317–21.

30. Richard Eaton, "Islamic History as Global History," in Adas, *Islamic and European Expansion*, 12.

31. Francis Robinson, "Knowledge, Its Transmission and the Making of Muslim Societies," in Robinson, *Cambridge Illustrated History of the Islamic World*, 230.

32. Janet L. Abu-Lughod, *Before European Hegemony* (Oxford: Oxford University Press, 1989), 216–24.

33. Andrew Watson, *Agricultural Innovation in the Early Islamic World* (Cambridge: Cambridge University Press, 1983); Michael Decker, "Plants and Progress: Rethinking the Islamic Agricultural Revolution," *Journal of World History* 20, no. 2 (2009): 187–206.

34. Arnold Pacey, *Technology in World History* (Cambridge, MA: MIT Press, 1991), 8, 74.

35. Robinson, "Knowledge, Its Transmission," 215.

36. Ahmad Dallal, "Science, Medicine, and Technology: The Making of a Scientific Culture," in Esposito, *Oxford History of Islam*, chap. 4.

37. David W. Tschanz, "The Arab Roots of European Medicine," *Aramco World*, May–June 1997, 20–31.

Chapter 10

1. Louisa Lim, "In The Land of Mao, a Rising Tide of Christianity," *All Things Considered*, NPR, July 19, 2010, http://www.npr.org/templates/story/story.php?storyId =128546334.

2. This section relies heavily on Diarmaid MacCulloch, *Christianity: The First Three Thousand Years* (New York, Viking, 2010), chap. 8.

3. Oleg Grabar, "The Umayyad Dome of the Rock in Jerusalem," in *Late Antique and Medieval Art of the Mediterranean World*, edited by Eva R. Hoffman (London: John Wiley and Sons, 2007), 166.

4. Quoted in Roger Boase, ed., *Islam and Global Dialogue* (Burlington, VT: Ashgate, 2005), 95.

5. Martin Palmer, *The Jesus Sutras* (New York: Random House, 2001).

6. Jack Weatherford, *Genghis Khan and the Making of the Modern World* (New York: Crown, 2004), 29.

7. Leonora Neville, *Authority in Byzantine Provincial Society*, 950–1100 (Cambridge: Cambridge University Press, 2004), 2.

8. Quoted in Deno John Geanakoplos, *Byzantium: Church, Society, and Civilization Seen through Contemporary Eyes* (Chicago: University of Chicago Press, 1984), 389.

9. Quoted in ibid., 143.

10. Quoted in A. A. Vasiliev, *History of the Byzantine Empire* (Madison: University of Wisconsin Press, 1978), 79–80.

11. Quoted in Geanakoplos, *Byzantium*, 362.

12. Quoted in ibid., 369.

13. Rowena Loverance, *Byzantium* (Cambridge, MA: Harvard University Press, 2004), 43.

14. Daniel H. Kaiser and Gary Marker, *Reinterpreting Russian History* (Oxford: Oxford University Press, 1994), 63–67.

15. Quoted in Patrick J. Geary, *Before France and Germany* (New York: Oxford University Press, 1988), 79.

16. Quoted in Stephen Williams, *Diocletian and the Roman Recovery* (London: Routledge, 1996), 218.

17. Peter Brown, *The Rise of Western Christendom* (London: Blackwell, 1996), 305.

18. Quoted in John M. Hobson, *The Eastern Origins of Western Civilization* (New York: Cambridge University Press, 2004), 113.

19. Clive Ponting, *A Green History of the World* (New York: St. Martin's, 1991), 121–23.

20. Judith M. Bennett, *A Medieval Life* (Boston: McGraw-Hill, 1998).

21. Bonnie Anderson and Judith Zinsser, *A History of Their Own* (Oxford: Oxford University Press, 2000), 1:210.

22. Anderson and Zinsser, *History of Their Own*, 393–94.

23. Christopher Tyerman, *Fighting for Christendom: Holy Wars and the Crusades* (Oxford: Oxford University Press, 2004), 16.

24. Elizabeth Hallam, *Chronicles of the Crusades* (New York: Welcome Rain, 2000), 127.

25. Edward Peters, "The Firanj Are Coming—Again," *Orbis* 48, no. 1 (2004): 3–17.

26. Quoted in Peter Watson, *Ideas* (New York: Harper, 2006), 319.

27. Quoted in Jean Gimple, *The Medieval Machine* (New York: Holt, 1976), 178.

28. Quoted in Stuart B. Schwartz, ed., *Victors and Vanquished* (Boston: Bedford/St. Martin's, 2000), 147.

29. Quoted in Carlo Cipolla, *Before the Industrial Revolution* (New York: Norton, 1976), 207.

30. Quoted in S. Lilley, *Men, Machines, and History* (New York: International, 1965), 62.

31. See Toby Huff, *The Rise of Early Modern Science* (Cambridge: Cambridge University Press, 1993).

32. Quoted in Edward Grant, *Science and Religion from Aristotle to Copernicus* (Westport, CT: Greenwood Press, 2004), 158.

33. Quoted in L. Thorndike, *A History of Magic and Experimental Science* (New York: Columbia University Press, 1923), 2:58.

34. Quoted in Edward Grant, *God and Reason in the Middle Ages* (Cambridge: Cambridge University Press, 2001), 70.

35. Grant, *Science and Religion*, 228–29.

36. Marcia L. Colish, *Medieval Foundations of the Western Intellectual Tradition* (New Haven, CT: Yale University Press, 1997), 128.

Chapter 11

1. Jack Weatherford, *Genghis Khan and the Making of the Modern World* (New York: Crown, 2004), xv.

2. Giovanni Carpini, *The Story of the Mongols*, translated by Erik Hildinger (Boston: Braden, 1996), 54.

3. Data derived from Thomas J. Barfield, "Pastoral Nomadic Societies," in *Berkshire Encyclopedia of World History* (Great Barrington, MA: Berkshire, 2005), 4:1432–37.

4. Quoted in Peter B. Golden, "Nomads and Sedentary Societies in Eurasia," in *Agricultural and Pastoral Societies in Ancient and Classical History*, edited by Michael Adas (Philadelphia: Temple University Press, 2001), 73.

5. Thomas J. Barfield, *The Nomadic Alternative* (Englewood Cliffs, NJ: Prentice Hall, 1993), 12.

6. Anatoly Khazanov, "The Spread of World Religions in Medieval Nomadic Societies of the Eurasian Steppes," in *Nomadic Diplomacy, Destruction and Religion from the Pacific to the Adriatic*, edited by Michael Gervers and Wayne Schlepp (Toronto: Joint Center for Asia Pacific Studies, 1994), 11.

7. Quoted in J. Otto Maenchen-Helfer, *The World of the Huns* (Berkeley: University of California Press, 1973), 14.

8. Carter Finley, *The Turks in World History* (Oxford: Oxford University Press, 2005), 28–37.

9. Ibid., 40.

10. David Christian, *A History of Russia, Central Asia, and Mongolia* (London: Blackwell, 1998), 1:385.

11. Quoted in ibid., 389.

12. David Morgan, *The Mongols* (Oxford: Blackwell, 1986), 63–67.

13. Weatherford, *Genghis Khan*, 86.

14. Chinggis Khan, "Letter to Changchun" in E. Bretschneider, *Mediaeval Researches from Eastern Asiatic Sources*, Vol. I (London: Kegan, Paul, Trench, Trübner, 1875), 37–39.

15. Thomas T. Allsen, *Mongol Imperialism* (Berkeley: University of California Press, 1987), 6.

16. Chinggis Khan, "Letter to Changchun," 38.

17. Quoted in Weatherford, *Genghis Khan*, 111.

18. Barfield, *Nomadic Alternative*, 166.

19. Peter Jackson, "The Mongols and the Faith of the Conquered," in *Mongols, Turks, and Others*, edited by Reuven Amitai and Michael Biran (Leiden: Brill, 2005), 262.

20. Quoted in Christian, *History of Russia*, 425.

21. This portrait is based on Jack Weatherford, *The Secret History of the Mongol Queens* (New York: Random House, 2010), 116–26, 274.

22. Quoted in David Morgan, *Medieval Persia* (London: Longman, 1988), 79.

23. Morgan, *Medieval Persia*, 82.

24. Guity Nashat, "Women in the Middle East" in *A Companion to Gender History*, edited by Teresa A. Meade and Merry E. Wiesner-Hanks (London: Blackwell, 2004), 243.

25. Charles J. Halperin, *Russia and the Golden Horde* (Bloomington: Indiana University Press, 1985), 126.

26. Charles H. Halperin, "Russia in the Mongol Empire in Comparative Perspective," *Harvard Journal of Asiatic Studies* 43, no. 1 (1983): 261.

27. Quoted in Christopher Dawson, *Mission to Asia* (New York: Harper and Row, 1966), 83–84.

28. Thomas Allsen, *Culture and Conquest in Mongol Eurasia* (Cambridge: Cambridge University Press, 2001), 211.

29. Quoted in ibid., 121.

30. John Aberth, *From the Brink of the Apocalypse* (New York: Routledge, 2000), 122–31.

31. Quoted in John Aberth, *The Black Death: The Great Mortality of 1348–1350* (Boston: Bedford/St. Martin's, 2005), 84–85.

32. Michael Dols, *The Black Death in the Middle East* (Princeton, NJ: Princeton University Press, 1977), 212, 223.

33. Quoted in John Aberth, *A Knight at the Movies: Medieval History on Film* (New York: Routledge, 2003), 225.

34. Aberth, *Black Death*, 72.

35. Quoted in Dols, *Black Death in the Middle East*, 67.

36. Andre Gunder Frank, *ReOrient: Global Economy in the Asian Age* (Berkeley: University of California Press, 1998), 256.

37. Arnold Pacey, *Technology in World Civilization* (Cambridge, MA: MIT Press, 1990), 62.

Chapter 12

1. Winona LaDuke, "We Are Still Here: The 500 Year Celebration," *Sojourners*, October 1991.

2. Brian Fagan, *Ancient North America* (London: Thames and Hudson, 2005), 503.

3. Quoted in Charles C. Mann, *1491: New Revelations of the Americas before Columbus* (New York: Alfred A. Knopf, 2005), 334.

4. Louise Levanthes, *When China Ruled the Seas* (New York: Simon and Schuster, 1994), 175.

5. Niccolò Machiavelli, *The Prince* (New York: New American Library, 1952), 90, 94.

6. Edward Dreyer, *Zheng He* (New York: Pearson Longman, 2007).

7. Christine de Pisan, *The Book of the City of Ladies*, translated by Rosalind Brown-Grant (New York: Penguin Books, 1999), pt. 1, p. 1.

8. Frank Viviano, "China's Great Armada," *National Geographic*, July 2005, 34.

9. Quoted in John J. Saunders, ed., *The Muslim World on the Eve of Europe's Expansion* (Englewood Cliffs, NJ: Prentice Hall, 1966), 41–43.

10. Leo Africanus, *History and Description of Africa* (London: Hakluyt Society, 1896), 824–25.

11. Quoted in Craig A. Lockhard, *Southeast Asia in World History* (Oxford: Oxford University Press, 2009), 67.

12. Quoted in Patricia Risso, *Merchants and Faith* (Boulder, CO: Westview Press, 1995), 49.

13. Quoted in Stuart B. Schwartz, ed., *Victors and Vanquished* (Boston: Bedford/St. Martin's, 2000), 8.

14. Quoted in Michael E. Smith, *The Aztecs* (London: Blackwell, 2003), 108.

15. Smith, *Aztecs*, 220.

16. Miguel Leon-Portilla, *Aztec Thought and Culture*, translated from the Spanish by Jack Emory Davis (Norman: University of Oklahoma Press, 1963), 7.

17. For this perspective, see Michael E. Malpass and Sonia Alconini, *Distant Provinces in the Inca Empire* (Iowa City: University of Iowa Press, 2010).

18. Terence N. D'Altroy, *The Incas* (London: Blackwell, 2002), chaps. 11, 12.

19. For a summary of this practice among the Aztecs and Incas, see Karen Vieira Powers, *Women in the Crucible of Conquest* (Albuquerque: University of New Mexico Press, 2005), chap. 1.

20. Ibid., 25.

21. Louise Burkhart, "Mexica Women on the Home Front," in *Indian Women of Early Mexico*, edited by Susan Schroeder et al. (Norman: University of Oklahoma Press, 1997), 25–54.

22. The "web" metaphor is derived from J. R. McNeill and William H. McNeill, *The Human Web* (New York: W. W. Norton, 2003).

23. Graph from David Christian, *Map of Time* (Berkeley: University of California Press, 2004), 343.

Acknowledgments

Chapter 2

Benjamin R. Foster. From *The Epic of Gilgamesh,* translated by Benjamin R. Foster. Copyright © 2001 by W.W. Norton & Company. Used by permission of W.W. Norton & Company, Inc.

Miriam Lichtheim. *Ancient Egyptian Literature, Volume II The New Kingdom* by Miriam Lichtheim, (University of California Press, 1976). Used by permission of the University of California Press.

Adolf Erman. "He has come unto us . . ." from *The Literature of the Ancient Egyptians*, translated by Aylward M. Blackman. Copyright © 1927 Methuen. Reproduced by permission of Taylor & Francis Books UK.

Pritchard, James B. (ed.). *Ancient Near Eastern Texts Relating to the Old Testament—Third Edition with Supplement.* © 1950, 1955, 1969, renewed 1978 by Princeton University Press. Reprinted by permission of Princeton University Press.

Chapter 4

Lao Tsu. From *Tao Te Ching*, by Lao Tsu, translated by Gia-fu Feng and Jane English, translation copyright © 1972 by Gia-fu Feng and Jane English, copyright renewed 2000 by Carol Wilson and Jane English. Used by permission of Alfred A. Knopf, a division of Random House, Inc.

Chapter 8

Edward H. Shafer. *The Golden Peaches of Samarkand: A Study of T'ang*, (University of California Press, 1963). © 1985 by the Regents of the University of California. Published by the University of California Press. Used by permission of the University of California Press and the Estate of Edward H. Schafer.

Chapter 12

Miguel Leon-Portilla. *Aztec Thought and Culture*, translated from the Spanish by Jack Emory Davis. Copyright © 1963 by the University of Oklahoma Press. Used by permission of the University of Oklahoma Press.

Miguel Leon-Portilla. *Fifteen Poets of the Aztec World*. Copyright © 1992 by the University of Oklahoma Press. Used by permission of the University of Oklahoma Press.

Index

Note: Names of individuals are in **boldface** and: (f) figures, including charts and graphs; (i) illustrations, including photographs and artifacts in the narrative portion of the book only, not in the docutext sections; (m) maps; (t) tables; (v) visual sources, including all illustrations in the docutext portion of the book; (d) documents in the docutext portion of the book.

Abbasid dynasty (Arab)
　Baghdad as capital, 294, 308, 310
　collapse of, 294, 298
　Mongol conquest of, 370
　Ottoman connection to, 401
　scope of, 290(m)
　Silk Road trade, 223
　slave revolts, 232
　time frame of events, 283(t)
　Turks, rise to power in, 360
Abd al-Malik (Umayyad caliph), 318
Abd al-Rahman III (Spain, 912–961), 305
Aboriginal Australians
　broad spectrum diet, 29
　and cultural diffusion, 385
　Dreamtime, 15, 18
　exchange networks, 387
　in fifteenth century, 385–87
　firestick farming, 385, 387
　male power among, 21–22
　modern status, 21(i), 23
　rock art, 15(i), 387
Abraham (Old Testament), 134, 284, 285
Abu Amir al-Mansur (981–1002), 305
Abu Bakr (caliph), 292
Academy (Plato), 138, 347
Achaemenid dynasty (Persia, 558–330 B.C.E.), 90
Adulis (African port), 186
Aeschylus (Greek playwright), 96
Afghanistan, early civilizations in, 53, 98

Africa. *See also* East Africa; North Africa; West Africa; *specific countries*
　Agricultural Revolution, 28(m), 32
　civilizations of. *See* African civilizations
　in fifteenth century, 386(t), 398(m)
　human beginnings in, 3–4, 12–14
　Paleolithic migrations from, 12–14, 17(m)
　slave trade. *See* Africa and slave trade
Africa and slave trade
　and Arab empire, 232, 241
　historical context for, 232, 241
　and Sand Roads, 241
African civilizations
　Axum (Ethiopia), 185–88
　Bantu cultures, 200–203
　development compared to other continents, 180–82
　earliest, 9(m), 54
　East African, 236–38
　Egyptian, 48–49
　environment, impact on, 183
　in fifteenth century, 386(t), 390, 398(m)
　Ghana, 211, 239–40
　Kush, 73
　locations/sites of, 8–9(m), 85(m)
　Mali, 211, 239–41
　Meroë, 183–85
　Niger Valley, 188–90, 239
　pastoral societies, earliest, 39–40
　population estimates, second-wave civilizations, 182(t)
　Sand Roads, 238–41
　second-wave, 183–90
　Songhay, 211, 402–3
　Sudanic Africa commercial centers, 241
　Swahili, 211, 236–38
　Ta-Seti civilization, 54
　third-wave, 236–41
　trans-Saharan trade, 182, 238–41
　West African, 238–41
Africanus, Leo (North African traveler), 403

afterlife
　Buddhist rebirth, 129
　Daoist view of, 126
　Egyptian belief, 67–68, 70
　Hindu rebirth, 127, 161–62
　Mesopotamian belief, 67–68
　Zoroastrian view, 133
Agaw language (Axum), 187
agricultural innovations
　earliest civilizations. *See* tools
　engineered landscapes, 192
　floating gardens, 406
　hillside terracing, 192, 199
　horses, use of, 38, 342(t), 343
　plows, 270(t), 342(t), 343
　raised-field system, 199
　three-field crop rotation, 343
　water-related. *See* irrigation
　wheeled plow, 343
Agricultural Revolution, 26–43
　artistic traditions, 33(i), 38(i), 40(i)
　breakthroughs leading to, 26–27
　chiefdoms, 42–43
　civilizations, emergence from, 6, 26–27, 43, 48, 54–55
　and climate changes, 24, 28–30
　domestication during. *See* animal domestication; plant domestication
　environmental damage from, 20, 37–38
　Fertile Crescent, 29(m), 31–32
　and globalization of agriculture, 28–29(m), 34–36
　health and illness, 35, 37–38
　population growth during, 36–37
　spirituality and worship, 30
　women, role of, 29, 40–41, 59
agricultural village societies, 40–43
　early modern era (1450–1750), 387–89
　features of, 32, 38, 40–43, 363–65
　as kinship societies, 40–42, 202–3, 388–89
　spirituality and establishment of, 30

agriculture. *See also specific foods*
  development of. *See* Agricultural
    Revolution
  expansion, Middle Ages Europe, 332,
    343
  innovations related to. *See*
    agricultural innovations
Ahura Mazda (Persian deity), 90, 92,
  133, 133(i)
Ain Ghazal (Jordan) statues, 33(i)
Ain Jalut (Palestine), Mongol defeat in,
  364
air pollution
  Chinese civilizations, 108
  Roman empire, 108
Aisha (wife of Muhammad), 296
Akkad (Mesopotamia), 67(m)
  features of, 72
  warfare for expansion, 69
alchemy, 156
alcoholic beverages, production,
  early, 39
Alexander the Great (Macedonia,
    d. 323 B.C.E.), 98(i)
  Aristotle as teacher of, 138
  conquests, scope of, 96–98, 97(m),
    111, 133, 222
  Greek civilization, expansion by,
    97(m), 97–99
  intermarriage of, 99
Alexandria (Egypt), sophistication of,
  98–99
algebra, 310(t), 311, 342(t)
Ali (caliph), 292
Ali, Sonni (Songhay ruler), 303, 403
Allah, Muslims relationship with,
  285–86
Almoravid empire, 361, 361(m)
Alopen (Persian Christian monk), 142
alphabet. *See* writing systems
American Indians. *See* Native
    Americans (of North America);
    North American cultures
Americas. *See also* Mesoamerica; North
    America; South America
  American Web trade and commerce,
    243–44, 244(m)
  civilizations, lack of contact, 242–43
  in fifteenth century/pre-Columbian,
    405(m)
  Paleolithic migration to, 8(m)
  pre-Columbia, groupings of people,
    203–4

second-wave civilizations. *See*
    Andean civilizations;
    Mesoamerican civilizations; North
    American cultures
Amitabha (Buddha), 274
Amos (prophet), 118
Amos (prophet, Judaism), 120(t), 135
Amun (Egyptian creator-god), 186(i),
    186–87
Analects (Confucius), 121
Ananda (Buddha's attendant), 130
Anasazi people. *See* Ancestral Pueblo
Anatolia
  agricultural villages, 30, 41
  in Byzantine Empire, 323(m)
  Christianity, spread to, 141
  Greek settlements in, 136
  Islam, spread to, 300–302, 301(m),
    360
  in Ottoman empire, 300–302, 301(m)
  Paleolithic settlements, 25(i), 25–26
ancestor worship
  Bantu cultures, 202, 203(i)
  Chinese worship, 123
  Dreamtime account of, 15, 15(i), 18
  Mongols, 361–62
  Paleolithic societies, 15, 18, 23
  Swahili civilization, 236
Ancestral Pueblo, 204(m), 204–6
  exchange networks, 205
  religious system of, 205(i), 205–6
al-Andalus, use of term, 304
Andean civilizations, 50(m), 84(m),
    195–200, 196(m). *See also specific*
    civilizations
  agriculture, 189–90, 197, 199
  American Web trade and commerce,
    244(m), 244–45
  Chavín, 196–97
  exchange networks, 199
  in fifteenth century, 386(t), 408–10
  Inca, 245, 408–10
  Moche, 197–99
  Norte Chico, 49, 50(m), 52
  Tiwanaku, 199–200
  Wari, 199–200
Angkor kingdom
  Angkor Wat (Hindu complex), 235,
    235(i)
  women, role in, 235
Anglo-Saxons, in Roman empire,
    109–10
Angra Mainyu (Persian deity), 133

animal domestication, 31–34
  animal husbandry, 39–40, 40(i), 354
  continental differences, 5–6
  herding nomads. *See* nomadic
    societies; pastoral societies
  impetus for, 33, 39–40, 41(i)
  secondary products revolution, 38–39
  and spread of disease, 37–38
animal extinction, Paleolithic era
    mammals, 18, 20, 22
animals
  domestication. *See* animal
    domestication
  Paleolithic depictions of, 10, 14, 23, 26
animism, 23
An Lushan rebellion (755–763), 275
Anselm (Christian scholar), 346
anthrax, 228
anti-Semitism, and Crusades, 339(m), 340
Aotearoa (New Zealand), 19
Apedemek (Meroë god), 185
Appian Way (Roman road), 167
aqueducts, Roman, 83
Aquinas, Thomas (Christian
    theologian), 347
Arab empire, 288–97
  Abbasid dynasty, 294
  caliphs, 292–94
  Christian communities within, 318–19
  collapse of, 298
  conquered people, policy toward,
    289–91
  dhimmis (people of the book) in, 290,
    319–20
  influence on other cultures, 291–92
  invasions by, goals of, 289
  Islam, conversion to, 291–92
  Islam and development of, 288–89, 359
  Islamic sects, conflicts, 292–95
  jizya (tax on non-Muslims), 290, 291,
    318
  Middle Eastern conquests, 318
  nomadic roots of, 356(t), 359
  scope of, 214, 231–32, 289
  slavery in, 232, 241
  Spain in, 289, 304
  trade routes, control of, 359
  Umayyad dynasty, 293–94, 318
Arabia
  empire-building. *See* Arab empire
  Islam, birth and development in, 212,
    282–88
  Islam and unification of, 288

pastoral societies, 356(t)
polytheism, pre-Islam, 283–85
strategic location of, 283–84, 284(m)
Arab Spring (2011), 281
Aramaic language, 141
architecture. *See also* ceremonial
centers; churches; mosques;
palaces; pyramids; temples
mound-builders, 43(i), 206–7
obelisks, 186, 188(i)
Paleolithic structures, 25(i)
aristocracy. *See* elites; nobility
Aristotle (384–322 B.C.E.)
key teaching of, 120(t), 138
Middle Ages interest in, 347
women, view of, 171, 173
Arius (Egyptian priest), 324
Arjuna (Hindu warrior), 131
armed forces. *See* military; warfare;
warrior societies
Armenia
Christian communities in, 318
Christianity, spread to, 142
*Arthashastra (The Science of Worldly
Wealth)*, 112
artisans
Mayan, 192
Meroë, 183–84
Moche, 197
Mongol empire, 365
women as, Middle Ages, 334–35
artistic traditions
Aboriginal Australian rock art, 15(i),
387
Agricultural Revolution era, 33(i),
38(i), 40(i)
Bantu, 203(i)
Black Death (plague) era, 378(i)
Buddha, depictions of, 129(i), 226(i)
building styles. *See* architecture
Chavín de Huántar, 196–97
Chinese bronze works, 53(i)
Chinese ceramics, 218(i), 219
Chinese painting, 116(i), 117, 122(i),
124(i), 155(i), 156(i), 169(i), 170(i),
264(i), 365(i)
Chinese terra-cotta army, 86(i), 87
Crusades era, 340(i)
Egyptian, 46(i), 47, 70(i), 186(i)
goddess figurines, 14–15, 23, 23(i)
Greek, 172(i)
Indian, 113(i), 128(i), 150(i), 352(i), 353
Islamic, 281, 285(i), 295(i), 296(i), 308(i)

Japanese, 266(i), 268(i)
Jenne-jeno terra-cotta statues, 189(i)
lost wax method, 388(i)
Luba statue (Bantu), 203(i)
Moche, 198
Mongols, representation of, 365(i),
370(i), 372(i), 373(i)
Niger Valley civilizations, 189(i)
Nok culture clay figures, 38(i)
Olmec monumental carvings, 54, 64,
64(i), 66
Paleolithic, 10(i), 14(i), 14–15, 15(i), 40(i)
Renaissance, 368(i), 393–94
rock art, 10(i), 11, 15(i), 40(i)
Roman, 98(i), 144(i), 164(i)
Spartan, 173(i)
Sunga era sculpture, 151(i)
Teotihuacán, 194–95
Turks, 360(i)
written word. *See* literature
Aryan peoples, 111, 159–60
Asarte (Phoenician goddess), 72
Ashoka (India, r. 268–232 B.C.E.), 113(i)
Buddhism, conversion to, 112, 130
enlightenment, legacy of, 112, 114, 144
Greek influence on, 98
Aspasia (Greece, ca. 470–400 B.C.E.), 172
Assyria (Mesopotamia), 67(m)
warfare for expansion, 69, 79, 134
astronomy
Ancestral Pueblo, 205
Chinese achievements, 248(i), 249
Greek achievements, 136
Indian civilizations, 113
Mayan, 192
Muslim achievements, 309, 309(i),
310(t), 376–77
observatories, 309, 309(i), 310(t)
Athaulf (Visigoths, r. 410–415), 329
atheists, 143
Athens, ancient. *See also* Greek
civilization
Athenian democracy, 94–96
disease/epidemics, 227
slavery, 164–65
Attila (Huns), meets Pope Leo I, 110(i)
Augustine (Saint, 354–430 C.E.), 142
on slavery, 165
Augustus (Rome, r. 27 B.C.E.–14 C.E.),
as first emperor, 103
Australia
Agricultural Revolution, absence
of, 29

early humans in, 4
in fifteenth century, 386(t)
gathering and hunting people of. *See*
Aboriginal Australians
Paleolithic migrations to, 15, 17(m), 18
population estimates, second-wave
civilizations, 182(t)
Austronesian-speaking peoples
Madagascar, settlement of, 19, 19(m),
230
Paleolithic migrations of, 19, 19(m), 35
Averroës. *See* Ibn Rushd (Averroës,
1126–1198)
Avicenna. *See* Ibn Sina (Avicenna,
980–1037)
Axum (Ethiopia), 184(m), 185–88
agriculture, 185–86
Christianity, spread to, 143, 181(t),
187–88, 231, 320–21
conquest of Meroë, 185
features of, 185–88
obelisks, 186, 188(i)
trade, 186, 188
Aztec empire, 404–7
capital of. see Tenochtitlán
(Mesoamerica)
emergence of, 212, 406
features of, 406–7
gender parallelism, 410
human sacrifice, 407
precursors to, 406
religious system of, 407
scope of, 405(m)
Spanish view of, 406
splendor and wealth of, 341, 406–7
trade and *pochteca*, 245, 407
Triple Alliance and power of, 406
women, status of, 406(i), 410

Babylon (Mesopotamia), 51(m), 67(m)
diplomacy with Egypt, 74–75
Hebrew exile from, 91, 134
warfare for expansion, 69, 79
Bacon, Roger (English scholar), 344
Bactria, Greek influence on, 99
Baghdad (Iraq)
as Abbasid capital, 294, 308, 310
Mongol conquest of, 370
women, segregation of, 297
Balkans
in Byzantine Empire, 322, 323(m)
Eastern Orthodox Christianity in, 327
in Ottoman empire, 400

ball game, Olmecs, 54
Baltic Sea region, Crusades in, 338, 339(m)
Banpo (China), agricultural village, 38
Bantu cultures, 184(m), 200–203
    cross-cultural encounters, 201–2
    expansion, method of, 200–201
    geographic origin of, 200
    Paleolithic migrations of, 35, 35(m)
    religious system of, 203
Ban Zhao (China, 45–116 C.E.), 123, 169
barbarians
    China, assimilation of, 107–8, 162,
        250, 260–61
    Germanic peoples viewed as, 110(i),
        329, 379–80
    nomadic peoples viewed as, 257–58,
        379–80
    Roman slaves viewed as, 165
Batwa (Pygmy) people, 201
B.C.E./B.C., defined, 6–7
Bedouins (Arab nomads), 282–83,
    356(t), 359
beer, 39
Beguines, 335–36
Beijing (China)
    as capital city, 391
    Khanbalik, Mongol capital, 367
Believers' Movement (Islam), 290
Berbers
    and Almoravid empire, 360, 361(m)
    conquest of Spain, 304
    as pastoral society, 356(t), 360
    trans-Saharan trade, 182
Bering Strait, Paleolithic migrations
    across, 18
Bernal, Martin, 73
Bernard of Clairvaux (French
    abbot), 340
bezant (coin), 326
Bhagavad Gita (The Song of the Lord),
    131–32
bhakti (worship) movement, 132
Bible. *See* New Testament; Old
    Testament
Bini people, 388
bin Laden, Osama, death of, 281
al-Biruni (973–1048), 310(t)
bishop of Rome. *See* pope and papacy
bishops, Eastern Orthodox, 324
Black Athena (Bernal), 73
Black Death (plague), 377–79
    as apocalyptic event, 378
    area of origin, 375(m), 377

artistic representations of, 378(i)
empires weakened by, 228, 379
during Mongol rule, 228, 377–79
population losses from, 227, 228
societal impact of, 378–79
spread of, 215, 221, 228, 375(m), 377
victims, handling and burial, 378(i)
bloodletting, Olmecs, 54
Boabdil (Muslim ruler), 306
boats. *See also* ships
    junks, 230
    Paleolithic era, 15, 19–20, 230
Boccaccio, Giovanni (Italy), on Black
    Death (plague), 228
bodhisattvas, 131
    Silk Roads Buddhism, 227
Bolivia, early civilization. *See* Tiwanaku
    civilization (Bolivia)
Bologna, University of (Italy), 346(i)
Bornu, Islam, spread to, 302(m)
Borobudur (Buddhist monument), 234,
    234(i)
Boudica (Celtic queen), 102(i)
Bouillon, Godefroi de, 340(i)
BP (before the present), 6–7
Brahman (World Soul), 127
Brahmanism, 120(t)
Brahmins, 159–61
    Buddhist rejection of, 129
    and Vedas, 126–27
Britain. *See* England
British empire, as new Roman empire,
    114
broad spectrum diet, 29
bronze art works
    Chinese civilizations, 53(i), 54
    lost wax method, 388(i)
bronze metallurgy, Chinese
    civilizations, 73
brothels, China/Mongol empire, 253
bubonic plague. *See* Black Death (plague)
Buddha
    early life (Siddhartha Gautama),
        128–29
    Greek-like depiction of, 99
    images, symbols in, 129(i)
    Jesus compared to, 139–40
    teachings of. *See* Buddhism
Buddhism
    bodhisattvas, 131, 227
    Chinese attack on, 275–76
    in Chinese civilizations, 107, 170–71,
        226–27, 250, 272–76, 273(m)

Chinese revival, post-Mao, 117
Confucianism compared to, 272–73
Diamond Sutra, 271
Greek culture and, 227
Hinduism relationship to, 129, 132,
    144–45
on impermanence, 174–75
Indian decline, 132
Indian origins of, 128–31
innovations and discoveries, 269, 271
Japan, 266–67
Mahayana, 131, 140, 227, 274
monasticism, 225–26, 274–75
nuns, 130, 168
printed texts, 269, 271
Pure Land, 274
sects and offshoots, 146, 147, 227
silk, use of, 225
Southeast Asia civilizations, 113,
    234–35
spread of, 112–13, 130, 143(m), 273(m)
supernatural elements, 274, 331
teachings and values of, 120(t), 129–31,
    139–40
temples and monuments, 227, 234(i),
    234–35
Theravada, 130–31, 274
trade and spread of, 226–27, 233–35,
    272
Vietnam, 264
wealth associated with, 226–27, 274
women, view of, 130
Bulgars, in Byzantine empire, 327
bureaucracy
    Chinese, 108, 110, 122, 123, 154, 391
    Inca, 408–9
    Japan, failure of, 266
    Korea, failure of, 262
    Mauryan empire, 112
    Mongol, 366, 371
    Vietnamese, 264
burials
    Agricultural Revolution, 32
    Chinese civilizations, 53, 64
    Egyptian civilization, 64
    Hopewell culture, 206
    Moche, 197–98, 198(i)
    mound-builders, 206–7
    Paleolithic, 23, 25
    Teotihuacán, 194
Burma, Pagan, 233(m), 235–36
bushido (Japanese way of the warrior),
    266

Byzantine empire, 321–28
  ancient civilizations within, 321
  Arab conquest of, 289
  architectural style, 325(i)
  Black Death (plague), impact on, 228
  Christianity, form of. *See* Eastern Orthodox Christianity
  Constantinople, conquest of, 315, 383, 401
  Constantinople as center, 316, 321
  Crusades, impact of, 326, 339(m), 339–40
  cultural influence of, 326–27
  decline of, 300–301, 323, 337, 401
  Eastern Orthodox Christianity, 324–28
  emperor, role of, 322, 324
  Greek texts preserved in, 138, 347
  icons, 324
  intellectual thought, 347
  Ottoman conquest of, 316, 323, 384
  Persian empire, conflict with, 326
  scope of, 323(m)
  state authority, features of, 322–23
  survival after Western collapse, 109
  as third-wave civilization, 316
  time frame of events, 317(t), 321
  trade, 223, 326
Byzantium. *See also* Constantinople
  Greek city of, 321

cacao beans, 244
Caesar, Julius (Roman ruler), 102
Caesar Augustus. *See* Augustus
caesaropapism, 324, 345
Caffa (Genoa), 377
Cahokia, 43(i), 204(m), 206–7
  as chiefdom, 42, 244
  exchange networks, 244
  time frame of, 181(t)
Cain and **Abel** (Bible), 40
calendars
  Islamic, 287
  Mayan, 192
  Olmec, 65
caliphs, 292–94
  first, 292–94
calligraphy, Islamic, 269
Cambodia
  Angkor kingdom, 211–12
  Khmer kingdom, 233, 233(m)
Cambridge University, 346

camels
  caravans, 218(i), 219, 223, 356(t)
  pastoral nomads, use of, 39, 182, 360
  and trans-Saharan trade, 182, 190, 239
  in warfare, 359
Cameroon, Bantu cultures, 200
canals
  Aztec, 406
  Chinese, 250–51, 253
  Persian, 92
cannibalism, Ancestral Pueblo, 205
cannons, 270, 343–44
canoes, 230, 244–45, 411
Canon of Medicine (Ibn Sina), 310(t)
Canton (China)
  as Islamic commercial center, 309
  massacre of foreigners, 272
capitalism, and Renaissance, 396
Caral (Peru), 49, 50(m)
caravan trade
  Silk Road, 218(i), 219, 223
  trans-Saharan, 182, 190, 239
Caribbean region, exchange networks, 244
Carolingian Empire, 329, 330(m). *See also* Charlemagne (Franks, r. 772–814)
Carpini, Giovanni DiPlano (Franciscan traveler), 355
Carthage
  Christianity, spread to, 144(i)
  Punic Wars, 100–102, 165
cartography
  Map of 1507 (Waldseemüller), 395(i)
  Muslim achievements, 310(t)
caste system, 158–62
  Buddhist rejection of, 130
  castes, levels of, 159–62, 160(t)
  early forms, 52, 113, 159
  Hindu teachings on, 127, 131, 161–62
  impact on Indian civilization, 162
  modern status, 151, 159(i)
  purity and pollution concepts, 159(i), 161–62
Çatalhüyük (Turkey), social organization of, 41
Catholicism
  blending local customs/beliefs. *See* syncretic (blended) religions
  institution of. *See* pope and papacy; Roman Catholic Church
  roots of. *See* Christianity, early
  Western European conversions (500–1000), 331

cave paintings, 14, 23
Cayuga people (North America), 388
C.E. (the Common Era), 6–7
Celts, Roman invasion of, 102(i)
Censorate (Chinese agency), 251
Central America. *See* Mesoamerica; *specific countries*
Central Asia. *See also specific countries*
  civilizations of. *See* Central Asian civilizations
  in fifteenth century, 386(t)
Central Asian civilizations
  Arab conquest of, 289, 360
  Black Death (plague), 228
  Buddhism, spread to, 226–27
  Christianity, spread to, 142
  as empire-builders. *See* Mongol empire; Mongols; Ottoman empire; Turks
  nomadic societies, 39–40, 356(t)
  oasis cities, 226
  Oxus civilization, 53–54
  people and culture of. *See specific civilizations by name*
  Silk Road trade, 222–28
ceremonial centers. *See also* temples
  Ancestral Pueblo, 204–5, 205(i)
  Hindu, 235, 235(i)
  Inca, 409(i)
  Mayan, 192
  Teotihuacán, 193–94, 194(i)
Chabi (wife of Khubilai Khan), 369
Chaco Canyon, 204(m)
  Chaco Phenomenon (Ancestral Pueblo), 204–5
  exchange networks, 244
Chalcedon, Council of (451 C.E.), 146
Champa kingdom, 233, 233(m), 235
Chang'an (Chinese capital), 262, 265
chariots, 73
Charlemagne (Franks, r. 772–814)
  empire of, 330(m)
  imperial bureaucracy of, 329–30
  reign, symbolism of, 314(i), 315
Charles the Bald, kingdom of, 330(m)
Chavín culture, 196(m), 196–97, 408
chess, 342(t)
chiefdoms, 42–43. *See also* kinship societies
  Bantu cultures, 201
  Cahokia, 244
  features of, 42–43

chiefdoms (*continued*)
  mound-builders, 206
  Olmec civilization, 54
  Pacific Ocean region, 20, 42
Chile, Paleolithic migrations to, 18
Chimu kingdom, 408
China
  Agricultural Revolution, 29(m), 34–35,
    38–39
  Austronesian language and, 19, 35
  civilizations/dynasties. See Chinese
    civilization, first; Chinese
    civilization, second-wave; Chinese
    civilization, third-wave
  dating system in, 7
  in fifteenth century, 390–93
  maritime voyages, 392–93, 396–400,
    398(m)
  religious revivals, post-Mao, 117, 315
Chinca people, 244
Chinese civilization, first. See also
    Shang dynasty (China,
    1600–1046 B.C.E.); Xia dynasty
    (China, 2070–1600 B.C.E.); Zhou
    dynasty (China, 1046–771 B.C.E.)
  class hierarchies in, 57–58
  decline of, 103
  innovations and discoveries, 38
  locations/sites of, 51(m)
  rulers, limits to power, 63
  silk industry, 223–24
  Son of Heaven ideology, 53
  spontaneous emergence of, 54
  writing system, 64, 65(t)
Chinese civilization, second-wave,
    103–6. See also Han dynasty
    (China, 206 B.C.E.–220 C.E.); Qin
    Shihuangdi (Chinese emperor,
    r. 221–210 B.C.E.)
  accomplishments of, 90(t)
  alphabet and language, 108
  assimilation of outsiders, 107–8, 162
  Buddhism, 107
  bureaucracy, 108, 110, 122, 123, 154
  Christianity, spread to, 106–7, 142
  civil service system, 108, 122, 153–54
  class hierarchies, 153–58, 162
  Confucianism, 106, 121–24
  Confucianism, decline of, 250,
    273–74
  Daoism, 124–26, 170–71
  education, 153–54
  empire building, 104–5

First Emperor. See Qin Shihuangdi
    (Chinese emperor, r. 221–210 B.C.E.)
  Great Wall, 105, 105(m), 109
  growth, domestic repercussions, 106
  inventions and discoveries, 82–83, 105
  Legalism, 121–22
  locations/sites of, 85(m)
  nomads, penetration by, 109, 170
  patriarchy, 168–71
  peasant revolts, 109, 157–58
  Roman empire compared to, 106–11
  Sea Roads, 228–32, 229(m)
  silk industry, 224–25
  Silk Road trade, 222–28
  slavery, 163–64
  Son of Heaven/Mandate of Heaven,
    106, 119
  unification, contributing factors,
    110–11
  unification, periods of, 103–5, 110
  warring states, era of, 103–4, 121
Chinese civilization, third-wave. See also
    Song dynasty (China, 960–1279);
    Sui dynasty (China 589–618);
    Tang dynasty (China, 618–907)
  Black Death (plague), 377
  Buddhism, attack on, 275–76
  Buddhism, spread to, 226–27, 250,
    272–76, 273(m)
  cities, sophistication of, 253, 254(i)
  civilized versus barbarian worldview,
    257–58
  civil service examination, 252–53
  commercialization of, 253–54, 271
  Daoism, 250
  elites, 253, 255
  Eurasia, influence on, 268–71
  global influence of, 249–50, 270–71
  as golden age, 251
  influence of other cultures on, 271–72
  innovations and discoveries, 231, 254,
    269–71, 270(t), 342(t), 376–77
  Japan, influence on, 265–67
  Korea, influence on, 261–63
  as middle kingdom, 257, 277
  in Mongol empire, 362(m), 367–68,
    373
  Nestorian Christianity during, 319
  nomadic people, assimilation of, 250,
    260–61
  north-south differences, 260, 271
  religions, assimilation of, 276
  Sea Roads and trade, 231, 271–72

  southward migration, 250
  state structure, 251–52
  time frame of events, 251(t)
  tribute arrangement, 257–60, 360
  tribute system, 257–60, 259(i)
  unification and revival, 231, 250
  Vietnam, influence on, 263–65
  waterways, 250–51, 253
  women, status of, 255–56
  xenophobic movements, 275–76
Chinggis Khan (Mongol ruler,
    1162–1227), 363–66. See also
    Mongol empire
  depictions of, 352(i), 370(i), 372(i)
  early life of, 363
  revival in Mongolia, 353
  rise to power, 363–64
  sons/grandsons of, 364, 367, 369, 372(i)
  warfare, style of, 365–66
Chinookan people (North America),
    387
Christ. See Jesus of Nazareth
Christianity
  Chinese revival, post-Mao, 117, 315
  conversions/spread of. See
    Catholicism; missionaries
  decline, and rise of Islam, 317–21
  founding and development. See
    Christianity, early
  Islam compared to, 287, 301
  Jerusalem, significance of, 318, 321
  among Mongols, 319
  mysticism, Islamic influence, 342(t)
  revival (1970s–), 315
  Roman Catholicism. See
    Catholicism; Roman Catholic
    Church; Western Christendom
  Western dating system based on, 6–7
Christianity, early, 140–46
  bishop of Rome as pope, 146
  in Chinese civilizations, 106–7
  councils, purpose of, 146
  Greek influence on, 138
  within Islamic communities, 318–19
  Jerusalem, as sacred location, 318
  Jesus of Nazareth, 139–40
  Judaism as influence, 135
  martyrs, 142, 144–45, 181
  monasticism, 142
  Nestorian, 290, 318–19
  nuns, 141, 168
  patriarchy, 141, 147
  rationalism versus, 345–46

Roman influence on, 145
Roman persecutions, 106–7
sects and offshoots, 146, 185, 324
silk, use of, 225
slavery, view of, 165
spread of, 106–7, 140–42, 141–43,
    143(m), 181, 185–88, 320–21
teachings and values of, 120(t),
    139–41
women, view of, 141, 145–46
Zoroastrian influence on, 133–34
Chumash (California), permanent
    settlements of, 26
chu nom (Vietnamese writing system),
    265
churches
of the Holy Sepulcher (Jerusalem),
    321
of Saint George (Lalibela), 321, 321(i)
St. Mark's Basilica (Venice), 325(i)
Church of North Africa, 142
Church of the East, 142
cities. *See also specific cities*
Chinese, third-wave, 253, 254(i)
decline, Western Europe (500–1000),
    329
in early civilizations. *See* city-states
Indus Valley, 6(i), 56, 56(i)
Middle Ages/Western Europe, 334,
    345
Niger River civilizations, 188–90
oasis, Central Asia, 226
Teotihuacán, 194–95
citizenship
Greek, 94–95, 96
Roman, 100, 107
City of Ladies (de Pizan), 395–96
city-states
African, fifteenth-century, 398(m)
Aztec, 406–7
of earliest civilizations, 49
features of, 55–56
Greek, 93(m), 93–94
Indus Valley civilization, 56
Italy, 334
Mayan, 192
Mesoamerican, 56
Mesopotamian, 67(m)
Middle Ages/Western Europe, 334,
    345
regulation of population in, 62–63
religion, utility of, 63
Roman empire beginnings as, 107

state authority in. *See* state authority,
    early civilizations
Sumer (Mesopotamia), 55–56, 68–69
Swahili, 237
civil engineering, Roman, 83
civilizations
continuities and changes over time,
    80–85, 276–77
defined, 6, 88
empires, emergence from, 6
global expansion of. *See* early
    modern era (1450–1750)
historical eras of. *See* civilizations,
    first; civilizations, second-wave;
    civilizations, third-wave; Fifteenth
    Century cultures and societies
use of term, 6, 48
civilizations, first, 8–9(m), 47–76,
    50–51(m)
Agricultural Revolution, emergence
    from, 6, 26–27, 43, 48, 54–55
Chinese, 53–54
cradle of, 48
cultural diffusion among, 73–74
decline of, 79
Egyptian, 48–49
environment, impact on culture,
    66–68
exchange networks, 71–73
Indus Valley, 52–53
interactions among, 70–75
Mesopotamia compared to Egypt,
    66–75
modern assessment of, 75–76
Norte Chico (Peru), 49, 52
Nubian (Africa), 54
Olmec (Mesoamerica), 54
origin, question of, 54–55
Oxus (Central Asia), 53–54
patriarchy, 59–61
people and culture of. *See specific
    civilizations by name*
rulers, limits to power, 63
state authority, 61–63, 68–70
Sumerian (Mesopotamia), 48–49
time frame of, 49(t)
warfare, 60
writing systems, 63–65, 65(t)
civilizations, second-wave, 84–85(m)
African, 183–90
Andean, 195–200
Chinese, 103–6, 110
class hierarchies, 80, 83, 152–67

collapse of, 108–11
continental comparisons, 180–82
disease, spread of, 83
features of, 90(t)
gender inequality, 83, 167–75
Greek, 93–99
importance, criteria for, 208
Indian, 111–13
innovations during, 82–83
interactions among, 89, 181–82
legacies of, 113–14
Mesoamerican, 190–95
North American, 204–7
patriarchy, 167–74
people and culture of. *See specific
    civilizations by name*
Persian, 90–91
population estimates, 182(t)
religious systems, rise of, 82, 118–20,
    120(t)
Roman, 99–103, 106–10
time frame of events, 89(t), 153(t),
    181(t)
transition from first civilizations,
    79–85
civilizations, third-wave, 216–17(m)
African, 236–41
Afro-Eurasian phenomenon, 232
American Web trade and commerce,
    243–45
Arab, 214, 288–97
Byzantine, 212, 321–28
Chinese, 82–83, 249–77
common themes across locations,
    212–13
emergence of, 211–12
historical eras following. *See*
    Fifteenth Century cultures and
    societies
interaction patterns among, 83,
    213–15
Islamic, 212, 298–311
Kieven Rus, 327–28
Mongol, 361–80, 362(m)
patriarchy, 215
people and culture of. *See specific
    civilizations by name*
and Sand Roads, 238–41
and Sea Roads, 228–38, 229(m)
and Silk Roads, 214, 222–28
Southeast Asian, 232–36
time frame of, 221(t)
Western Christendom, 328–48

civil wars. *See* revolts, rebellions, resistance
clans
    big men, 387
    confederations of, 389–90
    pastoral societies, 354
classes, social. *See* social class
class hierarchies, 152–67. *See also specific groups*
    caste system, 159–62, 160(t)
    Chinese civilizations, 57–58, 153–58, 162
    Confucian teachings on, 122–24
    estates (French), 345
    feudalism, Western Europe, 330–31, 336–37
    Greece, ancient, 94–95
    in kinship societies, 20, 41
    mound-builders, 207
    Oxus civilization, 53
    pastoral societies, 354–55
    Roman empire, 100, 102–3, 163–67
    slavery, 163–67
    stability and change in, 80, 83
    Sumerian civilization, 57–58, 64
    Swahili civilization, 237
    West African civilizations, 240
"Classic of Filial Piety" (painting), 122(i)
class structure, inequalities. *See* class hierarchies
Cleisthenes (Greek reformer), 95
clergy (Catholic), as first estate, 345
climate
    African, as environmental constraint, 183
    and Agricultural Revolution, 24, 28–30
    El Niño, 199
    Ice Age, 14, 18, 20, 24, 28–30
    Indian Ocean monsoons, 229(m), 230
    warming of. *See* global warming
clitorectomy (female genital cutting), 297
Clovis culture, 18
Code of Hammurabi. *See* Hammurabi (r. 1792–1750 B.C.E.) law code
Columbus, Christopher
    on Muslim defeat in Spain, 306
    racism/imperialism attributed to, 383
    voyages, global impact of, 384, 413–15
    voyages of, 382(i), 383, 397–99, 398(m)
commerce. *See also* trade, short-distance networks. *See* exchange networks

communion, Eastern versus Western Christianity, 325
compass, magnetic, 230, 231, 270(t), 271, 344
concubines, Chinese women, 169, 170, 256
Confucianism, 121–24
    Buddhism compared to, 272–73
    in China, decline of, 250, 273–74
    in China, post-Mongol restoration, 391
    "Classic of Filial Piety," 122(i)
    Han collapse and decline of, 107, 170
    Korea, 262
    Legalism replaced by, 106
    men, view of, 123, 168
    Neo-Confucianism, 251, 369
    revival of, post-Mao, 117
    teachings and values of, 120(t), 122–23, 156–57
    temples, 117, 391, 392(i)
    Vietnam, 264–65
    women, view of, 123, 169–71, 255, 255–56
Confucius (551–479 B.C.E.)
    Analects, 121
    birth, celebration of, 117
    key teaching of, 120(t)
    teachings of. *See* Confucianism
Constantine (Roman emperor)
    Christianity, conversion to, 143, 321
    Constantinople established, 321–22
Constantinople
    Crusades and fall of, 326, 339–40
    Eastern Orthodox Church, 142
    Ottoman conquest of, 316, 384, 401, 409
    population (in 1000), 334
Constantinople, Council of (533 C.E.), 146
consuls (Roman), 100, 103
Cook, James (explorer), 21
Coptic Christianity
    in Axum, 143, 185, 187–88, 231, 320–21
    in Egypt, 139–40, 142, 146, 319–20
Córdoba (Spain), 304–5
corn (maize)
    diffusion through Americas, 243–44
    domestication of, 5(i), 27, 33–34
    mound-builders, 206
    in Norte Chico, 52
Cortés, Hernán, 407

cotton
    Muslims cultivation, 309
    plantations, slave labor, 309
cotton textiles, 83
Council of Elders (Sparta), 95
courier networks
    Inca, 245(i)
    Mongol, 374
courtesans, Chinese, 256
Crete, Minoan civilization, 73
crop rotation, 343
crops
    production of. *See* Agricultural Revolution; agriculture
    of specific countries/regions. *See specific locations*
Crusades, 338–40
    anti-Semitism during, 339(m), 340
    Byzantine Empire, impact on, 326
    and cultural diffusion, 340–42
    modern references to, 340
    short and long-term impacts, 339–40
    time frame of, 326, 339(m)
cultural diffusion
    and Agricultural Revolution, 34–36
    and Arab conquests, 291–92
    and Crusades, 340–42
    cultural borrowing, 342–44
    and Egyptian civilization, 71, 73–75
    of Greek civilization, 98–99, 107, 138–39
    of language, 34–35
    of Mesopotamian civilization, 72–73
    and Mongol empire, 376–77
    and nomadic peoples, 222
    and religion. *See* syncretic (blended) religions
    of Roman culture, 108, 145
    and Sea Roads trade, 232–38
    and Silk Road trade, 221–22, 226–27
    of technology. *See* technology, diffusion of
culture. *See specific aspects of culture, for example religious systems or languages*
    environment, impact on, 66–68
    spread of. *See* cultural diffusion
cuneiform, 65(t)
currency
    Byzantine bezant, 326
    Chinese paper money, 254
    Persian coins, 103(i)
    silk as, 225

Cuzco (Inca capital), 408
Cyril (missionary), 327
Cyrillic alphabet, 327
Cyrus (Persia, r. 557–530 B.C.E.), 90–91

Damascus (Syria), as Umayyad capital, 294
Daodejing (The Way and Its Power) (Laozi), 125–26
Daoism, 124–26
    Chinese revival, post-Mao, 117
    dao (the way) in, 124(i), 125, 274
    female worship in, 255
    teachings and values of, 120(t), 125–26
    women, view of, 170–71
Darius I (Persia, r. 522–486 B.C.E.), 90–92
Darius III (Persia), 98(i)
Darwin, Charles (1809–1882), evolutionary theories, 3
dates, 232, 238, 239
dating systems. *See also* calendars, conventions used, 6–7
David, Jacques-Louis, 137(i)
da Vinci, Leonardo (Renaissance painter), 394
de Bry, Theodore (Flemish artist), 382(i), 383
deforestation
    Easter Island, 20
    Greece, ancient, 93–94
    Indus Valley civilization, 52
    Meroë, kingdom of, 185
    Mesopotamia, 68
    Roman empire, 108
    Western Christendom (1300), 332
deities. *See also* gods and goddesses
    Hindu, 128, 132, 299
    Japanese, 267
Delhi Sultanate (India), 298, 300(m), 391(m)
democracy
    ancient versus modern, 95
    Greek/Athenian, 94–96, 136
    Socrates critique of, 136
Democritus (Greek philosopher), 136
demography. *See* entries under *population*
de Pizan, Christine (1363–1430), 395–96
dharma (teachings of Buddha), 161, 274
dhimmis (people of the book), 290, 319–20

Diamond Sutra, 271
al-Din, Rashid (Persian historian), 371–72
al-Din, Safi (Safavid ruler), 371–72
Dionysus (Greek god), 135, 138
diplomacy
    Egypt-Babylon era, 74–75
    Mongol efforts, 375–76
    Teotihuacán, 195
direct democracy, Greeks, 95
diseases, Muslim identification of, 311
diseases, spread of. *See also* Black Death (plague)
    and animal domestication, 37–38
    globalization of disease, 375(m)
    and immunity, 227, 228
    and insects, 183, 201
    and Paleolithic migrations, 35
    Roman empire, 109
    in second-wave civilizations, 83
    and trade, 201, 227–28, 375(m)
divinity of kings
    Byzantine emperor, 324
    Japanese emperor, 267
    Mandate of Heaven/Son of Heaven (China), 53, 63, 106, 119, 264
    origin in Sudan, 71
    pharaohs (Egypt), 63, 64, 69, 71
    Roman emperor, 106
division of labor
    gathering and hunting peoples, 20–22
    Inca empire, 410
    Middle Ages/Western Europe, 330–31, 334–37, 336(i)
divorce
    pastoral societies, 355
    in Sparta, 173
Dome of the Rock (Jerusalem), 318(i)
domestication. *See also* animal domestication; plant domestication defined, 27
donkeys, 32
dowry
    Chinese women, 169, 256
    Greek women, 172
    Islamic women, 296
Dravidian language, 65(t)
Dreamtime (Aboriginal Australians), 15, 18
Dunhuang (China), Buddhist art and texts in, 226, 226(i)

early modern era (1450–1750)
    and economic inequality, 414
    features of, 413–15
    and globalization, 289–90, 413
East Africa. *See also specific countries and people*
    Black Death (plague), 377
    Sea Roads, 228–38, 229(m)
    Swahili civilization, 236–38
    trade, impact on, 236–38
Easter Island, deforestation, 20
Eastern Europe. *See also specific countries*
    in Mongol empire, 362(m), 365, 375–76
    southeast region. *See* Balkans
Eastern Orthodox Christianity, 324–28
    and Byzantine identity, 324
    caesaropapism, 324, 345
    establishment of, 142
    icons, 324
    Roman Catholic conflict with, 340
    Russian church. *See* Russian Orthodox Church
    theological features of, 324
    Western Christianity compared to, 324–26
Eastern Roman empire. *See* Byzantine empire
Eastern Woodlands people. *See* mound-builders
Ecclesiastes (Old Testament), 174
economic inequality, early modern era (1450–1750), 414
education. *See also* literacy
    Chinese examination system. *See* examination system (China)
    Confucian view of, 122–24
    Daoist view of, 125
    Greek, 138–39, 347
    institutions of. *See* universities and colleges
    Islamic system, 307–8, 310
    Korea, 262
    Middle Ages/Western Europe, 346
    Spartan women, 173
Egypt
    Black Death (plague), 377
    Christianity, decline of, 320
    Islam, spread to, 292, 320
Egyptian civilization
    afterlife, belief in, 67–68, 70
    Alexandria, 98–99
    cities in, 51(m)

Egyptian civilization (*continued*)
   Coptic Christianity in, 139–40, 142,
     146, 319–20
   cultural diffusion, 71, 73–75
   decline of, 79
   diplomacy with Babylon, 74–75
   emergence of, 48–49
   environment, impact on culture,
     66–68, 69
   exchange networks, 71–73, 181, 230
   gods and goddesses, 70, 107, 144,
     186–87
   Greek control of, 98–99
   Hebrew slaves, escape of, 134, 135
   kingship. *See* pharaohs (Egypt)
   location of, 51(m), 184(m)
   migration of foreigners to, 74–75
   New Kingdom, 49(t), 74(m)
   Nile, flooding of, 63, 66, 68, 69
   Nubian conquest of, 73, 181(t), 183,
     186–87
   Nubians in, 72(i), 73
   optimistic worldview of, 67–68
   political turmoil, 69–70
   political unity, period of, 69
   Ptolemaic period, 98–99
   pyramids, 67
   scribes, 46(i), 47
   state, power of, 62, 69–70
   Sumerian/Mesopotamian compared
     to, 66–75
   women, role of, 61
   writing system, 65(t)
elites. *See also* nobility
   Chinese civilizations, 53, 57, 154–55,
     224–25, 253
   Confucian view of, 122–24
   goods demanded by. *See* luxury goods
   Japanese, 267–69
   Korean, 262, 263
   special status, signs of, 57, 64
   in title societies, 41, 388
   Vietnamese, 264
   women, special status, 102, 169–70,
     172, 255–56
El Mirador (Guatemala), 191
El Niño, 199
emperors
   Byzantine, 322, 324
   divinity of. *See* divinity of kings
   Holy Roman, 329–30
empires. *See also specific empires*
   collapse, causes of, 108–9

defined, 88
emergence from civilizations, 6
modern analogies to, 114
modern fascination with, 88–89
pre-modern. *See* civilizations, first;
   civilizations, second-wave;
   civilizations, third-wave
energy production
   chain drive, 270(t)
   windmills, 343
England
   Angles and Saxons in, 329
   famine (1315–1322), 336–37
   Hundred Year's War, 393
   Roman invasion of, 100, 102(i)
   trade, Middle Ages, 332
Enheduanna (Mesopotamian
   priestess), 61
environment
   constraints, and African civilizations,
     183
   destruction of. *See* environmental
     damage
   impact on culture, early civilizations,
     66–68
   protection of. *See* environmentalism
environmental damage. *See also specific*
   environmental hazards
   in Agricultural Revolution, 20,
     37–38
   Chinese civilizations, 108
   deforestation, 20, 52, 68
   Greek civilization, 93
   from irrigation, 52, 68, 93
   Maya civilization, 193
   Meroë, kingdom of, 185
   Mesopotamia, 68
   Mongol empire, 370
   Paleolithic extinctions, 18, 20,
     22–23
   Roman empire, 108
environmentalism
   China reforestation, fifteenth century,
     392
   Islamic Green Revolution, 309
Epic of Gilgamesh, 56, 67, 68
epidemics. *See* diseases, spread of
Ericsson, Leif (Viking), 242
Eric the Red (Viking), 242
Eritrea, early civilizations. *See* Axum
   (Ethiopia)
estates (French), 345
ethics, Greek conception, 137–38

Ethiopia
   Agricultural Revolution, 32
   Christianity in, 320–21, 321(i)
   early civilizations. *See* Axum
     (Ethiopia)
   Islam, spread to, 302(m)
eunuchs, Zheng He, Chinese admiral as,
   392, 396
Eurasia
   Agricultural Revolution, 29(m)
   civilizations of. *See* Central Asian
     civilizations; Chinese civilizations;
     Eurasian civilizations
   Inner and Outer, 222, 223(m)
   Paleolithic migrations to, 14–15,
     16–17(m)
Eurasian civilizations. *See also* Central
   Asian civilizations; Chinese
   civilizations
   civilizations, early, 53–54
   civilizations, second-wave, 85(m), 88
   civilizations, third-wave, 221(t)
   common goals of, 88
   continental comparisons, 180–82
   interactions among, 222
   population estimates, second-wave
     civilizations, 182(t)
Euripides (Greek playwright), 96
Eurocentrism, Western dating systems
   and, 6–7
Europe. *See also* Eastern Europe;
   Western Europe; *specific countries*
   civilizations of. *See* Eurasian
     civilizations; Western European
     civilizations
   in fifteenth century, 393–400, 394(m)
   Paleolithic migrations to, 16(m)
examination system (China), 108, 123,
   153–54, 252–53, 391
   in Vietnam, 264
exchange networks. *See also specific*
   civilizations
   expansion of. *See* trade, early
     civilizations
   Paleolithic era, 13, 18, 19
exploration
   in fifteenth century. *See* maritime
     voyages
   technology for. *See* navigation
     technology
exports. *See* exchange networks; *specific*
   products
Ezana (Axum monarch), 187

fairs, Middle Ages, 332
faith versus reason, Middle Ages, 345–46
family. *See also* marriage
    Confucian view of, 122(i), 122–23, 169
    Daoist view of, 125
    Korean, Chinese influence, 262
farming
    large scale. *See* agriculture
    origin of. *See* Agricultural
        Revolution
Farsi (Persian language), 292
Faxian (Chinese traveler), in Gupta
    empire, 112–13
Ferdinand (Spanish king), 306
Ferdowsi (Persian poet), 292
Fertile Crescent
    Agricultural Revolution, 29, 29(m),
        31–32
    countries of, 31, 31(m)
feudalism
    class hierarchies, 330–31, 336–37
    political relationships in, 334
fictive kinship, 357
Fifteenth Century cultures and
        societies, 383–415
    agricultural village societies, 387–89
    Asia, developments in, 391(m)
    Aztec empire, 404–7
    China, Ming dynasty, 391–93
    connections, webs of, 410–11
    diversity within societies of, 410–11
    gathering and hunting peoples in,
        383–87
    Inca empire, 408–10
    Islamic empire, 400–404, 401(m)
    maritime voyages, 392–93, 397–400
    nomadic societies, 389–90
    non-global dimension of, 412–13
    religious systems in, 411, 412(m)
    Renaissance, 393–97
    time frame of events, 385(t)
    trade in, 411, 412(m)
    Western Christendom, 393–400
    world developments during, 386(t)
figs, 32
Fiji, 411
filial piety, Confucian view of, 122(i), 123
fire altar, Zoroastrian, 133(i)
firestick farming, 385, 387
First Civilizations. *See* civilizations, first
First Emperor, China. *See* Qin
        Shihuangdi (Chinese emperor,
        r. 221–210 B.C.E.)

fishing
    Andean civilizations, 197
    Paleolithic peoples, 15, 18, 25
Five Nations (Iroquois confederacy), 388
Florence (Italy), as trade center, 332
Florentine Codex, 406(i)
flu. *See* influenza
foods
    broad spectrum diet, 29
    Chinese, 253
    cultural diffusion, 360, 377
    production of. *See* Agricultural
        Revolution; agriculture; pastoral
        societies
foot binding, China, 255–56, 256(i), 369
Forbidden City (Beijing), 391
forest specialists, Batwa people, 201
Fotudeng (Buddhist monk), 226–27
France
    Arab conquest in, 289
    estates in, 345
    Franks in, 329
    Hundred Years' War, 393
    trading fairs, Middle Ages, 332
Franciscans, delegation to Mongols, 376
frankincense, 220, 230
Franks. *See also* Charlemagne (Franks,
        r. 772–814)
    in Roman empire, 109–10
    Romanization of, 329
Fulbe people (West Africa)
    Islam, conversion to, 390
    movement of, 398(m)
    as pastoral society, 356(t), 390
Funan, 233, 233(m)
fundamentalism, Islamic. *See* Islamic
        fundamentalism
fur trade, Siberian, 411

da Gama, Vasco, voyages of, 398(i),
        398–99
Ganges River region, civilizations of,
        111–12
Gao (West Africa), 241
gathering and hunting peoples
    affluent/complex cultures, 387
    agriculture, transition to, 24–30, 34
    boats during, 15, 20
    cave paintings, 14, 23
    conflicts, sources of, 21–22
    environmental damage by, 20, 22–23
    exchange networks, 13, 18, 19
    in fifteen century, 383–87

population, decline of, 35–37
    rock art, 10(i), 14(i)
    settlements, permanent, 24–26, 30
    societal rules, 22
    spirituality, 23, 26
    tools of, 3, 12, 14, 24
    in twenty-first century, 11, 35–37
    way of life of, 11–12, 20–22
    women, role of, 20–21, 59
Ge'ez language (Axum), 143, 186–87
Ge Hong (Chinese scholar), 156–57
Gelasius (Pope), 145–46
gender equality
    Chinese civilization, second-wave,
        170
    gathering and hunting peoples, 29,
        40–41, 59
    gender parallelism, 203, 410
    high-status women, opportunities
        for. *See* women in authority
    Paleolithic egalitarianism, 20–22
    pastoral societies, 40, 59, 355–56
    spiritual, *Quran (Koran)* on, 295–96
gender inequality. *See also* patriarchy;
        women
    Buddhism, 130
    change and consistency over time,
        167–68
    Christianity, early, 141, 145–46
    civilizations, second-wave, 83, 167–75
    Confucianism, 123, 169–71, 255, 255–56
    in earliest civilizations, 59–61
    female infanticide, 41
    Greek civilization, 170–72, 172(i)
    Hinduism, 127–28
    Islam, 295–98
    Middle Ages/Western Europe, 335,
        337
    patriarchal ideal, earliest civilizations,
        41, 59–61
    as regulation of female sexuality, 60–61
    and role assignment, 59
    in Roman Catholic Church, 335–36
    universities, male-only, 335
genital mutilation
    clitorectomy, 297
    eunuchs, 392, 396
Genoa (Italy), as trade center, 332, 345
geography
    map-making. *See* cartography
    Muslim achievements, 310(t)
    navigational tools. *See* navigational
        technology

Germanic peoples
   assimilation of, 329
   dominance in Western Europe, 329, 330(m)
   groups/tribes of, 329
   locations/sites of, 323(i)
   raids, decline of, 332, 333(m)
   Roman empire, invasions on, 109–10
   viewed as barbarians, 329, 379–80
Germany
   Holy Roman Empire, 330, 334
   Mongol invasion of, 375
   pogroms during Crusades, 340
Ghana, kingdom of, 211, 239–40, 240(m)
   gold as resource, 239–40
   Islam, spread to, 301(m)
al-Ghazali (1058–1111)
   law, writing on, 295
   on status of women, 297
Ghazan (Persian il-khan, 1295–1304), 371, 377
Ghaznavid nomads, 356(t)
Gilgamesh. See Epic of Gilgamesh
Gimbutas, Marija, 41
gladiators, slaves as, 166, 167
glassblowing, 83
globalization
   of agriculture, 28–29(m), 34–36
   beginning of. See early modern era (1450–1750)
   of culture. See cultural diffusion
   of disease, 375(m)
   early humans and, 4–5
global warming
   Ice Age, 24, 28–30
   interruption, and Agricultural Revolution, 32
goats, 356(t)
Göbekli Tepe (Turkey), 25(i), 25–26, 30
Gobir (West Africa), 241
goddess culture
   Daoist female worship, 255
   decline of, 61
   gathering and hunting peoples view of, 41
   goddess figurines, 14–15, 23, 23(i)
gods and goddesses. See also deities
   Andean, 179
   Arabs, pre-Islam, 283–85
   Aztec, 407

Egyptian, 70, 107, 144, 186(i), 186–87
   goddess, veneration of. See goddess culture
   Greek, 135, 138
   Kievan Rus, 327
   Mesopotamian, 61, 63
   Mongol, 353, 362
   Roman, 107
   worship, Roman ban on, 143–44
Golden Horde, Mongols in Russia, 372–74
gold metallurgy
   Meroë jewelry, 185(i)
   Moche ceremonial pieces, 197
   Scythian, 357(i)
gold trade
   early civilizations, 230
   third-wave civilizations, 232, 233, 238, 239, 240
Goths, 329
governments. See also bureaucracy
   in early civilizations. See city-states; state authority, early civilizations
   merchants and evolution of, 345
   Western Christendom, pluralistic, 344–45, 393
grains. See also specific grains
   alcoholic beverage-making, 38, 39
   domestication of, 30–33
   mills for grinding, 335, 343
Granada (Spain), 306
Grand Canal (China), 252(m)
Grand Mosque (Arabia), 317
Great Law of Peace (Iroquois Nation), 388
Great Mosque (Jenne), 303(i)
Great Suns (Natchez chiefs), 207
Great Vehicle (Mahayana Buddhism), 131
Great Wall of China, 105, 105(m), 109, 252(m)
Great Zimbabwe, 238
Greco-Persian Wars, 95–96
Greece, ancient civilization of. See Greek civilization
Greek civilization, 93–99
   Alexander the Great and expansion of, 97(m), 97–99
   in Byzantine Empire, 322, 323(m)
   citizens, status of, 94–95, 96
   city-states, 93(m), 93–94
   classical, time and location, 92, 93(m)
   democracy, 94–96

disease/epidemics, 227
   distinctive accomplishment of, 90(t), 94–95, 138–39
   environmental damage, 93–94
   features of, 93–95
   gods and goddesses, 135, 138
   Golden Age, 96
   Greco-Persian Wars, 95–96
   Greek scholarship, rediscovery of, 138–39, 325, 347
   Hellenistic era, 98–99
   homosexuality, 173–74
   influence on other cultures, 98–99, 107, 138–39, 325
   intellectual thought, 118, 120(t), 136–39, 325, 342(t), 345–48
   patriarchy, 171–74
   Peloponnesian War, 96
   in Roman empire, 101(m)
   slavery, 58, 163, 164–65
   Sparta, 94–95
   women, status of, 170–72, 172(i)
Greek fire (weapon), 326
Greek language
   of Byzantine Empire, 325
   diffusion of, 98–99
Greenland
   Paleolithic migrations to, 16(m)
   Viking colonization, 242, 338
griots (praise-singers), 189
Guam, in fifteenth century, 386(t), 411
Guatemala, Maya civilization, 178(i), 179, 191
Gu Hongzhong (Chinese painter), 169(i)
guilds
   Indian civilizations, 113, 161
   Middle Ages/Western Europe, 334, 335
gunpowder
   and Buddhism, 271
   Chinese invention of, 254, 270, 270(t), 342(t)
   stimulation of other inventions by, 270–71
Gupta empire (India, 320–550 C.E.), 112(m), 112–13
   distinctive accomplishment of, 90(t)
   features of, 112–13
   trade, 113
Guru Nanak (Sikhism, 1469–1539), 300
Gutenberg, Johannes, 269
Guyuk (Mongol ruler), 376

hadiths (sayings and deeds of Muhammad), changing versions of, 297

Hadza people (Tanzania), 11, 35

Hafiz (Sufi poet), 295, 308

Haitian Revolution (1791–1804), compared to Spartacus rebellion, 167

hajj (pilgrimage to Mecca)
Mansa Musa pilgrimage from Mali, 304–5
and sense of community, 281, 286, 308

hallucinogenic drugs
Andean shamans, 196, 197
Paleolithic societies use of, 18, 23

Hammurabi (r. 1792–1750 B.C.E.)
law code
inequality justified by, 64
punishment based on social status, 57–58
on restraint of power, 63

Han dynasty (China, 206 B.C.E.–220 C.E.)
beginning of, 106
civil service examination academy, 108, 153
collapse of, 107–9, 156, 158, 169–70, 250, 273–74
Confucianism, 106, 121–24
disease/epidemics, 227
emperors. *See* Wudi (China, r. 141–87 B.C.E.)
merchants, status of, 158
peasants, 155(i), 155–56
scope of, 105(m), 158(m)
slavery, 163–64
Wang Mang reforms, 155
Xiongnu raids/tribute, 109, 257–58, 359
Yellow Turban Rebellion, 157–58

Han Fei (China), on Legalism, 121

hangul (Korean writing system), 263

Hangzhou (China)
Marco Polo narrative on, 253, 341
population of (13th century), 334
Song dynasty growth, 253

Han Kuan (Chinese scholar), 356, 379

Han Yu (Chinese scholar), 277

Harappa, 51(m). *See also* Indus Valley civilization
collapse of, 111
features of, 56

Hatshepsut (Egypt, r. 1472–1457 B.C.E.), 61, 183

Hausa people (West Africa), 398(m)
city-states of, 239
Islam, spread to, 302(m)

Hawaii, chiefdoms, 20

Hazda people (Tanzania), 11

health care
innovations and discoveries. *See* medical science
Muslim achievements, 311

health status. *See* diseases; life expectancy

Hebrews
Babylon, freedom from, 91, 134
Bible produced by. *See* Old Testament
as chosen people, Arab view, 285
exile from Israel, 134
Judaism, birth of, 134–35
prophets of, 118, 120(t), 134–35
religious system. *See* Judaism
Yahweh, 134–35

Heian (Japan), 265, 267, 268

Helegu (Persian il-khan), 369, 371

Hellenes, 93

Hellenistic society. *See* Greek civilization

helots (Sparta), 95, 173

Herakles (Greek god), 227

herding. *See* nomadic societies; pastoral societies

heresy, Nestorian, 324

Herod (ruler of Galilee), 142

Herodotus (Greek historian), 91–92, 137

hieroglyphics, 65(t)

High Middle Ages
expansion during, 332–36, 333(m)
technological innovation during, 343, 343(i)

highway systems. *See* roads

hijra (journey), 287

Hildegard of Bingen (Christian mystic), 335

Hinduism, 126–28
Bhagavad Gita (The Song of the Lord), 131–32
bhakti (worship) movement, 132
Buddhism relationship to, 129, 132, 144–45
on caste, 127, 131, 161–62
ceremonial centers, 235, 235(i)
Indian origins of, 126–28
Islam compared to, 299–300
in Mughal empire, 403

reform version of, 131–32, 147
Southeast Asia civilizations, 113, 233–36
spread of, 235–36
teachings and values of, 120(t), 127–28
Vedas relationship to, 126–27
withdrawal in, 128(i)
women, view of, 127–28

Hippocrates (Greek physician), 137

Hispaniola (Haiti), Columbus landing in, 382(i), 383

Hittites (Anatolia), 73

hoe-based agriculture, 30

Holy Land. *See* Israel

Holy Roman Empire
political fragmentation, 334
scope of, 330

holy wars. *See* religious wars

hominid species, 3, 12–13, 22–23

Homo habilis, 3

Homo sapiens, 3, 12
societal development. *See* Paleolithic era

homosexuality
Greek civilization, 173–74
Spartan prohibition, 174

honor killing, 297

Hopewell culture, 204(m), 206
exchange networks, 206
time frame of, 181(t)

hoplites (Greek infantrymen), 94

Horace (Roman poet), 108

Horn of Africa, Axum (Ethiopia), 185–88

horses
agricultural use, 38, 342(t), 343
domestication of, 39–40
inventions related to, 270(t), 342(t), 358
military use, 73, 222, 257, 342(t), 357, 365(i)
nomads' reliance on, 257, 356(t), 358, 365(i)

horticulture, emergence of, 30

House of Wisdom (Baghdad), 310

Huitzilopochtli (Aztec god), 407

Hulegu (Persian il-khan), 371

humanists, 393–95

humanities, Byzantine study of, 347

human sacrifice
Aztec, 407
Chinese, 53, 64
Mayan, 192
Moche, 197, 198
Teotihuacán, 194

humors, 137
Hundred Years' War (1337–1453), 393
Hungary, Mongol invasion of, 375
Huns
    horses, use of, 356(t), 357
    Roman empire, invasions on, 110
    viewed as barbarians, 110(i), 379–80
hunter-gatherers. *See* gathering and
        hunting peoples

Ibn al-Arabi (1165–1240), 297–98
Ibn Battuta (1304–1368)
    on Muslims in Mali, 240
    on status of Islamic women, 302, 303
    on Swahili people, 237
    travels, scope of, 299(m)
Ibn Khaldun (1332–1406), 310(t), 379
Ibn Rushd (Averroës, 1126–1198), 310(t)
Ibn Sina (Avicenna, 980–1037), 310(t),
        311
Ibn Yasin (Islamic scholar), 361
Ice Age
    global warming, 24, 28–30
    human migrations during, 14,
        15–16(m), 18, 28
    land bridges during, 14, 15–16(m)
    megafaunal extinction, 18
Iceland, Viking colonization, 242
icons, symbolism attached to, 324
Igbo people (West Africa)
    exchange networks, 388
    in fifteenth century, 387–88
    lost wax method, 388(i)
    title society in, 41, 388
il-khans, in Persia, 369
imams (Shia leaders), 293
immigration. *See* migrations
immortality. *See* afterlife
immunity, to disease, 227, 228
Inanna (Mesopotamian goddess), 61
Inca empire, 408–10
    bureaucratic organization, 408–9
    conquered people, policy toward,
        408–9
    emergence of, 212, 408
    exchange networks, 245
    precursors to, 52, 200
    quipu, accounting system, 65(t), 245,
        408
    religious system of, 410–11
    road network, 245(i)
    scope of, 196, 214, 405(m), 408
    women, status of, 409–10

incense, 220
incest, rules against, 22
India
    Black Death (plague), 377
    civilizations of. *See* Indian
        civilizations
    Delhi Sultanate, 391(m)
    in fifteenth century, 386(t)
    innovations and discoveries, 342(t),
        343
    Islam, spread to, 298–300, 309, 360
    Mughal empire, 403
    Sikhism, 300
Indian civilizations
    achievements of, 113
    assimilation of outsiders, 162
    Buddhism, 128–31, 144–45
    caste system, 113, 158–62
    Christianity, spread to, 142, 231
    earliest civilizations near. *See* Indus
        Valley civilization
    Greek influence on, 98–99
    Gupta Empire, 112–13
    Hinduism, 126–28, 131–32
    influence on other cultures, 233–36
    Mauryan Empire, 111–13
    nomadic invasions on, 113
    people and culture of. *See specific
        civilizations by name*
    Sea Roads and trade, 231
    slavery, 164
    Vedas descriptions of, 126–27
Indian Ocean region
    China and, 402
    commerce, development of, 230–32
    Europe and, 406
    Indian civilizations and trade, 113
    monsoons, 229(m), 230
    Paleolithic migrations, 17(m), 19
    Portuguese voyages, 385(t), 398(i),
        399–400
    Sea Roads, 228–38, 229(m)
Indo-European language, 34
Indo-Europeans
    Greeks as, 92
    Persians as, 90
indulgences, 338
industrialization
    in early modern era, 413
    Middle Ages/Western Europe
        innovations, 343
Indus Valley civilization, 51(m), 52–53
    Aryan destruction of, 111

    decline of, 79
    exchange networks, 71–72, 230
    features of, 52–53
    Harappa, 51(m), 56
    modern practices derived from,
        52–53
    Mohenjo Daro, 51(m), 56
    writing system, 65(t)
infanticide of women
    agricultural village societies, 41
    Islamic prohibition, 296
Inner Asia. *See* Central Asia
innovations and discoveries
    Agricultural Revolution era, 38–39
    in agriculture. *See* agricultural
        innovations
    Chinese, 38, 83, 231, 254, 269–71,
        270(t), 376–77
    Indian, 342(t)
    metals, use of. *See* metallurgy; *specific
        metals*
    for military. *See* military innovations
    Muslim, 309–10, 310(t), 342(t)
    navigational. *See* navigation
        technology
    nomadic societies, 358
    Roman, 83
    stimulation of other inventions by.
        See technology, diffusion of
    for textile industry. *See* textile
        industry innovations
    tools, first. *See* tools
inventions. *See* innovations and
        discoveries; technology
investiture conflict, 332
Ionia
    Greek settlements in, 136
    Persian control of, 95
Iran
    early civilization. *See* Persian empire
    Islam, spread to, 291–92
    Islamization versus Arabization, 292
    Revolution of 1979, 281
Iraq
    early civilizations. *See* Baghdad
        (Iraq); Mesopotamia; Sumerian
        civilization (Mesopotamia)
    in Mongol empire, 369–70
    Nestorian Christianity, 290, 318–19
iron-chain suspension bridges, 83, 270(t)
iron metallurgy
    Bantu cultures, 201
    China, 253–54, 270(t)

Meroë, 184
Niger Valley civilizations, 188, 189
Iroquois people (North America)
in fifteenth century, 388–89
League of Five Nations
confederation, 388–89
irrigation
in earliest civilizations, 53, 68
environmental damage from, 52, 68, 93
Muslim system, 309
Persian empire, 92
Isabella (Spanish queen), 306
Isaiah (prophet), 118
Isaiah (prophet, Judaism), 120(t), 135
Ishi (Yahi people), 36–37
Isis (Egyptian goddess), 107, 144
Islam, 280–88. *See also specific topics*
Believers' Movement, 290
believers of. *See* Muslims
caliphs, 292–94
Christianity compared to, 288, 301
as civilization. *See* Arab empire;
Islamic empire
conversion to, 291–92
Crusades against, 338–39, 339(m)
dating system in, 7
and decline of Christianity, 317–21
early, conflicts within, 292–95
education system (*madrassas*), 307
European civilization, influence
on, 306
expansion of. *See* Arab empire;
Islamic empire; Islamization
founder of. *See* Muhammad
(570–632 C.E.)
fundamentalist. *See* Islamic
fundamentalism
hadiths (sayings and deeds of
Muhammad), 297
Hinduism compared to, 299–300
holy book of. *See* Quran (Koran)
Jerusalem, significance of, 318
jihad (struggle), 286
Judaism as influence, 135
laws of. *See* sharia (Islamic law code)
Mecca pilgrimage (*hajj*), 280(i), 281,
286, 308
modernizers versus fundamentalists,
311
Muslim identity, guidelines for, 294
origin, country of, 212
patriarchy, 296–97
places of worship. *See* mosques

second flowering of, 403–4
Shia, 293, 402
Sikhism derived from, 300
Sufi, 294–95, 295(i)
Sunni, 293
time frame of events, 283(t)
women, status of, 295–98, 296(i)
Zoroastrian influence on, 133–34,
292
Islamic empire, 298–312
Christian communities within, 318
in fifteenth century, 400–404, 401(m)
as global civilization, 306–12
Greek influence on, 347–48
Green Revolution, 309
influence on other cultures, 304, 306,
308–12, 311–12, 347
innovations and discoveries, 309–11,
310(t), 342(t), 347
Islam, integration with native
religions, 301–4
Jerusalem, conquest of, 318
jizya (tax on non-Muslims), 290–91,
299
networks of faith, levels of, 307–8
Ottoman empire, 400–401
scope of, 299(m), 302(m)
trade and expansion of, 302, 302(m),
308–9
Islamic fundamentalism, versus
modernizers, 311
Islamization
Anatolia, 300–302, 301(m), 360
versus Arabization, 292
early expansion, 213(m), 290(m),
317–21
East Africa, 237–38
India, 298–300, 309, 360
Mongol converts, 371, 376
Mughal empire, 403
and nomadic societies, 298, 300–302,
359, 359–61, 371
North Africa, 292, 319, 361, 361(m)
Nubia, 185, 320
Safavid empire, 402
Songhay civilization, 402–3
Southeast Asia, 404
Spain, 304–6, 361, 361(i)
Sufi contributions to, 299–302,
307–8
and Turkish conquests, 298, 300–302,
360–61
West Africa, 241, 302(m), 302–3

Israel. *See also* Palestine
ancient, cities of, 134(m)
founding of, 134
Hebrews exile from, 134
Issus, Battle of (333 B.C.E.), 98(i)
Istanbul (Turkey), Byzantine era. *See*
Constantinople
Istar (Mesopotamian goddess), 61, 72
Italy
Black Death (plague), 377–78
city-states, 345
Lombards in, 329
Middle Ages/Western Europe,
332–34, 345
trading networks, 332–34, 345

Jahangir (Mughal emperor), 295(i)
Jainism, 120(t)
Janissaries (Ottoman soldiers), 402(i)
Japan
early civilizations. *See* Japanese
civilization
Paleolithic societies, 25
proximity to China, 265, 265(m)
Japanese civilization
Buddhism, 266–67
Chinese influence on, 265–67
courtly culture of, 267–69
elites, 267–69
emperor, divinity of, 267
Mongol defeat in, 364
samurai, 266(i), 266–67
Seventeen Article Constitution (Japan),
265
Shinto, 267
women, view of, 267
Jasaw Chan Kùawiil I (Maya
r. 682–734), 178(i)
jatis (occupational caste), 160(t), 161,
162
Java
Islam, spread to, 404
Paleolithic climate change, 20
Paleolithic migrations to, 19, 19(m)
Sailendra kingdom, 234–35
Jenne (West Africa), 240(m)
Great Mosque, 303(i)
Jenne-jeno civilization (Niger Valley),
184(m)
iron-smithing, 189
terra-cotta sculpture, 189(i)
trade, long-distance, 190, 241
Jeremiah (prophet), 118

Jeremiah (prophet, Judaism), 120(t)
Jericho, 51(m)
Jerome, Saint (340–420 C.E.), 379–80
Jerusalem
　Christian holy places in, 321
　Ethiopian Christian relationship to,
　　320–21
　Muslim conquest of, 318
　Muslim holy places in, 318(i)
　seizure in Crusades, 338, 339(m), 340(i)
　significance, to three religions, 318
　temple, rebuilding, 91
Jesus of Nazareth
　birthday, symbolism of, 331
　Buddha compared to, 139–40
　Christianity, founding of. See
　　Christianity, early
　divinity of, 140, 146
　early life of, 139
　Sermon on the Mount, 139
Jesus Sutras, 319
jewelry
　Meroë, kingdom of, 185(i)
　Moche, ceremonial, 197
Jews
　ancient era. See Hebrews
　bias and persecution of. See
　　anti-Semitism
　Jerusalem, as sacred location, 318
　Muhammad, reaction to, 287
　religion of. See Judaism
　Spain, expulsion from, 306
Jie (nomadic society), 226–27
jihad (struggle)
　by Fulbe people, 390
　Islamic teaching, 286
Jin empire (China, 1115–1234)
　China tribute to, 260–61
　scope of, 252(m), 259
jizya (tax on non-Muslims), 290, 291, 318
Jomon society, 25
Jordan, Ain Ghazal statues, 33(i)
Judah, founding of, 134
Judaism
　Jerusalem, significance of, 318
　monotheism of, 134–35
　Zoroastrianism influence on, 133–34
Julian of Norwich (English mystic),
　336
junks, 230
Jurchen people, Jin empire, 252(m), 364
Justinian (Byzantine emperor,
　r. 527–565), 322, 323(m), 347

Juwayni (Persian historian), 369

Kaaba (Mecca)
　hajj (pilgrimage to Mecca), 281, 286,
　　293(i), 308
　Muhammad purification of, 293(i)
　polytheistic era, 283–84, 293(i)
　silk covering, 225
Kabîr (Indian poet), 300
kaghan (Turkic ruler), 359–60
Kaifeng (China), 254(i)
Kali (Hindu deity), 128
Kamasutra (Hindu text), 128
kami (Japanese sacred spirits), 267
Kaminalijuyu (Maya city), 195
Kanem civilization (West Africa), 239
　Islam, spread to, 301(m)
Kano (West Africa), 240(m), 241
Karakorum (Mongol capital), 365, 366,
　367, 374, 376
Karlsfeni, Thorfinn (Viking voyager),
　242–43
karma, 127, 129, 161, 233
Kazakhstan, 357(i)
Kenya, Bantu cultures in, 202
Kerela (India), Christianity, spread to,
　231
khanates, Mongol, 362(m)
Khanbalik (China)
　modern era. See Beijing
　Mongol capital, 367
Khayyam, Omar (1048–1131), 310(t)
Khitan, China tribute to, 259–60
Khmer kingdom, 233, 233(m)
Khonsu (Egyptian god), 186
Khotan (Central Asia), 226
Khubilai Khan (China), 364
　and Marco Polo, 368(i)
　policies of, 367–69
　religious tolerance, 372(i)
Khutulun (Mongol wrestler princess),
　370–71
al-Khwarazim (790–840), 310(t)
Khwarizm (Central Asia), 365–66
Kiev (Russia), Mongol invasion of, 373
Kievan Rus civilization (Russia), 211,
　327–28
　Crusades against, 338, 339(m)
　Eastern Orthodox Christianity in,
　　327–28
　Mongol conquest of, 372–74
　trade, 327
Kilwa (Swahili city), 237(m)

kings. See also emperors; pharaohs
　(Egypt); *specific names*
　divinity of. See divinity of kings
　in earliest civilizations, 62–64, 66
　Persian empire, 90–91
kinship societies. See also chiefdoms; clans
　Bantu cultures, 202–3
　features of, 40–42
　fictive kinship, 357
　in fifteenth century, 388–89
　Germanic peoples, 329
　Paleolithic societies, 25
　pastoral nomads as, 39–40, 257, 354
　state as replacement for, 42, 62
　title societies, 41, 388
Kipchak Khanate, Mongols in Russia,
　372–74
kivas, 204, 205(i)
knights, 334, 340(i)
Kong Fuzi. See Confucius
Kongo, kingdom of, in fifteenth
　century, 398(m)
Koran. See Quran (Koran)
Korea
　Chinese influences, 261
　Confucianism, 262
　tribute relationship with China,
　　261–62
　unification of (7th century), 262(m)
Koryo dynasty (Korea, 918–1392),
　261–62
Koumbi-Saleh (West Africa), 241
kowtow (in tribute system), 258
Krishna, Lord, 131–32
Kroeber, Alfred, 37
Kshatriya (warrior caste), 99, 159–61
Kumsong (Korea), 262
Kush (Nubia), 49(t)
　conquest of Egypt by, 73, 183,
　　186–87

labor
　gender-based. See division of labor
　Inca empire, 409
　Mongol empire, 365
　serfs, feudal era, 330–31
　shortages, and Black Death (plague),
　　377
　slaves as. See slavery
Labrador, Paleolithic settlements, 25
Lagash (Mesopotamia), 51(m), 63, 67(m)
lakshanas (Buddhist bodily symbols),
　129(i)

Lamu (Swahili city), 237(m)
land, owning. *See* property ownership
land bridges, Ice Age, 14, 15–16(m)
languages
    Agaw (Axum), 187
    Austronesian, 19, 19(m), 35, 230
    Chinese, 108
    Coptic, 142
    diffusion, and Agricultural
        Revolution, 34–35
    Dravidian, 65(t)
    Farsi, 292
    Ge'ez (Axum), 143, 186–87
    Greek, ancient, 98
    Indo-European, 34
    Latin, evolution of, 107
    Pali, 130
    Quechua, 212, 408
    Sanskrit, 126
    Swahili, 237
    Syriac, 141
    written. *See* writing systems
Laozi (Zhuangzi), 120(t). *See also*
    Daoism
Lapps, 356(t)
lateen sail, 344
latifundia (Roman estates), 166
Latin Christendom. *See* Roman
    Catholic Church
Latin language
    evolution of, 108
    and Roman Catholicism, 325, 331
laws and law codes
    of Hammurabi. *See* Hammurabi
        (r. 1792–1750 B.C.E.) law code
    Islamic. *See sharia* (Islamic law code)
    Laws of Manu, The (India), 128
    Legalism, China, 103, 121–22
    Roman, 108
Laws of Manu, The, 128
Leakey, Mary, 3
Lee, Richard, 21–22
Legalism (China), 103, 121–22
    Confucianism as response to, 121–22
    Han Fei on, 121
legions (Roman), 107
leisure, in gathering and hunting
    societies, 22
Leo I (Pope), meets Attila the Hun,
    110(i)
Lerner, Gerda, 61
Lessons for Women (Ban Zhao), 123
letters of credit, 254

life expectancy
    in Agricultural Revolution, 37–38
    in Paleolithic era, 22
lineage systems
    matrilineal descent, 389
    patrilineal descent, 41
literacy. *See also* education
    in earliest civilizations, 63–64
    and invention of paper, 342(t)
    Western Christendom, signs of, 331
literature. *See also* poetry
    Mesopotamian, 56, 67, 68
    Renaissance, 395–96
Liu Zongyuan (Chinese official), 250
livestock, raising/herding. *See* pastoral
    societies
llamas/alpaca, 33–34, 180, 199
Lombards, 329
long-distance trade. *See* commerce; trade
longhouses, 25
looms, 38, 83, 335
Lord of Sipan (Moche), 197, 198(i)
lost wax method, 388(i)
Lothar, kingdom of, 330(m)
Louis the German, kingdom of,
    330(m)
Luba statue (Bantu), 202, 203(i)
luxuriant inns, 253
luxury goods
    Mesoamerican civilizations, 192, 245
    Sea Roads items, 229–30, 231(t)
    Silk Roads items, 223–25
    Venetian merchants, 229
    Western Christendom demands, 341
Lycurgus (Sparta founder), 174

Macedonia, Alexander the Great, 96–98
Machiavelli, Niccolo (1469–1527), 395
Machu Picchu (Peru), 409(i)
Madagascar, Paleolithic migrations to,
    19, 19(m), 230
madrassas (Islamic schools), 307
Magyar people, invasions of, 332, 333(m)
Mahabharata, 131
Mahavira (Indian prophet), 120(t)
Mahayana Buddhism, 131, 140
    China, 274
    on Silk Roads, 227
Mahiya, Gudo (of Hadza), 11
maize. *See* corn (maize)
Malacca
    Islam, eclectic style in, 404
    strategic location of, 391(m)

Malacca, Straits of, and trade, 232–33,
    237
malaria, 201
Malay Peninsula (Malaysia)
    Islam, spread to, 404
    Srivijaya, kingdom of, 232–34
    and trade, 232–33, 233(m)
Malcolm X, 281
Mali, kingdom of, 211, 239–41, 240(m)
    Islam, spread to, 301(m), 303–5
mammoths, extinction of, 18, 20, 22
al-Mamun (Abbasid caliph), 310
Manchuria, 358
Mandate of Heaven (China), 53, 63,
    106, 119, 264
    Confucian teachings on, 124
    and Mongol rulers, 367
Manichaeism, 358
manors, feudalistic, 330–31, 336
Mansa Musa (West African ruler),
    pilgrimage to Mecca, 304–5
Mansur (caliph, r. 754–775), 297
manumission, 166
Mao Zedong (Chinese communist
    leader)
    Confucianism, view of, 117
    Qin Shihuangdi compared to, 114
map-making. *See* cartography
Maragha observatory (Persia), 310(t)
Marathon, Battle of (490 B.C.E.), 96
Marduk (god, Babylon), 63
maritime voyages
    Chinese (Ming dynasty), 391(m),
        392–93, 396–400, 398(m)
    in fifteenth century, 392–93,
        397–400
    motivations for, 399
    Portuguese, 385(t), 397–400, 398(m)
    religious connection to, 399
    Vikings, 242–43
Marius (Rome), 102
Marrakesh (Morocco), 361
marriage
    Christianity on, 141, 142
    Confucianism on, 125, 169
    Greek civilization, 172
    Hinduism on, 128
    Islam on, 296
    Japan, 267
    Korea, 262
    and matrilineal descent, 389
    Middle Ages/Western Europe, 337
    Mongols, 369, 371

marriage (*continued*)
   pastoral societies, 355
   plural, 262, 296
   San peoples, 21
   Sparta, 173
martyrs
   Christian, early, 142, 144–45, 181
   Islamic concept of, 293
Mary (mother of Jesus)
   devotional cult of, 141, 335
   Eastern Orthodox view, 324
Mary Magdalene, 141
Masai people, 356(t)
mathematics
   Greek achievements, 136–37
   Mayan achievements, 192, 310(t)
   Muslim achievements, 310–11, 342(t)
matrilineal descent, 389
Mauryan empire (India, 326–184 B.C.E.),
      111–12, 112(m)
   distinctive accomplishment of, 90(t)
   enlightened ruler of, See **Ashoka**
      (India, r. 268–232 B.C.E.)
   political philosophy of, 112
Maya civilization (Mesoamerica), 191(m),
      191–93
   collapse of, 82, 192–93, 212
   El Mirador (Guatemala), 191
   features of, 191–93
   Olmec influence on, 54, 65
   origins of, 191
   religious system of, 192
   state authority, 192
   temples and monuments, 66, 178(i),
      179, 191–92
   Teotihuacán incursions, 195
   Tikal, 66, 192
   time frame of, 181(t)
   trade, 192, 245
   writing systems, 192
Meander (Greek writer), 172
measles, 227
Mecca
   hajj (pilgrimage), 280(i), 281, 286,
      304–5, 308
   Kaaba, 225, 283–84, 293(i)
   Muhammad conquest of, 287
   Muhammed conquest of, 293(i)
medical science
   Chinese achievements, 376–77
   Greek achievements, 137
   Muslim achievements, 310(t), 310–11,
      342(t)

Medina (Arabia), *hijra* (journey) by
      Muhammad, 287
Mediterranean Sea, trade and
      commerce, early, 228–29
Menander (Bactrian king), 99
men and masculinity
   Aboriginal Australians, 21–22
   Aztec, 410
   Christian view of, 141
   Confucian view of, 123, 168, 255
   and dominance/power. *See*
      patriarchy
   in Greek civilization, 172, 174
   Inca, 410
   Middle Ages/Western Europe view
      of, 336
   in Roman empire, 102
   Spartan, 173–74
   West African civilizations, 240
merchants
   African, 236–38
   Aztec *pochteca*, 245, 407
   Buddhist, 226–27
   Chinese civilizations, 158, 220
   Indian civilizations, 113
   Muslims, 231–32, 308–9
   negative reputation of, 80, 158, 220
   state benefits to, 345
   as third estate, 345
   wealth of, 158, 220, 225, 231–32,
      308–9, 407
   Western Christendom, 335, 341, 345
   widows, role of, 335
Meroë, kingdom of, 183–85
   conquest by Axum, 185
   cultural influences on, 185
   location of, 51(m), 184(m)
   time frame of, 181(t)
Meru, Mount, 235
Merv (Central Asia), 226
Mesoamerica
   Agricultural Revolution, 28(m),
      33–34
   civilizations of. *See* Mesoamerican
      civilizations
   in fifteenth century/pre-Columbian,
      405(m)
   location of, 191, 191(m)
Mesoamerican civilizations, 84(m),
      190–95, 191(m)
   American Web trade and commerce,
      244(m), 244–45
   Aztec, 245, 404–7

development, compared to other
      continents, 181
   exchange networks, 244–45
   in fifteenth century, 386(t), 404–7
   Maya, 191–93, 245
   Olmec, 50(m), 54
   people and culture of. *See specific*
      civilizations by name
   population estimates, second-wave
      civilizations, 182(t)
   similarities among, 191
   Teotihuacán, 56, 193–95, 245
Mesopotamia, 55–76
   city-states, 67(m), 68–69. *See also*
      Akkad (Mesopotamia); Assyria
      (Mesopotamia); Babylon
      (Mesopotamia); Ur (Mesopotamia);
      Uruk (Mesopotamia)
   class hierarchies, 57–58, 64
   cultural diffusion, 72–73
   earliest civilization. *See* Sumerian
      civilization (Mesopotamia)
   Egyptian civilization compared to,
      66–75
   environment, impact on culture,
      66–68
   environmental damage, 68
   Epic of Gilgamesh, 56, 67, 68
   exchange networks, 71–72, 230
   gods and goddesses, 61, 63
   Greek influence on, 99
   Hammurabi law code, 57–58, 63
   invasions, vulnerability to, 66, 69
   Muslims reclamation of, 232
   other cultures, influence on, 73–75, 90
   Roman invasion of, 100
   slavery, 58, 58(i), 163
   Tigris and Euphrates, flooding of, 66
   warfare, 69
   women, veiled, 61
metallurgy. *See also specific materials, for*
      example, entries under bronze
   in Agricultural Revolution, 38
   development, continental
      comparisons, 181
   as environmental hazard, 93, 108
Methodius (missionary), 327
Metochite, Theodore (Byzantine
      scholar), 347
metta (loving-kindness), 140
Mexica people
   civilization of. *See* Aztec empire
   origin of, 404, 406

Mexico, early civilizations in. *See*
    Mesoamerican civilizations
Michaelangelo (Renaissance painter),
    394
micro-blades, 24
Micronesia
    Paleolithic migrations to, 19(m)
    trade network of, 411
Middle Ages
    feudalism, 330–31
    Western European civilization. *See*
        Western Christendom
Middle East
    Agricultural Revolution, 29, 29(m),
        31–32
    Arab Spring, 281
    Black Death (plague), 377
    civilizations of. *See* Middle Eastern
        civilizations
    crops of, 309, 377
    Crusades, lack of impact on, 339
    in fifteenth century, 386(t)
Middle Eastern civilizations
    Arab empire, 288–97
    cradle of, 48, 51(m)
    Islamic empire, 298–312
    Mesopotamian/Sumerian,
        55–76
    Ottoman empire, 300–302, 301(m),
        301–2, 400–401
    people and culture of. *See specific
        civilizations by name*
    Persian empire, 85(m), 90–92
migrations
    of Chinese within China, 250
    of Greeks, ancient, 98–99
    Paleolithic era, 4(m), 4–5, 12–20,
        16–17(m), 19(m), 28
Milan (Italy), as trade center, 345
military
    early civilizations. *See specific
        civilizations by name*
    innovations for. *See* military
        innovations
    methods of war. *See* warfare
    warriors. *See* warrior societies
military innovations
    bows and arrows, 365(i)
    Byzantine Greek fire, 326
    camels, use of, 359
    cannons, 270, 343–44
    chariots, horse-drawn, 73
    Chinese civilizations, 83

gunpowder, 270(t), 270–71, 342(t),
    343–44
horses, use of, 73, 222, 257, 342(t),
    357, 365(i)
iron suits of armor, 254
iron weapons, 185, 254
rockets, 309
mills
    as energy source, 343
    grains, grinding, 335, 343
    paper mills, 309
    windmills, 271, 343
Ming dynasty (China, 1368–1644),
    391(m), 391–93
    features of, 391–92
    maritime voyages, 391(m), 392–93,
        396–400, 398(m)
    Mongol rule, eradicating, 391–92
    Neo-Confucianism, 369
Minoan civilization, 73
missionaries
    Christian, early, 141–43
    Eastern Orthodox, 327
    Roman Catholic, 331
mita (Inca labor service), 409
Mithra (Persian god), 107
moa, extinction of, 20
mobility, social. *See* social mobility
Moche civilization (Peru), 196(m),
    197–99, 408
    features of, 197–99
    precursor to, 73
Modun (Xiongnu, r. 210–174 B.C.E.),
    358–59
Mohawk people (North America), 388
Mohenjo Daro, 51(m)
    features of, 6(i), 56, 56(i)
moksha (liberation), 127, 128
Mombasa (East Africa), 237(m)
monasticism
    Buddhist, 225, 226, 274–75
    Christian, Egyptian, 142
    Eastern Orthodox, 324
    Roman Catholic, 335
    and women. *See* nuns
money. *See* currency
Mongke (Mongol ruler), 364, 366
Mongol empire, 361–80
    Abbasid conquest by, 294
    Black Death (plague), 228, 375(m),
        377–79
    brutality and destructiveness, 365–66,
        370, 372, 373(i)

bureaucracy, 366, 371
China in, 362(m), 367–68
Chinese-Mongol society, 368–69, 373
Christianity during, 319
conquered people, policy toward,
    365–66, 370, 372, 373
courier network, 374
and cultural diffusion, 376–77
decline and rise of Europe, 379
decline of, 369, 371, 374, 377, 379
defeats, reasons for, 364
diplomacy, 375–76
Eastern Europe in, 362(m), 365,
    375–76
first ruler. *See* Chinggis Khan
    (Mongol ruler, 1162–1227)
invasions by, 362(m), 364, 367, 369–70
Iraq in, 369–70
Islam, converts to, 371, 376
under Khubilai Khan, 367–69
Marco Polo in, 362(m), 366, 370, 374
massacres, modern view of, 380
military tactics, 364–66
Mongol assimilation, 371–72, 373
origin of, 363–64
pastoralism continued within, 368–69,
    370, 372–73
Persia in, 369–72
pope and Christianity, outreach by,
    376
religious tolerance of, 319, 366, 368,
    368(i), 372(i)
Russia in, 372–74
scope of, 361–62, 362(m), 364
social structure, 364–65
successful conquests, factors in,
    364–66
taxation, 366, 369, 373–74
technology transfer, 376–77
time frame of events, 355(t)
trading networks of, 366, 374–75,
    375(m)
warfare tactics, 365–66, 370, 372, 373(i)
wealth of, 365
Western Europe, safety from, 375–76
women, status of, 369–71, 371–72,
    372(i)
Mongolia
    communist anti-religion massacre,
        353
    Mongols, origin of, 361, 362(m)
    Turks, origin of, 259, 359
    Xiongnu society, 358–59

Mongols
  empire-building. *See* Chinggis Khan
    (Mongol ruler, 1162–1227);
    Mongol empire
  origin of, 361, 362(m)
  spirituality, 361–62
  unification of tribes, 363–64
  women, status of, 355
monkey god (China), 272
monks. *See* monasticism
Monophysite, 146
monotheism
  Believers' Movement, 290
  Christianity, 140–46
  Islam, 280–88
  Judaism, 134–35
  Middle East, close relationships, 285(i)
  Paleolithic societies, 23
  rise, in second-wave civilizations,
    132–36
  Zoroastrianism, 103–4, 133–34
monsoons, Indian Ocean region,
    229(m), 230
Monte Alban (Maya City), 195
Morales, Evo, 179
Morocco, Almoravid empire, 360, 361(m)
Moscow (Russia), Mongol era, 374
mosques
  Dome of the Rock (Jerusalem), 318(i)
  Grand Mosque (Arabia), 317
  Great Mosque (Jenne), 303(i)
mound-builders, 204(m), 206–7
  Cahokia, 206–7
  Hopewell culture, 206
  military of, 207
  time frame of, 181(t)
Mount Olympus, 135, 138
movable type, 269
Mughal empire (India), 401(m)
  features of, 403
Muhammad (570–632 C.E.)
  biographical information, 284, 289,
    296
  Dome of the Rock symbolism, 318
  hijra (journey) to Medina, 287
  initial rejection of, 287
  on *jihad* (struggle), 286
  as messenger, 285, 286, 287
  military actions by, 287–88
  religious system of. *See* Islam
  revelations, 284–85
  successors to, 292
mullahs, Shia women, 298

musical instruments, 230
Muslims
  architecture of, 303, 303(i), 361
  as believers, 289–90
  commerce, positive view of, 308–9
  intellectual achievements of, 309,
    310(t), 310–11, 342(t), 376–77. *See*
    also specific disciplines, for example,
    medical science
  Islam, expansion of. *See* Arab empire;
    Islamic empire; Islamization
  Islamic identity, guidelines for, 294
  merchants/wealth, 231–32, 308–9
  Muslim (one who submits), 285
  religious system of. *See* Islam
  sects. *See* Shia Muslims; Sufi Muslims;
    Sunni Muslims
  as slave owners, 232, 241
  in United States, 281
  women, veiled. *See* veiled women
  world population (21st century), 282
Mussolini, Benito (Italy, 1883–1945),
    and new Roman empire, 114
Mut (Egyptian mother-goddess), 186
Myanmar. *See* Burma

Namarrgon (Aboriginal ancestor),
    15(i)
Namondjok (Aboriginal ancestor),
    15(i)
Nanna (Mesopotamian god), 63(i)
Nara (Japan), 265
Naram-Sin (Akkadian ruler), 58(i)
Natchez people (North America), 206
Native Americans (of North America)
  cultures of. *See* North American
    cultures
  diseases, impact on, 228
  in fifteenth century, 388–89
natural philosophy, Middle Ages/
    Western Europe, 346–48
nature. *See also* environment
  Daoist view of, 125
  women identified with, 61
navigation technology
  astrolab, 230
  Chinese innovations, 344
  compass, magnetic, 230, 231, 270(t),
    271, 344
  Western Christendom adoption, 344
navy, Roman, 100
Nazca civilization (Peru), 196(m), 408
Neanderthals, 23

Nenet nomads, 356(t)
Neo-Confucianism, 251, 369
Neolithic (New Stone Age)
    Revolution. *See* Agricultural
    Revolution
Nestorian Christianity, 146, 290,
    318–19
  blended doctrine of, 319
  Nestorian heresy, 324
  Nestorian Stele, 319(i)
Nestorius (bishop of Constantinople),
    324
New Guinea
  Agricultural Revolution, 29(m), 35
  in fifteenth century, 385
  Paleolithic migrations to, 19
New Jerusalem (Ethiopia), 321
New Rome, Constantinople as, 322
New Stone Age. *See* Neolithic
    Revolution
New Testament (Bible), miracles of
    Jesus, 140
New Zealand
  animal extinction in, 20
  Paleolithic migrations to, 17(m), 19
Nezahualcoyotl (Aztec ruler,
    1402–1472), 407
Nicaea Council (325 C.E.), 146
Nigeria. *See also* Igbo people (West
    Africa)
  Bantu cultures, 200
  Nok culture, 38(i)
Niger Valley civilizations, 184(m),
    188–90
  Jenne-jeno, 188–90, 239
  state structure, absence of, 189
  time frame of, 181(t)
Nile River region, earliest civilizations
    in. *See* Egyptian civilization;
    Nubian civilization (Africa)
Ninevah (Mesopotamia), 51(m), 67(m)
Nippur (Mesopotamia), 51(m)
nirvana (enlightenment), 129–30
nobility
  Middle Ages/Western Europe, 334,
    345
  as second estate, 345
Nok culture (Nigeria), artistic
    traditions, 38(i)
nomadic societies. *See also specific groups*
  Agricultural Revolution era, 39–40
  of Almoravid empire, 361, 361(m)
  Arabs as, 359

assimilation with conquered people, 250, 260–61, 329, 360, 371–72
Buddhist, 226
Central Asia, 39–40
centralized authority, 357, 359
China, early incursions by, 109, 170, 257–59, 359–60
China co-dependence with, 257
China tribute system with, 257–60, 360
class hierarchies, 354–55
confederations of, 357
and cultural diffusion, 222
as empire-builders, 214–15, 359–60
in fifteenth century, 389–90
Fulbe people, 390
Islam, conversion and spread by, 298, 300–302, 359–61
as kinship groups, 39, 257, 354
last conquest of, 389
locations/names of tribes, 356(t)
military of, 357–58
Mongols, 361–80
pastoral practices of. *See* pastoral societies
religious system of, 358
of steppes, 222, 228, 257
trade, early civilizations, 182, 222
trade routes, control of, 257, 260, 359
Turks, 359–60, 389
viewed as barbarians, 257–58, 329, 379–80
women, status of, 170, 369–71
Norte Chico civilization (Peru), 50(m), 196
decline of, 79
features of, 49, 52
quipa, accounting system, 52, 65(t)
North Africa. *See also specific countries*
Almoravid empire, 360, 361(m)
Christianity, spread to, 142, 144(i), 181
cities of, 184(m)
civilizations, early. *See* Egyptian civilization
Islam, spread to, 292, 319, 361, 361(m)
in Ottoman empire, 301(m), 401(m)
in Roman empire, 101(m), 181
North America. *See also* Mexico
Agricultural Revolution, 26, 28(m), 33–34
agricultural village societies in, 388–89

cultures of. *See* North American cultures
in fifteenth century, 388–89
in fifteenth century/pre-Columbian, 405(m)
gathering and hunting peoples in, 26, 35, 36–37
Paleolithic migrations to, 16(m), 18
Viking voyages to, 241–43
North American cultures, 84(m)
American Web trade and commerce, 243–44, 244(m)
Ancestral Pueblo, 204–6
Cahokia, 206–7
chiefdoms, 42, 206
Clovis culture, 18
complex/affluent gatherers and hunters, 387
in fifteenth century, 386(t), 387
Great Suns, 207
Hopewell culture, 206
Iroquois League of Five Nations, 388–89
mound-builders, 204(m), 206–7
people and culture of. *See specific cultures by name*
population estimates, 182(t)
Nubian civilizations (Africa), 51(m), 72–73, 184(m)
Christianity, decline of, 320
Christianity, spread to, 185
conquest of Egypt, 73, 181(t), 183, 186–87
in Egyptian empire, 72(i), 73, 181(t)
exchange networks, 72
Islam, spread to, 185, 320
Kush, 73, 183, 186–87
Meroë, kingdom of, 183–85
Ta-Seti civilization, 54
Nuer people, 356(t)
nuns
Buddhist, 130, 168
Christian, early, 141, 168
Christian mystics, 335
Roman Catholic, 334

oasis cities (Central Asia), 226
obelisks, Axum, 186, 188(i)
observatory
Maragha (Persia), 310(t)
Muslim innovation, 309, 309(i), 310(t)
obsidian blades, 56, 194
Oceania. *See* Pacific Ocean region

oceans
navigation of. *See* maritime voyages
regions. *See* Caribbean region; Indian Ocean region; Pacific Ocean region
Octavian (Rome). *See* Augustus
Odoacer (Germanic general), 329
Ogodei Khan (Mongol ruler), 364, 367, 374, 375, 415
Old Stone Age. *See* Paleolithic era
Old Testament (Bible)
Cain and Abel, 40
and decline of goddess culture, 61
Ethiopian Christian relationship to, 320–21
eye for eye principle, 72
on futility of existence, 174
Ten Commandments, 134
Yahweh, 79, 134–35
olives, 181
Olmec civilization (Mesoamerica), 50(m)
decline of, 79
exchange networks, 191
influence on other cultures, 54, 191
monumental heads, 54, 64, 64(i), 66
writing system, 54, 65(t)
Oneida people (North America), 388
Onondaga people (North America), 388
oracle bones
for predicting future, 53
as writing system, 65(t)
organized labor, guilds, 334, 335
Orthodox Christianity. *See* Eastern Orthodox Christianity
Osiris (Egyptian god), 70, 144
Otto I (Saxony, r. 936–973), 330
Ottoman empire
Abbasid connection to, 401
Byzantine Empire, conquest of, 316, 323
Constantinople, conquest of, 315, 383, 401
in fifteenth century, 400–401
global trade, impact on, 411
and Islam, 360
Janissaries in, 410(i)
military of, 402(i)
scope of, 301(m), 400, 401(m)
Turkic creation of, 301–2, 368, 400–401
Oxford University, 346
Oxus civilization (Central Asia), 53–54

Pachamama (Andean earth goddess), 179
Pacific Ocean region. *See also specific countries*
  Agricultural Revolution, 29(m), 35
  Austronesian-speakers, 19, 35
  chiefdoms, 20, 42
  in fifteenth century, 386(t), 411
  gathering and hunting peoples of, 20
  Paleolithic migrations to, 17(m), 19(m), 19–20
  population estimates, 182(t)
Pagan, kingdom of, 233(m), 235–36
Pakistan
  earliest civilizations in. *See* Indus Valley civilization
  Islamization versus Arabization, 292
palaces
  Forbidden City (Beijing), 391
  Persian, 92, 92(i)
Palau, in fifteenth century, 386(t), 411
Palembang (Srivijaya city), 233
Paleolithic era
  Africa, human beginnings, 3–4, 12–14
  animal extinction during, 18, 20, 22
  climate. *See* Ice Age
  human migrations in, 4(m), 4–5, 12–20, 16–17(m), 19(m), 28
  modern assessment of, 43–44
  people and culture of. *See* gathering and hunting peoples
  population growth, 20, 24
  sources of information about, 12–14
  time periods of, 24(f)
Palestine
  Christianity, spread to, 142
  Mongol defeat in, 364
Pali language, 130
Pallava writing system, 233
Paneb (Egyptian criminal), 70–71
papacy. *See* pope and papacy
papermaking, 83, 269, 270(t), 309, 342(t)
paper money, 254
Paris
  mills, in Middle Ages, 271
  population of (1300s), 334
  University of, 346
Parsis, 133
Parthenon (Greece), 96
Parthian dynasty (Persia. 247 B.C.E.–224 C.E.), 133

pastoral societies, 39–40, 354–58
  agriculturalists, relationship with, 40, 357–58
  animals of, 39–40, 40(i), 182, 354, 356(t), 358, 360
  confederations of. *See* nomadic societies
  contributions of, 357
  earliest, emergence of, 5–6
  features of, 39–40, 354–58
  in fifteenth century, 389–90
  geographic locations of, 354, 356(t)
  mobility pattern of, 356–57
  rock art of, 40(i)
  transportation, animals used, 182, 356(t)
  women, status of, 40, 59, 355–56
pater familias, 102
patriarch (Eastern Orthodox Christianity), 324
patriarchy, 59–61. *See also* gender inequality
  Chinese civilizations, 168–71, 255–56
  Christianity, 141, 147
  Confucianism, 123
  consistency over time, 168, 171, 175
  in earliest civilizations, 41, 167
  female infanticide, 41
  female sexuality, control of, 60–61
  Greek civilization, 171–74
  Hinduism, 128
  Indian civilizations, 127–28
  Islam, 296–97
  Middle Ages/Western Europe, 335, 337
  origin, question of, 59–60
  in second-wave civilizations, 168–74
  slavery, roots of, 163
  Sparta, 174
  third-wave civilizations, 215
  weakening, signs of, 170–71
patricians, 100
patrilineal descent, 41
Paul, Saint (10–65 C.E.), 120(t)
  on slavery, 165
  and spread of Christianity, 140–42
Paw Saw (Pagan queen), 235
pax Romana (Roman peace), 103, 106
peace treaties, first treaty, 73
peasant revolts
  Black Death (plague) era, 378
  Chinese civilizations, 109, 157–58

peasants. *See also* serfs
  Chinese civilizations, 58, 155(i), 155–56
  Egyptian civilization, 62
  revolts of. *See* peasant revolts
Peloponnesian War (431–404 B.C.E.), 96
Penifader, Cecilia (English peasant), 336–37
Pentecostal Christianity, Latin America, growth of, 315
pepper, 229
Pericles (Greek leader)
  Aspasia as mate, 172
  on Athenian democracy, 96
  reform efforts, 95
Perpetua (Christian martyr), 144–45
perpetual-motion machines, 343
Persepolis (Persia), 91(m), 92, 92(i), 97
Persia
  Arab cultural influences, 291–92
  Byzantine Empire conflict with, 326
  Islam, conversion to, 291–92, 318, 360
  Manichaeism, 358
  in Mongol empire, 369–72
  Mongol-Persian society, 371–72
  Nestorian Christianity, 318–19
  Safavid empire, 402
  Shia Muslims, 402
  Timur (Tamerlane) conquest of, 389, 391(m)
  Turkic empire, 360
Persian empire, 90–92, 91(m)
  Alexander the Great conquest of, 97, 133
  Arab conquest of, 289, 291, 318
  Christianity, spread to, 141–42
  distinctive accomplishment of, 90(t)
  Greco-Persian Wars, 95–96
  intellectual achievements, 309
  Sassanid dynasty, 133, 289
  Seleucid dynasty, 98, 133
  state authority, 91–92
  Zoroastrianism, 103–4, 133–34
Peru, civilizations of. *See* Andean civilizations
Perun (Rus god), 327
Petrarch, Francesco, on Black Death (plague), 378
pharaohs (Egypt)
  afterlife and, 67
  decline of power, 69–70
  divinity of, 63, 64, 69, 71

Philip II (Macedonian king), 96
Philippines, Paleolithic migrations
    to, 19
philosopher-kings, 138
Phoenicians. *See also* Carthage
    exchange networks, 230
    Mesopotamia, influence on, 72
pictographs
    Indus Valley civilization, 65(t)
    Mayan, 192
pilgrimages
    Muslims to Mecca. *See hajj*
      (pilgrimage to Mecca)
    to Sufi tombs, 308
Pillars of Islam, 286
Pillow Book (Sei Shonagon), 267
piracy, slave trade, 165
Pisa (Italy), as trade center, 345
pit houses, 204
pituri (psychoactive drug), 18
Piye (Kushite ruler), conquest of Egypt,
    186–87
plague. *See* Black Death (plague)
plantations, and slavery, 309
plant domestication
    in Agricultural Revolution, 5–6,
      30–34
    protein-rich crops, 34
    textiles, making from plants, 38
Plato (429–348 B.C.E.)
    Academy of, 138, 347
    rationalism, 120(t), 137–38
plebeians, 100
plows, 270(t), 342(t), 343
Plutarch (Greek writer), 173
pochteca (Aztec merchants), 245, 407
Po Chu-I (China, 772–846 C.E.), 153
poetry
    Aztec, 407
    Indian, 131, 233
    Muslim achievements, 342(t)
    Sufi, 308, 310(t)
    tanka (Japan), 267–69
    troubadour, 342(t)
pogroms, during Crusades, 339(m), 340
Poland, Mongol invasion of, 375
political systems. *See* governments
pollution. *See* environmental damage
Polo, Marco (merchant traveler)
    in China/Mongol empire, 253, 341,
      362(m), 366, 370, 374
    and Khubilai Khan, 368(i)
    travel, safety of, 215

Polybius (Roman writer), 106
polygyny/polygamy
    Islam on, 296
    Korea, 262
Polynesia
    chiefdoms of, 42
    Paleolithic migrations to, 19(m)
polytheism. *See also* deities; gods and
    goddesses
    Roman empire ban on, 143–44
Pompey (Roman statesman), 102
pope and papacy. *See also specific popes
    by name*
    beginning of, 146
    Crusades, impact on, 340
    Eastern Orthodox rejection of, 325
    investiture conflict, 332
population
    in Common Era, beginning of, 180
    in second-wave civilizations, 182(t)
    Teotihuacán (Mesoamerica), 193
population decline
    Black Death (plague), 377
    Roman empire, 109, 329
population growth
    Agricultural Revolution and,
      36–37
    China, third-wave civilization, 253
    and environmental transformation,
      37–38
    Middle Ages/Western Europe, 332,
      334
    Paleolithic era, 20, 24
    pre-modern, 81(t)
    second-wave civilizations, 182(t)
    years 1000–2000, 414(t)
Popul Vuh (Maya creation myth), 191
porcelain, Chinese, 83, 270(t), 271
Portugal, maritime voyages, fifteenth
    century, 385(t), 397–400, 398(m),
    405(t)
potatoes, domestication of, 5, 30
poverty. *See* peasants; serfs
Prajapati Goami (Buddha's foster
    mother), 130
priests
    Eastern Orthodox, 325
    Indian civilizations. *See* Brahmins
Prince, The (Machiavelli), 395
printing
    and Buddhism, 269, 271
    Chinese innovation, 254, 269, 270(t),
      271

    global impact of, 269–70
    Guttenberg's type, 269
promissory notes, 254
propaganda, in earliest civilizations, 64
property-ownership
    Chinese civilizations, 57, 154–55, 253
    in earliest civilizations, 57–58
    feudal, 330–31
    Middle Ages/Western Europe, 330–31,
      336–37
    and patriarchy, 60
prophets
    of Hebrews, 118, 120(t), 134–35
    Muhammad as, 285, 286, 287
protein crops, in Agricultural
    Revolution, 34
protests. *See* revolts, rebellions,
    resistance
Ptolemaic era (Egypt), 98–99
Pueblo Bonito (Ancestral Pueblo), 205,
    205(i)
Punic Wars, 100–102, 101–2
Pure Land Buddhism, 274
Purusha (Indian god), 159–60
Pyramid of the Moon (Teotihuacán),
    194(i)
Pyramid of the Sun (Teotihuacán), 193,
    194(i)
pyramids
    Egyptian, 67
    Maya, 191
    Moche, 197
    of mound-builders, 206–7
    Sumerian ziggurats, 55, 57, 63(i)
    Teotihuacán, 56, 193–94, 194(i)
Pythagoras (Greek philosopher), 136

qi (vital energy), 157
Qin dynasty (China, 221–206 B.C.E.)
    emperor. *See* Qin Shihuangdi
      (Chinese emperor,
      r. 221–210 B.C.E.)
    and unification of China, 103–5, 121
Qin Shihuangdi (Chinese emperor,
    r. 221–210 B.C.E.)
    brutality of, 64, 105, 121
    collapse of dynasty, 106
    empire building by, 104–5, 105(m)
    as First Emperor, 104
    human sacrifice by, 64
    Legalism, 103, 121
    Mao Zedong compared to, 114
    military power, 86(i), 87

Qin Shihuangdi (*continued*)
reunification of China, 103–5, 121
terra-cotta army funerary complex, 86(i), 87
Quechua language, 212, 408
Queen Mother of the West (Chinese deity), 255
queens. *See also specific names*
Chinese empresses, 170
Egyptian, 61
Meroë, kingdom of, 183
quipu (Andean accounting system), 52, 65(t), 245
Quran (Koran)
on Adam and Eve, 297
gender equality in, 295–96
laws based on. *See sharia* (Islamic law code)
madrassas (Islamic schools), 307
revelations of Muhammad in, 285–86
Quraysh people (Arabia)
Mecca, control by, 283–84
Muhammad as member, 284, 287

Rabia (woman Sufi), 297
Raherka and **Mersankh** (sculpture), 46(i), 47
raised-field agriculture, 199
Ramadan, 286
Ramayana (Indian epic poem), 131, 233
Ramisht (Persian merchant), 225
Rapa Nui (Easter Island), deforestation, 20
rape, Sumerian civilization, 61
Raphael (Renaissance painter), 394
rationalism, 136–39
Christian approach to, 346–47
contributions of, 118, 136–38
versus faith, Middle Ages, 345–46
Greek proponents of, 135–38
influence on other cultures, 345–48
and Islam, 138–39, 310
key teachings of, 120(t), 136
origin, question of, 135–36
al-Razi (Arab physician), 310(t), 311
rebellions. *See* revolts, rebellions, resistance
Red Sea, commerce, development of, 230
reforestation, China, fifteenth century, 392

reincarnation
Buddhism, 129
Hinduism, 127, 161–62, 233
reindeer, 356(t)
religious orders
Franciscans, 376
of monks and nuns. *See* monasticism
religious systems. *See also specific civilizations*
ancestor veneration. *See* ancestor worship
blended. *See* syncretic (blended) religions
divine kingship. *See* divinity of kings
emergence, rationale for, 82, 118–19
in fifteenth century, 411, 412(m)
formal organization of. *See* world religions
historians issue with, 147–48
monotheism, 132–36
polytheistic. *See* deities; goddess culture; gods and goddesses; polytheism
rise, in second-wave civilizations, 118–19, 119(t), 120(t)
wisdom traditions, 82
religious tolerance, Mongol empire, 319, 366, 368, 368(i), 372(i)
religious wars
Crusades, 338–40
Islamic, early, 289–91
Spain, Muslims and Christians, 305–6
ren (benevolence), 122
Renaissance, 393–97
artistic traditions, 393–94
intellectual thought, 394–96
Islamic interaction with, 394
literature of, 395–96
women, status of, 395–96
republic, Roman, 100, 102–3
Republic, The (Plato), 137–38
resistance movements. *See* revolts, rebellions, resistance
revolts, rebellions, resistance
An Lushan (China), 275
of peasants. *See* peasant revolts
of slaves. *See* slave revolts
Yellow Turban (China), 109, 126, 157–58, 158(m)
revolutions. *See also specific revolutions*
Iranian (1979), 281

rice, Chinese production, 253, 271
Rightly Guided Caliphs (632–661), 292–93
roads
Inca, 245(i)
Persian empire, 92
Roman, 83, 167
Wari civilization, 199–200
rock art
Aboriginal Australians, 15(i)
Sahara Desert pastoralists, 40(i)
San people, 10(i), 11
rockets, 309
Roman Catholic Church
Black Death (plague), impact on, 228
Byzantine Empire, decline of, 300–301
conversions/spread of Catholicism. *See* Catholicism; missionaries
councils, 146
Crusades, 338–40
early practices incorporated, 331
Eastern Orthodox compared to, 324–26
Eastern Orthodox doctrinal issues with, 340
empire-building discouraged by, 110–11
hierarchy of organization in, 331
Latin as language of, 331
maritime voyages, connection to, 399
nuns, 335
political independence of, 324, 346
political/secular connection, 332
pope/Vatican. *See* pope and papacy
Roman empire compared to, 331
supernatural elements, 331
wealth associated with, 331
women, limited role in, 335–36
Roman empire, 99–103, 106–10
assimilation of outsiders, 107
beginnings as city-state, 107
Chinese empire compared to, 106–11
Christianity, spread of, 141–42
Christians, persecution of, 106–7, 143, 144(i)
citizenship, 107
class hierarchies, 100, 102–3
collapse of, 108–9, 321, 328–29
disease/epidemics, 227
distinctive accomplishment of, 90(t)
eastern. *See* Byzantine empire

emperor, divinity of, 106
empire-building, 100–102, 181
environmental damage, 108
Germanic invasions on, 109–10,
    329–30
Greek influence on, 107, 138
growth, domestic repercussions,
    102–3
influence on other cultures, 108, 145,
    329–30
Latin language, evolution of, 108
laws of, 108
legacy of, 114
male dominance in, 102
military, 101, 102, 107
pax Romana (Roman peace), 103,
    106
population decline in, 109, 329
post-Roman history, 110
public works, 106
Punic Wars, 100–102
religious practices, 143–44
as republic, 100, 102–3
Rome, urban culture of, 107
scope of, 101(m)
slavery, 58, 102, 163–67, 164(i)
Spartacus rebellion, 167, 167(m)
trade and Silk Road, 222–23, 224–25
trade with Africa, 185–87
women, status of, 102
Rome (Italy), early civilization. *See*
    Roman empire
royal roads, Persian empire, 92
Rubaiyat, The (Khayyam), 310(t)
Rumi (Sufi poet), 308
Rus, early civilization. *See* Kievan Rus
    civilization
Russia
    early civilization. *See* Kievan Rus
        civilization
    Mongol contributions to, 373–74
    in Mongol empire, 372–74
    pastoral societies, 356(t)
Russian Orthodox Church, and
    Mongol rule, 373–74
Ryazan (Russia), Mongol invasion of,
    373(i)

sacrifice, human. *See* human sacrifice
Safavid empire
    features of, 402
    scope of, 401(m)

Sahara Desert
    pastoral societies, 356(t)
    trade routes. *See* Sand Roads
    trans-Saharan trade, early, 182,
        184(m)
Sailendra kingdom, 234–35
St. Mark's Basilica (Venice), 325(i)
saints. *See also specific saints by name*, Sufi,
    298, 308
Saka pastoralists, 40
Salamanca (university), 346
salt, 220, 269
Samarkand (Central Asia), 226, 389
Sami nomads, 356(t)
Samoa, 411
samsara (rebirth/reincarnation), 127
samurai (Japanese warriors), 266(i),
    266–67
    bushido (Japanese way of the warrior),
        266
San culture (South Africa), 21–22,
    184(m)
    rock art of, 10(i), 11
Sand Roads, 238–41
    Islam, spread of, 302
    slave trade, 241
    taxes on trade, 239–40
    trans-Saharan trade, 238–41, 240(m),
        302(m)
    West African civilizations, impact on,
        238–41
Sanhaja Berbers, Almoravid empire,
    360, 361(m)
Sanskrit language, 126
Sanskrit writing system, 233
Sanxingdui (China), 54
Sarai (Mongol capital), 373
Sassanid Empire (Persia, 224–651 C.E.),
    133
    Arab conquest of, 289
satraps (Persian governors), 91
Saudi Arabia. *See* Arab empire;
    Arabia
savanna grasslands, West Africa, 238
Saxons, 329
Scandinavia
    pastoral societies, 356(t)
    Vikings, 337–38
scholar-gentry
    Chinese civilizations, 155–57, 175
    Daoist view of, 126
    peasants, view of, 158

sciences. *See also specific disciplines, for
    example, medical science*
    Greek achievements, 136
    Muslim achievements, 310(t), 310–11,
        347
Scientific Revolution, rationality,
    influence on, 347
scribes (Egyptian), 46(i), 47
Scythians, as pastoral society, 357(i)
seals, woodblock printed, 271
Sea Roads
    China, transformation of, 231, 271–72
    cultural diffusion, 232–38
    East Africa, transformation by,
        236–38
    efficiency for trade, 229–30
    Southeast Asia, transformation by,
        232–36
    urban nodes in network of, 230
secondary products revolution, 38–39
second-wave civilizations. *See*
    civilizations, second-wave
Seleucid dynasty (Persia, 330–155 B.C.E.),
    98, 133
Seljuk Turkic empire
    ceramic tiles, 360(i)
    as pastoral society, 356(t)
    as sultanate, 360
Senate, Roman, 103
Seneca people (North America), 388
Septimus Severus (Roman emperor),
    144
serfs. *See also* peasants, in feudalistic
    system, 330–31
Sermon on the Mount (Jesus), 139
Seventeen Article Constitution (Japan), 265
sex and sexuality
    Greek civilization, 174
    Hindu view of, 128
    honor killing of women, 297
    Paleolithic era, 21
    Sumerian civilization, 61
    women's, male control of, 60–61
Shahnama (The Book of Kings)
    (Ferdowsi), 292
shamans
    Andean, 196, 197
    Mayan, 192
    Mongols, 361–62
    Paleolithic societies, 23
    San people, 10(i), 11
    Turkic, 301

Shanga (Swahili city), 237

Shang dynasty (China, 1600–1046 B.C.E.)
bronze metallurgy, 53(i), 73–74
features of, 53
writing system, 65(t)

sharia (Islamic law code)
Islamic law code, 294
origin of, 288
unifying function of, 294

shaykhs (Sufi teachers), 307, 308

Sheba (Ethiopian queen), 320

sheep, 356(t)

Shia Muslims
religious authority, view of, 293
Safavid official religion, 402
-Sunni conflict, 293, 402, 411
women mullahs, 298

Shihuangdi. *See* Qin Shihuangdi
(Chinese emperor, r. 221–210 B.C.E.)

Shikibu, Izumi (Japanese poet),
268–69, 269(i)

Shikibu, Murasaki (Japanese poet),
267, 269

Shi Le (Jie ruler), 226–27

Shinto, 267

ships
Chinese innovations, 230, 343
Islamic innovations, 344
sternpost rudder, 230, 270(t), 344
Viking, 242(i)

Shiva (Hindu deity), 132, 233, 235

Shonagon, Sei (Japanese writer),
Pillow Book, 267

Siberia
-Alaska land bridge, 14, 16(m)
in fifteenth century, 384, 411
Paleolithic migrations through,
16(m), 18
Turks from, 359

Sicily
Christianity restored to, 339, 345
and Crusades, 339

Siddhartha Gautama (566–486 B.C.E.),
118. *See also* Buddha
early life of, 128–29, 139
key teaching of, 120(t)

siege warfare, Mongols, 365

Sikhism, Indian origins of, 300

silk industry
Byzantine Empire, 326
China, 170(i), 223–25
demand for silk, 224–25
Middle Ages/Western Europe, 335

spread outside China, 215, 225
women, decline in role, 256, 335
women in, 170(i), 224

Silk Roads, 222–28, 223(m)
Buddhism, spread of, 226–27, 272
caravan trade, 218(i), 219, 223
and cultural diffusion, 221–22, 226–27
diseases, spread of, 227–28
in fifteenth century, 411
goods exchanged along, 223–25
impact on civilization, 214
nomadic societies control of, 257, 260
and relay trade, 222

Silla dynasty (Korea, 688–900), 261–62

Sima Guang (China, 1019–1086), 255

Skagit people, 387

slave revolts
Abbasid dynasty, 232
Haitian Revolution (1791–1804), 167
Spartacus rebellion, 167, 167(m)

slavery
consistency over time, 175
early civilizations. *See* slavery, in
first-second-third civilizations
historical context for, 163
and Muslims, 232, 241
revolts by slaves. *See* slave revolts
as trade/business. *See* Africa and slave
trade; slave trade
in West Africa, 240–41

slavery, in first-second-third
civilizations, 163–64
Aztec, 407
China, 163–64
Christianity on, 165
Greece, 58, 163, 164–65
India, 164
Korea, 263
living conditions, 166
Mesopotamia, 58, 58(i), 163
nomadic societies, 355, 365
revolts by slaves. *See* slave revolts
Roman empire, 58, 102, 163–67, 164(i)
supply, sources of, 165
West Africa, 240–41
of women captives, 58, 60, 163, 241

slave trade
and Africa. *See* Africa and slave trade
by early civilizations, 165, 230

smallpox, ancient era, 227

social class
inequalities among. *See* social
inequalities

poor. *See* peasants; serfs
upward trend. *See* social mobility
wealthy. *See* elites; nobility

social conversion, 291

social inequalities. *See also under specific
type of inequality*
class-based. *See* class hierarchies
consistency over time, 175
earliest civilizations, 57–61
gender-based. *See* gender inequality
second-wave civilizations, 151–75

social mobility
caste system and, 162
of merchants, 220

Socrates (469–399 B.C.E.)
death of (painting), 137(i)
death sentence, 136, 137(i), 138
rationalism, 120(t), 136

Sofala (Swahili city), 237(m)

Solomon (Hebrew king), 174
and Sheba (Ethiopian queen), 320–21

Song dynasty (China, 960–1279), 116,
251–55, 252(m)
economic growth, 253
filial piety, 122(i)
foot binding, 255–56, 256(i)
Mongol conquest, 367
Neo-Confucianism, 251
patriarchy, 255–56
peasants, 155(i)
unification and revival, 231
women, role changes for, 255–56

Songhay civilization (West Africa), 211,
239, 401(m)
exchange networks, 388
Islam, spread to, 301(m), 303, 402–3

Son of Heaven (China), 53, 63, 106, 119

Sophocles (Greek playwright), 96

Sorgaqtani (wife of Chinggis Khan),
372(i)

sorghum, 32

South America. *See also specific countries*
Agricultural Revolution, 28(m), 29,
32–33
civilizations of. *See* Andean
civilizations
in fifteenth century/pre-Columbian,
405(m)
Paleolithic migrations to, 16(m), 18

South Asia. *See also* India
earliest civilizations in. *See* Indus
Valley civilization
in fifteenth century, 386(t)

South China Sea, trade and commerce, 231

Southeast Asia. *See also specific countries*
  Agricultural Revolution, 29(m), 34
  civilizations of. *See* Southeast Asia civilizations
  in fifteenth century, 386(t)
  Islam, spread to, 404
  Mongol defeat in, 364

Southeast Asia civilizations, 232–36, 233(m)
  Buddhism, 113, 234–35
  Champa kingdom, 233, 233(m), 235
  early migrants to, 83
  Funan, 233, 233(m)
  Hinduism, 113, 233–36
  Indian influence on, 233–36
  Khmer kingdom, 233, 233(m)
  Pagan, 233(m), 235–36
  people and culture of. *See specific civilizations by name*
  Sailendra kingdom, 234–35
  Sea Roads trade, impact on, 232–36
  Srivijaya, kingdom of, 232–34

Southwest Asia. *See* Fertile Crescent

Spain
  Arab conquest of, 289, 304
  Christian reconquest (1200), 306, 338, 339(m), 384
  Crusades in, 338, 339(m)
  Islam, spread to, 304–6, 361, 361(i)
  Islamic contributions to, 304–6, 341
  Jews, expulsion from, 306
  maritime voyages, fifteenth century, 397–99
  Visigoths in, 329

Spanish America, Aztecs, Spanish view of, 406

Sparta
  homosexuality, prohibition, 173–74
  as militaristic society, 95, 172–73
  patriarchy, 171–74
  Peloponnesian War, 96
  Socrates view of, 136
  state authority, 95
  women, status of, 173(i), 173–74

Spartacus, slave revolt led by, 167, 167(m)

spice trade. *See also specific spices*
  and Southeast Asia, 404
  third-wave civilizations, 229, 233, 271

spinning wheel, 342(t)

spirit banner, 352

spirituality. *See* deities; gods and goddesses; religious systems; shamans; world religions

Srivijaya civilization (Sumatra), 211, 232–34, 233(m)

Staff God (Andean), 199

state authority, early civilizations. *See also* city-states; kings
  confederations, 388–89
  democracy, Greek-form, 94–96
  Mesopotamia, 61–63
  monumental structures signifying, 50, 54, 64, 66
  nomadic societies, 357, 359
  republic, Roman, 100, 102–3
  stateless societies. *See* kinship societies
  violence, use by state, 62

status, social. *See* social class

steppes
  Black Death (plague), impact on, 228
  Mongols in Russia, 372–74
  nomadic societies, 356(t), 359
  products and trade of, 222, 257

sternpost rudder, 230, 270(t), 344

stinkards, 207

stirrup, horses, 342(t), 358

Strabo (Greek geographer), 230

Subarctic Eurasia, pastoral societies, 356(t)

Sudan, divine kingship, origin of, 71

sudra (caste), 159–60

Sufi Muslims
  in Anatolia, 300–302
  beliefs and values of, 294–95, 295(i)
  and expansion of Islam, 307–8
  in India, 299
  other religions, contributions to, 342(t)
  poetry, 308, 310(t)
  Safavid empire, 402
  saints/friends of god, veneration of, 298, 308
  women, view of, 298–99

sugarcane
  crystallization, 83
  Muslim cultivation of, 309

sugar plantations, slave labor, 309

Sui dynasty (China 589–618), 110, 250–51
  Buddhism during, 274
  canal system, 250–51

founders, nomadic/Chinese ancestry, 260
  reunification of China, 107, 250–51

Sulla (Rome), 102

sultans and sultanates
  of Delhi, 298, 300(m), 391(m)
  Turkic rulers, 360

Sumatra
  Islam, spread to, 404
  Paleolithic climate change, 20
  spice trade, 271
  Srivijaya civilization, 211, 232–34, 233(m)

Sumerian civilization (Mesopotamia), 51(m), 67(m)
  city-states, 68–69
  class hierarchies in, 57–58
  divine kingship, 63
  Egyptian compared to, 66–75
  end of, 69, 79
  exchange networks, 71–72
  gender inequality, 60–61
  Hammurabi law code, 57–58, 63
  slavery, 57(i), 58
  Uruk, 55–56
  warfare, 58(i), 69
  writing system, 64, 65(t)
  ziggurats, 55, 57, 63(i)

Sunga dynasty, artistic traditions, 151(i)

Sunni Muslims
  religious authority, view of, 293
  -Shia conflict, 293, 402, 411

supernatural power. *See also* deities; gods and goddesses; shamans
  Bantu cultures, 202–3
  and Buddhism, 274, 331
  Jesus of Nazareth, 140
  oracle bones, 53

Susa (Persian empire), 91(m)

Swahili civilization, 211, 236–38, 237(m)
  Islam, spread to, 237–38

Swahili language, 237

syncretic (blended) religions
  Catholic-pagan blend, 331
  Islam, integration with native religions, 301–4
  Nestorian Christianity, 319
  Sikhism as, 300

Syria
  Christianity, spread to, 141–42
  Islam, spread to, 318
  Nestorian Christianity, 318–19

Syriac language, 141

Taino people (Haiti), Columbus greeted by, 382(i), 383
Taishi, Shotoku (Japanese elite), 265
Talas River, Battle of (China), 289
Tale of Genji, The (Murasaki Shikibu), 267, 269
Tamerlane. *See* Timur (Tamerlane)
Tang dynasty (China, 618–907), 252(m)
    civil service examination, 153–54
    diversity of groups in China, 260, 272
    features of, 110
    founders, mixed ancestry, 260
    Han era revival in, 322
    innovations and discoveries, 254
    nomadic raids/tribute, 259
    population growth, 253
    silk industry, 225
    Silk Road trade, 223
    unification and revival, 231
    Vietnam independence during, 264
    women, status of, 170, 255, 267
tanka (Japanese poetry), 267–69
Tanzania
    early humans in, 3
    Hadza people, 11, 35
Tartars. *See* Mongol empire; Mongols
Ta-Seti (Nubia) civilization, 54
Tata Inti (Andean sun god), 179
taxation
    Axum, 186
    Chinese system, 254
    Japanese system, 265
    jizya (tax on non-Muslims), 290, 291, 299, 318
    by Mongols, 366, 369, 373–74
    on pilgrimage to Mecca, 283
    on trade, 186, 233, 239–40, 366
technology. *See* energy production; innovations and discoveries; navigational technology; technology, diffusion of
technology, diffusion of
    and Chinese innovations, 269–71
    Middle Ages/Western Europe, 342–44
    and Mongol empire, 376–77
    secondary products revolution, 38–39
teff, 32
Temple of Heaven (Bejing), 391, 392(i)
Temple of the Feathered Serpent (Teotihuacán), 194
Temple of the Giant Jaguar (Tikal), 66, 178(i), 179

Temple on a Mountain Ledge (painting), 124(i)
temples
    Buddhist, 227, 234, 234(i), 274
    complex of. *See* ceremonial centers
    Confucian, 117, 391, 392(i)
    Greek, 96
    Mayan, 66, 178(i), 179, 191
    Paleolithic societies, 25–26
    Teotihuacán, 193–94, 194(i)
Temujin. *See* Chinggis Khan (Mongol ruler, 1162–1227)
Ten Commandments, 134
Tengri (Mongol god), 353, 362
Tenochtitlán (Mesoamerica)
    founding of, 406
    population of (1500), 334
tents, nomads, 357, 360
teosinte, 33–34
Teotihuacán (Mesoamerica), 56, 193–95
    collapse of, 195, 212
    Olmec influence on, 54
    pyramids, 193–94, 194(i)
    sphere of influence, 191(m)
    time frame of, 181(t)
    trade, 195, 245
terraces, for agriculture, 192, 199
terra-cotta army (China), 86(i), 87
Tertullian (150–225 c.e.), 142, 144, 345
Texcoco (Aztec city-state), 406–7
Texcoco, Lake, 400
textile industry
    cotton textiles, 83, 113
    India, 113
    innovations and technology. *See* textile industry innovations
    Middle Ages/Western Europe, 335
    silk. *See* silk industry
    and trade, 229
    weaving, earliest, 38
    women, decline in role, 256, 335
textile industry innovations
    looms, 38, 83, 335
    spinning wheel, 342(t)
Thales (Greek philosopher), 136
theater, Greek civilization, 96
Theodosius (Rome, r. 379–395 c.e.), 143–44
Theravada Buddhism, 130–31, 274
third-wave civilizations. *See* civilizations, third-wave
Thucydides (Greek historian), on plague, 83

Tibet, pastoral societies, 356(t)
Tigris-Euphrates river valley. *See* Mesopotamia
Tikal (Maya city)
    population estimates, 192
    Temple of the Giant Jaguar, 66, 178(i)
tiles, Turkish, 360(i)
Timbuktu (West Africa), 241
    as Islamic center, 303, 304, 403
    manuscripts of, 241(i)
time. *See also* calendars; dating systems
    Paleolithic measures of, 23
Timur (Tamerlane), 384, 389, 400(m)
title societies, Igbo people, 41, 388
Tiwanaku civilization (Bolivia), 199–200, 408
    as national symbol, 179
    precursor to, 52
    sphere of influence, 196(m)
    time frame of, 181(t)
Tlacaelel (Aztec official), 407
tlatelolco (Aztec market), 406–7
toga, 107
Toltecs (Mesoamerica), 406
Tonga, 411
tools
    Agricultural Revolution, 30, 32, 38–39
    Clovis point, 18
    digging sticks, 185
    of Jomon society, 25
    micro-blades, 24
    Paleolithic, 3, 5, 12, 14, 24
    stone age, end of, 38
trade
    and Byzantine Empire, 326
    early civilizations. *See* exchange networks; trade, second-third wave civilizations
    in fifteenth century, 411, 412(m)
    networks of (1300), 375
trade, second-third wave civilizations
    African civilizations routes, 184(m)
    American Web trade and commerce, 243–45
    Axum, 186, 188
    China, open to Europe, 341
    continental comparisons, second-wave, 181–82
    and cultural diffusion, 221–22, 226–27
    decline, and Black Death era, 377
    diseases, spread of, 228–29, 375(m)
    Greek, 94
    Gupta empire, 113

impact on civilization, 221–22, 225
Indian Ocean region, 230–32
Maya, 192, 245
modern trade compared to, 246
Mongol networks, 366, 374–75, 375(m)
Niger Valley civilizations, 190
nomadic people and control of, 257, 359
and patriarchy, 60
Persia, 92
political issues, 220–21
Roman, 185–87, 222–23, 224–25
Rus, 327
Sand Roads, 238–41
Sea Roads, 228–38, 229(m)
Silk Roads, 222–132
taxes on trade, 186, 233, 239–40
Teotihuacán, 195, 245
in third-wave, impact of, 220–21
Western Christendom, 332–34, 341
transatlantic slave trade. *See* Africa and slave trade
trans-Saharan trade. *See* Sand Roads
tribalism. *See* kinship societies
tribute system
  Aztec, 406
  China to raiding nomads, 257–60, 259(i), 360
  Korea to China, 261–62
Trinity (Christian doctrine)
  councils on, 146
  Eastern Orthodox view, 324, 325
  Islamic rejection of, 285
Triple Alliance (Mexica people), 406
troubadour poetry, 342(t)
Trung Trac and **Trung Nhi**, 104, 264
Tuareg people, 360
Tulalip people, 387
Tului (Mongol ruler), 372(i)
Turkana people, 356(t)
Turkey
  early civilization in. *See* Anatolia
  Islamization versus Arabization, 292
Turkmenistan, pastoral societies, 222
Turks
  Anatolia, conquest of, 301–2
  centralized authority, 359
  in China, assimilation of, 260
  China tribute to, 259
  empire-building. *See* Ottoman empire
  India, conquest of, 297
  Islam, conversion to, 289, 298, 360

Islam, spread by, 298, 300–302, 360–61
military, 359
Mughal empire, 403
origin of, 259
Seljuk empire, 356(t), 360, 360(i)
spirituality, 301
time frame of events, 355(t)
Timur (Tamerlane), 389, 391(m)
Uighurs, 259
turquoise ornaments, 205, 244
al-Tusi, Nasir al-Din (1201–1274), 310(t)
Twain, Mark, 47

Uighurs (Turkic people), 356(t)
  China tribute payments to, 259
Ukraine, Kievan Rus civilization, 211
ulama (Sunni scholars), 293
  and expansion of Islam, 307–8
Umar (caliph), 296
Umayyad dynasty (661–750)
  caliphs, 293–94
  Jerusalem, as sacred location, 318
umma (Islamic community), 286
  expansion of. *See* Arab empire; Islamic empire
United States
  early civilizations of. *See* North American cultures
  as new Roman Empire, 87
universities and colleges. *See also specific schools*, male-only, Middle Ages, 335
University of Paris, 346
untouchables caste, 113, 159(i), 160–61
Upanishads (Indian texts), 118, 120(t), 127
Upper River during Qing Ming Festival (Chinese painting), 254(i)
Ur (Mesopotamia), 67(m)
  ziggurat, 63(i)
urbanization. *See* cities
Uruk (Mesopotamia), 67(m)
  features of, 56
Urukagina (Mesopotamian ruler), 63
Uthman (caliph), 292
Uzbekistan
  pastoral societies, 222, 356(t)
  Timur (Tamerlane) from, 389

vaisya (caste), 159–60
Vajrapani (Buddha protector), 227
varnas (caste), 159–60, 160(t)

Vatican. *See* pope and papacy
Vedas (Indian texts), 126–27
veiled women
  Islam on, 296, 296(i)
  Sumerian civilization, 61
Venice (Italy)
  Islam, connection to, 325(i)
  population of (1300s), 334
  St. Mark's Basilica, 325(i)
  as trade center, 229, 332, 345
Venus figurines, 14–15, 23, 23(i)
Vienna, Ottoman invasion of, 401
Vietnamese civilization
  Buddhism, 264
  Champa kingdom, 233(m), 235
  Chinese influence on, 263–65
  civil service examination, 264
  Confucianism, 264–65
  expansion to south, 263(m)
  Funan, 233, 233(m)
  independence from China (938 C.E.), 264, 264(i)
  native religion, 264
  Trung sisters' revolt, 104
  women, status of, 264–65
Vijayanagara (Hindu kingdom)
  Mughal interactions with, 403
  scope of, 391(m)
Vikings
  invasions of, 332, 333(m)
  maritime voyages, 241–43
  North American colonies, 242, 337–38
village societies. *See* agricultural village societies
Vinland, Viking voyage to, 242–43
Virgin Mary. *See* Mary (mother of Jesus)
Vishnu (Hindu deity), 131–32
Visigoths, in Roman empire, 109–10, 329
Vladimir (prince of Kiev), 327

Waldseemüller, Martin, *Map of 1507*, 395(i)
Wang Mang (Chinese official), 155
Wang Shugu (China, 1649–1730), 116–17(i)
warfare
  Arab tactics, 289–90, 290(m)
  in earliest civilizations, 58(i), 60, 69
  innovations and technology for. *See* military innovations

warfare (*continued*)
　Mongol tactics, 365–66, 370, 372, 373(i)
　relationship to patriarchy, 60
　siege warfare, 365
Wari civilization (Peru), 196(m), 199–200
　precursor to, 52
　time frame of, 181(t)
warring states era (China), 103–4, 121
warrior societies
　Germanic peoples, 329
　Kshatriya caste, 99, 159–61
　Moche, 197–98
　Mongols, 364–66, 370–71
　nomadic pastoralists, 329, 357
　Roman, 102
　samurai, 146, 266, 266(i)
　Sparta, 173
wars. *See also* revolts, rebellions,
　　resistance; *specific wars*
　Greco-Persian, 95–96
　Hundred Years', 393
　Peloponnesian, 96
　Punic, 100–102
　of religion. *See* religious wars
water drilling, 309
waterways, man-made. *See also* canals
　Chinese system, 250–51, 253
wealth
　Aztec empire, 341, 406–7
　Buddhists, 226–27, 274
　maritime voyages in search of, 399
　of merchants, 158, 220, 225, 231–32,
　　308–9, 335, 407
　Mongol empire, 365
　Roman Catholic Church, 331
　and social class. *See* elites; nobility
weapons, development of. *See* military
　　innovations
weaving. *See also* textile industry
　in Agricultural Revolution, 38
　and women, 38, 41, 58, 170(i), 224,
　　256, 335
Wen (Chinese emperor), 359
Wendi (Chinese emperor,
　　r. 581–604 C.E.)
　Buddhist monasteries construction,
　　274
　reunification of China, 107
wen/wu (ideal men), 123
West Africa. *See also specific countries and
　　people*
　agricultural village societies, 387–88
　civilizations, second-wave, 211

crops of, 32
environmental variations within, 238
exchange networks, 238–39
Fulbe pastoral society, 390
Ghana, kingdom of, 240(m)
Igbo people, 387–88
Islam, spread to, 241, 302(m), 302–3,
　390
Islam/native religion, 303–4
Mali, kingdom of, 239–41, 240(m)
Niger Valley civilizations, 188–90
Sand Roads trade, impact on, 238–41
slave labor in, 240–41
slave trade, 241
Songhay civilization, 239, 388–89,
　402–3
trans-Saharan trade routes, 240(m)
women in authority, 240
Western Christendom
　agricultural expansion, 332, 342(t),
　　343
　Black Death (plague), 377–78, 378(i)
　Charlemagne's empire, 329–30,
　　330(m)
　Christian connection. *See* Roman
　　Catholic Church
　cities, growth of, 334, 345
　comparative backwardness of, 341,
　　377, 414
　Crusades, 338–40
　environmental strengths of, 328
　feudalism, 330–31, 334
　in fifteenth century, 386(t), 393–400,
　　394(m)
　Germanic kingdoms of, 329–30,
　　330(m)
　global dominance, emergence of,
　　414–15
　guilds, 334, 335
　High Middle Ages, expansion/
　　innovation during, 332–36, 333(m),
　　343, 343(i)
　Holy Roman Empire, 330
　industrialization during, 343, 343(i)
　intellectual thought, 345–48, 393–95
　invasions upon, 329, 332, 333(m),
　　337–38
　modern era. *See* Europe
　Mongol collapse, impact on, 379
　Muslim observations of, 341
　patriarchy, 335, 337
　political system, fragmented, 344–45,
　　393

population growth, 332, 334
Portuguese maritime voyages,
　397–400, 398(m)
power struggle, groups involved, 345
Renaissance, 393–97
Roman Catholic Church, 331–32
states, emergence of, 334
technology, borrowing from other
　cultures, 342–44
as third-wave civilization, 316
trade, 332–34, 341
universities and colleges, 335, 346
women, role of, 334–37, 336(i)
Western Europe. *See also specific
　　countries*
　cities, decline of (500–1000), 329
　civilizations of. *See* Western
　　European civilizations
Western European civilizations
　Greek civilization, 93–99
　people and culture of. *See specific
　　civilizations by name*
　Roman empire, 99–103, 106–10
　Western Christendom, 328–48
Western Hemisphere. *See also*
　　Mesoamerica; North America;
　　South America
　civilizations, first, 50–51(m)
　civilizations, third-wave, 212–13,
　　213(m)
　Paleolithic migrations to, 18–19
wheat
　domestication of, 5, 30, 32
　Egyptian cultivation, 68
　North Africa, 181
wheel, 73
wheelbarrow, 83, 270(t), 342(t)
Willendorf Venus, 23(i)
William of Conches (French scholar),
　346
windmills, 271, 343
wine
　Agricultural Revolution era, 39
　Mongol production, 253, 370
wisdom traditions, 82, 139
witches, Bantu cultures, 203
Woden (Germanic god), 329
women
　Black Death era, status of, 377
　elite, special status, 102, 169–70, 172,
　　255–56
　gender equality. *See* gender equality
　genital mutilation, 297

as historical force, 167–68, 215–16
honor killing, 297
identification with nature, 60
infanticide, 41
leadership roles. *See* women in authority
marriage. *See* dowry; marriage
monastic life. *See* nuns
and patriarchy. *See* gender inequality; patriarchy
slaves, captives as, 58, 60, 163, 241
status of, and culture. *See specific civilizations*
veiled. *See* veiled women
weavers, 38, 41, 58, 170(i), 224, 256, 335
women in authority. *See also* gender equality
African kingdoms, 240
Angkor kingdom, 235
Aztec, 406(i), 410
Bantu cultures, 202, 203(i)
Celtic, 102(i)
Chinese elite, 170–71
Egyptian, 60, 61
elites, 168, 169
gender parallelism, 203, 410
goddess worship. *See* goddess culture
Inca, 410
and matrilineal descent, 389
Meroë, kingdom of, 183
Mongol, 369–71, 371–72, 372(i)
nomadic societies, 170, 355–56, 369–71
Shia women mullahs, 298
Spartan system, 173(i), 173–74
Vietnamese, 104, 264
widows of merchants, 335
woodblock printing, 271
workers. *See* labor
world religions. *See also specific religions*
Buddhism, 128–31
Confucianism, 121–24
Daoism, 124–26
fifteenth century, global pattern, 412(m)

Hinduism, 126–28
Islam, 280–88
Judaism, 134–35
rise, in second-wave civilizations, 118–19
Shinto, 267
Zoroastrianism, 103–4, 133–34
writing systems
accounting function of, 64
Chinese, 65(t), 108
Cyrillic alphabet, 327
development, continental comparisons, 181
in earliest civilizations, 63–65, 65(t)
first, 65(t)
Islamic, 269
knowledge as threat to power, 64
Korean alphabet, 263
Mayan, 192
Mesopotamian, influence of, 73
Olmec, 54, 65(t)
Pallava, 233
Sanskrit, 233
Teotihuacán, 195
Vietnamese, 265
Wu (Chinese Empress, r. 690–705 C.E.), 170
Wu (Xia dynasty), flood control projects, 53
Wudi (China, r. 141–87 B.C.E.), 108, 153

Xenophon (Greek writer), 174
Xia dynasty (China, 2070–1600 B.C.E.), 53
Xian (China), terra-cotta army funerary complex, 86(i), 87
Xiongnu empire, 358(m), 358–59
centralized authority, 358–59
raids/tribute in China, 109, 258–59, 359–60
viewed as barbarians, 379

Yahi people (North America), 36–37
Yahweh
and decline of goddess culture, 61
Hebrew concept of, 134–35
yaks, 356(t)

Yap (Micronesia), in fifteenth century, 386(t), 411
Yathrib (Medina), *hijra* (journey) by Muhammad, 287
Yellow Turban Rebellion (China, 184 C.E.), 109, 126, 157–58, 158(m)
Yemen, village societies, 283
Yersini pestis. See Black Death (plague)
Yi dynasty (Korea, 1392–1910), 261–62
Yi Jing (Buddhist monk), 234
yin/yang, 125, 168
yoga, 52
yogurt, 360
Yongle (Chinese emperor, r. 1402–1422), 391–93
Yoruba people, 387–88, 398(m)
Yuan Chen (Chinese poet), 260–61
Yuan dynasty (China), 367
Yucatan, Maya civilization, 191(m), 193
Yuezhi nomads, 356(t)

Zapotec people (Mesoamerica), 195
Zarathustra/Zoraster, 118. *See also* Zoroastrianism
key teaching of, 120(t)
zero, Mayan concept, 192
Zheng He (Chinese admiral), maritime voyages of, 392, 396–97
Zheng Yin (Daoist master), 156
Zhou dynasty (China, 1046–771 B.C.E.)
beginning of, 119
decline of, 79, 121
emperor, limits to power, 63
features of, 53
Zhuangzi (369–286 B.C.E.)
key teaching of, 120(t)
teachings of. *See* Daoism
ziggurats, Sumerian, 55, 57, 63(i)
Zimbabwe, 202
Zion (Jerusalem), 134
Zoraster. *See* Zarathustra/Zoraster
Zoroastrianism, 120(t), 133–34
decline of, 133
fire altar as symbol, 133(i)
influence on other religions, 133–34, 292
Persian origins of, 103–4, 133

About the author

Robert W. Strayer (Ph.D., University of Wisconsin) brings wide experience in world history to the writing of *Ways of the World*. His teaching career began in Ethiopia where he taught high school world history for two years as part of the Peace Corps. At the university level, he taught African, Soviet, and world history for many years at the State University of New York–College at Brockport, where he received Chancellor's Awards for Excellence in Teaching and for Excellence in Scholarship. In 1998 he was visiting professor of world and Soviet history at the University of Canterbury in Christchurch, New Zealand. Since moving to California in 2002, he has taught world history at the University of California, Santa Cruz; California State University, Monterey Bay; and Cabrillo College. He is a long-time member of the World History Association and served on its Executive Committee. He has also participated in various AP World History gatherings, including two years as a reader. His publications include *Kenya: Focus on Nationalism*, *The Making of Mission Communities in East Africa*, *The Making of the Modern World*, *Why Did the Soviet Union Collapse?*, and *The Communist Experiment*.

"Strayer writes beautifully and clearly about complicated issues."

— Deborah Gerish, *Emporia State University*